WORLD HISTORY–
New Horizons

Jagdish P. Sharma

1993

LOW PRICE PUBLICATIONS
DELHI - 110052

ISBN 81-85557-43-8

Published by:
Low Price Publications
425, Nimri, Phase IV,
Ashok Vihar, Delhi - 110052.

Laser Set at:
Sita Composers Pvt. Ltd.,
Delhi - 110052.

Printed at :
D.K. Fine Art Press, Delhi-110052, Ph : 7116929.

PRINTED IN INDIA

Foreword

History is the record of socio-economic, politico-religious acts and decisions. It is concerned with the decisions and acts which arise out of men's need to make the least wasteful and most authentic or, as we say, the most scientific use of their ideas, political skill and historical resources. To some, history consists essentially in seeing the past through the eyes of the present and in the light of events and their problems. The main work of the historian is not to record, but to evaluate the day-to-day events in their historical perspective. It is rightly said that the past which a historian studies is not a dead past, but a past which in some sense is still living in the present. One can view the past, and achieve his understanding of the past, only through the eyes of the present. The predicament of the historian is a reflection of the nature—of man, events, facts, situations and circumstances. The relation of man to his environment is the relation of the historian to his theme of history. The historian and the facts of history are related to one another. The historian without the description of facts is rootless and futile. So also, the facts without their historian are meaningless. Hence in E.H. Carr's view, history is a continuous process of interaction between the historian and his facts, an unending dialogue between the present and the past.

This book by our young and brilliant scholar, Dr. Jagdish P. Sharma represents an important stage in the process of writing and reshaping the world history to enable it to meet the challenges of the historical future. The analysis and varied observations presented in this book make a valuable contribution to the understanding of world history. He has taken pains and devoted considerable time to piece together the important materials to write this book which would be helpful for, not only the students of world history but also for the general readers including the aspirants of civil services. It is a scholarly work.

AMBA PRASAD
Professor of History (Retd.)
University of Delhi

New Delhi

Preface

This book was conceived at a time when a series of changes were taking place around the world starting since the *Intifedah*, i.e. non-violent liberation struggle of the oppressed Arab-Palestinian people to the changes in Russia. To passionate observers, whose duty or interest it was to make a close study of upheavals in global atmosphere, the existence of a connection between different historical happenings had been apparent for a number of centuries. The great Reformation movement preceded by the Renaissance spirit along with the great geographical discoveries of the fifteenth and sixteenth centuries created or revived a sense of individual liberty. This helped to promote the growth of national consciousness, knowledge and awakening spirit. This in turn led to revolution in socio-politico economic, scientific, cultural, religious and diplomatic sphere.

The inspiration for writing this book has come from the sacrifices made by great reformers, revolutionaries and nationalists in the different stages of international history. The intention of this book is to develop to its logical conclusion a particular interaction between the different forces and happenings in history since the medieval times. It provides a useful overview of global history since the inception of Islam, Christianity, Renaissance, Reformation to the historical changes in inter-world war period and post-world war scenario.

I felt there is a need for a comprehensive and analytic elaboration of historical developments. This book is an attempt to simplify the same so that the student of world history can find his/her way around the subject without getting lost in the details.

Though the book should be considered as a whole, individual chapters are nevertheless self-contained. I have been greatly inspired in the study which led to this book by those who contributed to my historical bent of mind. I should like particularly to thank Prof. Amba Prasad (Delhi University), Dr. Attar Chand (Delhi University), Prof. Hiralal Gupta (Sagar University), Prof. Ram Rahul Sheel (Jawaharlal Nehru University), Prof. K.R. Singh (JNU), His Excellency Dr. Khalid el-Sheikh, Ambassador of the State of Palestine to India, Mr. Giridhari Gomango, Minister of State for Food Processing, Government of India, Prof. H.C. Verma (DU) Prof. A. Subbian (Annamalai University), Dr. M.L. Bhatia (DU), Prof. R.L. Shukla (DU), Prof. D.N. Jha (DU), Prof. B.P. Sahu (DU), Prof. A.H.H. Abidi (JNU), Prof. Muhammad Sadiq (JNU), Dr. Mohsin Usmani (JNU), Dr. Gulsan Dvetl (JNU), Dr. Girijesh Pant (JNU), Prof. Aparna Basu (DU), Dr. Suhas Chakravarty (DU), Dr. Mehmood Hussain (JNU), Dr. Dharmpal (DU), Prof. K.S. Behera (Utkal University), Dr. B.M. Das (Berhampur University), Prof. S.R. Sharma (Gwalior University), Dr. K.L. Tuteja (Kurukshetra University), Prof. Prasanna K. Mohanty (JNU), Dr. Harjinder Singh (DU), Mrs. Suraksha Kaushik (N.C. Jindal Public School), Mrs. Subhra Dey (DU) Dr. K.B. Panda (DU), Mr. Sujit K. Mohanty, Mr. R.S. Sabat, Mr. Mukul Kumar, Mr. Sanjay Pathak, Mr. S.N. Pattnaik and Miss Renu Uppal.

The staff of the Library of the Indian Council of World Affairs, particularly Mr. Shyam Singh and the Institute of Defence Studies and Strategic Analyses, the staff of Nehru Memorial Museum and Library, and Mr. B.R. Ajmani, have been cordial with me in spite of their day-to-day difficulties.

I am also thankful to several authors and scholars from whose books and articles I have heavily drawn opinions and interpretations to analyse and clarify my point of view on major issues involved in my studies.

In a work such as this the task of selection is necessarily difficult. I, therefore, ask the pardon of those readers whom I may, inadvertently, have offended by not including, or by passing over lightly, events which are of special interest to them.

Hence it is my duty to point out that I am alone responsible for its contents.

New Delhi
1993

Jagdish P. Sharma

Contents

1

World History : An Outline

Meaning

History as commonly used is the story of mankind in all its aspects. It has so often been misdescribed, as a story of successive events or an account of change. Unlike the natural scientist, the historian is not concerned with events as such at all. He is only concerned with those events which are the outward expression of thoughts, and is only concerned with these so far as they express thoughts. In a sense these thoughts are no doubt in themselves events happening in time. But the only way in which the historian can discern them is by rethinking them for himself. Therefore the historical knowledge is the knowledge of what mind has done in the past. At the same time, it is the redoing of this i.e. the perpetuation of past acts in the present. Its object is therefore not a mere object, something outside the mind which knows it. It is an activity of thought, which can be known only in so far as the knowing mind re-enacts it and knows itself as so doing. To the historian, the activities whose history he is studying are not spectacles to be watched, but experiences to be lived through in his own mind. The reconstruction of the past in the historian's mind is dependent on empirical evidence. But it is not in itself an empirical process. It cannot consist in mere recitor of facts. On the contrary, the process of reconstitution governs the selection and interpretation of the facts. This, indeed, is what makes them historical facts.

The philosophy of history is concerned neither with 'the past by itself' nor with 'the historian's thought about it by itself', but with the two things in their mutual relations'. History in general, connotes the entire human past as it actually happened. Besides, it also connotes man's attempt to describe and interpret that past. It is, in the words of Professor Barraclough, the attempt to discover on the basis of fragmentary evidence the significant things about the past. History is also concerned with change. Historian is primarily interested in the changing political, social, economic, artistic, philosophical, religious, scientific and diplomatic aspects of life. Nehru approached history in its abstract sense of past and then invested it with flesh and blood. To Nehru, it is historian who, through the process of selection, analysis and interpretation of facts, recreate the experience of the past generations. This is differently stated by E.H. Carr thus: "History can not be written unless the historian can achieve some kind of contact with the mind of those about whom he is writing". Thus history explains the evolution of man and the origin and progress of modern civilisation and culture. History is the study of man and his activities in all provinces of life in the past. It gives us an explanation of why, when and how our civilisation and culture originated and progressed from stage to stage till this day. It is thus the study of human societies, with the emphasis on the differences between them and on the change which have taken place in each one over time. It sketches as complete a picture as possible of everything that has influenced humanity directly or indirectly. Objectivity is the very soul of history.

Culture and Civilisation

History is the study of the origin and progress of the modern 'civilisation' and 'culture'. The word 'culture' is derived from the Latin word 'cultura' which means to cultivate mind. It is, therefore, "that refinement of the mind and intelligence", through which a person is able to appreciate all that is good, beautiful and true in life. It is the sum total of the values expressed through art, religion, literature, social institutions and mass action inspired by collective urge. 'Civilisation', on the other hand, is derived from the Latin word 'civilis' which means that which relates to city life. It implies the materialistic aspect of life. It stands for the material progress of human society from the most primitive to the modern times. It refers to the material, scientific and technological advancement which has made our life easy, convenient, comfortable, and luxurious.

In order to lead a better, secure, and comfortable life, men tried to understand and conquer the forces of nature and thus made numerous inventions and discoveries. This progress has continued through the ages and continues even today. Bettrand Russell, an eminent British philosopher, rightly observes: "Civilisation is the progress and predominance of science". It is this progress of man since his first appearance on earth which is the subject matter of history.

Value of the Study of World History

History is a store-house of wisdom. Hence, its study throws considerable light on the present and makes man wise, capable of foreseeing the future. The study of history enables the reader to understand the various factors responsible for the rise and fall of governments, nations, and empires. These factors are co-related, on the scientific principles of cause and effect.

Another valuable lesson of the study of world history is that failures are the pillars of success. The study of world history teaches us that the success or salvation of man depends upon his continuous and consistent toil to reach his goal, in spite of numerous difficulties, discouragements, frustrations and failures. The history of mankind is full of examples of such men, who reached their goal in the face of untold difficulties and frustrations. Columbus discovered the New World in spite of the great opposition and revolt of the crew of his vessel. Jesus ended his life on the cross and Gandhi braved the assassin's bullet without faltering in the pursuit of path of righteousness.

Our modern civilisation is the result of the spirit of inquiry and the passion for progress which made the ancient Greeks the pioneers of science. "It was this sense of wonder, this insatiable curiosity" which made the ancient Greeks study the earth and other planets and formed the basic principles of science and philosophy.

Superstition, conservatism and ignorance are the enemies of a nation's growth. A nation must be ever ready to welcome the "voice of reason and the light of truth", and to accept new ideas and ideals of the changing society. Whenever a country refuses to pay heed to the "voice of reason and the light of truth", it retrogresses and its civilisation may become static.

Whenever an individual, race, community or a nation is guided purely by self-interest, disregarding the interest of others, it digs its own grave and simultaneously causes much suffering to others. To take an example, had the native Rajputs not fought with each other and instead, had they presented a united front to the foreign invaders such as the Afghans, the Turks, Mughals, and the British, the history of India would have taken a different course altogether.

Whenever seeds of provincialism, communalism, linguism, terrorism and separatism are sown into the soil of a country, it, one day or the other, is bound to be torn to pieces. Its national unity is bound to receive a rude shock and suffer an irreparable loss. The division of Hindustan into India and Pakistan was the high price paid by us for our failure to bring about Hindu-Muslim unity. So long as we have not been able to uproot the deep-rooted provincial, communal, linguistic, religious, separatist and parochial elements from the soil of India, our national unity and national security are always open to grave danger.

World history is full of examples to teach a great lesson that no country in the world can indefinitely subject the people of other countries to its rule and thus to exploit them technologically, economically, and politically. The great ancient Roman empire, the empire of Alexander the Great, the conquests of Napoleon Bonaparte, and the colonial empires of the English, the Dutch and the French — all of them were torn to pieces, on the ruins of which came into being numerous independent nation-states. The growth of internationalism among the people as well as the nations of the world is the 'immediate need of the hour' in order to save mankind from the horrors that has flowed from the misuse of science and technology.

2

The Medieval Age

The expression "Medieval Age" stands for that period of Western European history which begins with the fall and break-up of the Roman Empire in the fifth century (476) and ends at the beginning of the Renaissance and the Reformation in the fifteenth century.

This period witnessed the full fusion of disparate historical and ideological strains. Precisely by virtue of this, a number of features came about which not only reflected the complexion of the age itself, but also, and perhaps more important laid the foundations of developments from sixteenth century onwards. Though the character of the age was certainly more static, there were nevertheless far more changes than is commonly assumed, both in the structure of the society and in the ideas which sustained it.

The Medieval Age can be divided into two periods: The Early Medieval Age and the Late Medieval Age. The period from the fall and break-up of the Roman Empire in the fifth century (476 A.D.) to about 1000 A.D. was known as the Early Medieval Age. This period was marked by invasions, robbery, violence and frequent wars and plunders. The barbarians swept into the Roman Empire for riches. The whole of Europe was sunk in chaos and anarchy. The beautiful and wonderful pieces of arts of all sorts and literature and all important works of science were either lost or destroyed and ruined. In brief, the whole of the Roman and Greek civilisation was swept away by the barbarians and the cultural change was in the direction of downward instead of upward.

The period running through the beginning of the eleventh century to the beginning of the Renaissance and Reformation in the fifteenth century was known as the Late Medieval Age in the history of Western Europe. During this period, life became more colourful. "Education changed and developed, towns grew, beautiful churches and castles were built, trade increased, nations developed and parliaments came into existence."

Europe during this time was no longer a mere geographical term but overwhelmingly an ideological notion. The unity of the Christian faith was largely responsible for bridging biological, linguistic and racial differences and for the emergence of a European Commonwealth from the Orkney islands to Sicily, from Sweden, the Prussian and Polish marshes to Castile and Aragon in the Iberian Peninsula. The inner core of this European community was religious and ideological and its structural organisation overwhelmingly ecclesiastical. Hence, this same period witnessed the split with Constantinople, because its religious and ideological principles did not accord with those of the West.

With this period there was progress in virtually all spheres of human, social and economic life. New techniques were acquired both in agriculture and domestic industry and in the production of the necessary implements. Missionary activity was given a new impetus with the missions penetrating as far as Central Asia. New lands were opened up by the new methods of cultivation. An orderly banking system emerged. Besides this, intellectual advances made great strides during this age. It was the time when some monastic schools reached their peak and when the universities came into being. Greek, Arabic and Hebrew were included in university studies as well as medicine and other related subjects.

This was also the age in which a great many heretical sects flourished. Means were devised to combat them, partly by persuasion and partly by the repressive measures. Throughout this age (thirteenth century onwards) there were symptoms that the traditional order of things no longer satisfied contemporaries. Moreover, this was a period of broadening of human perception, knowledge and inquiry which contributed to the veritable intellectual revolution. Man was shown to be capable not only of conquering nature but also of managing and manipulating his own affairs in public, that is of governing himself and through appropriate representative organs that is State. This age by making man's humanity a central topic of study gave rise to naturalism and humanism in all their facets, in scholarship, the arts, poetry, in vernacular products and so on.

Contributions of the Arabs

Arabia was the cradle of Islam and of Arab literature, culture and civilisation. In the 6th century A.D., it was a region with some sedentary agricultural and commercial life centered in Yemen and on the borders of Syria and Iraq, but the interior was the domain of camel-raising Bedouin nomads. The Bedouins were animists and polytheists in religious belief. They lived in small clans and recognised no authority outside the patriarchal leadership of the clan Sheikh. The name Arab was first used widely about the end of the 6th century, although it was known much earlier in 853 B.C. King Shalmanasar III had defeated a coalition of peoples, one of whom was led by Jindibu the Arab. The Arabs as mentioned were the nomadic, camel-owning tribes famous for their love of poetry and war. Arabia is a peninsula linked with both Africa and Asia. The Arabs were also essentially a commercial people. Further, the Arabs picked up different elements of culture from different pre-existing cultures. They borrowed something from the Greek, something from the Persian, something from the Roman, something from the Jewish, and something from the Indian cultures.

The Caliph, the successor of Mohammed, was both a secular ruler and a religious potentate. To question his authority amounted to questioning the authority of Allah. In the eighth century, several independent Caliphates were established at Gordova in Spain, at Cairo in Egypt, and at Baghdad in Asia Minor. These Caliphs ruled like oriental despots without any constitutions. A Caliph had three-fold functions: (i) To protect the Islamic faith; (ii) To promote and spread Islam even with the help of sword if need be; and (iii) To look after the welfare of his people.

The Arabs were essentially a commercial people, perhaps by instinct. Even their Prophet, Mohammed, was a caravan merchant. Through trade and commerce, the Arabs connected the three continents of Africa, Asia, and Europe, and the Arabic language became the language of commerce. Trade and commercial contacts were established through couriers. They were skilled industrialists. They were world-renowned for their manufactured products such as armour, steel weapons, glassware, rose water, leather goods, textiles, porcelain, textile fabrics, carpets, cushions, muslin, furniture, paper, pottery, etc. Baghdad, Bokhara and Samarkand were the leading centres of trade in their time. The Arabs soon became very wealthy and established universities in Baghdad, Cairo and Cordova. These universities earned such a reputation in the world that even some rich Christians sent their sons there for education. The Arabs also made substantial contributions in the field of literature. The literature was developed in three directions:

(i) Prose, (ii) Poetry, and (iii) Language. In prose literature, "The Arabian Nights" is a wonderful creation with which practically everybody is familiar. It is a fine source of entertainment. It is rich in proverbs, adventures, and fables, and is meant for people of all ages.

Poetry was a lovable and common form of literary expression. The Arabs loved poetry. The themes of their ballads were love and war. Among the world-renowned literary works of poetry of the Arabs are: "The Rubaiyat," composed by Omar Khayyam in the 12th century. "The Gulistan and the Bustan" (the mythical and philosophical odes) composed by Saadi in the late thirteenth century. In order to develop the Arab language scientifically, the Arabs produced works of dictionaries, grammars, and books on philosophy. They made great contributions in the field of science too. Different branches of science were taught in the Muslim Universities. Much progress was registered in medical science. Major operations were performed by the Muslim surgeons. Even insanity was scientifically treated. Besides, the Arab scientists made several discoveries in the fields of chemistry and physics such as nitrate of silver, nitric acid, sulphuric acid, potash, alcohol, and the principle of pendulum. They earned a great name in the field of mathematics. The Arabs are believed to be the founders of the Arabian numerals, 1, 2, 3, 4, 5, 6, 7, 8, 9, 10, etc. including Zero (0). These are much earlier than the Roman numerals. The Arabian mathematicians, however, borrowed this system of numerals, including zero from India. Further, they developed Algebra to second-degree equations. They also made great progress in the field of trigonometry.

The Arabs showed their artistic skill only in minor arts such as metal works, glass lamps, and decoration of manuscripts of Koran. These manuscripts were frequently written in a number of colours such as gold, blue, red, white, black and green, etc. Further, they produced wonderful works of embroidery on cottons, silks and satins. These were woven along with damasks in beautiful patterns and designs which found a ready market in the West. In architecture, the Arabian architects failed to produce anything new worth its name. Their chief works of architecture consisted of mosques and palaces of the Caliphs. They were marked by ornamentation with stained coloured glass, marble, glazed tiles, the free use of colours, and painting on the carved wood works. The greatest contribution of the Arabs is in the field of religion. Their Prophet, Mohammed, gave to the world a new religion known as Islam.

The Arabian civilisation was, thus a composite one. It continued, to some extent, the work of the pre-existing civilisations and passed it on to the West which served as "a part of the foundation of the renaissance".

Charlemagne

The period between the fall of Rome and the coronation of Charlemagne in A.D. 800, which was also the Golden age of Islam, is commonly called as the dark age of European history.

Among all the Germanic tribes who came into the Roman empire, the Franks were the most progressive tribesmen. Their leader, Clovis (565-511), brought the whole of Gaul or what is today called France, Belgium, the Netherlands and much of Western Germany under his control. As he was converted to Christianity in A.D. 506, it became the state religion of France. The successors of Clovis were weak-willed and were busy in a series of family conflicts which gravely weakened the crown.

Peppin the Short (A.D. 751-768), the last king of Merovingian dynasty, founded the Carolingian dynasty by establishing himself as the first king from that dynasty. In appreciation of the blessings of the Pope, Peppin gifted away some territory in Italy to

Pope over which he ruled as his own private property. Peppin conferred the Donation of Quierzy in A.D. 756 on the Pope as the legitimate representative of Imperial Power. This expedient resulted in the founding of Papal States, independent of any temporal power, upon which great papal ambitions were later based. These territories came to be known as papal states, and remained under the Pope from A.D. 756 to 1870.

The Franks regarded their king as the representative of God on earth and it became their political and religious duty to obey their king with a religious spirit which gave rise to the theory of Divine origin of kingship. Peppin the Short was king from 751 to 768. He was succeeded by his son Charles the Great in the year 768. Charles was perhaps the greatest, the wisest and the best ruler in the whole of Western Europe during the entire period of the early Middle Age. His great political ideal was to weld all the German people together into a "Christian Empire". Charles was a great warrior. He is said to have personally conducted as many as 26 campaigns during the course of first 30 years of his reign. In 773, when the Pope was harassed by the Romans, Charles, immediately, rushed to his help in Rome, divested the Romans and annexed their territory. A part of that territory, however, he gifted to the Pope. In 778, he attacked the Muslims in Spain and drove them away beyond Barcelona. Then he marched against the Avars and Bavarians in the east, conquered them, and annexed their territories to his empire. His empire extended from the North Sea to the central part of Italy and from the Atlantic Ocean to the Elbe River.

Throughout his life, Charles allied himself very closely with the Pope. He always acted as the Defender of the Pope and a fanatic of Roman Christianity in the western world. Like the Muslims, he made use of his shining sword for the purpose of propagating and spreading Christianity throughout his empire. As a reward for this, as Charles knelt in worship at the altar in St. Peter's Church at Rome, the Pope, Leo II, surprised Charles by placing a crown on his head on the Christmas Day, A.D. 800. The audience promptly and spontaneously hailed Charles as Emperor of the Holy Roman Empire. The crowd shouted, 'God bless and save Carolus Augustus, Crowned of God, the great', the peace bringing Emperor of the Roman's, and the Pope then fell at his feet to pay homage to him in the same manner as the bishops of Rome had formerly done to the Roman emperors at Constantinople.

Charles was perhaps the most brilliant, energetic and wise administrator and lawgiver in the Medieval Age. It was impossible for one single individual to govern such a vast empire, especially because of an acute shortage of coined money on account of a very few resources of gold and silver. He, therefore, granted great tracts, of land to those warriors who aided him in his military campaigns from time to time. They were to rule their respective tracts of land. These tracts were called counties, duchies and marches and their rulers were known as Counts, Dukes, and Marquises respectively. These were the germs of feudalism in Medieval Europe. Charles was a great law-maker. He used to summon assemblies of the Counts, Dukes and Marquises of his whole empire, sometimes in summer or spring.

The proposals for legislation, as formulated and submitted by Charles to the assembly, were called "Capitulas" or chapters of legislation. The Assembly always voiced its approval with one shouting; rarely it disapproved a capitula with a "collective grunt or moan". These Capitulas were framed purely on the principles of Christianity and the German tradition.

It was always the duty of the provincial bishops and administrators to report in this august assembly to the king any significant event that happened in his locality since the previous convocation.

Missi Dominici were the "emissaries of the master", sent by Charles to the Counties, Duchies, and Marches for the purpose of conveying his wishes to the local officials, reviewing their actions, judgments and accounts, checking bribery, extortion, nepotism and exploitation, receiving complaints and remedying wrongs, and protecting "the church, the poor and wards".

It is a matter of great surprise that Charles, although himself completely unlettered, was appalled by the illiteracy of his time. His first concern was to improve the standard of education among the clergy, many of whom were very ignorant. Hardly and ecclesiastics could read and write. He, therefore, invited foreign scholars to establish schools in France. In his own palace, he started a school, which "set a new standard of culture", under a very learned teacher, named Alcuin, a Yorkish Englishman. Besides Alcuin, Peter of Pisa, the grammarian, and Paul the deacon, the historian of the Lombards, were from Italy, while Theodulf the visigoth, the best writer of Latin verse of the day, was from Spain. Lectures, discussions on all sorts of subjects or riddles in verse became the fashion at his court. Charles himself delighted in theological discussion and his favourite book was St. Augustine's *City of God*.

Charles, soon, became known as "the Great". The Latin expression for Charles the Great was "Charlemagne".

Charles certainly deserved the title of "the Great" on all accounts. (i) After the fall and break-up of the Roman Empire, Charles, the first great empire-builder who, with his incessant military campaigns and dogged perseverance, successfully built a vast empire, the so-called Holy Roman Empire. In the second place, he halted the forces of disruption, anarchy and illiteracy and restored cohesion, law, order and literacy. In the third place, Charles was personally responsible for "a remarkable revival of intellectual activity". He proved himself a great and wise administrator. Like every great man, Charles valued time. According to Dr. Will Durant, "He gave audiences and heard cases in the morning while dressing and putting on his shoes". After the death of Charlemagne in 814 A.D., his vast empire was partitioned by his descendants. His system of government collapsed, its unity vanished and its prosperity declined. This decay of Charlemagne's empire exposed Western Europe to attacks from fresh invaders — the Arabs in the South, the Magyars or Hungarians in the east and the Scandinavians in the north.

3

Feudalism

Feudalism was the way of life in western Europe during the Middle ages. It controlled the politics, the financial affairs, the government, and the society of the times. The feudal form of society began to appear in western Europe about the middle of the 800's. It reached its height in the early 12th and 13th centuries, and had almost vanished at the end of the 15th century. The word *feudal* comes from the Latin word *feudum,* which means a landed estate or group of estates held by a person in return for military services to the recognised owner of the land. Feudalism was the system by which the nobles of the Middle ages kept the ownership and control of their lands. Feudalism had its roots in early German (Frankish) and Roman Institutions. The German *Comitatus* was a band of warriors who freely followed a chieftain in return for food, arms, and share of whatever booty might be won. The Roman Precarium was a temporary grant of land made by an owner to a tenant in return for service. Land granted in this way was later called a *fief.* The Lords also repaid the men who furnished these services by granting fiefs. A ceremony called *homage* established the feudal relationship between the Lord and men, i.e. between the Lord and the Vassal. The Vassal pledged himself to be faithful to his Lord in every way. The Lord pledged himself to support the Vassal with some of the goods produced on his land, and to provide for his protection in times of trouble.

In the late Medieval Age, when feudalism reigned supreme, society was divided into four social classes: (1) Barons or Lords, (2) Freemen, (3) Serfs, and (4) Slaves. The king was above the Lords or Barons. At the top of the social hierarchy were the Barons in the feudal Europe and the Lords in England. A Lord or a Baron had three-fold functions: to protect his lands and their inhabitants with the help of the armed forces; to supervise, direct and organise agriculture, industry, trade and commerce on these lands; and to render military aid to the King in time of war. He enjoyed enormous powers, perhaps, much more than those of the king. He was all-powerful with regard to his domains. He enjoyed legislative, executive, judicial and even military powers over his domains which were as good as his personal estates. The Lords had their own police force, armed forces, courts, and also minted their own coinage. For all practical purposes, they were sovereign in their respective feudatory domains.

Below the Barons and Lords in rank were the Freemen. They were nobles, professional soldiers, merchants, traders, businessmen, artisans and some peasants who owned their land without or with little obligations to any feudal Lord or Baron.

The serfs were more unfortunate than the Sudras in India. They were treated as chattel (movable possession). A serf cultivated a piece of land, owned by his Lord or Baron who granted him life tenure and afforded military protection to him. In return, a serf had numerous and divergent obligations towards his Lord. The Lord was virtually the master of the body and mind of his serf. The serf had to pay to his Lord an annual rent in products, labour and money if possible. He had to serve in the Lord's regiment in war. He could not send his child to school or church, for the Lord would lose a hand.

The slave trade was brisk, especially in Italy. The Muslims and Greeks were kidnapped and auctioned as slaves. They served as workers on the farm, domestic servants, prostitutes or concubines. However, slavery diminished as serfdom progressed.

Feudalism was practised in Europe in the most ceremonious manner. There were the elements or aspects of feudalism, namely, the land element and the personal element. Lord played the most significant role in developing and establishing the feudal relationship: (i) between Vassal or Serf and Lord, (ii) between Lord and Superior Lord, and (iii) between Superior Lord and the King. As it was impossible for a small land holder to protect himself and also his landed property, he surrendered it to a Lord and received it back from him for the purpose of cultivating it as a tenant at will.

The feudal system was developed on the basis of the land element but it functioned mainly on the personal element. Certain oaths of allegiance were taken by both the vassal and his Lord binding each other. First, the ceremony of Homage was performed in which the vassal declared, on both his knees before his Lord. "Sir, I enter your homage and faith and become your man by mouth and hands, and I swear and promise to keep faith with you against all others and to guard your rights with all my strength." This was followed by another ceremony called the "Investiture" in which the Lord handed over a fief to his vassal and promised to protect him and his property.

Further, the big landlords, called the "Superior Lords", frequently granted small portions of their holdings to lesser nobles, called the "Lords" on the same pattern and made the feudal system more intricate.

The Status of King

Theoretically, the king was sovereign in the feudal system, but in reality, "he stood an inch or two above the princes, dukes, marquises, and counts, and in practice, solely dependent in war and peace upon the military aid or diplomatic service of rich vassals... he was merely a great landlord.

The church became not only a religious but also social, economic, political and military institution. To ease tension and prevent loss of life and property caused by the frequent wars among the Lords, the church made an earnest appeal, through what came to be called the "Peace of God", against constant warfare.

The economic basis of Feudalism was the *manor*. In its simplest form this consisted of one village with one Lord, though a Lord often possessed a number of manors. Part of the manorial estate was reserved for the Lord and a small part of the rest was farmed by freeholders paying him rent. While the remainder was farmed by serfs, who formed most of the villagers. In return for their land, the serfs had to work two or three days weekly on the Lord's land with extra days at seed-time and harvest, besides providing him with fowls, eggs, pigs and other produce. However the serfs suffered the most during this time. Since the average manor had from 900 to 3,000 acres to be farmed by perhaps two dozen families, their toil was incessant. They had to suffer dangers and trials. The huntsmen ruined their poor crops, wild beasts killed their animals and even attacked their houses. Besides, serfs were 'bound to the soil', which meant that they could not leave the manor without their Lord's permission. Moreover, some took to the forests, which surrounded the villages and joined the bands of brigands and outlaws hiding there.

On the life scene, there was little trade and no large-scale manufacturing in feudal times. Almost all necessities were found in a feudal village. The largest house in the village belonged to the feudal Lord. It contained a hall large enough for all the freemen of the village. Here the Lord and the freemen would settle quarrels between neighbours and kinsmen. The revival of trade and commerce in the early part of 13th century took away some of the importance of the feudal landholding system and marked the beginning of its decline. The trading classes had wealth in cash to pay into national treasuries, and rulers were able to hire and assert their authority. Later, the development of strong, centralised governments further weakened the feudal system. Moreover, the *Crusades* weakened it even further. Many feudal Lords killed and their estates passed to the kings. But some feudal customs persisted for hundreds of years.

Estimate of Feudalism

Although not a perfect system, feudalism served the need of the time. "It was the best form of society possible in its time and place." It assured protection against general anarchy and confusion of the time. To a certain extent, it lessened if not removed, the constant danger of fresh barbarian invasions. Although it went against national unity, it did restrain the king from acting cruelly and arbitrarily. Slavery diminished and finally disappeared solely because of feudalism, for it recognised every person fit to enter into a contract. Chivalry, the flower of feudalism, functioned well "as a military, measure to organise local defence," writes Prof. A. F. Hattersley," economically to safeguard cultivation of the soil, and politically to provide machinery for local administration of justice."

Demerits of Feudalism

It was neither a well-organised society nor a well-established system. It was characterised by confusion and conflict in all provinces of life. The position of king was extremely weak and shaky, for he solely depended on the military aid of his wealthy Lords or Barons both in peace and in war. The condition of the common man, especially of the vassal or serf, was extremely poor, wretched, lamentable and miserable, for he was, in reality, solely dependent upon the 'whim and caprice' of his Lord, who was often cruel and immoral. The serf was often the victim of 'bad seasons, floods and epidemic diseases. It certainly delayed the emergence of national unity and consequent strong central government for a pretty long time. It gave rise to the privileged class of the nobles, lords, and barons who were all powerful and makers of the destiny of their serfs. It resulted in a tug of war between the State and the Church in the whole of Europe. The worst of all was the frequent private warfare amongst the nobles, lords, and barons, encouraged by feudalism. Finally, feudalism hampered all-round progress of an individual and the society.

The feudal system, being inherently weak and afflicted with numerous incurable maladies, was bound to decay and disappear soon. The advent of nationalistic and democratic forces, the unpopularity, impoverishment, and death of many feudal lords and barons, and the consequent rise of a powerful middle-class, which clamoured for the establishment of monarchy; the rise of money economy and the growth of towns—all these and other factors dealt a death-blow to feudalism.

4

Islam Through the Ages

As the decades of the seventies and eighties opened, the world witnessed one of the fastest socio-economic, politico-religious transformations in West Asian history. as it happened, the rise of radical, and not infrequently violent, vanguards of Islamic Values spread to several countries within the Islamic *Umma*. In its varied manifestations, the violent outbursts of adherents to radical Islam have constituted a challenge to the respective governments and state forms.

Ever since the popular uprising that led to the installation of an Islamic Republic in Iran, Popular Islam has tended to be exploited for launching offensive against Western oriented and other corrupt governments in the region. The legendary hostage crisis in Iran, the seizure of the grand mosque in Mecca, followed by the massacre of Iranian pilgrims there, the Iran-Iraq War, the assassination of President Anwar Sadat of Egypt by members of Islamic Jihad organisation, the radical Islamic threat to the Egyptian state, the civil wars in Lebanon and Afghanistan, the row over Salman Rushdie's book titled *The Satanic Verses* and the active Islamic challenge to the Algerian State were manifestations of the offensive by these rabidly assertive faithfuls to defend the faith. The enduring challenges posed by these developments necessitate the review of Islam as a religion, as a socio-politico movement and a way of life.

Origins of Islam as a Religion

The religion of Islam, which was given to the Arabs by Mohammad, the Prophet about thirteen centuries ago, is the religion of many countries at the present times. Millions of people live and die by it. The followers of this religion are called Muslims and their scripture is, the Quran (Koran). In order to understand it, an account of the circumstances and life of its Prophet is essential.

Circumstances

The later part of fifth and early sixth centuries of Christian era witnessed the decadence of ancient cultures and civilisations. But in the following century, the course of the socio-cultural history was suddenly changed by an unexpected people. The man who accomplished this change - the swiftest and most far-reaching in the whole history of the world (and within one generation) - gave the world a new religion, a new social system and laid the foundations of a new civilisation, was *Prophet Mohammad*.

Early Life of Mohammad

Little is known of the origin and youth of Mohammad. He was born about 20th of April, 570 or 571 A.D. at Mecca. He was the son of Abdullah, of the family of Hashim, and of Amina, of the family of Zuhra, both belonged to the powerful tribe of Quraish. His father died shortly after, and he lost his mother when he was still a child (about six years old). His relatives, particularly his uncle Abdul Muttalib, brought him up with loving care and affection.

During his youth he accompanied his relative with merchandise caravans to Syria. When twenty-five years old, he was employed by a rich widow named *Khadija,* to accompany her trading caravans to the fairs in Syria. He conducted Khadija's business with great success and later married her. He was fifteen years junior and she bore him two sons and four daughters (both his sons died young). Throughout his life, Mohammad devoted himself to meditation and kept himself singularly pure in a society where purity meant nothing.

The Social Evils

Contemporary Arab society was full of idolatry, corruption, day light murder, theft, adultery, unlimited polygamy, cruelty to women, oppression of the poor, usury, drunkenness, lying, superstition, infanticide, blood-feud, chaos and anarchy. Hence Mohammad looked with horror at the day-to-day happenings of the contemporary society and sought the solitude of the cave of Mount *Hira* (or Jabal Nur), near Mecca to devote himself to meditation and prayer. Then in A.D. 611, the Revelation of God, i.e. Allah suddenly came to Mohammad, imparted to him by Jibra'il (the archangel Gabriel). He and his wife Khadija were now convinced that he was the Prophet of Allah, and he began preaching a new knowledge, *Islam,* that is absolute surrender to Allah.

For three years the Prophet preached the new Faith secretly. He won some adherents in his own family. Amongst them were his friends *Abu Bakr* and *Omar,* his slave, *Zayd,* his daughter *Fatima,* his sons-in-law *Uthman* and *Ali* and also his uncle *Hamza.* His vigorous attacks on idolatry and his criticism of the power-position of the leading merchants caused ill feeling and his actions were outrightly condemned. Mohammad experienced set-back after set-back. His wife's death was followed by the demise of his uncle Abdul Muttalib. Meanwhile oppression at Mecca became intolerable and Mohammad had to emigrate to Medina (known as Hijra) on June 6, A.D. 622. This particular date forms the starting point of the Islamic era.

Hijrabat

On September 20, A.D. 622, the Prophet was received with respect and honour at Medina. This marked the beginning of the continuous external development of Islam as a new independent religion as well as a socio-political movement. Shortly afterwards, Islam began its triumphant march across the Arabian Peninsula and a large part of the world. This event (that is Hijri), the first historically dated and supremely important event, marked the beginning of the Islamic calendar.

Mohammad organised the new community of Muslims at Medina through his new religious revelations. The superhuman nature of his revelation established his authority as Prophet in Medina. Thus he consolidated his authority at Medina and concentrated on the second aim, the conquest of Mecca or centre of the new religion. After sometime, he and his followers succeeded in gaining a brilliant victory over the Meccans in the famous battle of *Badr* (about A.D. 630). Hence *Mecca* became the religious capital of the new religion and *Medina* remained the political capital.

Two years later, that is 8th June A.D. 632, when Mohammad, the messenger of *Allah,* died, almost the whole of the Arabian Peninsula had embraced Islam. Owing to insufficient research into the historical sources and the numerous traits and stories imputed to him in later times, it is difficult to obtain an accurate impression of the personal stature of the Prophet. Whatever there may be, his personality has remained central to Islam that is the creed which professed first the oneness of Allah and said that Mohammad is "the messenger of God". He is the most common proper name in the Muslim world today. His tomb in the great mosque of Medina is one of the most important places of pilgrimage to his believers. The influence of his teaching remains undiminished till this present day.

The Quran (Koran): The Holy Book of Islam

All that which Allah revealed to Prophet Mohammad is written down in the Holy scripture of Islam, the *Quran.* It is the fountainhead of all Islamic teachings and the basis of universal Muslim community. It is definite codification of the revelations of Mohammad, compiled and recorded from written annotation - on stone tablets, camels' bodies, on leather, parchment, papyrus and from oral sources, about 650 A.D. The revelations in the Quran vary in style and content.

The highest aim of Islam is the unity and realisation of *perfect oneness.* The Quran plays an important role in guiding the socio-politico-economic, cultural, national and international life of the Muslim people. It is written in rhythmic prose and the Arabic text, which is actually untranslatable, is considered authoritative.

Spiritual Teachings

The meaning of the Arabic term 'Islam' is "submission", "resignation" or "complete surrender to Allah", i.e. the highest state of "being" absolutely free from all attributes and opposites. Muslim, this very term is derived from the same root term and means "he who practises Islam".

Like the Bible, the Quran contains no systematic synopsis of the Islamic doctrine. The whole mansion of this religion is built upon the infallible doctrine of *Tawhid* or the Blessed oneness (mentioned above). The following are the different stages of arriving at this happy end: (a) believing in onesss, (b) seeking oneness, (c) knowing oneness, and (d) realising oneness.

Wealth, which has all along been regarded as a possession and an achievement, becomes the measure of charity and is freely spent in the service of humanity. The realisation of oneness as an action, attribute, faith and knowledge is based on the *Five Pillars of Islam.* They are: Belief in the *unity of God* and the acknowledgement of Mohammad and his predecessors as the inspired messengers of God, *prayer,* which begins "in communion" with God, *charity,* the evidence of one's having gained the desired object through the harmonised and successful soul, *pilgrimage* to Mecca and Medina to withdraw one from the busy materialistic life for a short time and to teach one the practical lessons of unity and universal brotherhood and *fasting* to administer the body under certain restraints of eating, drinking, and talking etc. The five pillars of Islam specified above, on which the whole mansion of Islam rests, make a man faithful, prayerful, charitable, altruistic and moderate. As per Quran life in this world must be regarded as preparatory to life beyond the grave.

Life in Islam

Based on the above points, life in Islam is divided into the following three sections: (a) to acquire and share with others worldly comforts and to promote the happiness and peace of the world by the increase of wealth, power and all the requisites of an unselfish culture, (b) to acquire and impart knowledge of religion, and (c) to explore spiritual realms on the basis of universal oneness.

Beliefs

The Muslims believe in the message and messengers of Allah. Besides, they believe in the books revealed by Allah and His Apostles. Four books are mentioned by name in Quran viz. : the *Tawrah* (the Jewish Torah) was given by Divine spirit to Moses: the *Zahur* (the Psalms) to David, the *Injil* (the Gospel) to Jesus: and the *Quran* to Prophet

Mohammad. More than any other cult, Islam postulates the unity, fearfulness, the sublimity of God and the direct contrast between God and man.

Like Christianity, Islam is universal. This religion has never identified itself with the Arabs, though the Arabs have identified themselves with Islam. The spiritual leaders of the Islamic Community and the jurists and the theologians (*the Ulema*) who compiled the holy Muslim Law from the Quran and tradition (Hadith). The realities are recorded in the Fiqh (law of moral obligations), which has undergone a process of historical evolutions from time to time. The ritual section of *Islamic ethics* contains the "five pillars" mentioned above.

Islam as a Socio-Judicial, Politico-Cultural Order

It is important to note that Islam is not merely a belief but also a social and juridical system, an all embracing religious way of life. The Islamic religious system is simple in its ritual, effective in its piety and is committed to learning. Owing to the absolute social equality which Islam introduced, there is no caste in Islamic society which may possess the day-to-day privileges. It is well known that Islam points the equality of man and woman and places duties on each towards the other and the Islamic law guarantees the wife's property rights. Although in practice, these duties are sometimes neglected, the retention of the established norms of the law of religious and moral obligations together with the deep significance attached to long standing traditions have, in the course of time, led to religious rigidity, a violent and reactionary social attitude among believing Muslims.

Political Expansion

As Mohammad did not appoint a successor, his obedient friend Abu Bakr (A.D. 632-634), a powerful figure took charge as the successor or deputy (that is Caliph) of the Prophet in spiritual and temporal affairs. He was the *first Caliph* (followed by Umar Ibn-al-Khittab, A.D. 634-644) and ending with Ali (A.D. 656- 661), of the Golden Age of Islam, which was to last for thirty years after the death of Mohammad (A.D.632). In this period, under the energetic leadership of Caliphs drawn from Mohammad's trusted band, State and religion combined to form a theocratic unit.

At that time, the Middle East and the present Arab Persian world was divided into two great empires, Byzantium and Persia. However, the two empires were unable to withstand the whirlwind Islam. With Islamic territorial and military expansion, one of the most inexplicate chapters of world history opened. As early as A.D. 633, one year after the death of Mohammad, various army detachments were sent to Syria in the north and Persia in the east. It was under the leadership of General Khalid ibn-al-Walid, *Iraq* (A.D. 633) and *Syria* (A.D. 634) were wrested from Byzantine hands. This was followed by the conquest of Damascus (the provincial capital of Byzantine empire) (A.D. 635), Jerusalem, Mesopotamia, Babylon, Hulwam (A.D. 640), Nihawend (642), Isfahan (A.D. 643), Persia, Alexandria (A.D. 642), Egypt (A.D. 639-641), Tripoli (A.D. 647) and Cyprus (A.D. 649).

The conquered people were treated fairly and the conquerors were received with a sense of liberation. In the early phase, no one was forcibly converted to the religion of Islam. This process of gradual Islamisation was to take many more generations. During the course of this process, the originally Arabian Islam, became internationalised.

Meanwhile, however, the murder of Third Caliph *Usman* and Fourth Caliph Ali, son-in-law of Mohammad was followed by a war of succession and split the ranks of Arab conquerors. The name *'Shi'ite* is derived from *Shi'at Ali*, that is the party of Ali.

It was the governor of Syria, *Muaawiya* (A.D. 661-680), succeeded by Abd-al-Malik (885-705) and his son al-walid (705-715), who emerged victorious from this conflict to found the new dynasty of Ummayads.

THE UMMAYAD CALIPHATE (A.D. 661-750)

During this Ummayad period, the centre of Islamic gravity had shifted northward. Muaawiya chose Damascus as the capital of his new caliphate. His generals crossed the Oxus, the Jaxartes and penetrated deep into central Asia and quickly resumed the tempo of Islamic expansion. In the west Tunisia, Algeria and Morocco and Turkey in Asia were occupied and towards the end of seventh century the Atlantic Coast was reached. In the south they penetrated into Spain and France. In the east, the Islamic armies occupied Transoxiana, Sind and the Indus which marked the eastern frontiers of the Muslim empire.

Social Organisation under the Ummayads and its Effect on Administration

Within about three or four decades of the Islamic revolution, the organisation of Arab 'society had changed considerably'. Society had definitely passed the clan and tribal stage and feudal elements had begun to appear in their rudimentary form. It took the whole of the Ummayad period to render the feudal organisation complete. Even under the Prophet, landed estates had begun to appear. The greatest warriors of Islam like Ali, Talhah, az- Zubayr and others received big estates under Abu Bakr, Umar and Uthman as *al-gata'i* (fiefs). The feudal organisation in Syria, Egypt and Persia was maintained. Thus the Arabs, who had lagged behind their neighbours in social evolution, by one sudden effect, overtook them. Naturally some of the glaring evils of feudalism were done away with by the early Muslim conquerors who were imbued with a spirit of equality and fraternity, and immense relief was afforded to the oppressed serfs, slaves and landless peasants who had so far been forced to work on land for practically nothing.

Abu Bakr and 'Umar I saw the danger in Muslim warriors becoming landowners to the exclusion of the people of the soil and exercised great control over the land-hungry Quraysh. But the social forces which the great revolution had released and hard facts and realities of the situation were too strong to be controlled or countered by the weak 'Uthman. The Quarysh were let loose on the vast Empire. Most of them received, or acquired by doubtful means, or purchased, big estates and converted them from *al-kharaj* lands to al-'ushr lands.

The revolution was brought about by the poor and the needy under the leadership of a scion of the upper class. But the fruits of the revolution went, as was the case with all such revolutions, to the upper class against whom the revolution had started. Within about thirty years after the demise of the great Prophet, we see his erstwhile enemies in control of the entire Empire with the son of Abu Sufyan at the top.

Against all the logic of social facts, against the opposition of some of the leading Companions, and even against the practice of giving away fiefs started by the Prophet, 'Umar wanted to avoid the birth of feudalism. Instead of a feudal aristocracy, he designed a military class of warriors (*al-mugatillah*) drawing regular pensions from the State. He was too much ahead of his times. So he had to make compromises. Even in this revolutionary enterprise he could not follow the logic to its extreme end. The ever-increasing mass of new converts could not be accommodated in his pension list based on Arabian tribes. Had he made it comprehensive enough to embrace all Muslims, it would not have worked. The productive forces had not yet reached a stage wherein the entire mass of the people could be equally or almost equally supported by the State out of its organised labour. Therefore, all that was physically possible was to ensure bread and vinegar for the entire Arab race and the early foreign converts. It was not an ordinary achievement. It had no parallel in the history of the world.

'Umar's effort was to avoid the inevitable, the conversion of the tribal into feudal society. As long as his strong hand was there the land-hungry Quraysh were held in check. But the weak and well-meaning 'Uthman could not control them. They migrated to the provinces and carved out estates for themselves thereby causing great resentment among the population of the provinces.

Thus the dictum, 'that out of every tribal society a feudal one is born, was again proved. The attempt at levelling and equalising failed; the brotherhood of all believers was jeopardised; racial differences, tribal distinction and even discrimination between the old and new converts entered the scheme of things. Under the Ummayads (except during the two-and half years under 'Umar II) it was not the religious consideration that played the strongest part but the considerations of revenue and income.

By the end of the Ummayad period, the following distinct classes had emerged:

1. The feudal aristocracy, Arab and non-Arab.
2. The military class (mainly Arabs) enjoying State pensions.
3. Small landowners.
4. New converts neither owning lands nor enjoying State pensions *(mawaliu-l-Islam).*
5. Artisans, labourers, etc.
6. The beggar class including the permanently sick, the incapacitated, the indolent and others.
7. Slaves.

Each one of these classes presented problems which the Ummayads had to tackle. A very honest and sincere effort was made by the saintly 'Umar II. But it was an uphill task, too big and too difficult for the conscientious *Khalifah.* He died in the effort, but the task remained unfulfilled. Those problems developed to such huge dimensions that they enveloped and destroyed the dynasty itself.

The Feudal Aristocracy

Feudalism with all its evils had existed in Syria, Persia and Egypt when the Muslims conquered these countries. Some of the glaring evils were removed by the conquerors. But the old system was allowed to continue in all the three lands. Estates deserted by the fleeing Patricians, former crown lands, lands of warriors confiscated for active opposition to the Muslim, lands belonging to the fire temples and those whose income was set apart for maintaining the postal service in Persian became State property, the income from which went to the central treasury. Other feudal estates under the Syrians, Egyptians and the Dihqans of Persia were allowed to continue under them in return for tax or tribute.

In Arabia proper, when the Prophet conquered the lands around al- Madinah, the estates belonging to Nanu Nadir were divided among the *Muhajirin* and two of the poor *al-Ansar;* and those of Banu Qurayzah were divided among those who were present. The Prophet also granted fiefs in all parts of Arabia. 1580 fiefs carved out of the estates of Khaybar were granted by 'Umar to the 1540 Muslims who had taken part in the treaty of al-Hudaybiyah. Under Abu Bakr and during the early part of 'Umar's reign many estates were given to the early heroes of Islam.

There was a clamour from all sides for more land. In the days of 'Umar I, after a very long sitting of the *Shura* and hot discussions, it was decided that no more conquered lands should be distributed among the Muslims. In spite of this, in the reign of Uthman, the Quraysh acquired private estates (*al- qata'i*). For instance, a large extent of the property left by the Patricians in Syria and the confiscated lands had passed on to the State. At the request of Mu'awiyah, 'Uthman assigned to him these estates or at least a part of them. He gave many more estates as fiefs to others also.

As the *Khalifah* Mu'awiyah retained the estates granted to him by 'Uthman and gave portions of them to his supporters, not in trust, but as alienable private property. 'Abdu 'l-Malik and other Ummayad *Khalifahs* did the same. Moreover, when the non-Muslim owners died heirless, 'Abu'l-Malik granted their *al-kharaj* lands to the Muslims as *al-'ushr* lands. Other Umayyad Khalifahs granted fiefs to their favourites and also allowed the Muslims to purchase the *kharaj* lands from non-Muslims. When the *kharaj* lands passed into the hands of the Muslims, they became *al-'ushr* lands; and hence, the revenue declined.

Not only in Syria but also in Iraq, Egypt and other parts of the Empire, the Muslims began to acquire great estates, by grant, by purchase, and by other means. The stern and wise principles laid down by 'Umar in the matter of acquiring lands were relaxed in so many individual cases by the weak 'Uthman that the democratic system of administration began to degenerate into a system based on the whim and fancy of the ruler. The Quraysh, and especially the Ummayads, took the maximum advantage of the weakness of 'Uthman. They established a monopoly over Babylon (as-Sawad), the most fertile region in the Empire, and claimed it as their private property to the exclusion of the Muslim community as a whole. The haughty Sa'id bin al-As went to the extent declaring: "The Sawad is nothing but the estate of the Quraysh. We take of it what we like and leave off what we choose to". The Quraysh had carved out many estates in this region. But 'Ali, on his election to the *khilafat*, took back most of the landed properties in Iraq which were granted by 'Uthman to his favourites and relatives.

In spite of what Ali was able to do in Iraq, by the end of the reign of Mu'awiyah, a form of feudalism was already established throughout the Muslim Empire. The evil which set in under the mild 'Uthman became more and more serious under the later Ummayads. The facts that many complaints of forceful possessions by the strong were brought before 'Umar II shows that the process of acquiring land was not fair in all cases. 'Umar II himself declared that more than half of the wealth was in the hands of Bane Marwan and that most of it was ill-gotten.

Thus was created a Muslim landed aristocracy which deprived the State of a large amount of revenue. The aristocrats were powerful men who could not be taxed strictly. The burden naturally fell on the poorer classes. In this way the evils of feudalism, rampant among the Romans and the Persians, which were abolished by the wise and strict rules of 'Umar I, reappeared under the Ummayads.

Ummayad *Khalifahs* like Mu'awiyah, 'Abdu 'l-Malik, al-Walid and Hisham and their powerful Viceroys like al-Hajjaj, Maslamah, and Khalid al-Qasri became the greatest landowners in the Empire. We have seen how 'Uthman granted most of the crown lands in Syria to Mu'awiyah. To this he added other estate like Fadak in Arabia, much bigger ones in Persia and the East and those confiscated from the Romans in Egypt and other parts of Africa. These estates were, in theory, the property of the Muslim community as a whole; but Mu'awiyah began to dispose them off as if they were his private property. Of course, a large part of the income went towards the State expenses; but the great part of the Shaykhayn (Abu Bakr and 'Umar) disappeared.

This accumulation of huge estates continued under the successors of Mu'awiyah. Abdu-l'-Malik accelerated this process. When feudalisation was at its climax, the saintly 'Umar II was elected the *Khalifah*. 'Umar realised that the vast estates of the Ummayads were accumulated at the expense of the State and the poorer subjects. Nevertheless, he was determined either to succeed or die in the attempt. He made a beginning with himself. He had inherited vast estates from his father. He returned all of them to the State. Even cash and jewels in the house including those of his wife, the noble Fatimah, he surrendered to the State treasury.

Thereafter 'Umar II assembled the common people in the mosque and addressed them. 'Umar II undertook a task too big for him, a task which was counter to the historical process. He fought the feudal aristocracy heroically; but he could not succeed. The princes of the royal blood, finding the saint too much against them, removed him from their path by poisoning him. Thus even the great Ummayad saint could not put an end to vast estates accumulating in the hands of the princes. After him the process was set on the move with a vengeance by his unworthy successors and the climax was reached under Hisham.

Hisham and his Governor at - Iraq, Khalid bin 'Abdillahi'l-Qasri were the two great landlords in 'Iraq who monopolised huge quantities of grains. They could raise the price by withholding the stock and lower it by releasing it. They could force others to sell before them and then sell their own stocks at a price to be dictated by them. It is interesting to note that a keen business rivalry developed between these two great landlords which ended in the political and financial ruin of the state.

The Military Class

The rise of the military class in Arabia, is a unique feature in the history of the world. There is no parallel where the entire population of a sub-continent, unable to support itself any more on the limited resources of the land, rises as one man, and dominates the surrounding countries, and subsists on the income of the conquered lands by a system of universal pensions.

Their own lands could support the Arabs no more. So they rose and carried everything that lay before them. If they settled in the adjoining countries, there was the fear of their getting merged in the population of those countries. They had to retain their identity as conquerors and yet maintain themselves. Therefore, as a result of the inexorable economic causes, the entire nation and the early non-Arab Muslims had to be converted into a military class with pensions from the revenues of the Empire. If Arabia had been economically self-sufficient, a feudal monarchy would have emerged. Feudalism could be only based on productive land; there was not much of it in Arabia; so it could not thrive there. The tribal forces swelled, burst as under the tribal structure, overflowed into the adjacemt land and again sank back into the old tribal bounds. As there was not sufficient productive land in Arabia to support a feudal or any other form of society more advanced than the tribal one, the country could not have anything but tribalism.

Even as early as the days of 'Umar I, all Arabs were liable to military service and received State pensions. Military service was compulsory for all those subjects of the Empire who received pensions. They were bound, at stated periods, to attend the courses of their respective *al-jund* or legion for the necessary training. Under the Ummayads, thousands of *mawalis* had to fight in the ranks of the Muslim armies without receiving any pension. This injustice was brought to the notice of 'Umar II. He ordered that all Muslims, Arabs or non-Arabs, who took part in the wars, should receive pensions. This generous policy did not last long.

From the beginning, there was no uniformity in the military pensions. As we have already seen, political and military pensions were clubbed together. Pensions were reduced or increased at will. The custom of giving pensions also, to the wives and children of the *muqatilah* had already been restricted by Mu'awiyah and altogether discontinued by 'Abdu l'Malik. 'Umar II reintroduced the practice.

The Small Landowners

In the early Muslim Empire, feudalism was completely divested of military obligation. If the old feudal order was retained, it was done so only for the purpose of collecting taxes and not to serve military ends.

Those lands which were conquered from the feudal order by force (*'anwatan*) were given to the actual tillers of the soil and those estates which were conquered by peace (*sulhan*) were allowed to be retained by the old landlords. Thus there were three categories of lands:

1. Estates vacated by the former rulers and the nobility, the endowed estates of fire temples, estates belonging to the postal department and lands left behind by those who were killed on the battlefield, etc. These estates became crown lands from which the State took the landowners' share of the produce.
2. Those lands which were conquered by force and given back to the peasantry in return for *al-kharaj* without any obligation to render military service. On these lands flourished the smaller peasantry.
3. Those lands which were conquered by peace and left under the old feudal lords in return for a stipulated tribute or *al- kharaj* to be paid by them in a lump sum.

The conversion of the peasants to Islam deprived the State of *al-jizyah* and *al-kharaj*. When such conversions began to take place on a mass scale, they created a very serious financial problem for the rulers.

The Mawali

Very large number of the landless new Muslims migrated to the towns and attached themselves to Arab families as their clients (*al-mawali*). Further, prisoners taken in wars, who subsequently became Muslims, were also thus attached to the families of their masters.

Under the Ummayads, the influx into towns of these categories of men became so great that the countryside suffered for want of labourers. Moreover, mass conversion caused very great financial loss to the government. Most of the Ummayads were more particular about the revenue than about conversion to Islam. Hence al-Hajjaj collected *al-jizyah* from the *mawali* as well and collected *kharaj* from those *mawali* who, after their conversion to Islam, continued in possession of the *kharaj* lands. He "even reimposed it upon those who had before been freed from it. He forebade *hijrah* (immigration into the centres of Islam) to the *mawali* and drove back to the towns under their jurisdiction.

There was very great discontent among the *mawali*. They were Muslims, but they had to pay the *jizyah* and the *kharaj*. 'Umar II, realising the injustice done to the *mawali*, cancelled Hajjaj's order forcing them to pay the *jizyah* and ordered annuities to be given to those who served in the army. But the good and just rule of 'Umar II did not continue long. After him the *mawali* were treated with contempt and injustice: and they played an important role in bringing about the downfall of the Ummayad dynasty.

Artisans and Labourers

Islam gave a stupendous fillip to arts and sciences. Though the zenith was not yet reached under the Ummayads, many industries had begun to appear. The textile industries kept large numbers well occupied. The manufacture of clothes, carpets (*al-bisat*), curtains (*as-stir*), long strips (*an-nakhkh*), prayer-rugs (*al-musalla*), quilts, pillows, various sorts of cushions, etc., gave employment to many. The perfume industry was especially paying under the Ummayads. Jewellers and manufacturers of valuable vessels and costly clothes of silk and of gold and silver embroidery made heaps of money. Shipbuilding and arms manufacture employed a very large number of workers.

Artisans, both Muslim and non-Muslim, thrived and prospered. They were not much affected by the civil wars; and life went on smoothly in spite of the civil strife. Mu'awiyah and, after him, Abdu 'l-Malik and al-Walid I were very much interested in the prosperity of the industrial classes. Al-Walid had a special taste for architecture and constructed many magnificent buildings which gave employment to thousands. We do not find any evidence of large-scale unemployment under the Ummayads.

The skilled non-Muslim artisans who earned large incomes had a very great advantage over their Muslim co-professionists. While the Muslims had to pay *zakat* on gold, silver and animals, the non-Muslims escaped by paying *jizyah* alone, which never exceeded four *dinars* per year on the richest class. This advantage, which the non-Muslims enjoyed over the Muslims, the Ummayads were not slow to perceive. Their Governors taxed the rich non-Muslim artisans in ways other than those prescribed by the *shari'at*. For example, under *Muawiyah*, the presents received by his Governor of 'Iraq on a Nawruz alone amounted to 10,000,000 *dirhams*.

The Beggar Class

The beggar class consisted of the incapacitated and the indolent. 'Umar I fixed pensions for all early Muslims; and the charities were administered in such a way that there was no necessity for begging. But things degenerated after him. The system of pensions and charities could not embrace all Arabs and non-Arabs; Muslims and non-Muslims. Therefore begging became a common thing. Al-Walid I made elaborate arrangements to support the blind, the aged, the maimed and the other incapacitated. Hundreds of public kitchens were established where the poor could take their meals. This indiscriminate charity and the system of caring gave rise to a class of lazy persons who made begging and visiting mosques as a profession. This class not only depended on the State for its support, but also paid no taxes. Non-Muslim beggars belonging to the above categories were exempted from *jizyah*.

The Slaves

The teachings of the Prophet and his example decidedly discouraged slavery. As a result, under 'Umar I, it was completely abolished as far as the Arab nationals were concerned. The Arab upper classes, even in those days when their resources used to be very slender, were accustomed to have slaves. In many families male slaves were a boon. As long as they were young, they served as domestic servants. When they came of age, they earned their own livelihood as artisans but were always attached and devoted to their masters' families. Thus a childless widow or a brotherless girl could always depend on the slaves of the family (in bondage or freed) to attend to all her needs.

After the emergence of Islam, the resources of the Arabs multiplied on the one hand, and, on the other, all Arab slaves were emancipated. The rich could not get slaves to serve their needs. Slaves were imported from far and wide.

Thus we see that by the end of the Ummayad period, feudalism had been firmly established in the entire Islamic Empire. A feudal aristocracy of Muslims had sprung up in addition to the already existing non-Muslim one; the strong socialistic and equalitarian tendencies of Islam had been drowned in mutual jealousies and the race for more and more land. Instead of a uniform society based on equality and brotherhood, a stratified society had appeared among the Arabs. While the old stratification continued among the non-Arabs; the feudal aristocracy was growing richer and richer by defrauding the Government on the one hand and the peasants and others on the other; and each of these new classes presented a set of problems for the Ummayads to solve.

THE UMMAYAD CENTRAL GOVERNMENT

The Khilafat

Under the Ummayads the *Khilafat,* of the holy Prophet was converted into a *de facto* kingship. From the beginning there were no fixed rules regarding the election of a *Khalifah.* The Qur'an is silent on the point and the Prophet left the matter entirely in the hands of the Muslim community by leaving no clear instructions. The election of Abu Bakr, though generally approved, cannot be called a regular one.

The Prophet did not make any rules concerning elections, for no one under the circumstances could have have done it. Modern methods of election could not have been practised in those days in any country of the world, and least of all, in Arabia. The old Arab custom was that the most influential members of the clan or tribe proposed a man to be the chief and the others acknowledged him. If there was a serious difference of opinion, only the sword could decide. A similar procedure was adopted in the election of Abu Bakr. A small section of the *Ansar,* assembled in the meeting place of Banu Sa'dah, and agreed to elect Abu Bakr. Then he was acknowledged by others. 'Ali genuinely felt injured that his claims were ignored and did not pay homage to Abu Bakr till after the death of Fatimah. As yet a civil war among the Muslims was out of the question. The general sense of the Companions of the Prophet including that of 'Ali and the much chagrined Sa'd bin 'Ubadah who refused to pay homage to Abu Bakr till his death was that the sceptre of the young State should not be split. So any undeserving man could have easily got himself elected and demanded obedience in the name of the unity of all the Muslims. To avoid such a contingency Abu Bakr proposed 'Umar. But he declined the honour and immediately nominated Abu Bakr and paid homage to him. The agreement against splitting the sceptre of Islam prevailed; and those like 'Ali and sa'd who were dissatisfied with the election, had to yield in the general interest of the young community.

Before his death Abu Bakr nominated 'Umar after consulting some of the leading Companions. The insurgent mob hailed him as the *Khalifah,* and practically thrust the office on him. There was no other way. Electing one more candidate would have meant civil war.

A feudal society was being born from a tribal one and it required feudal overlords. The Ummayads supplied it with them. As to the method of appointing the successors, the experience of the preceding half a century had clearly shown Mu'awiyah that the method of nomination was the best. He also knew that in the case of earlier nominations it was not personal merit alone that counted. For instance, by no stretch of imagination could it be considered that 'Uthman was the best qualified person for the Khilafat on the ground of personal capacity to rule a martial race and a rising empire. Family, wealth, position, relationship to the Prophet, tribal backing, past services were all taken into account. When family, position, wealth, tribal backing, etc., counted in nominating a successor and not services to Islam or personal merits, it was quite natural that Mu'awiyah should nominate his son for the great office.

Under the Sufyanids succession was determined by the rule of primogeniture. Mu'awiyah was succeeded by his eldest son, Yazid, who, in his turn, was succeeded by his eldest son, Mu'awiyah II. Although in practice, the Khilafat passed father to son under the Sufyanids and descended down in the same family under the Marwanids, the office in theory continued to be elective. The authority of the *Khalifahs* was based on the homage done to him by every Muslim citizen and never was the *Khilafat* looked upon as hereditary.

The nomination of a single successor under the Sufyanids gave place to the nomination of two under the Marwanids. Marwan nominated his two sons to succeed him one after the other, 'Abdu 'L-Malik and 'Abdu 'L-Aziz. The latter having predeceased the former, 'Abdu 'L-Malik nominated two of his sons, al-Walid and Sulayman. Sulayman nominated a cousin and a brother, 'Umar bin 'Abdi 'L-Aziz and Yazid bin 'Addi 'L-Malik. Yazid II nominated a brother and a son, Hisham and al-Walid II. Besides, under the Marwanids the rule of a son succeeding the father was not strictly followed. The rule of Mu'awiyah II was a failure. No boy could rule the unruly Arabs. Therefore Marwan started and others followed the practice of nominating two grown-up persons to avoid a minor's rule. But throughout, the successors were chosen from the descendants of Marwan I.

The choice of two successors at a time by the last reigning prince gave rise to a new kind of evil. At the time of al-Walid II, Yazid and Ibrahim, the sons of al-Walid I, the eldest son of 'Abdu 'L-Malik, were left out of power, while al-Walid II, the third son of 'Abdu 'L-Malik ruled over the Empire with the possibility of his son succeeding him. This made the sons of al-Walid I murder al-Walid II. This murder divided the Ummayads into two camps, and become one of the causes for the downfall of the dynasty.

The Shura

From the beginning the Shura was not an elected or representative body. It consisted in effect of a few topmost men. It was more a Council of Elders of the pre-Islamic days than a parliament. Since its meetings took place in the mosque, less important persons also could take part in it. Such presumptuous spirits were only few and the earlier Khalifahs tolerated them. Under the first two *Khalifahs* the most important leaders were constantly consulted. Under 'Uthman even this semblance of a council disappeared. His relatives were his chief advisers. During his governorship of al-Hijaz, 'Umar II established a council and consulted it on all important affairs of the province. When he succeeded to the office of the Khilafat, he endeavoured his best to get as many of the best men among scholars around him as possible. But his reign was so short and eventful that he could not accomplish anything definite in this direction.

The Court

It was quite natural that with wealth and absolute power a court should spring up. The great 'Umar I, even if he wanted a huge court, could not have afforded the luxury out of his 5,000 *dirhams* per year (about Rs. 100 per month) with his several wives and numerous children. It was under 'Uthman that the beginnings of a court appeared. His pompous life and costly surroundings, so vehemently denounced by Abu Dharri 'L-Chifari, were the precursors of the Ummayad court. Even in 'Umar's days, Mu'awiyah, his young Viceroy in Syria, could afford to maintain a small money for his conscientious master. After the attempt on his life, Mu'awiyah instituted a guard and even in the mosque, he constructed a small partition wall known as the *hujrah* (room) to protect himself from intending assassins. It was this very same *Khalifah* of the holy Prophet who set up a throne and sat on it like a king. From these beginnings a veritable royal court developed at Damascus under the worldy Ummayads with all the attendant evils. Thus the great successorship of the holy Prophet of God was, under the Ummayads, converted into a grand monarchy with absolute powers and all its accompaniments.

The heroic and saintly 'Umar II did a good deal to eliminate the rot that had entered the sacred institution. He returned all his wealth and that of his wife to the State treasury, led a simple life and was content with the meal served in the State kitchen for the poor and the helpless. The courtiers, songsters, poets, musicians, and others were turned out of the court. He sat on the floor as his great-grandfather 'Umar I had done. He tried to get round him as many scholars and divines as possible to advise him, and kept himself in touch with great scholars like al-Hasan al-Basri.

After the death of 'Umar II the grand court of the Ummayads was revived. The old pomp and gay life of the palace was restored. Poets, musicians, songstresses and others returned and the Ummayad royalty was restored with great pomp and ostentation. The ruler of the Muslim Empire was no more the *de facto Khalifah* of the holy Prophet of God, but he became a worldly emperor like the Caesars with unlimited power over his subjects.

The Central Boards

There were five Boards at the Centre -*Diwanu 'l-Jund* (The Military Board), *Diwanu 'l-Kharaj* (The Board of Finance), *Diwanu 'r-Rasa'il* (The Board of Correspondence), *Diwanu 'l-Khatam* (The Board of Signet) and *Diwanu 'l-Barid* (The Board of Posts).

Diwanu 'L-Jund

It was the same great *Diwan* established by 'Umar I which assigned annuities to all Arabs and to the Muslim soldiers of other nationalities.

Diwanu 'L-Kharaj

This Central Board directly administered the revenue side of as-Sawad, the richest region of the Empire, and also administered the entire finance of the State. It was the Central Finance Board where all receipts and disbursements were made and records relating to them maintained. The surplus of the provinces was paid into this Board. Still, huge sums were kept in the provincial treasuries for local purposes and emergencies.

Diwanu 'r-Rasa'il

The Prophet employed several persons to maintain the records of the State. During the Khilafat, the machinery at the Centre was almost the same as far as correspondence was concerned. Individual Companions were employed to record the various activities of the State.

Under the Ummayads, a regular Board of Correspondence (*Diwanu 'r-Rasa'il*) was established. Literally, it means a Board of Letters or Pamphlets. As a matter of fact, this Board issued circulars and pamphlets giving instructions to the provincial officers and the subjects in general. Some of these circulars and pamphlets have been copied in the book of al-Jahshiyari. This Board dealt with all correspondence, issued circulars and pamphlets and coordinated the work of all the other Boards. Political correspondence under the early Khalifahs was very brief and to the point.

Diwani 'L-Khatam

Mu'awiyah established a Chancery Board which bore the title of *Diwanu 'L-Khatam* (The Board of Signet). Every order issued by the Khalifah was registered by the Board; and then the original was sealed and despatched. Before the establishment of this Board, unsealed orders were sent out or delivered to the persons concerned. Mu'awiyah gave a letter to 'Amr bin az-Zubayr ordering Ziyad bin Ablhi to give the bearer 100,000 *dirhams.* 'Amr opened the letter, altered the figure to 200,000 *dirhams* and received the amount from Ziyad. The fraud was however, detected when the Viceroy sent his account. 'Amr was arrested for fraud; but his brother, 'Abdullah bin-as-Zubayr, paid the extra amount to Mu'awiyah and secured his release. The keeping of office copies and the sealing of orders before despatching them were not confined only to the Central Government; the Governors also adopted the system.

Diwanu 'L-Barid

Mu'awiyah was the first Muslim ruler to establish the postal system. It was originally designed to serve the purpose of the State; and later, it was used by the subjects also. The main highways were divided into stages, and each state had horses ready to carry the post. In Arabia and Syria, camels were used. Thus by a system of relay, the State messages and, later, all posts were carried from one part of the Empire to another. The system was known as *al-Barid*.

Under 'Abdu 'l-Malik the postal system was considerably improved. Not only was the post carried through a relay of horses, but also State officials used the postal system for swift journey. In times of emergency the postal carriages were used for swift transport of troops. They were able to carry 50 to 100 men at a time. Under Yusuf bin 'Umar, the Viceroy of Iraq, the postal department for that province alone cost 4,000,000 *dirhams* a year. The postmasters, in addition to their postal duties, had to keep the *Khalifah* informed of all important happenings in the territories under their jurisdictions.

The Currency

Before Islam the Arabs were using the Persian and Roman coins. Neither had they a Central Government nor a common currency. Of course, in the south, where a high standard of civilisation and a stable government had prevailed, some coins bearing Himyaritic inscriptions and the Attic owl also had been under circulation. The Meccans accepted all coins of pure gold and silver and determined their value by weight. Under the Prophet and Abu Bakr, only the Roman and Persian currencies were used.

Under 'Umar I the Muslim Empire expanded by leaps and bounds and all kinds of coins poured in, some of which were defective. On an examination it was found that the *dirhams* were of three different weights. Some weighed 20 carats, some 12 and some only 10. 'Umar struck the average and minted *dirhams* each weighing 14 carats which equalled 7/10 *mithqal*. The model adopted was that of the Persian *dirham*. Some had "All praise is to Allah" inscribed on them, some bore "Muhammad is the Messenger of God," and others, "There is no God but Allah." He fixed the ratio of the *dinar* and the *dirham* as 1 : 10. 'Uthman issued some dirhams with the inscription "Allah is Great."

When 'Abdu 'l-Malik became the undisputed master of the Muslim Empire, he took up the problem of coinage. According to al- Balandhuri, the Romans got paper from Egypt and the Muslims got dinars from the Romans. (Up to the days of 'Abdu 'l-Malik, the Egyptian paper bore Christian inscriptions and the sign of the cross as water mark. Under 'Abdu 'l-Malik the verse "Say, He alone is God" was substituted. The Romans threatened to retaliate by increasing some blasphemy against the Prophet on the *dinars*.

When Yazid bin 'Abdi 'l-Malik became the *Khalifah*, his Viceroy in 'Iraq, 'Umar bin Hubayrah, minted the Hubayriyah *dirham* on the standard weight of six *dawanig*. When Hisham, who was a great hoarder, succeeded Yazid, he ordered that the standard should be raised to seven *dawanig*. So his Viceroy, Khalid al-Qasri, minted and issued the Khalidiyan coins containing seven dawanig. All the previous coins were withdrawn and all mints except the one at Wasit were closed down. Khaild was deposed and his successor reverted to the old standard of six *dawanig*.

Weights and Measures

From the very beginning of the Muslim State, great care was taken to see that merchants and dealers used proper weights and measures. Of all the pious *Khalifahs* 'Ali was most particular about it. He used to go round the market of Kulfah, to see that proper weights and measures were used and no one cheated the public. Under the Ummayads police officers were in charge of the supervision of weights and measures. Al-Walid I was also in the habit of visiting markets. Sometimes he even reduced the prices of articles.

Often local areas had their own weights and measures. The following weights were in general use:

The Habbah (Grain): It was equal to the weight of two grains of barley. The word was of purely Arabian origin.

The *Qirat* (Carat): It was equal to 4 habbahs of 8 grains of barley. The word is of Greek origin.

The *Danig:* It weighed 2-1/2 *cirats*. The word is of Persian origin. Its weight was equal to 20 grains of barley which was equal to 1/6 of the weight of a *dirham*.

The Mithagl: Each dinar weighed one *mithgal*. The weight of a *dinar* was 10/7 of that of a *dirham*. The weight of the *dinar* was equal to that of half of modern English guinea.

The *Ugiyah* (Ounce): The word is of Greek origin and it weighed about 1/12 of an English pound. Its exact weight was 1.312 English ounces.

The *Ritl:* A ritl weighed 15.75 ounces, i.e. about one pound. Its exact weight was 38.4 tolas.

The Mann: A mann weighed two *ritls*. Roughly it was equal to an Indian *Ser*.

The Nuwat: It was a weight employed to weigh gold and silver. It weighed 20 *Ugiyahs* which equalled 64 *tolas*.

The Qintar: This weight was used to weigh a very large quantity of the precious metals. Reports vary as to its exact weight.

The Buhar: The word literally means weight; and is evidently an Arabicised form of the Persian word *bar* (weight).

Liquids and grains were mostly measured and not weighed. The following measures were prevalent:

1. *The Mudd* (Modius): It was Greek in origin and measured 1.15 litres.
2. *The Sa:* 4 mudds made one *sa.*
3. *The Qafiz*: 12 *sa's* made one *qafiz.*
4. *The Wasq:* (ass load): It was equal to five *gafizes* which equalled 60 sa's.
5. *The Kurr:* 6 wasqs made one kurr which equalled 300 sa's, nearly 4-1/3 cwt. of wheat.
6. *The Jarib:* 40 *gafizes* made one *jarib.*

Units for Measuring Lengths

1. *The Usbu':* Six grains of barley lined up breadthwise made one *usbu'* or inch.
2. *The Bishr:* A span is called a *bishr.*
3. *The Dhira:* 24 *usbu's* made one *dhira* (cubit).
4. *The Ba':* A fathom was called a *ba.*
5. *The Mil:* 4,000 cubits made one mil. The *mil* was equal to 1.44 English miles.
6. *The Farsakh:* This word is of Persian origin and is the same as the Persian *farsang* or *para-i-sang.* A *farsakh* was equal to 3-3/4 English miles.

The unit for measuring lands was the *jarib.* A *jarib* was equal to 3,600 square yards.

Under the Ummayads, weights and measures were standardised and they used to be sealed by the Government. Al-Hajjaj seems to be at the bottom of this reform. The picture of a Byzantine weight, validated by al-Walid I, bearing on the obverse IB, i.e. two ounces, and on the reverse a Kufic inscription stating that the *Khalifah* has recognised it as equivalent to two *ugiyahs,* is published by Hitti. He is of the opinion that probably it is "the earliest inscribed Muslim weight thus far found".

The Change of the Language of Administration

When 'Abdu 'l-Malik consolidated the much distracted Muslim Empire under his sway, he desired uniformity in the administration. In Persia most of the crucial administrative posts were occupied by the Persians, in Syria by the Greeks and in Egypt by the Copts. Most of these administrators were non-Muslims. Arabic was the language of the Bedouins, and, as such, had not yet possessed the terms necessary for running the administration of a huge civilised empire. Most of the Khalifahs and their Governors thought—that the administration could not be carried on in Arabic. It is due to the genius of the great intellectual Al-Hajjaj, that this insurmountable difficulty was mastered.

The man in charge of the Syrian *Diwan* in the days of Mu'awiyah was Sarun (Sergius) bin al-Mansur the Greek, and he was followed by his son al-Mansur. The man who translated the Syrian Diwan from Syriac to Arabic was Sulayman bin Sa'id, the *Katibu 'r-Rasa'il.* The translation of the Syrian *Diwan* took place in the days of al-Walid.

The Diwan of Egypt was translated into Arabic by Ibn Yarbu' al- Fazari of Hims during the reign of al-Walid.

Thus were all the records of the Government translated into Arabic; and the language of Arabia became the medium of administration throughout the Muslim Empire. In spite of this change, Persians, Greeks, and Copts were not completely excluded from the administration. They picked up Arabic and continued in the service of the Government in large numbers.

Religious Organisation under the Ummayads

Although it has become a fashion to paint all the Ummayads except the 'Umar II as irreligious and to call the Ummayad period, a period of reaction against Islam, the main factors of the Islamic religion continued unaltered under the Ummayads. It is a lack of historical sense that makes critics consider Islam a sudden jump in the historical evolution of Arabia and the Ummayad period as a recoiling after that sudden jump. A careful study of all the available material will show that throughout the historical process was consistent and natural and that the dialectical process has worked as consistently as in any other country of the world.

It is true that the thesis and antithesis in pre-Islamic Arabia found a synthesis under Islam, that under the Ummayads, this synthesis developed into a thesis and antithesis for which a new synthesis was found under the 'Abbasids which again, in its turn, got resolved into a thesis and antithesis.

The religious organisation under the Ummayads remained almost the same as under the *Khalifahs*. Religious dogmas still remained elastic; and if people were executed for their views, they were done so because their views were dangerous to the dynastic interests of the Ummayads, and not because they held religious views different from the common ones. The spirit of toleration was admitted into the fold of Islam and employed usefully. Even rival prophets like Tulayhah continued under the Ummayads.

Muslim laws were not as yet codified; much less the Muslim tenets. The judges possessed wide discretionary powers and the practice of denouncing people as *Kafirs* on the slightest pretext had not yet come into vogue. The term used to denounce the shocking behaviour of Yazid I was *fisg* (transgression). In spite of all the profane acts attributed to Walid II, including the testing of the Qur'an to pieces with arrows, he was not denounced as a *kafir*. He was only dubbed a *fasiq*e (transgressor), and curiously enough it is recorded that this monarch, like one of his predecessors, 'Uthman, suffered death with the Qur'an in his hand.

The same arrangement for the conduct of prayers and the care of the mosques, which had existed under the *Khalifahs*, continued under the Ummayads. New mosques were built in very large numbers and the old ones enlarged and beautified. The *zakat* and other alms were collected and distributed to the poor exactly as they were done under the Khalifahs. Every year the *Khalifah* appointed a person to lead the Hajj ceremonies as the previous rulers had done, and very often Ummayad rulers lead the pilgrimage in person. The other most important duty of waging war against the infidels and inviting the non-Muslim nations to embrace Islam was as faithfully and zealously performed by the Ummayads as done by the *Khalifahs* before and the 'Abbasids after them. On the whole, the form of religious organisation, the spirit of religious performances and ceremonies and the guarding of Muslim interests, as opposed to those of the non-Muslims, remained the same as under the immediate successors of the Prophet.

PROVINCIAL ADMINISTRATION UNDER THE UMMAYADS

The Easterners in general, and the Muslims in particular, loved local autonomy. In the matter of administration the provinces were autonomous to a very large extent. All provincial expenses were met from the revenues of the respective provinces. All works of public utility, such as roads, canals, public buildings, mosques, schools, etc., were raised and all essential services run from the treasury of the province where they were required.

After meeting all the charges and paying the State annuities, the provincial treasuries contained huge amounts. When Mukhtar conquered Kufah, the treasury contained 9,000,000 *dirhams*. Ibn Zīyad left 19,000,000 at Basrah, and Yazid bin Muhallab captured the treasury of the same city with 10,000,000.

Another important feature to be noted in the Ummayad administration is the separation of financial, from political administration. Formerly, the *Amir* or *Wali*, as the chief of the whole administration, had both these departments, under his charge. Mu'awiyah was the first to see the evils of the system although as early as the reign of 'Umar we see separate treasury officers being appointed in certain provinces. Mu'awiyah desired that these two branches of of administration should be separated completely.

The appointment of subordinate Governors or administrators was in the hands of the major Governors. The Governor of Africa appointed the *'Amil* of Spain and the Governor of Iraq, the *Amils* of Khurasan, Sind, etc. The intimation of the appointment used to be given to the *Khalifah*. Sometimes the *Khalifah* himself suggested the dismissal of certain *'Amils* and the appointment of certain others. In all the major towns of the provinces 'Amils were appointed. When 'Ziyad bin Abihi became the Viceroy of Iraq, he divided Khurasan into four districts and appointed an 'Amil over each of them. Similarly under Hijjaj *'Amils* were appointed over Karman, Sijistan, Sind and other districts. Later, when the Governors of Khurasan became practically independent, they appointed their own *'Amils* over the various districts of that country.

The Provinces and Districts of the Empire

At the end of the Ummayad period, the Muslim Empire was divided into 14 huge provinces. Each of them was subdivided into several large districts. To give an example, the whole of Arabia, a subcontinent larger than the Indian peninsula, formed a single province and the whole of Spain one district.

The Province of Arabia

The Arabian province was divided into four districts: 1. Hijaz, comprising the whole of Hijaz, the entire Arabian region north of Makkah and the whole of Wadiu '1-Qura. It contained the towns of Makkah (which was the capital of the district and also of the province), Madinah, Tayma', Yanbu', Jar, -Ta' if etc.

It comprised the whole of north-western Arabia and a portion of the north-east.

Yaman: This district comprised the whole of Yaman (consisting of Tihamatu '1-Yaman with its capital Zubayd and Najdu '1-Yaman with its capital San'a'), Hadramawt and Mahra. It contained the famous towns of San 'a', Ma'rib, Shihr, Zafar, etc., and the ports of Hudaydah, Mukha and 'Adan.

'Uman: Comparatively it was a smaller district comprising the south- western part of Arabia, and its capital was Suhar, a port on the Arabian Sea.

Hajr: The capital of Hajr was Ahsa'. This district comprised the whole of Yamamah also. Hajr was that area most of which was formerly covered by Bahrayn.

The Province of Iraq

This province was divided into six districts.

Kufah: It encompassed the area around al-Kufah including Qadisiyah and 'Aynu 't-Tamar.

Basrah: The district of Basrah included Ubullah and 'Abbadan also in addition to Basrah.

Wasit: This district had Fammu 's-Sulh also in it.

Mada'in: The district of Mada'in included, in addition to the town of that name, Naharwan, Jalula, etc.

Hulwan: This district encompassed Khanigm and as-Sirwan also.

Samarra: Besides Samarra this district had in it the towns of Karkh, Anbar, Hit Tarkit, etc.

The Province of Jazirah

It comprised the ancient Assyria. It was the region that lay between the Tigris and the Euphrates. It consisted of three districts.

The Region of Rabi'ah with Mawsil as its headquarters included the towns of Nasibin, Ra'su '1-Ayn, etc.

The Region of Bakr with Amad as its capital.

The Region of Mudar with ar-Raqqah as the capital of the district.

Mawsil was the capital of the province.

The Province of Syria

It contained six districts:

Qinnasrin: Its capital was Halab and it comprised in it the towns of Qinnasrin, Mar'ash, Iskandarunah, etc.

Hims: It comprised Salamiyah, Tadmur, and Ladhiqiya also.

Damascus with Beirut, Tripoli, etc.

Urdunn: Its capital was Tiberias and it included the important port of Acre.

Filastin: With its capital ar-Ramlah, this district had in it the towns of Ma'ab, Tabuk, etc.,

The Province of Egypt

Egypt was divided into seven districts.

Jifar which had Farama as its capital.

Hawf with Bilabays (also Balbis and Bilbis) as its capital.

Ar-Rif: It had Abbasiyah as its chief town.

Alexandria with the surrounding area.

Maqduniyah with Fustat as its capital.

As-Sa'id: This district had Aswan as its capital.

Wahat: The Oases.

The Province of Maqhrib (The West).

This province comprised the whole of North Africa, West of Egypt and also Spain, Sardinia and the Balearic Islands. It had seven districts:

Barqah.

Ifrigiyah with Qarawan as the capital.

Tahirat.

Sijilmasah

Fas: Also known as the Nearer Sus

The Farther Sus (as-Susu '1-Aqsa).

Its capital was Tarafanah.

Spain: Its capital was Cordova.

The Eastern Province

It consisted of two big divisions divided by the river Oxus (Jayhun or Amu). The fertile region that lies on the east of the river was called (a) Ma Wara'u 'n-Nahr or

Haytal and that which lies on the west, (b) Khurasan. The former was divided into six districts and the latter into eight.

The Province of Daylam

This province comprised the region on the south and south-east coast of the Caspian Sea. It had five districts:

Qumis: Its capital was Damighan.
Jurjan having Shahristan for its capital.
Tabaristan with Amul as the capital.
Ad-Daylaman: Its capital was Bardan.
Khazar with Itil as the capital.

The Province of ar-Rihab

It comprised the region on south-west of the Caspian Sea.

The Province of Jibal

Its consisted of three districts
Ar-Rayy
Hamadhan which was also the capital of the province.
Isfahan

The Province of Khuzistan

It contained seven districts:
As-Sus.
Jundaysabur: It was also the capital of the province.
Tustar.
'Askar Mukram.
Ahwaz.
Ad-Dawraq.
Ramhurmuz.

The Province of Ears

It had six Districts:
Arjan.
Ardashir Kharrah: Its capital was Siraf.
Daralifird.
Shiraz: It was also the capital of the province.
Sabur.
Istakhr.

The Province of Karman

It comprised five districts:
Bardsir (also Sardsir).
Narmasir.
As-Sirjan: It was also the capital of the province.
Bamm.
Jirut.

The Province of as-Sind

Mukran: Its cpaital was Banjbur (Panjpur).
Turan with Qasdar as the capital.
As-Sind Proper: Its capital was Mansurah.
Wayhind.
Qanuj.

Although Syria was a province of the Empire, no separate Governors were appointed for that country under the Ummayads. Mu'awiyah, who had been its Governor for twenty years, became the ruler of the whole of the Muslim Empire. Even after he became the *Khalifah,* he kept the provincial government of Syria in his own hands appointing deputies over the various districts.

The most important viceroyalty of the Empire was that of Iraq. From the days of 'Umar, that is, since the foundation of the two military towns of Kufah and Basrah each had a separate Governor. But during the most critical periods of Ummayad history, these two governorships had to be combined under one very able administrator. Mu'awiyah combined these two governorships under Ziyad bin Abjhi and Yazid combined them under 'Ubaydullah bin Ziyad. Similarly, 'Abdu 'l-Malik combined them under Hajjaj whose viceroyalty comprised the whole of Iraq, Tabaristan, Jurjan, Khwarizm, Khurasan, Sijistan, Karman, as-Sind, etc.

Spain was under the Viceroy of Africa. It was governed by a series of *'Amils* who were subordinate to the Viceroy of Africa. The duration of the office of the Viceroy of Africa was subject to the caprice of the *Khalifahs* who themselves changed very fast. The *'Amils* of Spain were changed at the whim and fancy of the Governors of Africa. So no capable *'Amil* could continue in Spain for long time. It was one of the reasons for the failure of the Arabs in Spain.

About Egypt, a great mass of details in addition to the accounts given by the later historians is available from the papyri. Mu'awiyah had promised the whole revenue of Egypt to 'Amir bin al-'As for his support against 'Ali. When further conquests in North Africa were made, Mu'awiyah did not like that the revenue of the new territory should also go into the pockets of 'Amr. So he incorporated the newly conquered African territory into a separate province.

The Provincial Diwans

There seem to have been only three Boards in the provinces.
Diwanu 'l-Jund (The Military Board).
Diwanu 'r-Rasa'il (The Board of Correspondence).
Diwanu 'l-Mustaghillat (The Finance Board).

Diwanu 'l-Jund administered the military affairs of the province. Diwanu 'r-Rasa'il was the Chief Secretariat which dealt with all correspondence and coordinated the work of all departments. The entire correspondence of this department from the very beginning was carried on in Arabic. *Diwanu 'l- Mustaghilat* was the finance department of the province where accounts of all receipts and disbursements were kept.

A register containing the copies of all orders emanating from the Governor was maintained in all the provinces.

Diwanu 'l-Barid at the Centre was represented in the provinces by *Sahibu 'L-Barid* (The Pcstmaster).

The Provincial Officials

The provincial officials under the Ummayads were almost the same as under the *Khalifahs*.

The Amir or Wali

The duties of the *Khalifah* were to conduct the daily prayers, to command the Muslim armies, to collect taxes and charities and spend them as they should be spent and to administer civil and criminal justice.

In the province all these duties devolved on the Governor if he was appointed with general powers. The *Wali* himself conducted prayers in the chief mosque of the provincial headquarters and made arrangements for the conduct of prayers throughout his province.

The Governors with general powers were permanent officers subject to good conduct. They had almost absolute powers. Such Governors in Iraq were Ziyad, his son 'Ubaydullah, Hajjaj bin Yusuf, 'Umar bin Hubayrah, and Khalid bin 'Abdillahi '1-Qasri. Of all these Hajjaj was the most firmly established *Wali* and he continued till his death.

The primary reason why such absolute powers had to be given to the Governors was the difficulty of communication. If every case had to be referred to the *Khalifah,* it would have involved very long delay, and sometimes delay would have been dangerous.

Under the later Ummayads, princes of the royal blood were appointed Governors. Some of them preferred to remain at the court appointing substitutes to administer their provinces for them, concerning themselves with filling their pockets from the revenues of the provinces. Thus when Hisham appointed Maslamah Governor of Armenia and Ajharbayjan, the prince preferred to remain at the court. Later, when he took charge of the province in person, he failed to send the balance of the revenue to the central treasury.

The 'Amil

The *Amil* was in charge of the revenue of the province.

Sahibu 'L-Kharaj

The person in charge of the collection of the land-tax was called *Sahibu 'l-Kharaj.* In the days of the Prophet, there was not much *kharaj* to be collected. *Zakat* was the chief source of revenue; the officer collecting it was called an *'Amil.* Later on, when *kharaj* became the most important source of revenue, the revenue officer was called *Sahibu 'l-Kharaj.* Very often an 'Amil took over the duties of an *Amir* also and appointed a separate individual to collect the *kharaj.*

The Katib

The chief of a *Diwan* was known as the *Katib.* While the *Wali* was in charge of the entire administration, military and fiscal, the *Katib* administered certain departments thus relieving the Wali of a great amount of work. Later, when the administrative machinery developed further, it was not possible for the *Wali* to attend to all the details of administration by himself. So he had to appoint several *Katibs* to assist him.

Early in the Ummayad period, revenue administration was separated from the executive business. The Finance Secretary of the province (*Sahibu 'l-Kharaj*) was in charge of the collection and disbursement of the entire revenue of the province. He had to collect the *kharaj*, the *zakat*, the *Jizyah*, the tribute from the tributary princes, and other *ma'muls*, such as presents on the Nawruz and Mihrgan festivals, and meet all the expenses of the province—pensions, salaries, public undertakings, etc.

Sahibu 'L-Ahdath

Each of the chief police officers of the provinces and of the provincial towns was known as *Sahibu 'l-Ahdath*. His function was half military and half police. He had to maintain law and order: if necessary, engage the rebels in the battle and take the policing of the province. *Sahibu 'l-Ahdath* was the officer responsible for the prevention of rebellion and other crimes like theft.

Under Ziyad, Kufah alone had a military police force of 40,000 men. Perfect order prevailed throughout the province. No one dared even to pick up a thing left on the road till the owner returned and recovered it. Lonely women could sleep in their houses without locking the doors. Ziyad declared that if a citizen lost anything through theft, he would hold himself responsible for.

Under Mu'awiyah all the suspects in Damascus were registered and watched. Ziyad appointed Ja'd bin Qays to watch the activities of the suspects.

The Qadi

The Arabs in general and the Muslims in particular hated becoming Judges. In pre-Islamic days, eminently just people were appointed *Hakim* or *Qadi* to decide particular cases of dispute. The terms *Hakim*, and *Qadi* were continued under Islam. In the early days only a few *Qadis* were appointed. Later, as Muslim colonies sprang up throughout the length and breadth of the Empire, a network of *Qadis* had to be established to decide disputes among the Muslims.

In those good days most of the disputes were settled by the parties themselves and the *Qadis* did not have much work to do. So they were given a lot of other duties to perform. Many of them administered the properties of orphans and the insane and also the endowments (*awqaf*).

The rules of Muslim jurisprudence not having been codified till then, the *Qadi* had a large measure of freedom in deciding cases. Sometimes the Qadi wrote to the *Khalifah* for elucidation of certain points of law.

As the law was not yet codified, there was a lack of uniformity in its administration. Since a good deal depended on the discretion of the Qadis, it is obvious that they should have held different views on several questions.

During the days of Mu'awiyah, his *Qadi* in Egypt, Sulaym bin 'Anz, decided a dispute relating to inheritance. The parties refused to abide by the decision and again came to him quarrelling. This time the *Qadi* wrote down his judgment and took the signatures of army officers.

Distinctive Features of Certain Major Provinces

Iraq

Iraq was the richest and most populous of all the provinces. The most important cities of this province were the two military stations of Kufah and Basrah. Their entire population was bound to render military service. As early as the days of 'Umar I, they became restive and troublesome; and even that great *Khalifah* had to change his Governors constantly on the demand of the citizens. Under 'Uthman things became much worse, and the citizens of these two cities had a hand in the revolution which brought about his murder. After 'Uthman, the long service of civil wars and the dependence of one party or another on these mighty military settlements destroyed all discipline and law in them.

When 'Abdu 'L-Malik succeeded in consolidating the whole of the Muslim Empire under him he placed the province of Iraq under the able and ferocious Viceroy, Hajjaj bin Yusuf. By a series of most drastic measures, Hajjaj re-established order and enforced the old compulsory military service on the part of all those who received State annuities.

Egypt

Financial administration in Egypt was carried on by the Copts who had been trained in the Byzantine system. Some records seem to have been kept in Greek, but the bulk of the records was maintained in the Coptic language till it was translated into Arabic under Walid I.

The province of Egypt was divided into Upper and Lower Egypt. Each of these units was divided into districts. Each district consisted of a town or village with the surrounding territory. These districts, in their turn, were divided into villages each under a headman.

Syria

Syria, being the seat of government, was governed by the *Khalifah* himself with the help of the Deputy Governors of the four districts. It was the first foreign province to come under the Arab rule, and was governed according to the rules originally laid down. Since the Ummayads had to depend on this province for the continuance of their power, the Syrian subjects were usually kept contented.

Spain

When the Muslims conquered Spain, the system of feudalism was prevalent in that land. The Muslim administration swept away the unjust rights and privileges of the governing classes—nobles and the clergy. In the place of grinding imposts, the Spaniards had now to pay taxes like *kharaj, jizyah,* etc.

Of course, the estates of the nobles and others, who fought the invaders, were confiscated and distributed among the Muslim soldiers. The slaves and serfs, who had been treated worse than as animals, were raised to the status of free human beings with a permanent right in the lands they tilled.

Spain was subdivided into five large sub-districts; Andalusia, Central Spain, Galicia cum Lusitania, the area east of the Douro to the Pyrenees, and the territory beyond the Pyrenees. The Arabs converted Spain into a garden and gave to the Spaniards a civilised government.

THE ABBASID CALIPHATE (A.D. 750-1258)

The year 750 witnessed the fall of the Ummayad caliphate due to the revolt in the Persian Province of Khurasan, and led to the rise of the Abbasid caliphate, so named after an uncle of Mohammad that is Abbas, with capital at Baghdad. The last of the thirteen successors of Mu'awiyah were more interested in women and wine than in state affairs. Hence the Abbasids exploited the general discontent to seize control. The capital of this vast empire was removed from ancient Damascus (Syria) to the new city of Baghdad (Iraq), founded on the West bank of the Tigris river and thus opened a new chapter in the history of Islam.

Unlike the Ummayad caliphs, those of Baghdad were Persian oriented. Persian Vizers, wives and wines became conspicuous in court. They appeared more eastward than westward and began to surround themselves with a host of courtiers and palace attendants. At the same time, however, the five centuries of Abbasid or Baghdad caliphate were characterised by an unparalleled and momentous flourishing of cultural and social life. Particularly under the rule of *Harun al-Rashid* (A.D. 786-809), and his son Mamun (A.D. 812-833) the Abbasid state reached the plateau of its might and influence. The luminous reigns of these two caliphs gave the entire Abbasid court a halo in popular imagination, intellectual creativity and rendered it the most celebrated in Muslim annals. With more fiction than fact, the *Arabian Nights* have immortalised the splendour, luxury and intellectual achievement of the period. The capital, Baghdad, developed into an international trade and industrial centre.

Social structure in the Abbasid period underwent a radical change. The traditional Arabian aristocracy based on blood and sword was no more in prominence. Instead of the Military men, the merchant took his position as Muslim trade became international, covering from China to Western Africa. The new aristocracy of businessmen, scholars, craftsmen replaced the earlier one.

Trade and Commerce

Under the Abbasids, economic life also thrived. The market and post systems were well organised with Baghdad as centre. The most important trade routes ran eastwards overland via Rayy, Nishapur and Merv to Bukhara and Samarquand and from there further on to central Asia and China or along Tigris to Basrah and so by sea to India and China. The westerly routes followed the Euphrates and Tigris to the Syrian harbours or passed overland through Asia minor to Constantinople, or through Syria and Palestine to Egypt and thence to North Africa.

The chief ports for trade to India, the Indonesian archipelago and China were Basra, Sirat and Aden. Voyages were made to far-off places. Among the most important commodities were milk, fine woods, camphor, indigo, precious stones, pepper and other spices. The main items of export were costly tapestries and carpets. The leading centres of production and trade were Iraq (Baghdad), Fars (Shiraz), and Egypt (Cairo) followed by Syria (Damascus) and Transoxiana (Bukhara and Samarquand). Agriculture and market gardening brought a wide range of fruit and food to the market. The towns were not only the centres of trade and industry but also the staple market of their products.

Decline of the Abbasids

The cycle of life ascribed by the Abbasid state did not differ from that of the Ummayad except in the duration of the period of decline. As time passed, the Abbasid caliphs lost much of their independence to Persian and Turkish sultanate dynasties. Local dynasties sprang up. However, during the Abbasid period there was practically no further expansion of Islam. Islam expanded to Africa, Asia Minor, Northern India, followed by Southern India. But it was no longer possible to speak of the Muslim empire as a political entity. In A.D. 1258, Baghdad was sacked and its inhabitants were massacred by *Hulaqu*, the great grandson of Chengiz Khan of Mongol race. Besides this, the rise of the local dynasties which succeeded in making themselves independent of the Abbasids, such as the Aghalabids in Tunisia, the Fatimids in Egypt, and the Samanids in Transoxiana furthered this disintegration. Out of this chaos, emerged two new forces: the Ottoman Empire and a reborn Persia and they were followed by the European invasion of the Islamic empire in the nineteenth and twentieth centuries.

The early part of twentieth century, however, witnessed the rise of nationalism in the Islamic world which culminated in the struggle for independence and later to revolution and national liberation in Turkey, Jordan, Iraq, Lebanon, Egypt, Libya, Sudan, Tunisia, Morocco, etc.

Islamic Revivalism

The Islamic movements in the 1920s particularly the Muslim Brotherhood (Egypt) played an important role in shaping the national liberal struggles of the Islamic nations. *Ikhwan Al- Muslimun* or the Muslim Brotherhood organisation was founded by an Egyptian called Hassan al-Banna in 1928. It had branches in Sudan, Syria, Lebanon, Jordan, North Africa and other Islamic states. The main principles of this organisation are the precise explanation of the holy Quran, to unify Arab nation, the growth of national wealth and its liberation, the struggle against poverty and vice, liberation of Arab countries including Palestine and the promotion of universal peace through the principles of Islam etc.

During President Nasser's period, the great majority of the people supported his charismatic and nationalist leadership and opposed the Muslim Brotherhood. A major reason for this support was Nasser's political philosophy which represented a combination of nationalist objectives, liberation of Palestine or Pan-Arabism and Islamic symbolism.

However, the 1970s witnessed the growth of radical Islamic organisations and ideologies, which aimed at establishing strict Islamic society and to enforce *Shariat* (Islamic Law). In contrast to the moderate Muslim Brotherhood organisations, the militants of the 1970s and 1980s are aggressive and do not shy away from violence. They, like the moderate Islamic movements take a hostile view towards Zionist Israel and Western Imperialism. Since the 1979 Islamic revolution in Iran, the revivalist Islamic movement is being made a basis for a new radical national identity in the Islamic countries.

The current trend of Islamic radicalism is largely due to the disillusionment in the Muslim world with other ideologies such as Marxism, Zionism, Capitalism and Socialism, none of which appeared to the Muslims as a way of meeting their day-to-day demands, or finding a solution to the ongoing political conflicts within the Arab sphere or solving their basic socio- economic problems. On the contrary, the economic crisis and social problems that have resulted from these ideologies and conflicts have only deepened and become more complex. In desperation, Muslims have therefore sought a solution derived from and steeped in their faith, Islam.

The resurgence of Islam as a living and influential faith seeking to meet the needs of the present day is one of the great features of this century. The greatest need of the moment is a better understanding of the Islamic values and rectifying mistakes through a process of intellectual discussion and persuasion.

5

The Renaissance

The late fifteenth and sixteenth centuries form a fascinating period in the history of the world. This is not only because of the great intellectual, artistic, religious and economic forces that arose within it but also because it was the first period of history where one can visualise history with any clarity. It was a time when many people voiced feelings recognisably akin to their own. The mastery of realistic techniques in painting and sculpture along with the survival of personal correspondence, the growing habit of writing self-revealing autobiographies and the preserving effect of the printing further enriched the knowledge of the way in which people lived during this time.

The Renaissance marked a shifting of emphasis in the socio-politico, religious-economic culture of the people. In the first place, the men of Renaissance substituted a worldly point of view for a religious point of view, with reference to art, literature, and the state. The centre of reference became man rather than God. Secondly, the men of the Renaissance sought in the past the kind of society which they wished to substitute for the medieval society with its emphasis on religion. They found the society they sought in the classical culture of ancient Greek and Rome. Hence they protested against the religious character of education in the Middle ages. This phase of the Renaissance is known as *Classicism* in history. Thus the Renaissance was the early cultural expression of a new age which emphasised the supremacy of the civil authority and the prime importance of the natural man. People in this age began to think for themselves rather than accepting the authority of scholars.

Meaning of Renaissance

"Renaissance" literally means rebirth. This word 'Renaissance' was first used by the great French historian, Jules Michelet, in 1855. In its Italian form, *rinascita*, it can be traced back to a work of 1550 by the Italian artist and art historian Giorgio Vasari. It means revival of the ancient culture of the Greeks and the Romans. The past, however, cannot be revived, for, past is past. What the people in the age of Renaissance did was to develop a fresh culture, based on that of Europe in the Medieval Age, to which they added fresh "ideas and inspirations" acquired by them through and by the study of the Greek and Roman literature, arts such as architecture, painting, sculpture, music, philosophy, science and technology. In the Medieval Age, human activities were controlled and guided by the paramount authority of the church. Anything approved and accepted by the authority of the Church was regarded as the Gospel's truth, and the influence of the church was paramount in practically all educational institutions, including some of the universities such as the Oxford, the Cambridge, the Paris, and the Naples Universities. No one could question the authority of the church. Human mind was virtually enslaved by the papal authority. The Renaissance, however, ushered in the age of reason and scientific temper. The people of Renaissance began to question the authority of the church and worked out their new theories and doctrines. They subjected everything that was taught to be true by the church to scientific investigation.

The Renaissance was characterised by humanism. The medieval writers and artists concentrated their energies on theological subjects, whereas the Renaissance scholars and artists focussed their mind on humanities. "The natural, the human, and the sensual were given precedence over the ascetical, the supernatural and the logical." Renaissance was, thus, a great movement for the revival of man's power of clear thinking on scientific basis and expressing himself in all provinces of life freely and fearlessly.

To sum up, "The Renaissance was an era of striking accomplishment in painting, sculpture, architecture, music, literature, philosophy, science, and technology. It also was an age of change in the economic foundations and in the basic structure of European society and in the organisation of states. And last but not least, the Renaissance affected the Christian church, which for generations had presided at the formation of European civilisation.

A number of factors were responsible for ushering in the age of Renaissance in Europe. The most important of them are explained below: Human mind and human activities were fettered in the Medieval Age by the Church authority. But with the passage of time, some scholars began to think independently and subjected everything to scientific investigation. Such original thinkers were chiefly responsible for ushering in the age of Renaissance. Peter Abelard, Roger Bacon, Albertus Magnus, Thomas Aquinas, St. Francis, and Dante were the "moving spirits of the new era". All of them injected a new spirit of enquiry, a scientific temper into the people.

Before the discovery of the printing press, books were copied by hand and, therefore, it was extremely difficult to spread knowledge far and wide. But the discovery of the printing press and the consequent wide circulation of books produced an immeasurable change. Towards the middle of the 15th century, John Gutenburg successfully operated the first printing press with movable types at Mains in Germany. This was followed by William Cazton in England in 1477. They were also set up in Italy and Hungary.

The city of Constantinople was the capital of the Eastern Roman Empire. In the year 1453, it fell into the hands of the Ottoman Turks, as a result of which the Greek scholars and thinkers of that city migrated, along with their original manuscripts, to various parts of Europe. The majority of them went to Italy, where they instilled in the people the spirit of enquiry and an enthusiasm for the study of the classics. This, naturally, provided a fresh impetus to the Renaissance.

Another significant effect of the fall of Constantinople into the hands of the Ottoman Turks in 1453 was that it closed down the last window through which the eastern articles reached west. The European merchants and navigators, therefore, explored new sea-routes to the east. Further, the Europeans came into contact with the Asians through the Crusades in the Medieval Age. The coming together of the Westerners and the Easterners through the Crusades and also through the newly-discovered sea-routes brought about not only wealth but also an inner urge and a broader vision to reorient life which to a great extent provided an impetus to the Renaissance.

Lastly, progressive rulers, popes and some noble families became patrons of this new movement. European rulers such as Francis I of France, Henry VIII of England, Charles V of Spain, Sigismud I of Poland, Christian II of Denmark wholeheartedly patronised the Renaissance and invited scholars and men of new learning to their courts. Further, some of the popes of the Roman Catholic Church gave every encouragement to the revival of the Graeco-Roman classics. Pope Nicholas V, being himself a great scholar, began the collection of old manuscripts in the Vatican. Another Pope named Leo X was a great lover of Classical art, sculpture, painting, music and literature, and, therefore, wholeheartedly patronised the Renaissance. Finally, some wealthy, noble, and influential families patronised artists, scientists and literary men of the Renaissance age. The Medici family of Florence, for example, founded an academy in Florence, which was solely devoted to the study and research of Platonic philosophy.

Thus, these were, in general, the factors that contributed to the rise, growth and spread of the Renaissance.

Origins of Renaissance

Every European state contributed something to the Renaissance, but Italy proved to be the "well-spring," "the school of Europe", like Athens in ancient Greece, from which the other European nations drew inspiration and life. "Italy had re-discovered ancient Greece and Rome". She rediscovered her own language and soul, applied new standards of diction and form to the vernacular, and composed poetry classical in spirit, but indigenous and 'modern' in tongue and thought. It was in Italy that most of the wonderful masterpieces of literature, architecture, sculpture, painting, music and science were first produced which became the perennial source of inspiration for others. Practically, all other European states invited and welcomed the masters and teachers of the "new learning and new art" from Italy. Finally, students and scholars from all other parts of Europe went to Italy.

The following factors were responsible for ushering in the Renaissance in Italy:

Dr. H.A.L. Fisher is of the view that it is natural that the Renaissance of European art and literature should have taken place in a land "where the marbles of antiquity still gleaned among the cypresses and olives, and the tradition of humane learning, descending from classical times, had never been wholly interrupted."

Italy was the centre of the glory of the ancient Romans. As such, all historical remains and relics of the ancient Romans in Italy were inviting and attracting the scholars and the artists. The ancient civilisation had never entirely disappeared in Italy. Much of Latin literature was preserved or hidden in monasteries.

With the fall of Constantinople in 1453 into the hands of Ottoman Turks, the Greek scholars and thinkers, with their original manuscripts and art treasures of the distant past, migrated mainly to Italy where they instilled in the people the spirit of enquiry and an enthusiasm for the study of the classics. This naturally fired the imagination of the Italian artists and men of letters who could then produce wonderful masterpieces of arts and literature, essentially modern in spirit and tone.

The Italian cities, through their enormous and brisk trade with both Asian and European countries, amassed enormous wealth. "Never before had there been so large a middle class with so much money". This provided sufficient leisure to them to encourage and spread the new learning.

Finally, there was much burning desire and buoyant spirit on the part of the Italians for the new learning. Some of the Popes such as Nicholas V (1447-55), Julius II (1503-13) and Leo X (1513-21), and some royal Italian families such as Medici family of Florence championed the cause of those who had love for the new learning.

This robust creative age in Italy came to an end around the middle of the sixteenth century when the country came under the political domination of Spain. However, the renaissance spread throughout Europe.

Growth and Spread of Renaissance

The Renaissance literature reflected the spirit of humanism and secularism. Further, it was written not in Latin but in the languages of the people, i.e. the vernacular languages which actually developed in the late Medieval Age.

Italian Writers

Among the Italian vernacular writers, the name of Nicolo Machiavelli stands out. He produced many historical works and amongst them, his "Prince" really proved to be an excellent guide for princes all over the world. Dante's "Divine Comedy" was translated and published in Italian language. Ariosto composed "Orlando Furioso," a poem in Italian, and Tasso, too, composed his epic, "Jerusalem Delivered."

German Writers

In Germany, Martin Luther made significant contribution to German literature by his works of translation of the Bible.

Spanish Writers

Cervantes, one of the most brilliant writers of all times, produced his immortal work, "Don Quixote", which is considered to be "the most beautiful and wonderful gift of the Renaissance to the literature of the world". Further, Lope de Vega and Calderon composed dramas and poems respectively in Spanish.

Portuguese Writers

At the same time, the Portuguese literature witnessed its glory in the "Lusiads", an immortal epic by Camoens, narrating the wonderful voyages and exploits of Vasco Da Gama.

French Writers

Michael De Montaigne (1533-92), through his essays, and Francis Rabelais (1490-1553), through his poetry, particularly the "Gargantua", inaugurated the Golden Age in French literature in the 17th century.

Dutch Writers

Desiderius Erasmus (1466-1536) produced his immortal work, "In Praise of Folly."

English Writers

The English literature reached its highest pinnacle of glory in the sixteenth century. There was a continuous flow of great literature in English. Geoffery Chaucer, Father of English poetry, wrote "Canterbury Tales"; Francis Bacon, "the greatest, wisest, and meanest of mankind", wrote a variety of essays; Sir Thomas Moore produced his "Utopia"; Milton composed his immortal epic "Paradise Lost"; Crammer wrote his "Book of Common Prayers"; Ben Johnson, Christopher Marlowe, and Shakespeare created wonderful, thrilling and lovable plays and dramas.

Thus, throughout Europe, there was much continuous outpouring of vernacular literature which was much enjoyed by the regional peoples. This, ultimately, led to the development of national literature and also national political institutions.

The Renaissance in Arts

Art in all its forms was dominated solely by the Christian church in the Medieval Age. It dealt with and depicted only the moral virtues and mysteries of the Christian faith. It was completely devoid of the spirit of humanism and naturalism.

The creative age of Renaissance sharply reacted against the domination of the Church. The Renaissance artists and architects, first in Italy and then in other parts of Europe, created arts and architecture which were graceful, elegant, realistic, lifelike and peerless in their beauty, harmony of shades and balanced form. The Renaissance art reflected the spirit of humanism and naturalism.

The Art of Architecture

The medieval towns and buildings were constructed mainly for defence and security and not for luxuries, comforts, and conveniences of their owners. The ancient Greek architectural orders—Doric, Ionic, and Corinthian—were revived and freely employed for all varieties of buildings. It reached its climax in St. Peter's Church in Rome, built in the 16th century under the personal guidance and supervision of two great artists and architects named, Raphael, and Michelangelo. Likewise, in the 17th century, St. Paul's Cathedral was constructed by Sir Christopher Wren. These two and also St. Mark's and the Doge's palaces in Venice, were the most beautiful architectural creations of the age of Renaissance.

The Art of Sculpture

In the art of sculpture, too, the spirit of humanism and naturalism was very much depicted in the period of Renaissance. There were four outstanding and peerless sculptors in Florence in Italy.

Lorenzo Ghiberti (1378-1455)

The first high priest of the new sculpture was Lorenzo Ghiberti in the 15th century. He chiselled his most magnificent and wonderful doors for the Baptistery at Florence, which were considered by Michelangelo as "worthy of being placed at the entrance to paradise".

Donatello (1386-1466)

Slightly younger than Ghiberti was Donatello whose art of sculpture was marked by the quality of intense realism, and naturalism. He fashioned with his chisel the life-like statues of St. George and St. Mark in Venice which are probably his best-known works.

Luca Della Robbia (1399-1482)

He founded a new school of sculptors in glazed terra cotta. He was renowned for his classical purity and simplicity of style.

Michelangelo

A revolutionary sculptor, a most celebrated architect and painter, Michelangelo was, an omni-competent and a versatile genius. He had a magic in his chisel. He chiselled out the gigantic statue of David in Florence which is "a masterpiece of anatomical study and suggests, in the massive head, intellectual superiority". His another gigantic statue of Moses has been described as "half prize-fighter, half Jupiter". Finally, "deep emotion is expressed with stirring realism" in his sculpture called, the "Pieta". The Italian sculptors became so much world renowned that Henry VII of England and Francis I of France warmly invited them to their respective countries. The new sculpture became the order of the day throughout Western Europe in the 16th century.

The Art of Painting

The art of painting was more original, and attained a "higher degree of perfection than did any of the other arts" in the creative age of Renaissance. New artistic methods such as frescoes for wall painting, oil colours, and woodcuts were invented, improved and perfected to a very large extent. Italy produced in the 16th century world's four most remarkable and greatest painters, Leonardo da Vinci, Michelangelo, Raphael, and Titian.

Leonardo da Vinci (1452-1519)

A Florentine by birth, Leonardo da Vinci was an omni-competent, versatile genius. He was a musician of the highest order, a great painter, a competent engineer, an ingenious craftsman, and a poet-cum-philosopher. He was considered to be a "scientific painter, carefully studying the human body, the problems of perspective and mastering the values of light and shade and colour." His "Mona Lisa", "The Last Supper", "The Virgin of the Rocks", and "The Virgin and Child with Saint Anne" are recognised as the most marvellous masterpieces of art. These paintings are peerless in their inward beauty, grace, psychological effect, mysterious charm, well-balanced colour, shade, light, and background.

Michelangelo (1475-1564)

Michelangelo, like Leonardo, was an omni-competent genius, a bright painter, a matchless sculptor, an architect of the first rank, an eminent engineer, a great poet, and a very serious-minded student of anatomy and physiology. His most remarkable achievement in the art of painting was his most magnificent and wonderful frescoes on the ceiling of the Sistine Chapel, in all there are 145 pictures in it with 394 figures, a few of which are 10 ft. high.

Raphael (1483-1520)

Sanzio Raphael was a revolutionary painter, an eminent sculptor, and a remarkable architect of the 16th century. He was an architect of St. Peter's Church at Rome. His "Sistine Madonna" was his most marvellous achievement in the art of painting. "Its beauty of composition and its lifelike charm have made it one of the most famous paintings in the world."

Titian (1477-1576)

Titian was the chief representative of the Venetian School of painting which is characterised by the secularisation of the Renaissance art. Their paintings "reflected the pleasure, the voluptuous beauty, and the strongly secular spirit of life in Venice". Titian's greatest gift was that of oil painting.

The new art of painting, although originated, developed and perfected in Italy, soon became the heritage of the whole of Western Europe. In Germany, Albrecht Durer and Holbein; in Spain, Velasquez Murillo and El Greco; and in Holland, Rubbens and Van Dykes, produced excellent and magnificent works of painting.

The Art of Music

Italy witnessed the Golden Age in the art of music in the 16th century. The old and outdated crude instruments of the Medieval Age were substituted with new, sweet and melodious ones. The harpsi-chord, the forerunner of piano, and the Violin gained popularity and pre-eminence. Great attention was paid to harmony, rhythm and symmetry. The musicians introduced a combination of different melodies and polyphony and also numerous independent voice parts. Giovanni Palestrina, the chief representative of the Roman school of music, Giovanni Gabrieli and Adrian Willaert of the Venetian school of music—all of the 16th century—were great musicians of the age.

The Renaissance art, thus, depicted life in all its aspects. Pleasure and pain, worldliness and saintliness, wealth and poverty, were all vividly expressed in the Renaissance art.

The Renaissance in Science

In the Medieval Age, the feudal society was marked by confusion, disorder, poverty, blind faith in magic superstitions, supernaturalism and mysteries. Further, the church condemned the scientists, branded their methods and approach as "heathenish", and physicians, in general, were looked down as atheists. All these factors were most unfavourable for carrying on scientific pursuits.

Man, in the 15th century, was more concerned with the life and things of the world on which he lived rather than with those of the next. Intellectuals engaged themselves in humanism. The Reformation challenged the authority of the Pope. The geographical discoveries brought new ideas. Roger Bacon strongly recommended, as early as in the 13th century, experiments in laboratory in science. Descartes, in the 16th century, taught that everything must be questioned. The experimental method of Roger Bacon and the idea of doubt as recommended by Descartes, ultimately developed into the modern scientific spirit. The scientific spirit led to a number of bewildering inventions and new scientific processes which revolutionised the then social, economic, cultural and political life.

Astronomy

It is a science of heavenly bodies. Until the middle of the sixteenth century, the "Ptolemaic system" reigned supreme in the science of astronomy. Ptolemy, a Greek astronomer of Egypt, propounded this system, under which, the earth was considered to be the centre of our planetary system, and therefore the sun, the moon and the stars revolved around the earth. This theory was almost held sacred.

Nicholas Copernicus (1473-1543), a Pole, after scientific study, observation and reflection, discovered the truth that the sun, and not the earth, is the centre of our planetary system. The earth, the moon and other stars revolve in a circle around the sun. The Copernican theory was quite revolutionary in nature, as it challenged the authority of the Church. His book, "The Revolutions of the Heavenly Orbs", was published only after his death. This truth, in fact, was long discovered by Aristarchus of Samos who declared that the earth revolves around the sun, and that at the same time, it itself rotates daily on its own axis. But nobody believed him.

The Copernican theory was popularised in the 17th century by two great astronomers, John Kepler, the German scientist, and Galileo, an Italian scientist.

John Kepler (1571-1630) made mathematical laws to prove the conclusions of Copernicus but pointed out that the planets revolve round the sun not in a circle but in elliptical orbits (= paths).

Galileo (1564-1642) brought fresh evidence, by his invention of telescope, to support the conclusions of Copernicus. According to him, there are mountains on the moon and rings around Saturn. However, the Inquisition (=Papal court for trying heretics) compelled him, at the pain of death, to deny publicly what he had affirmed openly. Even then, he murmured that Truth shall prevail.

Sir Issac Newton (1642-1727) discovered that movements of all heavenly bodies were controlled by the forces of gravitation.

Physics

In the science of physics, numerous inventions were made. Gilbert (1540-1603), one of the greatest physicists before Galileo, made experiments with magnetic properties. He, thus, made way for the study of electricity.

Stevin (1548-1620) discovered the law of the parallelorgram of forces and made experiments with the pressure of liquids.

Galileo (1564-1642) was a versatile genius. He was an outstanding astronomer and the greatest of the early physicists. By scientific study and close observation of a swinging lamp in the Cathedral of Pisa, he discovered the law of pendulum. Further, by dropping heavy and light balls from the leaning tower of Pisa, he discovered another law of physics that the speed of a falling body solely depends upon the distance it falls and not upon the weight of the body, as was taught by Aristotle. Galileo, thus, laid the foundations of modern dynamics. Galileo also invented the air thermometer, the hydrostatic balance and an astronomical clock. Other important inventions included the barometer and the balance scale for determining weight.

Chemistry

In this period, alchemy gave place to chemistry. Paracelsus (1493-1541) affirmed that reactions in the body of a person involve chemical changes. He also used chemicals for medicinal purposes.

Cordus (1515-1544) made ether from sulphuric acid and alcohol.

Helmont (1577-1644) discovered carbon dioxide and affirmed that there are gases different in kind from the atmospheric air.

Medicine

Great progress was registered in the science of medicine. Vasalius (1514-1565), a scientist of Netherland, wrote a treatise on anatomy in which the skeleton, cartilage, muscles, veins and arteries, digestive and reproductive systems, lungs, and the brain—all of them were dealt with in minute detail.

William Harvey (1578-1657) discovered that the circulation of blood begins from the heart to the arteries and from there to the veins and back to the heart. This is a revolutionary contribution to the science of medicine.

Mathematics

In the science of mathematics, the west received a rich gift from the east through the Muslims. The rudimentary principles of algebra and the Arabic numerals came from the Muslims, who, in turn, learnt from the ancient Indians.

Tartaglia (1500-1557), Ferrari (1522-1565), Vieta (1540-1603) and Kepler (1571-1630) devised different kinds of equations. Desargues (1593-1662) systematized modern geometry. Esscartes devised a practical system of analytical geometry. Stevin (1548-1620) recommended a decimal system of coinage, weights, and measures. Finally, Napier (1550-1617) invented logarithms in which he made use of the decimal point.

Other Inventions and Discoveries

Printing Press: In the beginning, printing was invented in China. However, later on, it was also invented in Western Europe independently.

In the Medieval Age, the kings, princes, and nobles got their signatures cut on blocks of wood or metal and used them very conveniently for signing or sealing documents. Later on, someone somewhere invented the process of making letters on separate tiny pieces of wood and metal—all of the same size and then setting them in any order for the purpose of printing. This movable type proved to be of immense importance, for the movable types could be set and reset again and again in the desired order. The person who was responsible for the change from the composite blocks to the movable type, is still shrouded in mystery. What is certain is that about the year 1450, John Gutemburg was using movable types in his printing press in Germany.

Gunpowder: It was originally invented by the Chinese and used by them and the Arabs. In the 14th century Europe, bronze cannon came to be manufactured from which stone cannon balls were fired. Later on, they were replaced by iron cannon and iron balls. Hand guns were also manufactured.

Mariner's Compass: Its early history is very obscure. As early as the 5th century A.D., it was known in a crude form to the Chinese.

Alexander Neckam wrote in his work of the 12th century that "Mariners at sea .... touch a needle with a magnet which will turn round till on its motion ceasing, its point will be directed towards the north". This was the earliest known reference in literature.

Chaucer, a great English poet, wrote in 1391 of the division of the compass card into thirty-two points.

Thus were laid many of the foundations of modern science in the robust age of the Renaissance.

Results of Renaissance

The Renaissance produced consequences of immense importance:

The Spirit of Enquiry

One of the greatest boons of the Renaissance to the modern world is the revival of the spirit of enquiry, the scientific temper, and the curiosity to know the unknown and to explore the unexplored. Human mind was chained and enslaved under the Papal authority in the Medieval Age. It was liberated from such a slavery in the age of Renaissance. It, then, engaged itself in inventing and discovering the things and processes which have made human life richer, fuller, more secure, more convenient and more comfortable than what it was in the distant past.

The Spirit of Humanism

Human intellect, energy and time in the Medieval Age were devoted solely to the study of theological subjects. The Renaissance inaugurated a revolt against this and promoted human interest in everything concerning the happiness and welfare of man. The apostles of new culture came to be known as the "Humanists" and their subjects of study were called the "Humanities".

Enriched Curriculum

It enriched the curricula of schools, colleges and universities by adding Caesar, Cicero, Virgil and Homer and also the Latin and Greek languages to it.

Stimulus to Vernaculars

Humanism provided an impetus to the growth of vernacular literatures. Writers began to write in vernacular languages such as Italian, French, English, German, etc.

Church Weakened

As the spirit of enquiry gained currency, everything preached by the church was questioned and anything that failed to appeal to reason was rejected. As a result of this, many revolted against the established authority of the church.

Monarchy Strengthened

On the one hand, the Papal authority was weakened and on the other monarchy was strengthened. People were utterly tired of confusion and anarchy of the feudal society. Hence, they supported, in the Renaissance age, a strong monarchy to enjoy life in peace, security, and political stability.

Intellectual Revolution

The invention of printing press accomplished an intellectual revolution, for, without it "books would still be luxuries for the rich, newspapers would be unknown and universal education hardly possible".

Triple Revolution

The invention of gunpowder caused a triple revolution. First, it revolutionised the art and science of warfare. Second, it revolutionised the social conditions by breaking down the feudal barons and lords and lifting up the common man. Third, it caused political revolution by championing the cause of the autocratic monarchs.

Navigation, Colonisation and Commerce

The invention of the Mariner's Compass with the magnetic needle caused almost a revolution in navigation, which facilitated colonisation and overseas commerce which in turn caused several bloody wars in the human history.

Arts and Sciences Encouraged

The Renaissance provided a tremendous impetus to the growth of various kinds of arts, learning and literature. It also encouraged the study of sciences and patronised the scientists who made numerous scientific inventions and discoveries. It also led to geographical discoveries.

Thus, Renaissance was the specific epoch in history which followed the middle ages and introduced, what we considered the modern times in history. This movement was by no means confined to art and architecture but found its expression in all spheres of human life including philosophy, literature, religion, geography, natural science and astronomy. Since the term 'Renaissance' is now generally used in different senses, any general consideration of the subject must today be reasonably flexible. It must recognise cultural achievement and the revival of antiquity. It should try to determine the novel elements in all aspects of life.

6

The Reformation (1517-1555)

By far the most momentous event of the early modern period was the *Reformation.* It started as a reform movement within the catholic church. Its original objective was to purify the Roman Christian church and to revivify the Christian morals in European life and society. It resulted in the emergence throughout Europe of several new churches or religious traditions—Lutheran, Calvinist (Reformed), Anglican, Anabaptist, Antitrinarian—all anticatholic in orientation and collectively known as Protestanism. Two developments, however, characterise the history of the Reformation viz:- a theological debate about the proper understanding of the Christian church and a political understanding of the legal status of new Reformation churches. But the Reformation was more than just a religious struggle. It was part of a broader stream in which other powerful currents of the time moved that is economic, social, and political. Many historians prefer to speak of a "Revolution" rather than a "Reformation".

The Reformation, as noted above, led to the establishment of a number of protestant churches in England, Germany, Italy, Scandinavia, Scotland, France and Switzerland etc. It was a sequence of reformatory movements that reappeared throughout Europe. The term 'Reformation' (from Latin reformare, i.e. to renew) was employed in the sixteenth century by the adherents of the movement to express the notion that theirs was an effort at returning the church to its biblical sources. The term "Protestant", soon the broad name for all followers of the Reformation, stemmed from the "protest" voiced at the Diet of Speyer (1529). Historians have been tempted to speak of the Reformation as a broad, international revolution—a term that has a measure of justification on the basis of the wide effects of the Reformation.

The urgent need of a reform in existing religious institutions was generally recognised outside as well as within the Catholic church. For more than 1,000 years after the fall of the Roman Empire, the Christian or Catholic church of Rome held a supreme position. It was the centre of all culture, the defender of christianity, and the mainstay of the people. At the height of the church's power, under Pope Innocent III, who reigned from 1198 to 1216, all European rulers accepted the Pope's spiritual and temporal sovereignty. In the course of the 1300's and 1400's the church began to fall from this position of universal power struggles with rulers, religious schisms, and corruptions it. The catholic church in particular was seen as suffering from various abuses both moral and theological. These abuses that penetrated all parts and layers of catholic Church threatened its entire structure. The public was quite indignant and expressed serious concern at the decline of the morals and values of the clergy.

The Catholic hierarchy seemed ill equipped to deal with the spiritual needs of the people. The higher clergy, notably the bishops, were recruited from the nobility and saw their office mainly as a source of power, prestige and wealth. Equally precarious was the condition of the lower clergy—the Parish Priests. The qualifications for becoming a priest were minimal. Remuneration was low. Anarchy reigned within the church. Among Popes and bishops, corruption of morals existed. Many enjoyed and practised worldly interests, allowed nepotism and simony, and proved greedy. Immortality and sexual promiscuity was the order of the churchmen. A large section of the clergy were interested themselves in secular affairs, in science, art, materialism and economics, rather than in the salvation or purification of the souls. Besides this, constant rivalries and jealousies among the members of the church, between monks and priests existed. Bishops tried to hold as many lucrative church offices as possible without fulfilling the corresponding responsibilities. Moreover, errors of faith had developed, which led to errors in conduct. Pope misused indulgences and abused their power to censure and excommunicate.

The growth of heretical sects further weakened the church. Since the 1200's, the number of Christians who rejected official church doctrines had grown alarmingly. Reformist sects included the Albigenses and waldenses in the 1100's and 1200's and the Lollards and Hussites in the thirteenth and fourteenth centuries. In this setting many voices pleaded for church reform. The humanists, especially those led by *Erasmus* voiced their opposition to the status-quo. They were convinced that the Church was leading the people away from the pure and simple religion of Christ.

Furthermore, during the middle ages, the kingdoms of Europe were not really nations. They had shifting boundaries and constant civil wars. But a *new force of nationalism* gradually spread throughout Europe. Rulers tried to gain absolute sovereignty for themselves. They began to look jeolously at the power and vast material wealth of the church.

The Revival of Learning was another factor that led to the Reformation. At one time, only nobles and churchmen could be educated. But during the Renaissance, universities and schools sprang up everywhere and students crowded into the towns. Many protestant leaders came from the ranks of those students. New interest grew in original texts of the Bible and the classics of the ancient world. Humanists thus began to criticise church teachings and doctrines. The invention of the *Printing Press* spread the above new ideas.

Finally, the decline of feudalism, the poverty of peasants, the growth of commerce and the rise of a middle class also led to Reformation. The new middle class which was made up of businessmen and merchants opposed the church, because it represented the mainstay of an order that had blocked their rise to power.

The greatest figure of the Reformation was an Augustinian monk, *Martin Luther* (1483-1546). He was the greatest figure in 16th century Reformation. He was also the composer of commentaries on scripture, theology and ecclesiastical abuses. Today, hundreds of years later, the immediate and direct influence of his work is continuously felt. Luther was not, however, a great originator but was a great accomplisher. Many men before Luther like Ockham, Marsilins, Bradwardine, Wydiffe, Wessel, Huss, Savonarola etc., had urged reform of the organisation of the church. Luther based his thinking on the Epistles of St. Paul. They led him to conclude that only faith in the sacrifice of Jesus Christ, rather than in that of priests, sacraments, or good deeds, could ensure salvation. He also concluded that only the *Bible*, not the Pope, was infallible, or free from error. He believed that the institution of Pope was not of divine but of human origin and every Christian was directly responsible to God and did not need the mediation of a priest. Thus he broke down the distinction between the religions and secular.

Luther's outrage at the way *indulgences*, or spiritual Pardons, were sold in Saxony led him to speak out against the church. On 31 October 1517, he posted his *'Ninety Five Theses"* church in Wittenberg. He had no intention of starting a movement to destroy the authority of the church. He meant only to reform abuses within it. But when the theses were circulated throughout Germany, it caused a major upheaval. Humanists throughout Germany responded enthusiastically to Luther's attack on indulgences. Also, Luther had inadvertently touched a politically sensitive matter. By attacking the sale of indulgences, Luther had infringed on fiscal interests of both the Papacy and Elector Albert of Brandenburg.

In 1518, Pope Leo X declared Luther a heretic. In 1519, Johann Eck challenged Luther to debate at Leipzig. In 1520, Luther took a further decisive step by publishing three fundamental Pamphlets viz:- *An Address to the christian Nobility of the German Nation, The Babylonian Captivity of the Church, and The Liberty of a Christian man.* The Pope threatened a ban of excommunication against Luther; but, in the presence of applauding Wittenberg university students, Luther publicly burned the Pope's bull and thereby protested on behalf of the individual's inalienable right, as a Christian, to be subject to God alone. Then Emperor Charles V ordered him to appear before the Imperial *Diet at Worms*. Once there, Luther refused to retract any of his statements. The emperor ruled against him and forbade him to preach. Luther defied the Pope and emperor and began to organise his Lutheran church in 1522.

Lutheranism spread rapidly throughout Germany, The Netherlands parts of Switzerland, Denmark, France, Scotland, Hungary and Czechoslovakia. In Switzerland, the thirteen cantons, torn by internal strife, were receptive to protestantism. Huldreich Zwingli, a priest from Zurich, began preaching a reformed religion in 1519. His views spread to Strasbourg, Constance, Memmingen, and Lindan in South Germany. *John Calvin* dominated the later part of the Swiss Reformation. His *Institutes of the Christian Religion*, written in 1536, was the most profound protestant treatise of the Reformation. Aided by William *Farel*, Calvin established a powerful centre for his teachings in Geneva. His views on the Bible, the church government made him famous. Calvinism spread to Germany, France, Scotland, England and The Netherlands.

In *France*, protestantism found many supporters among the people. In *Scandinavia*, King Frederick I of Denmark took the lead in introducing Lutheranism. A Danish translation of the New Testament appeared in 1524. In *England*, the Reformation began with Henry VIII's quarrel with the Pope over his right to divorce his first wife, Catherine of Aragon. The Pope refused to allow the divorce, and Henry broke with the church at Rome. The Act of supremacy of 1534 made the king, not the Pope, head of the Roman catholic church in England. In *Scotland*, John Knox led the Reformation. He persuaded the parliament to adopt a calvinist confession in 1560. In *Ireland*, the established church followed all the changes that took place in England during the reign of Henry VIII Edward VI, Mary I, and Elizabeth I.

Protestants viewed the Reformation as the restoration of Biblical Christianity against the utterly perverted church whereas Catholics saw it as a rebellion against truth. However, the Reformation entailed the repudiation of authority and therefore, as scholars opined, was the direct forerunner of the French Revolution and all other changes in the modern world.

Foremost among the consequences of the Reformation was the division of western Christendom into several religious factions. The centrality of the Catholic church was destroyed. The concept of universal church gave way to the idea of national churches. Protestantism, became the chief religion of the countries of north-western Europe. Protestantism made the Bible the centre of a simpler church service in the vernacular, or language of the people. The Roman catholic church conducted its own counter Reformation.

Economically, the Reformation greatly strengthened the position of the mercantile and industrial class, but it lowered that of the peasants. Politically, Lutheranism promoted a belief in absolute monarchy based on powers attained by Divine right. But calvinism encouraged self-determination and the right of revolution against tyranny. Protestantism in general led to the subordination of the church to state, and strengthened the system of national territories, independent of each other.

Thus, the Reformation provided a host of stimuli for all areas of human life. It left a deep imprint upon the western world. This affected their intellectual trends, their economy and their national developments. The Reformation stimulated education, changed social relationships, and led to new legal concepts and new laws. Indeed, the cause of individualism, which the Renaissance, humanism, and capitalistic enterprise had fostered, was also advanced by the Reformation.

7

Geographical Discoveries

The second part of the fifteenth century and the first half of the sixteenth century, the span of about hundred years, in world history witnessed the Age of Discovery. During this period, the Europeans learned with the confidence of experience to think of the world as a whole. They discovered that the world was larger by far, and more diverse, than any the then accepted authority, ancient or medieval had taught. The enlargement of geographical knowledge which Europeans achieved in the above hundred years was prodigious in its extent and in its speed. The enlargement of geographical knowledge, however, was not the primary purpose of the explorers. The great discoverers were not Renaissance humanists consumed by intellectual curiosity. They were practical commercial minded men. Distant unknown islands and continents, unless productive of gold or other precious things, were of little interest to them. They set out to discover not only new lands but also new routes to old lands. Their main purpose, and that of the rulers and investors, who sent them out, was to establish direct contact with areas of commercial interest and importance in Asia and Africa, and to link them with the individual centres in Europe. They were, to a great extent, interested in establishing the predominance of European commerce in the discovered world. In all this the significant factor was not simply discovery but the determination with which discovery was exploited and capitalised for their own benefits.

The newly discovered and explored world had been largely undergoing a process of Europeanisation. There were a variety of factors that were responsible for the discovery of new lands by the Europeans and also for Europeanisation of the new world. Those factors were as follows:

Europe-Hungry of Commerce: In the Medieval Age, there existed a flourishing trade and commerce between Europe and Asia through Constantinople, the capital of the Eastern Roman Empire. The city of Constantinople, however, fell in the year 1453 into the hands of the fanatical Ottoman Turks who immediately closed the trade routes within their empire for the European traders. Hence, the Europeans were compelled to discover new sea routes for the purpose of trade.

Europe - Hungry of Eastern Luxuries: The rich and the well-to-do in Europe developed a taste for the luxurious articles obtainable from the East by trade with Africa and Asia such as silk from China, and cotton goods and precious stones from India. "Besides species", all kinds of precious stones, drugs, perfumes, gums, dyes, and fragrant woods came from the East. The demand for such articles, day by day, went on increasing on the part of the Europeans. Hence, they were compelled to find new sea routes to the East.

Europe - Hungry for Adventure and Gain: Europe was also hungry for adventure and gain. Many young Europeans were inspired by the spirit of adventure to sail into the unknown and thus to discover the undiscovered lands. Many were prompted by the idea of gain in the form of wealth, land, and luxurious articles.

Europe was, thus, hungry in more than one sense. The Europeans were hungry for commerce with the East, hungry for the Eastern luxurious articles, hungry for adventure, for conquest of land, and for gain.

To Spread Christianity: Christianity has been, since its inception, one of the most intensely missionary religions in the world. There began in Europe in the fifteenth century a powerful Christian missionary movement, the leaders of which were prepared even to run the risk of their lives as soldiers of Christ to convey the holy message of the Christ in every nook and corner of the world. At the same time, the European traders were determined to find out new routes to the East for purposes of trade. Hence, many a time, European traders, merchants, and missionaries sailed together to the unexplored lands.

Growth of Geographical Knowledge: The growth of geographical knowledge greatly contributed to the geographical explorations and discoveries. Several books, such as "A Merchant's Handbook" by a Florentine, which dealt with all the known trade routes between the West and the Far East, and "Secrets of the Faithful Crusader", written by a Venetian, narrated Asiatic cities, and also other books on travel such as, "The Far East", "The Holy Lands", and "Africa" improved the geographical knowledge of the Europeans.

Mariner's Compass: Finally, even if all the factors narrated above were present, there would have been no geographical explorations and discoveries but for the invention of Mariner's Compass with a magnetic needle. It showed in the darkness of the night the direction towards the north when the navigators lost the knowledge of the quarter of the world, to which they were sailing. Thus, the Mariner's Compass, the Astrolabe, the improvement in the ship-building, and the art of map-making with greater accuracy supplied new impetus to geographical explorations and discoveries.

Portuguese Explorations

The little state of Portugal ranked first among the powers as a pioneer in geographical explorations and discoveries.

Henry, the Navigator (1394-1460): Prince Henry, the styled Navigator, founded a school for seamen, and provided every possible help and encouragement to them in their voyages. The portuguese ventured out into the Atlantic Ocean. Under the patronage of Henry, the navigator, annual expeditions were organised to explore the West Coast of Africa and for that purpose he called for the services of the learned geographers, map-makers, sailors, and ship-designers. His another achievement was that he got built a greatly improved sailing ship, named the "Caravel", capable of long voyages in stormy weather through the open sea, which was later on imitated by most of the maritime powers. The expeditions, under the patronage of Henry, explored several islands on the Western coast of Africa and claimed the Maderia Island, the Azores, and the West African Guinea Coast. Here were established the Portuguese settlements.

Bartholomew Diaz (The Cape Route to the East) : After the death of Prince Henry, navigational spirit continued unabated with the Portuguese sailors. Under the royal patronage, a very able and ambitious Portuguese sailor named Bartholomew Diaz sailed south of the African coast in 1487. He named it the Cape of Storms, as he himself was caught in one of such storms. However, its name was later on changed by his royal patron, from the Cape of Storms to the Cape of Good Hope, thereby implying that it provided a good hope for the Portuguese to reach India.

Vasco Da Gama (A.D. 1469-1524) (The Cape Route to the East): After more than a decade, another ambitious and adventurous sailor named Vasco Da Gama was given a commission to proceed farther the Cape of Good Hope. He sailed the African continent for ten months and twelve days and landed in Calicut on the west coast of India in the year 1498 and returned home with the eastern spices and precious stones, worth the amount sixty times more than the total cost of his expedition. Thus was realised the dream of the Portuguese navigators. This was followed by the building of a vast commercial empire by the Portuguese, which included India, Ceylon, Sumatra, Java and the East India. In 1517, they went to Canton in China, and in 1542, they arrived in Japan. Vasco Da Gama's discovery of a new sea-route to India was most significant event in the history of the world.

Spanish Explorations

The Spanish geographical explorations proved to be of far-reaching consequences in human history. They discovered America, i.e. the new Continent.

Christopher Columbus (The Atlantic Route to America) : In 1490, Columbus, an Italian sailor from the city of Genoa, after a careful study of globe prepared by the German geographer, Martin Behaim, reached more quickly and easily by sailing due west across the Atlantic Ocean. Financed by Queen Isabella of Spain, Columbus sailed on 3rd August, 1492, at the head of three ships, *The Santa Maria, The Nina,* and *The Pinta*, with 88 men on board to reach the Far East. After a long, tedious, and dangerous voyage of two months and nine days, the happy cry "land, land!" came from the lockouts. On 12th October, 1492, he landed on an island which he believed to be the East Indies, just off the coast of Asia. Columbus named the natives "Indians". He discovered the coasts of the Carribean Sea, Venezuela, the Central America. Later on, it was discovered that it was not Asia but altogether a new continent, a new world of North and South America.

Amerigo Vespucci (The Atlantic Route to South America) : The explorations of Columbus inspired others to follow him. An Italian named Amerigo Vespucci made several voyages after 1497, explored further areas, supplied geographic details about the land and its people discovered by him, and recognised it altogether a "new world", entirely different from Asia. The German geographer, Waldseemuller, suggested that the "new world" would be named America in honour of Amerigo.

Vasco Nunez de Balboa: Another Spanish sailor, Balboa, in the hope of discovering gold in the New World, crossed the Isthmus of Darien (Panama) in the year 1513. Besides Balboa, Ponce de Leon discovered Florida.

Ferdinand Magellan (1519-22) (The South-West Route to South America): A Portuguese sailor, Ferdinand Magellan, under the service of King Charles I, the grandson of Isabella, of Spain, sailed from Spain with five ships - *San Antonio, Trinidad, Conception, Victoria,* and *Santiago* at the head of 267 crew, in September 1519. He crossed the Atlantic and rounded South America through the Straits which have been named after him, the Straits of Magellan, and saw a new ocean. He named it Pacific. Magellan sailed across the Pacific Ocean and landed on the Philippine Islands. Magellan, however, lost his life in a fight with the natives of the Philippine Islands on April 27, 1521. Out of the total five ships, only *Victoria* reached Seville harbour, returning via the Cape of Good Hope (Africa) and thus back to Europe. "That was the first voyage around the world, and one of the greatest in all history."

Hernando Cortez Conquers Mexico (1519): Cortez proved to be one of the greatest Spanish explorers of the early sixteenth century. He with his soldiers landed in Mexico and fought the natives. He drove out their ruler and became the Spanish Governor.

English Explorations

In 1497, King Henry VII of England employed an Italian from Genoa, John Cabet, to sail the North-west route to China and India and "to seek out, discover, and find whatever isles, countries, regions or provinces which before this time have been unknown to all Christians". He crossed the Atlantic and reached the shores of the North East of North America, and named one island New Foundland, without knowing that he had discovered a new continent. This enabled England to assert her first claim over the mainland of North America. The subsequent explorers, particularly those of Sebastiah Cabot, strengthened the British claim over Canada and the U.S.A. During the last quarter of the sixteenth century, the English explorers like Drake, Gilbert and Raleigh further explored the east coast of North America.

French Explorations

In 1524, an Italian, Verrazano, under the service of the king of France, explored the bays and mouths of rivers along the coast from North Carolina to New York. A decade later, i.e. 1535, the Frenchman Jacque Cartier explored the St. Lawrence River, and founded the city of Montreal. Later on, Samuel de Champlain, Marquette, Joliet, and La Salle extended French claims to Canada and the Mississippi and St. Lawrence river valleys.

Effects of Geographical Discoveries

The geographical explorations and discoveries produced consequences of immense importance in human history.

The Commercial Revolution: It caused, what has sometime been called with some exaggeration, the "Commercial Revolution". It gave rise to the brisk maritime trade between the Europeans and the Easterners and also the Americans. The Europeans imported not only the eastern spices and other items which they used to import in the past but also new luxurious articles such as Indian textiles, Persian carpets, etc. and several other eastern commodities like potatoes, chocolate, cocoa, tobacco, maize, quinine, cane sugar, tea, coffee, dye-woods, whale oil, indigo, porcelain, etc. Huge quantities of fish, fur, and timber were shipped from America to Europe. They also explored several European manufactured goods to Asia, Africa, and America where they founded European colonies. Thus, commerce underwent a remarkable change, both in quantum and in variety of goods, articles, and commodities, imported and exported. However, there was no corresponding change in quantity, and variety of the manufactured articles. Such a change had to wait until a great revolution called the Industrial Revolution. This naturally led to a remarkable improvement in the "mechanism of the exchange of goods," including credit institutions, commercial banks and other instruments known to the modern system of capitalism.

The Mercantile System: The economists of the age widely thought that total international trade was limited, and that, that country was the richest which possessed the greatest supply of bullion. This resulted in what is known as the "mercantile system". Accordingly, every commercially-minded European monarch aimed at increasing his country's overseas trade at the expense of foreigners. This system prescribed exports as much as possible but not the raw materials, and imports as little as possible. The European government, therefore, subsidised home industries; they erected high tariff walls; they passed Navigation Acts to boost shipping industry; and extorted trade concessions from the defeated enemy. "If a monarch controlled no gold or silver mines of his own", writes Dr. Steward Easton, "and if piracy on the high seas to steal the products of the mines of foreigners proved insufficient to allay his thirst for the precious metals, he had only one alternative - to win a favourable balance of trade". This could be possible only if his subjects exported more than they imported so that they could receive the balance in bullion.

Colonialism, Imperialism, and Exploitation: The geographical exploitations and discoveries led to colonialism, imperialism, and exploitation. The Europeans emigrated from Europe in vast numbers to the newly explored areas where they founded their colonies, ruled over the natives, and exploited them all-round. Practically the whole of the East was, thus, brought under the domination of the West. There sprang up the Portuguese, the Spanish, the Dutch, the French, and the English colonial empires in Asia, Africa, and America.

Commercial and Colonial Wars: The geographical explorations, discoveries, and colonial settlements caused commercial and colonial wars amongst the European powers, as they carried their rival national flags into distant lands. So there were frequent such wars between the Dutch and the Portuguese, between the Spaniards and the French, between the French and the English, and others, in many lands for many years.

Civilisation Enriched: The Europeans, by coming into close contact with the peoples of Asia, Africa, and America and their luxurious articles and goods, metals and precious stones, and many more things which were previously unknown to them, enriched their own civilisation.

The Atlantic - The Main Highway: In the Medieval Age, the Mediterranean and the Baltic Sea served as the only sea routes for commerce, which made Italy and Turkey Prominent commercial powers. But with the exploration of America and another sea-route to the East, the Atlantic Sea became the chief highway of commerce, therefore, the ports of this sea in Lisbon, London, Amsterdam, and in other countries became the capitals of commercial activity. This, naturally, caused setback to the ports of the Mediterranean and the Baltic Seas.

All-round Progress Stimulated: Geographical explorations and discoveries went a long way in broadening the general outlook of the Europeans. This, accompanied with material prosperity and the spirit of Renaissance, profoundly influenced the arts and sciences of Europe, which in turn made possible an all-round progress of man.

Spread of Christianity: One of the factors responsible for geographical explorations and discoveries was the zeal of Christian missionaries for the spread of Christianity. That was fulfilled when the colonies were founded in Asia, Africa, and America, and the missionaries followed the trader and the flag and started their activities and made converts.

Growth of Absolute Monarchy: The geographical explorations and discoveries produced favourable conditions for the growth of absolute monarchies. With the full support of the middle class, the powerful monarchs destroyed the power of the feudal lords and enjoyed absolute powers in many European countries such as England, Spain, etc.

Superiority of the West: Finally, the European voyages of explorations and discoveries proved the superiority of the West to the East. In most areas of Asia, Africa, and America, their indigenous civilisations were practically uprooted and the European civilisation along with Christianity were imposed upon them. With the dawning of the 20th century, however, the East began to revive from its lethargy and slumber.

Thus to the Europeans, the new world particularly Asia and Africa was fabulously wealthy and of precious interest. Among the travellers, men such as Marco Polo, ventured to the East and brought back accounts of what he found there. However, this limited source of factual knowledge left the average educated European entirely ignorant of the real conditions, important and superior cultural realities of the East particularly India.

8

The Glorious Revolution of 1688

About the nature of Glorious Revolution, Trevelyan significantly observes, "For many generations to come the Revolution of 1688-89 was spoken of by our ancestors as the Glorious Revolution. Its glory did not consist in any deed of arms, in any single act of heroism on the part of the Englishmen, nor in the fact that a whole nation proved itself stronger than one very foolish king. There was indeed a certain ignominy in the fact that a foreign fleet and army, however welcome and however friendly, had been required to enable the English to recover the liberties they had muddled away in their frantic faction feuds. The true glory of the British revolution lay in the fact that it was bloodless, that there was no civil war, no massacre, no proscription and above all that a settlement by consent was reached vis-a-vis the religious and political differences that had so long and so freely divided men and parties. The settlement of 1689 stood the test of the time." The very wording of the resolution of the parliament showed the nature of the revolution. The resolution was "James II-, having endeavoured to subvert the constitution of this kingdom by breaking the original contract between king and people and by advice of Jesuits and other wicked persons having violated the fundamental laws and having withdrawn himself out of the kingdom, has abdicated the government and that the throne is thereby vacant."

The revolution only consolidated the achievement of the past constitutional struggles between the two central institutions—King and Parliament, and it was definitely too conservative, for the ostensible object of the revolution was not any fundamental change but protection of the rights and privileges of the parliament. Nonetheless the revolution stands as a landmark in the whole history of England. Its glory consisted not in the shouting and tumult but in the still smaller voice of wisdom that prevailed throughout the din. Thus Marriot's opinion that the revolution was conservative in nature stands true, for all the old values were kept intact. It was also liberal in the sense that it did not change the old monarchical system even in the face of despotic exercise of regal powers. Hence Macaulay's opinion that the revolution was more defensive as well as parliamentary seemed reasonable and justified. It defended the rights of the people and acknowledged the supremacy of the general will in the administration of the country. On the whole the revolution was the spontaneous outcome of the general will which defended the democratic evolution of the country as against the despotism of the Stuart monarchs. Anyway it was the masterpiece of the political wisdom of the people. It was more brilliant than the defeat of Armada. It was an achievement of all the religious and political parties so much so that it became "the object of superstitious reverence." By the peaceful settlement of political disputes, it prevented the occurrence of another civil war in the country.

There is another set of scholars who held the view that the revolution was not a great revolt or breaking with the past traditions but it was a rebellion of handful rich parliamentarians who were anxious to control the administration of the country. "It certainly led to the rule of a few rich Tory and Whig families. In fact it did very little to associate masses in the government." But all historians agree that the revolution was of great significance. As Ramsay Muir remarks, "Moreover, the solution had to be sought in very difficult circumstances. These lands were divided and they were threatened by the greatest power in the world. They had to fight for their unity which was less than a century old, they had to fight for their freedom and for the freedom of Europe. Their own leaders were anything but confident and it was in these critical circumstances that the new principles of government were brought into operation." It was very difficult for all the people to bring about such a revolution in the political administrative structure of the country. Only a band of adventurous politicians brought about the significant change. Trevelyan also writes, "The Englishmen who made the revolution were not heroes. Few of them were even honest men. But they were very clever men and taught by bitter experience they believed at this supreme crisis as very clever men do not always behave with sense and moderation."

As compared to other revolutions of the world, the English revolution did not result in violent upsurge or bloodshed accompanied by social and economic changes. On the other hand nothing was brought about by force but it was only the unity of the people of all shades of opinion, Whigs and Tories, Anglicans and Dissenters, against despotism that brought about significant changes. It was an unqualified agreement in which both the parties, the king and the people, mutually respected each other's limitations. Thus the settlement might be treated as a compromise but it revealed the attachment of the parties to the different political philosophies propounded by Hobbes, Locke, and Halifax. The forces were largely influenced by the views of Hobbes who denied the competence of the people to depose their king. On the other hand, the Whigs inculcated the spirit of Locke who believed that there existed a contract between the king and the people in the government of the country. But ultimately the Tories and the Whigs compromised and declared the throne vacant after the flight of James II. It was due to Locke that the settlement of 1688 was looked upon as an agreement which prescribed limited powers of the government. The idea of separation of power, as advocated by Locke, was accepted in practice, and hence a series of specific laws were framed to solve the respective problems of the state. Another important personality Halifax challenged the despotism of the Stuarts and fought successfully for the victory of Common Law which was "not the king's laws nor the Parliament's laws but the laws of England."

The revolution settlement explicitly showed the attitude of the two political parties - Whigs and Tories - which was essentially of the nature of compromise. The Tories gave up their defensive attitude towards Jacobitism, confirmed the Protestant succession through Act of Settlement, and took up a compromising attitude by lending their support to the Toleration Act. This led to mutual respect between the two parties, and that was a common sight during the time of Queen Anne. The economic policy of the Whigs led to the passing of the Navigation Act and a similar Act like the Bank of England; and the reaction of the Tories to these Acts was to be seen in the Bounty Act which "marked the transition of political power from Tory to Whig."

Another important and significant characteristic of the settlement was the conservation of the settlement. The settlement unfolded the fulfilment of the legislations of the Long Parliament and of the Restoration period. The declarations of Star Chamber and High Commission was made illegal and the assertion of the freedom of speech by the House of Commons were simply the repetition of the work of Long Parliament with emphasis. The monarch still possessed real powers like the appointment of ministers, but he did not possess the power of dispensing with the services of such ministers unless the Parliament expressed disapproval of their actions through vote of no-confidence. The king did not revive the divine right theory but he did not hesitate in suspending the Habeas Corpus. But the victory of Common law was recognised by all. Further, the Clarenden Code and the Test Act was not repealed throughout the eighteenth century on account of the deep-rooted conservatism of the People. Macaulay wrote, "It is because we had a preserving revolution in the seventeenth century that we have not had a destroying revolution in the nineteenth, it is because we had freedom in the midst of servitude that we have order in the midst of anarchy."

But the revolution had a great impact upon the position of the king. According to the Bill of Rights, the king was dispossessed of the right of suspending or dispensing the laws, promulgate ordinances, set up arbitrary courts like Star Chamber, High Commission, Council of the North and Wales etc. He must call the sittings of Parliament before levying fresh taxation or framing laws. He could neither imprison any person without due process of law or rule the country on the basis of hereditary right. The Act of Settlement expressly had not only secured the independence of judiciary but it also settled that the future claims to the throne of England would be decided by the Parliament. Even the ministers securing royal pardon for their acts of omission and commission could not free themselves from the clutches of Parliamentary control. William and Mary and subsequently Queen Anne were not asked to recognise that their powers had been curtailed, but the emergence of Parliament as supreme body compelled them to act under certain limitations.

The Parliament emerged victorious over the monarchy and the church as a result of the revolution settlement. The House of Commons had become supreme in matters like succession, justice, army, trade and finance, and the House of Lords was relegated to a subordinate position. Its influence over religion could be guessed by the famous enactment, Toleration Act, which recognised the supremacy of the established church. Mowat informs that though the scope of toleration was narrow yet it recognised the important principles governing the diversity of religious opinion. Maitland is of opinion that the Toleration Act holds the same place in the history of the relations of the church and state which the Bill of Rights holds in the history of the relations of the king and people. Thus the Glorious Revolution weakened the king and strengthened the Parliament.

9

The Industrial Revolution

The term Industrial Revolution was first circulated by Arnold Toynbee and is now generally used to indicate those economic changes which transformed England from agricultural to industrial country. Trevelyan regards the term completely a misnomer for it was not in fact an event but a process which continued in a gradual and evolutionary process throughout the eighteenth century and it is still continuing in one or other form. Pollard also has laid stress that "the period during which these changes took place cannot be definitely fixed, but usually it is taken to extend from about the middle of the eighteenth century to the close of the reign of George III". Thus upto the Industrial revolution, economic and social change though continuous has the pace of a slow moving stream but in the days of Watt and Stephenson, it has acquired the momentum of water over mill dam, distracting to the eye of spectator.

Thus the term Industrial revolution is used to express the change which was responsible for the adoption of the system of making things on a large scale in large factories with the aid of steam power, as opposed to the old system, which was generally followed up to the middle of the eighteenth century, of making goods in the cottages or shops of the workers. It was thus fundamentally the replacement of handicraft by power driven machinery. In its broader aspects the revolution involved the development of a large scale capitalistic enterprise, changes in the status of the labour, population shift and increase and new social, economic and political problems.

It has been suggested by some scholars that the word 'evolution' should have been used in place of 'revolution', because the changes were not accompanied with violent or sudden changes in the method of production. The process of change is still continuing, and it will go on in the years to come. However, the word revolution is more appropriate in as far as the fact that the changes completely changed the industrial shape of England. Formerly, the things were manufactured by hand and in the house of the workers, but after the revolution there was a substitution of hand labour by power driven machinery. The manufacturing work was transferred from the cottage to the factories.

Why did the revolution occur in England and not elsewhere - it is to be noted that when the whole of Europe was convulsing by a whirlwind of revolution, England was undergoing significant social and economic changes. While the countries of Europe were engaged in war and preparation of armaments, in England people were engaged in revolutionising their economic situation. There were many factors responsible for this economic transformation.

The political stability combined with the popularly elected institutions made the industrialisation of the country easier. While Germany, France, Holland and other advanced countries of Europe had not yet evolved perfect political institutions, England after 1688 had moved on the path of parliamentary democracy. The people had been free to shape their internal and external policies; and even the slightest attempt by the

Jacobites to change the political set up of the country proved a failure. Such a situation was totally absent in European countries.

In England the people possessed personal freedom since sixteenth century. Serfdom was completely absent in England whereas in the European countries, it still persisted. The people in England believed in cooperation, and hence they singly or jointly invested money in the development of industry. Comparatively speaking they enjoyed enough social and political freedom, which factors helped the growth of industry in England. People could freely move from one place to another, and hence the population was not fixed to the profession of agriculture. There was plentiful supply of labour to the new factories where goods were manufactured at cheap rates.

England was free from external invasions, and while the revolutionary and Napoleonic wars ravaged the whole of the European continent, on the English soil there was no war. The people of England directed their efforts towards the development of agriculture and industry. The freedom of the country from foreign invasion materially contributed to the prosperity of the people. France remained all along busy with the Napoleonic wars, and other European countries were in constant danger of the threats of war and invasion. But England warded off this factor by fighting wars not on her own soil but in the continent; and diplomatically outwitted France and defeated her. Thus her prestige in the international politics had also increased immensely.

There had been steady growth of population in the second-half of the eighteenth century and onwards. There was a sharp decline in the death rate and there was, thus, a plentiful supply of labour. While the people of the continent were more war conscious, the people of England had ample opportunities to improve their standard of living. The earlier capitalists emerged "without a lower middle class". It has rightly been observed without a rapidly lower middle class with sufficient education and technical background, the industrial revolution could have been impossible.

The demand of English goods had been rapid and tremendous and to cope with the increasing demands, it was essential to invest capital in inventing machinery, for it was not possible to meet the demands of the world market by producing goods on a small scale. This important factor was absent in the continent. The trade of England in the eighteenth century had increased by leaps and bounds, and the merchants found abroad an ever increasing demand for English goods. Thus the industrial capitalists in England encouraged and patronised the investors who reduced the use of labour by making new machines.

There was ample wealth in the country due to the expansion of trade and commerce. The wise financial measures of Walpole brought great prosperity to England; and the people realising the financial stability and political permanence, invested large capital in setting up large scale factories. The foundation of Bank of England led the investors to borrow money for the purpose of investing in industries. The traders were harvesting enormous profits from the colonial trade and they also re-exported goods to world markets. Thus the capital gained was invested in setting up new factories or in making new inventions.

The most predominant factor which the other countries of the continent did not possess was that England enjoyed colonial and naval supremacy which provided further incentive to the rapid development of industry. The colonies provided the raw materials at cheap rates, and those were converted into manufactured goods, and exported to world markets. Holland was the only country which had some connection with the English ships in carrying goods from one place to another. But she had no colonies or supremacy of the sea. Hence Holland could not compete with England. France too remained busy with wars, and by the time she recovered, England was already the workshop of the world. France had colonies, but the lack of efficient navy and supremacy of the sea hindered her progress in the field of industry.

It is indeed significant to note that the English people had accumulated enormous capital, the source material for the expansion of industry. The trading companies provided enormous profits as well as colonies to the people of England, these were invested in the industrial development of England. Profits accrued from world trade was likewise invested in setting up factory, industry, which experienced no shortage of either raw materials or labour. Thus wealth was bound to accumulate, and it was profitably invested in industry, but she invested her capital in fighting wars or in producing armaments. Hence she did not evolve factory industry.

Great Britain possessed many natural advantages which the other countries of Europe did not possess. The geographical position was suitable for world trade. Being centrally situated, no part of the world was inaccessible to her ships. England possessed excellent harbours and her canals and rivers provided the internal communication for transhipment of goods. Her climate was suitable for the growth of industry and above all, the coal and iron mines lay in close proximity.

Reference may also be made to some of the most important inventions which were responsible for the industrial development of England. John Kay invented in 1733 'the flying shuttle' which increased production. In 1765 James Hargreaves invented Spinning Tenny, which did the job of eight spinners. In 1769, Arkwright invented Waterframe which was run by water power or horse power. It ushered in the factory system. In 1779, Samuel Crompton invented the Mule which combined the uses of Spinning Jenny and water-frame. In 1785, Edmund Cartwright invented the power loom which helped to weave with speed. In 1793 Whitney invented a machine through which seeds could be separated from the cotton fibres. In 1785, the cylinder printing was invented for bleaching and dyeing purposes. The invention of steam engine brought a radical change. Newcomen was the first to invent steam engine, and after him James Watt introduced some good change. It replaced the water power, and much advantage was gained by the textile and iron industries.

Ramsay Muir, therefore, remarks, "these tremendous new forces which were to revolutionise the conditions of human life, were at first a British monopoly and the long wars which were soon to begin extended the period of this monopoly because other countries strained and ravaged by war, could not immitate these British inventions. Moreover, the command of these new and cheap commodities immeasurably increased the resources of British foreign trade."

Trevelyan has summed up the causes in the following sentences: "the great changes in man's command over natural and consequent manner of life, which began in England under George III and have since spread with varying degree of intensity over almost the whole inhabited globe, make bewildering work for the historians upto the Industrial Revolution, economic and social change, though continuous, has the pace of a slowly moving stream, but in the days of Watt and Stephenson it has acquired the momentum of water over a mill dam distracting to the eye of spectator. Nor for all its hurry, does it ever react any pool at the bottom and resumed its former leisurely advance. It is a contract still. The French revolution occupied a dozen years at most, but the industrial revolution may yet continue for as many as hundred, creating and obliterating one form of economic and social life after another, so that the historians can never say - this or that is the normal state of modern England."

The effects of the Industrial revolution are numerous. According to Ramsay Muir, the Industrial revolution was a mighty but silent upheaval. No wonder it brought about momentous changes in English society. It increased the national wealth, led to the growth of population and redistribution of population, marked the advent of capitalist class, inaugurated the system of factories, employing women and children and lastly made it necessary for parliamentary reforms.

It is a fact that the industrialisation of the country led to the increase of national wealth of England. Agriculture was replaced by industry, and slowly a large number of textile mills, iron and steel factories were set up. All these factories produced goods on a large scale, and found market not only in the colonies but in the whole world. British ships went everywhere. This made it imperative for the setting up of factories. The factory towns like Lancashire, Manchester and Sheffield came into existence. According to Hall and Albion, "the new cities grew with astonishing rapidity and without direction". Consequently the problems of health and sanitation cropped up; and later it indirectly helped the growth of planned cities.

The Industrial revolution led to the establishment of capitalist society in which the rich grew richer and the poor became poorer. The labourers were exploited to the utmost, and the employers cared little for them. Their sufferings were painful. Women and children were employed for long hours and their conditions of work were depressing. Most of the factories were cramped, dirty, unhealthy places merely to work in and often causing the working people to catch disease of various kinds. In short, the workers were just like canon fodders, and the employers cared more for profits.

Another effect was that the revolution was instrumental in shifting the population from the south and east of England to the north and west of England, where the factories were situated. There was concentration of labour in those places and consequently the factory owners employed them on nominal wages. Consequently there was demand of representation in the Parliament, for the new towns did not constitute a constituency from where representatives could be elected to the parliament. Thus the clamour for the reorganisation of constituencies on the basis of population began. The establishment of factories also led to the formation of Trade Unions, and the old personal bond of relationship between the worker and the employer was gone for ever. The struggle between capital and labour ensued, which had impacts upon the development of the country.

The group of Englishmen, the enterprising and often self made men who created, owned and operated the factories, foundries and mines profitted greatly by the Industrial revolution. Some of such people built up fortunes rivalling those of landed aristocracy. As time went on they forgot their antecedents and thought of themselves together with the merchants and middlemen who also grew richer with the new industry as men of the middle class. The middle class grew soon powerful during the following centuries, and acquired political power side by side with their increasing volume of wealth. Between the bourgeoisie and the working class beneath, a social chasm developed, one different but not impossible to bridge. The working class no longer owned the tools with which it worked. Without land and without property, without guarantee of employment it sank to the social scale and later came to be known as proletariat.

It would not be wrong to say that the Revolution brought the play of nationalism and internationalism. The inventions linked and made all the countries inter-dependent. Similarly without the Industrial revolution, international linking would not have been possible. Each and every country came closer and closer, and their dependence upon each other became a paramount feature of the new order of things.

Another important effect was the growth of the philosophy of individualism and the writers like Bentham and Mill emphasised the need of living of individuals on their own resources to work out their own salvation. It was pointed out that competition was the prominent feature of trade, and the only way of achieving prosperity was through the adoption of *Leissez faire* or free trade policy.

Pollard remarks, "political emancipation was but one of the results of the industrial revolution, commercial expansion was another. England had now definitely and decisively specialised in certain industries, she could only do so by relying upon external sources for her supply of other wants. The more her new industries gave her to export, the more she required to import from customers upon whose wealth her own prosperity depended. In particular, England became dependent upon foreign producers for her food supplies". Pollard again says, that its most general effect was to emphasise and exaggerate the tendency towards specialisation. But the specialists lack of all round capacity is natural and notorious. Again the problems of poverty local government and sanitation had been created or intensified by the Industrial revolution.

Thus the Industrial revolution was not merely an economic change, it was on the whole a social revolution. The old settled stable order existing in Britain in the middle of the eighteenth century was being wholly transformed. The most momentous change in the conditions of human life which history records was fairly afoot, and Britain was the country of its origin. It can be rightly concluded that the inventors of the eighteenth century were every bit as important in English history as the politicians, in fact they did more than the politicians to create the country they live in.

10

The Progress Made in the Field of Transport on Account of the Industrial Revolution between 1700-1830

England in the years 1700-1830, witnessed a considerable increase in the number of mills, mines and factories. This implied that large quantities of raw materials had to be transported to the manufacturers, and that great amounts of finished articles had to be distributed both at home and overseas. To make this possible, it was essential, that the methods of transport by road, river and coastal navigation, must be improved.

Britain's natural waterways had served as trade routes from the Middle Ages. Some of the most important trading and industrial centres, were situated on navigable rivers—London, York, Chester, Newcastle and Bristol. Few rivers, however, mere sufficiently deep and unobstructed, to permit to navigation for great distances. Hindrances to navigation were many, created both by nature and man. The depth of water was in some places insufficient, due to silting up, to rapids, or to an inadequacy of the flow. The tortuous loops of some lowland rivers increased the travelling distance between points. The construction of weirs across rivers, in connection with water-driven fulling and flour mills, created barriers to navigation. The existence of fords sometimes involved the artificial rising of the river-bed, making the ford shallow. Low built medieval bridges, while not actually preventing navigation, sometimes obstructed the passing of large boats. Moreover the susceptibility of some lowland rivers to flooding meant, that any change in the interests of improved navigation, might increase the liability to flood. Some of these problems could be dealt with easily, while others were hard to overcome.

Towns could not be easily persuaded to pull down their fine medieval bridges. Nor were the mill owners with long established legal rights to their weirs, willing to sacrifice their means of livelihood. However, as a first step towards increasing the depth of water, attempts were made to increase the rate of flow of the water. This action by making use of the natural movement of the water to scour the river bed, helped to increase the depth of the water without much expense. The distance to the river's mouth was shortened, thus increasing the angle of the fall. This was achieved by the elimination of long weanders by short cuts across the neck of the loops. Thus inconvenient sharp bends with their accompanying shallows were avoided. Commonly, however, the depth of water was increased artificially by holding up the water behind weirs, which were then by-passed by short loop cuts and the difference in level was negotiated by means of a pound-lock, which became the key to successful river navigation.

In the 18th century, therefore, these and many other schemes were carried out, to improve river navigation. In 1721, the proprietors of salt-works in the neighbourhood of Middlewich, secured an act of Parliament, giving them authority to deepen and clean the river weaver, which flowed northwards into the navigable lower stretch of the river

Mersey. This brought the coal of south Lancashire more cheaply to the salt-works and reduced the marketing cost of manufactured salt.

The improvement of river navigation, had important results for industry. By the middle of the 18th century, it had opened up many new areas to heavy industry. This permitted the development of the coal-fields of Derbyshire and south Lancashire by the extension of the navigable portions of the rivers - Trent, Derwent, Mersey and their tributaries, and of the woollen-cloth manufacturing districts of Gloucestershire and the West-Riding of Yorkshire by the upper Thames and Aire.

But in spite of improved rivers navigation, several growing industrial districts still lay beyond any hope. Construction of canals, quite independent of existing water courses, became necessary, although financial and technical difficulties were involved in this.

In the circumstances, was needed the construction of one or two successful canals, which would demonstrate to engineers and manufacturers all over the country, that canals would solve their transport problems and could be made to pay. The first to be built was the Sankey Brook Navigation completed in 1757. It connected the south Lancashire coal-field around St. Helens with the navigable river Mersey near Warrington. It secured a cheap outlet for Lancashire coal, and completed the process of taking the coal to the salt of North Cheshire.

The second pioneering canal was built by the Duke of Bridgewater at his own cost to link up his colliery at Worslay with Manchester, and it was opened in 1761. As Manchester needed some better communication with the sea, the Duke built a second canal, connecting Manchester with Runcorn and so with Liverpool. This greater canal was not finished until 1776 and was called the Bridgewater Canal.

There followed a great boom in canal building, lasting until the early years of the 19th century. The pottery, salt manufacturers and other who were hampered by want of good transport, combined to finance several canals in the Midlands. They were the Trent and Mersey (otherwise the Grand Trunk Canal, the Staffordshire and Worcestershire Canal authorized in 1766, the Birmingham Coventry in 1768 and the Oxford Canals in 1769). The Grand Junction Canal connecting London with the Midlands, was authorized in 1793. The great river systems were linked up by new canals, such as the Thames-Sevem Canal in 1799, the forth Clyde Canal in 1790 and the Selles Canal in 1793. In the last decade of the 18th century, England was rapidly covered with a system of inland waterways, built by numerous private companies. These companies had to obtain an Act of Parliament in order to have compulsory powers to take land for the purpose of the canal. Before granting the power to take land, Parliament laid down certain maximum rates of change for the use of the waterway.

These canals and inland navigations were an enormous improvement on anything that had existed before. The carriage of goods was not merely rendered much cheaper, but they were more expeditiously conveyed. It becamc possible to transport raw materials in quantities, bulky goods like coal and building materials, received a new mobility, and a further stimulus to the movement of bulky goods was given, when iron tramways or wagonways were laid down after 1767, to connect up the coal mines or quarries with the canals, making coal easily available at reasonable prices. The pottery manufacture received a new impetus from the increased facilities for getting China clay from Cornwall, as well as for distributing the breakable wave and the pottery district developed rapidly. The products of each and every industrial region were made available to consumers in all parts of the country, while the newly acquired accesses of many important industrial areas to sea-ports, greatly assisted the growth of export trade.

There was another aspect of the consequences of canal construction. In the days when digging had to be done entirely by the spade, many thousand men were employed in the construction of a simple canal. They were the beginnings of a growing army of unskilled labourers, a type of workmen hitherto uncommon in Britain. On the other hand, canals also bred another important class of workers, the skilled engineers a group which was to grow enormously in importance, in the 19th century.

The heavy investment in canals and improvements in river navigation, was the result of the failure of roads to cater for the growing volume of traffic in the 18th century. In manorial times all landowners had been theoretically responsible for the highways adjacent to their own lands. But only when the maintenance of law and order was at stake, did the medieval state intervene, by enforcing the responsibility and levying rates on those who failed to repair the roads. After some time the maintenance of roads became the responsibility of the parish in which they lay. This caused little difficulty in a country parish, where roads were used mainly by local inhabitants. But matters were different in a poor agricultural parish, which had the misfortune to bestride a main road. In this case, the road users were mainly those who lived outside the parish, and it was natural for those who bore the expense and the labour of road- maintenance in the parish, to resent the heavy burden of repair for the use of others. In this situation invariably, the duty of maintaining roads in a good condition was neglected and even the busiest of main roads remained without any form of hard surface.

The problem of road maintenance was tackled by Turnpike Trusts. A turnpike road was usually planned and financed by a group of people, interested in improving a certain road, often due to their local industrial activities. They secured permission by Act of Parliament, to collect tolls from all users of the road in question, on condition that they maintained the road in a good state of repair. As in the case of canals, as soon as it became evident that investment of money in a turnpike road could be very profitable, there was no shortage of money coming forward and much of this was put to very good use during the 18th century.

The first turnpike trust was established in 1706 in Buckinghamshire. Throughout the early decades of the century, there was a steady growth in the number of member of turnpike trusts, but the rapid increase in their numbers began only after 1748. Between 1748 and 1770, the number of turnpike trusts rose from 150 to 530. In 1773, Parliament passed a General Turnpike Act, which regulated the actions of turnpike trustees everywhere. This act with some modifications, later on, remained the basis for the administration of all turnpike roads. The turnpike trusts spent a great deal of money on road maintenance, and hand-in-hand with these trusts, developed the science of road-engineering, three great pioneers in road construction being John Metcalf, Thomas Telford and John London McAdam.

Yet although the turnpikes effected a great deal of improvement in the road system of the country, they were far from offering the perfect answer to the demand for better roads. There was no obligation on the trustees to spend any fixed proportion of their revenue from tolls on the maintenance of their stretch of road. As a trust was rarely given authority over more than a comparatively short stretch of road, travellers on long journeys, found themselves obliged to pay a considerable number of tolls in the course of their journeys. Again the system did not sufficiently recognize the needs of the local traveller, whose daily journey to work might take him past a toll-bar. This problem led first, to considerable evasion of tolls, and then to local hostility to the turnpikes, which occasionally took the form of rioting and the destruction of toll bars. The turnpike trusts failed to meet the needs of the times, because they were a piecemeal and a purely local answer to the problem. Where roads crossed many parishes and even countries on the way from one large town to another, only a truly national system of road administration could have answered completely.

Anyway, the improvement of roads made possible by the turnpike trusts and the technical contributions of the road engineers, led to a great acceleration of coach traffic. The stage coach enjoyed a spell of popularity. Travel though still an expensive luxury, became less of a physical hardship. But the railways coming hard on the heels of the stage-coaches, gradually displaced this form of road traffic.

All these transport changes covered a period of more than a century. Their combined effect was twofold - to reduce substantially the cost of carriage of industrial products, and to permit an enormous increase in the quantities of goods carried. Apart from this, resources hitherto completely sterilized by their location away from water carriage or market, were mobilized for production. Quarries, mines and manufacturing plants sprang into life along the lines of the new canals. Towns like Stourport or St. Helens were also a product of improved transport. Canal made them import transit centres and manufacturing centres, because they allowed economic activity generally to be expanded. Moreover, the canal system and the turnpike roads, did more than stimulate the exchange of goods inside the island; they hastened the growth of overseas trade. Goods from Europe, America, Asia and Africa could now be distributed in much greater quantities, through the length and breadth of England. They could be more readily purchased abroad, by the increased export of coal and manufactured goods. In this way, helped by changed and improved modes of transport in the 18th century, the whole character and scope of British production and commerce, began to assume its modern form.

11

The Agrarian Revolution

The first half of eighteenth century effected no change in the agricultural condition of England. The method of agriculture and the system of cultivation remained the same as it was in the seventeenth century. Agriculturally England was a backward country, and it had not adopted any scientific method in the system of cultivation. But the second half of the eighteenth century witnessed revolutionary changes in the field of agriculture. As Ramsay Muir says, "In the second half of the eighteenth century, scientific farming became a fashionable hobby in which many great landowners from the King downwards took a keen interest, and a school of agricultural writers such as Arthur Young did a great deal to spread this useful fashion."

Thus agriculture was no longer looked upon as a profession of labourers but it became a hobby of squires and nobles patronised by the King. The small farmers could only till their lands their fathers had left to them, and they carried on the traditional system of farming. The method had become old and it did not yield sufficient production. Thus the rich people began to invest their money in agriculture and adopted scientific methods to improve production. Thus a proper atmosphere cropped up for improving agriculture on account of the patronage given by the king and the rich people like Bedford and Holkhann.

Thus the agricultural revolution had two important aspects: Firstly, there was the system of Enclosures which comprised big plots of land and where machinery could replace the age-old system of cultivation. Secondly, there was the increasing use of machinery in the system of agriculture. The two factors combined to bring about a green revolution in England, Scotland and Wales. It was all due to the fact that the population of England had increased and if the system would not have been changed, the people of England might have had to face starvation and famine. Thus it was considered essential to improve the system of agriculture in order to feed the increasing population. Hence they preferred large enclosures than the small holdings scattered in the villages.

The need for consolidating the scattered arable lands was felt by the scientific cultivation, and during the reign of George III steps were taken to do away with the small holdings. The various Enclosure Acts were passed, and it overcame all the difficulties in the way of transforming the small holdings into big enclosures. There was no opposition and everyone believed that enclosures meant the increase of country's material progress. But the enclosures made the rich farmers more rich, and the poor became labourers and daily wage-earners.

Trevelyan remarks, "It was, therefore, the reign of George III that the Midlands and East Anglia and much of the North England and Scottish landscape took on their present appearance of a chess board pattern, made up of innumerable fields enclosed by hedges or stone-walls. The extreme south-east corner of the islands and many western countries had displaced those familiar features for centuries past."

Thus the enclosures were of two types; the first were the waste land enclosures which tilled the land so far unused, and the other ones were the consolidated strips of land owned by large number of farmers. The former type did not bring any harm but the latter affected the poor farmers badly, and they were ultimately forced to give up the habit of cultivation and become mill-workers. The system also deprived the poor owners of their land, and left them completely at the mercy of factory owners. Arthur Young also admitted that the Enclosure system deprived the farmers of their simple village life and even their bread which was granted by their forefathers.

In the first-half of the eighteenth century the Parliament passed nearly 112 Enclosure Acts which mainly dealt with private enclosures; and in the second-half of eighteenth century, the Parliament passed nearly 3000 Enclosure Acts. The increased number of enclosures enhanced the production of agricultural commodities. But it adversely affected the life of the poor farmers, and numerous petitions were filled in the Parliament to ventilate the grievance of the poor farmers. But Enclosures became a blessing in disguise. As Trevelyan remarks, "the enclosures had not brought equal benefits to all. The share of the poor had been inadequate. The loss of their village industries accounts for half their distress - Arthur Young was himself horrified at some of the results of the movement of which he had been the chief apostle. The condition of the agricultural labourer deprived of the industries previously conducted by his wife and children, was indeed most unhappy." But on the whole it must be admitted that the enclosures mechanised the method of production and consequently increased agricultural produce.

The Agricultural Revolution made great progress due to the inventions of three persons, Jethro Tull, Townshend and Robert Bakewell. Tull was a gentleman farmer of Berkshire and he studied the conditions favourable for the healthy growth of plant life. He invented new methods of drilling and hosing. The machine made the channels, sowed the seeds into them and covered them with great exactness and precision. Townshend was the landowner of Norfolk and introduced the system of rotation of crops. By this system, the fertility of the soil was increased, and there was no need of leaving one-third of the land uncultivated if the farmer followed the system of rotation of crops. Blackwell was a Liecestershire farmer who brought about great improvements in the breeding of sheep and cattle.

The numerous improvements in agriculture and stock breeding put an end to the traditional open field system which, according to Southgate, "had served the country well but it had existed for some hundred of years. It was antiquated and while it remained, no improvement was possible". Though the progress made in the field of agriculture was peaceful, its speed varied from place to place. But the changes on the whole were gradual and at the same time uncertain. Machinery was introduced in the cultivation of more and more lands, cattle was breeded on scientific lines, and the land was enclosed with unlimited speed. The farmers invested more money in agriculture, and the necessary stimulus for these changes was provided by the high prices which made improved and mechanised farming profitable. Thus like industry, agriculture became capitalistic.

Green significantly observes, "Despite the social evils which resulted from enclosure, it was economically expedient and necessary." Economically it was justifiable but socially it was disastrous. Socially, the old system had some advantages, e.g. the open field system encouraged community spirit, spirit of co-operation, and rights over waste lands; and the above factors enabled the farmers to exchange their instruments of farming at times of need. The landless people had also the right to settle in the unclaimed and waste lands. But the Agrarian revolution completely destroyed the above spirit of co-operation. The numerous Enclosure Bills were passed at the initiative of the big landlords who exploited and deprived the poor peasants of their inherited landed properties.

The small free holders were ruined for they had to bear a part of the expenses of enclosing the land, which was beyond their means to bear. He had also to pay for the fences, and in case of default the land remained mortgaged to the big landlord. He was also deprived of the common pasture lands and also the right of cutting wood for fuel and fire. The position of the lease holder was similar to the free holders. Above all the village autonomy was also gone for ever. Thus the small farmers were destroyed and the land was now owned by few wealthy people. A landless Proletariat was created, and the whole rural society of England was destroyed and the misery and distress of the poor people increased.

But the economic consequences of the Agrarian revolution could not be minimised. Besides removing the economic evils of the old system, it must be admitted, the enclosure movement had its own advantages. It replaced the system of sporadic farming by the system of big holdings. Farming was thus made easier and productive. The farmers were now free to cultivate their land with improved methods. It also increased the area of cultivation and more waste lands were reclaimed for the purpose of agriculture.

Thus the agricultural revolution increased the production of the country, and ultimately the wealth of the country multiplied. The scientific inventions changed the fate of the country. However, it had mixed blessings. As Ramsay Muir remarks, "A wide gap such as had not previously existed, was opened between two big landowners and the capitalist farmers on the one side and the wage earning labourers on the other and the landowners ceased to be the natural leaders of the rural community as they had been in days when nearly all the members of that community, had once interest in the land on which they worked."

According to Hall and Albion, "Such was the agricultural revolution. The former happy inefficient population of the villages dwindled away to a fraction of the old number; yet that small remainder following the new methods of Tull, Townshend and Bakewell made the village acres far more productive than they had ever been before. Bread and beef were thus supplied to meet the demands of the rapidly increasing industrial population. Between 1761 and 1801 there were exactly two thousand Enclosure Acts affecting nearly a tenth of the total area of England and the following forty years saw nearly as many more".

Further he says, "the enclosures were far from being an unmixed evil. Without them it is difficult to see how England would have made good use of the new agricultural discoveries or how she could have led a larger population or even how in later years she could have defeated Napoleon. To some extent, therefore, most Englishmen benefitted but most of all the landlords who being rich became richer still. A certain part of the new wealth percolated down to the intelligent farmer, a term always used in England to denote a person who rents a farm and who tills it in person: an agricultural labourer working for wages never being called a farmer. But the lesser folk at the bottom paid the penalty for the advance of science."

12

The American War of Independence (1776)

It is somewhat surprising that some scholars call the American War of Independence simply a Civil War for the colonies enjoyed no kind of sovereignty and formed a part of British Empire. But it should not be forgotten that at that time in the colonies and in England there were a large number of loyalists who wanted to retain the rule of the British. While there was a large section of people who clamoured that the British authorities had no right to tax the American people. Still all the colonists joined together to oust the English from their soil. The colonists' grievances regarding the levy of taxation from the American people was simply an accession rather than a cause of the revolt of thirteen English colonies in North America.

The first and the foremost cause of the American revolution could be found in the composition of the people inhabiting the British colonies. The Englishmen who left England just in the beginning of the Stuart period had no sympathy for the mother country. The pilgrim fathers left the country out of fear of being prosecuted on account of their religious beliefs. They bitterly resented anti-Puritan policy of the Catholic James I who refused to introduce reforms in the religious system of the country. The Form of Apology and the Hampden Court Conference could not solve their religious problems and so most of the settlers left the mother country out of disgust and fear. Later, the Dissenters too left the country on the same score, and the Catholics of the days of Charles II who felt the rigors of Clarendon Code, left the country out of their own accord, and some of such people were sent or deported to these colonies as bad characters. Thus, these two categories of people were—people who left on account of religious persecutions or disabilities and people who were sent by way of punishment—had little sympathies for their mother country. These settlers as well as others in search of better living and adventure, were initially encouraged by the British government. The British Government also encouraged the Dutchmen to settle in the English colonies. Such settlers had little sympathy for the British Government, which on account of lack of transport facilities and better communication was to enforce authority in the interior part of the country. Hence when the revolt took place, the English got little support even from her own people settled with colonies. Southgate has remarked, "the thirteen colonies were entirely distinct and separate from one and another. No sort of federation existed among them. They happened to be situated in close proximity to one another but there was no closer political connection than would have existed if they had to be scattered about the five continents. A good deal of jealousy and friction existed among them."

It is said the American colonist were mostly adventurous people and they loved liberty more than anything. Since their settlement in the colonies they had established representative institutions. It is also said that the colonist had more liberty and democracy than the English people possessed in their country. The common people of the colonies had a taste of democracy and there was nothing like an English oligarchy which had monopolised all power in the country. Their assemblies were independent, and each member took a lively interest in the internal administration of the colony. They, therefore, did not tolerate any outside interference in the matter of administration. Because of their domineering spirit as well as their desire to remain independent, they regarded England as less progressive but more reactionary.

The government system in the colonies was far from satisfactory. The English government appointed Governors to rule the colonies, but besides the Governors, there were military Captains and Colonels who had enough powers to rule over the people. But the colonists had their own assemblies to whom the Governors were not at all responsible. Many attempts were made to attach the Governors to the assemblies, but they bore no fruit. But the Governor's salary was determined by the assemblies which in order to make themselves responsible, sometimes took recourse to reducing their salaries. Even the judges nominated by the British government had to meet the same fate. But the most important aspect on which there had been conflicts between the British nominated Governors and the assemblies were the subjects of taxation and legislation. The colonists always questioned the right of imposing laws by the British government, and they even disputed British Parliament's right to tax them. The colonists always resisted such attempts, but the problem was never solved. The English Governor of New York once remarked, "If once they can clothe themselves without the help of England, they would soon think of putting onto execution designs they have harboured in their breasts."

The thirteen English colonies were subject to untold economic exploitations and hence they defeated the very idea that the colonies existed for the prosperity of the mother country. Even the industries and trade of these colonies were subject to severe restrictions. As for example, the various Navigation Acts had placed numerous restrictions on trade and production in the colonies. These restrictions were never liked by the colonists who depended upon the mother country for imports and exports. Tout has significantly observed, "the colonies had real cause for dissatisfaction at the commercial policy of the mother country." The Navigation Acts were a source of certain amount of friction. The strict execution of commercial laws which gave Britain a monopoly of American trade was responsible for the cabinet. The colonists had no right to enter into direct trade relations with other country and they had first to export their goods to Great Britain, and then those goods were re-exported to other colonies. The result was that England enjoyed the profits of their export trade. But these restrictions never called for protests in the beginning of the 18th century; for all such restrictions were never strictly enforced by the Whig oligarchy. Their trade and productions went on untampered. But with the advent of George III, such imposed restrictions were enforced strictly, and this excited protests from those who had been disobeying such regulations for decades.

There was temperamental difference between the colonists and the British subjects. As Trevelyan observes, "English society was old, elaborate and artificial, while the American society was new, simple and raw." From the point of view of religion also, the colonists were mostly Puritans, and their outlook was different from the English people who belonged to the established Church of England. The Puritans never believed in compromise, and being extremists they always disliked the English who had deprived them of being the son of the soil on account of religious difference. But in their blood there were germs of English traditions, and they liked the English beliefs in equality and freedom. Thus it was not unusual for the colonists to demand freedom when the English themselves fought with the King for their rights. Further the English in the colonies wanted to be rich like their counterparts in the mother country. But the trade restrictions, imposed by the British Government made it impossible for them to amass fortunes. Therefore they resented this partisan attitude of the mother country.

The Seven Years War indirectly incited the colonies to break away from the mother country. Till this War, the colonies were unable to defend themselves against the French in Canada, and they always looked forward for their protection upon the mother country. But in the liquidation of the French power in Canada, the danger of external aggression was gone for good. They now thought it futile to depend any longer for their protection upon the mother country. Thus the conquest of Canada was followed by the revolt of the American colonies and England had to repent for the removal of the only checking force, i.e. the French power in Canada. Pollard has significantly observed, "The conquest of Canada led to the loss of the thirteen American colonies. Their original bias towards separation had never been eradicated, and the recurrent quarrel between the various legislatures and their Governors had only been prevented from coming to a head by fear of the Frenchmen at their gates and disunion among themselves."

It had been argued at that time that England had spent enormous money on the defence of her colonies in North America during the Seven Years War and as such the colonies should contribute money to the mother country which was on the verge of bankruptcy. The British statesmen had no idea of the storm that was slowly and gradually brewing up in the colonies. They still regarded the colonists as Englishmen; and as every honest Englishman felt, they expected help from such people. But the colonies were not prepared to let a farthing to the mother country, and even for the defence they were quite unwilling to pay. The problem of local defence was more acute after the Seven Years War. North America passed into British hands, and the original inhabitants—the Red Indians—who liked the French still, nourished the feeling that the British would soon ruin them. They rose in revolt in 1763 and 1764, but they were suppressed. Thus the idea originated with the British statesmen that the colonies should contribute towards local defence. The attempt of the mother country to raise money for such a defence created the crisis. The French who had suffered a humiliating defeat at the hands of English in the Seven Years War also incited the colonies to revolt.

But George III and his ministers made the matters worse. It was in 1763 that Grenville opened colonial despatches and found everything in mess. He thought to set matters in right direction, and revised some of the duties in order to encourage colonial production. He also increased the bounties of the British Government on the export of colonial goods, and tried to check smuggling by reducing duties on various commodities. Grenville was prepared to relax the restrictions but at the same time he rightly enforced the laws. A Court of Admiralty was set up to try cases dealing with infringement of Navigation Acts and Trade Acts. In 1764, the Stamp Act as proposed requiring the colonists to purchase stamps for legal documents. It was passed in 1765, and it was declared that the money received from this tax would be utilised in the defence of the colonists. Some of the colonies met at Virginia to protest against the Act. The questions were raised as to the principle of taxation by the British Parliament. In 1776, the Stamp Act was repealed but a Declaratory Act was passed which announced that the British Parliament had right to tax the colonists. Against it, slogans were raised: No taxation without representation. During the ministry of Townshed, the colonies were asked to pay duties on tea, paper, glass and colours. But it soon evoked riots and consequently led to boycott of British goods by the colonists. It led to Boston Massacre by way of retaliation of British authority.

An attempt was made in 1770 by Lord North to pacify the colonies. He abolished all duties except on tea, and permitted the East India Company to send tea from India to America. A nominal duty was imposed on such imports. But the colonies objected to England's right to tax them. They soon formed the Boston Tea Party and at Boston threw into the sea all the tea-chests sent by the East India Company directly from India. The Boston port was soon closed by the British Government. The colonists met at Philadelphia and declared that the British Government had no right to tax them. It was decided to send 'Olive Branch Petition' to the British Government requesting the repeal of all laws passed by the British Parliament in respect of the colonies. But the mother country was not ready to listen to their grievances. Hence the revolt started.

Results

The American War of Independence put a setback to the colonial aspirations of the English people temporarily, but it did not curb the superiority of the British Government in the establishment of colonies. According to Green, the Americans were descendants of English settlers and hence they had imbibed the English traditions and language. The feelings and thoughts were quite akin to the Englishmen, and like the Englishmen they exercised tremendous influence over the social, economic and intellectual life of the people of the world. The combined influences of the Americans and the English led to the establishment of the superiority of the English race which moulded the western civilization.

The American War of Independence doomed the old colonial idea of exploitation. The English statesmen realised that it was impossible to exploit the colonial people without giving the least concession to their aspirations; and this idea led to the modification of all colonial policy in the nineteenth century and this modification led to the establishment of British Commonwealth of Nations.

The American War of Independence led to the breaking up of the personal ambitions of George III who realised the futility of pursuing his own schemes of the revival of the royal power. The blame for the entire defeat in America was put on George III and his unworthy ministers. This led George to abandon his policy; and the normal evolution in the sphere of constitution was thus restored. The Cabinet system and other political institutions progressed according to the general will expressed in British Parliament.

The loss of American colonies put a temporary set-back to the British prestige abroad. The loyal colonists numbering 20,000 left America and migrated to Canada. There was no place for the British Government to send her convicts by way of exiles. Besides, England lost a very good market for her manufactured goods, and she lost her trade fortunes. It was under these circumstances that Englishmen colonised Australia and Newzealand, and vigorously struggled in India to compensate her losses in America.

Another noticeable change was brought about in the relationship that existed between England and Ireland. The American War of Independence gave a fillip to Irish people who were fighting for independence. The Irish like the Americans demanded full legislative independence in the matter of taxation and legislation. The English statesmen conceded their demands in 1782. English people were very conservative in granting of any kind of independence. But the American War of Independence and the Irish question led them to modify their old colonial policy, and they granted economic independence, i.e. the right to trade freely, to the new colonies.

According to Green, "whatever might be the importance of American independence in the history of England, it was of unequalled moment in the history of the world.

The American Independence speeded up the revolution in France. The French armies which fought side by side, on the American colonies against the British imperialists returned to France with new ideas, and they soon plunged themselves in the War against Lious. They played a leading role in the French Revolution."

Commenting upon the emergence of United States of America, Trevelyan remarks, "It was well that America was made. It was tragic that the making could only be effected by a war with Britain. The parting was perhaps inevitable at some date and in some form, but the parting in anger and still more the memory of that moment's anger fondly cherished by America as the starting point of her history, have had consequences that we owe to this day." But J.H. Plumbs is more realistic when he says, "There is no doubt that the American revolt led to a new attitude towards the empire. A considerable body of opinion believed that the colonies were lost through indifferences, through a failure to realize that colonies were like children who grew to maturity.

It should be noted that the English started the war with better resources and favourable circumstances, and the colonies laboured hard under several strains and hardships. The colonists had no organized army, and all that they possessed was the strong will to oust the English domination. This very factor enabled the colonists to gain success, and the English failed on account of several factors.

One of the causes of British failure was that they underestimated the strength, resources as well as the strong determination of the colonists. The British government felt that they would conquer America with an army of four regiments only, and hence they did not make the requisite preparation. The British officials as well as the military officers were incompetent people who least bothered to read carefully the colonial despatches. They did not work with a coordinated plan of operations, and it resulted in mismanagement. The colonists also got sufficient time to recoup their strength, and they then fought with renewed vigour and strength. The British officers never took the necessary precautions of blocking the way of the French who were helping the colonists with reinforcements. The British also suffered on account of the lack of positive idea about the land, climate and vegetation. This difficulty was magnified by the lack of communication and transport. The colonists in this respect were in superior position. Further, the colonists were determined to defeat the English soldiers whose line of communication was always broken by the colonists, who were fighting for their cause under the unified leadership of George Washington. Washington's leadership was unequalled, and he thoroughly understood the strength of the English forces. The British officers on the other hand were not independent and they had to submit to the interferences of the ministers of George III. The failure of British causes was not due to king's enemies but to the king's friends who were largely instrumental in furthering the personal rule of George III. The people in England were also not enthusiastic about the success of British cause on account of their hostile attitude towards George and his ministers. It is said that they prayed for their failure, for only that would bring the ruin of George's ulterior motives. Keith Feiling has rightly observed, "No war was ever worse handled in British military history than the American War of Independence."

13

The French Revolution (1789)

If the economy of the nineteenth century world was formed mainly under the influence of the British Industrial revolution, its politics, social attitudes and ideology were formed mainly by the French. Britain provided the model for its railways and factories, the new economic shape which replaced the traditional socio-economic, and political structures. Whereas France made its revolutions and gave them the socio-politico and ideological inspirations. The world politics of 1789 to 1917 were largely the struggle for and against the principles of 1789. France provided the basic material for issues of liberal and democratic politics of the contemporary world. It provided the concept and importance of nationalism. It provided the codes of law, the model of scientific and technological organisation. This was rightly the work of the French revolution.

The French revolution spread far and wide new principles of government, new ideas of socio-politico organisation, new theory of the rights of man and a great challenge to the established customs and institutions of Europe. The old regime in Europe was based on politico-religious authority, class privilege and absolutism. It had become out of date and anomalous. Hence the new ideas and principles promulgated by the French Revolution permeated the whole of Europe and gave a rude shock to their prevalent socio-politico-religious and administrative order. The later part of eighteenth century was an age of crisis for the old regimes of Europe and their socio-politico and economic systems. Its last decades were filled with political agitations sometimes reaching the point of revolt, of colonial movements for autonomy, sometimes reaching to the extreme point of secession. The above analysis shows that the European states like Germany, Austria, Prussia, Russia, Italy, Spain etc. were devitalised powers, crippled by prolonged struggles among themselves as well as by rotten political and financial systems. It was the socio-politico-religious and economic weakness of these European states that prevented them from stemming the tide of the French revolution. The French revolution remains the true revolution of its time, and not merely one, though the most prominent of its kind. And its origins must therefore be sought not merely in the general conditions of Europe, but in the specific situation of France.

France on the eve of the revolution had become decadent. Her military prestige had been shattered when she was crushed in the seven years' war (1757-63). This disaster caused the loss of her colonies, trade and commerce and almost irreparable damage to her finances. King Louis XV, sunk in vice, immorality and sex, did nothing to restore the prestige of the crown. The French royal monarchy which owed its strength to the military glory it had given to the nation, became discredited. Murmurs of discontent became increasingly vocal and the monarchical institution became the target of bitter criticism. The immediate cause of the revolution was a financial crisis originating with the war in America. The two successive ministers Turgot and Necker had financed the American War of Independence by borrowing, and their successor, Calonne, had used the same method to pay off arrears. The deficit grew to such proportions that on August 20, 1786, Calonne sent Louis XVI a note declaring state reform imperative.

The administrative and fiscal structure of the kingdom was grossly obsolete. It was so confused that the situation can be described through the following rough example. A statement of financial expectations drawn up in March, 1788, the first and last budget of the old regime, estimated expenditures at 629 million livres and receipts at 503 million, leaving a deficit of 126 million, or 20 per cent. Contemporary records attributed the deficit to court wastefulness and financiers. Profits Servicing of the debts alone required 318 million, more than half of expenditures. The government could have reduced the expenses only by repudiating the debts. The attempt to remedy the economic and fiscal ills by the reforms of 1776-88 failed. For though the extravagance of Versailles palace has often been blamed for the crisis, court expenditure only amounted to 6 per cent of the total in 1788. War, navy and diplomacy made up one quarter, the servicing of the existing debt one-half. It has been rightly said that the revolution was precipitated by the economic factor, and "the train which had been laid by philosophy was fired by finance". It was the financial question that led to the crisis in 1789.

To some the French Revolution of 1789 was much less a rebellion against despotism, a rebellion against inequality. It actually sprang from a combination of intellectual ferment and material grievances and it was the intellectual forment that made the material grievances more fiercely resented. There was prevalent social inequality making clear cut distinctions between the privileged and unprivileged classes of the French society. The privileged part consisted of the nobility and clergy which formed a small fraction of the total population of the country. But in rank, possession and privilege, the position of the Third estate was comparatively at the lowest ebb. The nobles had appropriated all the jobs in the administration, church and army to themselves; and flocked round the king for all kinds of patronage. They were exempted from most of the taxes, the other taxes which they paid were nominal only. The nobles were divided into two sections—Nobles of the Sword and Nobles of the Robe. The nobles of the sword were a hereditary caste whose titles went all the way back to the feudal system of the middle ages. But the nobles of the robe at one time held judicial offices which carried the right to wear a pompous gown. But in matter of privilege, the nobles of the sword enjoyed the position of upper hand.

Like the nobles, the clergymen occupied a privileged position. They possessed wealth, land, luxuries, and some of them had fixed annual income like the nobles. They were also divided into classes. The hither clergies comprised the regular clergies who were supposed to live in the monasteries and conduct the spiritual services. They lived a luxurious life and simply exploited the people in the name of religion. The lower clergies came from lower classes and hence they were not unpopular. But they enjoyed the same privileges as the landed aristocracy. In matters of privilege they enjoyed all political and social privileges which the third estate did not possess. Gardiner has significantly pointed out, "Not only were the bishops and higher clergy rolling in wealth and living worldy and sometimes vicious lives, whilst the poor parish priests who did the work were in great poverty, but the bishops cried out for the persecution of Protestants and sceptics, although some of them were themselves sceptic".

The nobility and clergy constituted the upper strata of the social order, and the middle classes, workers and peasants constituted the lower class who represented the Third Estate. The middle class was better off but socially, their position was humiliating. They constituted the unprivileged class and their lot socially, economically and politically was unhappy. The middle class was denied any control in their own affairs and their enterprise was hampered by irritating bureaucratic regulations and an unfair burden of taxation. The peasants and workers were no longer serfs but they lived in a state of extreme poverty, bore the whole weight of national taxation and suffered much at the hands of the upper classes. There was the French maxim: "the nobles fight, the clergy pray and the people pay". The middle class which suffered most revolted against the oppressive order but their leadership was taken by the most prosperous and enterprising bourgeoisie. They resented the social superiority and the lavish extravagance of the nobles as well as the court; and from this class arose the leaders of the French Revolution. The social order could be well presented by the remark, "class was divided against class, group against group, and each one was dissatisfied, distrusting the class above and despising the class below".

The whole political system in France was confounded with confusions. It was a prodigal anarchy on account of excessive centralisation of power as well as despotic and incompetent monarchy. The monarch was the head of the state, and Louis XIV had once declared, "the sovereign authority is vested in my person, and legislative power exist in myself alone. My people are one only with me, national rights only rest in my hands". There was no contact between the king and the people, for he always remained in the capital where the nobles participated in the frivolties of the royal court. Queen Marie Antoinetti interferred in the politics and administration of the country and the king was virtually under her influence. The administration, therefore, became unsatisfactory, and the nobles and the clergies made most of the bargains in their own favours. There was no uniformity in the legal system and the people were governed under different system of law. "The power of despotism was irresponsible and unlimited; it was above the law. But it had not used its power to redress abuses; it had not created a single uniform system of law, it seemed to be the source and buttress of all the evils from which France suffered", remarks Ramsay Muir.

The French philosophers did not attack the monarchy directly but there is no doubt that they sharpened the discontent which many serious Frenchmen already felt and they hastened that resounding collapse of the old political and social fabric of France which is usually known as the French Revolution. Important among those philosophers were Montesquieu, Voltaire and Rousseau besides others. They prepared the ground for the French revolution. Montesquieu who has been given the highest position among the French philosophers was influenced by the writings of John Locke and Newton of England. Essentially he was not a revolutionary rather he was a supporter of monarchy. But he was all out for limited and constitutional monarchy and he never supported the divine rights of kings. His main doctrine—separation of powers—the details of which he analysed in 'the Spirit of Law'. He advocated the separation of executive, legislative and judicial powers for the proper functioning of the government. Another philosopher Voltaire was a product of the middle class. He advocated the supremacy of reason and mercilessly attacked everything that failed to convince him. He denounced the abuses of the state but directed his criticisms against the church. According to Hazen. "Voltaire was one of the masterminds of European history whose name has been the name of an era. His significance to his tunnes is shown in the title men gave him—King Voltaire. He was a pillar of cloud by day and of fire by night for all who enlisted in the fight for the liberation of mankind". Rousseau was another intellectual giant who "began where Voltaire left off; the latter harnessed the horses of reason, the former unchained the triggers of emotion". Voltaire aimed at destroying the existing institutions while Rousseau came forward with a plan of social reconstruction. His fundamental theory was that of the inherent virtue of the natural man whom civilisation had corrupted and deprived of his natural rights to liberty and happiness. 'Man is born-free but everywhere he is in chains'. He advocated that the government must rest upon the general will. He propounded the Social Contract theory, the gospel of democracy. Rousseau may be considered to be the pioneer of French Revolution for he put forward a solid programme which was put into operation by the French people. Besides these writers, there were a number of writers of smaller eminence who contributed much towards enlightening the French people. Diderot and a group of editors brought forward Encyclopaedia in order to acquaint the people with the correct knowledge. "All the more did it make excellent gun-powder for destroying the state and never before was a revolution so around with words and phrases" remarks Ketelby. Helvetius, Holbach, Quesmai and Turgot were all great enthusiasts of reform. Hence Mallet remarks, "The seed sown by these remarkable writers fell upon fruitful soil. An enthusiasm for the natural greatness of man and boundless contempt for the society in which he lived pervaded the thought of the time. Almost every European country witnessed a change which most people were prepared to welcome.

Character of the French Revolution

Although largely inspired by English political ideas and practices the French Revolution was quite unlike the English revolutions of the seventeenth century. The aims of the English revolutions (the Puritan Revolution of 1641 and the Glorious Revolution of 1688) were in the main political. The risings in England were directed against the arbitrary power of the Crown and the illegal exercise of the royal prerogative. In the result the people were satisfied when their rights and privileges were safe-guarded by constitutional checks imposed by Parliament on the royal power. The motive force of the French Revolution on the other was social in the first instance and political in the second. It was social inequality which pinched the French people most. In France the cleavage between class and class was much wider than in England, and the privileged classes enjoyed exemptions and advantages wholly disproportionate to their services to the state. The result was that there was glaring inequality, at once irritating and oppressive, in the social structure of France. The French people, long accustomed to centralised despotism, complained not so much of the evils of absolutism as of the unjust privileges enjoyed by the upper classes. It was privilege which polluted justice by making invidious distinction between man and man and shifted the main burden of taxation on to the shoulders of the poor. So the French people wanted to abolish privilege more than anything else.

Another feature of the French Revolution was that it was thoroughly destructive in character. The people in France sought to abolish the old Regime root and branch. They made a violent breach with the past by attempting a wholesale reconstruction of their old social and political systems. The English Revolution of 1688 on the other hand was defensive and conservative. The people vindicated their ancient rights and demanded nothing new. They wanted to reform and not to destroy.

The Summoning of the States-General and Fall of the Old Regime

After Necker's fall came a succession of worthless and incompetent finance ministers who mismanaged matters and thereby hastened the catastrophe. Bankruptcy was impending and there was no alternative but to impose new taxes. The Parliament of Paris opposed any scheme of taxation and demanded the convocation of the States-General which, it was declared, was the only body legally competent to impose taxes. The king attempted to overawe the Parliament which in its turn defied the king. Riots broke out in many places and the demand for the summoning of the States-General increased. The king having no other resources to fall back upon, at last in despair summoned the States-General in 1789.

Every member of the States-General brought from his constituency a statement of grievances or Cahiers. All the orders agreed in asking for a constitution and reforms in taxation, but the Third Estate likewise demanded the abolition of the feudal rights. The State-General or the feudal Parliament of France was a three-chambered body composed of the elected representatives of the three orders, the clergy, the nobles and the commons. It had not met for 176 years and so it was as good as a dead institution. So when it was revived at a time of great national crisis, the question of its constitution assumed paramount importance. Previously, each of the three orders had an equal number of delegates and each order voted separately. The first two chambers being composed of the privileged classes (the clergy and the nobility), the Third Estate, i.e., the commons were left in a permanent minority and so the action of the privileged orders had always been decisive. At the time of summoning the States-General, Necker had allowed the Third Estate as many members as the two other orders combined.

As soon as the States-General met (May 5, 1789), the members of the Third Estate held that it was not a feudal assembly but one representing the whole nation. Hence they demanded that the three orders were to meet as a single chamber in which each individual should have a vote. As the Third Estate had been permitted to send twice as many members as either the clergy or the nobility, the substitution of individual votes for vote by border meant the transference of power from the privileged classes to the communality. The clergy and the nobility offered a stubborn resistance but the Commons remained firm. At last after much contention the Third Estate took the momentous step of declaring itself the National Assembly (June 17, 1789). By this the Commons claimed the right to speak and act for the whole nation even though they were not supported by the privileged orders. The action was no doubt revolutionary for it was not sanctioned by the constitution of France. It brought matters to a crisis and led to the other steps in the development of the revolution. The king under pressure from the court sought to oppose the revolutionary proceedings of the Third Estate. He closed the hall in order to prevent the session of the National Assembly. The members in anger rushed to a neighbouring tennis-court and all assembled and took an oath not to separate till the constitution of the realm had been definitely established. Next in a royal session the king declared the acts of the Third Estate as illegal, tried to pressurise the Commons to submit to the old procedure, viz, meeing in three separate chambers and ordered the Third Estate to keep out of the hall. At this Mirabeau, a noble who had cast his lot with the people, gave vent to a very strong expression hurling defiance at king's orders. The king perceiving the firm resolution of the commoners, gave way and ordered the clergy and nobility to join the Third Estate. Thus the three orders formed a single chamber and the formation of the National Assembly was completed. The people had scored their first triumph over the king. Hence, at the very outset of the revolution, power passed out of the hands of the king and the privileged orders, into those of the people. Having recognised the National Assembly, the king, urged on by his courtiers, sought to suppress it. Considerable bodies of soldiers began to appear near Paris and Necker, the popular minister, was dismissed. These measures alarmed the people. They believed that the king was determined to use armed force in order to suppress the National Assembly. The mob of Paris rose in fury against the king whom the popular orators denounced as a tyrant. The enraged populace stormed the state prison called the Bastille, which to the mob was an odious symbol of tyranny and abuses of the Old Regime. After a bloody encounter with the royal troops it was razed to the ground (14th July, 1789). The fall of the Bastille was regarded in France as a triumph of liberty and produced a wide-spread enthusiasm.

The Parisian mob followed up the fall of the Bastille by assuming control of the city. A new form of municipal government was established in Paris and a city militia called the National Guard was organised to maintain order. Lafayette was made the commander of the new military force. The revolution had entered upon a municipal phase.

Alarmed at the critical state of affairs the king at once yielded to the storm. He sent away the troops, recalled Necker and recognised the National Guard. Order was for the time being restored in Paris, but the news of the fall of the Bastille spread like a wild fire and excited popular feeling in the province to a high pitch. Other cities set up municipal government like that of Paris and organised provincial national guards. Outside the towns, the Revolution took the form of a rising against feudalism. The peasants rose everywhere, sacked the castles of the nobles and destroyed records of their feudal services. The revolution was now in full tide.

The rising of the peasants in the provinces produced immediate and startling effects. In a memorable session of National Assembly on the 4th August, 1789, the nobles voluntarily surrendered their feudal rights and privileges. Rights of hunting, corvees, and other customary services were abolished, the guilds and similar corporations were swept away and titles were abandoned. Offices cease to be purchasable and were thrown open to all. Thus, class distinctions were abolished and the principle of equality was declared to be the basis of the state and society. The last relics of fedualism were swept out of France and the overthrow of the Old Regime was completed. Meanwhile the renewed intrigues of the court excited. The suspicion was intensified by the terror of the famine due to the scarcity of bread in Paris. On the 5th October a large number of women, pale and haggard, long suffering, set out for Versailles to fetch the king, drawing cannons with them. The king was frightened at this demonstration, agreed to leave Versailles and came back to Paris escorted by the fierce women. Henceforth the king was practically a prisoner in the hands of the mob. The monarchy was all but ruined.

Effect of the French Revolution on England

Southgate has remarked, "The course of the French Revolution was followed with greatest interest in this country. For a time much sympathy was felt with the French. But as the movement grew more violent and extreme, British opinion became less favourable". In the beginning the English welcomed the Revolution and change that was being brought about by the destruction of old arbitrary government in France. The people of England were sympathetic towards the French, for the Declaration of the Rights of Man greatly appealed to them. Even the poets like Wordsworth, Coleridge, Southey, Landey etc. drew inspiration from this great event. Burns, the poet of Scotland, was very much thrilled by the Revolution. The French Revolution gave an impetus to the movement for parliamentary reform.

Burke the English statesman and philosopher, published a book, *Reflections on the Revolution in France,* and in that work he pointed out the impact of the French Revolution on English people. He believed that anarchy in France was bound to affect the English people. State was an organism and changes should be brought about in a gradual process. But the views of Burke were challenged by some English writers. One such writer was Tom Paine who in his book, *Rights of Man,* pleaded a revolutionary gospel and attacked the philosophy of Burke, Paine asked the people to set up new institutions in which the corrupt politicians should not find any place. Similarly William Godwin in his work, *Political Justice*, enunciated revolutionary ideas which however, could not become popular on account of rigid style. According to Plumb, "In literary and artistic circles and in the wilder living sections of the autocracy the revolution was at first immensely popular. It seemed to mark the end of that medieval obscurantism in institutions and beliefs associated with the ancient regime. It symbolised the destruction of despots in church and state and the chance of an era in which human personality breed from the shackles of the past, could achieve a new fulfilment. In literary and artistic circles and in the wider-living sections of the aristocracy, the Revolution was very popular.

14

Reign of Terror (June 2, 1793 - July 1794)

The spring which followed the execution of Louis was crowded with disasters (Jan. 21, 1893) for the negicide French state. With England, Spain and Holland added to the circle of her enemies, with her armies withdrawn from Belgium, with Dumouriez, her best general, gone over to the enemy, with insurrection ablaze in the Vendee the Republic was fighting with its back to the wall. It was the stress of these terrible anxieties which swept the Girondins clean out of the political scene, and founded that firm and terrible instrument of autocratic rule which succeeded amidst much bloodshed and cruelty in restoring the military situation. It was the darkest and most terrible period of the Revolution. It was also an emergency despotism—"a dictatorship of distress". It was founded on the theory that only by establishing a despotism could civil war be ended, unity restored, and the country put in a condition to defend itself against the enemy at its doors.

To understand the atrocities committed during this period it is necessary to bear in mind that the condition of France was desperate about this time and so desperate remedies were necessary for national salvation. If men would not fight from love or loyalty they must fight from fear. Hence the machinery of capital punishment was used to destroy all elements of opposition, and all potential traitors. The joy of life was not abolished by the terror. The theatres were well attended. But the majority of the middle class did well to keep out of politics.

It was obviously an abnormal regime but the times themselves were abnormal. It was also an unconstitutional regime for it was felt that the government's hand must not be fettered by a constitution. For the time being the French people had to put their liberties in storage and forget the principles of the Revolution. One does not deny the fact that it was an unwholesome regime and that many were far from happy in an atmosphere of suspicion. Yet it is difficult to see how without the terror France could have pulled herself out of anarchy and civil war and mobilised the strength to beat back the foreign foe. It was thus a period of marvellous product of practical statesmanship. And it saved France.

The cornerstone and the very soul of the Terror was the *Committee of Public Safety.* It consisted of twelve members with almost unlimited executive power. There were ministers in it who were hardly more than clerks. There was a legislature too, which in actual fact was a mere creature of the body it had created. Though the members of the Committee were elected for one month, they were at almost always reelected. Besides the deputies also wielded despotic power, though like the intendants of old, they were responsible to the government. Thus France was centralised once more.

The system of terror which emanated from the government was wielded by various committees and tribunals. Throughout France was established a network of revolutionary committees "whose chief business was to enforce the Law of suspects—a terrible law which rendered suspect all persons who might in any way be identified with the old regime: it might even be applied to anyone who could not show a positive service to the Revolution. In Paris, a central committee, known as *Committee of General Security*, examined cases of suspicion and decided who should be hailed before the Revolutionary Tribunal. A number of courts were established to handle the cases. For most of the persons brought before these courts *the guillotine was in store.*

Such were the principal organs of the Terror. Some of its machinery—the committee of public safety, the revolutionary tribunal, and the deputies on mission—had come into being before the system was fully evolved. By September 1793 the "Reign of Terror" was supposed officially to begin. *The law of suspects* authorised the arrest of any and every person suspected of being attached to the cause of Monarchy or unfavourably disposed towards the cause of the Republic. These suspects were to be detained in prison till the establishment of peace. The second part of the machinery, the *Revolutionary tribunal* was created for the speedy trial of the criminals or suspects. In the square of the Revolution the heads of the unfortunate victims fell under the stroke of the guillotine.

The first activities of the Terror were directed against internal uprisings. The *vendean revolt* was put down with ruthless severity which resulted in the burning of villages and the butchery of some two thousand people. Besides revolting towns were also suppressed. Meanwhile in June there was a harvest of executions in Paris. The most prominent of the victims were Marie Antoinette, the captive queen, Madame Roland, the guiding spirit of the Girondists who oftured, "Liberty, how many crimes are committed in thy name?" Bailly, Barnave, "Philip Egalite", and several eminent Girondist leaders. The blood thirsty Marat was stabbed to death by a Norman girl, Charlotte Corday who wanted to rid her country of this hideous monster.

The whole machinery of terror was handled by a small group of Jacobins whose patron was—Robespierre. This group intended that the Terror should go on until the Republic should be founded on an entirely new pattern. It should be a regime, inspired by *"civic virtue"*—a policy eminently practicable on the part of a government as despotic as that of the terror.

Along with the measures taken to avert internal dangers, the committee took energetic steps to encounter external enemies. The war department was in the hands of Carnot who performed almost Herculean feats in organising and equipping armies. On the basis of the *Levee en masse* he created and equipped the biggest army till now known to history. The Girondist generals were replaced by the generals chosen from amongst the Mountain, and Carnot had a special gift for selecting the best men. The result was that the French armies were successful everywhere. The English were beaten at Handschoote and compelled to raise the siege of Dunkirk. The Austrians were defeated at Wattignies. The Allies were forced back on the Rhine. Holland was occupied and transformed into the Batavian Republic, and made a close ally. Belgium was recovered by the French victory at Fleurus over the Austrians, and Toulon was recaptured from the English. Prussia and Spain concluded peace with France by the Treaty of Basle in 1795. These astonishing successes won for Carnot the appellation of "Organiser of Victory". The great coalition was broken up. Only England and Austria remained in the field against France.

The regulative policy, necessitated by the war, could now be supplemented by measures in the interest of reform. The sending of most of the significant elements to the guillotine in March, 1794 put the commune into immediate eclipse. But Robespierre for his own purposes had still one obstacle before him. That was Danton.

Robespierre and Danton were said to be two men of contradictory qualities between whom cooperation was inconceivable. Danton the "Incorruptible" was a practically minded easy going libertine but Robespierre was a man of fixed ideas who never bent to realities and seldom temporixed. The military success of the French army brought about the downfall of the Reign of Terror. Danton along with the radical Hebertists declared that the terror must be relaxed. The country was pacified, the invader had been beaten back. His soul had begun to revolt against the interminable executions and wanted the return of normal times in order to enjoy the fortune he had amassed from the Revolution.

Besides, to complete their separation from the royalist party, the Hebertists the extreme section of the Jacobins abolished the old calendar and replaced by a new one which divided the year according to the natural change of seasons. Thus, July became *Thermidor* or the period of heat, April was called *Germinal* or the building time, etc. The new era hence began from the birth of the new Republic, September 21, 1792 instead of from the birth of Christ.

The demand of Danton and Hebertists for a return to a more humane policy made Robespierre very much critical of Danton's position. Mercy to him and his satellites was treason and they denounced Danton as the representative of the dangerous policy of moderation. Finally, in April 1794, he and his followers were arrested, hastily tried on trumped-up charges, and met their fate on the guillotine. "Show my head to the people", Danton had said to his executioner; "it is worth it." It was mainly owing to his splendid energy that France was saved from the Prussian invasion in 1792 and got a strong government. He had the gift of a statesman. He tried to smooth over the differences between the Jacobins and the Girondists and to keep all Republicans working together for the welfare of France. To the very end he protested against the needless severity in France and the reckless policy which banded and armed whole Europe against her. With his fall France lost a statesman who could possibly have dominated the course of events.

The elimination of Danton and the "Indulgents" left Robespierre to all appearances supreme. Now at last he was in a position to usher in his "reign of virtue". But his ideas were quite nebulous. He dominated all the three houses of the Terror. He overthrew the worship of Reason and at his instance the convention passed a decree recognising the existence of the Supreme Being and immortality of the soul." He then took steps to make the Revolutionary Tribunal more murderous in its activity. It was stripped of its last vestiges of legal form. By the Law of 22nd prairial (drafted by Robespierre himself) the Terror was so intensified that any sort of evidence was admitted in trials. The number of executions was multiplied. The Tribunal thus reorganised was responsible for 1,376 executions in the course of 45 days. And yet the great victory at Fleurus on June 26—one of the decisive battles of the war seemed to prove beyond a doubt that the Terror was no longer needed.

But fortunately Robespierre overreached himself. At last an opposition was organised against Robespierre and the convention outlawed him, and his adherents. They were arrested on the 27th of July and Robespierre was executed on the 10th Thermidor, July 28, 1794. The terror had come to an end in the blood of its principal champion.

Though not the author of the Reign of Terror, Robespierre was undoubtedly the most active promoter of it. But he resorted to terror not for its own sake but as a means of attaining his fanatical ideals. His great ambition was to set up a reign of virtue, through the medium of democracy, and he regarded the Terror as the best means of establishing it.

The fall of Robespierre was followed by a milder regime. The Reign of Terror gradually came to an end, because the system was thoroughly discredited. Moreover, the public opinion was now strongly against it. The commune of Paris was dissolved, the Revolutionary Tribunal suspended, the functions of the public safety were restricted and the Jacobin Club was closed. The critical period of the Revolution was not yet ended for the reaction which now set in threatened for a short time to end in a return to monarchy; but thanks to the terror, the most acute dangers were past. Terror had done its work and there was nothing to justify its further continuance.

15

The Directory Government

The fall of Robespierre was followed by a milder regime. The Reign of Terror came to an end. The general run of the bourgeoisie which was now able to return to politics and to dominate public opinion decided to stick to the Republic and it was this class which impressed its character on the new regime.

The so-called constitution of the year III was framed and promulgated during the summer of 1794. The executive was entrusted to a Directory consisting of five members. The legislative power was entrusted to two Houses called the council of Five Hundred and the Council of the Ancients. This new executive was to be chosen (one each year) for a term of five years by the legislature. The administration of the country at large was a compromise between the centralisation of the old regime and decentralisation of the constitutional monarchy. There were to be resident commissioners in each department appointed by the central government to see to the enforcement of the laws. In its electoral requirements and its weak Executive the new policy resembled the constitutional Monarchy. Also, like the Constitution of 1791, it put political power into the hands of the middle class. The former regime was bourgeois monarchy, this one was bourgeois republic.

This new republican experiment, which is commonly known as the "Directory", expressed well the national desire for an order stable enough to preclude any violent changes. To avert the possibility of a monarchist legislature the convention further decreed that two-thirds of the new legislature should be chosen from amongst the deputies of the present convention. This measure was unpopular and the bourgeoise and the royalists organised an insurrection against the convention known as the resurrection of the 13th Vendemiaire (October 5, 1795). Napoleon Bonaparte was then at Paris and he was entrusted with the task of defending the Convention against the Parisian mob. He crushed the mob and the convention was thus sustained. On October 26, the convention declared itself dissolved. And—what is still more important—Bonaparte had retrieved his shattered fortunes and had good hope of winning some tangible recognition of his service.

The following month the new regime began to operate. The rule of Directory, though it lasted four years, proved to be one of the most vicious governments that France had ever endured. It was ill-fated from birth. The Directors except Carnot were a group of corrupt, disreputable and self-seeking politicians of little ability. Many of them were speculators and profiteers who seemed to care for nothing but the enjoyment of power and wealth. These new rich, vulgar in taste and unscrupulous in habits, wanted above all to consolidate and increase their gains. Opposed to the royalists, their aims were a constitutional parliamentary system on a narrow social basis. They succeeded in preventing a repetition of Robespierre's revolutionary dictatorship only at the price of producing Napoleon's military dictatorship. Explanation of how this came about lies in their success in crushing rebellion at home and their failure to produce victory abroad.

The peculiar tone of the society was due to the moral reaction which followed the harsh discipline and dangers of terror. People felt that they had a right to enjoy life to the full without any need to think at all of private virtue or public duty.

The misgovernment of the Directory was chiefly the result of the peculiar factors mentioned above. It was aggravated by the faults of the constitution. Since the executive was not responsible to the legislature, it deliberately tried to control the public Institution by bribery and intimidation. The continued issuance of Paper Money had plunged the government once more into financial ruin and the country into misery of unstable prices. The wealthy people were exploited through forced loans and the poor were almost driven to desperation. At home the directory more and more openly relied upon the army to defend it against revolt. The Convention had already in 1795, destroyed the main instruments of revolutionary action, closed the Jacobin club, ended the commune and executed the communards, reorganised its own committees, and abolished the Revolutionary Tribunal. There was not even external peace, for the Directory needed war to enable it to bleed conquered countries and thus rescue it from bankruptcy. By the spring of 1795 the severe winter, dislocation of trade, and increase in social distress bred a series of revolts. In April, when Parisians rioted and demanded 'bread and the Constitution of 1793' the troops under General Pichegru promptly crushed them. The Directory was then mainly a continuation of the Thermedorian reaction under the convention. With an army of more than 800,000 men—the largest ever raised until then by one European power—it felt able to make up for its lack of popularity by frequent use of armed force. The last episode of the French Revolution was not the fall of Robespierre but the strange and extravagant episode known as the Babeuf plot of 1796. In 1795, The Society of the Pantheon—a new political club was formed. It circulated its own paper, The *Tribume* edited by Francois-Noel Babeuf, an embittered and fanatical agitator. It was attacked by the Directory, which in February 1796 sent General Bonaparte in person to close the meeting place and dissolve the society. It was thus to be the final battle for the forgotten revolutionary ideal of equality—the ideal most blatantly derided by the existing conditions of inflation, distress and corruption. Yet the event became of considerable historical importance because of the mythical and legendary character it acquired. The trial of the plotters, staged in 1797 before a Special Court and intended to frighten waverers into support of the Directory. The execution of Babeuf made him the last famous martyr of the White Terror. Perhaps he has acquired greater renown than he deserved or than the importance of the plot in 1796 merited. But in revolutions legends are powerful and ghosts can walk.

In foreign affairs, too, the army assumed an ever greater role. By the beginning of 1796 France's only active enemies on land were Austria, Sardinia and Great Britain (at sea). The convention had made peace with Holland, Spain and Prussia. The British refusal to make peace even after the break-up of the first coalition, kept active the war at sea. Peace had also been made with Portugal, with the German states of Saxony and the two Hesses, with the Italian states of Naples, Parma and the papacy. By the beginning of 1796 the Directory was able to concentrate all its efforts on the war against Austria. Austria signed the peace of Campo Formio on 17th October 1797. She thereby abandoned Belgium to France and recognised its annexation; recognised the new French creation of a Cisalpine Republic in northern Italy; surrendered the Ionian islands of Greece. The Austrian Emperor promised to cede to France large districts of the Rhine Land, and in return was promised part of Bavaria, the ecclesiastical stage of Salzburg, and the exclusion of his rival, Prussia, from any territorial gains. It was a settlement as characteristic of sly Napoleonic diplomacy as the campaign had been of Napoleonic generalship. Only Britain now remained at war with France.

At home the Directory faced its first political crisis with the elections of 1797. Only 13 out of the 216 retiring members of the elected councils were returned. In September 1797 the Directory forestalled the action of the new hostile and mainly royalist majority. With the help of Bonaparte it expelled the newly elected members from the Assemblies. By this *coup d'etat* of Fructidor the Directors forfeited their last shreds of legality, and henceforth relied more openly on armed force. Bonaparte's own seizure of power was brought one step further. In the further elections of May 1798, the extremists held the field and the Directory resorted to the further *coup d'etat* of Floreal, in which it annulled 98 elections. The political system was as bankrupt as the treasury. The elections of May 1799 brought into the legislative Assemblies all the Directory's most active opponents. Of the five Directors, Barras and Sieyes were resolved to resort to the ultimate sanction. Open alliance with Bonaparte, the most popular personality in France.

The public dissatisfaction with the Directory was an asset for Bonaparte as soon as his political ambition was awakended but it was the war which gave him a chance to display his genuis and to capture the public imagination.

The fall of Directory was brought about as much by the inherent defeat of its constitution as by its blundering foreign policy. The Directors could not agree among themselves as well as with the legislature. Again, there were constant plots and intrigues hatched by the royalists and extremists in the legislature. The Directory stood between the two and sought to suppress them both. The result was constant friction leading to a series of *coup d'etat* or appeals to force, with the object to keeping the ruling party in power. The foreign policy of the Directory was as unprincipled and aggressive as its domestic policy was weak and unpopular. Besides this, it was losing its hold on the public mind on account of want of harmony among the Directors themselves as well as between the legislature and the government of the Directory was tyrannical without being efficient. It had alienated every class of society. Taking advantage of the unpopularity of the Directory Abbe Siyes, one of the Directors, sought to overthrow the government and set up a new constitution. He was looking for a suitable agent and it was in the nick of time that Napoleon returned to France from Egypt. Sieyes and Napoleon put their heads together, organised a *coup d' etat,* dispersed the legislature by military force and overthrew the Directory on Christmas eve, November 9, 1799. This is known as the *coup d' etat* of 18th Brumaire. Thus the Directory was replaced by the Consulate. And Napoleon dazzled France and Europe with the achievements of dictatorship.

16

Rise of Napoleon Bonaparte

The history of Napoleon has often been written by his enemies. Nepoleon is admired because he merited the sovereignty to which the suffrages of a grateful nation elevated him. He abhorred war, he consecrated the most extraordinary energies to promote the prosperity of his country. He was regardless of luxury, had a high sense of honour, revered religion, respected the rights of conscience and truly advocated equality of privileges and the universal brotherhood of man. Such was the true character of Napoleon Bonaparte.

Napoleon Bonaparte was born on August 15, 1769 on the island of Corsica about a year after it had been acquired by France on the morning of 15th of August 1769. Letitia gave birth to her second son Napoleon. Had the young Napoleon seen the light two months earlier he would have been by birth an Italian not a Frenchman, for those eight weeks had elapsed since the island had been transferred to the dominion of France.

His father Charles Bonaparte died soon after Napoleon's birth. He was said to have appreciated the remarkable powers of his son. Madame Bonaparte was left a widow with eight children, Joseph, Napoleon Lucien, Louis, Jerome, Eliza, Pauline and Caroline. Rousseau had once truly predicted that "I have a presentiment that this little island will some day astonish Europe'. This prediction came true with the birth of Napoleon in Ajaccio. He ever regarded his mother with the most profound respect and affection. He often said, "My opinion is that the future good or bad of a child depends entirely upon its mother." When placed at the head of the government of France he immediately established schools for female education, remarking that France needed nothing so much as to promote its regeneration as good mothers.

His father was fortunate enough to obtain for him a scholarship in a military school in France where officers were made after several years of training Napoleon emerged as a sub-lieutenant of artillery. He loved to hear from his mother's lips, the story of her hardships and sufferings. "My mother", said Napoleon at St. Helena, "loves me. She is capable of selling everything for me, even to her last article of clothing." This distinguished lady died at Marseilles in the year 1822, about a year after the death of her illustrious son upon the island of St. Helena.

When the island of Corsica was surrendered to the French, Count Marbouef was appointed by the court at Paris, as its governor. The beauty of Madame Bonaparte, and her rich intellectual endowments attracted his admiration. When Napoleon was about ten years of age Count Marbouef obtained for him admission to the military school at Brienne, near Paris. The ardent and studious boy was soon established in school. His companions regarded him as a *foreigner*, as he spoke the Italian language and French was to him almost an unknown tongue. While they were wasting their time in dissipation and in frivolous amusements, he consecrated his days and nights with untiring assiduity to study and elevated himself above his companions and by his superiority, commanded their respect. In a letter written to his mother at this time he says, "With my sword by my side, and Homer in my pocket, I hope to carve my way through the world." He was seldom seen upon the playground but every leisure hour found him in the Library. But he had early shown a taste for martial sports. In some respects the works of philosophers affected some of his later viewpoints but most of his ideas were probably the product of experience and observation. His first aspiration was to free his native island from France. He remained in the school of Brienne for five years, from 1779 till 1784. His great superiority was universally recognised. In September 1785, Napoleon then but sixteen years of age, was examined to receive an appointment in the army. In September 1791, Napoleon then twenty-two years of age, had been promoted to a first lieutenancy. He in 1793 gave up his hope of liberating Corsica and made up his mind to serve his government. He established a debating club, composed of several officers in the army upon the island to discuss the great political questions which were then agitating Europe. At this time he warmly espoused the cause of popular liberty. He was promoted steadily due to his gift of strategy and for this service he was promoted to the command of a Brigade. Soon after this he became involved in the disgrace of the Robespierre faction with whom he had been playing politics. He was too valuable an officer to be sent to the guillotine and he suffered nothing worse than an eight day imprisonment. He first distinguished himself at the siege of Toulon. In 1795 he refused to accept an assignment in the Army of the West because he felt himself to be worthy of something better. For this insubordination he was suspended from rank. But by sheer luck he got the chance to redeem himself in the incident of the 13th Vendemiaire.

The reaction which followed the Reigns of Terror is historically known as the *Thermidorean Reaction.* The fall of Robespierre was followed by a milder regime. The Thermidorians got the upper hand in the state and they swept away the last traces of terrorism.

The convention took up the long neglected task of framing a constitution for Republican France. The so-called constitution of the year III was framed and promulgated during the summer of 1795. The executive power, instead of being placed in the hands of one King, or president was entrusted to five chiefs, who were to be called Directors. The legislative powers were committed to two bodies, as in the United States. The first corresponding to the US Senate was to be called the Council of Ancients and the second was called the Council of Five hundred, corresponded with the American House of Representatives. It was framed by the moderate Republicans who wished to establish a Republican government, protecting France on the one hand from the Royalists and on the other hand from the misrule of the violent Jacobins, who wished to perpetuate the reign of terror.

The city of Paris was divided into ninety-six sections or wards. When the constitution was tendered to the several sections of Paris, forty-eight of them voted in its favour, while forty-six rejected it. The opposing sections, now aroused, began to arm, resolved upon violent resistance. The Parisian mob ever ready for an outbreak joined most heartily with their aristocratic leaders and all Paris seemed to be rousing to attack the convention. The Convention was now on the utmost state of trepidation.

Here Napoleon was immediately introduced to the Convention. This rising of October, 5, 1795 of the 13th Vendemialine was crushed by Napoleon and the Convention was thus sustained - And what is still more important - Bonaparte had retrieved his shattered fortunes and had good hope of winning some tangible recognition of his service.

Thus Napoleon established the new government of France, called the Directory from the five Directors who composed its executive. Immediately after the quelling of the sections, Napoleon was triumphantly received by the convention. His friend Barras became one of the Directors and Napoleon was appointed Commander-in-Chief of the army of the Interior and entrusted with the military defence and government of the metropolis.

The defeat of the Insurgents was the deathblow to all the hopes of the Royalists and seemed to establish the Republic upon a firm foundation. Napoleon manifested the natural clemency of his disposition very strongly in his hour of triumph.

The situation of Napoleon was now flattering in the extreme. He was but twenty-five years of age. The distinguished services he had rendered, the high rank he had attained and the ample income at his disposal gave him a very elevated position in public view. This eminence of Napoleon was the result of long years of previous toil. He was now reaping the fruit of the seed which he had sown in his incessant application to study in the military school; in his continued devotion to literary and scientific pursuits after he became an officer, in his energy, and fearlessness and untiring assiduity of Toulon in his days of wintry exposure and nights of sleeplessness, in fortifying the coast of France, and in his untiring toil among the fastnesses of the Alps.

The public dissatisfaction with the Directory was an asset for Bonaparte as soon his political ambition was awakened, but it was the war, which in the meantime gave him a chance to display his genius and to capture the public imagination. After "Vendemiaire" he received what he had long desired, the command of the Army of Italy. The appointment was due to Carnot, who had seen a plan which Bonaparte had once drawn up for the conquest of Italy and who recognised the general's unusual gifts. During the year 1796-97 Bonaparte won a series of striking victories, which ended the first coalition and brought peace with all the powers except Britain. No commander in the field had acquired so distinguished a reputation. On the 6th of March, 1796, he married a lady of Paris, i.e. Josephine Tascher Beauharnais who was rendered quite prominent in society by her social attractions; her personal loveliness and her elevated rank. She was a widow, twenty-eight years of age, born on the island of Martincio, in the West Indies. She lost her husband Viscount Beauharnais in the storm of terror in France was survived with two children, Eugene and Hortense. He defeated the Sardinians at Turin and compelled them to sue for peace by a cession of Savoy and Nice. Then he turned against the Austrians, crossed the bridge of Lodi in the teeth of a murderous fire and entered Milan in triumph. The Austrians were driven out of Lombardy. Then he besieged Mantua. The Austrians were again beaten at Bassano, Arcola and Rivloli Mantua fell and Venice was conquered. Then he invaded Italy and the papal territory. He forced upon the Pope the Treaty of Tolentino by which the latter agreed to maintain a neutral attitude to cede territories and recognise the newly formed Republics in Italy. The Emperor Francis II of Austria concluded a peace with Napoleon by the Treaty of Campo Formio (1797). By this treaty Austria ceded Belgium to France and recognised the French possession of the Ionian islands and the extension of the French frontiers up to the Rhine. The Treaty of Campo Formio initiated the process of changing the map of Europe which was to be carried on several times in the years to come.

On his return to France after the Italian campaigns, Napolean was received with immense enthusiasm. Austria being humbled, only one power remained at war with France, namely England. The Directory appointed Napoleon to the command of army meant for the invasion of England. But a direct invasion of England seemed impossible without a powerful fleet, so Napoleon advised the Director to fit out an expedition for the conquest of Egypt, the key to the east. He left Toulon and set sail for Egypt in May 1798.

This Egyptian campaign was the outcome of his comprehensive Eastern design which aimed at destroying British power in India, as well as taking Europe in the rear by way of Constantinople. The first indication of his Eastern design was to be found in the occupation of the Adriatic port of Ancona during his campaign in Italy. The conquest of Egypt would give him an invaluable base for operations both against Turkey whose dismemberment he sought and against India from which he sought to expel the English.

Eluding the vigilance of the British fleet, Napoleon managed to reach Egypt conquering Malta on the way. He won the famous battle of the Pyramids which made him the master of the basin of the Nile. But the English admiral Nelson followed him closely and in the battle of Abukir Bay, i.e. the Battle of the Nile, he completely destroyed the French Fleet. This victory entirely cut off Bonaparte from communication with France and he was as good as imprisoned in Egypt. He then invaded Syria but failed in his attempt to take Acre. He then returned to France leaving his army to its fate.

Bonaparte returned from Egypt in October 1799. It was a puzzled and dejected France that received him. The radicals had managed to turn the tables on the moderates and had now the control of the government. The new directors had only deepened the public discontent, first by their policy of bleeding the rich (alienating the wealtheir middle-class and also by the law of Hostages which compelled each dept. to give hostages to the govt. for its loyalty. Abroad French armies had sustained defeat. Public opinion was so dissatisfied that already a plot was on foot to invoke the aid of the army and reorganize the state under some military leader. This conspiracy was organised by one of the directors, i.e. Abbe Sieyes.

Bonaparte carefully took soundings of the situation and plunged into the conspiracy, became both its instrument and its leader. Made commander of the troops in Paris he delivered a public speech. The Directory speedily broke up, three of the members being accomplices in the plot, the other two were arrested. The chief obstacle was the Council of Five hundred. Luckily Lucian, Napolean's brother was president of the five hundred and 'he managed during the din to fetch some soldiers who were persuaded that their general had been maltreated and forthwith invaded the hall. The outcome was the expulsion of the deputies by armed force. Thus was executed the *coup d'etat* of the 18th Brumaine (November 9, 1799).

The cards were now in Bonaparte's hands. A fraction of the Council, got together, adopted under Bonaparte's auspices the constitution of the Year VIII which established the Consulate. The executive was composed of three consuls, but practically all its power was vested in the hands of the First Consul, i.e. Bonaparte himself. In 1800 the government was completely decentralised in the manner of the old regime. Bonaparte was now the absolute master of France. The new arrangements were submitted to a Plebiscite and ratified by an overwhelming majority. On December 15, 1799, a Proclamation was issued in these words, "Citizens, the Revolution is established upon the principles which were its origin. It is at an end."

Bonaparte represented thus and safeguarded the new social order. Under the existing constitution Bonaparte enjoyed a ten-year term (8th May 1802) as first Consul. After he had achieved new glories for France - recovered the lost conquests, crushed the IInd coalition, effected a general peace (which included Great Britain), and restored religious tranquility - he was awarded in 1802 with position - he was now more of a monarch than the head of the Republic and henceforth he signed all documents by his Christian name - "Napoleon".

The conspiracy of French princes for the assassination of Napoleon roused republican France to increased efforts to consolidate the government. In abolishing the old feudal system and in limiting the royal authority, it was felt that now the dignity and the safety of France required that Napoleon should be invested with regal power. The Senate of France on 18th of May 1804, by unanimous acclamation, without a single dissentient voice passed the decree, "That Napoleon Bonaparte should be named Emperor, and in that capacity, be invested with the government of the French Republic."

The establishment of the empire meant that there was a revival of court etiquettes and ceremony. Although he himself cared little for pomp and ceremonies, because he felt it to be a waste of valuable time, he always had an eye for serene effects. The new regime was not one of privilege. In 1802 was constituted the Legion of Honour in which men were enrolled who had performed conspicuous service for the state. Thus Napoleon was emphatically a national leader.

Much of his success was due to the fact of understanding to sell the temperament of the French. He realised their vanity as a people. He gave them a well ordered administration. Besides, he respected the principle of equality. He personified also himself as the revolution.

But he said on another occasion, "I destroyed the revolution and this was equally true. The French got wearied of the political features of the revolution. Napoleon as a strong ruler was able to protect the more valued fruits of the revolution. Moreover, there burnt in him the flame of genius. These achievements were made possible by hard and incessant work. It is unreasonable to assert that Napoleon could have made out of France a republican empire. The despots of Europe would not even permit him to make out of France a republican empire. Had Napoleon neglected to surround his popular institutions with imperial energy, France would immediately have been overwhelmed by her assailants. The rise of Napoleon was thus inevitable in the logic of European history.

17

Napoleon Bonaparte as First Consul 1799-1804

France had tried Republicanism (1799-1804) and the experiment had failed. There was neither intelligence nor sufficient virtue among the people to enable them to govern themselves. Physical power alone was recognised. The strongest grasped the helm and with the guillotine, confiscation and exile endeavoured hopelessly to cripple their adversaries. Ten years of such anarchy had weakened the nation. France longed for repose. Napoleon was the only one capable of giving her repose. The nation called upon him to assume the reigns of government and to restore the dominion of security and order. If we compare Napoleon with the leaders of the armies, the founders of dynasties and with those who have ascended the throne in the midst of popular commotions we find he stands without a rival.

He from the very brink of outlawry was raised to power by the gesture of a younger brother who had told him to "hold his tongue". As first consul with plenary powers and plenty of work he had virtually been made dictator. The overthrow of the Directory by Napoleon necessitated the revision of the constitution. In the sense the Revolution stood for the principle of equality of opportunity it appeared to have finished its work on December 15, 1799, a proclamation was issued in these words, "Citizens, the Revolution is its origin. It is at an end." Bonaparte represented and safeguarded the new social order. Under the existing constitution Bonaparte enjoyed but a ten year as first consul and he had to share the honours with two colleagues - Ducos and Sdayes. Such a position could hardly accord with his ambition. After he had achieved new glories for France - recovered the lost conquests, crushed the Second Coalition, effected a general peace (including Great Britain) and restored religious tranquility - he was awarded in 1802 with position of consul for life. This new constitution made him the sole executive. In this position he was now more of a monarch and signed all documents by his Christian name - "Napoleon". But even this second run on the ladder was not enough. His vanity demanded the trappings and grandeur of power. On May 18, 1804 he was accordingly proclaimed "emperor of the French", his rule being made hereditary under a new constitution and approved by the people in a plebiscite.

The popularity which he enjoyed at the time of the consulate - it was as first consul that he began his role of autocrat - was not only enhanced by the victorious peace which he secured but also by the products of his statesmanship. Thus he consolidated his position by the reforms which he enacted, given below:

National Reforms

The motives for Napoleon's reforms are as following: He wished the gratitude of the nation to strengthen himself. Besides, he had a practical mind which required the Institution of an orderly - stable government. Moreover he had a steady care for his own fame. Bonaparte was a child of the revolution equally in the sense that like so many other brilliant men he was enabled by reason of that great social convulsion to come into forefront of affairs. Between 1800 and 1803 as First Consul he was free to devote his energies mainly to the Internal reorganisation of France. In general, the principle of election was replaced by that of appointment. The general structure of the judiciary remained, but judges were now appointed by the first consul. After the experiment of decentralisation under the constitutional Monarchy and the half centralisation of the Directory we return to the rigid centralisation of Napoleon. The consulate was thus in fact a restoration of the despotism of the later Bourbon dynasty but with a difference. It was a popular despotism. Napoleon provided for a centralised system of public services. The unification and codification of the laws was made a fact under Napoleon. The finances were set in order for the first time in a decade. He strove to make his people understand that payment of taxes was a public duty and must not be shirked from. Few new taxes were instituted, but the old ones were carefully supervised and collected and all the revenue was economically administered. The national credit was also restored very soon and France enjoyed a degree of stability and she had never known before. The Bank of France was founded in 1800, its constitution drafted by a leading Paris Banker, Perregaux, designed to give manufacturers the benefit of loans at a low interest. In 1803 this Bank was given the monopoly of issuing bank-notes. The system of taxation was made more efficient by Gandin. Indeed Napoleon made every effort to rebuild the shattered industrial life of his country and won a large measure of success. He also constructed the finest thoroughfares in Europe largely in order to promote internal trade. Local government at the same time was centralised by putting a prefect, appointed by the first consul in sole charge of each department. Local elected councils were left with only advisory powers and even the mayor of each commune was centrally appointed. These measures virtually restored the centralised authority of the old Regime with its powerful intendants, since the prefects we know were all in turn completely under the direction of the central government.

The enormously complex task of codifying French Law was completed. The unification and codification of the laws was as a matter of fact studied by the various Assemblies. The powerful council of state, itself a revival in modern form of the old curia negis or royal council was the machine through which Bonaparte remodelled the laws. It held by sessions to discuss various drafts of the new codes, with Bonaparte himself presiding over 36. It hammered out a synthesis between the liberal, customary, and natural theories of the revolution and the Roman law theories which under the Directory had been revived in reaction against the Revolution. The synthesis which was embodied in the 2287 articles of the Napoleonic code of 1804, was itself made possible by Bonaparte's readiness to employ men of talent whatever their past. The code gave prominence to the principles of Roman law and acceptable to other European countries in later years. This basis affected the especially the laws of the family, marriage and divorce, the status of women, paternal authority, and property. Under the new codes, the authority of the father was strengthened, wives were subjected to husbands, divorce was made more difficult and property upto a quarter of the whole could be bequeathed away from the family. Equality of civil rights was preserved. The Code confirmed the rights of the private property and the land settlement of the Revolution. Bonaparte ensured above all that there would be no counter-revolution - and this rallied middle classes and peasants alike behind the consulate.

In the midst of all these cares, Napoleon was making strenuous efforts to restore religion to France. It required great moral courage to prosecute such a movement. He was constitutionally serious, thoughtful and pensive. His inquisitive mind pondered the mysteries of the past and the uncertainties of the future. Educated in a wild country, where the peasantry were imbued with religious feelings and having been trained by a pious mother, the sight of the hallowed rites of religion revived in his sensitive and exalted imagination the deepest impression of his childhood. He had collected for himself a library of well known books relating to the organisation and the history of the church and to the relations of church and state. To declare the catholic religion the religion of the state is impossible. It is contrary to the prevalent ideas of France, and will never be admitted. In place of the declaration was avowed the fact that the catholic religion is the religion of the majority of the French men. The question of the re-establishment of Christianity was very earnestly discussed in the council of state. A general religious peace was established in France. He realised that only through reconciliation - with the papacy could religious unity be restored and religious wants of the nation be satisfied. Agreement was reached as a result of negotiation. The religious treaty with Rome called the *'Concordat'* was signed on the 15th of July 1801. On 11th of April, 1802 the event was celebrated by a magnificent religious ceremony in the Cathedral of Notre Dome. By this Instrument the higher clergy appointed by the State must receive the confirmation of the Pope. The lower clergy were to be appointed by the bishops with the sanction of the government and were to be paid by the state on compensation for the church's renunciation of the confiscated lands. Thus Napoleon restored the religious peace.

He then exerted all his energies for the elevation of France. He sought out and encouraged talent whenever it could be found. No merit escaped his princely munificence. Authors, artists, men of science were loaded with honours and emoluments. He devoted most earnest attention to the education of the youth. The navy, commerce, agriculture, manufactures, and all mechanical arts, secured his assiduous care. He laboured to the utmost and with a moral courage of discountenance. Whatever was loose in morals or enervating in amusements or tastes.

The theatre was the most popular source of entertainment in France. He frowned upon all frivolous and immodest performance and encouraged those only which were moral, grave and dignified. In the grandeur of tragedy alone he took pleasure. In his private department he exhibited the example of a moral, simple and toilsome life. Thus by his works of reorganisation Napoleon purged the Revolution of the features which seemed to make for chaos and retained those which might be calculated to bring out merit and to render the state a more efficient machine. In that sense he harnessed the revolution to the chariot of autocracy. But he also capitalised the patriotism born of the revolution to lead his soldiers on the path of territorial aggrandisement. It was here that self Interest and vanity came to mar the soundness of his judgment and led to the downfall of France.

Having set his house in order Napoleon proceeded against the enemies of France. Bonaparte, like many English men and Austrians, regarded the Peace of Amiens of 1802, as bound to be only a truce. He planned to rival British supremacy and pressed on with the expansion of ports and dockyards. He began extensive ship-building and fitted out colonial expeditions to Mauritius and Madagascar, defeated the Austrians in the historical battle of Marengo in June 1800. He reorganised the Cisalpine Republic in northern Italy, the Batavian Republic in Holland and the Helvetic republic in Switzerland. In 1803 with the consent of Tsar of Russia he devised a new imperial constitution for Germany which recast the old map of tiny principalities. These are thus the achievements of the Consulate.

A child of the Revolution, he combined the substance of old absolutism with the new sanction of popular approval. He was even more of a challenge to other monarchs than was the Revolution itself, a crowned and anointed Jacobin, a usurper legitimized by the will of the sovereign people. The Consulate dictatorship of Napoleon in France was a utilitarian, efficient, industrious, hard headed government. Its oppressiveness must not be exaggerated. It lacked the fanaticism and passion of the rule of Robespierre and the brutality of twentieth century dictatorships. He won his victories chiefly because he possessed a deeper grasp than his opponents offered by natural calamities, handled his army with extraordinary facility and was ever on the alert to catch his enemy and to expose it to an overwhelming blow. The last of the series of benevolent despot he was at the same time one of the great modern Statesmen. Whatever may be his statesmanship, it is a matter of regret that his history has often been written by his enemies. T.S.C. Abbot puts three questions to get the justified answer on behalf of Napoleon. They are viz.: 1) Did Napoleon usurp the sovereignty of France? 2) Having attained the supreme power, was he a tyrant, devoting that power to the promotion of his own selfish aggrandisement? 3) were the wars in which he was incessantly engaged provoked by his arrogance?

Abbot justified the power of Napoleon. To the first question the answer is that Napoleon did not usurp the sovereignty of France. It was the result of popular plebiscite, all he did. Secondly, he was not selfish about the utilisation of powers vested in him. He wanted trustworthy men and that's why he appointed his brothers to look after his kingdoms. Finally, of the sixty wars he fought, the majority of them were compelled on him by Great Britain. It was Britain which can be termed as the devil of the Europe.

18

Congress of Vienna (1815)

The years intervening between 1815 and 1923 are something more than a period of time. They possess the unity essential to great drama: with prologue, successive acts and Epilogue. The prologue is enacted, with a superb stage setting, at Vienna, the scene of the epilogue is in Paris. At Vienna we see a group of great personages, emperors, kings, statesmen and diplomatists, whose decisions will lay down the Lines of International politics for a generation. In this group the Czar Alexander, the Duke of Wellington, Lord Castlereigh, Metternich and Talleyrand stand out conspicuous.

The first Act of the drama is dominated by the European settlement which emerged from the hands of the diplomatists at Vienna. As Paris danced Thermidor, and London after the 1918 armistice, so through that autumn and winter Vienna danced while the Corsican was safe in Elba.

The new map was shaped by statesman for whom revolution emanating from France was the greatest of all dangers to the well being of mankind. As in 1918 the exhausted peoples of the Victorious Entente said with one voice, "No more Prussian militarism". So in 1815 the conquerors came to a common resolve that there must be no more French revolution and that every germ of liberal opinion must be promptly killed lest it might develop into the malignant revolutionary ferver.

To the Congress of Vienna the principles of President Wilson would have been anathema guided by Metternich, Telleyrand and Casterleagh; it held that the well being of Europe was to be secured not by compliance with the assumed wishes of the peoples concerned, but only by punctual obedience to legitimate authority.

After Napoleon's abdication for himself and his family in the first days of April 1815, the Allies sat down to mould the map of Europe anew, according to their heart's desire. Their task was not an easy one. As all the nations of Europe had been profoundly affected by his fall, the immediate and one of the main problems before the allies was the question of government of France. A cartoon represented Louis XVIII mounted on a horse beside the Cossack, and trampling on the body of a dead Frenchman. Louis established the restored Bourbon dynasty. Certain arrangements had been agreed upon by the allies before going to Vienna, in the First Treaty of Paris on May 30, 1814 and needed now to be carried out. The work of Congress of Vienna foreshadowed in a number of treaties concluded before the Congress by the powers. The work of the Congress was guided by the following three principles - viz., Legitimacy, balance of power and compensation. Legitimacy meant the restoration of the pre-revolutionary dynasties and governments overthrown by Napoleon. By Balance of Power means a balance or parity of strength was to be maintained between France and her neighbours. By the application of balance of power it was hoped that France would no longer be able to disturb the peace of Europe by attacking her neighbours. The third principle which moulded the work of the Congress was the principle of compensation to the victors who had suffered huge loss of man power and money in the war against Napoleon. Besides these above three principles there were two other principles adopted for future peace of Europe were contempt of revolution and revolutionary ideas and international cooperation. By the Treaty of Charimont and the quadruple alliance the big powers pledged to protect the system of Vienna at least for twenty years and maintain International cooperation. By the doctrine of legitimacy in Italy the Pope was restored to his throne. The Bourbon Ferdinand was restored to the kingdom of two Sicillies (Naples and Sicilly in South Italy). Besides the Habsburg princes were restored the central duchies of Italy. Again, the Bourbon King was also restored to his kingdom of Spain. Moreover, the legitimate dynasty was restored to the throne of Portugal. The House of Orange was restored to the Kingdom of Holland. The Swiss confederation was restored with most of its territories. Moreover, in Germany the doctrine of legitimacy was applied with great flexibility in order to suit other demands. The Austrian hegemony upon Germany, i.e. Holy Roman empire had also to be restored according to legitimacy. Metternich faced opposition from Czar Alexander and the German nationalists. Ultimately the decision was made that those states which were destroyed by Napoleon before 1803 were not to be restored and Germany was to have 38 states under Legitimate princes. These 38 states were organized in a confederation or a Bund with Austria as President.

The principle of Balance of Power was adopted by the peace makers to ensure the future peace of Europe. It had two objects, viz: To protect Europe from the danger of future French invasion by strengthening the neighbouring states of France and to divide the territories among the victors in such a way that one would not be stronger than the other. According to the arrangements on the north-eastern border of France, Belgium (an Austrian province) was joined Holland under the House of Orange so that the United Kingdom of Netherlands could resist successfully future French thrust. On the eastern border of France the Rhenish provinces of Germany were given to Prussia. Besides, on the south eastern border of France, Switzerland received three Cantons. And on the south of France piedmont received Genoa. Moreover on the other frontiers of France there were natural boundaries like the Mediterranean, the provinces and the Atlantic.

The Vienna settlement restored with modifications, some safeguards, where restoration was possible; it sought to protect Europe against a revival of French militarism; it provided a guaranteed order and initiated a policy for settling future disputes; and it built broadly on Metternich's principle of a balanced European society of five major powers, and so well distributed were its stresses that no major war disturbed it for forty years.

Thus Russia, Prussia, Austria, Great Britain and in some measure Sweden were recompensed for the efforts they had put forth in the defeat of Napoleon. Russia received Central Poland as a constitutional kingdom allied in personal union to her crown, and the ratification of Finland and some small conquests from Turkey; Prussia was given Western Pomerania (taken from Sweden), part of Saxony and valuable Rhenish provinces; to Austria was restored most of what she had lost, save Belgium and some lands in south Germany which she renounced in exchange for Venetia; Great Britain acquired Malta, Heligoland, a protectorate over the Lonian islands, the Cape of Good Hope and other imperial advantages. Sweden was granted Norway (taken from Denmark) in exchange for Finland and Western Pomerania, which she had ceded to Russia and Prussia respectively. Saxony was allowed to keep her royal title, but with Denmark she paid in territorial losses the penalty of having supported the unvictorious side. The Grand Duchy of Warsaw and the kingdom of West Phalia were abolished. The return of the Pope to Italy and of the Bourbons of Naples, Spain and France was sanctioned. In some respects the arrangements of Vienna embodied the profound changes in political relationships and values which had taken place during the previous twenty years.

The settlement of Italy and Germany made in the Congress of Vienna deserves special mention. The settlement of Italy was done according to particular wish of Metternich. He was determined to prevent Italian unity and establish Austrian domination on the land. Austria received Lombardy and Venetia as compensation, the King of piedmont was restored and the Pope was restored to the papal Kingdom. The Habsburg princess including the second wife of Napoleon were restored to central duchies. No central government was created in Italy at the instance of Metternich. Italy became "a geographical expression" and ceased to exist in political sense.

As regards Germany, the balancing power was fairly carried out. Prussia complained that she got less than the 1805 standard. But she had a great deal of Polish territory in 1805, and she exchanged this for half of Saxony and for the Rhine province, German in blood and speech. It is singular that Prussia showed no special desire for this last acquisition, which made her ultimately the national champion of Germany against France.

"Criticisms"

"It has been customary to denounce the peace makers of Vienna as reactionary and illiberal in the extreme." In the year 1815 Alexander may be said to have attained his apogee. He was the conqueror of conquerors, the Liberator of Europe, the soldier of God whose sword had been blessed by the peoples and sanctified by the Lord."

The Congress of Vienna was heralded by lofty sentiment and high sounding phrases and much criticism has been directed towards the cynical commentary afforded by its achievements upon its protestations. "The great phrases such as 'the reconstruction of the social order; the regeneration of the political system of Europe were used by powers to deceive the people. Their real object was to divide the spoils of victory among them." Gentz, the secretary of the Congress remarked, "Men had promised ... the return of the Golden ages. But the Congress resulted in nothing but restorations."

The change is also brought against the Vienna powers that they ignored the challenge of the French revolution; that they failed to see that the new forces of democracy and nationalism were becoming determining political factors - or that they saw it too well and were determined to keep them under. They accepted the criterion of the Balance of Power, not the measure of popular sentiment; thought in terms of traditional diplomacy, of dynasties and states, nor in those of popular sympathies and national self-expression. It is true that when they talked of the "rights, freedom and Independence of all nations they did not mean to draw political frontiers round every group of articulate nationalists. They were bent on preventing another European cataclysm, on putting restraints upon potential tyrants. They had seen aggression not only in the interests of political aggrandisement; but also in the name of the "Rights of men". They had discovered what the twentieth century rediscovered. "The Vienna settlement of 1815 is commonly stigmatised as the work of obscurantists and reactionaries, who failed to appreciate the strength and direction of the forces which had been liberated, if not generated, by the French revolution and by the wars and conquests of Napoleon, with the result that their handiwork was not destined to permanence. They made mistakes and ignored latent forces destined to operate powerfully in the near future. Besides, the settlement of 1815 was branded as "a great deception and betrayal". The Germans were treated most unjustly in the Congress. General Blucher, the Conqueror of Napoleon compared the Congress to an annual cattle fair. Again, the Vienna Congress bore the stamp rather of a temporary agreement than the work destined to last for centuries." The settlement of 1815 was too artificial to be permanent." In this settlement there was little that was permanent and much that was temporary. Within half a century, the work of the Congress was undone. Belgium became independent of Holland in 1830. Italy was united between the years 1861-66. Germany was united in 1870. The Union of Finland with Russia was dissolved in 1917 and that of Norway with Sweden in 1905. Besides, the Congress did not show any respect to the new born principles of liberalism and democracy. Venice which had a republican constitution for many years was deprived of it. Genoa also lost her constitution. When the Venetians sent a representation to the Congress seeking restoration of their constitution they were curtly replied. "Republics are out of fashion." It was a mean and hypocritical policy of the treaty makers not to extend the doctrine of legitimacy to the republics", remarked Cruttwell.

"Besides, though the settlement was supposed to be in favour of the old order and existing rights, the smaller states were ruthlessly sacrificed for the benefit of the larger. For this side of the activities of the peace makers, there is little excuse and it is the gravest criticism of their actions."

The principle of legitimacy, balance of power and compensation were old and outmoded doctrines of the eighteenth century. They did not fit with the swiftly changing ideas of the nineteenth century. The doctrine of legitimacy was not even consistently applied. Moreover, the decisions at the Congress of Vienna were made by the great powers and were imposed upon the small powers of Europe without their Consent. Grant and Temperley opine that the Congress represented only old regime and the aristocrats. They blocked the entry of new ideas. Hence the settlement of Vienna has been branded as a reactionary settlement. Thus it has been customary to denounce the peace makers of Vienna as reactionary and illiberal in the extreme. It is indeed true that they represented the old regime and were, to a large extent, untouched by the new ideas.

Justification of the Vienna Settlement

But whatever may be the criticisms, the diplomats of Vienna settlement represented the best and not the worst of the old regime, and their settlement averted any major war in Europe for forty years. According to them the settlement was a fair one. Dr. Thomson has also remarked that, "It was, on the whole, a reasonable and statesmanlike settlement." Standing on the boundary line between the two ages, the legislation of Vienna forms a landmark in history. Compared to other epoch-making settlements concluded before and after the Vienna settlement was not an unjust one. Along then with profit-seeking and self-protection, the settlement generally known under the Vienna title did embody certain definite principles. It restored, with modifications, some safeguards, where restoration was possible; it sought to protect Europe against a revival of French militarism; it provided a guaranteed order, and initiated a policy for settling future disputes: and it built broadly on Metternich's principle of a balanced European society of five major powers.

France was treated with leniency, and the adjustments of the Balance of Power and territory were carried out with the scrupulous nicety of a grocer weighing out his wares, or of a banker labouring his accounts.

The Treaty of Utrecht, 1713 caused a lasting bitterness in the heart of the Habsburgs. The Versailles treaty of 1919 was branded by Germany as "a dictated peace" dipped in the blood of the Germans. The Vienna Treaty of 1815 was a much more liberal treaty viewed in this light. Castlereagh, the British statesman, was particularly careful that the revenge attitude against France was avoided.

If the work of the Congress of Vienna was not permanent, it was not a vital defect. No treaty is permanent. So also the Vienna settlement is no exception to it. In some respects the arrangements of Vienna embodied the profound changes in political relationships and values which had taken place during the previous twenty years. They marked the aggrandisement of Russia and her intrusion into western affairs; they acknowledged the disappearance of the Holy Roman empire, with withdrawal of Sweden into a comparative scandinavian isolation and the abandonment of her trans-baltic ambitions. If it restored disunion to Italy and gave no permanent settlement to Germany, yet it showed both moderation and political wisdom. It also provided a real foundation on which later Europe was to build and preserved forty years of International stability.

It is true that the new born ideas of nationality and democracy were ignored by the peace makers of 1815. But David Thomson has remarked, "It would be wrong to blame the makers of the settlement for failing to appreciate the power of nationalism and liberalism, which few realised in 1815." The new ideas like democracy and nationalism were born of the womb of the revolution. They came through red, ruin and terror. Their constructive aspect was not yet visible. It was therefore natural for the conservative peace makers to ignore the new ideas and forces of anarchy and revolution. They feared that acceptance of the ideas would plunge Europe into a catastrophe of war when peace was the most cherished thing.

Besides, peace makers should not be unjustly blamed for their conservatism and neglect to new ideas. No statesman can write on a clean slate. The hands of the peace makers were tied by previous treaties viz.: the treaties of Abo, Kalisch, and Toplitz etc. The diplomats had to accept them in the body of the general treaty. Again, it was not an easy task to build up an European system on the ruins of Napoleonic empire. The peace makers had to consider the question of balance of power for the sake of International peace. They had to do justice towards the dynasties overthrown by Napoleon. If the peace makers did some injustice to nationalist demands by uniting Belgium to Holland and Norway to Sweden, they had to do it under pressure. On the whole the settlement of 1815 was a "Just Settlement."

Moreover, the historical changes that had taken place during previous 20 years to be respected by the Congress. Russia had taken Poland and made an entry in European politics: the Holy Roman empire had been liquidated by Napoleon; Sweden retired as a northern power, the map of Germany was simplified by Napoleon. All these and similar other facts of historical development were acknowledged by the Congress.

Last but not the least, it may be said that the Vienna settlement was not altogether an unjust settlement. But it proved to be short-sighted work by ignoring the ferment of nationality and democracy. The decades that followed the Congress saw repeated onslaughts by these forces on the dam created at Vienna and the attack did not cease till the dam was broken.

The work of Vienna, interrupted by Napoleon was completed by two treaties signed at Paris, on November 20, 1815. Of these one, the IInd Treaty of Paris, bound France to carry out the new arrangements imposed in consequence of the return of Napoleon, to submit the frontiers of 1790, to pay an indemnity, and to return the works of art to foreign capitals. The second treaty was *Quadruple alliance* between the four Great Powers. They bound themselves to maintain the arrangements of Chaumont, Vienna, and Paris by armed force for twenty years, both as regards the territorial boundaries now fixed and as regards the perpetual exclusion of Bonaparte and his dynasty from the throne of France. Finally, by Article VI, they agreed to 'renew' their meetings at fixed periods to discuss matters of common interest". In the last article lay the germ of future International government.

The germ of its destruction lay in a solemn declaration by which Alexander sought to bound all monarchs together in a Christian union of charity, peace and love, issued on September 26, 1815. It was to be signed by kings alone. The Regent of Great Britain was unable to sign it, though he sent a private letter to Alexander, expressing his sympathy with the sentiments. With this exception it was signed by every king in Europe and by the President of the Swiss Republic. Its importance was, in a sense, fortuitous, for it came to be regarded by European liberals as a hateful compact of despots against the liberties of mankind. It was not that, nor had it any diplomatic or binding force. Charity and love are not capable of being defined in diplomatic terms, and no one except Alexander thought seriously of the treaty. Castlereagh called it a 'piece of sublime mysticism and nonsense'. Metternich made profane Tests about Christianity in connection with it. Neither regarded himself as in any way bound by it.

(Failure of the Congress)

"The Congress system died because despotism was not reconcilable with the opposed system of parliamentary freedom. The League of Nations survived, until it was destroyed in a world at war. Both were weakened by the fact that they were never universal; in neither case did the powers learn the secret of reconciling national interests with the common good. It is too soon yet to judge whether the secret has been found by the makers of the third great experiment in International organisation.

The congressional experiment was partly a tribute to a positive ideal of International peace which has proved of more than ephemeral value; but it was largely a by-product of the Napoleonic wars, a transient impulse arising from a unique historical and psychological experience. It was the fruit of the common uprising against the common enemy, a fading spark from the glowing inspiration of what had been, for a short time, a single-minded Europe.

The following points may further be added to both the merits and demerits of the Vienna Settlement of 1815:

Merits

(1) "Although the work of the Congress was retrograded reactionary, nonetheless, it marks not only the close of an epoch but also the beginning of a new."

(2) If the Congress of Vienna was guilty of neglecting nationalism and liberalism, it did succeed in reconstructing the framework of the European family of nations in such a manner that it stood fast for a century despite localised wars and political tumults. In those hundred years the mother continent of Western civilisation grew in wealth, influence and prestige to such an extent that the world became her debtor spiritually, culturally, and, of course, economically.

(3) If the Congress of Vienna failed to satisfy the aspirations of Poland, if it ignored the population of Belgium and yoked Norway to an uncongenial partner, whom she endured nevertheless for 90 years, if it restored disunion to Italy and gave no permanent settlement to Germany, yet it showed both moderation and political wisdom, and it proved a real foundation on which later Europe was to be built. It preserved internatio-

nal stability at least for 40 years, i.e., uptil the outbreak of the Crimean War in 1856. (Prof. C.D. Hazen)

(4) Harold Nicholson, C.D.M. Ketelbey and Grant and Temperley are unanimous in their views that the powers at Vienna did indeed a creditable deed by averting the outbreak of any major war in Europe for half a century by means of their settlement. According to them the settlement was a fair one. France was treated with leniency.

(5) Harold Nicholson denies the allegation that the makers of the Vienna Congress were mere lucksters (meaning dealers in small articles in the diplomatic market, bartering the happiness of millions with scented smile.) L.C.B. Seaman finds justification in Nicholson's denial of such a charge against the authors of the Vienna Settlement. But he differs from Nicholson in denying that the direct credit for the avoidance of any major European war should go to the makers of Vienna peace arrangements. He had substantiated his stand-point by arguing that none of the provisions of the settlement itself had contained any seed of a future war. All the major European powers were fully satiated by the territorial adjustments. Their desires had totally been fulfilled and they had nothing to grudge or grumble. Thus no clause of the Peace Settlement was hostile enough so as to conflagrate the post-settlement situation leading to a war. He continues to defend that the Vienna settlement must be rated a better peace than either Utretch or Versailles. Utretch rankled in the hearts of the Habsburgs and its commercial and colonial clauses were an encouragement to the British to embark in due course on new wars against France and Spain. Versailles humiliated the Germans, disappointed the Italians and inflated the French. The disregard of liberation and nationalism by the Vienna Congress peace makers did not cause war. They were right in thinking in 1815 that before revolutions can make wars, there must first be the wars that encourage the revolutions. Thus the peace arrived at the table of the Congress of Vienna was the most ideal peace amidst the chaos and confusion which had occupied Europe during the Napoleonic era.

(6) L.C.B. Seaman does not approve of Woodrow Wilson's casting aspersions specifically on the principle of restoration reached at the Vienna Settlement. He refutes Wilson's charges by arguing strongly that the powers assembled at Vienna had not the desire of universalising the principle of restoration. They had only one country in view to which this principle was to be strictly applicable and that country was none other than France.

(7) As a counter-charge to the criticism that the Congress of Vienna ignored popular sentiment, Seaman advocates that by withholding autonomy to Belgium and Italy at that time the makers of Vienna peace indeed did a commendable deed. Because if Belgium and Italy were allowed to function as independent states then, they would either have been grabbed by or remained subservient to France.

Thus the peace makers at Vienna rather suspended an impending catastrophe for Italy and Belgium by withholding the grant of autonomy to them. As regards the settlement of Germany was concerned, the principal authors of Vienna peace did the right thing by binding Germany into a loose federation of 39 states and by not granting complete independence to her. Because by that time Germany had not been actuated by the spirit of national self-determination. It was an amalgamation of more than 300 states before the Vienna Settlement. These were all positive steps with an eye to the future.

(8) Commenting on the territorial settlements of the Congress of Vienna, W. Alison Phillips, a very noted historian on European history observes, "Of course, even had the map of Europe been an absolute blank, the wisest diplomacy could not have rearranged its boundaries so as to satisfy every national ambition."

(9) The Congress of Vienna also took to her credit some other notable achievements. It accelerated the pace of Industrial Revolution and improved to some extent the status of women in society. According to Prof. Fyffe, "standing on the boundary line between two ages, the legislation of Vienna forms a landmark in history."

(10) Certain special provisions of the peace settlement reflected the humanitarianism of the 18th century "enlightenment. For example, it included a declaration favouring the abolition of the slave-trade arrangements for the free navigation of international rivers, and additions to international law." (Prof. Hayes)

Demerits

(1) The one goal common to all the partners was the overthrow of the common enemy. Once that was achieved, it became easy to forget promises made to the people. Inertia set in and the war-weary people avidly clutched at the prospect of peace—peace at any price. Dominating both the domestic and foreign scenes was a compelling desire on the part of the ruling classes to return to the status quo ante bellum. This was an understandable wish, but it meant turning back "the clock of history", a manifestly impossible task. Yet so strong was this determination that anything which threatened it had to be destroyed.

(2) The disregard for a force which had already shown its tremendous power and which was destined to dominate world affairs throughout the 19th and 20th centuries was both callous and injudicious. The force was nationalism. The failure of the peace-makers in respect to it is demonstrated by the quick collapse of their settlements in various countries like Netherlands, Belgium, Germany and Italy.

(3) Absorbed in squabbles over the division of the soils, the monarchs and statesmen assembled at Vienna gave but cursory and passing attention to proposals for the establishment of a new European order in the possibilities of which law of them believed, observes Michael T. Florinsky, a renowned Russian historian.

(4) The Vienna Settlement was essentially reactionary and conservative in character. The Congress of Vienna was a Congress of aristocrats to whom the ideas of nationality and democracy as proclaimed by the French Revolution were incomprehensible or loathsome. To them the Congress was a passing storm (Hazen) and their sole aim was to maintain and preserve conservatism on a sound footing which had already been shaken to its foundations by the violent convulsion of liberal ideas unleashed by the French revolutionary upsurge. The authors of Vienna Settlement believed that the clock of change was moved by Napoleon much in advance through revolutionary ideas and it was now their duty to bring it back to its proper place.

(5) According to Prof. Hayes, "the Vienna settlement was, defective, in so far as the people were regarded as so many pawns and chattels in the game of dynastic aggrandisement."

(6) The powers rearranged Europe according to their desires, disposing of it as if it were their own personal and private property. The ignorance of the popular sentiment had lately been so wonderfully aroused that it proved a force strong enough in toppling the pillars of the Vienna Settlement till its final decay. "Thus the history of Europe from 1815 onwards has been the history of rectifying the cardinal errors of the Congress of Vienna." (Prof. Hayes).

(7) Critics have pointed out that the Congress of Vienna failed to provide a satisfactory solution to the Eastern Question.

19

July Revolution of 1830 in France

No revolution happens in history without factors working for its outbreak. The July Revolution of 1830 had also many causes:

No country of Europe had undergone between 1789-1815 so sweeping and so vital a transformation as had France. The French people were ideologically divided into four camps—the aristocratic and the democratic with daggers drawn at each other. The former believed in the rights and privileges of three Institutions—the monarchy, the nobility and the church. The latter wanted to preserve the fruits of the French Revolution; the land settlement of the Revolution, the code Napoleon, equality, and secularism and Individual freedom. The adherents of the new order were determined to protect the valued changes brought by the Revolution at all cost. This contest between the adherents of the old and supporters of the new made the revolution inevitable.

Besides, the Restored Bourbon monarchy which reigned in France from 1815 failed to ingratiate itself with the nation as a whole. Louis XVIII was virtually imposed on the French throne by the victorious Allies. This gave a stamp of unpopularity to the dynasty. The French could not forget the inglorious scene of Louis XVIII entering Paris accompanied by the allied army. It was said that Louis XVIII came "in the baggage of the Allies".

The Bourbons had a tradition for despotism. Most of the French men believed that a Bourbon can never change. Despotism was his life. Besides, in spite of his extraordinary commonsense Louis XVIII could not sacrifice his belief in hereditary divine right of monarchy. When a messenger announced to Louis that Napoleon had abdicated and that Louis was now the King of France, Louis fanatically replied, "Have I ever ceased to be?" He himself was a by-product of royalisms believed on dictatorship, ruthlessness and savagery. All these factors made the dynasty unpopular and unacceptable to the liberals.

Secondly, Louis XVIII had returned to France with a constitutional charter (1814) granting an elective chamber, personal equality, freedom of religion and the press, and certain other desiderata of liberalism. Like Charles II of England, he had no wish to go on his travels again, and was disposed to pursue a moderate and concillatory policy. He tried to maintain a balance between opposing interests. He appealed for unity, declaring he would not be the "King of two peoples". But he was unable to control the ultra-Royalist forces which pressed upon the ministry and the country, or to bring the liberals into constitutional play.

The constitutional charter which he granted incorporated in it some of the fruits of the revolution like the civil code, legal equality and an elected legislature. On the other hand the charter retained all the essential powers in the hands of the King according to the ideas of the ancien't regime. This proved Louis was not a true constitutional king.

Again, Louis was half hearted in his loyalty to the charter. Cobban has remarked, "Louis XVIII's English exile had not taught him the virtues of parliamentary government."

He adopted the policy of selecting his own ministers and dismissing them at his own will without caring to know whether they had majority support in the chamber or not. He appointed and dismissed Talleyrand. Talleyrand was followed by Richilieu. He was forced to resign in 1818 and was followed by Decazes. The latter had to quit this ministry after the murder of Duke de Bury in 1820. Rochelieu came again and left in 1821. Louis now Villele at the recommendation of his mistress Madam du Cayala. The policy of appointing and dismissing ministers without caring for the sentiment of the people, created confusion among the liberals.

Further, Louis exercised his prerogative by frequently dissolving the chamber before its term was over. Cobban opines, Louis cut the very root of parliamentary government by dissolving the chamber whenever he felt it necessary. In 1816, he dissolved the Ultra royalists dominated chamber to save his moderate policy and moderate ministry. In 1824 he dissolved the moderate chamber in order to satisfy his ultra royalist minister Villele. Such frivolities with the chamber created the impression that the king was essentially a despot.

Besides, Louis never thought of making his government popular by extending the voting right to all the people. The charter of 1814 gave voting right to men paying tax of 300 Francs per year. The wealthy people only got the right of franchise and the poor were denied this fundamental right. This shows the right of equality was denied in matters of voting. This was too inconsistent to be overlooked by Frenchmen.

All political omens pointed in a favourable direction, and seemed to promise an enlightened administration, when a new turn was unexpectedly given to the course of events by the murder of the Duke of Berry in 1820. He was the younger son of the Comte d'Artois, the heir to the throne; and as his brother was childless, his assassination involved the prospect that the Elder branch of Bourbons would become extinct. The crime was the work of a fanatic, Louvel, but it was immediately seized upon as a pretext for discrediting the Liberal ministry, and Decazes was over-thrown. His fall from power changed the current of French history; it proved the starting point of a reaction which fathered increasing strength until it provoked the revolution in 1830.

The tenure of Villele, the leader of Ultra royalists lasted from 1821 to 1827, and afforded him an opportunity to carry out the programme whose main features were purely reactionary. His methods were more subtle and astute than those which had wrecked his party in 1816. He did not wish to alarm the country by an open manifestation of his far-reaching designs. He curbed the headstrong impertinence of his followers, who had learnt nothing and forgotten nothing, and who still believed it possible to ignore all the changes which had taken place in France since the revolution. In his campaign to undo the work of the Revolution, Villele relied upon two powerful forces: the church and material interests. With the aid of the first, he designed to utilise religious instruction as a vehicle for political propaganda, to uproot the members of the revolution, and to inculcate those principles of public morality which would serve as his justification for restoring the old order. With the aid of the second, he hoped to conciliate national opinion and to divert the energies of the people from political channels to the pursuit of material welfare.

From the standpoint of reactionaries the project was well conceived, and showed an intelligent grasp of the situation, while in the execution of it Villale - adopting expediency as his guiding principle - withstood the temptation to employ hasty and ill-considered measures. The policy of the ministry, was to regain for the royalists their lost privileges by slow and imperceptible stages; accordingly the reaction was gradual. In 1822 the censorship of the press was strengthened, and the conduct of trials for offences against the Press Law was taken out of the hands of Juries. This measure shifted public opinion. It invested the government with the control of all anti-clerical and anti-aristocratic publications, and enabled it to suppress any writings which might serve to keep alive the revolutionary spirit. At the same time heavy tariffs were levied on imported commodities, to the satisfaction of landed proprietors and wealthy manufacturers, and the direction of education was given over to the church. While Villele by the prudence of his financial and economic administration was thus consolidating the power which the rash act of a fanatic had conferred upon the royalist party, Chateaubriand insisted that to make their position impregnable something more was needed i.e. to revive the glories of the empire. The French people must be compensated for the loss of their revolutionary heritage - equality and political rights - by the revival of French ascendancy on the continent. Chateaubriand held the opinion that France, like Rome would be content to sacrifice liberty for empire. With this conviction he forced Villele's hand and at the beginning of 1823 a French army was sent across the Pyrenees to the assistance of the Spanish King, whose subjects were on open revolt. Like Walpole, whom Villele resembled in his caution and in his reliance upon the fruits of a sound financial system, to build up the strength of the ruling dynasty, he was averse from war and foreign enterprises.

An application began to form itself; the secret revolutionary society of the Carbonari - which was spreading through Italy, Spain, and Germany, opposed itself to the clerical organisation known as the congregation. There were insurrections in the army and protest from the academic Francoise, and the Napoleonic legend was beginning to hallow the name of the dead emperor. But Louis XVIII died peacefully in his bed (1824); there was even a faint stirring of patriotic pride in the Lilies when the Duce d'Angouleme successfully invaded Spain. It was the old incorrigible Comte d'Artois raised to the throne in 1824 as Charles X, who drove the opposition to a rebellion. Charles X began well by announcing his attachment to the parliamentary institutions and by appealing to the French Love of ceremonial. But he soon became unpopular. He was ultra reactionary and clerical to the core. France became bored, and the boredom of the people became dangerous to the rulers of France. Secure for the moment of his parliamentary majority, and strengthened by the accession of Charles X Villele could now bring forward the measures embodied in the ultra-Royalist programme. The most important was the indemnification of the emigres, who had gone into exile at the outbreak of the Revolution and had fought in the ranks of their country's enemies. The rate of interest on the National debt was reduced from 5 to 4 per cent (1825), and the economy thus affected enabled the government to compensate the old nobility for the losses they had sustained by the sequestration of their possessions. This was followed by other measures relating to the foundation of religious bodies and the admission of Jesuits into France. But the open alliance between the 'altar and the throne', and the growing pretensions of the priest party awakened the apprehensions of the nation and the chamber of peers. The stronghold of liberalism- began to display more determined powers of resistance. The ministerial defeat was acclaimed with enthusiasm; and, when the king reviewed the National guard, cries were raised from the ranks: "Down with the ministers". It was a portent of the future. Undaunted by the setback which his policy had suffered, Villele replied by disbanding the civic militia, re-establishing the censorship of the press, and nominating seventy six new members from the chamber of peers in order to swamp the liberal opposition. A majority adverse to the ministry was returned at the general election (1827), and Villele, overthrown by the combined efforts of his opponents, resigned office.

The successor of Villele was Martignac, who attempted to conciliate public opinion by opportune concessions. He abolished the censorship of newspapers, and deprived the Jesuits of the power to give public instruction. The policy of compromise met with no support either from the *Liberals* or from the ultra Royalists. There was no longer any room for moderate men. Martignac, in trying to please both parties, pleased nobody, and so fell between two stools. The Liberals demanded that the basis of the franchise should be broadened. Martignac professed to meet the liberals half-way, and to soothe the administrative ambitions of the nation, by extending the Franchise in provincial assemblies. His proposal was rejected by the extremists on both sides of the chamber on the plea that it was not progressive enough for one party, it was too progressive for the other. Accordingly the two parties, while unable to agree on any constructive programmes, again united to overthrow the ministry (1829).

Matters had now reached a crisis. Charles X found himself confronted by the dilemma which had faced Louis XVIII, thirteen years before, the claims of the present and the claims of the past. He could accept once and for all the role of a constitutional ruler, and openly dissociate himself from the insidious attempts of his supporters to subvert the principles of the revolution, or he could definitely throw in his lot with the ultra royalists, and make a final bid to emancipate himself from the checks imposed upon his power by the charter. Shrewdness and observations were alike denied to the elderly bigot i.e. Charles X. Charles X differing from his pleasant, easy going brother, was a man of strict, autocratic and clerical principle. "I would rather chop wood", he said, "than reign after the fashion of the King of England." He was deaf to all the calls of the future, obedient only to the voice of the past.

The issues for which the political parties had been contending in France since the Restoration were aristocratic pretensions and clerical domination on one side, equality and secularism on the other. The king had always been the mainstay of the reactionary party, a thorn in the side of his temporizing prudent predecessor. "What can you expect?" Louis XVIII, had said when the Comte d'Artois forced him in 1821 to accept Villele as his minister: "he conspired against Louis XVI; he conspired against me, he will end by conspiring against himself." To a generation which held the theory of popular rights Charles X now opposed the doctrine of divine right; to progress he opposed reaction; to the charter he opposed the prerogatives of Louis XIV. "I told you", he said to Martignac, "there is no way of dealing with these men; it is time to call halt." The idea spread, fomented by the unconcealed desires of the ultra royalist papers, that the King mediated a *coup d' etat* to overturn the constitution and to bring back the ancient regime. That this was in effect his design was made plain to all, when dismissing Martignac, an adroit and moderate statesman, who might have saved the crown, Charles summoned Jules de Polignac to his side. Polignac was an uncompromising partisan of the old order, whose action proclaimed to the world that he had burnt his boats behind him. He had been one of the original emigres, had been imprisoned under the emperor and had refused to swear to the charter in 1815. Men began significantly to recall the fate of James II. "There is no such thing as political experience", declared Wellington; "With the warning of James II before him, Charles X was setting up a government by priests, through priests, for priests." Bourmont, the general who had betrayed Napoleon before Ligny, was to be Polignac's minister of war, a mark of ignominy was added to the general distrust inspired by his cabinet. Yet it is notable that under the last and weakest minister of her last and weakest legitimate king, France captured Algiers. The Liberal deputies had protested in an address to the Crown against a ministry holding office when it was not backed by a parliamentary majority. The king interpreted the protest as one insult to the monarchy, and dissolved the chambers (1830). This was an occasion appointed for *coup d' etat*. Charles issued on July 25, 1830 three ordinances: (1) setting aside the recent elections as null and void, and summoning a new chamber; (2) narrowing the franchise; and (3) silencing the press and altering the electoral law. The next day Paris, at the instigation of the Journalists, broke out in revolt and erected barricades.

To the royalist *coup d'etat* Paris responded by three days of fierce fighting, which drove the king from his throne and sealed the fate of the ancient monarchy of France. The king now sought to revoke the ordinances, but it was too late. And after a futile attempt to save his dynasty by abdicating in favour of his grandson, he passed on to exile.

The Revolution of 1830 was an event of great significance in the history of France. On the surface of it appeared to involve no considerable changes. This July Revolution is notable as the act of a single city, i.e. Paris decided the fate of France. A large share of street fighting had been done by men like Cavaignac, who wanted republic, or else by the Bonapartist supporters of a second empire. The revolution which occurred was due largely to Lafayette and to Talleyrand, two men who were not often found in agreement, and their agreement on this occasion was suggestive. Their plan was a constitutional monarchy of the English type, with Louoi Philippe (the Orleanist Bourbon) as a good solid bourgeois and constitutional king. Despite the change of dynasty, the monarchy itself was not overthrown, thanks to the skill with which the politicians manoeuvred the course of events. A French republic in 1830 would have been interpreted as a challenge to Europe; and with the memoirs of 1789 still fresh in their minds, the Allies would have taken the immediate step to ward off the threatened danger.

Moreover, not only did the insurrection of 1830 failed to destroy the monarchy, but the modifications, effected in the constitution were insignificant. They hardly made even a pretence at giving substance to the lip-professions of the politicians in favour of popular sovereignty.

The July Revolution of 1830 resembled the English Revolution to the extent that its significance was negative rather than positive. Alike in 1688, and in 1830, no real advance was made in the direction of democracy, since the political changes were unaccompanied by parliamentary and economic reforms, without which democracy must remain a transparent fiction. Once for all, France rejected the principle established at the Vienna Congress - the principle of 'legitimacy'. The excesses of Charles X completely obscured the great benefits which the early years of Bourbon administration had conferred upon France.

The downfall of the Bourbon dynasty involved also the final rejection of the ultra royalist programme. In short, the Revolution of 1830 was the complement of the Revolution of 1789 for the future, the achievements of the revolutionary spirit - the principles of equality, secularism, and constitutional liberty - rested on secure foundations. The Charter of 1814 was no longer a royal concession, it had become the inalienable birthright of the nation.

The Revolution of 1830 was felt all over Europe - in Poland, Germany, Italy, Switzerland, England, the Netherlands. It was the signal and encouragement for widespread popular movements which for a short time seemed to threaten the whole structure erected in 1815 at Vienna.

As a direct result of the July Revolution in France, the Long rumbling revolution in Belgium broke out in August. The Dutch were hated by the Belgians and movement was essentially one for national independence. The Belgians declared their Independence and rejected the union with Holland imposed on them in 1815. They sought French help against Dutch King William I. A Liberal constitution was promulgated in Belgium. Russia wanted to intervene to restore the status quo of 1815. But the French warning and the outbreak of Polish revolt prevented her. England summoned a congress of five powers in London to settle the Belgium problem. In this congress the Independence of Belgium was recognized and she was declared neutral. It was a triumph of nationalism and liberalism.

Besides, the impact of the revolution was felt on Switzerland leading to liberalisation of the Swiss constitution. Again, Norway got the recognition of her autonomy from the Swedish King.

The rulers of Brunswick, Hanover, Hesse, Bavaria, Baden, Saxony etc. were forced to grant liberal constitution. But Metternich reimposed the Carlisbad decree and stamped out the seeds of liberalism in Germany.

The Italy revolution broke out in Parma, Modena, and some other papal states. But Austrian intervention led to its failure. Further, Poland revolted against Russian rule. But the Russian army suppressed the Polish rising and the Polish constitution was revoked.

The July Revolution led to a civil war in Spain and Portugal. The problems in Belgium, Italy, Germany, Poland were political in nature but in Spain and Portugal the problem was of succession. Ferdinand VII, the ruler of Spain, died while he had only one daughter named Isabella. After her father's death there ensued a conflict between Isabella and her uncle Don Carlos. Don Carlos was the brother of Feridinand VII. Ultimately due to intervention of England and France, the cause of Isabella and her liberal policy was saved in Spain.

In case of Portugal the Queen was Donna Maria, daughter of Pedro I and similarly, under such a situation Donna Maria was challenged by her uncle Don Migupl and therefore Maria granted a liberal constitution to the people and secured the help of England and France and gained the cause of succession.

Thus in France, Belgium, Spain, Portugal, Norway, Switzerland and England the revolution altered the territorial and political systems erected in 1815. Legitimacy, balance of power and conservatism were set aside, Liberalism and nationality became triumphant. In Italy, Germany and Poland, the July revolution at least temporarily upset the political and territorial systems enforced in 1815. Moreover, Europe was politically and ideologically divided into two camps by the impact of the July Revolution.

The July Revolution in France had been bloodless, and it had set up a solid constitutional monarchy. It seemed to hail the approach of the millennium, when all nations would be endowed with parliaments and carry Magna Carta written on their hearts.

20

The Revolution of 1848 and Its Ethos

The Revolution of Intellectuals

Prof. E. Lipson opines, "The Revolution of 1848 constituted an epoch in the history of political democracy because the extension of the suffrage transferred power from the middle class to the community at large. It was also an epoch in the history of economic democracy because it witnessed a remarkable, though tentative, experiment in socialism. The populace of Paris had not overthrown the monarchy merely in order to establish a republic."

"For forms of government
Let fools contest;
Whatever is best administered
is best."

The revolution is a landmark in the history of Europe. According to Hazen, "the revolution of 1848 in France was extraordinary swift entirely unexpected and extremely radical." In the words of A.J. Grant and Harold Temperley, "The French revolution of 1848 was the work of Paris alone, and of only a small part of the population of Paris. There had been agitation in the provinces against the narrow character of the franchise, but in the movement which sent the orleanist monarchy 'on its travels' the provinces had taken no part. It can hardly be doubted that the great majority of French men were opposed to what happened."

The February Revolution

The July Monarchy - as the government of Louis Philippe was called because the Revolution of 1830 had taken place in July - was only a shade better than its predecessor. Though the King was an astute politician and knew the value of wearing the tricolour and dressing in citizens' clothes like the bourgeois King he was, his government was very far from liberal and while the number of voters was now increased from 100,000 to 200,000, the change was not impressive seeing that the population of France was over 30,000,000. Power had merely shifted from the landless aristocracy to the rich bourgeoisie. "It was a franchise question", writes Prof. C.D.M. Ketelbey, "which precipitated the crisis by which in February 1848 the Orleanist monarchy was overthrown and Louis Philippe driven into exile. The Revolution of 1848 was a composite movement showing clearly the various hostile elements which had been gathering against the Government."

During most of the period the nation as a whole was prosperous, for it was natural that such a regime would show considerable interest in industry and commerce. But generally speaking, "the policy of the July monarchy was negative." (T.W. Riker). It did nothing to relieve the workers of the evil conditions which had come in with the Industrial revolution; it was governed in its later years by a political machine whose corruption was flagrant and shameless, and its foreign policy was negative and humiliating. It is true that it accomplished the conquest of Algeria, though this was largely an accident, as the Algerian adventure had been a last coup de theatre of the late Bourbon monarchy. Due to its Algerian policy, it lost respect of all French patriots and when, it tried in its last days to pursue a stronger policy, it singularly bungled. The French will forgive any thing of a government that gives them glory. Conversely, loss of prestige is a government's worst sin. As Lamartine, one of the Liberals, acutely observed, "France is bored".

Causes in General

Louis Philippe's fall was not unexpected. His fall did not come over the franchise question in 1848. The discontent which was smouldering for a long time among various groups converged together in 1848 to lit the flame of the revolution.

The fundamental cause of unpopularity of Louis Philippe was *his support to the upper middle class people* i.e. the Bankers, the merchants and the manufacturers and he was regarded by them as the "Bourgeoise emperor." The middle class people alone enjoyed the exercise of political rights since the franchise was limited to those who paid 500 francs. Wrapped up in the pursuit of wealth, they engrossed public offices and devoted themselves to material interests. In these circumstances the Assembly had no claim to be regarded as representative of the nation; and it exposed its weakness still further by barren party conflicts, which laid bare the futility of its discussions.

Besides, Louis Philippe's Pacific foreign policy also contributed to the collapse of his movement. Further the French people had not forgotten the humiliation which France had suffered in the hands of Congress of Vienna. The nation aspired for a vigorous foreign policy. They aspired that French influence in European politics should be revived. Louis Philippe completely disappointed them. "He followed a drab and colourless policy of 'peace at any price'." He sacrificed golden chances of augmenting French influence in Belgium, Egypt and Spain. "It also hastened the collapse of a regime, whose policy abroad and at home was based on 'timid resistance' to all political innovations." (E. Lipston). *History was repeating itself* and burning with zeal for republican propaganda. France as in the days of the Convention was prepared to issue a challenge to the monarchical system and bid subjects everywhere rise up against despotism.

Again, Louis Philippe supported the cause of the Belgians who were struggling to make themselves free from the oppression of the Dutch. The Belgians achieved their independence and in 1831 Belgium was made a separate kingdom. After achieving their independence the Belgians offered the crown to Duke of Numcurs, the son of Louis Philippe. But due to determined attitude of the British Prime Minister Palmerston, Louis had to decline the offer. He also extended no support to the popular insurrection in Poland and Italy.

The Social Problems

Besides, the dawning consciousness that economic issues are the controlling factors in society, and that true democracy must rest on economic as well as on political foundations, marked in itself an epoch. The grievances of the working classes attracted the attention of republicans, whose energies in the past had been absorbed in pre-mature outbreaks and vain appeals to revolutionary traditions: accordingly they began to concentrate upon social and parliamentary reform as the starting point of the new order.

The Beginnings of Socialism

The beginnings of socialism date from this period, and if only a few were prepared to accept Proudhon's maxim, "property is theft", there were many approved of Louis Blanc's principle, "the right to work". As early as 1834 the workmen of Lyons had taken up arms in defence of their trade unions, whose existence was menaced by a law directed against Industrial associations. A few years later (1842) a contemporary remarked: "The time for purely political movements in France is past, the coming revolution can not but be a social revolution." To all this seething mass of political and social unrest the government, content to steer its course midway between reaction and revolution, and devoid of any constructive programme, presented an impenetrable front. Thus in the eyes of the French nation the July monarchy ceased to justify itself. It did not prevent the isolation of France in the councils of Europe, nor spare her the shame of diplomatic humiliations.

Further, the French intervention in the Eastern question also proved to be ineffective. Both France and England had supported the revolt of the Greeks against the Turkish misrule. But hostility began to develop between these two powers due to their conflicting interests in the Balkan region.

Mehmet Ali, the pasha of Egypt, who was a vassal of Turkish Sultan invaded Syria in 1839 and he was backed by France. Theirs, the French minister championed the cause of Mehmet Ali with the aim of reviving the influence of France in Egypt. The great powers like Russia, Austria and Great Britain demanded the immediate withdrawal of the pasha from Syria. But Mehmet Ali being backed by France refused to comply with the demand of the great powers. Mehmet Ali gave up his claim over Syria by the Treaty of London in 1841. Thus the French policy again received a setback. Louis Philippe's muddle headed policy with regard to Spain also made him unpopular. His foreign policy was timid, inconsistent and inglorious. In his tortuous diplomacy the Nation found little occasion for pride or satisfaction.

The Influence of Saint Simon

The course of a revolution, when once it has broken out, inevitably follows the impulse of the ideas of the time. Paris before 1848, and to a smaller extent France, had been full of political and social speculation. The chief influence came from *Saint-Simon*, who had died in 1825. This strange man and powerful thinker had thrown out a great mass of ideas, partly scientific and partly utopian. His proposals rested on a general view of human history. Critical and constructive epochs had he believed, alternated, and the French revolution of 1789 had marked the end of the last epoch of criticism and destruction. He believed that if men were left to organise themselves freely they would fall into 'natural' groups, with special aptitudes and likings for different occupations, and thus the necessary work of the world would be performed freely joyfully and efficiently.

Louis Blanc's Theory of Right to Work

More immediately important than either of these views, but closely connected with those of Saint Simon, was the socialist movement, which for the first time during the Revolution of 1848 becomes a great force among the peoples of Europe. Its meaning has changed much since then, especially through the influence of Karl Marx. Its chief exponent for France at this epoch was Louis Blanc, an immensely voluminous writer on political and economic subjects. He was sure of victory, for he believed in the essential goodness of human nature and he believed that the transformation to the final stage would come easily and without bloodshed. All that is necessary is to provide workmen with money, form a co-operative workshop and success will come inevitably." 'We will work and live or we will fight and die' was the watchword of those who thought themselves Louis Blanc's followers. He proposed also the formation of a Ministry of Progress.

The King Shall Reign Not Rule

Its inherent weakness was revealed in the manner of its overthrow, which came with startling suddenness. Louis Philippe was not content to reign without ruling; to enjoy the semblance of power without its reality. From the outset of his reign, he had opposed a strenuous resistance to the efforts of the conservative leaders to establish a virtual dictatorship over the monarchy as the price of their assistance in dethroning Charles X. While keeping up the appearance of parliamentary government, and the fiction of ministerial responsibility, he had no intention of being a *roi faineant* or resigning his authority to "these princes of the tribune." On more than one occasion the dissensions between the King and his ministers had provoked an open rupture, and in 1837 he had sacrificed Guizot for Mole, an opportunist in policy, and a more complaint instrument, whom he maintained in office for two years in face of parliamentary opposition.

Opposition Parties United in 1848

"By 1846, however the Bourgeois liberalism as exemplified in France by Louis Philippe were numerous and determined. At last six groups, viz. the Legitimatists, Republicans, Socialists, Catholics, Patriots and Reformers, were highly critical, if not openly hostile." (C.J.H. Hayes) In the words of Riker, "Opposition to the July monarchy developed from three directions. The Liberals representing the intellectuals, the Lower bourgeoisie, and some from the upper ranks of the latter class who were wearied of a humdrum rule, endeavoured in spite of the fettering of the press to create a public opinion in support of wider sufferage. Some of this element were secretly republican. A second group of malcontents were the Socialists who represented the cause of the exploited proletariat. A third element looked hopefully abroad to the head of the house of Bonaparte, Louis Napoleon, nephew of the late emperor." The forces opposed to Louis Philippe converged in 1848. Public opinion in Paris was mobilized by reform banquets held in various parts of the city. On February 22, 1848, the day appointed for the demonstration, the democracy of Paris poured into the streets, and the national guard, called upon to maintain order, openly betrayed its sympathy with the demonstrators.

The Revolution which most people seemed to want but no one seemed to expect finally occurred. In February 1848, economic stress combined with political agitation easily overthrew a regime that in the end proved singularly hollow, and the King, like his unlamented predecessor, took the road to exile. As few seemed to want his infant grandson, a republic was proclaimed.

Significance of the Revolution of 1848

In the words of Prof. C.D.M. Ketelberg, "So far as it was a 'revolution of contempt', it was followed by the genuine Republican movement that had been baulked in 1830, and looked back to 1792 which drove Louis Philippe from the throne, abolished monarchy and set up a provisional government." The Revolution of 1848 naturally invites *comparison* with the earlier movements engineered against arbitrary monarchy, the second against middle class government; in other words, legal equality was established in 1789, social equality in 1830, and political equality in 1848. The ascendancy of the bourgeoisie in the government of France was destroyed by the institution of manhood suffrage; and political power was now extended to the people. This Revolution of 1848 constituted an epoch in the history of political democracy. The watchword of the Revolution was "the right to work" and Louis Blanc's 'Organisation du Travail' (published in 1839) was the gospel of 1848, just as the contract Social of Rousseau was the gospel of 1789.

According to De Tocqueville, "Though the February revolution was of all our revolutions the shortest and the least sanguinary, yet far more than any other, it filled the minds and hearts of men with the idea and feeling of its omnipotence."

Results of the Revolution of 1848 in France

Firstly, the February Revolution buried the experiment of bourgeois constitutional monarchy initiated a republic.

Secondly, the Revolution brought in its wake universal franchise for Frenchmen which had outlived many ups and downs of French history and continues to this day. The introduction of universal franchise swelled the electorate from 1/4 million to 9 millions over night.

Thirdly, the Revolution led to the abolition of slavery in the French colonies.

Fourthly, the provisional government of the second republic made experiments with socialism by opening national workshops for the unemployed and issued a decree guaranteeing employment to all. It recognised the principle of 'right to work'.

Fifthly, the Revolution of 1848 destroyed the privileges of the bourgeoise by destroying their exclusive right to vote. Moreover, the February revolution of France turned into an *International Revolution.* The waves of the revolution crossed the French frontier and devastated the political structure in Europe erected in 1815. The Metternich system collapsed for the time being under its impact.

The Revolution of 1848-49 in Germany, and in Austrian Empire and in Hungary

The spark which set Germany and Austria alight came from France and the flame was fanned by the revolutionary breeze from Italy. Indeed revolution might have triumphed throughout Germany and Austria had the French republic lent positive aid to the struggling liberalism of Germany and had the King of Sardinia successfully crushed the Austrians in Italy. Unaided as they were, the inexperienced revolutionaries in Germany, in Austria and in Hungary were ultimately subdued by the reactionaries.

The character of the revolution assumed different forms in the various parts of central Europe. In Germany, the movement was based on a strong desire for national unity linked to a strong belief that liberalism would achieve this end. These impulses united professors and students, who dreamed of unity, to the workers who wished for the suffrage and to peasants who wished to abolish feudal rights. In the German part of Austria the movement was similar, but the population as a whole was liberal rather than national in its outlook. In Hungary and the non-government parts of the Austrian empire the impulse, though sometimes liberal on the surface, was in essence always national. A wholly different set of forces was there put in motion. The Czechs of Bohemia sturdy patriots from the days of Huns, fought fiercely for their rights against the hated Austrians. The Magyars, proud of an old constitution and a parliament, struggled to free themselves to place under their own radical domination a mass of Slavs and

Rumans, who formed more than half of their population, and were fiercely insistent on their own rights. The paradox therefore emerged in Hungary that Serbs, Croats and Rumans ultimately fought for Austria against Hungary to secure their national rights. And, greater paradox still, the Czar of Russia came to their assistance. Thus Austria was saved partly by the division of her enemies, partly by aid from outside. And the recovery of Austria brought with it the success of reaction in Germany. The course of events indeed exceedingly dramatic. In March 1848 every throne in Central Europe was tottering and revolution was everywhere triumphant. Before the end of the year the prospects of revolution were dark and in 1849 reaction again prevailed everywhere.

21

Foreign Policy of Napoleon III

A student of European history will never fail and falter to commemorate the most enigmatic and puzzling character and figure of Napoleon III. How the sheer Roman culture governs the course of history was vividly manifested in the personage of Napoleon III. In the name of democracy he became a dictator. It would be tantamount to calling Napoleon 'the Little' as a misnomer because in none of the occasions he can be equated with his great uncle. Yet he became the president and emperor of France. This is the miracle of history, through Bonapartism he wanted to dazzle France and puzzle Europe. But in the long-run he was neither believed nor understood. He was his own architect and destroyer. The abrupt rise of the second empire saw its own downfall before the death of its creator. For all these things Napoleon III was responsible. He posed himself as an ardent lover of democracy but he was the most diehard autocrat. Prof. Ricker opines, "He lacked the foresight that would have saved him from some of his blunders, and he lacked the insight that would have enabled him to discern the merits and failings of others." He was magnanimous and not naturally vindictive. He was like Napoleon I in wishing to attract to his service all elements in the population. In his rise to power he had shown himself a dexterous politician and he often displayed this quality in his diplomacy. He was the product of circumstances and he was never able to outgrow its grim and exactions. He was too much some times the victim of his own imagination. Sometimes the second empire was itself an adventure. It was an attempt to revive benevolent despotism on a Napoleonic pattern, an attempt to impress the world—and especially France herself—with Napoleonic triumphs. Prof. C.D. Hazen writes, "The period of 1860 to 1870 witnesses the gradual transformation of the empire from autocracy to Liberalism, the rise of a vigorous party of opposition, a disastrous foreign policy, a growing democratization within the state, and a final tragic collapse. In the words of E. Lipson, "Napoleon recognised the importance of indulging the national pride by adopting a resolute and vigorous attitude in his relations with other countries; yet whether he had any coherent design mapped out in his mind may be doubted." He was vaguely aware, as Otto said "that he needed a war", for he confessed his determination never to fall, as Louis Philippe had done, by clinging at all costs to an ultra pacific policy. Prof. Grants Temperley writes, "Despite his claim that "the Empire means peace' he was constantly pushed by his name and Napoleonic tradition into a policy of demonstration and adventure. France would forgive him much or all if he gave her glory and prosperity; but failure of any sort would be fatal to him." Today, Napoleon wrote before coming to power, the rule of classes is over, and you can govern only with the masses". "His efforts", remarks Prof. Thomson, "to govern with the masses led to a series of disasters in foreign policy, for he believed (not entirely without justification) that the masses wanted glory and were intensely nationalistic." 'Halfpint Napoleon' Victor Hugo had scornfully dubbed him. The second empire, judged in terms of military glory or original achievement was indeed only a pale shadow of the first. But it has considerable importance for the material development of France and for the shaping of modern Europe.

Objects of Napoleon III's Foreign Policy

The foreign policy of Napoleon III was influenced by several factors. As a champion of Nationalism he genuinely sympathised with national aspirations. Secondly, he wanted the stability of the government and therefore wanted a chain of military. Besides, the wrecking the settlement of 1815 was the sheet anchor of his foreign policy. He believed that his position would never be secure until the Treaty of 1815 was removed. His policy in Italy, Germany, Poland and his role in the Crimean War prove his hatred for the Treaty system of 1815. Fourthly, he had a sympathy for the down-trodden nationalities of Europe. Besides, Napoleon III desired to create a new balance of power in Europe revolving round France by establishing the moral hegemony of France on Liberated nations, particularly Italy and Germany. Moreover, in his colonial policy he was an imperialist out and out. Finally he wanted to support the cause of catholic religion.

Policy of English Friendship

"If the third Napoleon was un-Napoleonic in appearance, he was no less dissimilar from his uncle in other ways." He had meditated a good deal on the Lessons of the First empire of his uncle. He was determined to avoid the mistakes of his uncle. While England was Napoleon I's great enemy, Napoleon III sought to base his policy on English friendship.

In the words of Prof. E. Lipson, "Napoleon's autocracy after 1859 was unassailable while France was absorbed in the spectacle of great feats of arms and he was able with ease to silence opposition. But, as the tendencies of his foreign enterprises were gradually disclosed, the political instinct of the nation reasserted itself, discontent once more raised its head, and the possession of sovereignty began by degrees to slip from his grasp." An account of these enterprises will serve to indicate the nature and scope of his policy abroad.

The Crimean War

It is the paradox of Napoleon's career that his first diplomatic venture was expressly designed to propitiate those very interests which his subsequent actions were destined in later years hopelessly and fatally to antagonize. On behalf of the catholic party in France he laid claim to the possession of the Holy places in Jerusalem, a claim contested by Russia as the representative of the Greek or Orthodox church. Out of this obscure controversy, developed the Crimean War, which cost the lives of over half a million men. This Crimean War occupies a peculiar place in the history of Europe in the nineteenth century. (Grants Temperley). It was the last war on a large scale to be fought without the help of the modern resources of science. Prof. Ricker writes, "It is doubtful if there was ever a more unnecessary war than the Crimean war, and the dreadful sufferings from cold and cholera which added to its horrors are a commentary on the lightness with which diplomats play with crisis."

Besides, the above religious conflict which resulted in the culmination of the Crimean war, Napoleon III had a personal quarrel with Czar Nicholas I of Russia. Nicholas could not take him as one belonging to his own class. He refused to address Napoleon as Mon Frere (My Brother) according to the custom of International Law. Napoleon III felt humiliated by the Czar's conduct. Moreover, Napoleon wanted to resist the Russian aggression in the Near East. When the Czarist army occupied the principalities of Moldaria and Wallachia, belonging to Turkey, England and France joined Turkey against Russia. This led to the outbreak of the Crimean War. Napoleon III won applause of Liberals for humbling the power of conservative Russia. It is now generally recognized by historians that the questions at issue could have been settled without resorting to war; and the results of the conflict afforded no adequate compensation for the blood and treasure expended on it. The Treaty of Paris (1856) which brought the war to a conclusion, neutralized the Black Sea, opened the navigation of the Danube to all countries, emancipated the Danubian principalities from Turkish control, admitted Turkey to the Public Law of Europe, and pledged the European powers to maintain her integrity; in return the Sultan promised to his Christian subjects religious toleration and equal rights with Musalmans. The Treaty was short-lived, its terms being violated about as soon as the ink on the parchment was dry. Turkey did not carry out her undertaking and her integrity had not remained intact, while the neutrality of the Black Sea lasted only till 1870. Above all the Crimean war shattered the peace of Europe after it had been maintained for forty years; it ushered in a succession of wars which transformed the world into an armed camp, and made destruction the goal of human effort and the summit of national ambition. At the moment however, the outcome of the Russian campaign was acclaimed by the French people with an outburst of enthusiasm. It was undoubtedly a great personal triumph for the emperor, who presided over the Congress of Paris held to discuss terms of peace and posed in the eyes of the nation as the arbiter of European destinies. He had emerged successfully from the ordeal of arms, and had preserved from extinction, as it seemed, the traditionally ally of France. In wiping out the stains of 1815 and 1840, he had covered France with glory and had attained the pinnacle of his greatness, from this time onwards his fortunes gradually declined, until he was completely overwhelmed by the catastrophe of 1870.

The Treaty of Paris gave to Napoleon a new lease of power; stimulated by success, he at once began to devise ways and means to turn his prestige to account. The career of Napoleon I had shown that the passion for glory begets in a nation an inordinate craving which is only quenched by defeat and suffering; the career of his nephew in his turn engulfed in a flood of boundless ambitions, was to demonstrate the same lesson. The moment now seemed ripe to undertake the supreme task bequeathed to him by destiny as part and parcel of his heritage. The Napoleonic idea foreshadowed the most farreaching designs; to remould the map of Europe, to break up the settlement of 1815; to extend the frontiers of France to the Rhine, and to emancipate the oppressed nationalities.

Results

The Crimean war was the first glorious event in the foreign policy of Napoleon III. It removed the stains of 1815. Secondly, Russia was humiliated in the war. The balance of power in the Near East was preserved. Thirdly, the Anglo-French entente was strengthened in the Crimean war. Queen Victoria paid an official visit to Paris after the war. Besides, within France Napoleon earned great popularity with the catholics. Fifthly, yet the French success in the Crimean war, was a barren victory; France did not get a single inch of territory nor a single penny as compensation though she spent huge sums on the war.

The first fruits of his nationalist programme were seen in the creation of the Roumanian state out of the Danubian principalities, which had been rendered autonomous at the Congress of Paris. A more ambitious project soon unfolded itself in the schemes for the Liberation of Italy. Napoleon's Italian policy by its half-hearted measures succeeded in satisfying no one and marked the beginning of the end of the empire.

Italian Policy

Napoleon III also sympathised with the national aspirations of Italian people. During his youth, Napoleon III had fought as a revolutionary in Italy and he was the member of Carbonary Secret Society. Besides, he was by degrees an Italian as his uncle Napoleon had migrated from the Italian city of Corsica. Further, he believed that by helping the Liberals of Italy, he would gain the support of the Liberals of France. He also aimed at for some territorial gain. Above all his ambition was to tear up the treaties of 1815, treaties that symbolised the humiliation of the Napoleonic dynasty. The unification of Italy involved the complete rearrangement of the political system of Europe made in the Congress of Vienna.

Prof. Ricker opines, "The years following the Congress of Vienna were years of an uphill struggle in pursuit of aspirations. The Italians or more correctly - an active minority - yearned for liberty and unity. "Liberty" means freedom from the oppressive rule of petty tyrants and "unity" carried with it the expulsion of Austrians". The chief weapon in the cause was Insurrection, plotted by secret societies, first the Carbonary and later 'Young Italy'.

"Whether we like it or not" said Cavour, "our destinies depend upon France." During the Crimean war Cavour, the prime minister of Sardinia-piedmont made a risky alliance with France and England in 1855, and fought against Russia. He could gain the friendly alliance of France. In 1858 Cavour met Napoleon III at *Plombiers* and the Franco Sardinian alliance was concluded. According to this alliance the French emperor promised to come to the assistance of Sardinia in case of war with Austria. As the price of help Napoleon III was to get Nice and Savoy. Naples and papal states should be united into an Italian Confederation under the presidency of Pope.

In 1859 there was the outbreak of war between Austria and the state of Sardinia piedmont. Napoleon III came to the assistance of Sardinia-piedmont and their combined armies defeated the Austrian army successfully in the battles of Magneta and Solferino. The Austrian power was on the point of total collapse. Napoleon suddenly called a halt and concluded the Truce of Villafranca (1859). According to the terms of the treaty of Villafranca Austria promised to cede Lombardy to piedmont. Austria was allowed to retain Venetia. She also agreed for the restoration of the princes in Tuscany and Modena. The Pope was to be president of Italian Confederation. The terms of the Truce of Villafranca were ratified by the Treaty of Zurich. Shortly after the Treaty of Zurich the people of Parma, Modena and Tuscany revolted and demanded their incorporation with piedmont. After a plebiscite the states were incorporated with piedmont and Napoleon III recognized the annexation of these states. As the price of his help he got Nice and Savoy.

The reasons for Napoleon's action i.e. to stop the war were various. He had wanted an enlarged Sardinia as a convenient buffer state against Austria - one that would be small enough, to remain a satellite of France. The clericals opposed his policy in Italy because they apprehended that his policy would imperil the position of the Pope. Besides, when it came to the making of a nation which by revolution might soon compromise the whole of the peninsula, Napoleon was dubious. It was also clear to Napoleon that his victories had not really crushed the Austrian strength and that to enter Venetia would be exceedingly hazardous, whereas if he withdrew from war now, he could do so at a time when France had covered herself with glory. The Italians would feel outraged, but after all, the Emperor had some reason to be disappointed at the scant welcome his troops had received in Lombardy and at the failure of the Tuscans to send recruits; and moreover, being a man of gentle mould, he was convinced as never before, of the brutality of war—which he had seen at close range. But above all, he was greatly disquieted at the threatening conduct of Prussia on the Rhine. Hence he told the King to think no more of ceding Savoy and Nice. Palmerston had declared that he ought to have offered his aid out of Philanthrophy alone. But one may question whether he or any Britisher would have done that, and further more, Great Britain had kept her neutrality throughout this critical phase of the Revolution. In any event, Napoleon had thus gained nothing but "glory".

However, the Italian Policy of Napoleon III was half-hearted and inconsistent. The French Legitimists protested against the expulsion of the Napolitan, Bourbons from Southern Italy and the "French radicals were estranged because the emperor's abrupt withdrawal from the war left the Italians in the lurch. His Italian policy thus struck the first serious blow against Napoleon III for it offended the clericals and the French Liberals did not forgive him for upholding the power of the Pope.

After the Crimean war the two Danubian principalities, Moladavia and Wallachia, had been granted autonomy in their internal affairs. In 1860 the people demanded for the union of these principalities into a single state called Romania. Napoleon III persuaded the powers to recognise the union of these two states under Prince Alexander Cuza at their head.

In a short time Napoleon also deeply offended Russia by intervening in support of Poland during the insurrection of 1863. The Polish Insurrection, remarks a French writer "gave Napoleon a unique opportunity of rallying all parties. The catholics considered that nation a martyr to its faith, for democrats, its independence was a dogma, while conservatives remembered the historic role of Poland as the ally of France against Austria." The people of Poland revolted against the Russian Czar in the year 1863 and appealed for French help. All sections of French people including the Catholics and Liberals supported the nationalists movement. Napoleon III felt reluctant to extend help to the Polish people, because he was apprehending a war with Russia in which Austria and Prussia would help the later. In April 1863, the French emperor addressed strong remonstrances to Russia, but the Russian Czar, being supported by Bismarck, ignored them. The Czar crushed the Polish Insurrection in a ruthless manner and with relentless severity. The failure of Polish rebellion led to the disappointment of French Liberals and Catholics.

Mexican Expedition

Napoleon III's success in the Far East and the Middle East induced him to jump on a more ambitious project in Mexico. It was just this time, when various difficulties were arising him more troublesome than any which he had previously encountered that Napoleon chose for another enterprise most unnecessary, most reckless, and in the end most disastrous. He undertook to erect an empire five thousand miles away, in a country of which he knew but little and in which political institutions had for half a century rested on a very shifting basis, Mexico. He had hoped that he would be able to compensate his failure in Italy and Poland by achieving success in Mexico. He always considered that his uncle had made a mistake by selling away Louisiana in America to USA. Napoleon III wanted to rectify his uncle's mistake by establishing a French protectorate in Mexico.

Mexico, a north American state was distracted by a political strife and for some years it was in a state or chrnoic disorder. The republican leader Benito Juarez had overthrown the President Miramon, the leader of the Catholics and the monarchists. Miramon appealed to the leading Catholic powers of Europe for help. The Mexican government under its president Juarez was oppressing the catholics and had confiscated the ecclesiastical property. The English and Spanish and French people residing at Mexico were badly treated by the government. Above all, the Mexican government owing to its financial embarrassment repudiated the debt which it owed to France, Spain and Great Britain and suspended all payment to foreign creditors. Great Britain, Spain and France signed the Treaty of London in 1861 to interfere in the affairs of Mexico and to protect the interests of European residents. But the president of Mexico promised to discharge and settle all the financial obligation of his country. So Spain and Great Britain did not exert further pressure on Mexican government. But Napoleon III to glorify France to gain the support of catholic party and to revive his popularity, aimed to overthrow the Mexican republic and to establish a monarchy. For him the moment was most opportune as USA was involved in a great civil war. The emperor was determined to place Arch duke Maximillan brother of Austrian emperor as the king of Mexico. In 1864 Napoleon III set up a Roman Catholic monarchy with Maximillan as its sovereign. But by this time the civil war in USA was over and the American government asked France to quit Mexico. Napoleon complied with the demand of the American government and French troops were withdrawn from Mexico. Emperor Maximillan was left to the mercy of the Mexicans and was killed ultimately (June 19, 1867).

The Mexican expedition inflicted a terrible blow to the prestige of Napoleon III. "The Mexican war was as disastrous for Napoleon III, as the Spanish war had been for Napoleon." According to Lipson, "the Mexican incident served to illustrate the unstable imagination of the emperor, his passion for grandoise and fantastic schemes, and lack of fore-thought and iron resolution to carry his schemes to a successful conclusion."

Napoleon III and Franco-Prussian War

The Mexican adventure prevented the French emperor from playing a part in the decisive events like the Danish war and the Austro Prussian war in 1866. Prussia after these wars emerged as the most ambitious, aggressive and powerful military state in Europe.

Otto Eduard Leopold, Prince von Bismarck Schonhaussen (1815-98), the astute diplomat of Prussia had met Napoleon III at Biarritz in October 1865 and according to the agreement the French emperor agreed to be neutral in case of war between Prussia and Austria.

The relations between France and Prussia had been unfriendly ever since Napoleon I inflicted on the latter the crushing defeat of Jena (1806). Bismarck was not influenced by traditional feuds and what he called "stagnating antipathies", and he had no scruple in utilizing with subtle craft any foreign power, whose assistance at the moment might contribute directly or indirectly to the end which he so sedulously pursued. The Austro-Prussian war broke out in 1866 and the rapidity and the completeness of the Prussian victory upset the calculations of Napoleon III who had thought would intervene in an opportune moment and dictate peace to the powers extracting favourable terms for France. Thus due to his pre-occupation in Mexican affairs, Napoleon failed to take advantage of the war between Austria and Prussia. The battle of Koniggratz or Sadowa, July 3, 1866, was decisive. Even then it was not too late for an intervention. Napoleon could have played a commanding part in determining the terms of peace had he threatened to come to the aid of Austria, as Austria desired. His minister of foreign affairs said to him on July 5th:

"Let the emperor make a simple military demonstration and he will be astonished at the facility with which he will become arbiter and master of the situation without striking a blow." King William later said that the war of 1866 was the ruin of France, "because Napoleon should have attacked us in the rear." This was what Bismarck most feared. Austria was defeated at Sadowa. The French people considered it to be a humiliating defeat for France because it was the traditional policy of France to keep Germany weak and divided. The French people clamoured for the revenge of Sadowa.

"It was France that was defeated at Sadowa". (Theins) Napoleon III had remained neutral during the Austro-Prussian war according to Biareitz agreement with Bismarck with the hope of some territorial gain on the bank of the river Rhine or Belgium. After the end of the war Napoleon demanded some territorial compensation for his neutrality in the war. But Bismarck refused to comply with his demands. At last Napoleon decided to purchase Luxemburg from the King of Holland. The King of Holland was prepared to sell but he was prevented by Bismarck. Thus Napoleon III was outwitted by the diplomacy of Bismarck. At last to regain his popularity and to gratify the desire of people, Napoleon III decided to go to the extent of war against Prussia. Bismarck also had said, "a war with France lay in the logic of history." He believed that the unification of Germany would not be completed without a war with France.

War between Prussia and France became inevitable and the question of succession to Spanish throne provided the immediate pretext for the war. The Spanish throne was offered to prince Leopold, a relative of the king of Prussia. But Napoleon III put pressure on the King of Prussia to withdraw the candidature of Leopold. The demand was complied with but the French emperor demanded an assurance that in future the candidature of Leopold should not be renewed. All these factors finally culminated in the Franco-Prussia War (1870) in which Napoleon III was defeated in the battle of Sedan. This led to the fall if IInd empire and the establishment of the Third Republic in France.

The German policy of Napoleon III was muddlesome and muddle-headed. It contributed largely to his downfall. He was impelled by popular pressure to declare war against Prussia, knowing fully well that his army was ill-organized and ill-equipped.

Estimate

After his intervention in the affairs of Poland the emperor came to be treated as a dangerous firebrand, whose restless energy, impulsive temperament and incalculable moods were frought with serious menace to the stability of the existing political system. Napoleon III was a prisoner of indecision though the world knew him to be the "most designing" ruler. He earned the hostility of the Czar. During the Austro-Sardinian War he supported Sardinia but in a half-hearted manner. The Italian liberals condemned his policy. At the same time Austria became his enemy. Throughout his period he remained as an enigma both to France and Europe.

In short, the second empire was a very active regime, not always successful, but very often so, and chiefly important for its economic achievements and for its deliberate promotion of *Nationalism* in Europe.

22

American Civil War (1861-65)

The civil war was the conflict between the Northern States (the Union) and the eleven southern states which seceded to form the confederate states of America. It was the most climatic event of nineteenth century American history. Measured by numbers engaged and casualties in proportion to population, it was the biggest American war and indeed, the biggest war anywhere in the century from 1815 to 1914. This war between the above two combatants is also known as the war between the states or the war of the Rebellion and the war of secession. Historians have coined a number of other designations, such as war for Southern Independence", "Brothers war", "American Hiad", and "Second American Revolution". Each of these has merit in calling attention to some aspect of the struggle. Still, the term civil war remains the most appropriate, because of its sense as well as usage. This indeed was the term typically used by both North and South during the war period.

The precise nature of the civil war remains a subject of disagreement and debate. From the southern point of view, the confederate state of America formed an independent country with a constitutionally legitimate government. From the Predominant Northern Point of view, states had no constitutional right to secede and set up a separate government. Secession therefore was rebellion, and the adherents of the confederacy were rebels. However, southerners took pride in calling themselves rebels while they repudiated the charge of rebellion.

The war aims of both the above sides were simple. At the beginning the North fought only to preserve the union. The South fought to win recognition as an independent nation. After 1862 the long troublesome slavery problem became an additional issue of vast importance. A victory to the North would mean ultimate freedom for slaves whereas a southern victory would ensure the protection of slavery in all confederate states. This civil war was immensely costly in both lives and dollars. It left the South devastated. Its most important consequences were to preserve and strengthen the American nation, to speed the rise of American industrial capitalism and to bring about the end of the treacherous slavery system. It has also appealed to the popular imagination more than any other war the Americans had fought.

Factors Responsible for the Outbreak of the Civil War

The war's basic causes, like its essential nature, continue to be controversial. Historians of both North and South seldom have succeeded in escaping the influence of their respective sectional backgrounds. During the first generation after 1865 Northern writers generally treated the war as a "necessary and righteous undertaking to put down the aggressive intention of a "slave power conspiracy", which had aimed at first to dominate and then to disrupt the union. Southern writers saw the conflict as equally righteous on the part of the South, which was said to have sought only to defend itself against abolitionist threats, economic exploitation, and encroachments upon state rights. By the end of the nineteenth and the beginning of the twentieth century, historical interpretations on both sides had gained in sophistication and opinions on the causes and nature of the war were, accordingly revised. In the 1920s revisionism reached a climax. Charles A. Beard and many others stressed the economic aspects of the pre-war sectional controversy, to the exclusion of the ethical aspects. Of real importance, in Beard's view, were the shift in political power from Southern planters to Northern industrialists, and the change in the essential nature of the federal government, which gained in authority at the expense of the states. Avery Craven, J.G. Randell, and others described the war as unnecessary and unfortunate—the work of a blundering generation". According to this group of revisionists, the war came chiefly because of excitements engendered both North and South by agitators, fanatics, and self-seeking politicians.

After the coming of the world war II, the revisionists interpretations declined in popularity. *"Counter revisionists"*, such as Arthur M. Schlesinger Jr; now held the view that the traditional view of Northerners was essentially correct. That is to say, right and wrong were involved in the conflict, the South as the defender of slavery was basically wrong, and the war was necessary and desirable as a means of overcoming a social evil and preparing the way for social stability, progress and justice.

The civil war came as a climax to a long series of quarrels between the North and South over the interpretation of the United States *constitution*. In general, the North favoured a loose interpretation that would grant the federal government expanded powers. The South wanted to reserve all undefined powers to the individual states.

During the colonial period Southern colonies were more agrarian, had more plantations, depended more on staple crops and possessed more slaves than did the colonies to the north. Although these differences were frequently troublesome during the revolutionary period (1776), independence was possible only through cooperation. Union, however, did not eliminate sectionalism. As the Republic grew older and stronger, differences between the North and the South grew more pronounced. Besides, the North as well as the West, wanted internal improvements sponsored by the federal government roads, railroads, canals etc. The South, however, had little desire for these projects.

Another source of conflict was the opening of public lands in the west. The distribution of such lands in small lots speeded the development of this section. But it was opposed in the South because it aided the free farmer rather than the slave-holding plantation owner. A similar difference of opinion developed over the tariff. A high tariff protected the Northern manufacturer. The South wanted a low tariff in order to trade its cotton for cheap foreign goods. Another important issue that overshadowed all others, was the right of the federal government to prohibit slavery in the western territories. Such legislation would severely limit the number of slave states in the union and would multiply the number of free states. Thus many Southerners feared that a government increasingly dominated by the free states might eventually endanger existing slaveholdings. Thus the South opposed all efforts to block the expansion of slavery.

More and more Northerners became convinced that slavery should not be allowed to spread to new territories. At the same time Southerners were becoming equally determined to create new slave states. For forty years (1820-60) this issue created an ever widening cleavage between the South and the rest of the nation. The slave states had long been a separate section economically. Now they began to regard themselves as a separate social and political unit as well. The first clear evidence of political "sectionalism" came in 1819 when Missouri sought admission to the union as a slave state. This issue provoked a passionate debate. After months of wrangling the US

Congress finally passed the *Missouri Compromise* (1820) which admitted Missouri as a slave state and Maine as a free state and stipulated that all the remaining Louisiana territory north of the Southern border of Missouri would be free. Although the South won Missouri, only two potential slave states remained in the Louisiana territory while the North could carve numerous free states from the vast area of north and west of Missouri.

The "Missouri compromise" did preserve an uneasy place for almost a generation, however, the differences over slavery became sharper. Frequent tendencies to disrupt the government prevailed from time to time, but they increased materially after 1850s, chiefly on account of the passage of the *Fugitive Slave Law* and the incidents connected with its enforcement. It became serious when Senator Stephen A. Douglas of Llionis persuaded Congress to repeal the Missouri compromise in 1854. His new measure, the *Kansas - Nebraska Act*, led to the first armed conflict between North and South i.e. the fighting for control of Kansas. Three years later the tension between the two regions was heightened by the Dred Scott Decision (1858), which held that Congress had no right to prohibit slavery in federal territories. In the North and West many people now began to accept the fact that slavery was morally wrong and that a start should be made toward its extinction. The moderate point of view was best expressed by a tall gentle lawyer from Llinois, Abraham Lincoln. In 1859, Extremists such as John Brown wanted direct action and led a futile raid on *Harper's Ferry*, planning to start a Negro insurrection in the South.

Meanwhile, a new political party, the Republican had been formed in 1854 to combat the extension of slavery. This party gained strength so rapidly that Southern leaders threatened to secede from the Union if the "Black Republicans" came to power. When the new party did win the elections of 1860 and Lincoln was chosen President, the Southern states led by South Caroline (Dec. 20, 1860) carried out their threat by February 1, 1861, six other states of the Lower South—Alabama, Florida, Georgia, Louisiana, Missiccipi and Texas—had seceded. The confederate states of America were organised on February 4, 1861, at Montgomery, and the four states of Arkansas, North Caroline, Tennessee, and Virginia joined the confederate states by July of the same year. Kentucky, Maryland and Missouri were divided and were represented in both armies. The western part of Virginia remained loyal to the union and later organised as the state of West Virginia.

Many efforts were made to preserve the union and to prevent bloodshed. The outgoing President, James Buchanan, was devoted to the Union but he believed the constitution forbade his taking any action against the South. For several weeks President Lincoln also followed a "wait and see" course. But when the confederates fired upon Sumter, in the harbour of Charleston, S.C., on April 12, 1861, it precipitated the conflict. President Lincoln immediately called for 75,000 volunteers to enforce the authority of the union and declared a blockade on the coast of the Southern states. The confederate states likewise called for volunteers and issued letters of reprisal. The North was rich and had a greater variety of industries than the South, where agriculture was the only large industry.

In comparison of the Northern and Southern nations, the union seemed to possess every advantage. Twenty three Northern states and seven territories, containing about 22 million people, were arrayed against eleven Southern states with 9,105,000 people. About 3,654,000 of the above Southerners were Negro slaves—of doubtful value to the Southern cause. Besides this great difference in population, a steady flow of European immigrants into the Northern states gave the union a tremendous advantage in man power. The North's economic superiority was almost incalculable. Natural resources abounded, from midwestern diary products to new England timber. At Union's disposal were 110,000 manufacturing plants and 1,300,000 industrial workers. Whereas the confederacy could rely only on 18,000 manufacturing establishments and 110,000 skilled workers. The commodities manufactured annually by the state of New York alone were four times greater in value than those produced by the entire confederacy.

Moreover, the North produced 97% of all firearms in America and 96% of the national railroad equipment. Over 70% of America's 31,300 miles of railroads were located in the North. The North not only possessed 81% of the country's bank deposits, the pre-war South's banking and foreign exchanges were in New York city. Finally, the North possessed an established government with inherited foundations, proven machinery, and functioning diplomacy. The South had only hope to substantiate its experiment in confederation.

The civil war from April 12, 1861, when Ft. Sumter was bombarded, to May 26, 1865, when Trans-Missiccippi army surrendered, covered a period of about four years. It was the costliest war in American history with over a third of the combined union and confederate forces casualties. The view of the civil war was horrible. Dead dead dead everywhere in every imaginable position and most of the dead soldiers were stripped or naked. Besides, the dead, there were hundreds of poor wounded who had been on the field without food or water for innumerable days. The confederates had about 500,000 men and lost 95,000 in killed and wounded, while the Federals had 2,666,999 men and lost 359,258. It is not certain what number of confederates were killed by accident or disease, but it is estimated that the total was nearly 200,000. The war cost the confederate states about $2,000,000 and the US (Union) about $3,500,000,000. It is estimated that the total cost, counting both sections of the country, aggregates $9,000,000,000.

At the beginning of the civil war, the Federal Congress had resolved that its primary purpose was to preserve the union, not to conquer the South or free the slaves. But as public opinion became more and more radical, Congress in 1862 abolished slavery in the district of Columbia and the adjoining territories. Finally in September 1862, President Lincoln felt in a strong enough position to make a preliminary announcement about *emancipation* of slaves. His great proclamation stated that on the following New Year's day all slaves in states still in rebellion would become free. On January 1, 1863, accordingly, the President issued the Emancipation proclamation. This proclamation actually did not free a single slave because it did not apply in the border states (they were not "in rebellion") and could not be enforced in the confederate states. It's moral effect, however, was widespread, and by 1865 several states—Missouri, Tennesse, West Virginia, and Maryland had gone ahead and freed their slaves.

At the end of the civil war, slavery still existed in the confederacy and Kentucky. But as the war was grinding to a close, Congress proposed the *Thirteenth Amendment*, which stated that "neither slavery nor involuntary servitude - - shall exist within the United States - - -. When this amendment was ratified in December, 1865, Slavery was finally ended throughout the United States. In 1870, the fifteenth amendment gave the *Negro* the right to vote. President Lincoln in 1865, urged his countrymen to treat the defeated with charity rather than hate. But his dream for a harmonious reunion of the nation was shattered by the assassin's bullet that took his life less than a week after the surrender of the confederates. The ruling class of the *Old South* was destroyed by the new government, which forbade any officer or politician who had served the confederacy from taking up a post of any responsibility.

Consequences

The civil war provided the deepest and most lasting emotional experience for the American people in all their history.

Political

The post-war period was marked by a debasement of public morality. Corruption, characterised the *Grant administration* of the federal government (1869-77). The civil war left the Republican party as the dominant political organisation for several decades. The war and post-war Reconstruction also produced the solid South with its Democratic, one party system.

Economic

While impoverishing the South, the war stimulated the growth of industry and the rise of big business in the North. Before the war, economic enterprise had been highly individualistic. Afterwards, it became increasingly a large scale operation.

New Status for the Negro

The war brought to an end the slavery, with adoption of the Thirteenth Amendment to the constitution in December 1865. Moreover, a constitutional basis had been laid for the ultimate acceptance of the Negro as a true freeman and citizen.

Strengthened National Power

The war not only preserved the United States but also gave the country a new unity and strength. What had been a federal union was converted into the American nation.

Victory of Democratic Principle

Above all, the war resulted in vindication for the principle of self-government.

Thus, the civil war subordinated the rights of the divided states to the rights of the nation, abolished the institution of slavery and organised the American industry. Hence, it represented the greatest collective experience of the American people.

23

The Rise of Democracy and the Extension of Political Representation and Civil Liberty in Britain

Characteristics of the Period

This period was remarkable for the triumph of democracy and liberal principles in central and local government and legislation. It saw the extension of political franchise and the growth of full civil and religious liberty in the United Kingdom of Great Britain and Ireland. It witnessed the expansion of the new British Empire and its system of federal and responsible government. It was also characterised by a great number of liberal and humanitarian laws and reforms relating to economic, social, religious, and educational matters. Thus we find that monarchical and aristocratic control yielded to democratic control, regulation and interference, the principle of limited property suffrage to that of democratic suffrage, the principle of privileges to that of equality and the principle of irresponsibility to that of responsibility and political freedom. "A great moral change was coming over Europe, the principles of freedom were in full operation" observed Lord Castlereagh in 1814. The principles of nationality and independence, of constitutional government and all-sided reform were the forces which inspired and guided human activities. There was a fourfold revolution in process. It covered political, social, economic, and intellectual activities and institutions of the people.

Two Revolutions

(1) The French Revolution which created new values in social and political matters and (2) the Intellectual and Mechanical Revolution which created new methods in the organisation of agriculture, industry and commerce changed men's minds and men's ways of life. The first emphasised democracy and the other new standards of living. Both needed reform of old aristocratic ideals and standards. The spirit of individualism and humanitarianism was the guiding spirit of a large part of the nineteenth century. It disturbed and destroyed the old order of a status society and close class privileges and exclusions. It encouraged the common man and gave him the rights and liberties of a common national citizenship. The hopes of the working classes for attainment of political and economic rights were raised and helped by liberal and socialistic movements, and by trade unionist and democratic organisations.

New Movements in England

From 1820 the stagnation which had set in with 1789 in political progress and reform began to disappear. There came the new Whiggism of Lord John Russell and Brougham and the new Toryism of Canning, Huskisson and Peel. There appeared the democratic Radicalism of William Cobbett and the utilitarian Individualism of Bentham, the Trade Unionism of Francis Place and the Utopian Socialism of Robert Owen. The politicians and reformers of the period were greatly influenced by the ideas of Bentham and his followers.

George III's Reactionary Policy

The English parliamentary system as it prevailed in 1820 had lost its democratic features under the personal influence and intrigue of George III, the fear of the French Revolution and Napoleonic wars and the corruption and bribery of an unrepresentative parliament. The monarch and aristocratic classes dominated in the government and parliament of the country. They had repressed every attempt at political reform and economic relief. A great thinker like Burke who in 1770 in his Thoughts upon the *Present discontents* had complained that the House of Commons was beginning to exercise control *upon* the people, whereas "it was designed as a control for the people", and had advocated the influence of public opinion on the House of Commons and wanted it to be "express image of the feelings of the nation", protested against the evils of French revolutionary ideas. Both the parties in the country had become apathetic towards reform and relief. Therefore till the death of George III Tories who administered the affairs of the country stemmed the advance of democracy and reform in the country by suspending laws of personal liberty and by passing laws of repression.

New Conditions and Discontents

A new generation however, arose. It was oppressed by other evils than those of war. It was distracted by new social and industrial problems. It became an ardent supporter of reform. The enormous burden of national debt caused by the Napoleonic wars weighed heavily on the workers' necessaries of life and means of production. The misery, grievance and discontent it caused were the chief motive power of democratic movements after 1815. The artificial prosperity brought by the war in agriculture, industries and commerce could not be kept up during the time of peace. There was a social crisis also. The mechanical and scientific inventions and the resulting agricultural and industrial revolutions had disturbed the old systems of production and standards of living. Those who worked in the old way could not compete with the products of factories. Many had either to give up their old pursuits and remained unemployed or were reduced to the position of wage-earners clustering round factories. The agricultural revolution also ruined the farmers and dispossessed the peasants of small but invaluable rights over common fields and common pasturage which were now being enclosed. The result of these enclosures was that a number of peasants who had eked out their livelihood on the produce of their arable plots and pasturage rights and on the products of their spinning wheels and handlooms lost it. These half manufacturers and half farmers who could not specialise in skilled industry or agriculture became wage-earners in the factories or daily-labourers on the land possessing no share in the ownership of the means of production, and losing their industrial independence. These changes also led to the rise of discontent amongst these classes against the new methods. The Combination Law of 1799, the Corn Law of 1815, the Suspension Act and the Six Acts of Lord Sidmouth made their life miserable and their liberty of person, opinion and association impossible. The Radical Reformers who advocated advanced democratic principles wanted to annul the harsh legislation of the war period. The working-men also wanted to get relief from them and to secure bread at its natural price. Therefore they became interested in a drastic measure of electoral reform. Their agitation increased in proportion to their misery and discontent.

William Cobbett, a Radical Reformer

William Cobbett promoted the cause of democracy. His paper, the Weekly Register, caught the ear of the people and made the press a permanent power. He was a prolific and vigorous writer. He led the popular demand for a complete reform of parliament. He demanded that the House of Commons should be elected annually by all the tax-payers of the land. His determined and continuous agitation made the Radicalism of the nineteenth century. Working-men started Hampden Clubs in towns and villages. Their delegates drew up a political programme which demanded annual parliaments, exclusion of all placemen, adult tax-payer's suffrage, one member for every 20,000 inhabitants, and talent and virtue to be the sole qualification for members. This radical movement of 1816-1819 was however suppressed under the repressive laws. But the democratic feeling continued to exist, and the pent up enthusiasm found expression at the time of the Reform Act of 1832.

Jeremy Bentham's Influence

There were other influences which discredited the old political system and increased the demand for reform. The radical and utilitarian philosophy of Jeremy Bentham which was a great force from 1800 to 1830 advocated the promotion of the greatest happiness of the greatest number. This new creed proved itself subversive of old modes of thought and of institutions which rested only on prescription and tradition. He condemned monarchy and aristocracy and pronounced democracy to be the sole form of rational government because as each man sought his own happiness, the government of the majority would necessarily pursue the interests and the happiness of that majority. He advocated parliamentary reform. According to him man was a reasoning creature engaged in a constant pursuit of happiness. His followers like James Mill and John Mill carried a crusade in and out of parliament against the abuses of the Georgian regime.

Francis Place and Robert Owen

Francis Place was a great upholder of individual liberty of the laissez faire type. He was a great organiser and possessed a tenacity of purpose. He prepared the way for the abolition of the odious Combination Law of 1799 which had prevented the formation of trade unions of working-men. He was a decided opponent of state interference. He agitated for an advanced measure of reform. His influence was great. Robert Owen also inspired hope amongst the workers of a better political and social order by his socialistic ideas and cooperatives schemes.

George IV's Character

After the death of George III in 1820 the Regent ascended the throne as George IV. He was not a man of good character. He was thoroughly selfish and did not care for the prosperity of the nation. His manners were courtly. His accession however did not mark a break in English history. He had acted as Regent since 1811. His reign opened with the controversy relating to Queen Caroline's behaviour. There was a Bill of Pains and Penalties against the Queen for the purpose of dissolving her marriage with the king. Lord Brongham defended the Queen. It was however abandoned by the government amidst popular rejoicings. The result of the Queen's trial was the alternation of the middle classes from the government which was forced to strengthen itself by the admission of more liberal statesmen into its body. In 1822 Peel became the Home Secretary in the place of Lord Sidmouth. Castlereagh who was now Lord Londonderry committed suicide. Canning became the Foreign Secretary. These appointments marked the liberalising of Liverpool's Cabinet which was continued in 1823 by the appointment of Robinson as Chancellor of the Exchequer and Huskisson as President of the Board of Trade. Castlereagh had very little sympathy with the lowest classes. He had supported the policy of repression adopted by the Liverpool ministry and shared with Sidmouth the responsibility for Six Acts. The moderate conservatism of the new ministers, namely Peel and Canning, was in favour of advance and reform. Huskisson followed the policy of free trade and removed (1823) a number of restrictions on foreign vessels imposed by the Navigation Acts of 1651 and 1660 and on foreign trade. He adopted the principle of reciprocity of duties in his new measures. He reduced duties on some goods imported and exported.

In 1827 Lord Liverpool fell ill. Canning became the Prime Minister, but seven of the old ministers like Wellington, Peel, and Eldon refused to serve under him and therefore resigned. They were opposed to Catholic emancipation and Repeal of the Corn Laws. Thus there was a great schism amongst the Tories. Canning was in favour of Catholic emancipation and the improvement of Corn Laws, but he was opposed to parliamentary reform and repeal of Test and Corporation Acts. He was however helped by the Whigs like Brougham and Burdett some of whom took office under him. Though he relied on Whig support he was one of the founders of the new Toryism which was not opposed to social reforms. His Corn Bill was rejected by the Lords at the instigation of Wellington. He died in 1827. He was not a consistent member of either party. He thus stood "half-way between the new and old" in a time of transition. The Goderich (formerly Robinson) ministry continued till 1827. He was unable to control the cabinet. Then the Duke of Wellington formed the ministry which lasted till 1830.

Wellington's Ministry

Mr. Robert Peel became the Home Secretary. The Canningites Huskisson, Palmerston Dudley joined him. Wellington was the last of the old Tories. He was opposed to all reform except as an alternative to civil war. In 1828 the Test and Corporation Acts were repealed on the motion of Lord Russell, though there was opposition from extreme Tories. The Canningites later on resigned from the ministry, and began to advocate parliamentary reform. The ministry became purely Tory and strongly anti-Catholic. The question of Catholic emancipation became very acute. The early attempts of Pitt in 1801, of Granville in 1807, of Canning in 1812 and Grattan in 1819, the Roman Catholic Relief Bills of 1821,1822 and 1823, had all failed because of the king's and Tory opposition. The questions had led to great disorders in Ireland between the Protestant Orangemen and the Catholic White Boys. Wellington was afraid of civil war and Peel of the danger to Union. Both incurred great unpopularity. Peel resigned his seat at Oxford. The Act provided that the Roman Catholics should be eligible for all public offices, except those of Regent, Lord Chancellor of England and Ireland, Lord-Lieutenant of Ireland and judicial appointments in ecclesiastical courts. The members of parliament were no longer required to abjure Roman Catholic doctrines. The Jesuits and Monks were not to enter the country without licence. At the same time another act was passed, raising the qualification for the franchise in Ireland from 40s. to £10 in the hope of weakening the power of the Catholic peasantry. It was thus a measure of disfranchisement. The Emancipation Act however did not solve the problem of Ireland. It did not provide an endowment for the Roman Catholic clergy. O'Connell who was reelected began his agitation for the repeal of the union.

The King and Parliament

George IV and his ministers had continued to rule supreme over parliament and public opinion. Mr. Brougham's resolution of 1822 which stated that the influence of the crown had greatly increased and that it was destructive of the independence of parliament and inconsistent with the well-governing of the realm was thrown out. The influence of the crown over parliament enabled any party ministry to command a majority. But there was a gradual decline of the personal influence of the king in the work of administration. It practically ended when the king had to yield to Wellington in the matter of Catholic emancipation. The king himself had not much interest in matters of government, nor did he possess much knowledge about it.

William IV's Character

William IV succeeded to the throne in 1830. He was not much conversant with public affairs. He was more inclined towards liberal measures and reforms. He did not want to interfere in the working of the constitutional government. He respected the wishes of the House of Commons and accepted ministries which had a majority in it. There was a new parliament which met in October. There occurred an unfortunate reference in the king's speech to the determination of the government to repress by force all disturbances in England. There was however no sympathy expressed in it for the distress in the country which cause disturbances. The king's speech was followed by a declaration of Wellington resisting all measures of reform. The July Revolution of 1830 in Paris against the unconstitutional acts of Charles X of France had encouraged reformers in England, and strengthened constitutional government. In November the ministry of Wellington resigned owing to a defeat on the reform of the Civil List. Although the Whigs supported him in 1829 he could not secure their permanent support because of his opposition to parliamentary reform. Thus he failed as a party leader. He kept his position mainly because he alone could manage George IV.

Lord Grey's Ministry

The Tory ministers were weakened and discredited by the split in the party. The death of George IV also weakened their position. William who was personally popular and favourable to reform restored the Whigs to power. Lord Grey became the prime minister, Lord Althorp the Chancellor of the Exchequer and leader of the House of Commons and Brougham, Lord Chancellor. The Canningites, Palmerston, Grant, Goderich, joined the Whigs.

The desire for parliamentary reform was due to the political awakening of the people and to the existence of defects in the old system of parliamentary representation. Firstly, the seats in the House of Commons were not distributed according to population. Boroughs which had decayed in importance still sent members to the House of Commons. Old Sarum which was "a green mound and a wall with two niche's in it" sent two, and thirty-five constituencies with hardly any voters returned seventy members. On the contrary, towns which had greatly increased in population owing to the influence of the industrial revolution and the growth of trade were not properly represented. The country of Middlesex, including London, sent only eight members, and Manchester, Leeds, Sheffield and Birmingham which were thickly populated sent none.

Secondly, the House of Commons was largely composed of members under the influence of great landowners who controlled the pocket or nomination boroughs which were considered by them as their personal property.

Thirdly, the franchise was limited and based on no uniform system. In counties all 40s. freeholders could vote. But non-freeholders were excluded. The freeholders who were the country gentlemen and independent yeomanry were however susceptible to the social influences of great nobles and local landowners. The expenses of election contests were enormous.

In boroughs the franchise was not uniform and was limited. The privileges which gave a man a right to vote differed from borough to borough. In some the holders of certain houses or players of scot and lot (local rates), in others, freemen or holders of corporate office were entitled to vote.

Fourthly, the evils of the borough system of franchise were its complexity which caused considerable disputes in a borough as to who really had the right to vote, and the prevalence of bribery and corruption which obstructed the freedom of choice of members. There were two types of boroughs. In the pocket or nomination boroughs the inhabitants were very few in number. They looked up for patronage and protection to the crown or great landlords. These boroughs obediently returned the nominees of their patrons. Thus the House of Commons largely consisted of the nominees of the Crown and the House of Lords. In the rotten boroughs the electors were sufficiently numerous to be independent of a patron, they sold their votes. They made the right of voting a valuable privilege. They owed no allegiance to political parties or principles. They wanted to serve personal ends and satisfy social aspirations. Bribery at elections had become a systematic abuse in the reign of Charles II when the political importance of parliament had increased in the constitution. The Revolution of 1688 increased that influence still further. The accession of Hanoverians and the rise of the cabinet made it necessary to secure the support of parliament for government's policy and measures. Therefore in spite of bribery being an offence at common law and of the various Bribery Acts the evil continued. Both the crown and ministers bought seats from patrons and constituencies with a promise of titles, places, pensions or hard cash. Thus the sale of boroughs became a general practice. It was open and undisguised. Attempts made to check corruption between 1768 and 1786 failed. Legislation, statesmanship and public opinion all tolerated it. In larger boroughs and seaports corruption was more difficult, but the government influence was great owing to the presence of petty officers of customs and excise who supported the government candidates. In 1782 the Place Act disfranchised a number of revenue officers. Rockingham himself admitted that 11,500 of these collectors had votes and they chiefly determined the issue of 70 elections. It was only in a few great cities that the corruption was less. But there also a number of vexatious contests and obstacles had to be overcome. There were often riots and use of violence.

Fifthly, the representatives, who secured their seats by a general system of corruption, themselves got corrupt and readily sold their votes to the crown and his ministers. George III personally examined the voting list and awarded peerages and titles of honour places, pensions and pecuniary bribes. This method of managing the House of Commons developed from the time of Charles II and became a system during the reigns of the first four Georges. The Plact Acts of 1708, 1742 and 1782, however restricted a large number of place-holders, from sitting in parliament, and revenue and judicial officers were altogether disqualified.

House of Commons Tried Election Petitions

Scandalous as were the electoral abuses, still more was the conduct of the House of Commons in trying election petitions. There was injustice in these trials. The majority of the House of Commons connived at the purchase and sale of votes and seats, and at bribery, partiality and corruption at elections when committed by their own party. It only condemned them in the case of its political opponents.

Character of the Representative System

Thus the representative system was thoroughly corrupt, venal and dependent. The crown and the dominant political families could therefore command a majority in the House of Commons. The decayed and rotten boroughs where the private property of noblemen, the close corporations openly sold the seats at their disposal to members who in turn sold their votes to the crown and the ministers. From the early times there was no rational theory of representation. Its main object was to gather representatives from the places best able to give aids and subsidies to the crown. The crown and its officers selected places for representation as they liked. Hence inequalities of representation continually increased. They were not corrected by the use of the royal prerogative of enfranchising and disfranchising boroughs. The new boroughs which were enfranchised by the Tudors and the Stuarts were not places of importance or great size. They were more or less nomination boroughs created for the purpose of adding to the power of the crown.

The Revolution of 1688 though favourable to parliamentary government did not rectify the inequalities of representation. The prerogatives of the crown were limited, and the powers of the parliament increased. But their responsibility to the people was not secured. The House of Commons was largely beyond the reach of the public opinion and was not representative and accountable to the people. It was managed by the government by a system of bribery and corruption which continued till the Reform Act of 1832.

Character of the House of Commons in Practice

In spite of all these defects parliament attracted the best men to the service of the state like the Pitts, Fox, Burke, Russell. There were also some popular elements in the House of Commons. It recognised its responsibility to the people and was not insensible to the public opinion which was awakened by the influence of the press. The small class which returned a number of members was the most enlightened in the country and a part of them was generally inclined to favour principles of freedom and parliamentary government. Again the division of parties led to the party in opposition to preach popular principles and to act as restraint over the government and the majority in parliament. Walpole's fall in 1741, Elder Pitt's entry into the cabinet in 1756, Fox's loss of supporters in 1784, Younger Pitt's continuance in office in 1783, the passing of Catholic Emancipation Act of 1829, Earl Grey's triumph in 1832 were all indicative of the influence of the public opinion.

Prior Attempts at Parliamentary System

There were a number of attempts made at reform from 1766 and 1770 when Chatham advocated parliamentary reform. He had said "Before the end of this century either the parliament will reform itself from within or be reformed with a vengeance from without." In 1776 Wilkes introduced a comprehensive scheme of reform in a bill. He wanted to disfranchise rotten boroughs, to enfranchise large towns and to give more members to large counties. In 1782 and 1783 Pitt submitted three resolutions affirming (1) the necessity of preventing bribery and expense at elections, (2) the expediency of disfranchising, a borough whenever the majority of its voters should be convicted of corruption and transferring the unbribed minority to the county constituency and (3) the desirability of increasing the number of country and metropolitan members. In 1785 he introduced a Reform Bill which proposed to disfranchise corrupt boroughs and to increase the number of members for London and counties. All these proposals were rejected. In 1792 was formed the Society of the Friends of the people for parliamentary reform. It consisted of Whig-Liberals who were persons of rank. From 1800 to 1820 there were a number of motions made in 1809, 1818, and 1819, by men like Grey and Burdett. But the reaction against the French Revolution continued. There was a concentration of national energy against Napoleanic wars. The Tories who were in power were not inclined towards reform. The king did not favour it. The violence of extreme reformers and the Cato street conspiracy whose object was to assassinate the ministers weakened the movement for reform. From 1820 to 1830 there was again a revival of reform movement due to the moderate reformers like Burdett supported by the Whigs, especially Lord John Russell, and relying upon the desire of the middle classes to secure reform. Lord John Russell made motions in 1820, 1822, 1826, 1828 and 1830. Attempts were also made by others. Reform Associations were formed, especially the Union of Birmingham. In 1821 Grampound a notorious rotten borough in Cornwall was disfranchised and its two members were given to Yorkshire. The Tory party was opposed to parliamentary reform.

First Reform Bill

Earl Grey's ministry was pledged for parliamentary reform. There was agitation by the people in favour of reform. There were numerous public meetings held, political unions started and petitions presented for reform. The ministers had to encounter the vested interests of the proprietors of boroughs, the opposition of the House of Lords and of a majority of the House of Commons, the conservative spirit of the king who disliked and feared the measure at first and of the Tories in the country. The First Reform Bill was presented by Lord John Russell in the House of Commons on March 1, 1831. It passed the second reading by a majority of one in the largest House on record up to date. It was thrown out in the committee. Parliament was then dissolved by William IV in person. There was a great upheaval in the country. The election cry was "the Bill, the whole Bill and nothing but the Bill." The Tory candidates were routed and overthrown. The elections secured a large majority in favour of ministers and reform. On June 24, 1831 the second Reform Bill was introduced by Lord John Russell. The third reading was carried in the House of Commons by an overwhelming majority of 109 on September 21. On October, 8, it was however rejected by the Lords. The ministry refused to resign. Public excitement ran high. There were riots in favour of reforms. On December 12, the third Reform Bill was introduced by Lord John Russell. On March 23, 1832, the third reading was passed by the Commons. On May 7, a hostile amendment to the third Reform Bill was carried in the committee of the House of Lords. The king refused to create a majority of Whig peers in order to carry the Bill through the Lords. The ministers resigned. The king was obliged to promise to create Whig peers if necessary to secure the passing of the Reform Bill and to recall Grey on May 5. On June 4, the king requested Wellington to withdraw his opposition to the bill. Consequently Wellington and a hundred of his supporters retired from the House and the remaining peers passed the Bill. It became the Reform Act of 1832.

The Reform Act of 1832

The Act provided firstly the redistribution of seats by the abolition of a number of nomination and rotten boroughs. Fifty-six boroughs having less than 2,000 inhabitants and returning 111 members were disfranchised. Thirty boroughs having less than 4,000 inhabitants each lost one member. Two more boroughs lost two members. Thus 143 seats were made available for distribution by these changes. Sixty-five seats were given to the counties, forty-four to large towns like Birmingham, Manchester, Leeds, and Sheffield, each receiving two; twenty-one to smaller towns, each receiving one, eight were given to Scotland and five to Ireland. Reform Acts were also passed for Scotland and Ireland. Secondly, the Act extended the franchise. In the boroughs householders paying an annual rent of £10 received the franchise, and the old system of unequal and restricted qualifications was replaced by a uniform qualification. In the countries the 40s. freeholders retained the franchise. Thirdly, the Act was a reform of electoral machinery registration and corrupt practices. Detailed regulations for the conduct of elections were laid down. Excessive expenses were checked by a reduction of the days of polling and other means.

The Reform Act completed the revolution of 1688 in two ways. In 1688 political power had been transferred from the king to the landed classes, that is, the Whig landowners. In 1832 the landed classes were forced to extend their privileges to the commercial and industrial middle classes. From 1688 parliament had been manipulated by the government. It was largely subservient to the crown whose influence was supreme. From 1832 the members of the House of Commons were drawn from a large electorate and became greatly independent. Since then the House became the dominating element in the constitution. The period between 1832 to 1867 was the period of the rule of the middle class. The Act was passed owing to the alliance of the aristocratic Whigs with the moderate Liberals. It continued the work of the Revolution of 1688 by giving the chief power in the Commons to the middle class. It however did not create new political ideas or forces in the country. It is stated that it was not so much a reform act as it was an act to make reform possible. The reformed parliaments between 1832 and 1867 began to give a new social order, a new economic policy and a new political life. The reformed parliament was more liberal and progressive. It was more active and susceptible to the influence of public opinion.

Many of the Whigs supported the Reform Bill in the hope that it would check the growth of democratic sentiment. They would have resisted the extension of franchise to artisans and labourers. The extension of franchise did not diminish the influence of the landed gentry and wealthy men who formed the great majority in the parliaments after 1832. The Bill was however not a final settlement. The radical democrats wanted a broader franchise but failed. The exclusion of artisans from the franchise let to the development of chartism. It was the later Reform Bills of 1867 and 1884 which extended the franchise to urban and rural labourers.

The Whigs and Radicals

After the Reform Act of 1832 the Whigs supplanted the Tories in power and used their ascendancy for passing a number of great measures for the liberty and welfare of the people. Radicals had no ties with the Whig aristocracy and no respect for their constitutional traditions. Their principles were democratic. They wanted every political and economic grievance of the common classes to be immediately redressed and were against any delay. Earl Grey and his followers were however against their extreme democratic ideas and individualistic measures.

Measures of Reformed Parliament

Earl Grey remained prime minister from 1830 to 1834. In 1832 parliament was dissolved. The new parliament (1833) under the Reform Act began to reform abuses. It passed the Affirmation Act allowing affirmation instead of an oath. The Act for the emancipation of slaves in colonies by passing compensation to slave owners and the Factory Act prohibiting the employment of children in factories under nine and restricting the work of women and young persons under eighteen to ten hours a day and of children below twelve to eight hours a day. The government made a grant to education and threw open the eastern trade under the influence of *Laissez faire.* In 1834 the poor Law Amendment Act was passed under Melbourne ministry. It restricted outdoor relief, imposed a workhouse test in the case of ablebodied seeking indoor relief and abolished the law of Settlement which hindered the movement of labourers from place to place.

The First Ministry of Melbourne lasted from July to November 1834. Viscount Melbourne had been a follower of Canning. He held office under Wellington but resigned with other Canningites in 1828. He was the home secretary in the ministry of Grey and helped in the Reform Bill. It was he who trained Queen Victoria in the principles of constitutional government. He depended largely upon the support of Althorp in the House of Commons. Melbourne however thought his position insecure and wished to retire from it. The king disliked Melbourne. He therefore dismissed him with his consent.

Peel's First Ministry

The king sent for Sir Robert Peel. He had been home secretary in 1822 and had resigned in 1827 on Canning's becoming the prime minister. He had no following in the House of Commons and failed to get support in it. He therefore advised the dissolution of parliament. At the time of the general election Pitt issued his manifesto or address to his constituents at Tamworth. It was a definite statement of the principles of the Peel's conservative party. He said that he was neither "a defender of abuses" nor "an enemy of judicious reform" and that the Reform Bill constitutes a new era" and is the final and irrevocable settlement of a great constitutional question. He advocated "a careful review of institutions, civil and ecclesiastical, undertaken in a friendly temper" to secure "the firm maintenance of established rights, the correction of proved abuses and the redress of real grievances." The election however returned a liberal majority opposed to Peel. In the King's speech Peel promised "to advance soberly and cautiously in the path of progressive improvement." He also made promises of certain definite reforms. Peel could not continue a struggle against the hostile majority in the House of Commons and was compelled to resign. Thus the constitutional result of the Reform Act was seen. Henceforth the minister ruled only with the support of the House of Commons.

Second Ministry of Melbourne

The second ministry of Lord Melbourne lasted from 1835 to 1841. Its first measure of importance was the Municipal Reform Act of 1835. The Act provided that all towns should have a uniform system of government, consisting of a town council, elected by the rate payers in each ward who had resided three years in the borough and including a mayor, aldermen and councillors, that the town council should administer accounts which were to be daily audited and published and that all old trading privileges should be abolished. This act extended the municipal franchise and put it on a uniform basis. It did for the government of towns what the Reform Bill had done for the government of the country. It greatly diminished jobbery in municipal affairs, abolished privilege, and introduced representative self-government in municipalities. In 1836 the House of Commons issued the Division Lists which were published. Thus the public got to know how its representatives voted. The Stamp Duty which was levied on newspapers was reduced from four pence to one penny per issue. It cheapened the newspaper and removed financial restrictions on its free circulation. In 1817 the king died.

Queen Victoria Succeeds

Queen Victoria was only eighteen when she ascended the throne in 1837. She got married in 1840 to Prince Albert of Saxe-Coburg Gotha and died after a long and eventful reign of 64 years in 1901. Her reign was remarkable for the triumph of democracy, the extension of the Empire, the grant of responsible government to the colonies and the progress of the country in social, economic and educational matters. She was the daughter of Edward, Duke of Kent, son of George III. Lord Melbourne whose ministry continued till 1841 became her confidential adviser and inculcated in her the principles of constitutional government. He was a man of sterling character, great tact and wisdom.

Work of Melbourne Ministry

The period between 1837 and 1846 was one of discontent and danger. In 1837 there was a rebellion in Canada owing to the mismanagement of the Home Government. Lord Durham who was sent in 1838 to Canada took rigorous measures to establish order. In 1838 the People's Charter was published. It demanded annual parliaments, manhood suffrage, vote by ballot, equal electoral districts, abolition of property qualification for members of parliament and payment of members. All the demands except the first have been now achieved. One of the causes of the discontent amongst the working classes was the ousting of hand labour by machinery without a corresponding lessening of the price of commodities. The dearness of raw materials, the increasing growth of the population and the illegality of trade unions had enabled the manufacturers to keep down the wages of labourers. The second was the existence of Corn Laws of 1815 which had raised artificially the price of the necessities of life. The main object of the chartist movement was the amelioration of the condition of the poor to be brought about by means of the points in the charter. The moral-force-chartists believed in employing methods of persuasion in achieving their demands and the physical-force-chartists in employing methods of violence to do it. The condition of the lowest classes was miserable. The immediate effect of the introduction of machinery was diminution in the demand for manual labour in the towns. The migration of workers from country districts to towns increased the competition among workmen and diminished their wages. The Reform Act had not put an end to their miseries. The new Poor Law caused much hardship in the beginning.

In 1838 Cobden and Brigitht formed the Anti-Corn Law League in Manchester. Its aim was to alter economic rather than political conditions. It was mainly a middle class and not a working- class movement. In 1841 Lord John Russell's proposal to repeal the Corn Laws, to impose a tax of eight shillings a quarter instead of the sliding scale and to reduce the sugar duty was not carried.

Bed-Chamber Question

In May 1839, Melbourne resigned because the Jamaica Bill which related to questions arising out of emancipation was carried by only five in the Commons. Peel was invited to form a ministry but he refused to take office unless the Whig ladies of the royal household in attendance on the queen resigned their posts. They had all been appointed from the parliamentary supporters of the ministry. Nearly all the ladies were related to the ministers themselves or their political followers. Peel thought that their influence was hostile to the ministry. The queen refused to adopt a course which she thought to be "contrary to usage and repugnant to her feelings." Melbourne supported her. She therefore continued the Melbourne ministry till 1841 when it was defeated on the question of reduction of sugar duty and free trade and on a vote of want of confidence by the vote and parliament was dissolved.

The Position of Parties in 1841

In 1841 the Whig rule of eleven years ended. Though they had a majority in the Commons and passed many important laws, they were not a united party. Melbourne was not strong enough to enforce discipline. He did not give his party a strong lead. There were serious differences of opinion in the party. Earl Grey had little sympathy with the Radicals. Mr. Stanley and Lord John Russell differed entirely as to the appropriation of Irish ecclesiastical revenues. Brougham quarrelled with his colleagues. On the other hand the Conservative party was consolidated by Peel. There was a permanent Conservative majority in the House of Lords which often rejected or modified the bills which the ministry supported. In the election of 1841 they got a majority in the House of Commons. Dread of democracy converted many to conservatism. The Whigs had failed to appreciate the grievances of the working classes and the importance of the anti-Corn Law movement.

Peel's Second Ministry

The second ministry of Peel lasted from 1841 to 1846. It was important for the softening of class hatreds. This was partly the work of Peel who by his financial reforms ushered in a period of prosperity and who educated the Tory party to see the necessity of conciliating the labouring classes, showed sympathy for the demands of the charter in founding the Complete Suffrage Association in 1842.

Peel was a great statesman. He saw that old Toryism which resisted all progress had been rendered obsolete by the new conditions arising from the Industrial Revolutions and the demands of democracy. He accepted the Reform Bill and organised the Conservatives on the lines of the Tamworth Manifesto of 1834. He would not sacrifice the interests of the nation to those of his party. Twice he broke up his party when its principles seemed at variance with national needs, once in 1829 when he introduced the Catholic Emancipation Bill, and then in 1846 when he repealed the Corn Laws. As a prime minister he exercised close supervision and authority over his colleagues. He had great sympathy with the poor and looked after their welfare. He was an eminently just man.

The First Russell Ministry

The period between 1846 and 1867 was one of consolidation of parties. The first Russell ministry lasted from 1846 to 1852. It was the last Whig government. Lord John Russell had identified himself with the causes of religious equality and parliamentary reform. To him the question of reform was finally settled by the Reform Act of 1832. Palmerston was the foreign secretary. In 1847 the Factory Act was passed, for bidding the employment of women and children in textile factories for more than ten hours a day. In the same year Disraeli became the leader of the Conservative party. 1848 was "the year of Revolutions" in Europe. It led to the revival of chartism in England under Feargus O'Connor, when Louis Philippe in France abdicated and a French republic was set up. A million chartists proposed to march to parliament to present a petition signed by two million men in favour of chartism. Considering this to be an attempt to overawe parliament by physical force the home secretary declared the meeting of the chartists to be held at Kennington Common illegal. They were not allowed to cross the Westminister bridge. Chartism failed but many of its demands were met later on by the adoption of various measures for the amelioration of economic suffering and for extending democracy.

Derby's First Ministry

In February 1852, Lord Stanley, Earl of Derby formed his first ministry, and Benjamin Disraeli became the Chancellor of the Exchequer. As the colonial secretary in Lord Grey's ministry he had carried the Bill for the Abolition of Slavery. He however left the Whigs in 1834 owing to his opposition to the appropriation of the revenues of the Irish church. He joined the Conservative party under Peel. On Peel's adopting free trade, he resigned office and became a leader of the protectionists. He was a man of great vigour and known as the 'Rupert of debate.' Parlmerston's resolutions on free trade were accepted by Disraeli and were passed by a large majority. In December, Disraeli's budget was introduced and defeated by the opposition of Gladstone who strongly objected to the increased house duty. The ministry consequently resigned.

Aberdeen Ministry

The Aberdeen ministry lasted from 1852 to 1855. It was a coalition ministry of Whigs and Peelites who were now united for the first time.

Palmerston's First Ministry

The first Palmerston ministry lasted from 1855 to 1858. Gladstone joined it. It was defeated on the conspiracy to murder reform Bill.

Derby's Second Ministry

The second Derby ministry included Disraeli as the chancellor of the exchequer. It lasted from 1858 to 1859. It was maintained because of disunion in the Liberal party. In 1858 Jews were admitted as members of parliament. Disraeli introduced a Reform Bill in 1859 and the government was defeated on it. The elections returned a Liberal majority and the ministry was defeated on amendment to the address and resigned.

Palmerston's Second Ministry

The second ministry of Lord Palmerston lasted from 1859 to 1865. Mr. Gladstone became the Chancellor of the Exchequer and Lord John Russell, the foreign secretary. The Peelites now finally left the Conservatives and united with the Whigs to form a very strong ministry.

Russell's Second Ministry

Palmerston was succeeded by Lord John Russell as prime minister. The second ministry of Russell lasted from 1865 to 1866. Gladstone remained the Chancellor of the Exchequer and the leader of the Commons. The government brought a Reform Bill in 1866 lowering the franchise. It was defeated on an amendment and therefore resigned in June 1866. The time was unfavourable for reform. There was a pressure of other questions. The House of Commons was not anxious and there was not a strong general demand outside. Gladstone said that by introducing the bill the government had adopted the cause of democracy. The bill was too moderate for extreme Liberals and too advanced for Conservatives. It was an attempt to make a compromise. The Conservatives and a group of Liberals under Robert Lowe opposed the bill. The opposition to the bill caused discontent among the working class especially among the Trade Unionists who now began to take an active interest in political questions. A London reform mob pulled down the railings of Hyde Park on July 23, 1866. Their violence made Lord Derby the new prime minister and Disraeli, the Chancellor of the Exchequer realise the urgent need of reform.

Derby's Third Ministry

The third ministry of Lord Derby lasted from 1866 to 1868. In 1867 Disraeli introduced his Reform Bill. The Liberals wanted the lowering of the franchise still further. The extreme Liberals desired to get the widest measure of reform. John Stuart Mill wanted to secure extension of franchise to women. Many Conservatives strongly objected to the measure and called it "A Leap in the Dark" and a political betrayal. The bill was amended and passed in 1867 with the addition of clauses dealing with redistribution. It was carried by a combination of both parties. It enfranchised all occupiers of houses or rate-payers in towns and also occupiers of lodgings having resided there one year and paying ten pounds rent. In the counties occupiers at twelve pounds rental were given the vote and the old freehold suffrage of 40s. was retained. About one million new voters were added by the Act. The artisan class in the towns got representation. In the redistribution of seats fifty-two seats were taken from smaller boroughs and given to others. The bill was passed in the Lords by Lord Derby's influence. In 1868 similar Reform Acts for Scotland and Ireland were passed.

Disraeli's First Ministry

In 1868 Lord Derby had resigned on account of ill-health. He was succeeded by Disraeli as prime minister. Disraeli's first ministry was defeated in the general election of 1868. The Liberals got a majority in the House of Commons and the ministry of Disraeli resigned. Lord John Russell had withdrawn from active political life after the defeat of his Reform Bill in 1866. He was a champion of liberty. In the matters of religious liberty he did a great deal in removing religious disabilities of Protestant non-conformists by moving successfully for the Repeal of the Test and Corporation Acts (1828) and by introducing the Marriage Act which legalised marriages in non-conformist chapels, of Roman Catholics by supporting the Roman Catholic Emancipation Act (1829) and Peel's Maynooth grant, and of Jews by supporting the bill for admission of Jews to parliament. He supported the cause of national liberty in Italy. He favoured the extension of constitutional liberty to the colonies and was sincerely anxious to improve the condition of Ireland. He has been called 'Lord John Reformer'.

Gladstone's First Ministry

In 1868 the first ministry of Gladstone was formed. It lasted till 1874. Robert Lowe became the Chancellor of the exchequer, William Ewart Gladstone had been trained in the school of Canning and Peel. He was the President of the board of Trade in Peel's second ministry but had resigned office on the question of Maynooth College grant which Peel had increased in 1845. It was a Roman Catholic College. In 1846 he returned as colonial and war secretary. He was the chancellor of exchequer under Aberdeen, Palmerston and Russell. He was the great democratic and Liberal statesmen of this period. He hated oppression, trusted the people and was a master of finance. In 1868 compulsory church rates on non-conformists were abolished. In 1869 the Irish church was disestablished. In 1870 the first Irish Land Act was passed, obliging landlords to give their tenants compensation for improvements. The Elementary Education Act established school boards. By an order in council all public offices in the civil service except those of the Foreign office were thrown open to public competition. There was army reform, establishing the supremacy of parliament over the army through the secretary of state for war to whom the commander-in-chief was made subordinate and reorganising the war office into three departments, the enlistment and regulation of the army and abolishing the system of purchase of commissions which did not secure competent officers. In 1871 religious tests in the Universities were abolished and they were thrown open to non-conformists. The Trade Union Act recognised the legality of Trade Unions and made their officials liable to legal penalties for the misuse of union funds. It was further amended and extended in 1875 and 1876. In 1872 was passed the Ballot Act. Ballot meant secret voting. Franchise could not be publicly and freely exercised because the richer and power classes forced the electors to vote for them against the free-will and opinions. Therefore the system of secret voting was necessary to check this intimidation or under influence. It was also to be a safeguard against bribery. There was strong opposition to the ballot. Mill denounced it as "unmanly." The Whigs held that suffrage was a public trust and that public voting was necessary to see that it was properly fulfilled. But open voting had led to bribery and intimidation and the public nomination of candidates on the husting caused frequent riots. The Act provided that voting at parliamentary elections should be by ballot and that the candidates should no longer be publicly nominated on the hustings. It diminished the bribery of electors and disturbances at elections and the illegitimate influence of landlords and employees.

Gladstone's Resignation and Return to Power

In 1873 Gladstone's Irish University Bill was rejected by three votes. The University of Dublin was to be a teaching and examining body, was to be separated from the Protestant Trinity college and was not to teach modern history, theology, and philosophy in order to avoid religious difficulties. The bill pleased no one. Disraeli strongly opposed the bill. A combination of Roman Catholics, Conservatives and moderate Liberals defeated it. Gladstone resigned on March 13. But Disraeli refused to take office on the ground that the question was not of first rate importance. He was unwilling to take office with a Liberal majority in the Commons. On March 18, Gladstone resumed office. In the same year the Supreme Court of Judicature Act was passed. It established one Supreme Court of Judicature, divided into a High Court of Justice and a Court of Appeal.

Supreme Court of Judicature

The Courts of Queen's Bench, Common Pleas, Exchequer, Chancery, Admiralty and Probate and Divorce, which were independent, now became divisions of the High Court of Justice. The representatives of the old courts of Appeal, namely, the Court of Exchequer Chamber, the Court of Appeal in Chancery, the House of Lords, the Judicial Committee of the Privy Council were admitted to the new court of Appeal whose decisions were to be final. All judges were empowered to administer equity as well as law. Thus the act consolidated the administration of justice and terminated the separate administration of law and equity. In 1876 however further appeal was allowed to a committee of the House of Lords, which included the Lord Chancellor, two Lords of Appeal holding life peerages, and peers who have been lawyers.

Effects of Liberal Measures

In 1874 parliament was dissolved. The general election returned a Conservative majority. Therefore the ministry of Gladstone resigned. Gladstone's first ministry carried out for the first time its liberal principles. His policy was of active liberal reforms in domestic affairs. Hence it differed completely from the policy of the Conservatives. The ministry however had become unpopular. The country was not anxious for reforms. Its policy had upset vested interest amongst landlords, the Army, the Church, the non-conformists, and the working classes. Disraeli exaggeratedly put it that it had "harassed every trade, worried every profession and assailed or menaced every class, institution and species of property in the country."

There was a general belief that the foreign policy of the government was weak and had lowered the British prestige abroad. The queen personally disliked Gladstone. However the Liberal government had done much in the way of reform in administration and judiciary and of advance of liberty by removing restrictions and providing securities.

Disraeli's Second Ministry

The second ministry of Disraeli lasted from 1874 to 1880. His position was very strong. He had a majority in the House of Commons, a large majority in the House of Lords and very able colleagues. He had no special mandate from the country. There was no desire for domestic reform. The queen trusted him fully. The merchants and employers of labour who were liberals were beginning to favour the Conservatives owing to the growing dependence of the Liberals upon the working classes. Disraeli's home policy was however not of any importance. It did not disturb the work of the previous ministry. It had no desire for reform. Its foreign policy was vigorous and actuated by the ambition of making the influence of Great Britain supreme in Europe and of consolidating and extending the Empire and of developing imperialism. In 1876 the Royal Titles Bill conferred on the queen the title of the Empress of India and a proclamation of the queen as Empress of India was issued at a magnificent Durbar at Delhi in 1877. This action of Disraeli strengthened the regard of the queen for him. In 1876 the Education Act was passed which made elementary education compulsory. In 1880 parliament was dissolved and the Liberal's returned in majority. Disraeli's ministry resigned. It fell because of the unpopularity and heavy expense of the Afghan and Zulu wars. There was also commercial and agricultural depression in 1879. Gladstone's Midlothian campaign attacked the general policy of government in a series of brilliant speeches which had great influence on public opinion.

Disraeli's Character and Work

Disraeli who died in 1881 was at first a strong advocate of protection. He violently attacked Peel for repeating the Corn Laws in 1846. He was the chancellor of the exchequer in all the three Derby's ministries. In 1876 he was created Earl of Beaconsfield. He is called the second founder of the Conservative party. He at first believed that "the natural rulers of England are the aristocracy supported by the people", but later realised the importance and energies of an educated and enfranchised people and took up the cause of reform. He in 1852 approved the policy of free trade and committed the Conservative party to a new policy. He had real sympathy with the poorer classes. Reform Bill of 1857 showed that conservatism was no longer the exclusive creed of the privileged and wealthy classes. He was the most distinguished member of the "Young England Party" which took a deep interest in the "condition of England question". He regarded the aim of the Conservative party as "the maintenance of our institutions, the protection of our empire and the improvement of the condition of the people." These principles guided the Conservative party. He did little to put his theories of politics and imperialism into practice. He possessed little constructive ability and no administrative capacity. His sympathy with the working classes did not result in any measure of social amelioration. His Reform Bill of 1867 was taken from the Whigs. He did nothing to remedy Irish grievances.

Gladstone's Second Ministry

Gladstone's second ministry lasted from 1880 to 1885. He included Chamberlain and Dilke, two Radicals, in the cabinet. Chamberlain advocated unionism, direct taxation and the cause of the labourer. He said he preached 'the gospel of political humanity.' In 1883 he openly advocated disestablishment of the church, manhood suffrage, payment of members and free education. He attacked the House of Lord, saying "they toil not, neither do they spin". He championed the new radicalism. He had established in many towns a Liberal caucus, that is, a meeting of party voters. This had helped largely in the victory of the Liberals in 1880. Many of the Whigs did not like his democratic policy and principles. Similarly at this time there arose a new fourth party, besides the other three Liberals, Conservatives and Irish Nationalists. It was led by Lord Randolph Churchill and included Sir Henry Drummond Wolff, Sir John Gorst and often Mr. Arthur Balfour. Churchill advocated Tory democracy. He sympathised with popular government. He wanted to win over the working men by a policy of social reform and the Parnellites by denouncing coercion. This party stood in the same relation to the Conservatives as the Radicals did to the Liberals. In 1880 Mr. Charles Bradlaugh a professed atheist claimed to make an affirmation of his allegiance instead of an oath on taking his seat. In 1881 the judges decided against Bradlaugh's claim as oath would have no binding effect on his conscience. He was reelected but the Commons expelled him. In this year the Irish Land Act established a court to which tenants could apply for fixing fair rent. Rent so decided was to remain for 15 years. The Burials Act (1880) removed a non-conformist grievance by allowing burials in parish churchyards without any service and with any orderly form the mourners chose. The Education Act (1881) made education compulsory.

Third Reform Act of 1884

In 1884 the Third Reform Bill was introduced. It provided (1) that the county franchise, like the borough franchise, should be extended to all occupiers of houses and £10 lodgers, (2) that persons who, though otherwise qualified, were neither tenants nor £10 lodgers should have the right to vote (the service franchise) and (3) that the Bill should apply to Scotland and Ireland as well as England. Gladstone wanted to bring the Redistribution Bill separately. The Reform Bill intended to enfranchise the agricultural labourer and thus remedy the deficiency of the Bill of 1867. It placed the county and borough franchises on the same footing. It added the service element to the electorate and thus made a great advance in democratic representation. The Act of 1832 had added about half a million electors, that of 1867 about one million and that of 1884 about two millions. The franchise was however attached not to individuals but to property. There was still the early idea of the House of Commons, being a gathering called by the crown, of the representatives of owners of property who might after or before the redress of their grievances grant some part of the property of those whom they represented for public purposes. But women as owners of property were not represented. Lord Coke had condemned such practice. The new theory was that the right of vote was a natural right and the every citizen who paid rates, or taxes to the public revenue or gave labour to the public wealth was entitled to participate in public affairs. In 1866 Mill had advocated the cause of women's franchise and had petitioned parliament to remove the anomaly by which some holders of property were given the right to vote while others equally qualified were excluded. He had also moved an amendment to the Reform Bill of 1867 to substitute the word 'person' for the word 'men' in respect of franchise. But it was defeated.

Movement for Reform

There had been a movement for further extension of franchise from 1872. The suffrage was no longer regarded as a trust committed to those whom the state thought to be the best qualified to exercise it. It came to be considered as a right which "every man not presumably incapacitated by some consideration of personal unfitness or of political danger" was morally entitled to enjoy. Mr. Trevelyan made a number of proposals for the fresh extension of the suffrage from 1873 to 1879 and for a uniform parliamentary franchise for borough and country constituencies and for a redistribution of political power in order to obtain a more equitable representation of the electoral body. His proposals, however, failed. There was also a reform movement in the country. In 1883 Mr. Chamberlain, Sir Charles Dilke and Mr. John Morley championed the cause of reform. No man who was expected to fulfill the duties of a citizen was to be exclude from the suffrage. They wanted equal electorate districts, and payment of members. They pressed for a uniform borough and country franchise. The Conservatives though they had their doubts did not oppose the principle of the Bill. But they wanted a redistribution of seats accompanying reform. Otherwise they feared a defeat at the elections. The Conservative majority in the House of Lords threw out the Bill and demanded a complete scheme of reform and re-distribution together. Gladstone denied the right of the Lords to force a dissolution and refused to dissolve the parliament. The action of the Lords caused great resentment and led to an agitation to mend or end the Upper House. A compromise was however arrived at under the influence of the Queen. Gladstone agreed to bring in a Re-distribution Bill also. Its provisions were to be arranged between the leaders of the government and the opposition. On December 6, 1884 passed the Reform Bill. The Re-distribution Bill passed in the Commons in May 1885 and in the Lords in June 1885. In the same month Gladstone resigned owing to his defeat on the budget proposals. The Irish had voted against the government.

Divisions in the Liberal Party

From now on we see the beginning of the break-up of the Liberal party. It was only Gladstone's influence which tended to keep the party together. Divisions were however slowly appearing. The extreme Radicals led by Chamberlain became more powerful owing to the extension of franchise.

Period from 1885-1901

The period from 1867 to 1885 had been one of an increased number of legislative measures. It was a period of unrest. There were Irish troubles and colonial and imperial troubles. There was agricultural revolution and a movement for the improvement of agricultural labourers. There was also reform agitation. From 1885 to 1901 the electorate became more democratic. There was also a reorganisation of local government and extension of suffrage in counties and parishes. There however took place splits in the Liberal and Irish parties and the movement for Irish Home Rule collapsed. The Conservative party got strengthened.

Salisbury's First Ministry

Lord Salisbury's first ministry lasted from 1885-1886. He was a member of Lord Derby's cabinet in 1867 but had resigned on the government bringing its Reform Bill. He was at first Secretary of State for India in Disraeli's cabinet and then Foreign Secretary from 1878 to 1880. As prime minister his rule was marked by the decrease of Irish agitation. He worked also as the Foreign Secretary. The fourth party became very powerful. Randolph Churchill became the leader of the Commons and Gorst and Balfour obtained office. In 1881 Lord Ashbourne's Act was passed to encourage tenant ownership in Ireland. In 1885 there was a general election in which 335 Liberals, 249 Conservatives and 86 Home Rulers were returned. In 1886 Breadlaugh took his seat in parliament. The speaker Brand refused to admit any valid objection to the taking of the oath of allegiance by a lawfully elected member. The government resigned on the amendment of Jesse Collings, regretting the absence from the Queen's speech a mention of measures for the relief of the agricultural labourers, being carried with the support of the Irish members.

Gladstone's Third Ministry

Gladstone's third ministry of 1886 was important for the introduction of the first Home Rule Bill for Ireland. This led to a split in the Liberal party. Leaders of the Liberal unionists like Lord Harington, Chamberlain and others refused to take office and combined to form the party of the Liberal unionists, ninety-three Liberals voted against the Bill and thus broke the Liberal Party. In the general election of 1886 the Liberals were defeated.

Salisbury's Second Ministry

Lord Salisbury's second ministry lasted from 1886 to 1892. Seventy-eight Liberal unionist members did not at first join the Conservative government but supported Lord Salisbury. The Conservatives in order to win over the Unionists gave up the ultra-conservative principles and adopted a more Liberal policy somewhat on the lines of the Tory Democracy of Churchill. There did not take place any reconciliation between the Liberals amd Unionists. Gladstone and Chamberlain could not agree.

Gladstone's Fourth Ministry

In the general election of 1892 the Liberals secured a majority. Therefore Lord Salisbury's ministry resigned. Gladstone's fourth ministry which came into power lasted from 1892 to 1894. In 1891 the Liberals had accepted the unwieldy Newcastle Programme. It included Welsh and Scottish Disestablishment, local veto and the limitation of hours of labour. Consequently it alienated the established church, the liquor interest and many employers. Gladstone's interest was however confined to Home Rule for Ireland. He was not favourable to Welsh Dis-establishment. It was in this parliament that for the first time the representatives of the Independent Labour Party were returned to parliament. In 1893 the second Home Rule Bill was passed by the Commons and rejected by the Lords. But Gladstone denied the right of the House of Lords to force a dissolution and refused to dissolve. He felt bound to carry out a part of the Newcastle Programme. He brought in the employer's Liability Bill which increased the liability of employers for injuries to workmen. He however withdrew the Bill as the Lords insisted on allowing workmen to "contract out" from the advantages of the Bill if they wished.

In 1894 was passed the District and parish Councils Act which was complementary to the County Councils Act of 1888. The Common Law had recognised the right of all rated parishioners to assemble in a vestry and administer parochial affairs. But in many parishes this popular principle gradually fell into disuse, and a few inhabitants who were self-chosen and irresponsible claimed a right of administering parochial affairs. The Act of 1894 divided each administrative country into urban and rural districts, and every district into parishes. Each district was given a council which was elected by the county electors within the district. This district council, urban or rural, was given the power of administering the poor law and high ways and was to act as sanitary authority. There were to be parish councils elected in all villages with more than three hundred inhabitants and to act as "secular vestries" with the civil powers of vestries of enforcing rights of way, of preventing enclosures, of managing parochial charities which were not ecclesiastical. There were also set up parish meetings consisting of persons in the parish whose names were enrolled as electors on the parliamentary or local government registers and which had a population below three hundred. The vestry still retains control over purely ecclesiastical matters including ecclesiastical charities. The parish councils and meetings were also given the duties of appointment of overseers, custody of parish books and registers, management of parish property, lighting, watching establishment of baths and wash-houses and the provisions of burial grounds. These local government acts extended self-government to localities in all the lesser details of ordinary common life. They also removed the chaos which had existed before.

Gladstone's Character and Work

On March 3, 1894, Gladstone resigned owing to age, health and differences of policy over naval estimates. The Queen chose Lord Rosebery as his successor without even consulting him. The Liberal party which was already broken by the Home Rule controversy was further weakened by the retirement of Gladstone, by the want of union between the Imperialist Liberals who supported Rosebery and those Liberals like Harcourt who were more interested in social reform and by personal jealousies. Gladstone died in 1898. He was very Conservative in principles at first, but later he evolved as a great Peelite and a Liberal, tolerant in religion and favourable to reform, freedom and progress. But he never accepted radicalism. He was a great orator and a brilliant debater. His budget speeches were considered as "masterpieces of financial exposition." He was very earnest and serious in his work. He was a great scholar.

The Rosebery ministry lasted till June 1895. He was an Imperialist. Sir William Harcourt became the Chancellor of the Exchequer. The increased naval expenditure made increased taxation necessary. Harcourt's budget imposed Succession Duties on the whole of the estate, that is, on real and personal property alike on a graduated scale rising from one per cent to eight per cent according to the value of property. This budget was popular with the middle and lower classes but was strongly opposed by the wealthy and property owners. The government also introduced several measures according to the Newcastle Programme. Local Velo Bill and Welsh Dis-establishment however did not pass in the Lords. It was defeated on a snatch vote on the army estimates. Rosebery resigned. In the general election of 1895 the Liberal Party was defeated. The Unionists got a majority of 152 votes.

Salisbury's Third Ministry

Lord Salisbury's third ministry lasted from 1895 to 1902. This was the twentieth ministry of the reign. The Conservatives and Liberal Unionists now became united. Joseph Chamberlain became the colonial secretary. His influence led to the development of imperialism. Disraeli was the advocate of the imperial idea. He wanted the closer union of the empire. He had advocated colonial self-government accompanied by an imperial tariff. He wanted to define the military responsibilities of the colonies towards Great Britain and the establishment of a colonial council in England. Imperialism was strongly supported by Lord Rosebery also. Mr. Chamberlain was a great advocate of a closer union between the colonies and the mother country. During his tenure of colonial office from 1895 to 1902 he strengthened the idea in the conferences of colonial delegates who attended the Diamond Jubilee of Queen Victoria in 1897 by discussing the questions of imperial trade and imperial defence. The workmen's compensation Act of 1897 extended compensation to workmen (excluding agricultural labourers and domestic servants). It, however, allowed workmen to contract out of its provisions. In 1899 was passed the government of London Act. The Act of 1888 had made London a separate administrative country under a county council but the city of London was to retain its own rights and to be governed by the corporation. The new Act retained the privileges of the city of London and transformed the vestires into metropolitan boroughs. The administrative county of London was divided into 28 boroughs, each with its council of a mayor, Aldermen and councillors like any other country borough. The number of councillors was not to exceed 70 and to be fixed by the number of wards in the borough. The number of aldermen was to be one-sixth of the councillors.

Queen Victoria's Period

The result of all these acts was a distribution of all the functions of local government between county councils, district councils and parish councils. They were coordinated under the supervision and control of the central authority. Trained officials took the place of local magnates in the administration of local affairs. Queen Victoria died on January 22, 1901. Her death closed a long eventful reign of 64 years. It is stated of her "although she resolutely opposed any attempt to lessen the power or prestige of monarchy in Great Britain, she was the first occupant of the throne who could be called a genuinely constitutional monarch". She took active interest in domestic politics. She believed in the liberty of the subjects and religious toleration. But she believed in class distinctions and in not changing the great institutions of government. She was in favour of the established church.

The Two Parties

During her reign developed the two great modern parties, namely, Liberals and Conservatives. The Liberals advocated ideas of liberty and progress. They believed in the extension of suffrage, local self-government in the colonies, and other social, religious, economic and educational reforms. Their sympathies were with the people. The Conservatives advocated the maintenance of the constitution against the encroachments of democracy. They would improve institutions but would not destroy or change them. The land, the church and the law were their strongholds. Their sympathies were with authority and traditions, classes and national institutions. Disraeli had stated in 1867 "in a progressive country change is constant and the great question is, not whether you should resist change which is inevitable, but whether that change should be carried out in deference to the manners, the customs, the laws and the traditions of a people, or whether it should be carried out in deference to abstract principles and arbitrary and general doctrines. The one is a natural system. The other is a philosophic system". They had accepted however the postulates of democracy.

Party Organisation

Owing to the obstructionist tactics of the Irish party the House of Commons introduced new rules of procedure in 1882. This led to the rigidity of party ties. On every division party members had to vote for the party. Every question became a question of vote of confidence in the party. Independent action of members had no place. The opposition only opposed or embarrassed the government. There was no question of cooperation. Consequently party organisations strengthened. The Union of conservative and constitutional Associations was founded in 1867. Its object was to strengthen the hands of the local associations. Its work was to help in forming such associations and in giving them information. It met annually in different places. It was reorganised after 1880. Party funds were placed in the hands of the central committee which was a body created in 1880 and consisted of the whips and certain other members appointed by the official leaders. In 1877 was organised the Liberal Federation. It did similar work. In 1883 Chamberlain who was its active spirit advocated, while he was a minister, an extensive scheme of radical reform comprising dis-establishment, manhood suffrage, equal electoral districts and payment of members. His colleagues however did not agree with it. The Newcastle Programme of the Liberal Federation was formulated in 1886. It consisted of Home Rule for Ireland, Dis-establishment of the church in Wales, electoral reform, payment of members, land reform, local veto, taxation of land values, and the ending or mending of the House of Lords. There was however nothing in this programme which went directly to help the welfare of the working classes.

Modern Conservative Party

The modern Conservative party believes in protection. It revolted against the free trade proposals of the old Conservative government. In 1903 Mr. Joseph Chamberlain who was a Liberal Unionist and had joined the Conservative party advocated economic imperialism and imperial preference. His programme was not however authorised by the party. He wanted to bind the empire by a system of preferential tariffs and to protect British industries by general and penal tariffs against foreign competition. Mr. Chamberlain's proposals broke up the Unionist party just as Mr. Peel's proposals to adopt free trade and to repeal the Corn Laws had broken up the Conservative party in 1846. The Conservatives dislike change but reluctantly accept it when compelled by circumstances to do so. They believe in slow and evolutionary change.

Labour Party

The third party of Labour which is now important and permanent in English politics owes its rise to the activities of trade unions and socialist associations. In 1893 an Independent Labour Party was formed in order to unite the various socialist organisations in the country for common action. Their aim was "the collective ownership and control of the means of production, distribution and exchange." Their political method was that of parliamentary action, that is, representation of the people in the House of Commons "by men in favour of the object of the party and rigidly pledged to its policy." Their immediate programme was eight hour's day, unsectarian education, work for the unemployed, abolition of piece-work, or overtime-work, and of employment of children under fourteen, extinction by taxation of unearned incomes, universal disagreement, women's suffrage, municipal control of the drink, traffic and hospitals and triennial parliaments. The Independent Labour Party and the Trade Unions in the Trade Union Congress of 1899 founded the Labour Representation Committee when there was felt the need of sending more representatives to parliament. A conference of delegates of Trade Unions and Socialist Associations met in 1900 to devise means for securing an increased number of labour members to parliament. The name of the Labour Representation Committee was changed to that of the Labour Party in 1906 when a large number of labour members were returned to parliament. The organisation of labour is known as the federation of trade unions, trade councils, socialist societies and local labour associations. Its object is "to organise and maintain a parliamentary Labour Party with its own whips and policy" and to promote the election of candidates for whose candidature an affiliated society has made itself financially responsible.

24

The Eastern Question

The Turkish empire which had once threatened Europe with subjection began to show signs of dismemberment from the beginning of the 19th century. The decay of this once mighty empire was due mainly to the weakness of the Government. The central authority was weak. The Sultan was at the mercy of his guards. Besides this, the intrigues of the nobles of the court formed a constant source of trouble. Lastly the hold of the Sultan upon the provincial governments was very weak, the Pashas or provincial governors being practically independent.

In the 19th century the Eastern Question entered upon a new phase. Previously the question had reference to the attempts of Russia and Austria to partition Turkey between themselves. Now the question became more complicated. In the 19th century besides the designs of Russia, the question had reference to the revolt of the subject kingdoms of Turkey, many of which inspired by the new idea of nationality sought to throw off the hated Turkish domination. Turkey was threatened from within and without, by Russia and her own subjects, by aggression and disintegration.

The Greek War of Independence

The oppressiveness of the Turkish rule coupled with the spirit of nationality which had been awakened by the uprising of the nations against Napoleon, led the people of the historic land of Greece to rise in revolt to secure their independence. The war began in 1821 and both parties were guilty of savage atrocities. At first the Greeks were left to themselves. The rulers of Europe under the influence of the reactionary policy of Mellernich remained apathetic. They looked upon this movement as revolutionary similar to those in Spain and Naples. In England opinion was divided. The Tory Government distrustful of Russia's designs and fearing to involve England in European entanglements, remained indifferent. But though the Governments did not sympathise with the aspirations of the Greeks for independence, the people of Europe were enthusiastic in their sympathy for the Greek cause and many were the volunteers who joined the Greek ranks to defend the historic land of Hellenic culture. The Greeks maintained a heroic resistance for 5 years but they began to lose ground when the Sultan called to his assistance, Mehmet Ali, the Pasha of Egypt. The Greeks were almost subdued.

From the extremity of their misfortune the Greeks were rescued by foreign intervention. The English minister Canning succeeded in persuading Russia and France to join Great Britain in interposing on behalf of the Greeks by the Treaty of London (1827) it was agreed to demand of Turkey that Greece be made a self-governing state under Turkish suzerainty. As Turkey refused this demand a combined Anglo-French fleet attacked and completely destroyed the Turkish fleet in 1827. This battle practically secured Greek independence. But the English Government considered it an "untoward event" and was opposed to further measures of coercion against Turkey. Consequently Russia Declared war against Turkey, invaded her Danubian provinces and forced her to sign the Treaty of Adrianople (1829). By this the Sultan recognised the independence of Greece and agreed that the provinces of Servia, Moldavia and Wallachia should have Christian governors. A conference of powers at London confirmed this treaty. The crown of Greece was offered to Prince Otto of Bavaria. This agreement temporarily settled the Eastern question.

This successful revolt of Greece was a great blow to the Holy Alliance and was the first victory of liberalism and the principle of nationality since the Congress of Vienna.

In the words of Lord Morley, the Eastern question may be described as a "shifting, intractable and interwoven tangled conflicting interests, rival peoples and antagonistic faiths." The question was a composite one. In part it was the result of the rise of a feeling of nationality among the Balkan peoples, in part it was the problem of the declining Turkish empire and of the divergent interests of the great powers in the Near East. The problem took different shapes at different times but one of its constant factors was the ambition of Russia at the expense of Turkey. What was to take place of Turkey in the event of her disappearance from Europe? The crux of the whole situation lay in the answer to this question.

It is evident, therefore, that powers like Russia, England, Austria, France and even Germany were interested in the Balkans in 19th century. But Germany was aloof from the Balkan complications. Austria was Russia's rival in the Balkans. In 1878 at the Congress of Berlin Bismark posed as an 'honest broker' and administered a check to Russia in order to befriend Russia. So Germany delayed fraternising with Turkey, drilling her army and securing permission for German capitalists to build the Baghdad Railway.

The Greek war of Independence had already opened the channels of Turkish weakness. This weakness was exploited by Mehmet Ali of Egypt and it was his ambition that opened the next episode in the Eastern Question. In the previous time the powers had championed the cause of Greeks by dismembering Turkey but now from self interest they posed championed the integrity of Turkey.

Mehmet Ali of Egypt was rewarded for his ex-services in Greek war the Governorship of Crete. Ambitious as he was he proceeded in 1831 to tear away Syria from suzerain. His soldiers threatened to march upon Constantinople, the Sultan appealed to the powers for help but no response came except from Russia who was ready to help. The Sultan accepted Russian help like a drowning man catching a serpent. But the pouring of Russian troops in Turkey produced reaction in the minds of England, France and Austria who pressurized the Sultan to bury off hostilities by cession of Syria making Russian help unnecessary. But Russia demanded as price of their help and Turkey agreed to give Russian warships free passage through the Straits and to close all other war ships except Russia. So, the Black Sea became a Russian lake. Russia now got the protectorate over Turkey. The Treaty was high watermark of Russian influence in the East. But England in particular was nervous of Russian designs. She was determined to upset the Treaty. Her opportunity came when the Sultan was beaten for the second time in his premature attempts to recover Syria from his Egyptian vassal. At this point the powers intervened. France supported Mehmet Ali to secure her interest in Egypt and Syria and reducing British influence in the Mediterranean. Palmerstone, the British Prime Minister, saw the danger of Britain between Russian and French influence in Turkey. So he wanted to maintain the integrity of Turkey by preventing the isolated interference of any single power. Russia was now placed in a false position. Dreading the designs of Mehmet Ali and France, Russia, drew closer to England, offering to renounce her special position and agreeing to collective intervention. The result was the Convention of London by which Britain, Russia, Austria and Prussia agreed without the knowledge of France to force terms on Mehmet Ali. The successful operation of the allied fleet compelled Mehmet Ali to submit and to accept the Treaty of London (1841). By this Mehmet Ali agreed to be a vassal of the Sultan. The Black Sea was to be closed to all warships of nations to save Turkey from dangerous position. The Treaty of London was a triumph of Palmerstone. It gave a rebuff to France and a check to Russia and made it clear that England would tolerate neither the Russian protectorate over Turkey not the French protectorate over Egypt. It also preserved the integrity of the Ottoman Empire which was threatened with dissolution by the ambition of Mehmet Ali, the success of the previous intervention in Turkish affairs and the extension of Russian influence which resulted from it emboldened Czar Nicholas I to attempt to extend Russian influence still further. This attempt precipitated the reopening of the Eastern Question and led to the Crimean War.

Czar Nicholas I regarded the Sultan of Turkey as the 'Sickman of Europe' and wanted to inherit the Turkish empire before the death of the sick man. Conflict between Greek Christians and Latin Christians as to the protection the holy places at Jerusalem. Russia demanded protection of all Greek Christians resident in the Turkish empire. The Sultan accused Russia as interfering in the domestic affairs of Turkey, led Russia to mobilise her troops. England and France later on Sardinia joined against Russia. In 1856 Russia was defeated and Nicholas having died, his successor Alexander II made the peace of Paris in 1856.

After the Treaty of Paris (1856) Russia had to abandon all claims to a protectorate over the orthodox Christian subjects of Turkey. The Black Sea was neutralised. Russian aggrandisement in the east came to an end. Turkey gained much from this war. Her territorial integrity was guaranteed and she was admitted as a member of the concert of Europe from which she had been excluded. From these points the peace of Paris may be regarded as offering a satisfactory solution of the Eastern question. Russia was checked and the 'sickman' was set on his legs again. But the spirit of 1856, the terms of peace lasted for just 14 years. Russia threw to the winds the provision concerning the neutrality of the Black Sea and in 1878 completely wiped away the Crimean humiliation by recovering Bessarabia. Thus as a solution of the Eastern question the treaty of Paris was a flat failure.

From 1856 to 1878 the after effects of the Paris Peace Conference was felt and there had been a series of glaring infractions of the Treaty of Paris which the powers had to connive at.

The first of these was the union of Wallachia and Moldavia into one kingdom i.e. of Rumania. Both these principalities were inhabited by a people who came from the same stock and spoke the same language and applied to themselves the same term Rumanians. Animated by the prevailing impulse towards national unity the people wanted a union of the two under one national government. By the peace of Paris however the two principalities were to be autonomous but were to remain separate. This separation they challenged in 1859 by each electing the same person Alexander Couza as their Hopsdar or Prince. England, Austria and Turkey opposed this Union as it was a breach of the Treaty of Paris, but Napoleon III showed himself sympathetic to the nationalistic aspirations of Rumanians. In 1861, the powers led to recognize the union as an accomplished fact and the nation of Rumania came into existence.

Secondly, in 1867 Serbia aided by Austria and England secured the evacuation of her fortress by the Turkish garrison. Serbia thus practically became independent of Turkey. Lastly Russia as soon as she had recovered from the blow of the Crimean War, began to interfere in the affairs of the Ottoman empire. Thus in 1865, she encouraged the

Cretan rebellion and in 1870 helped the Bulgars to obtain ecclesiastical independence. In the midst of the Franco-Prussian War Russia was encouraged by Bismark to repudiate the Black Sea clauses of the Treaty of Paris. This she did, and thus recovered the right to fortify Sebastopol and maintain a fleet on the Black Sea. England protested but in vain. Finally in 1871 she decided to make war upon Turkey.

Russo-Turkish War (1877-78)

In 1875, the Eastern question once more entered upon an acute phase. Two things had become clear in the Balkan peninsula. One was the increasing restlessness of the subject states of Turkey, due to their growing nationalist aspirations and race-consciousness. The spectacle of Serbs, Greeks and Kumanians winning their partial or complete freedom inevitably around the other non-Turkish inhabitants of the Balkans to attempt a like movement for freedom. This feeling was specially strong among the different Slav peoples of the Balkans who now began to be conscious of their racial kinship with the Slavs of Russia, Poland and Austrian dominions. This pan-Slavic feeling was encouraged by Russia whose agents carried on an unceasing propaganda among the Balkan Slavs of the South to stir up racial consciousness and national hostility. Nationalism was thus becoming tinged with racialism. The leadership of the South Slav agitation seemed about to be assumed by Serbia who began to dream of uniting under herself all the Serbs, and their close relations, the Croats, in one kingdom.

Besides pan-Slavism and the growth of national feeling, there was another factor in the Balkans which precipitated the crisis. This was the disappointment of all hopes of Turkish revival and reform. The Sultan had not carried out his promised reforms for his Christian subjects. On the contrary, his incompetence and extravagance had imposed upon them a burden which was almost past endurance. As a protest against the rapacity and extortion of his tax collectors the peasants of Bosnia and Herzegovina rose in revolt in 1875. Their fellow Serbs of Montenegro and Serbia sympathised with them in their distress and helped them. The movement threatened to be widespread and so to localise the conflict the powers presented the *Andrassy Note* (of the Austrian Chancellor Count Andrassy) protesting against Turkish misgovernment. The Sultan accepted the protest and promised reforms but the insurgents demanded more substantial guarantee than elusive promises. Meanwhile Bulgaria caught the contagion and so the powers to prevent a general conflagration issued another note the Berlin memorandum calling upon to make concessions and threatened armed intervention in case of default. But as Britain refused to be a party to any measure of coercion against Turkey the Sultan was encouraged to ignore the protest of Europe. As the Bulgarian rising threatened Turkish rule nearer to Constantinople it was put down with horrible cruelty. The atrocities committed by Turkish irregulars thrilled all Europe with horror.

In England, Gladstone thundered against the Turks declaring that they should be cleared out 'bag and baggage from the province they have desolated and profaned'. But it was Disraeli, the Jew and not Gladstone, the ardent Christian who was then the Prime Minister and Disraeli's concern was more for what Russia might do in the Balkans than for the oppressed Christians of Bulgaria. As Disraeli's attitude made joint action impossible Russia resolved upon independent action and declared war against Turkey in 1871. She could not ignore the sufferings of her co-religionists and fellow Slavs.

The Sultan of Turkey was defeated by Russia and agreed to conclude the treaty of San Stefano with Russia. This treaty practically declared the dissolution of the Turkish empire. Several States were declared independent of Turkey while in others Russian influence preponderated.

The extension of Russian influence in the Balkan States was prejudicial to England's interest and so she demanded a revision of the treaty of San Stefano by a Congress of European powers. Austria joined hands with England in asking Russia to submit the Eastern question to the collective decision of the powers for the question affected them all. The war-like attitude of England at last forced Russia to agree to refer the settlement of the Turkish question to a Congress of European powers.

The Congress met in Berlin in 1878 under Bismark's presidency. It grew up the treaty of Berlin by which the following arrangements were made: 1. Montenegro, Serbia and Rumania were declared independent. 2. Bulgaria was divided into two parts, one part was made a self-governing principality subject to the payment of an annual tribute to the Sultan, while the other part (southern part) was constituted as the province of East Roumelia with an independent administration under Christian governor but under Turkish suzerainty. 3. Austria was allowed to 'occupy' and administer Bosnia and Herzegovina which nominally remained dependent on Turkey. 4. Russia received Bessarabia and a number of territories in Asia Minor, England, by a separate treaty with Turkey secured the control of Cyprus.

If the treaty of Paris had guaranteed the territorial integrity of the Ottoman empire, the treaty of Berlin decreed its dismemberment. The diplomats of Berlin revised the treaty of San Stefano, not in justice and equity rather than to secure the interests of Austria and Britain. They did not see to the interest of Balkan people but they sought to harmonise the conflicting interests of England, Austria and Russia by a policy of balance and compromise. Austria was allowed to occupy Bosnia and Herzegovina and England Cyprus. The principle was based upon selfish principles at the cost of the national sentiment of the Balkan people. The Serbs were detached from their own people of Bosnia and Herzegovina.

Russia could not be checked in her expansionist policy in the Balkans by the Berlin Congress of 1878 as she could get Bessarabia and the Black Sea was open to her for her war vessels. The Russian menace to British interests was transferred to Asia from Europe but not removed. So the treaty had no effect of weakening Russia and strengthening Turkey.

The Berlin Congress lacked farsightedness. Though Bismark posed as an 'honest brother' was obliged to take sides between Austria and Rissia and alienated Russia. The bad feeling and rivalry which this state of affairs engendered eventually led to the Great War of 1914. The Macedonian problem led to the Balkan War of 1912-13.

The following are the developments of the Eastern question after the treaty of Berlin.

1. Bulgaria was the first state to challenge the Berlin settlement. The separation between Bulgaria and Eastern Rumalia effected it. The Congress was an arbitrary and artificial one as it corresponded no racial divisions. It was due because the powers feared that a big Bulgaria brought into existence by Russia would be a mere tool in the hands of the latter. But racial kinship is stronger than Treaties and people of Eastern Romelia effected in 1885 a bloodless revolution and proclaimed their political union with their kinsmen of Bulgaria. The Bulgarian King, Prince Alexander Battenburg, responded to their call and declared himself prince of the united Bulgaria. The Sultan protested against this violation of the Treaty of Berlin, the Czar in anger recalled his officers from the Bulgarian army, but the British Government approved the union which was then accepted as an accomplished fact by the powers.

The only state to actively oppose this union was Serbia who out of jealousy declared that the Bulgarian aggrandisement threatened the balance of power in the Balkans and went to war with Bulgaria. In the war that ensued Serbia was badly beaten by the

Bulgarians who were however stopped in the midst of their victorious career by Austria who forced a treaty on the combatants on the basis of status quo.

2. The Armenian subjects of the Turks were exposed to periodical outrages throughout the 19th century. Armenia was England's protegé and in the Treaty of Berlin as well as in the Cyprus Convention between Turkey and England, the latter had extracted from the Sultan promises of better treatment of the Armenians. But the contrary happened. The Armenians were badly treated. The Turks feared that England like Russia would set up another independent Bulgaria in Armenia and so were resolved upon exterminating the Armenians. Throughout 1894 and 1895 the massacre of the Armenians went on amidst scenes of indescribable horror. In 1896 the scene of carnage was transferred to Constantinople itself where 6000 Armenians were killed in a single day. These were inspired by the Turkish Government. In response the great powers had the following feelings: Russia would not stir because she did not like to set up another ungrateful Bulgaria in Armenia and because she wanted to have her revenge on England who had thwarted her in Bulgaria. Disraeli had cared little for the Bulgarian atrocities and so Russia now cared less for the Armenian massacre. Germany now fishing for Turkey's friendship and so instead of putting pressure on the Sultan displayed his good intentions towards him. Austria followed suit, England left alone, protested and threatened in vain. She realised her mistake in having hitherto supported Turkey in making herself responsible for the good conduct of the Sultan. Hence Lord Salisbury remarked that in trying to uphold the integrity of the Ottoman empire England had hitherto 'put her money on the wrong horse.'

3. *Greeco-Turkish War (1897)*: Greece had high hopes of obtaining a rectification of her frontier at the Congress of Berlin. But as nothing was done in the direction the Greeks threatened war with Turkey. The powers held her back as they were not inclined to tolerate another Balkan war. But in 1881, the Sultan was persuaded by the British Government to cede Thessaly and a portion of Epirus to Greece.

The acquisitions of the island of Crete next engaged the attention of the Greeks. The island was inhabited mostly by the people of the Greek race, who wanted to throw off Turkish sovereignty and to unite themselves with Greece. Agitation for union grew stronger and insurrections against Turkish rule became chronic in the island. But nothing came to these except empty promises of reform from Turkish Government. In 1896, the flame of rebellion flared up worse than ever and the revolutionaries in Crete headed by Venizetos, proclaimed their union with Greece. This time Greece yielded to the popular enthusiasm sent an expedition to help the Cretan insurgents. Thereupon Turkey declared war upon Greece, easily defeated her and compelled her to abandon the project of annexing Crete and to cede a portion of Thessaly. After long negotiations among powers it was decided that Crete should be an autonomous state under Turkish suzerainty. The island was placed under an International Commission of four powers with prince George, a son of the King of Greece as Governor. This arrangement did not satisfy the Cretans who made several attempts at union with Greece but were held in check by the powers. It was not until the Balkan War of 1912 in which Turkey was smitten hip and thigh that they permitted the union of Crete with Greece in 1913.

4. *The Young Turk Movement*: The Eastern question entered upon a new and startling phase in 1908. The Young Turks, a revolutionary constitutional party, effected a bloodless revolution and forced the Sultan. Abdul Hamid II to grant a constitution.

The prospect of Turkey rejuvenated and reformed made European states uneasy and there followed a series of infractions of the Treaty of Berlin. Austria annexed Bosnia and Herzegovina—provinces which under the Treaty of Berlin she was authorised only to "occupy" and administer. Bulgaria declared her complete independence of Turkey. The Treaty of Berlin was openly floated and the violent infractions of the treaty produced nothing but ineffective protests from England, France and Russia. But the state most aggrieved by these occurrences was Serbia. Bosnia and Herzegovina were mostly inhabited by the people of Serbian race and the Serbians had long entertained the ambition of annexing them. The annexation of these provinces by Austria not only dashed their hopes to the ground but also prevented their expansion to the sea. So the action of Austria made the Serbians highly indignant, a situation which gave rise to future trouble.

Policy of the Young Turks

Though professing constitutional principles the Young Turks disappointed popular expectations. Their policy was on of 'Turkification' i.e. they sought to maintain uncontrolled domination of the Turks over the various peoples of their composite empire. The subject races were cruelly persecuted like in Macedonia and Albania. This produced widespread dissatisfaction which brought Turkey to the point of extinction. Italy declared war against Turkey in 1911.

But in 1912 four Balkan states, viz. Montenegro, Serbia, Bulgaria and Greece declared war against Turkey as a protest against the cruel persecution of the Christians of Macedonia in which large number of their countrymen had lost their lives. They desired to liberate Macedonia from the hated Turkish rule. The Turks were defeated and within six months, Ottoman empire was reduced to Constantinople. At this point the powers intervened and by the Treaty of London in 1913, Turkey was allowed to retain Constantinople with some territories to hold it safe.

By the treaty of London 1913, the new state of Albania to the south-west of Serbia was created. This rendered Serbia completely land-locked country. This was what Austria needed Serbia to be to prevent Serbia from having access to the Adriatic Sea. The Serbian feeling was highly inflamed against Austria but the Serbians could not do anything. They sought compensation elsewhere in Macedonia. They were opposed by the Bulgarians who treacherously attacked Serbia and Greece. The action of Bulgaria roused the other Balkan states against her. Turkey joined the allies to recover some territories recently lost. The Bulgarians were defeated and submitted to the treaty of Bucharest (1913) by which they lost considerable territory.

Thus it is clear that these prolonged Balkan wars from 1908 to the treaty of Bucharest (1913) were prelude to the Great War of 1914.

25

Italian Unification

The making of the new Italy was to some extent a popular movement and in that sense we may speak of the "Italian revolution", but the problem of leadership was all-important as we shall see, writes T.W. Ricker.

In the leisure of St. Helena, Napoleon wrote, concerning Italy: "Italy is surrounded by the Alps and the sea. Her natural limits are defined with as much exactitude as if she were an island. Italy is only united to the continent by one hundred and fifty leagues of frontier and these one hundred and fifty leagues are fortified by the highest barrier that can be opposed to man. Italy, isolated between her natural limits, is destined to form a great and powerful nation. Italy is one nation; unity of language, customs and literature, must within a period more or less distant, unite her inhabitants under one sole government. And Rome will, without the slightest doubt, be chosen by the Italians as their capital." (C.D. Hazen)

No movement in the 19th century of European history was so much blessed with patriotic leadership as the movement of Italian unity. Cavour, Mazzini and Garibaldi are names to conjure with. Cavour was the brain, Mazzini was the pen and Garibaldi was the sword of the Italian unification movement. "Italy was the first to erect a national state and Italian patriotism during the era was closely associated with Liberalism." (C.J.H. Hayes) Prof. C.D.M. Keetleby observes that, "No cause was more blessed in leaders of devoted patriotism and of excellent though dissimilar parts than that of Italian Risorgimento. But Mazzini, its fervent though unpractical apostle, and Garibaldi, its soldier and knight-errant, might have been martyrs of a barren hope without Cavour, the real "creator of Italian unity."

For centuries Italy, in the phrase of Metternich, was nothing more than a geographical expression. One attempt after another to weld the peninsula into a United kingdom had failed. With the expedition of Charles VIII, across the Alps, Italy now became the cockpit of Europe, where foreign powers contended for mastery.

In the nineteenth century more than one obstacle impeded the path of Italian unity. The most important was the fact that Italy lay under the heel of foreign domination. Austria was entrenched in the north; her Satellites—princes of Austrian birth—ruled in Tuscany, Modena and Parma; while in the south a bourbon dynasty governed the two Sicilies (Naples and Sicily). From the Mediterranean towns and Western Europe had left the Italian people a prey to slow decay. Prof. Riker writes, "In truth there was no Italian people, but only various groups, under several governments, speaking a variation of the same tongue, and only a few intellectuals looked back to a happier past." A new epoch began when Italy was drawn into the vortex of Napoleonic conquest. The effects of French rule were evanescent or transcient: "Throughout Italy one stroke of pen erased all our Liberties, all our reforms, all our hopes. The old regime reappeared, pernicious as before but surcharged with vengeance. Yet the lesson that Italy was a nation, once learnt was never forgotten." At the Vienna Congress national aspirations were ignored and Italy was treated merely as a pawn in the diplomatic game. Metternich confessed that "general dissatisfaction was prevalent." "In Italy", he wrote, "provinces are against provinces, towns against towns, families against families and—men against men." The restoration of 1815 were followed by reactionary or demoralising administration. The government of Modena was extremely tyrannical. In Lombardy and Venetia Austria always followed the policy to "Austrianise" the political life of the people. The Italian patriots and liberals inspired the people to rise against the oppressive and tyrannical rule of their rulers." But confronted with arbitrary and suspicious governments debarred from freedom of political discussion, jealousy and rigorously controlled in all their movements, Italian patriots could only find an outlet for their energies in secret societies or sets which now everywhere sprang up, but were particularly formidable in Naples." Thus, secret societies began to spread over Italy and the most important was the Carbonari which aimed for the achievement of constitutional freedom." "We Italians", cried Mazzini, "have neither parliament, nor hustings, nor liberty of the press, nor liberty of speech, nor possibility of lawful public assemblage, nor a single means of expressing the opinion stirring within us." Italy did not escape the effects of the French Revolution of 1830, which was the cause of outbreaks in Modena, Parma and Papal states. The price of Austrian protection was the Austrian tutelage. Hence to extirpate the grinding oppression of arbitrary and capricious despots, and to reap the golden harvest of a freer life, the first and indispensable step was to drive the foreigner from the soil.

Unity of aim is not incompatible with diversity of opinion as to how the aim shall be accomplished. A common liberalism likewise characterised the foremost Italian champions of political union, though at first these were divided into three factions on the question of national union.

Mazzini's (1805-1872) Republicanism

One faction, radically liberal was republican. "The republicans were followers of Giuseppe Mazzini, the prophet of Italian movement." (E. Lipson), the chief exponent of republicanism was a native of Genoa and son of an university Professor.

As a young man he joined the revolutionary society of the Carbonari and was jailed and exiled for participating in one of its riots. In 1831 he promoted a non-secret organisation "Young Italy", which composed of intellectual under forty years of age, should conduct an incessant campaign among the classes of Italians for the purpose of instilling in them the duty of liberating their country and unifying it under a popular "Roman republic." At least, 50,000 young men were enrolled in Mazzini's 'Young Italy", and though its republicanism proved ineffectual, the patriotic and liberal idea in back of it became a major factor in Italian developments from 1831 to 1870. It is the peculiar merit of Mazzini that more than any other man, he grasped the vision of a United Italy and set himself with all the ardour of one who preaches a new religion to make his countrymen share in that vision. "Italy", he wrote, "wills to be a nation". His task was to educate the Italian nation to realise that it was a nation, and not a geographical expression. His propaganda broadened the political horizon of Italians and created a vigorous public opinion in favour of national independence, hence amongst the makers of modern Italy he holds an imperishable place.

But while Mazzini gave to the Italian world the ideal of united Italy it was reserved for other men to translate his ideal from theory into fact.

The most celebrated disciple of Mazzini was Joseph Garibaldi (1807-1882), a native of Nice, who as a sailor in the royal Sardinian navy was attracted to "Young Italy"—its nationalism and republicanism, and especially its incentive to heroic feats in which by temperament he revelled. Condemned to death for participating in a mutiny on his warship, he escaped and fled to South America, where he got enlisted in an "Italian Legion" and for 14 years fought valiantly in revolutionary wars on that continent.

The Federalists

A second faction seeking to reconcile traditional conservative religion with Modern Liberalism, was led by Vincent Gioberti (1801-52), a piedmontese priest, who like Garibaldi's Mazzini, lived many years in exile, but, unlike them was never a republican. His chief book, "The Moral and Civil Primacy of the Italians" (1843), urged a confederation of existing Italian states, each provided with a Liberal constitution, and all presided over by the Pope. A considerable number of upper middle class persons, including patriotic members of the catholic clergy, shared Gioberti's dream, and for a brief time Pope Pious IX appeared to sympathise with it. Prof. Grant and Temperly write, "Free and united Italy was born of the Kingdom of Sardinia."

The third faction, and the one which eventually predominated was that of Liberal royalists, those who looked for leadership to the kingdom of Sardinia. The personalities in the Sardinian government of the 1850s made significant contributions to the royalist cause. One was the honest king Victor Emmanuel II who succeeded his father Charles Albert on 1849. The other was Count Camilo di Cavour (1810-1861). "Count Camilo di Cavour was a noble man, who like his contemporary, Bismarck had also a practical business head." (Riker) Born in the very year 1810 in which Metternich became chancellor of Austria and belonging to a noble piedmontese family, Cavour was to become a greater, at least a more permanently successful diplomat than Metternich and to acquire fame as the foremost Liberal nation builder of the nineteenth century.

Cavour's first thought was to make Sardinia worthy, both materially and morally for the cause she had before her. The material problem was that of making her strong enough to hazard another war. Under his imporation as finance minister Sardinia promoted the Industrial revolution. Cavour came to the head of the government in 1852, and with one short interval of few months enjoyed a tenure of power which lasted eight years. His achievements in the domestic sphere merit some notice, for they not only served to rally round the Minister the important body of Liberal opinion, but they laid the foundations of an organised and consolidated state—the necessary prelude to an efficient foreign policy. Prof. Kettleby writes, "a keen constitutionalist of an English type—his enemies called him sarcastically "Milord Cavour"—he set himself to maintain and develop parliamentary government in Piedmont; he built railways, promoted trade and expanded commerce, stabilised finance, reorganised the army, abolished antiquated inequalities and reduced the clerical power". One of their first measures had been the dissolution of the monasteries. He had made himself known as a Liberal in the sense in which the word was then used, and his liberalism was genuine; but it was the cause of Italian nationalism that claimed all his devotion. His goal was the same as Mazzini's the same as that of most great Italians for a long time past, Italy free and united. He did not believe that Italy could win her goal single handed or by enthusiasm alone. He looked round for allies and employed all the methods of a skilful and unscrupulous diplomacy. Cavour's whole policy was dominated by an inflexible ambition to effect the emancipation of Italy from Austria and her union under the House of Savoy. Mazzini did not believe in Cavour's honesty. He called him "the ministerial liberator who taught his master how to prevent the union of Italy. He had dreamed of a new earth but Cavour only gave a rearrangement of the old one.

Cavour's first step was taken when he intervened in 1853 on behalf of the political refugees from Lombardy and Venetia, whose property had been sequestrated by the Austrian government. The intervention failed in its, immediate object, but it was approved by England and France and revealed Piedmont as the champion of the oppressed Italians. "He was well known in both Paris and London." The real turning point came in 1855 with the momentous decision of Cavour to participate in the Crimean War, a decision which enhanced the prestige of the Sardinian monarchy and gave it a claim upon the gratitude of its allies. At the same time it completed the isolation of Austria, which lost the friendship of Russia by her ingratitude and estranged the western powers by her vacillation. At the Congress of Paris (1856) Cavour denounced the evils of Austrian oppression in Italy, and his disclosures shamed Austria into moderating the harshness of her rule. Daniele Manin, the eminent patriot, voiced the general sentiment when he declared: "We do not want Austria to mend her ways in Italy; we want her to go".

Napoleon III and Italy

The Italian war for liberation began in April 1859, and lasted less than three months. The French emperor Napoleon III was sympathetic towards the cause of the Italians. During his early career he was a member of the revolutionary society. He had also his imperialistic designs in the Italian cause. Above all, he found in the Italian question an opportunity to discredit the Vienna settlement of 1815 which stood as a symbol of humiliation on the part of France. Moreover according to E. Lipson "He was the inheritor of the Napoleonic traditions". As early as 1855 he had given an inkling of his intentions by his famous question to Cavour " What can be done for Italy?" In July 1858 Napoleon III invited Cavour to meet him at, Plombiers. According to the terms of the pact of Plombiers Napoleon III promised to help Sardinia-Piedmont in expelling Austria from Italy. Northern and central Italy were to be united under the House of Savoy and Nice as the price of his help. Napoleon III urged for the marriage of his cousin Prince Jerome Bonaparte and daughter of Victor Emmanuel II.

True to his word Napoleon sent an army into Italy (April 19, 1859), and together the French and Sardinian forces defeated the Austrians at Magenta and Solfernio and drove them out of Lombardy. The effect on the Italians was electrical. Once more the people of Modena, Parma, Tuscany and Romagna revolted against their rulers; and central Italy was prepared to profit by the war and join Sardinia. Tuscany once hesitant member of the group, had been brought into line by a patriot, hardly less staunch than Cavour—the Tuscan statesman Ricasoli. The Italian revolution had more than commenced; it was rapidly spreading. And then to the consternation of all patriots. Napoleon abandoned the war and concluded a separate peace i.e. the truce of Villafranca with the Austrian emperor.

The reasons for Napoleon's action were various. He had wanted an enlarged Sardinia as a convenient buffer state against Austria, one that would be small enough, however to remain a satellite of France. The terms of the truce of Villafranca were notified by the treaty of Zurich. The state of Sardinia Piedmont acquired Lombardy and this was the first step towards the unification of Italy.

Popular Revolt in Central Italy

During the Austro-Sardinian war the National Society had fomented rebellion in central Italy. The motto of this society was unity, independence and Victor Emmanuel. The expulsion of Austria from Lombardy was followed by popular insurrections in Parma,

Modena and Tuscany. In these states the rulers were driven out from their dominions. The people demanded their annexation with the state of Sardinia Piedmont. Cavour resigned office and his work seemed hopelessly compromised, but again he returned to office in January 1860, satisfied that central Italy was worth the price. He persuaded Victor Emmanuel to assent to the cession of Savoy and Nice. But the progress of the above movements mainly depended upon the attitude of the foreign powers. Palmerstone and Russek, the Whig ministers of England supported the popular movements in these Italian states. Cavour reopened the offer of Nice and Savoy to France and secured the support of Napoleon III for annexation of central states to Sardinia. After popular voting the central Italian states like Parma, Modena, Tuscany and Romagna were incorporated into Sardinia Piedmont.

Cavour had said, "they have stopped me from making Italy by diplomacy from the north; I will make it by revolution from the south. Garibaldi (1807-1882), the warrior, was to share with Cavour the diplomat, the chief honour in the making of Italy. The Sicilians rose in revolt against the despotism of their King Francis II of Naples. The eyes of the Italian world were now fixed upon Sicily where an astonishing panorama was unfolding itself before their gaze. In some respects the "Garibaldian epic" was most striking, as it certainly was the most dramatic episode of the Italian movement. The Sicilians appealed to Garibaldi, the man of sword was born at Nice. He was a member of "Young Italy" and had taken part in the unsuccessful insurrection organised by Mazzini in 1834. At the head of his 'Thousand' he landed at Marshala on May 11, 1860 and defeated the Neapolitan troops. He conquered Sicily and assumed the position of a dictator in the name of Victor Emmanuel II (August 1860), Garibaldi was on the point of marching towards Rome. But Rome was the seat of the Pope and was occupied by a French garrison. The invasion of Rome meant an open war with France which may endanger the cause of the Italians. At this critical juncture, Cavour declared that, "Italy must be saved from foreigners, evil principles and mad men." Cavour sent the King Victor Emmanuel II to check the march of Garibaldi against Rome. Victor Emmanuel II defeated the Papal army and occupied the two Papal states namely Umbria and Marches. Garibaldi was checked and surrendered all the newly conquered territories to King Emmanuel II. After plebiscites Naples and Sicily were annexed with Sardinia Piedmont (Sept. 1860). Victor Emmanuel II was proclaimed as the King of United Italy on 7th March 1861 and in the same year the first Italian parliament met at Turin. With the exception of Rome and Venetia the rest of Italy were annexed to the Sardinia-Piedmont.

On June 6, 1861, Cavour died at the age of fifty-one, worn out by his long exertions, "We have made Italy", he murmured in his last moments. It was an extraordinary achievement, in which Cavour himself had been the leading personal factor and to a large extent the brain that made it possible. "A people", as one observer expressed it, "who had seemed dead, had arisen to new and vigorous life, breaking the spell which bound it and showing itself worthy of a new and splendid destiny. Venice was acquired as a result of the seven weeks war, in 1866, when the outbreak of the Austro-Prussian war furnished Italy with an opportunity to strike a blow at her traditional enemy. Rome came into Italian possession in 1870, when the Franco-Prussian war compelled the retirement of the French garrison. This completion of his life work Cavour did not live to see. But he lived long enough to create Italy of the Italians, and to earn the undying gratitude of the Italian people.

26

Italy Since 1919

The Great war of 1914-1918 had dramatic effects on the Italian economy. It was a 'war of exhaustion', which would be won by the side with the most men, arms and resources.

But the costs were real none the less, and had to be paid later. One calculation is that the State spent about 41 billion lire, at pre-war prices, on military supplies, pensions, food subsidies, etc. The State budget went heavily into deficit: from 2.9 billion lire in 1914-15 to 23.3 billion lire in 1918-19. Governments could only pay for the war by borrowing, and so the National Debt rose five-fold from 15.7 billion lire in June 1914 to 84.9 billion lire in June 1919, including war debts of over 15 billion lire to Britain and 8.5 billion lire to the USA. There were almost six times as many bank notes in circulation in June 1919 as five years previously. Inflation was the inevitable result, or cause. The wholesale price index rose from 100 in 1913 to 412.9 in 1918, and even this probably understated the real position.

There were other disadvantages to the 'industrial mobilisation' system and to the 'war economy'. Only a few regions enjoyed a war boom. Most of the arms firms were in the 'industrial triangle' of Piedmont, Liguria and Lombardy. The war worsened the already grave regional imbalance, especially as Southern savings in government stock were used to finance Northern industrial investment.

There was, therefore, much discontent among the Northern workers. Most soldiers of whom had opposed the war from the outset. They knew their employers were making huge profits, and they knew many shopkeepers were selling only on the black market. By May 1917 the chief of police recognised that the workers of Turin were 'in a state of compressed effervescence'. Their unrest could probably be contained by firm discipline and regular pay rises, but only if food supplies were readily available. In August bread shortages in Turin caused major rioting. Barricades were built, and troops had to be rushed in. About fifty people were killed before order was restored. The riots showed how morale in the cities had fallen to dangerously low levels, and they shocked politicians and generals alike. Economic grievances and class antagonism remained acute in the Northern cities in 1918.

The Great War also had sudden and dramatic effects in the countryside. Over $2\frac{1}{2}$ million peasants and labourers were taken into the army, leaving only the older men, women and adolescents to till the fields. In some areas women had always done farm work while the men went off to foreign building sites, so the position was not much different from usual. But in other regions - e.g. Latium, Apulia, Sardinia—a woman's place was in the home, and families suffered accordingly.

Ambiguity also prevailed within the political movements—the Catholics, Socialists and Nationalists. Catholic attitudes to the war ranged from nationalism to pacifism with pro-war feeling more common in the South. Most bishops thought the war was a divine punishment, to be borne as patiently as possible, i.e. they thought the same as most soldiers. The faithful were urged to do their duty, but there was not much enthusiasm.

The Catholics took part in the war effort, but they kept their distance. They took a longer view. When the war was unpopular, they appeared as 'neutralists', seeking to mitigate disaster; when men rallied to the flag, the Catholics rallied too.

There was, on the face of it, less ambiguity about the Socialists' attitude to the war. They were opposed to it. Militarism was widely detested; and skilled industrial workers, natural Socialist supporters, had no contact with the troops of their experiences. As the war went on, many Socialists inevitably became involved. Socialist local councils organised rationing and welfare payments; Socialist Co-operatives helped to keep down the cost of living and to prevent profiteering.

Thus many Socialists leaders and institutions did little to oppose the war, and much to support it. However, there were exception. The party's formal leadership, the Directorate, remained in the hands of the party's 'revolutionary', 'intransigent', 'maximalist' wing; and the Directorate appointed the editor of the party's newspaper, *Avanti*. So Socialist propaganda, under *Avanti's* new editor Serrati, remained firmly anti-war. The paper was much censored, but in October 1915 it managed to publish the resolutions of the international anti-war conference at Zimmerwald.

The Nationalists, of course, had no doubts about the virtues of war, although they too were divided about war aims. They took part in the 'Congress of Oppressed Nationalities in 1918.

The war left other major legacies. They included a thirst for justice ('land for the peasants') and a transformed industrial economy. The very bases of the Liberal State were being questioned. The government was dominated by Nitti, who welcomed State intervention in economic and social affairs and encouraged demands for a 'broader democracy'. The war also produced tens of thousands of new officers, drunk with patriotism and greedy to command. They had won the war, and did not intend to let anyone forget it. The Great War, like the Resistance of 1943-45, provided a whole generation with patriotic credentials and a claim to reward. But perhaps the greatest legacy of the war was psychological, or medical. It left men utterly exhausted. The overwhelming impression given by the letters and diaries of this period is of strain, of not being able to cope any more. Perhaps that was why almost as many Italians died from influenza in 1918-19 as were killed in the whole war. This was the people that had to deal with Italy's post-war crisis.

One major reason for the strange death of Liberal Italy was that her statesmen lost at diplomacy, just when the game mattered most. Italy had won the war but it was bungled at the peace. Orlando and Sonnino went to the Versailles peace conference in 1919, demanding the full terms of the 1915 Treaty of London, i.e. Trent, Trieste, the South Tyrol to the Brenner, Istria and Northern Dalmaria. Most of these demands were granted, even though they ran counter to the 'principle of nationality' dear to the American President, Woodrow Wilson. But Wilson drew the line at Dalmaria, and the atmosphere was not improved when the Italians asked for Fiume (Rijeka), the former Hungarian port on the Croatian coast. Fiume had not been mentioned in 1915.

The Fiume question revealed again the differences among Italian politicians about Italian war aims. Did Italy want the Treaty—a good old-fashioned document of secret *Realpolitik* giving her control of the Adriatic—or did she want to embrace the new 'democratic' ideals and claim Fiume on national grounds. The answer, it seemed, was that she could not make up her mind.

The result was a disastrous rebuff. President Wilson refused to 'concede' either Fiume of Dalmaria to Italy, and published his arguments in a leading Paris newspaper. Sonnino and Orlando, affronted, went back home and were greeted as popular heroes.

Conversely, Wilson became the arch-villain—a great change from the virtual adulation he had received in Italy a few months previously. The collapse of 'Wilsonism' had very important consequences for Italian politics: it destroyed the credibility of the 'democratic interventionist' as well as of the Allies. Two months later the Orlando government fell. Italy had acquired Trent and Trieste, and the Italian army occupied Istria and Northern Dalmaria *de facto*, but her Allies had failed her over Fiume—and also over the ex-German colonial territories in Africa, which the British and French carefully kept out of Italian hands. It seemed, in D'Annunzio's phrase, a 'mutilated victory'. 'Interventionists', Nationalists and even many ordinary Italians, greatly resented the sanctimoniousness of the Americans, the selfishness of the British and the French, and the feebleness of their own government - especially when in June 1919, Francesco Severio Nitti became Prime Minister.

Nitti was an economist. Like most devotees of the Dismal Science, he overrated both its importance and its dismalness. Nitti issued an amnesty to the wartime deserters, which affronted all right-minded patriots. He also cut down military spending, and this infuriated all the Right, especially the many new army officers. Soon the loyalty of some army units was dubious. Throughout the country a host of 'interventionist' groups railed against the 'renouncing' government.

In September D'Annunzio agreed to lead a military coup organized by prominent Nationalists, top army officers and one or two industrialists. He marched into Fiume with 2,000 'legionaries', mainly deserters or mutineers from the army. The '*Commandante*' remained there for fifteen months, hurling defiance at '*Cagoia*' and at Nitti's successor Giolitti. Fiume became a symbol of patriotic fervour and youthful vitality. Futurists, ex-servicemen, Nationalists, syndicalists, anarchists and adventurers flocked there from all over Italy. Long rhetorical speeches from balconies to the eager crowds below, punctuated by massive acclamations.

Initially there was not much that Italian governments could do. Nitti could not expel D'Annunzio by force, for the 'invasion' was very popular in Italy. Giolitti, who succeeded Nitti as Prime Minister in mid-1920, was more effective. He began negotiating directly with the Yugoslavs, an in November 1920 the two countries reached agreement. The Treaty of Rapallo declared that Fiume was to be independent. Italy kept Trieste and Istria. In Dalmatia, Zara and four islands were to go to Italy, but the rest was to be Yugoslav. This treaty was generally welcomed in Italy. On Christmas Day 1920 Giolitti took the final step, and sent the navy in. D'Annunzio surrendered almost immediately. The '*Commandante's*' regime was no more.

Yet Fiume was an important episode, or rather an important symbol. D'Annunzio had held the city, in defiance of Italian governments and international opinion, for over a year. He had proved that the Italian state was weak, and that the Armed Forces might prove disloyal. He had also pioneered a new style of 'mass politics', adopted by later demagogues in Italy and elsewhere. The plight of Fiume and Dalmatia provided slogans for all kinds of super-militant patriotic groups; it kept the spirit of 'interventionism' alive throughout the post-war years.

Economic Problems

Another major reason why the Liberal regime collapsed was its failure to cope with the transition to a peace time economy. The problems were, indeed, intractable. The Nationalists, and some wartime 'technocrats', argued that there should be no transition at all. Some industrialists, especially those in heavy industry, electricity and shipbuilding, agreed; it was their only chance of survival in the post-war world. They could never sell all their guns, aeroplanes and ships on the open market; nor could they easily sell them to peaceful governments anxious to cut public spending.

In the meantime Italy suffered all the ills of hasty adjustment. As millions of men left the army, unemployment reached a peak of 2 million in November 1919; as industrialists 'reconverted' their plant to peacetime production, share prices halved. Above all, there was inflation. The wholesale price index (1913 =100) rose from 412.9 in 1918 to 590.7 in 1920. The lira fell from 30 to the pound sterling in March 1919 to 50 in December of that year, and to 100 in December 1920. This post-war inflation was almost as bad as in the war itself. It wiped out the middle-class, savings, crippled the huge rentier class, and drastically reduced the wages and pensions of State employees. And civil servants had suffered enough already—senior administrative salaries in 1918 were less than half what they had been in 1914, in real terms.

These dark economic prospects were worsened by intense labour militancy. For $3\frac{1}{2}$ years severe factory discipline had been enforced on recalcitrant workers. Suddenly a new era dawned. Socialist and anarchist leaders came out of prison or exile. Socialist trade unionists began organizing again; although—or perhaps because—most of them were 'reformists', they needed to prove their virility. Much of the militancy was defensive, for inflation hit workers' income as much as anyone else's. But much was not defensive at all. Many workers were convinced that revolution was imminent, 'as in Russia', and at least some of the agitations were designed to 'prepare' or help carry out the revolutionary task. Strikes, lockouts, riots, factory occupations and gang welfare became commonplace. Over 1 million people went on strike in 1919, and more again in 1920. Membership of the Socialist Unions in the General Confederation of Labour rose from 250,000 in 1918 to 2 million by the late 1920's; the recently founded Catholic confederation claimed 1.2 million, mainly in textiles and agriculture; and the anarcho-syndicalists of the Italian Syndical Union claimed 300,000 members in September 1919, with much support in the steelworks and shipyards of Liguria. Industrialists nervously bought of trouble whenever they could, and governments seemed helpless.

Food riots broke out spontaneously in Central and Northern Italy in June 1919, provoked mainly by a sudden sharp increase in prices. The rioting was 'revolutionary' in the old-fashioned style: granaries were plundered, shops were looted, trees of liberty were planted, little local republics were set up. When riots or strikes broke out, government sought to compromise, to settle, to 'absorb' or buy off popular discontent. The policy worked, in the short run; but it fatally antagonized the middle classes. They complained it was not just the workers they had to contend with, but also the government.

The most famous example of labour militancy was the 'occupation of the factories' in September 1920. It started as part of a normal wage dispute in the engineering industry. The unions feared an employers' lockout, and occupying the factories seemed the logical way to prevent one. In addition, the anarchists and syndicalists had long advocated 'direct action' of this kind as a prelude to revolution. So over 400,000 workers took over their factories or shipyards, expelled the managers, ran up the Red (or Black) Flag.

In the late 1920 an economic recession hit Italy, and deepened the industrialists' gloom.

Political Breakdown

All these problems were serious, but not insuperable. Liberal Italy might have weathered the storm, given time and a stable political framework. But post-war Italy did not have a stable political framework. It had been precarious enough in 1913, but by 1919 it was weaker still. The old ruling class had been bitterly divided by the war: 'interventionists' against neutralists, Salandrians against Giolittians. The 'democratic interventionists' - Republicans, reformists Socialists, pro-war syndicalists - were also divided among themselves, and in any case were discredited by President Wilson at Versailles. The Nationalists, proud of their victorious war, trumpeted that a stronger State and a warlike economy were necessary. Indeed, in early 1919 there was much agitation, especially by the 'democratic interventionists', for a Constituent Assembly' to draft a new Constitution and push through thorough-going political and social reforms.

The two major groups of 'outsiders' were also more troublesome than ever. The Catholics, building on their wartime efforts, founded their own political party. The Popular party (*Partito Populare Italiano*, PPI) was an uneasy fusion of Right, Centre and Left-wing Catholics, supported mainly by the small peasant proprietors and tenants of Northern and North-Central Italy, and anxious to win over the Southern peasantry too.

The Socialists were, apparently, even more threatening. However, the Socialists' revolutionary slogans were purely verbal. They had no idea how to lead a revolution, and by the late summer of 1919 they were totally absorbed in election campaigning.

The Rise of Fascism

This complex crisis clearly offered immense scope for paranoid patriots. Continuing the hysterical traditions of 1917-18, they founded various movements—the '*Fasci* of Resistance', the 'Italian *Fasci* of National Defense', the 'Association of Italian Volunteers' and so forth; the term 'Fascio' (which literally meant 'bundle', and came to mean 'group') was deliberately reminiscent of the '*Fasci* of National Defense' as well as of the revolutionary Sicilian *Fasci*.

The most prominent 'interventionist' group was that of D'Annunzio's legionaries, whose sights were set on Rome as well as on Fiume. After Fiume had fallen, D'Annunzio's supporters founded a 'National Federation of Fiume Legionaries', both patriotic and syndicalist. Former members of the '*Arditi*' (shock-troops) also founded a semi-political movement after the war, it soon had 10,000 members-men who had been chosen in war specially for their murderous qualities, and who enjoyed a good fight. The Futurists were also still active, and indeed Marinetti was the acknowledged leader of the *Arditi*. He, too, founded '*Fasci*' throughout Italy, the '*Fasci Futuristi*', loosely co-ordinated by a 'Futurist Political Party' with a programme based on 'total and intransigent anti-clericalism'.

These 'interventionist' movements had much in common. They attacked the same targets: parliament, government, Nitti, Giolitti, Socialists, Catholics, bureaucrats and war-profiteers, they were urban, and strongest in Northern and North-Central Italy; they were paramilitary in organization and style; and they relied heavily on patriotic myths and bellicose sentiments. They appealed to students, both those who had fought in the war and those who had, unhappily, been too young. And they all recruited ex-officers. At least 130,000 officers were discharged from the army in 1919. All the 'interventionists' were active. They were available for political adventures like D'Annunzio or Marinetti.

The most formidable Right-wing demagogue in Italy was Benito Mussolini, thirty-five years old in early 1919 and with varied experiences behind him. Born in Romagna, the son of a blacksmith and a schoolmistress, he soon became the classic figure of Italian society. He read voraciously especially in literature and philosophy; he kept himself by a series of short-lived jobs—school teaching, building worker; and he joined a revolutionary political movement, the PSI. He served his time in Switzerland, as all good revolutionaries should; he wrote an anti-clerical novel. Mussolini was intelligent, yet impatient of complexities; he was energetic, yet anxious for instant panaceas; he was inconsistent, yet always convinced of his own righteousness.

In short, he was a born journalist. Journalism was how he—and many others—made his way to the top; and he remained a journalist at heart all his life. From the local Socialist paper at Forli, *Lotta di Classe*, he became editor of the official Socialist daily *Avanti* in 1912, at the age of twenty-nine. This was a post of great political influence, and he was popular and successful in the job. Two years later, however, he broke with the PSI over the intervention issue. He had made sure he had funds enough to found another paper, the *Popolo d' Italia*, but even so his action was not that of a calculating careerist. On the contrary, Mussolini was a violent and impulsive man, and he enjoyed living dangerously. War seemed desirable and exciting to a man of his temperament. Naturally he went off to fight, and was honourably wounded; and naturally he came back to battle against 'the internal enemy' in the columns of his newspaper. He never forgot those glorious years. He had campaigned for the war, wrecked his Socialist career for the war, and fought in the war: the war was the great ennobling experience of his life, indeed the great ennobling revolution of the twentieth century.

When peace came Mussolini, too, founded a political movement, the *Fasci di Combattimento*, whose inaugural meeting was held in a building on piazza San Sepolcro, Milan, on 23 March 1919. The *Fasci* were often indistinguishable from *Arditi*. Captain Ferruccio Veechi of the *Arditi* was chairman of the Fascists' inaugural meeting. The *Fasci di Combattimento* had the usual radical programme—a Constituent Assembly, abolition of the Senate, land for the peasants, seizure of Church property and major tax changes. But there was not much of a market for all this, and what there was had been cornered by the Socialists. The movement remained strident but ineffective in 1919-20, restricted to a few major centres, like Milan, Bologna, Trieste. It had only 870 members in December 1919. In November Fascists, Futurists, and *Arditi* stood together in the parliamentary elections in Milan: they won a derisory 4,657 votes, out of 270,000.

It was the *Popolo d'Italia*, not the *Fasci*, that kept Mussolini in the limelight; it was in the newspapers, not in 'interventionist' politics, where his word was law and no rivals like D 'Annunzio could challenge him. Mussolini remained an editor, first and foremost, long after he had become the'*Duce*' (leader) of Fascism. He successfully turned the paper into the spokesman for all the discontented extreme 'interventionists'. But the newspaper continually needed money, money which could only be provided by industrialists—sugar barons, steel magnates, or ship-builders. For nearly two years Mussolini struggled to keep his newspaper alive, and to find a political opening.

It came, eventually from setting up armed 'squads', real para-military organizations run by Fascist ex-officers. Trieste, where national passions ran deep, was soon dominated by these groups, well-armed and enjoying army help. In late 1920 the Fascist para-military movement—'*squadrismo*'—really took off, rather to Mussolini's surprise. The 'occupation of the factories' frightened many people; the local election results in October-November frightened even more. It was time to stand and fight.

The really important breakthrough came not in the North, nor in the cities, nor even in centres of nationalist excitement like Trieste. It owed little to Mussolini or to his newspaper. It came in the 'red' provinces of Central Italy, in Emilia and Tuscany, where landlords and leaseholders, reacted against the victorious Socialist labour leagues, against the new local councils and against government agricultural policy. Fascist squads were the ideal instrument for breaking up Socialist or *Popolare* dominance in the countryside. A lorry-load of ex-officers or students would descend on some villages at night, beat up the local unionists, 'purge' them of their iniquities by making them drink castor-oil, burn down the local party offices, and depart. The police would stand by.

Yet *'squadrismo'* was not just class conflict, nor was it just thuggery. Many ordinary peasants were sick of the petty Socialist dictatorships too, and joined the squads willingly. The squads were convinced of their own righteousness. They were restoring law and order, they were rescuing their country from tyranny, and they were avenging their fallen wartime comrades. That was why so many respectable Liberals wished them well. Mario Missiroli described Fascism as 'the emergence of a besieged army'. And it was victorious. The 'red' provinces of the Po valley and of Tuscany were transformed, sometimes in only a few weeks, from being the home of the most powerful peasant unions in Europe to being the main strongholds of the Fascist squads.

All this transformed the Fascist movement too. The initial stereotype of Fascism, the 'revolutionary', 'interventionist', 'Fascism of the first hour' in Milan and the big cities, the Fascism of Mussolini, syndicalists, ex-officers and students, was replaced by another stereotype *squadrismo*, reactionary and rural. Mussolini was the *Duce* of Fascism. He and his paper acted on the squads' behalf, as national organizer, financier and propagandist.

For most of 1921 Mussolini played the squad-tamer, reassuring his city followers that Fascism had not sold out to the rural bourgeoisie, and reassuring the Establishment that he was respectable at heart. He proclaimed that land should be leased out to the peasants. Mussolini also reaffirmed his republicanism, to console his more radical supporters. Even so, the Fascist movement was clearly becoming more conservative. By July 1921 Mussolini had become the peace-maker. He proposed a 'pact of pacification' between the Fascists and the Socialist unions.

Mussolini kept his hold on the movement. But he managed, in October 1921, to put Fascism on a proper footing as a formal political party, the National Fascist Party (*Partio Nazionale Fascista*, PNF). The new party founded local branches, welcomed 'respectable' recruits, collected regular dues. It was obviously designed to be a centralized body under Mussolini's control. With over 200,000 members by the end of 1921, and over 300,000 by May 1922, the party gave Mussolini a real political base other than his newspaper. It greatly improved his hand in negotiations with other politicians. The PNF rapidly became the party of the middle classes, filling the vacuum left by the collapse of Liberalism.

By late 1921 'Fascism' already meant quite a distinct phenomena. To many, it meant strike-breaking—seen either as a vicious attack on workers' rights, or as a heroic, patriotic duty. To others, it meant the 'national' unions, a new way of disciplining and mobilising labour. To a few, it was still a revolutionary, republican movement. To most people, and to most Fascists, 'Fascism' now meant squadrismo—a number of different para-military groups, fiercely independent, somtimes in league with large landowners, sometimes more 'syndicalist', but always recruiting from the urban middle class or from landholders and small owners, always run by local bosses.

Fascism was a typical militant student movement, except that these students knew how to fight, and their parents approved of their activities. The only indisputable conclusion is the Fascism was a number of complex local movements, linked by patriotic sentiment, by hatred of Socialism and by the myth of the *Duce*.

The opponents of Fascism helped Mussolini too. In January 1921 the Socialist party split, and therefore Italy had a real Communist Party, sectarian and financed by 'Russian gold'. It was too small to be a threat, but its existence was excellent propaganda for the Fascists.

By mid-October 1922 Mussolini could insist on becoming Prime Minister himself, unless the politicians used force against the massed Fascists. The Facta government, still formally in office, was obviously reluctant to do so. But early on 28 October, after much hesitation, it finally asked the king to sign a decree establishing martial laws. The king, after initially agreeing, refused. More probably he thought resistance was not worth it. Why risk a blood-thirsty civil war, when the only question was how many Fascist ministers were to be included in the next coalition government? And the Fascists had already taken over most of the country—the 'March on Rome' of 28 October was actually a successful 'March on the provincial capitals'. So the king refused to authorise martial law. Two days later Mussolini arrived on the overnight sleeper from Milan, summoned by the king to form a new government.

Thus Mussolini did not really seize power. He did not, by 28 October, need to use force. He won by threatening to use it, and by having the squads ready to obey. Formally, he became Prime Minister constitutionally, appointed by king; the 'March on Rome' happened afterwards, when hordes of Black-shirts were allowed to roam around the capital exulting and rampaging in the rain. Mussolini won by being 'brought into the system' by a king and a governing elite that could see no other way of containing organised violence. Although it is right to stress the longer-term causes of his victory—the 'mutilated victory' of Versailles, agrarian class conflicts, ex-officers seeking social promotion, proportional representation and so forth—there was nothing inevitable about it.

On 28 October 1922 a new era of Italian history began literally so, for the Fascist regime dared its documents thereafter from the March on Rome. Mussolini formed a coalition Cabinet—a 'National Government', as he called it—including himself and three Fascists in the key post, but also including two *Popolari*, four Liberals of various types, a Nationalist (Federzoni), and three prestigious names —Marshal Diaz at the War Ministry, Admiral Thaon di Revel at the Admiralty, and the philosopher Giovanni Gentile at Education. The talk was all of 'normalization' and restoring law and order.

In January 1923 the Fascist Militia (MVSN) was formed, 'to defend the Fascist revolution'. The Militia was recruited from party members. It was paid out of public funds; and it was answerable directly to the *Duce*. The Militia had few functions. It guarded public buildings, and it allowed Fascists to parade around in uniforms; but its main purpose was to exist. It provided the *squadristi* with rewards, both in cash and glamour. It was an outward and visible sign that the Fascist Revolution had succeeded.

The *Duce* set up a new Fascist body, the 'Grand Council'. Like the Militia, it did little—most political decisions were still taken by the government coalition—but it created a formal Fascist 'Cabinet', parallel to the constitutional one, and it gave the top Fascist bosses the opportunity to look important while the party beneath them was slowly transformed.

Mussolini's major political achievement in 1923 was also geared to this aim. In April the PPI Congress was very much divided on the party remaining in the Fascist-led government, and ten days later Mussolini brusquely dismissed the *Popolari* ministers. Clearly the government's parliamentary majority was now at risk, so Mussolini immediately proposed a new electoral system. This was a shrewd move. The Fascists proposed a 'corrected' proportional system, in which the party grouping with the largest number of votes, provided it amounted to at least 25 per cent of the valid votes cast, would receive two-thirds of the parliamentary seats. This would ensure, in theory a stable government majority. In practice it would mean that Mussolini could form a 'national bloc' of pro-government groups.

Soon came the elections, to consolidate it still further. In April 1924 the '*listone*' of approved candidates—Fascists, former Nationalists, Right-wing Liberals including Salandra, Orlando and Dr. Nicola, Agrarians, even a few *Popolari*—won 66.3 per cent of the valid votes, and was thus entitled to two-thirds of the seats. Of the bloc's 374 victorious candidates, about 60 per cent were 'Fascists'. These parties had little in common, and they squabbled ceaselessly. Mussolini had succeeded in his aim. He had brought Fascism under control, and had made it respectable and parliamentary. He had destroyed and discredited the main opposition parties, especially the Socialists and Catholics.

The Fascist State

Mussolini's speech of 3 January 1925 was a foretaste of things to come. He had made three main promises, or threats. He had promised that press freedom would be curbed and that the opposition parties would be disciplined; he had promised a 'strong State'; and he had promised that the Fascist squads would not be unleashed. So the outlines of a new 'regime' were already discernible. It would be non-liberal and authoritarian. It would strengthen the institutions of High Politics; and it would do its best to abolish the trivial concerns of Low Politics.

Mussolini's first aim, to curb the opposition, was achieved with remarkably little fuss or protest. The two Liberal ministers, Casati and Sarrochi, resigned after the 3 January speech, as did Salandra from his post as head of the Italian delegation to the League of Nations.

The government tightened up press censorship immediately after 3 January, and unflattering papers were regularly seized. In 1925 the leading Liberal journals were brought under government control. Only the strictly party newspapers— the Communist's *L'Unita*, the Socialists' *Avanti* and so forth—provided alternative viewpoints (until November 1926), and even they were rigorously censored and available only in the big cities.

In 1926 amid a clamour for law and order, it withdrew all passports, banned all opposition parties and their journals, declared that the mandate of opposition deputies had expired (so they lost their parliamentary immunity), and set up a 'special tribunal' to repress anti-Fascist activity. Thus the classic Liberal institutions of informed public opinion were brought down. 'Public opinion' henceforth would be what the government said it was: the newspapers, like the radio, would be under the 'Great Editor'.

Mussolini's second promise on 3 January had been to strengthen the traditional machinery of High Politics. This presented even fewer problems. The repression of 1925-26 was repression by the police and the courts. From November 1926 the police were allowed, once again, to banish suspected persons to remote provinces or Southern islands.

As for the courts, the only real innovation was the 'Special Tribunal for the Defense of the State', set up in November 1926 to try terrorists and other political criminals. The tribunal was run by Militia consuls presided over by military judges, and it applied military law. Usually it imposed prison sentences or '*confino*'. Its most famous victim was the Communist leader Antonio Gramsci, who was sentenced to twenty years' imprisonment. The legal system remained unchanged and 'un-Fascist'—although admittedly no more independent of the executive than before 1922. Judges simply joined the party, and kept their jobs.

In April 1925 Mussolini on the post of War Minister himself, and new army regulation were pushed through the following year. Mussolini also became Navy Minister in May 1925, and Air Minister in August.

Fascist Ideology

There were many strands in Fascist thought. The syndicalists, revolutionary and anti-capitalist, were anxious to build a new kind of 'producers State'. The provincial radicals, populist and impatient, yearned to sweep away Church, king and parliament. There were spiritual revivalists, preaching national pride and a 'new Rome'; and there were ex-Nationalists, royalists and anti-democratic, drawing up blueprints for a strong State and a planned economy. Fascists knew whom they were against: Bolsheviks, Freemasons, international bankers—anybody, in short, engaged in a secret conspiracy against the nation. These ideas were mainly a legacy from pre-war days. The Fascists may not have had a coherent doctrine, but they had a powerful one. They had won the war, and vanquished the Bolsheviks after it; they had built a new State and a new economy. They would spread civilization and order throughout Mediterranean and North Africa, as their Roman forefathers had done. Indeed, this cult of ancient Rome was perhaps the most striking feature of the regime. The word '*Duce*' itself came from *Dux*; the Fasci were, of course, the Roman lictors' symbols of office; the Militia and the youth organizations all had a pseudo-Roman hierarchy and titles - legions, cohorts, centurions and so forth.

Furthermore, this ideology was not just for Fascists. To achieve their noble purpose, the Fascists had to 'mobilise' every Italian to the cause. 'The thoughts and wishes of the *Duce* must become the thoughts and wishes of the masses. Theirs was a mass regime, founded on war: 'real' Italy had vanquished 'legal' Italy, in 1922 as in 1915. The Fascists never forgot their origins. Mussolini 'considered the whole nation in a permanent state of war', and so the morale and fighting spirit of the masses had to be constantly maintained.

They had numerous instruments to hand. The press, for example, was not merely censored, but primed. Government subsidies were increased, in return for fulsome praise of the regime. Despite his militarism, Mussolini always believed the pen was mightier than the sword. His press office sent out detailed instructions on what to print and how to print it. Foreign words were Italianized—'cocktail' became 'coda de gallo' - and even the word 'Mezzogiorno' was banned. Reports of crime, or suicide, or traffic accidents, disappeared from the newspapers. Nothing was allowed to disturb the national harmony.

He founded both a National Fascist Institute of Culture and a Royal Italian Academy, on the French model, to mobilise the intellectuals. The first radio stations were set up in 1924-25; there were over 300,000 registered sets in 1932, and over 1 million by 1938. Each set was listened to by numerous people. And broadcasting was State-controlled.

So, too, did the cinema. The regime built an 'Experimental Centre of Cinematography' training 100 students a year, including Michelangelo Antonioni; and it took over *Cinecita*—Italy's Hollywood—in 1938. After 1934 many Italian films were subsidised.

Fascist Syndicates and Corporations

The Fascists' key achievement was to 'discipline' labour. The Fascist movement had taken off in 1920-21 as a reaction to trade union militancy. The Fascists had destroyed the existing trade unions and co-operatives. But that was not enough. To avoid renewed trouble in future the Fascists needed to 'represent the workers' interests' within their own organizations. So the Fascist unions—'syndicates' is the Italian term—had to be reasonably successful in negotiations, if they were to attract some working-class support. The Fascist syndicalists built up their empires rapidly after 1921. Mussolini needed all the working- class support he could get, if only to put pressure on wavering businessmen; so he backed the syndicates. In 1925 there were several major strikes led by the Fascist union, sometimes supported tacitly by the government. In October 1925 the industrialists were forced to recognise the new facts of industrial and political power. The industrialists' confederation and the Fascist syndicates' confederation recognized each other's right to represent exclusively their respective side's interest, and pledged themselves not to negotiate with any other body. It was a triumph for the Fascist syndicalists.

In 1930 a National Council of Corporations was founded, to act as a joint consultative body on the economy. It met and deliberated regularly.

The Catholic Church was the greatest obstacle to any 'totalitarian' regime in Italy. All the others—parliament, press, opposition parties; union—could be smashed or emasculated; but not the Church. Nor could she simply be ignored, for she had immense influence in education and welfare, and she proclaimed values quite incompatible with those of Fascism. Mussolini, therefore, needed all his political skills. He had to reassure the hierarchy of the Church by material concessions.

Mussolini did not attack the Church as such. On the contrary, he wooed her.

By 1926 the Vatican Secretary of State, Cardinal Gasparri, was confident that Mussolini was going to stay in power. A major long-term deal could be done. On 11 February 1929 Mussolini and Gasparri signed the 'Lateran Pacts' a treaty, a financial convention and a Concordat. The treaty set up a separate sovereign State of 'Vatican City', with forty-four hectares of land and full diplomatic rights. The financial convention gave the Pope 750 million lire, plus a further 1,000 million in Italian State bonds, as compensation for the loss of his pre-1870 territories. And the Concordat granted various privileges to the Church. Religious education was brought into secondary as well as primary schools, seminarists were exempted from military service, and church marriage were deemed legally valid - they no longer had to be followed by a civil ceremony. The Concordat also guaranteed the future position of Catholic Action organizations 'in so far as they carry out their activities independent of all political parties, and immediately subordinate to the Church hierarchy.

The pacts were a triumph for the *Duce*. The cost was negligible, the benefits huge. Mussolini had 'solved the Roman question', which had baffled even Cavour and Crispi; he could count on world-wide prestige and a chorus of admiration. He was 'the man sent by providence', as Pius XI called him. His regime was sanctified and blessed by Mother Church. At home. nobody could touch him now; abroad, he could assume the agreeable mantle of Defender of the Faith. The Church, too, could rejoice. She had achieved sovereign territory at last, financial security, above all recognition and immunity for her work.

Thus although the Church undoubtedly contributed to the Fascist consensus between 1926 and 1938, she was also a rival, and a rival who was building up strength.

The Economy and Society Under the Fascists

Mussolini's economic and social policies, like his other policies, were geared to political propaganda rather than to real achievements. In his first years in office Mussolini tried, as always, to balance 'Fascists' demands—syndicalism, etc,—with the need to win over the Establishment. He appointed an orthodox financier, De'Stefani, as Treasury

Minister; and he made many concessions to business interests. The telephones were handed back to private companies; private life insurance was also reintroduced. The huge shipping and steel firm of Ansaldo, owned by Perrone brothers, was reconstructed with government cash, and the (Catholic) *Banco di Roma* was reduced. Furthermore, these were boom years. The index of manufacturing production rose from 54 in 1921 to 83 in 1925 (1938 = 100); not until the late 1950s were similar rates of growth achieved in Italy. Many Businessmen were delighted by the new government's policies.

By 1929 Italy had become self-sufficient in Chemicals; and steel production was up to 2,122,000 tonnes, compared with 982,000 tonnes in 1922. So the Fascist economic pattern was becoming set. Italy was turning away from her export markets, and boosting instead the industries which stood to gain most from Empire and re-armament.

In the Depression years of 1929-33 this policy was continued. The government lowered money wages in November 1930, by around 12 per cent, and encouraged price-fixing and cartel agreements. Mergers became common. The Fascist government boosted total demand and employment by public works and welfare benefits: the money spent on road-building doubled in four years. Even so, the general policy remained deflationary. Money supply declined from 19 billion lire in 1929 to 16 billion lire in 1932, and to 15.3 billion lire in 1934; the cost of living dropped by 16 per cent between 1927 and 1932.

The main thrust of government policy was directed towards the banks. The major banks—the *Credito Italiano*, and the *Banca Commerciale* and *Banco di Roma*—had lent large sums to industry and commerce on the security of shares in the debtor firms.

The State took over much new industrial investment, and did so to public acclaim. Millions of small savers were protected, and confidence was restored. Italy weathered the storm of 1929-35 rather better than some other industrial countries. Gross national product fell 5.4 per cent between the 1929 peak and the 1931-33 trough, and industrial production fell by 22.7 per cent; the figures for Western Europe as a whole were 7.1 per cent and 23.2 per cent. This relative success was a boost for Fascist propaganda. Liberal economics seemed to be discredited by events world-wide; government intervention seemed to work in Italy.

Agriculture

The Fascists took over a country where there were $3\frac{1}{2}$ million landowners, many of them 'new' peasant-owners anxious to keep newly acquired land. Furthermore, it were the peasants who had fought the war, and who contributed to the state. So the Fascists backed the peasantry, or rather they backed the new landed peasantry. In some Liberal or Catholic areas Fascist syndicates even took over big estates after 1922, selling them or leasing them out to landless peasants. 'Land to the peasants' was a constant propaganda cry throughout the regime, justifying reclamation schemes in Italy and imperial dreams in Africa. Mussolini proclaimed the need to 'ruralise Italy', and told the Prefects to give particular attention to agriculture, 'in precedence over all other forms of economic activity... the regime is predominantly rural, and intends to remain so'. This was not just rhetoric. In many regions the small farmers were the backbone of the Fascist regime. Mussolini's rural conservatism had a solid basis in fact.

The government would 'free the Italian people from the slavery of foreign bread', so that the people would not starve in the time of war. In 1925, after a poor harvest had made it necessary to import 2.3 million tonnes of wheat, he proclaimed a 'Battle for Wheat'. A high tariff was put on imported grain, thus raising food prices and discouraging consumption. By 1933 the tariff was 750 lire per tonne, and the Italian farmer was benefiting accordingly. Landowners grew wheat even on unsuitable soil, using all the advances of modern science—selected seeds, chemical fertilisers, farm machinery and so forth, most of them subsidised by new government grants. The Fascists made an intense effort to spread knowledge of new farming techniques, and even the priests were expected to play their part. The archbishop of Reggio Calabria, for example, instructed his clergy to be model farmers and to spread technical skills - be therefore true apostles also in this respect; and you will have the blessing of your parishioners, of the national government and, above all, of God.'

The 'Battle for Wheat' undeniably produced more wheat. The average harvest rose from 5.39 million tonnes in 1921-25 to 7.27 million tonnes ten year later, and imports fell off markedly. The same was true of Fascism's other major agricultural policy, the famous land reclamation and improvement schemes. Such schemes were not new in united Italy—over 500,000 hectares of marsh land had been drained before 1911—but the Fascists decided to do it on a larger scale. In 1928 the so-called 'Mussolini Law' promised to throw huge sums of public money into reclamation.

Social Change and the Population

Perhaps the most significant economic change in the Fascist period was in the civil service and public agencies. The number of public employees doubled during the 1930s from 500,000 to 1 million, quite apart from the extra jobs in the Fascist Party, Militia or syndicates. Fascism offered the middle classes security - not just against trade unions, socialism or inflation, but also against unemployment. There were more jobs for them, more prestige, and more power, and the salary-wage gap—the middle class's differential—widened for the first time since figures began. The Italian middle classes (unlike the German) held on to their money and their privileges after the early 1920s.

The economic changes also widened the gap between North and South. The industries which grew fastest in the Fascist period were mechanical engineering, steelmaking, chemicals and hydro-electricity supply. They were all in the North, indeed mainly in the famous 'industrial triangle' of North-West Italy. In the other southern regions 'Industrial workers' were artisans or, at best, engaged in food-processing or in the building trades.

Fascist Population Policy

Mussolini did not merely want more people in the countryside; he also wanted more people. The 41 million Italians of 1931 were not enough. Indeed, one of the main reasons for trying to 'ruralise' Italy was the fact that rural people were more fertile. Family allowances, introduced in the 1930s, became an important part of a wage-earners's income and there were also tax reliefs - although you had to have had ten children before you were finally exempted from income tax. Some of the new measures were imaginative. 'Marriage loans' cost 89 million lire in 1939. Part of the loan was cancelled every time the happy couple produced another child. 'Marriage grants' to newly-weds cost a further 55 million lire, and 'birth grants' to the newly fecund came to 86 million lire; there were special prizes for the super-prolific. Jobs and promotions in the civil services were reserved for the fertile married; after 1938 university professions had to be married. Over 1 million Italian bachelors paid a 'celibate's levy'. In 1936 a thirty-year-old bachelor had to pay *double* his normal income tax plus 155 lire p.a.

Population policy - *la politica della razza* - was closely linked to other major policies - ruralisation, land improvement, and the 'Battle for Wheat' - and also to more general issues, such as religious observance, autarchy and *italianita*. Ultimately they were all geared to Empire and to war. Mussolini wanted '60 million Italians' by 1950, enough to populate on Empire or to fight a major European war of attrition; without births 'there will be no Empire, we will become a colony'.

The Fascist attitude to women was, basically, male chauvinist. Women were to be 'exemplary wives and mothers', 'guardians of the hearth', subject to 'the legitimate authority of the husband. 'War is to man what motherhood to woman' proclaimed the *Duce*.

More women stayed on at school or even began to go to university. In the long run the Fascist regime probably helped, rather than hindered, female emancipation. It mobilized women into public organizations - 500,000 'Rural Housewives' by 1939, another 500,000 'Fascist Women' in the party. It helped with summer holidays and advice on child-rearing, it encouraged female sport in general and women athletes like Ondina Valle in particular, and it kept girls out of dead-end jobs. In 1925 it even gave the women vote at local elections. Besides, it greatly expanded the educational opportunities for women. By 1935-36 17.4 per cent of university students were female, compared with less than 4 per cent before 1914. Women were not allowed to apply for the most competitive jobs in senior secondary schools, but that simply meant that Latin, Italian, History and Philosophy were taught by men, whereas Mathematics, Physics and Chemistry continued to be taught by women.

27

Significance of the Reform Act of 1832

The object of the Reform Bill of 1832 was to remove the defects of the political life of the people. The Napoleonic wars had brought a tremendous upheavals in the social and political life of the people of England, and the wealthy people exploited the poverty of the people for getting a seat in the Parliament and even the government officials also took recourse to bribery and corruption to meet their ends. But the people who were greatly influenced by the doctrines of the French Revolution and July Revolution demanded a reform in the political life of the country. Trevelyan aptly remarks, "From squire to position, from cotton lord to mill-hand, everyone was talking of the need for reform". It is a fact that the system of representation before 1832 was defective and hence the demand for reform in parliamentary representation was justified.

Since 1688, the Parliament had been supreme but it did not truly constitute a representative body. The situation in the country had changed on account of the Industrial Revolution which led to the steady migration of the villagers to the new industrial towns. These towns had no representations in the Parliament, and the old constituencies which returned members to the Commons remained the same. The Counties and Boroughs sent two representatives each to the Parliament irrespective of their areas and population. As for example, Cornwall had same representation in the Parliament as Scotland had had at that time. Similarly the new industrial towns like Birmingham, Manchester, Sheffield, Leeds, had no representatives in the Parliament. On the other hand, uninhabited places like Old Sarum, Gatton and Dunwich had still the right to send two representatives to the Parliament. There was also great disparity in the matter of representation among the three different categories of Boroughs - Independent Boroughs, Pocket Boroughs, and Rotten Boroughs. All such Boroughs had right to send two hundred representatives to the Parliament irrespective of the fact that these represented small areas of England. Even the Pocket Boroughs, owned by the feudal lords, sent representatives to the Parliament. They were mostly nominees of such Lords.

There was no uniformity in the system of franchise, and only the rich had the right to vote. The number of voters was not proportionate to the population. The Counties and Boroughs had different systems of voting. In some Boroughs, the Mayors nominated the members, and in some others, only the owners of buildings had right to vote. In the Counties, the free-holders had right to cast vote. But such free-holders must pay forty shillings by way of tax to the government. Thus a large section of people like the copy-holders and the peasants had no right of franchise.

The House of Commons had a long career since the time of Edward I but it was not representative of people. Pitt the Younger was also of the opinion, "the House is not true representative of the people of Great Britain; it is the representative of nominal boroughs, of ruined and exterminated towns, of noble families, of wealthy individuals and foreign potentiates." Truly speaking, the wealthy and landlord classes had full control over the House of Commons, and the membership of the House was based on the principle of wealth. Only seeing the dominance of wealthy people, Sydney Smith remarked, "The country belongs to the Duke of Rutland, Lord Lonsdale, the Duke of Newcastle, and about twenty other holders of boroughs. They are our masters."

Bribery and corruption was rampant in returning members to the House of Commons. The voters were openly intimidated, the labourers and peasants were not allowed to cast their votes according to their own will. They always feared unemployment if they did not accept the dictates of their masters, and even in the newspapers, advertisement was given by the respective Boroughs that their seats could be purchased on the payment of specified amount. To get a seat in the Parliament, one was expected to spend amounts upto two lacs pounds. After being returned to Parliament, such members tried their best to cash as much as they could. Marriot has remarked, "A seat was as much a marketable commodity in the eighteenth century as an advowson in the nineteenth, and the legitimacy of transaction was recognised alike in Pitt's Reform Bill of 1785 and the Act of Union of 1800."

There were other defects too which made it essential to introduce reforms in the systems of representation. The system of voting was not secret, and hence the voters did not go against the wishes of their masters. The members of the Parliament did not receive any salary and hence there was no scope for ordinary people to occupy the seat in the Commons. The constituencies were also not constituted either on the basis of area or on the basis of population. The tenure of the membership was seven years and so the direct relation between the representative and the common people was nonetheless little. Lastly, it can also be said that the House of Commons and the House of Lords stood on equal footing in matters of power. These were the defects which needed removal, and hence a demand arose for effecting reforms in the political life of people.

A demand for reform grew up everywhere. According to Ramsay Muir, the people of London conducted meetings in the different night clubs; the people of Birmingham formed political union, the people of North England staged strikes and demonstrations, and the people of South England revolted under the leadership of Captain Swing. All these movements were diverted towards effecting speedy reforms in parliamentary representation. At this juncture Lord Grey came to power and formed a committee to suggest reforms. Several proposals were formulated, and the Tories nicknamed them as 'A new Constitution'. But nobody inside or outside the Parliament expected from the Whigs any drastic proposals of change. Everybody was, therefore, startled, and either delighted or horrified by the magnitude of the reforms."

The special features of the Reform Bill were: firstly nearly sixty Boroughs were disfranchised. Such Boroughs had a population of even less than two thousand, and they returned nearly one hundred and nineteen members to the Parliament. Only those forty-seven Boroughs who had a population between two thousand and four thousand, were given right to send one representative to the Parliament. Weymouth and Melcombe Boroughs were given right to send two representatives instead of four representatives. The seats of the Parliament were distributed as follows - England 97, Wales 1, Scotland 5 and Ireland 3. Seven big industrial towns got the right to send two representatives, and London got four seats in the Parliament, Yorkshire got six seats and Isle of Wight got one seat. Twenty six Counties were given double representations. In the Boroughs and the Counties those who paid ten pounds yearly rent were give the right to vote. These proposals were supported by the people, and after few modifications, it was placed in the newly elected Parliament on 24, June 1831, and it was passed by the House of Commons. But the House of Lords rejected the Bill. Again change was made for the third time in the Bill, and after great storm and stress, the Bill was passed by the

House of Lords also; and on 6 June 1832, the King gave his assent. With the passage of the Bill, the death warrant of the Lords was signed and the Crown itself realised its own limits.

The Reform Act of 1832 was mainly directed towards, firstly, the redistribution of parliamentary representation in such a way that places with few or no inhabitants were to loose their seats and those with more inhabitants were to get them, and secondly to liberalise the voting qualification in such a way that more persons became voters. For the realisation of the first objective, towns were divided into four classes; the first category comprising fifty-six towns which were to have no representation in Parliament; the second category consisting of thirty towns got the right to send one representative to the Parliament; the third category comprised such towns which had earlier no representation, got the right to send one representative; and the fourth class comprised such towns which received the right of returning one member to the House. The remaining seats were distributed among the Counties. The right of franchise was given to all males of full age owning or occupying a house worth ten pounds a year. This was for people of Boroughs. But in the Counties, all men were given the right to vote if they held land for the term of their life or on a lease for sixty years.

The Reform Act of 1832 has been called the modern 'Magna Carta' by Trevelyan. It brought about a constitutional revolution in England, and it shifted the political power from the aristocracy to the middle classes and thereby paved the way for democracy. The evils of the rotten Boroughs were done away with and the new industrial towns got representation in the Commons. According to Kier, "the effect of the Reform Act was to deepen the cleavage, thus manifested, between the two Houses. That harmony which had been naturally created when so many members of the Commons were nominees of the Lords was destroyed with the abolition of so many nomination Boroughs and the enlargement of the franchise. If members of the Lower House were in the political confusion which preceded the hardening of the party organisation and discipline, largely free to oppose the Lords. The Lords responded to the challenge. It was under difficulties overcome only by Wellington's influence that they yielded to the repeat of Corn Laws. They regularly opposed measures threatening vested interests." Again he says, "the principle of popular sovereignty which the Reform Act had grudgingly but irrevocably accepted was bound in the end to do more than merely diminish the weight of the Crown and the Lords in Government and enhance the powers of a ministry reposing on a property organized majority of votes."

To quote Trevelyan again, "It is incorrect to say that the Bill gave all power to the middle class. Power which had previously resided in a privileged section of the landlords was now divided among all the landlords on one side and a portion of the middle class on the other. The ten pound house-hold franchise was not set up in the Counties at all. Even in the Boroughs it did not affect the poorer classes. It was because half the middle class were still left without votes that they eventually joined with the working men to demand a further extension of the franchise under Bright Gladstone. If the first Reform Bill had given full representation to the Middle class, the politics of the Victorian era would have taken a more distinctive class character than they actually did." According to another historian, the Reform Act made possible a series of political and administrative reforms that laid the foundations of modern Britain.

According to Carrington, the Reform Bill of 1832 did not establish democracy in England, it did not give votes to the masses of the people. But it ensured that the franchise was evenly distributed among the upper and middle classes and it destroyed the powers of the ruling families who had controlled the pocket Boroughs for so many years. It was, no doubt, a boon from the Parliament. According to Trevelyan, "the nation was henceforth master of its own House. But the political extent of the nation would yet need to be defined by a succession of franchise struggles, each less violent indeed than the great original." Describing the effects of the Reforms Bill, Ramsay Muir aptly remarks, "It destroyed the entrenched power of the land-owning oligarchy which had governed Britain since the fall of the Stuart Monarchy and it gave to a large electorate the opportunity of recasting the political and social system. The section of the nation to which controlling power now passed was in the main middle class together with the more prosperous artisans."

According to Hall and Albion, the Reform Act of 1832 did accomplish a revolution, more genuine than the revolution which occurred in France in 1830. The Act did not dethrone a dynasty but it did destroy what amounted to a semi-feudal monopoly of the British Government in the hands of the landed aristocracy. Further, "the Act was a compromise. The poor had supported the middle class mainly by riots actual or threatened and had helped it to win a secure footing in the British constitutional system. The bill set a precedent and was an important landmark in advance towards democracy." According to Gregg, "the Reform Act was a middle class measure, yet was sponsored by a cabinet with a majority of peers. It was intended to benefit the manufacturers and industrialists, yet was supported by the very workers to whom they begrudged the Factory Acts." But on the whole, as Semellie remarks, "the Act is an excellent example of the British skill of muddling through. An aristocracy muddled through a democracy, taking many of the aristocratic virtues with them and they muddled through from an age of privilege to an age of numbers." In concluding the importance of the Act, the opinion of Ken may be quoted that "one of the effects of the Reform Act was that the King in future could not choose his ministers at his sole discretion and furnish them so long as they enjoyed his confidence with a parliamentary majority generally reliable under normal conditions. Another effect was that it enabled the House of Commons to establish its supremacy over the House of Lords. The change came slowly but it did come. The result was that the ministers in future were increasing to derive their strength from the support of the electorate and less from that of the Crown and House of Lords."

28

The Making of a New Germany

The respective movements of Italians and Germans towards unity had gone on coincidently, but the Germans had to wait longer for a state to place itself at their head and the movement proceeded more placidly than that in Italy — perhaps an index of the difference in temperament between the two peoples. This unification of Germany was one of the outstanding events of the 19th century history of Europe. It sealed the triumph of Nationalism, one of the heritages of the French revolution and the Napoleonic era. Germany achieved her political unification under the astute leadership of Bismarck. The completion of the German unity under the leadership of Prussia completely altered the balance of power which had been established since the Congress of Vienna.

German nationalism may be said to have begun with the symptoms of resistance to Napoleon. It is true that Germans had felt a certain sense of nationality during Luther's quarrel with Rome, but divided as they were among so many princes who were more often than otherwise in league with an outside power. There was nothing calculated to keep alive that spirit of self-defence out of which nationalism is born and so there was little in the way of a trend towards unity before the nineteenth century. This Germany of princely states, who were always fighting among themselves for supremacy over one another, was given some semblance of a united country by Napoleon Bonaparte when he formed the confederation of Rhine. Nationalism was a fairly spontaneous movement of redemption, and as Prussia had led the way, it seemed as though Prussia should assume the leadership after the war, utilizing this nascent movement to create a German Nation. The idea of French revolution had aroused nationalist aspirations among the Germans. The settlement of Congress of Vienna upset all chances of the German unification. The ousted princes were restored to their states and all nationalist aspirations were curbed by strong reactionary measures. Thus, the old local divisions were once again established and Austria was given to control Germany by a federal Diet. The Diet was a mere sham. It lacked executive power and was useless as an organ of government.

The three decades which followed the Vienna settlement were, in fact, dreary years for Germany, but one important movement stands out. Prussia established little by little— the *Zollveriin* which by 1842 included all the German states but Austria. This phenomenon of economic policy taught two things, viz. the merits of close relations; for in place of the multitude of tariff which divided thirty-six states from one another. Merchandise was now able to circulate freely from one end of Germany to the other. Economic union foreshadowed the political union. Secondly, Prussia excluded Austria from membership in the Zollverein. It tended to draw the Germans towards the leadership of Prussia. Austria fomented division among the princely states to safeguard her own interests. As yet Prussia took no advantage of her position, for the Hohenzollerns allowed themselves to be dominated by Metternich, but if ever the break should come between Austria and Prussia some of the German states would probably rally to Prussia's leadership. The Prussian King William III also adopted reactionary policies and helped Austria in suppressing liberals in Germany. Thus a keen sense of disappointment prevailed over the German liberals.

Gradually the twin ideas of Liberalism and Nationalism developed in Germany and it was in the universities that these two elements found their richest soil. The university of Jena became the centre of Liberalism and agitation and the university students "determined to found a society which should combine the highest ideals of personal life with a great patriotic purpose and sobriety. Chastity and German unity were their watch words. The students held their patriotic demonstrations and at one such demonstrations in 1819 at Wartburg, a reactionary journalist, Kortzebune, was murdered because he was suspected to be a secret emissary of the Czar. Metternich, the reactionary genius of Europe, took full advantage of these developments and called a conference of the German princes at Carlsbad and the famous Carlsbad decrees which were passed by the Federal Diet in 1819 inaugurated a period of repression, suppression and strict control. Restrictions were imposed upon press. The July revolution of 1830 in France sent a new thrill of hope to the Liberals of Germany. The rulers of small German states like Nassau, Burnswick, Hanover, Saxony and Hrse-Cassel were forced by their rulers to grant them liberal constitution. But ruler of Prussia did not concede to the demands of Liberals. The third stage in the progress of German Nationalism was partly a result of the March revolution and of the general upsetting of the political order in 1848. Democracy was a slow growth in Germany. It may perhaps be attributed to the slow development of the middle class, which is the element that ordinarily promotes it. The idea of unity was definitely propagated in two ways. The student societies like the Burschenschaft, clamoured for German unity and wore the colours red, black and gold, as symbolic of this idea. More important were the teachings and writings of university professors, who expanded German history with special emphasis on Prussia's capacity for leadership and on the unhappy disintegration of Germany in a world of national status. The plea for a common sentiment of unity especially against France, the historic foe, and for a fatherland which still existed only in patriotic dreams was reflected in the composing of martial songs, Die Wacht and Rhein (1840) and Deutschland Deutschland uber alles (1841). In 1847, some intellectuals brought the question to the forefront; and after the February revolution in Paris an informal assembly was constituted to plan the meeting of a national constituent assembly. A famous body of princes, elected by a very broad suffrage, met at Frankfurt in May 1848. Historically it is known as the *"Frankfurt Parliament"*. No doubt the February revolution acted as a catalytic agent to precipitate widespread discontent in Germany. The people of Prussia, Austria, Saxony, Hanover and Baden, Schleswig, Holstein rose in revolt and the rulers hastened to grant constitutional reforms. At Frankfurt the crown of united Germany was offered to Frederick William IV, the King of Prussia who declined to accept the offer. The King of Prussia considered Frankfurt to be rebellious and revolutionary and was not in favour of antagonising Austria. Prof. Riker writes, "the Hohenzollern King could not pick up a crown from the gutter", (as he expressed it); he preferred to rule a smaller state by divine right and the power of the sword than to govern all Germany as a constitutional monarch. Moreover Austria was opposed to union, and when Austria recovered her grip on Central Europe, it would be necessary, perhaps to meet her challenge - which might well mean war, not only with Austria herself but with many of the lesser states, at heart opposed to Union. Thus Prussia shirked the issue which Sardinia had just seized. It did not mean that Germans lost their chance to become united on anything like a democratic basis. Liberalism was not to march with nationalism, as in Italy.

The reaction which swept over Germany in 1849 finished not only the Frankfurt Parliament but also the institutions which had been hastily granted during the crisis. The King of Prussia had. promised a constitution establishing manhood suffrage, but when in 1850 the Constitution was promulgated, it was seen how wantonly he had pricked his people. The men of wealth was supposed to dominate the popular chamber. The press was rigidly controlled; public meetings were closely watched and at the least pretext dissolved; and arbitrary arrest and imprisonment were not infrequent. Men supposed to be Liberals were treated almost like outlaws, for all professions were virtually closed to them, and they could hope to get justice in the courts. With the question of German unity, on the other hand, Frederick William had some sympathy, but he merely envisaged a federation of princes looking to Prussian rather than Austrian hegemony; and to this, Austria would not submit. When he started to found such an organization, Austria forced him to give it up in an agreement signed at *Olmutz*; and the old Germanic confederation, was revived "in all its glory". The humiliation of Olmutz as Prussians called this episode, seemed more than ever to prove the moral unfitness of Prussia for leadership. In 1857 William IV became insane and died in 1861 and William I became the King of Prussia. On the accession of William I, new chapter began in the history of German unification. William I had the qualities of firmness and evenness of mind. He was brave, honest, pious, practical and was a Prussian to the core, sensitive to the humiliation of his kingdom and confident in its destiny. It was during the fifties, that the Industrial revolution came to Prussia and modern capitalism founded an enduring structure. Banks multiplied, railway mileage increased and electric telegraph was now for the first time pressed into the service of the business. "Germany", said Bismarck. "does not look to Prussia's liberalism but to her power... Not by speeches and majority votes are the great questions of the day to be decided (therein lay the blunder of 1848 and 1849), but by blood and iron." All that apparently was needed was a man to guide the policy and such a man Prussia produced. - Otto Von Bismarck.

J.A.S. Grenville opines that, "In the transformation of the German States into Germany we can see two forces at work. In one respect unification was the outcome of a traditional struggle between dynastic states, with the populations of the state following their rulers in war. These dynastic conflicts had been common since the Reformation. When viewed from this point of view the struggle for supremacy in Germany was a conflict between German rulers with the most powerful, the King of Prussia, coming out on top after defeating his weaker rivals... In the process of unification there was also another force at work which was revolutionary and anti-particularist. It had surfaced in '1848' and gradually became dominant in twentieth century Germany. This was popular nationalism which found its focus not in particularist state institutions, rulers, administrations or parliaments, but in German institutions, the Kaiser, the Reichstag and the combined German armies." German unification was far more complete than Bismarck in a sense ever intended or imagined it to be. This was because it was the German people who decided that their individual states counted for less than Germany as a whole and the local allegiance and associations were cultural or largely sentimental of historical relics. Only united could Germany be a great power militarily and industrially among other powers; indeed united she would be the leading European power. The needs of Industrial growth and the climatic development of German nationalism burst the nineteenth-century shackles which Bismarck believed he had to ingeniously place on his creation. Thus the story of German unification and Bismarck's role in it is analogous to that of the sorcerer's apprentice. Bismarck released powerful forces and in the end found they had a life of their own, too strong for his successors to control.

From the moment Bismarck became the first minister of the Prussian crown in September 1862, his words, his actions, his conflicts and alliances, dominated first the Prussian, then the German and later European affairs for nearly three decades.

Bismarck himself was always conscious of the limitations of what it was possible for one man to achieve and how dependent the future was on the unpredictable reactions of others as well as on mere chance: 'Politics is neither arithmetic nor mathematics; Bismarck wrote many times; To be sure, one has to reckon with given and unknown factors, but there are no rules, and formulae with which to sum up the results in advance; and he added with characteristic scorn, 'only professors can create scientific laws'. 'By himself the individual can create nothing; he can only wait until he hears God's footsteps resounding through events and then spring forward to grasp the hem of his mantle - that is all." Bismarck's Christianity was Lutheran; he believed in free will. When applied to International affairs this meant that success and failure were not predestined. The diplomat, he believed, must make use of all his talents to assume a successful outcome for his own state in the continuing struggle between nations. He believed in morality as something that certainly applied to private life, but equally looked on moral considerations as having no relevance to politics. He distinguished between questions that concerned individuals and those that affected the interests of groups, be they social classes, political parties, or nations. Bismarck believed that provided he could show that an action served the interests of the state no further justification was needed. A lust for power characterised Bismarck's own political life though he was kept on periphery of political power away from Berlin until the King entrusted him at the age of forty-seven with the Principal ministerial office in 1862. He was a wealthy Junker. Like many of this class he had held a post in the Prussian bureaucracy and was even for a time a delegate of Prussia to the federal diet. Later he served as ambassador to St. Petersburg and Paris and thus acquired a useful knowledge of two important countries with whom he was ultimately to deal. He merged Prussia with himself, and was almost as much of an autocrat as Frederick the Great had been. But he was worthy of his presumption. A less engaging figure than Cavour, he had all the latter's dexterous opportunism, and perhaps more than the latter's daring.

Bismarck was one of those dominating personalities that have shaped the course of history to suit their ends, and it was his luck that he belonged to an age when he did not have to wresttle with the caprices of public opinion. On his mother's side, his forbearers were intelligent middle class professionals, many of them educated, professors of law and civil servants. Although Bismarck reacted against efforts to impose an education on him in his youth, he became a master of the German language spoken and written. He was a good linguist, fluent in French and good in English and had taught himself Russian. As a student he lived a rather dissolute life, but passed his law examination with ease. He spent a short time reluctantly in army service at the age of 24, after his mother's death, helped his father run the family estates.

Ambition and a thirst for power transformed Bismarck and enabled him to subordinate the defects which stood in his way even though he never entirely overcame them. He suffered from periods of excessive eating and drinking, hypochondria and nervous prostration. Clever, self-assured, incapable of playing second fiddle, always determined to be the leader, to have everything revolve around him, these were some of the characteristics of the 'Iron Chancellor'. In the end all these characteristics and others, were typical not of a class, the "Junkers", or of Prussians in general, but were uniquely combined in the make-up of an individual, Bismarck. Bismarck became involved in politics as a representative of the landed gentry to the United Landtag in session in Berlin in 1847. The revolution of 1848 found him back on his estate all ready to rescue the King from the popular mob and the barricades. As a parliamentary representative to the parliament elected in 1850 under the three class system he soon became notorious as an extreme reactionary. What mattered to him was Prussia. In 1851 Frederick William IV chose Bismarck to serve as Prussia's ambassador to the revived German Diet. He travelled to Vienna and Paris widening his experience and meeting Francis Joseph and Napoleon III. The knowledge he gained of Russia and the respect for its potential power was to influence him throughout his later career. William I did not like him much. In his wildest dreams William I could not have imagined in 1862 that the man he had appointed temporarily as chief minister was not to relinquish that office for twenty-eight years, out lasting the King's own long life. Nor with all his self confidence could Bismarck have foretold what lay before him.

His appointment aroused general indignation. A day before proroguing parliament, which refused to pass the estimates, he had bombastically declaimed to the finance committee of the lower house. "It is not by speeches and majority resolutions that the great questions of our times are decided. That was the great mistake of 1848 and 1849. It is by Iron and Blood." Later the phrase in reverse order, 'blood and iron' became famous. At the time it was regarded as a wild and provocative challenge to domestic and International tranquility.

The first step to Prussia's renewed rise to great power status Bismarck saw quite clearly was *to make Prussia* the master of Germany north to river Maine. Prussia should assume this leadership of the German states and Germany should merge in Prussia and not Prussia in Germany. In dealing with the various chessmen on the European diplomatic board Bismarck showed his cleverness and total lack of scruple during the early years. To each he presented—Prussian interests and policies in the light most likely to appeal. To the emperor Napoleon III, Bismarck intimidated that both France and Prussia were dissatisfied powers who cared not a fig for the Vienna treaty settlement of 1815. They should support each other to suitably redraw the map of Europe. To Francis Joseph, Bismarck presented Prussian policy as being based on the tradition of the old alliance between Prussia and Austria and the equality of the two states in German affairs as against the pretensions of the smaller German sovereigns; Prussia like Austria, so Bismarck assured the Austrian ministers, cared nothing for the public opinion or national sentiments and would make policy according to its dynastic interests. To the Tsar of Russia, Bismarck emphasized Prussia's traditional friendship and the interests the two monarchies shared in the suppression of Polish nationalism. During the first years of office Bismarck's aim, far from strengthening 'German' institutions was to attempt to discredit the German Confederation in every possible way, to show its impotence when faced with 'real' states such as Austria and Prussia. Bismarck knew his country men, knew how readily they leant to militarism, and he was prepared to take the risk. By 1863 he had his army—his main instrument for the achievement of German unity.

Since the beginning of his career as Minister-President Bismarck tried to prevent France or Russia from interfering in the internal affairs of Germany. To expel Austria from German Confederation he tried to gain the diplomatic support of other foreign powers. His main objective was to isolate *Austria diplomatically*. In 1863 the Polish insurrection broke out. Both France and England supported the cause of the people of Poland but Bismarck promptly offered his assistance to Russian Czar Nicholas I and earned the Russian gratitude. Russia assumed her neutrality in case of conflict with Austria. In 1863 the Austrian emperor Francis Joseph summoned a conference of the German princes to consider the proposals to reform the federal constitution. Bismarck apprehended that this would strengthen the hold of Austria in Germany and he induced King William I not to attend the congress of princes summoned by the Austrian emperor and the scheme of Austria to introduce reforms in the confederation ended in failure. Bismarck was waiting for an opportunity to pick up a quarrel with Austria. The *Schleswig Holstein question* gave him the chance and he exploited it in such a manner that ultimately it led to war between Prussia and Austria.

Origins of the Seven Weeks War

The Schlewig-Holstein Question and the War with Denmark

Whatever enemies he must meet on the road to German unity, he knew that Austria was one that he could certainly reckon with. In 1863, writes Prof. Thad W. Riker, "he could hardly have foreseen how this war was to tread was opened in this year by the Schleswig-Holstein Question."

Schleswig and Holstein were two duchies attached to the Kingdom of Denmark by a purely personal union - i.e. the tie of common sovereign. There had been a good deal of trouble over their relations to Denmark, since the duchies were mostly German and wished to be ruled by the Duke of Augustenburg who had legally a better claim than the King of Denmark and was besides a German; but in 1852 the concert of Europe, including Austria and Prussia had signed the protocol of London, guaranteeing Danish rule on the basis of a personal union. Thus matters rested for some time. Again in 1863, the Danish parliament precipitated a crisis by adopting a new constitution incorporating Schleswig as an integral part of Denmark. The act at once aroused an outcry in Germany. Schleswig was two-thirds German and was being forced under Danish yoke. Yet, as Schleswig unlike Holstein, was not a member of the German Confederation and as the confederation itself had not been a party to the protocol, this body had no case for interference.

Bismarck at once determined to fish in these troubled waters. He had no intention that the duchies should be won by the confederation and become the spoil of the Duke of Augustenburg. He was resolved that Prussia should have them; especially he coveted Holstein, with its important position between North and Baltic Seas and the excellent harbour of Kiel. In any case he intended that in the solution of an important German question Prussia and not the unwieldly conclave of princes should take the lead. Instead of defying the whole confederation, including Austria, he proposed that Prussia and Austria should jointly intervene. They were to constitute themselves the self-appointed mandatories of Europe to uphold the protocol of London. Sure of international situation, it only remained for Bismarck to give Denmark terms that she would certainly reject and to head off the federal army. He knew that German opinion was against him, but with Austria on his side he did not care. If the Danes should back down, his plan was ruined.

Prussia and Austria demanded a withdrawal of the new constitution within fourty-eight hours, and since only a parliament could do that and since the present parliament had just been dissolved. Everything turned out beautifully for Bismarck. War was declared; the invaders were naturally successful; and only Great Britain blustered. By the treaty of Vienna (1864) Denmark handed over Schleswig and Holstein to Austria and Prussia to dispose of as they pleased. It was in the uncertainty of this settlement—

the assumption that these two rivals could agree on the disposal of the duchies—that one might have found the germ of the Seven Weeks' War. Nothing better showed the hollowness of public law in Europe than the Danish affair. The war might have broken out in 1865. Instead was signed the convention of Gastein. The duchies were divided, Austria administering Holstein, Prussia Schleswig; but nothing was said of their permanent disposition, and Augustenburg was doing all that he could, with Austria's backing to get possession of them. "We have", said Bismarck, "just prepared over the cracks." From the time of the convention of Gastein Bismarck began preparing for war. The army was in readiness but he had to pay heed to Europe, for whenever a war of aggression seemed to be planned between the great powers, outsiders felt that they should be paid for keeping quiet. With Italy he intended to make an alliance, but hardly less important was the neutrality of France; hence the famous interview of Biarritz, at the termination of which Bismarck was satisfied that Napoleon would not bother him. It has always been something of an enigma why the emperor did not demand "pound of flesh"; but these are some reasons. In the first place he wanted the war between Austria and Prussia to take place, for he hoped in the final results to get the left Bank of Rhine (what a unique way of smashing what was left of the Vienna settlement) but he was apparently afraid that by being too grasping now he might drive Bismarck to patch up differences with Austria - he was ignorant of Bismarck's policy. In the second place, Napoleon was in no position at this moment to risk the chance of a possible check and of being drawn into war himself, for he had foolishly embarked on a project outside Europe which not only involved his prestige but had seriously depleted his military resources. Napoleon had converted an effort to collect debts from the Mexican Republic into veritable war of conquest, setting up as emperor of Mexico, Francis Joseph's brother, Maximilan, presumably as a sort of dependent of Imperial France. Napoleon was therefore somewhat in the position of a man who could not pay his legitimate debts because his money is tied up in stocks. Besides Napoleon was already suffering from a malady which eventually carried him off. Besides the Napoleon of Biarritz was no more the Napoleon of Plombieres. Besides his mental sluggishness, there is one blunder that convicts Napoleon of extraordinary want of perception. Like British statesmen of the same period, he had failed to take accurate measure of Prussia. He believed that Austria would win, and that it was with Vienna that he must traffic. And Austria was willing to pay him for his neutrality by promising to cede Venetia to Italy—a return to the Emperor's flair for nationalities.

With Italy, Bismarck made an alliance, using Venetia, of course as the bait. And now that Bismarck had Italy to attack his enemy in the rear, he was not afraid of having to fight the south German princes. Bismarck raised the question of reform of the Germanic Confederation. According to Bismarck's scheme, now laid before the Diet, the assembly of the confederation should be henceforth chosen by universal manhood suffrage, and he allowed the inference that Austria was not to be included in the organisation. But it did exasperate Austria, and enabled Bismarck to mask his real objective in the coming conflict. Here it may be simply be stated that Bismarck used the Schleswig Holstein question to goad Austria into war. On June 11, 1866 Austria pressed the Diet for federal action against Prussia, and the proposal was carried. Prussia then declared the confederation at an end.

The Seven Week's War was won by Prussia because Austria had to fight on two fronts, because she had to face disaffection at home, and because Prussia was incomparably superior in military technique and skill—*Helmuth Von Moltke,* her chief of staff, being one of the greatest strategists of the nineteenth century. Austria suffered a crushing defeat at the hands of Prussia in the *Battle of Konoggratz* or Sadowa. The South German states were, meanwhile, also worsted and soon after Koniggratz sued for peace. Moltke, with an army flushed with victory, resolved to crown his triumph with the capture of Vienna. Thus Bismarck triumphed. The reason for his moderation were three fold. In the first place Bismarck knew that he had accomplished the purpose of the war - there would be no longer any question of the elimination of Austria from Germany—and he did not wish to make a bitter and vengeful enemy. For this, by the Treaty of Prague, Austria was not required to cede an inch of territory to Prussia but only to pay a small indemnity. Prussia satisfied himself with various annexations—Hanover, Hesse, Schleswig, Holstein and with the stipulation *that Austria should exclude herself from all German federations*. To Italy, went Venetia and to please Napoleon the Danes of northern Schleswig were to be allowed to vote their own disposition. In the second place, Bismarck did not wish too utterly to alienate the south German states whose inclusion, would be needed for a united German nation. A third reason for Bismarck's policy was Napoleon. The Seven Weeks' War with Austria had produced these following results: Prussia had aggrandized herself territorially; and people of the territories annexed were not at all consulted as to their fate. Besides, Austria was thrust out of Germany and Prussia was able to form her own free will i.e. the *North German* confederation embracing the German states north of the river Maine. The constitution of this organisation, became the model of the constitution for the future German empire. Moreover, Prussia's hegemony in Germany was thus established. Besides, the war also resulted in the furtherance of Italian unity, since Italy acquired Venetia. Finally, it led to a reconstitution of the Hapsburg monarchy. There never had been such an upheaval in central Europe, and henceforth though Austria remained a great power, there was no question but that the centre of political gravity in central Europe had shifted from Vienna to Berlin. Perhaps another result of the war was the discomfiture of France. German unity was half won.

Napoleon's calculations had been upset. When he asked among other things for a large slice of the Rhineland, here Bismarck remarked that he was talking as though Prussia had been beaten. When after the armistice Napoleon renewed his demand, his ambassador made the mistake of putting it into writing. Bismarck declined it, but pocketed the document. Later Benedetti the French Ambassador asked for Belgium, and the same procedure followed except that Bismarck simply gave an evasive answer. Bismarck worked according to the basic maxim of, "Whenever you sup with the Devil you need a long spoon." Bismarck had one important thing on his mind, i.e. the problem to conciliate the south German paving their way for their inclusion in German empire under Prussia; and he knew the possibility of their inclusion in France, their historic protector. He proceeded then to publish the French demand for territory on the Rhine (which included a province of Bavaria). Now it was possible on the part of North German Confederation to sign a series of treaties with the south German states which put their respective territories under Prussia's military control.

A crucial stage in the unification of Germany was thus brought about, not because the German states wanted unity under Prussian leadership or because the spirit of the German people had manifested itself irresistibly as in 1848. J.A.S. Grenville truly observes, "What had been achieved under Bismarck's leadership in 1866 was the exclusion of Austria from the future development of German affairs. Without Austria Prussia was bound to dominate because of her overwhelming size and strength, Bismarck believed that in good time the southern German state would fall like ripe fruit into the Prussian basket. The Prussian victory of 1866 transformed the politics of Prussia.

The Franco-Prussian War and the Completion of German Unity

By December 1866 Bismarck became decidedly less friendly to France. He now referred to Luxemberg as 'German' and privately wrote that the French alliance would be "too dearly bought" if purchased 'by a humiliating injury to German national feelings'. Bismarck now believed the best way to consolidate the North-German Confederation with the south was 'through the excitement of national feelings' and that could only mean the encouragement of anti-French prejudices. At the same time, he posed as the injured friend when talking to Napoleon-III's emissaries, blaming the emperor for his clumsy diplomacy.

Napoleon III, scathingly attacked by the opposition at home was desperate to prove that his friendly policy towards Prussia, and his sympathetic attitude towards German national consolidation, would pay dividends for France. He also boasted in Paris that Prussia had been halted at the gates of Vienna by France in 1868. The emperor was promptly answered by Bismarck in Berlin. Bismarck considered France as the traditional enemy of Germany. It was the policy of France to keep Germany weak and divided. Bismarck was convinced that France would strenuously resist all efforts to unify Germany under Prussian leadership. He apprehended that Napoleon III would interfere in the deliberation of the treaty of Prague and for this reason Bismarck treated Austria most leniently. He also thought that without a national impulse he would not be able to prevail upon the south German states to join the German empire. It was next achievement of Bismarck's statesmanship to bring these two aspects together to use their estrangement with France to bring these remaining four states into one Prussian system and complete the unification of Germany. A war with France lay in the logic of History, declared Bismarck and prepared his country for that occasion.

Napoleon III was losing his popularity at home, specially after the failure of his Mexican adventure. He remained neutral during the Austro-Prussian War with the hope of some territorial gain. He had thought that a war between Austria and Prussia would be a prolonged one and he would be in a position to play the role of an arbiter of peace. But the sudden and amazing victory Prussia completely upset his plans. The startling growth of Prussian power however demonstrated a challenge to France. It was France, said Theirs, "who was defeated at Sadowa." The French people clamoured for war and revenge for Sadowa. At last Napoleon III intended to have some territories on the bank of river Rhine and Bismarck refused. Napoleon now returned to Belgium as mentioned above, but the neutrality of Belgium had been guaranteed by the European powers in the London Conference of 1831. The French emperor at last made his last bid for compensation and proposed to purchase Luxemberg from the King of Holland. The King of Holland was on the point of transferring Luxemberg to Napoleon III but Bismarck conveyed it to the King of Holland that he would not agree with the proposal. "A land that is essentially German must not fall into the clutches of our hereditary enemies" cried the Germans. Napoleon III was disappointed when the King of Holland refused to sell Luxemberg to France. Napoleon III decided to go to the extent of war to enable France to have some territorial gain and to glorify her in European politics.

But Bismarck had made the necessary diplomatic preparation for the war against France. He had earned the goodwill of Czar, Alexander II of Russia. Since the Crimean War the relations between France and Russia were quite hostile and Bismarck exploited this situation to his greatest advantage. Bismarck treated Austria leniently after the war and imposed on her very moderate terms. Austria, thus, even after the war remained friendly to Prussia. Italy with the prospect of recovering Rome from France to complete her unification agreed to help Prussia in case of war with France. Bismarck thus secured the goodwill and diplomatic support of European powers. He was in search of a pretext for a war with France and the question of succession to the Spanish throne provided the immediate excuse for the war between France and Prussia.

In 1858 the Spanish people expelled their Bourbon queen Isabella and the vacant Spanish throne was offered to Leopold, a relative of the King of Prussia. Leopold had declined to accept the offer due to the protests of France. France opposed this idea because this would lead to the union of Spain and Prussia under a single dynasty. The offer was renewed again and it created a feeling of indignation in France. Napoleon III demanded an assurance that the Crown should not be offered to Leopold again in future. The French ambassador Benedetti met the Prussian King William at Ems to convey the demand of his government. The candidature was withdrawn on 12th July 1870. But Benedetti was asked by the French government to secure the assurance from Prussian King that the candidature of Leopold would not be renewed again. King William I refused to comply with this French demand. In the meantime Bismarck received a telegram from the King who was at Ems regarding his discussion with the French Ambassador, Bismarck exploited the situation and war broke out between France and Prussia.

The French were inflicted with crushing defeats in the battle of Urorth Graveloth and Sedan. The battle of Sedan signalised the overthrow of Napoleon III. During this war the southern states joined hands with Prussia. The Treaty of Frankfurt was concluded with France. According to the terms of the treaty France ceded Alsace and Lorraine to Prussia. She was also asked to pay a huge war indemnity. German troops were to remain in occupation on French soil till the payment of this indemnity.

Ketelbey remarks, "The Franco-German War made Germany mistress of Europe and Bismarck master of Germany." For Napoleon III it was a question of 'prestige' on which the survival of his regime depended. For Bismarck the war with France enabled him to complete the work of unification at one stroke. His particular genius lay in creating situations which afforded opportunities for decisive action. He was like a tiger waiting to spring. Riker opines that, "The Franco-Prussian war was one of the most one-sided conflicts in history. In numbers, generalship and military organisation and equipment Prussia had an overwhelming supremacy. Napoleon himself was taken prisoner along with more than 80,000 men. No one was surprised when Paris proclaimed a republic, September, 4, 1870. The Second empire had collapsed ingloriously in a national crisis. In the second period of war, Paris finally capitulated after a siege of over four months; the preliminaries of peace were ratified by a national assembly and the Treaty of Frankfurt was signed.

Results of the War:
The Establishment of the German Empire

As Bismarck had intended, the unity of Germany was consummated by the war. On January 18, 1871, in the Hall of Mirrors in the famous palace of Versailles, William I was proclaimed German Emperor. (1) There was not a murmur in the general acclamations with which Germans now accepted the leadership of Prussia. (2) And since in the enlarged federation Prussia would continue to hold the dominant position, the German nation would soon adopt the Prussian standard of a militarised and paternalistic state. Germany was not only unified but Prussianized. Italy also completed her unification. (3) For when France had withdrawn her garrison from Rome to aid in the national defence, the Italians entered Rome without any difficulty and made it their capital. (4) Another result of the war was the emergence in International politics of the question of Alsace-Lorraine without sympathising unduly with France for the loss of the provinces. (5) It was in flagrant violation of the new principle of nationality. Furthermore, this action from the practical standpoint to the French, a punishment like this bound to affect the general peace of Europe. Finally, a result of the war was the disturbance of the balance of power. The German empire was so powerful that without a make-weight her position in Europe, especially under the military traditions of Prussia, was ominous for the future. Besides, it was the end of Bonapartism, the system of monarchy based upon the plebiscite which after uniting all Europe under the spectre of Napoleon, ended by leaving France shorn of territory and prestige and faced by a new and formidable rival. Moreover, Russia took advantage of the Franco-German rivalry and violated the Black-Sea clauses of the treaty of Paris. Because of her friendly terms with Prussia she was encouraged again to interfere in the Balkan affairs.

Thus a mere quarrel between Prussian and French ministers had been turned into the great German patriotic war in defence of the fatherland. Of course it was a 'sham' to use one of Bismarck's favourite phrases. Had the Germans wished it, Germany could have been unified without a war with France.

29

Bismarck's Germany

Historians place Otto von Bismarck (1815-1898) beside other great Germans: Luther, Fredrick the Great and Goethe. A talented person, Bismarck is commonly hailed as the architect of modern Germany.

Bismarck was a product of the stalemate produced by the abortive revolution of 1848 in the German-speaking world. This revolution was but a link in the series of revolutionary movements unleashed by the Great French Revolution of 1789. The French Revolution, wrote on its banner the inspiring catchwords of liberty, equality and fraternity. The impact of the historic event can be correctly gauged by the symbolic meeting of Napoleon, the harbinger of the new age and Goethe, the greatest man of letters in Germany. It is also not without significance that Beethoven, the biggest figure in western music, also a German and contemporary, was so profoundly affected by the French Revolution that he dedicated his Eroica symphony to Napoleon as the symbol of this revolution. That both Goethe and Beethoven were subsequently disillusioned with Napoleon when he became emperor and a tyrant.

The revolution in France dealt a moral blow to the era of dynastic rule in Europe. In the dynastic politics which dominated Europe after the decline of feudalism there was no place for the people and the exercise by them of their rights. The people were treated like inanimate matter, like a piece of real estate or movable property. The 1848 revolution sought to introduce a new principle of political organisation derived from the Great French Revolution. The principle of popular sovereignty was sought to be substituted for the personal rule of the monarch.

Impact of the French Revolution

Under the stimulus of the French revolutionary wars, and, more especially, the defeat of Prussia by Napoleon in 1806 at Jena, nationalism became a force in Germany. It deeply affected all Germany, and, especially Prussia. The Prussian statesman Stein introduced important reforms which had the effect of transforming the Prussian hereditary serfs into emancipated peasants. The land-owning class of Prussian aristocrats, called the junkers, saw the new reforms as directed at their power. This class therefore became an ardent enemy of reformist impulses and liberal principles. Nevertheless there could now be no return to the old order. The ferment had gone too deep, and could not be stilled completely.

What was the nature of this mid-nineteenth century convulsion? It was a bourgeois democratic revolution whose avowed aim was to replace dynastic states by nation-states, and politics based on absolutism by liberal parliamentary constitutions. It was both a struggle of social classes and divergent philosophies and principles. The old order was based on the rule of hereditary princes and landed aristocracy. Legitimacy and birth were the characteristic features of the old ideology. The new order was represented by the rising cities, the third estate, the new industrial and trading middle class and to a certain extent, also the common people. It sought to achieve power in the state on the ideological platform popularised by the Great French Revolution. The revolution of 1848 prospered in the original home of the Great Revolution of 1789. It succeeded overthrowing the monarchy in France; but the revolution did not culminate in the establishment of a stable constitutional democracy as it was known in Britain. The outcome was, first, a "plebisicitary democracy" and, finally, the new empire of Louis Napoleon, the nephew of the great Napoleon.

The French bourgeoisie did not have the strength of their counterpart in Britain and could not establish their direct rule. The weakness and timidity of the liberal bourgeoisie in other countries, especially Germany, was much greater. Its lack of revolutionary fervour and its obsessive fear that the revolution would go too far in the direction of mass democracy and socialism resulted in its defeat. The victory of reaction had disastrous consequences.

Old Order Restored by Vienna Settlement

The German revolutionaries wanted nothing less than the upsetting of the post-Napoleonic Vienna settlement of 1815. This settlement was based on the principle of legitimacy. The historic monarchies and the ancient dynasties had been restored by the Vienna arrangements—inspired by the conservative Austrian statesman, Metternich. The German liberals wanted to put an end to absolutism and inaugurate constitutional monarchy patterned after the English model. Their objective was a German national state. Germany was then split up into many sovereignties and the loose German confederation did not exercise any effective central authority. Austria and Prusssia were the two largest units of the confederation. But instead of giving the Germans a purposeful central administration the two frustrated each other.

The presidency of the German Confederation was held by Austria. But Austria was not a national state. Its foundation was dynastic. Its very existance was the negation of the national principle. Apart from the German portion of its population, Austria embraced within its territorial limits people belonging to different nationalities, races and linguistic groups. The Austrian statesmen, not surprisingly, saw in linguistic nationalism total dissolution of their historic monarchy.

The other major German power was Prussia. However after Frederick the Great had fallen on evil days, the Austrians did not treat the Prussians on a footing of equality. The Deutscher Bund (Confederal German Assembly) had given way to a National Assembly in the course of the revolution of 1848. It offered the crown of united Germany to William I, King of Prussia. The Prussian King was not prepared to accept the crown from the people's representatives. The conservatives did not want a unified Germany based on liberalism. They knew that the currents of national unity were running strong and could not be resisted. They therefore accepted reluctantly a united Germany. But they were determined to preserve the social *status quo*. They sought to perpetuate a Germany of princes and aristocratic classes; they offered staunch resistance to the British type constitutional monarchy where real power would reside in the people's representatives.

The bourgeoisie in Germany was very weak. It did not have the strength which the industrial middle class displayed in Great Britain. Germany's aristocratic classes also did not have the foresight of their British equivalents. British bourgeoisie had pioneered the Industrial Revolution. The wisdom of the English land-owning middle class made a genuine compromise (embodied in the various reform acts) possible in England. In Germany the bourgeoisie had neither the confident English strength nor the energy and the revolutionary *elan* of the French bourgeoisie. The landowning classes in Germany were not prepared to make any compromise in the interest of national unity and progress either.

German Unification

There were three ways of uniting the badly splintered German-speaking people: the first alternative was a popular revolution and "eviction of all the princes, and the establishment of a united German republic;" the second alternative was to bring together the German territories under "Austrian overlordship;" and the third way of accomplishing this task was for Prussia to push Austria out of Germany and unite the German people under Prussian leadership.

Popular revolution proved to be beyond the strength and resources of the German bourgeoisie. The failure of the revolution resulted in the restoration of a reactionary and divided Germany. Austria was Roman Catholic and had very little affinity with the Protestant German states. Besides, Austria, which was launched on a course which led to multinational dynastic configuration, was not really interested in the unification of the German-speaking people in a powerful nation-state. The only alternative that remained was the exclusion of Austria from Germany and the securing of German unification under Prussian hegemony. And this is what Bismarck tried to do after his king appointed him Prime Minister of Prussia.

Bismarck began his career as an elected member of the United Prussian Diet. He was looked upon by his class as the most effective champion of its ideas and interests. He gave expression to the most conservative and reactionary views and enjoyed conveying them in a most "offensive manner" (*Bismarck and the German Empire,* by Erick Eyck, p.19). However his attachment to the interests of his class was not sincere. For him it was a kind of posturing. He was trying to secure the junker support to promote his own career.

Bismarck is not unjustly credited with the creation of a united Germany. In order to accomplish this mission Bismarck underwent a period of preparation. His first important assignment was as Prussian envoy to the revised German Diet. It was from his Frankfurt days that the outlines of Bismarck's German policy became fixed. The German Diet was not a representative assembly. The members were not elected by the people, and were not accountable to them. They were delegates of several sovereign states. Bismarck definitely wanted German unification, but he was wary about arousing popular enthusiasm to achieve it. He was for a summit unity among the German princes. Bismarck feared a popular upheaval. Secondly, as a member of the Prussian ruling class Bismarck wanted this unification, to take place not under Austrian leadership but under Prussian auspices. He wanted the Prussian king to become the German Emperor. A united Germany established from below would have resulted in a strong centralised state. This would, undoubtedly, have facilitated the economic development of the United nation. But Bismarck distrusted even moderate liberalism and desired top arrangements among the German princes even if it entailed a degree of autonomy for the princes. Thirdly, Bismarck wanted a conservative constitution to be established in Germany. He viewed with scorn a constitutional monarchy based on parliamentarianism. It is true that Bismarck did not much relish interference by the Emperor in the high affairs of the state, but he wanted interference of people's representatives even less'. His ardent desire was to dominate both the Emperor and Parliament in the name of what he conceived to be the interest of the state.

It was during his term in the confederal assembly at Frankfurt that Bismarck learnt the intricacies of German politics. He soon became convinced that Austria would not treat Prussia as its peer. The high and mighty attitude of the Austrians offended him. Because Austria had filled the office of "Holy Roman Emperor of the German people " the Austrians had come to look upon their primacy among German states as a matter of right. They thought it natural that other German states should show the utmost deference to Austria. There was a convention in the German Diet that other delegates should not smoke in the presence of the Austrians. Bismarck resented this. He thought that both in terms of strength and dynamism Prussia was at least an equal of Austria if not its superior. But in dynastic terms the Hapsburgs had precedence and priority. In an effort at self-assertion on behalf of his king and state Bismarck took out his pipe and defiantly smoked in the presence of the Austrian President. This was a typically Bismarckian method of signalising the new equality of Prussia and Austria in German affairs.

Bismarck's Ambition

It was Bismarck's ambition to be the minister President of Prussia but the Prussian king was not, yet "ready" for him. Before taking the supreme office in the Prussian state he filled the posts of ambassador of Prussia to the Court of St. Petersburg (Russia) and the Court of Napoleon III in France. Both these appointments were a training ground for Bismarck. The experience he thus acquired of international affairs and the strengths and weaknesses of the leading figures of European politics stood him in good stead.

Bismarck's ambition was from the beginning directed towards seizing the supreme power in the state, and from that position lead the state to strength and glory. Bismarck likened the Prussian administration to an orchestra. But he did not wish to play a minor role in it.

When a constitutional conflict developed between the Prussian Assembly and the ministry, the king, William II, was persuaded by the minister of war, Roon, that Bismarck alone could successfully pilot the ship of Prussian state in the stormy days ahead. It was at this point that destiny beckoned to the chief ministership of the Prussian state. As a great servant of the state Bismarck remained in power till his resignation as Reich Chancellor in 1890.

Bismarck's Limited Wars

The period of Bismarck's service can be divided into two parts. In the first period he consolidated the position of Prussia in Germany and Europe as the foremost German state. To establish this supremacy he waged three short but decisive wars. The first, against Denmark was in alliance with Austria over the issue of Schleswig-Holstein. Denmark was beaten swiftly and decisively and was divested of the possession of these two provinces in which German-speaking people preponderated. After settling this question, Bismarck moved towards a conflict with Austria. Bismarck and the Prussian military organisation made meticulous preparations for a decisive and speedy victory. The Prussian army was superior to the Austrain Army in training and organisation, equipment and tactics. By skilful diplomacy Bismarck secured Austria's isolation. After the defeat of Austria at Sadowa Bismarck did not allow the war to be expanded further. He brought it to a speedy conclusion without imposing onerous conditions on the Austrians. The objective was to establish the primacy of Prussia in German affairs.

The leadership of Germany was now captured by Prussia and retained by it hereafter. Bismarck had now taken great strides forward towards the realisation of his dream of German unity under the Hohezollern leadership. He had no doubt about the popular sentiment in favour of unity. Only two obstacles now remained. To expel French influene from south Germany and, simultaneously, overcome the reluctance of German princes to submerge their sovereignties and privileges in a United Germany. The controversy over Spanish succession provided Bismarck with an opportunity to make war on France. He was aided by the stupidity and cupidity of Louis Napoleon. If the latter had played his cards well Bismarck's wishes would have been frustrated. Later, on Bismarck fostered a legend that the Franco-Prussian war was planned in advance by Bismarck with meticulous care. But nothing of the kind had really happened. Bismarck understood human limitations very well. He did not believe that statesmen, no matter how foresighted, could create events. However, he knew that a wise statesman could take advantage of the unfolding events and the mistakes of others and use them for his own purpose. This is exactly what he did. The blunders of Napoleon III played into his hands.

The French started the war with high expectations. Despite their vaunted valour and their glorious military tradition, the French were not really prepared for the new kind of war which drew strength from science, invention and industrial organisation. The Germans had drawn the necessary lessons from the American civil war, the first of the modern wars. They had learnt to make use of railways for transporting armies and supplies; they had equipped their arms with the artillery pieces made by the steel works owned by the Krupps. The French suffered a most humiliating defeat.

Bismarck was not in favour of imposing a peace on France. But now a mass hysteria had been roused in Germany, and Bismarck could not overrule the preemptory demands of the Prussian General Staff and the king. Thus Alsace and Lorraine were annexed to Germany. A huge indemnity was imposed on the defeated French nation. Bismarck tried to reduce its rigour somewhat. But he was now a prisoner of the chauvinism which military success had bred in Germany. Nevertheless Bismarck was nervous about inviting fierce resistance among the French people. He was afraid of awakening in France. He had to make superhuman exertions in the next twenty years to keep the peace of Europe and to preserve the ascendancy which Germany had acquired. He regretted that circumstances had prevented him from making a generous peace with France.

Marx had described the first phase of the Franco-Prussian war as a "war of defence," but contended later that it had "degenerated into a war against the French people." (*Selected works* Vol.2, p. 192). Both Marx and Engels were critical of the terms of the peace imposed by Bismarck on the French people. Marx denounced Bismarck as a "Prussian Shylock" and a "bully." (*Selected works* Vol.2, pp. 208 & 234).

Friedrich Engels, himself a German, strongly disapproved of Bismarck's annexation of Alsace and Lorraine. He remarked that although the major portion of these two provinces was German- speaking, they had become French field in spirit. It was the French Revolution which had liberated these two provinces from feudal shackles and had given them liberty. The people had become French by choice. So much so that subsequently they "selected only staunch Frenchmen to represent them in the Reichstage and rejected everyone who was suspected of even the mildest pro-German sympathies." (*Ibid.*, Vol. 3, p. 415.)

Marx was right in predicting that Germany's annexation of the two provinces would force France into the arms of Russia. But his fears of Russian domination of Central Europe were groundless. It was not France which played the Russian game. It was the skilful French diplomacy in the post- Bismarck period which lured both Tsarist Russia and Britain into an alliance with France. It was therefore completely wrong for Marx to assert that as a result of the peace treaty Germany would become "the avowed tool of Russian aggrandisement." (*Ibid.*, Vol. 2, p. 199). In fact it was the subsequent reversal by Germany of Bismarck's policy of friendship with Russia that enabled France to win over a reluctant Russia for the policy of creating a Franco-Russian military alliance.

Franco-German War

Marx found it difficult to curb his prejudice against the Slavic peoples in general and the Russians in particular. He was of the view that the estrangement between France and the new Germany would make the Tsar the "arbiter" of Europe. This was not correct. At that point of time Russia was an industrially backward country, whereas both France and Germany, especially the latter, were much more advanced. Russia began to industrialise speedily, with the help of European capital, several years after the Franco-Prussian war, and it emerged as a super-power only at the end of the Second World War. Bismarck's policy of friendship with Russia helped to preserve peace and did not bring Russian overlordship as Marx had feared. In other respects Marxist evaluation of Bismarck was penetrating.

Marx was a product of his environment and despite his pretension to universality and genuine flashes of insight, his judgment was sometimes clouded by his West European bias. It is significant that in his first address to the General Council of the First International he quoted with obvious pride the manifesto of the German Social-ist-Democratic Workmen's party. The manifesto said: "We protest against the annexation of Alsace and Lorraine. And we are conscious of speaking in the name of the German working class. In the common interest of France and Germany, in the interest of peace and liberty, in the interest of *Western civilisation against Eastern barbarism*, the German workmen will not patiently tolerate the annexation of Alsace and Lorraine..." (Ibid., Vol. 2, p. 199.)

The German Empire Launched

The Prussian victory at Sedan sent a wave of enthusiasm throughout the German nation. Bismarck was not able to persuade the princes of Germany to offer the crown to the Prussian King. The king had refused the crown in 1848 when offered by the popularly elected National Assembly. Now the king's condition had been fulfilled. The princes themselves conferred this honour on the Prussian king. The popular representatives also expressed their hearty approval of the act.

Bismarck wished to set up a Germany united on the federal principle. To overcome the attachment of some of the more important German princes to their separate sovereignties, Bismarck offered them autonomy and certain privileges. However, for the purposes of defence, foreign policy and economic development Germany, on Bismarck's insistence, effectively became a single unit.

Germany's industrial growth, now vastly stimulated by unity, made rapid strides. This industrial advance, in turn, made Germany a cohesive centralised state. But this was not Bismarck's doing. The forces released by unification were so strong that neither the assurance of Bismarck to the German princes to preserve their rights nor the desire of these princes for autonomy could prevail against the strong centralised tendency set in motion by German unity and rapid industrialisation.

Bismarck, thus, objectively became the foster mother of nationalism: although he did not like the blind fury of an aggressive German nationalism, it was he who provided it with a concrete framework of a powerful militarised state.

The constitution of the united German Empire was not a liberal constitution. Bismarck never accepted the principle of parliamentary responsibility. However, he insisted on the principle of collective ministerial responsibility: when the new emperor, twenty years later, began to develop direct relations with his ministers Bismarck did not like this. Bismarck treated the Reichstag with contempt. He repeatedly sought to rule without parliament, especially in the matter of military budget.

Parliament in Imperial Germany

Bismarck nevertheless desired a representative Reichstag to mirror the moods of the German nation, and provide him with a platform, a means of moulding German public opinion.

Karl Marx and Friedrich Engels were not unimpressed by the work of the "German magician". Engels praised the introduction by Bismarck of the universal franchise, and said that despite his conservative claims Bismarck had put into the hands of the German working class a weapon to secure which, it had been described in the Communist Manifesto, as "one of the first and most important tasks" of the proletariat.

Bismarck first introduced the principle of universal franchise as Engels noted, in elections to the North German Reichstag. After the establishment of the German Empire in 1871 this principle was applied to elections to the Reichstag of United Germany. Engels characterised universal franchise as '"revolutionary", and devoted the bulk of his introduction to Marx's work, *the Class Struggle in France,* to its impact on the methodology of revolutionary transformation. This introduction bears the date 6 March 1895, which, significantly, was the fag end of both his life and that of Bismarck.

Bismarck Since 1871

After the foundation of the German empire he considered Germany a satisfied power. Although he waged no less than three wars after he became Prussia's chief minister, he turned into an upholder of the *status quo*. He had two supreme objectives: to preserve stability and order and maintain Germany's primacy in the concert of Europe. The strength and central situation of the German empire plus its economic dynamism made it easy to preserve Germany's leadership. Bismarck had no urge for military adventures. Even the colonial empire he acquired for the sake of prestige, without great exertion. In fact his horizon did not extend beyond Europe. He thought that the Hapsburg empire (Austria-Hungary) was an essential factor in the European order. A Europe reorganised on the principle of nationality would open a Pandora's box. In order to preserve European peace he pledged support to Austria-Hungary. It was not designed to encourage Austrian expansionism, it was designed to check it. Similarly, the Reinsurance Treaty with the Czar assured German neutrality in a war in which Russia was a victim of aggression. He gave these apparently contradictory guarantees with a view to preventing wars of aggression which, he feared, would destroy the precarious balance in Europe.

His alliance with Austria-Hungary and the Reinsurance Treaty with Russia were not wholly based on duplicity. Bismarck wanted to ensure Germany's security and European peace. He never claimed that he was leading a moral crusade. Bismarck's peace policy could in the circumstances be secured only methods of Realpolitik. His Reinsurance Treaty with Russia was intended to prevent a line up of France and Russia, and also ensure that Austria-Hungary did not engage in a war of aggrandisement against the Russian empire. In one of his perceptive speeches before German Parliament (Reichstag) in 1888 Bismarck put his theme succinctly; "...I advance the proposition that, on account of our geographical position, we must make greater efforts than other powers would be obliged to make in view of the same ends. We lie in the middle of Europe. We have at least three fronts on which we can be attacked. France has only an eastern boundary, Russia only its western, exposed to assault. We are, moreover, more exposed than any other people to the dangers of a hostile coalition because of our geographical position, and because, perhaps of the feeble power of cohesion which, until now, the German people have exhibited when compared with others." (*The world's great speeches*, p. 122)

While Bismarck's policy was directed towards keeping British influence out of Europe he was wise enough not to do anything that would excite Britain's opposition and envy. He had no pretensions to a world policy and world domination. He did not enter into any rivalry with Britain in naval power. His colonial ventures also did not challenge Britain's overseas empire. Not only were his successors brash, aggressive and impetuous, they also allowed Russo-German relations to be exacerbated. On the top of this, by undertaking an ambitious naval programme they challenged Britain's sea power. These moves ensured that eventually a great coalition would be formed against Germany.

To ensure German national security, Bismarck laid down the principle that in a company of five great European powers, it was essential for Germany always to be one of a grouping of at least three. When the Slavo-phile elements in Czarist Russia mounted a campaign against the treaty bond between Russia and Germany, Bismarck became apprehensive about Germany's security. But he wisely persevered in a policy of great prejudice and reserve, professing continued confidence in the treaty relationship between Germany and Russia. Apart from the signs of hostility towards Germany among the chauvinist sections in Russia, what made Bismarck even more fearful was the immaturity of William, then crown prince, but who, as everybody knew, would, soon became the emperor. The crown prince had begun to take an increasing interest in the affairs of the state, especially Germany's foreign relations. In a despatch from the German ambassador in Vienna a mention had been made of the Austrian foreign minister's observation that it would be desirable to destroy Russia's military power before it could become too dangerous. In the margin of this despatch the crown prince expressed his assent. William's opinion expressed flat opposition to Bismarck's line in foreign relations. The initiatives of the young prince gave Bismarck great alarm. It was the settled policy of Bismarck to avoid a war with Russia. He was prepared to do everything in his power to retain the Russian tie. He wanted to retain alll levers that would permit him to obstruct the conclusion of a Franco-Russian alliance. He was in favour of mediating differences between Russia and Austria. He also tried to bind Italy in his own country. He further sought to promote a closer entente with the British.

When William became emperor, the young sovereign and his new set of advisers began to question the rationale of Bismarck's policy. And so a clash between the two became inevitable. Bismarck soon departed from the European political scene which he had so completely dominated as the German Chancellor. The new Emperor destroyed one by one the bases of Bismarck's European system. It was finally Germany which decided not to renew the treaty with Russia.

Thus Russia was driven by the combined actions of the German emperor and Russian chauvinists into the embrace of France, relations with Italy were allowed by the new rulers to deteriorate, and, with the ambitious programme of German naval construction, the fear and enmity of the British nation was roused. An awful prospect of war on several fronts which Bismarck had tried to avoid—was thereby opened. Bismarck's European order collapsed.

Bismarck's was an old world outlook. He did not understand that new forces of mass-democracy and national feeling were struggling for dominance and that nothing could stop these forces from sweeping everything in its path away. For Bismarck did not realise in time that these forces, which had a destructive potential, could be contained and moderated only within the confines of the steam engine of a genuine parliamentary government.

If despite Bismarck's effort to curb nationalist fervour an extreme form of nationalism in the end swept Germany off its feet, there was nothing that he could have done to prevent the resurgence of Polish, Hungarian and Italian national feeling. The same upsurge of nationalism overwhelmed the Balkan nationalities also. The unification of Germany under Prussian leadership fuelled the engine of industrialisation in Germany. Introduction of the principle of universal suffrage and social insurance, designed by Bismarck to fight the liberal bourgeoisie, whetted the appetite of the German working class. Bismarck's anti-socialist laws could not stem the rising tide of socialism either.

Western Response

The western states have been aggressive from their very inception. The three leading European nations, the French, the British and the Germans have been the most warlike of them all. The English first wasted their super-abundant energies in the subjugation of France. This provoked a fierce French national resistance, and in the next three centuries Europe had to spend its vitality in curbing France. Britain wisely withdrew from the contest for domination in Europe, and acquired a vast overseas empire. By achieving a strong and united Germany Bismarck built her into a dynamic power. Nationalism, industrialisn, mass hysteria, and popular democracy, coupled with the innate warlike spirit of the western states, steadily undermined the Bismarckian system based on moderation and checks and balances.

In domestic politics Bismarck sought to preserve the two foundations of his constitution. He was averse to the principle of ministerial responsibility to parliament. He said he was responsible alone to the sovereign. However, he really did not permit any freedom of action to the emperor. The emperor was to be solely guided by his Chancellor, especially in the sphere of foreign relations.

Germany was sharply divided on religious lines, between the Catholics and the Lutherans. The prolonged wars of religion devastated Germany. Finally, a stalemate had been reached in these wars which was in a way documented by the Treaty of Westphalia. Only then was the principle of toleration firmly established in Germany and Europe. Bismarck revived the old controversies to attain his own ends. He detested not only liberal democracy but also mass parties. This brought him into a "cultural" conflict with the Roman Catholic Church. In this he did no service to the cause of religious toleration, the absence of which had brought so much harm on Germany.

What were then the solid achievements of Bismarck? Although Germany's position in Europe and his personal ascendancy were based on three short and decisive wars which Prussia waged under his direction, his greatest achievement, was the maintenance of the European balance of power, limitation of all conflicts and their speedy termination without letting these disturb the peace of Europe. This was no mean achievement in a world where great powers were engaged in a fearful arms race. This long spell of peace was made possible because of the solid reconstruction of Europe which the greatest statesman of the 19th century (Bismarck) worked out in the seventies of the last century.

To sum up, Bismarck checked and moderated the drive of the unified, and aggressive German nation towards its territorial expansion. Neither Kaiser Willian II nor Hitler could do this, and, therefore, brought the German state to total desolation and collapse. Bismarck limited and restrained the unlimited programme of German unification. He did not seek to bring the entire German-speaking people, the whole German nation under one sovereignty. He knew that if the principle of nationality was allowed unfettered sway, this would result in the disintegration of three powerful empires (Romanov, Hapsburg and Hohenzollern) and a general conflagration. Bismarck never sought to absorb German-speaking Austria into the German Empire. Hitler could not resist the temptation and thereby paved the way for another World War.

Bismarck, the "conservative", was really an innovator. He was the harbinger of the welfare state. It was he who gave the German proletariat a stake in the social order. He could not stop them from making a bid for power.

Last Days

After Bismarck began to clash with the young emperor, the German statesman began to reconsider his anti-liberal positions. Forced with the constant interference of the emperor, he declared that absolutism was bad and bureaucracy worse. He now began to appreciate the liberal virtues: "Perhaps my dutiful behaviour has been the cause of the deplorable backbone in Germany," he lamented. He regretted that the German Parliament was not powerful enough and was in no position to restrain the brash new leaders. Having fought the principle of ministerial responsibility to Parliament, he now repented his all too successful effort to perpetuate the weakness of the Reichstag.

However, it was now too late. The collision between the Chancellor and his emperor was inevitable. But 40 years in the service of the state, 28 years in supreme power, had spoilt Bismarck for retirement, one of his biographers remarked. His retirement was a period of intense disillusionment. One by one the elements in his balanced system of foreign policy were being undermined: moderation, Russian link, England's non-hostility, nothing remained.

Kissinger has remarked that operating the Bismarckian system of balance of power needed a man of Bismarck's genius and ability (Kissinger in *Daedalus*, Summer 1968, vol.9, No. 3, pp. 906-7). A succession of statesmen of such calibre is well-nigh impossible. This was the fatal weakness of the Bismarckian construction. When the control of the ship of state was taken away from his masterly direction the system did not survive for long.

30

The First World War

The international crisis since the Vienna settlement of 1815 vitiated the political atmosphere and widened the gulf between the Great Powers. In the political atmosphere of 1914 surcharged with suspicion, ill-will and provocation propaganda, it was not difficult to create another crisis. The murder of Archduke Francis Ferdinand on 28 June 1914, provided the great powers with the 'occasion' to test their respective strength, and this precipitated a world war.

General Causes of the First World War

Division of Europe into two Armed Camps

During the course of last 50 years uptil 1914, on account of the diplomatic activity of the Great Powers, Europe had been divided into two armed camps—the Triple Alliance (Germany, Austria-Hungary and Italy) and the Triple Entente (Great Britain, France and Russia). The relations between these two blocs were most antagonistic as was clear from the attitude they took in the settlement of various political crisis from 1905 to 1913. Consequently, the armed peace that reigned in the last decade was not likely to last long.

Growth of a Militant Germany

Germany from the very outset was a military state. She was the product of the "blood and iron" policy of Bismarck and the same policy continued even after the achievement of German independence and unity. The German army was the strongest and most powerful engine of war in Europe. But German ambition was not confined to Europe alone. Her expanding trade and the demand for "a place in the sun" required an equally powerful navy. Britain's greatness was mainly due to her naval supremacy. Hence Germany must be equally strong at sea if she wanted to be a world power. Therefore she must have as great and powerful navy as Great Britain. To achieve this end, she launched two ambitious programmes of naval expansion in 1898 and 1907. This led to the British hostility and competition.

So long as Germany had not challenged British naval superiority, the relations between the two had remained cordial. Bismarck had taken special care not to offend Great Britain. But after his exit, German foreign policy also changed. English friendship was thrown to the winds and a programme of naval expansion was launched, and consequently relations between the two became intensely strained.

Competition in Armaments

The increased German military and naval development evoked a race in armaments and all the great powers of Europe started raising the strength of their armies and naval forces. This unhealthy competition further accentuated the bitterness that had already existed among the members of the two blocs and brought the war nearer. In spite of the two Hague Conferences armaments could not be limited.

German Jingoism - Kaiser's Provocative Attitude

Administration in Germany was dominated by the army. The civilian authority was definitely subservient to it, as the Kaiser invariably supported the latter if there was a conflict between the two. The army often used hostile language and exhibited a bellicose attitude towards the members of the Triple Entente. The Kaiser himself has asserted on a previous occasion that if he had not kept his people under control there would have been a war with England long ago. His attitude in the Moroccan crisis was most provocative. German admirals and generals followed in the footsteps of their master. Admiral Tripitz and General Von Moltke claimed that they could sweep England, France and Russia aside if they had their way. This sabre-rattling of the German army and naval officers overawed the politicians in their own country and created a good deal of distrust abroad. Consequently every political move of Germany was watched with great suspicion.

Franco-German Rivalry over Alsace and Lorraine

France had not forgotten her defeat in 1870-71 and had not reconciled herself to the loss of Alsace and Lorraine. The German annexation of these provinces was a running sore in the body politic of France and sooner or later a war of revenge was bound to follow. The strained relations between the two countries were mostly responsible for the formation of the Triple Alliance and the Dual Alliance (between France and Russia).

The Balkan Problems

No single event influenced the outbreak of the war in 1914 more than the Balkan wars of 1912-13. The clash of interests of the great powers in the Balkan peninsula was the most outstanding cause of the First World War.

The pre-1914 scene of Europe shows how relations between Austria-Hungary on the one side, and Serbia and Russia on the other hand reached a breaking point. Serbia sufficiently enlarged after the Balkan war of 1912-13, was in a much stronger position in 1914 than in 1908. She had not forgotten the Austrian usurpation of Bosnia and Herzegovina, two predominantly Slav provinces. She had been dreaming of uniting all the Slav peoples in one state. The only country that stood between her and the realisation of her dream was Austria-Hungary. If she could be humbled her object would be achieved. Austria-Hungary too regarded Serbia as her chief enemy. The existence of an independent Serbia talking of pan-Slavism and dreaming of a Greater Serbia, was a perpetual source of nuisance to the solidarity of the Austro-Hungarian empire. A large number of Slavs within her empire, pining to join Serbia and amenable to Serbian propaganda, were a constant headache to her. Moreover, it was Serbia which stood in the way of the realisation of Austrian designs of expansion as far as Salonika and even Constantinople. Hence the cry was that Serbia must be crushed.

The Balkan tangle was further complicated by the unqualified support of Russia to Serbia. Russia, a Slave nation herself encouraged Serbian nationalism and pan-Slavism. She hoped that the Slavs, and Croats living in the Austro-Hungarian empire would one day unite under the Serbian banner. Could Serbia not play the same part in the unification of the Slavs as was played by Piedmont in the case of Italian unity? Surely she could, with Russian support. So the crux of the Balkan problem lay in the rival aspirations of Austria-Hungary and Serbia supported by Russia.

Since the Bosnian annexation of 1908, both Russia and Serbia harboured the most evil designs against Austria. A bitter press campaign had been unleashed in Serbia where there was no censorship, inciting the Slav subjects of the Emperor to rise against him and to help Serbia in achieving a Greater Serbia or Yugoslavia. In addition, secret societies with the object of assassinating Austrian officials had been established in Serbia. Their membership transcended the Serbian borders and many young Slavs abroad were their active members. Several attempts had been made to assassinate high Austrian dignitaries including the heir to the Austrian throne.

The hostile Serbian press campaign and the subversive activities of the Slav terrorists had in turn caused extreme hostility in Austria and Hungary. Count Berchtold, the Austrian foreign minister, and Count Stephen Tisza, the Hungarian premier, were itching to have an opportunity to crush and silence Serbian nationalism for ever.

Nor was the conflict in the Balkans confined to Austria, Hungary, Russia and Serbia. The relations between Austria and Rumania were also strained and had almost reached a breaking point. The cause of friction was the maltreatment of the Rumanians in Hungary and Count Tisza was mainly responsible for their oppression. As a result of the suppression of their brethren in Hungary, there was great unrest and anti-Hungarian feeling in Rumania. Consequently, both Germany and Austria-Hungary were perturbed lest Rumania which had friendly relations with them, might forsake her allegiance to the Triple Alliance.

The Balkan problem was further complicated by the fact that Germany had been expanding her influence in the Ottoman Empire. Her generals were training the Turkish armies and she had obtained valuable economic concessions from the Sultan. Her Turkish policy, particularly the construction of the Berlin-Baghdad Railway, was bitterly resented by Russia.

Moreover, both Austria-Hungary and Germany had been trying to isolate Serbia in the Balkans. Rumania and Bulgaria had kings of German descent and the queen of Greece was a German princess. The only country which was out of their fold and was hostile to them was Serbia. Her extinction would put an end to pan-Slavism and open the way to Salonika and Constantinople. The whole of the Balkan peninsula would be in their grip. Russians as allies and kinsmen of the Serbs could be bullied into submission as they had been in 1908. So the Austrian statesmen waited for a suitable occasion to achieve their objective.

The Immediate Cause

The murder of Archduke Francis Ferdinand and his consort in the streets of Serajavo, the capital of Bosnia. The assassin, Gavrilo Princep, a Bosnian revolutionary, was an Austrian subject, but Slav by race. A storm of indignation broke out in Austria-Hungary and a bitter anti-Serbian propaganda was unleashed. Serbian hostility was the root cause of the tragedy and Serbia was accused of the conspiracy to murder the heir to the Austrian throne.

Historical research in recent times has tried to prove that the assassin and his accomplines had their training in Belgrade and they used Serbian weapons and were members of the Serbian secret terrorist society of 'Black Hand'.

However to the anti-Serbian party in Austria headed by Count Berchtord, no better occasion than this could present itself to have a final reckoning with Serbia "Politically, the murder of the Archduke served admirably the purpose of the war party at Vienna."

The news of the dastardly murder of the Archduke and his consort cast a gloom over all Europe. It was unequivocally condemned by the great powers. But at the same time there was apprehension that it might lead to a war between Austria-Hungary and Serbia since the feelings between the two had been running high. Such a catastrophe would certainly bring in Russia and was very likely to spread to other European countries, which were bound to each other by alliances. Hence there was feverish diplomatic activity to "localise the conflict".

Diplomatic Activity in European Capitals

Austrian Attitude

Berchtold had already decided to crush Serbia. He would not miss the opportunity. He also knew what the implications of a war with Serbia would be. Russian intervention was certain. So he wanted to arm himself with the German promise of support before he took the next step against Serbia. He prepared a memorandum for the Kaiser and the Austrian ambassador had secret meetings with him at Potsdam on 5 and 6 July. The Kaiser was flabbergasted and were greatly moved by the Emperor Francis Joseph's appeal for support against Serbia. Moreover, the Kaiser would not let down his only ally in Europe and so he gave a "blank cheque" to Austria. He was certainly aware of the fact that a war between Austria and Serbia would mean a war with Russia also, because Serge Sazonov, the Russian foreign minister had publicly announced that, "under no pretext would Russia admit an Austrian aggression against Serbia."

The Austrian Ultimatum to Serbia (23 July 1914)

Having obtained the unqualified support of Germany, Berchtold won over his colleagues in the cabinet to his point of view and sent an ultimatum to Serbia on 23 July, to be accepted within 48 hours. Serbia was accused of violating the solemn promise "to live on good neighbourly terms" given in 1909.

In the "ten point" ultimatum, Austria had demanded a guarantee of good behaviour in the future, dissolution of secret societies with the collaboration of Austrian officials and immediate suppression of anti-Austrian propaganda.

The Serbian government sent a judicious and conciliatory reply on the 25th accepting 8 points out of ten and appealed to Austria to refer the disputed points either to the International Court of Justice at the Hague or to an International Conference. Simultaneously in view of the tense situation Serbia issued orders for mobilisation. Austria regarded the Serbian reply as "evasive" and unsatisfactory and ordered partial mobilisation.

Russian and French Attitude

French support to Russia - Russia was an ally of Serbia and watched the political developments in Austria with great anxiety. Sazonov had already warned Austria on 18th July that she would stand by Serbia if Austria declared a war on her. Poincare, the French President and Viviani, the French premier were on a friendly visit to Russia from 20 to 23rd July and they affirmed French support to Russia in the crisis. Poincare remarked to the Austrian Ambassador in Russia, "Serbia has very warm friends in the Russian people, and Russia has an ally, France." But both the Czar and Sazonov did not want a war and on the 28th sent a note to Austria suggesting friendly discussions on the Austro-Serbian dispute. Austria rejected the offer. On 29th July, on hearing the news of the declaration of war on Serbia by Austria, Russia got ready for mobilization.

The British Attitude

Throughout the period of suspense, the British attitude was one of watchfulness and preparedness. Consequently the British fleet was not dispersed on the 25th after the annual manoeuvres which were being performed at this time on the North Sea.

On 27th Sir Edward Grey, the British Secretary of State for Foreign Affairs proposed a four-power conference of Great Britain, France, Germany and Italy to prevent further complications and deterioration in international relations. But the Kaiser's reaction was not favourable because he had a bitter experience of such conferences at Algeiiras (1906).

Grey then asked Germany to advise moderation to Austria and to restrain her "from a foolhardy policy." He strongly recommended that the dispute should be "localised" between Austria and Serbia. While diplomatic notes were exchanging among the Great Powers, Berchfold declared the war on Serbia on 28th July "to cut the ground from any attempt at intervention on hearing the news of the Austrian declaration of war on Serbia, the Tsar agreed to mobilise Russian forces.

Last Minute Effort by the Kaiser

The Kaiser made a last-minute effort to localise the conflict. He told Bethmann Hollweg, the German Chancellor, to advise Austria to have direct talks with Russia. But when there was no response, the Chancellor wired to the German ambassador at Vienna. "As an ally we must refuse to be drawn into a world conflagration, because Austria does not respect our advice. Tell Berchfold with all emphasis and great seriousness." Berchfold ignored the warning and was confirmed of German support in the struggle. Russian mobilisation meant a war between Russia and Austria which in turn meant a war between Germany and Russia.

German Ultimatum to Russia and France

On 31st July 1914 Germany sent an ultimatum to Russia and France demanding their demobilisation within 12 hours (Russia) and demanding France's neutrality in a Russo-German war. On Russian refusal to comply with the German ultimatum, Germany declared war on Russia.

Meanwhile on the 29th, Germany tried to secure British neutrality in the event of a Franco-German war but failed.

On 31st Grey demanded an assurance from France and Germany that if hostilities broke out between them, they should respect the neutrality of Belgium. On 2nd August the threat of war between Germany and France grew very grave. On 3rd August Germany declared war on France. Germany sent an ultimatum to Belgium demanding passage for German troops through her territory. Belgium rejected it. On 4th August Great Britain declared war on Germany. Japan declared war on Germany on 23rd August and Turkey joined the central powers (Germany and Austria) on 29th October and declared war on Russia. On 5th November England and France also declared war on Turkey.

Who was to Blame?

The first world war had broken out in its naked fury in spite of the assertion that "no nation willed the war and statesmen blundered into it rather than sought it."

Austrian Responsibility: Count Berchfold, the foreign minister of Austria, was certainly the immediate villain of the peace. He exploited the situation created by the murder of

Archduke to crush Serbia, the inveterate enemy of Austria in the Balkans. Firstly, he assured himself of the Kaiser's unqualified support. Secondly, he sent a strongly worded ultimatum to Serbia convinced that it would be rejected by her. Thirdly, when he found the Kaiser's attitude getting lukewarm on receipt of the Serbian reply, he precipitated the crisis by declaring war on Serbia on 28th July and, finally, he ignored the last minute warning of German Chancellor.

Russian Responsibility: If the general mobilisation in Russia had been halted, perhaps the efforts of the Great powers to localise the conflict might have succeeded. Russia was also smarting under her loss of prestige in 1909.

Germany could not escape the responsibility for causing the war: The Kaiser's blank cheque to Austria on 6th July was a major factor in allowing the crisis to deepen into a world-wide conflict. The Kaiser knew full well that a war between Austria and Serbia would mean a war with Russia too and hence it was a blunder of great magnitude to extend unqualified support to a war which was bent upon wreaking her vengeance on Serbia.

Then again Germany was primarily responsible for forcing Great Britain to enter the war. The violation of Belgian neutrality by Germany made it certain that Britain would join the conflict.

British Responsibility: The probable course of events in Britain was not correctly gauged in Germany.

Serbian too must share the responsibility of precipitating a world-wide conflict together with Great Powers of Europe. Emboldened by the promise of Russian support in a conflict with Austria she allowed unbridled anti-Austrian propaganda in the country and encouraged the violent activities of the terrorist society known as the "Black Hand".

The fact remains that events moved too fast to allow any control over the mutual jealousies and hatreds of the Great Powers, which made the war inevitable. "The ambitions, the fears and the hatreds of the two groups had plunged the world in a darkness." Grey very significantly remarked, "The lamps are going out all over Europe; we shall not see them lit again in our life time."

31

The Russian Revolution

In March 1917, in the third year of the Great War, the political system that had prevailed in Russia for several centuries - namely the Tsarist autocracy - suddenly collapsed. Signs of its disintegration had been mounting for a year or two; the likelihood of its early demise had been widely sensed. Yet no one expected it to come just at that moment. For a century in the past, its overthrow had been the dream of liberal and radical oppositionists, some of whom had schemed, worked, even suffered martyrdom, to bring it about. Yet its collapse, when it came, was not the immediate result of any such efforts.

The trouble began when irregularities in the food supply led to street disorders in the capital city. Compared to ones that had occurred in the past, these disorders were not of an unusual or particularly dangerous nature. Nevertheless, the regime proved incapable of controlling them and restoring order. The war had taken its toll of the best units of the old army, with their relatively high morale and good discipline. The garrisons in the neighbourhood of the capital, to which appeal had to be taken in the effort to restore order, were now manned by raw and semi-demoralized recruits. They refused their collaboration, disobeyed orders, fraternized with the unruly crowds and declined to support the police. In this development, the hollowness of the authority of the regime was at once revealed. It suddenly became apparent to everyone that "the king was naked" - naked, in this instance, of effective support from any quarter. In the short space of a few days, the monarchy, lacking effective defenders, fell of its own weight.

Even today, it is difficult to assess the meaning of this collapse. Was the Tsarist autocracy so largely an anachronism, were its weaknesses and failures of such gravity, that it was bound to fall in any case at an early date, and did the war merely hasten its end? or was it Russia's participation in the war that destroyed what would otherwise have been, for the regime, a reasonable chance of adjustment into another age?

The question is hypothetical. There can be no authoritative answer. But it will be useful to have glance at some of the background circumstances and, in the first instance, at certain of the more basic weaknesses of the regime.

Russia, at the outset of this century, was still predominantly an agricultural country. The agrarian system was unsuitable and inadequate to the needs of the modern age. The regime was well along, by 1914, in the implementation of an extensive program of modernisation, designed to shift the weight of agricultural production from the landed estate and the village commune to the small, independent farmer-proprietor. There are many who felt that this was the most promising approach ever taken to the great problems of rural and ownership and of the organisation of agricultural production that confronted Russia as the legacy of serfdom. But in 1914 this program was still only partially completed in the physical sense. And what had been accomplished here had scarcely begun to affect as yet the most dangerous aspect of the problem, which was the state of mind of the peasant himself. This class was bitter, skeptical, withdrawn, and alienated not only from the regime itself but from the entire educated Russian society.

No less disturbing were the deficiencies of the political system. In 1906 the effort had been undertaken by the Tsar, under heavy pressure, to modernise the political institutions of the country by adding to them a representative legislative branch in the form of the State Duma. The Duma survived formally as an institution down to 1917; but restrictions on the franchise, evoked by a combination of the Tsar's timidity and the provocative and defiant behaviour of many of the deputies in some of the initial sessions (1906 and 1907), had so narrowed its representative quality as to render it incapable of functioning as a really effective bond between people and government. In earlier times the need of such a parliamentary bond had not been great. Now, with the rise of literacy and particularly with the growth of a large professional and technical intelligentsia, its absence was keenly felt.

Closely connected with this imperfection of the political system was a situation that might well be viewed as the most deep-seated and ominous of all the weaknesses of the autocracy. This was the extensive alienation from its spirit and purposes of large parts of the intelligentsia generally, and of the youth in particular. This situation was not of recent origin. The disaffection of these elements had been a prominent feature of Russian political life for at least a half-century. From the standpoint of the prospects for survival of the autocracy, its importance could scarcely be exaggerated. It worked in two ways. It operated on the one hand to enrich the ranks of the revolutionary opposition. But by the same token it served to impoverish the bureaucracy - to impoverish it in talent, in intelligence and in imagination. Had the talents and enthusiasms of those many brilliant youths who early found their way into the revolutionary movement been enlisted in the constructive undertakings of the regime, instead of being rejected, the achievements of the Tsarist government might have been of a different order.

Closely connected with this problem of the alienation of the intelligentsia was the problem of national minorities. It is obvious that the romantic nationalism of the late nineteenth and early twentieth centuries, so closely linked to language, tended to disintegrate the great multilingual empires, particularly the Austrian and the Russian, just as it tended to unite peoples of a common tongue. In Russia the effect of this nationalism was felt, again, in two directions. Among the Great Russians it stimulated cultural chauvinism, anti-semitism and demands for the forceful russification of the national minorities. Among the minority peoples it provoked precisely those feelings, sensitivities and ambitions most calculated to make them resent such pressures and to demand cultural and political autonomy.

The extent to which this national unrest fed the revolutionary movement may be judged from the fact that a majority in the Social-Democratic Labor Party, out of which the Bolshevik faction emerged, was made up of members of the national-minority groups. At a time when nationalism was rapidly becoming the dominant political emotion of the age, and in a country where the majority or near majority of the population was made up of national-minority elements, no government could expect to have an easy time of it. But the Tsar's government, showing itself in the final decades of its power disgracefully receptive to all manner of chauvinistic and anti-Semitic influences, seriously disqualified itself for the promulgation of any hopeful approach to this problem.

To all these weaknesses there must be added the personal failings of the Tsar, Nicholas II. How long fate would have given it to him to continue to bear the crown, had the vicissitudes of the war not intervened, one cannot know. But to have had favourable chances for survival, war or no war, the system of autocracy could not have waited long for a more capable autocrat - one better educated, wider in outlook and more seriously motivated. But one could not run a great empire on tact, charm and good manners alone. His limitations, fatal under the stress of a great war, were such as to constitute a danger to the dynasty even in time of peace.

The picture was, of course, not all dark. The positive features and achievements of the Tsarist autocracy have tended to be lost from sight behind the dust and clamour of the Revolution. Soviet historians, in particular, have been at no pains to draw attention to them. The rate of industrial development in the final decades of Tsardom was impressively high. So, also, was the progress made in the direction of general education. Improvements in social legislation were not negligible. The judicial system was far from perfect, but it was well in advance of the political system in which it was embedded. Russian cultural life enjoyed, in the final decades and years of Tsardom, a feverish vitality. The Russia of those years was truly a great battleground of negative and positive forces, working and contending within the same political framework. What, then, the outcome might have been had there been no war is most unclear.

The Russo-Japanese war of 1904-05 had already brought the system to the verge of collapse. How anyone seeing this - be it the Tsar's minister or his French allies - could have imagined that it could with impunity, only ten years later, take upon itself the far greater strains of a war with Germany, remains one of the mysteries of the age. Perhaps the autocracy, all unknowing, was already doomed to an early demise when the Tsar gave the order for mobilisation in July 1914.

The fall of the autocracy in February 1917, leaving Russia not only without a government but without any acceptable and traditional procedure for choosing a new one, could be no more than the first phase of the great process of the Russian Revolution. There remained to be endured a long agony of contest to determine who and what should take the place of the Tsars as the rulers of the traditional Russian lands. Even the so-called October Revolution - the seizure of power by Lenin and his associates in the major urban and industrial centres at the end of 1917 - was not the final answer to this question. A further three-year ordeal of civil strife, embracing the various allied interventions, the civil war in all its phases and even the bizarre Russo-Polish war of 1920, had still to be lived through before it could be said that the Russian Revolution was complete. And if the first great question of the Revolution concerns the reasons for the decline and fall of Tsardom, the second - no less complex and no less baffling - concerns the chain of causes and events by which there finally emerged, as Tsardom's successor, the extreme radical wing of the Russian Social Democratic Labour Party - a faction whose members , then known as the Bolsheviki, were soon to appropriate to themselves, and to establish in world usage, the designation of communists.

The success of the Bolsheviki could not possibly be explained by their numbers. The membership of the faction of the party, as we call it - as of March 1917 was tiny. Elections held in December 1917, at a time when the party was already in control of the main centres of population and enjoying the prestige of a dramatic political success, showed it to have the support of about one-fourth of the voters.

Here there were both positive and negative factors that proved decisive for the Communist victory. On the negative side there was the fact that none of the major rival factions or parties was well situated to establish itself in power. The monarchists and reactionaries disqualified themselves from the start and forfeited every possibility of adequate popular support, particularly among the peasantry and the intelligentsia.

The Liberals were of course the first to attempt the governing of Russia in the immediate aftermath of the February Revolution. The moderate socialists, including both Socialist-Revolutionaries and the remainder of the Social Democrats were briefly the successors to the Liberals in the Provisional Government. After that, they constituted over the period of the civil war the main political opposition to Communist power. They lacked military and administrative skills, vigor of leadership and unity of popular appeal. The Socialist-Revolutionaries lacked support in the big cities, the Social Democrats in the countryside.

Not only were the various non-Communist elements handicapped individually as candidates for the succession, but they were unable even to collaborate effectively in opposing the Bolsheviki bid for power. The hatreds and suspicions that divided moderate socialists from the monarchistic and conservative ex-officers with whom they were ostensibly allied in the effort to unseat the Bolsheviki were no whit less intense than those that divided them from the Bolsheviki themselves. The reactionaries were already discredited. The unnatural alliance with them tended to discredit the socialists in the eyes of the masses. At the same time, the mutual antagonism of the two elements frustrated the effectiveness of their joint military-political action against the Communists.

So impelling were these realities that it is tempting to say that Bolshevism triumphed because no unity existed among it major political opponents, and none of those opponents, in any case, would have been remotely capable of ruling the country. No less central to it were positive factors as well: the extraordinary discipline, compactness and tightness of the Communist Party; the magnificent political leadership - bold, determined and imaginative—given to it at all times by its dominant figure, Vladimir Il'ich Ulyanov-Lenin: and the driving, unrelenting military leadership which the party gave to the Red Army units in the civil war. In the confusion that followed the breakdown of the old order, the cutting edge of these qualities was of a far greater effectiveness than any of the shifting, undependable winds of popular sympathy. The Bolsheviki came out ahead very largely because they were the only political force that had hardness; sharpness, disciplined drive and clearly defined purpose.

But the feelings of the popular masses were not wholly irrelevant to the outcome. These masses had been insufficiently attached to Tsardom to defend it in its moment of trial. They were insufficiently opposed to Bolshevism to oppose it in its moment of challenge.

This, in outline, was the Russian Revolution: the passing of power in the traditional Russian lands from the enfeebled hands of the Tsarist autocracy to "dictatorship of the proletariat". And as one tries, from the perspective to review the significance of this great transition, three features of it stand out.

The first of these is the essential altruism of purpose that underlay this revolution. For nearly a century in the past, the greatest public issues of western society had resolved around the problems of the distribution of wealth in an economic environment not yet one of plenty. The initial effect of the Industrial Revolution had been to sharpen old injustices, to create new ones, to open up new forms of hardship, suffering, exploitation and degradation. These effects made themselves felt in Russia some decades later than in England and Germany. As problems in Russian life they were reaching their peak around the turn of the century and in the immediately ensuing years. The outlook that inspired the Bolsheviki and brought them finally to power was founded on an understandable desire to correct these anomalies, to eliminate social injustice and economic exploitation, to assure to the servant of the machine the comfort, security, dignity of status and sense of community of which the Industrial Revolution and the workings of the capitalist system were conceived to have robbed him.

In 1917 millions of people across the continent of Europe had been reduced to desperation by social distress or by the sufferings of the World War or by a combination of the two. One cannot understand the meaning of the Russian Revolution unless one recalls the vast thrill of excitement and anticipation that went through great portions of the world public as the news of this event reached them. Tsardom, in its helpless ineptness, had permitted itself to stand before the eyes of the world as the symbol of an obsolescent an oppressive feudalism. To many millions beyond Russia's borders the Russian Revolution appeared as a great breakthrough of hope. Here were boldness, grandeur of concept and elevation of purpose bursting through the crust of tradition and privilege in one of the most backward and miserable of European countries. Here was the first great attempt to defy the evils of modern industrialism by setting against it a political system founded on the dignity and social innocence of the common working man - dedicated to the realisation of his needs, his dreams, and his aspirations.

Whether one sees this revolution as a hopeful breakthrough or only as the onset of new misunderstanding, conflict and misery - one is obliged to concede to the Russian Revolution the status of the greatest political event of the present century. It deserves this description by virtue of the profound exemplary effect it had across great portions of the globe, of the alteration it produced in Russia's relations with the great powers of the West, and of the changes it brought to the life of one of the world's great peoples.

It was in its exemplary effect beyond Russia's borders that the Bolsheviki themselves saw the greatest importance of the Revolution. The Russian Revolution had important political repercussions in the West and the Third World. It served, in the first place, to split the socialist and labor elements in all the advanced countries. The split had actually begun during the war. It had begun in the form of a division of opinion as to which of the two principles, socialist internationalism or national patriotism, was to be the dominant force in wartime socialist policy.

Those in Western Europe had opposed the war as an unworthy contest, conducted among imperialists for the benefit of imperialists. They tended, once the war was over, to cling to the association with Russian Communism into which this wartime affinity had thrown them. They accepted the Bolsheviki example as authoritative. They made themselves the spokesmen for the same sort of revolution in their own countries that the Bolsheviki had carried out in Russia. It was out of these groups of dissident radical socialists that the Western Communist parties were formed. And it was from the exemplary power of communist success in Russia that these parties continued to draw strength in ensuing decades. Increasingly, as the years went by, they became gathering points for all those elements in the Western countries whose discontent with their own societies could find no adequate outlet in normal democratic political activity.

Initially, most Western communists felt themselves in a sense parties to the Russian Revolution. They shared in its enthusiasms, its excitements and its international political goals. To the extent that physical proximity and ease of communication permitted, they remained in touch with the Russian Communist leaders, had a part in their councils and regarded the Russian Revolution as only the first phase of their own. It was not long, however, before the Russian Communists, proud of their own triumph, began to view their success in Russia as a proper source of authority over like-minded people elsewhere.

Meanwhile, Western society had been importantly affected by the "backlash" of international communist activity. Extremism on the left of the political spectrum was bound to breed extremism on the right. All the activities of the Western Communist parties had an important effect in stimulating fascist tendencies in the West. Many features of the international communist movement - the addiction to conspiratorial methods, the bewildering mixture of legal with illegal methods of operation, the use of "front" groups, combined to invite the attribution to it, of a certain demon image. Particularly was this true in Germany, where the powerful communist threat in the years of the 1920s not only weakened moderate political forces by confronting them with constant attacks from the left, but served as a pretext for the build-up of fascist forces.

The effect of the examples of the Russian Revolution in the West had much to do, in the end, with the failure of the post-Versaillies order and the origins of World War II.

Of even greater significance than the exemplary effect of the Russian Revolution on the advanced countries of the West was its similar influence on the underdeveloped peoples of the non-European world. The Russian Revolution occurred at a time when Europe's hegemony over the underdeveloped parts of the world was already passing its peak. This hegemony, a function of the great technological disparity between Europe and the rest of the world that had arisen since the opening of the world trade routes, was bound eventually to be modified by natural processes; but the First World War, draining Europe of much of its vitality as well as its capital, accelerated the process.

It was against this background that the Russian Revolution burst forth spectacularly as the first great example of successful revolt.

The Russian Revolution unquestionably hastened the disintegration of Europe's colonial empire and of her political influence in other parts of the world. For the non-European countries themselves, the exemplary effects of the Russian Revolution were of enormous importance. The effect it had on China's political development would alone be enough to justify this conclusion, and this was only a part of the whole. In India, in Turkey and at a later date in Africa, the example of Russia's revolution was one of the outstanding environmental factors of the nineteen-twenties and thirties.

The Russian Revolution did work a fundamental and extremely important change in this state of affairs in the Afro-Asian, Latin American world. It was not the issue of socialism versus capitalism that was the heart of difficulty. There was no reason why great countries could not go different ways in this respect; and increasingly over the course of the years, as the two systems evoked toward each other, this dichotomy came to lose significance. The trouble was that the Bolsheviki leaders brought to their conquest of power in Russia a complex of attitudes toward the Western governments. Among these attitudes were a fundamental challenge to the legitimacy of the Western governments, a pervasive cynicism about the parliamentary and democratic sources of their power.

Soviet historians have tended to place the blame for the tensions and conflicts of the ensuing decades on the Western side. The Western statesmen, they allege, saw in the Russian Revolution the rise of a force bound to threaten their capitalistic and imperialistic interests. All of these things were present, in one degree or another, in the pattern of Western statesmanship.

The most momentous of the consequences of the Russian Revolution was of course the internal one. A political system of eight hundred years' standing was swept away. An entire upper class, in part the heritage of ages, was sloughed off, its members were driven to emigration, disenfranchised or degraded in status. In place of all this came the Communist party, whose dictatorship with changes in personality and with successive phases of development, was never to be essentially relaxed. The nationalisation of industry, that cherished goal of all Marxist striving, was carried to completion, only to have its significance thrown into question in recent times. By drastic methods, and at the cost of much sacrifice and suffering, Russia was driven into the ranks of the major industrial powers. A half-century after the Revolution, living conditions for industrial workers were better than they were before it. The peasantry, after a brief respite in the 1920s when it was permitted to enjoy the fruits of the expropriation of the landlords, found itself subjected to new exploitation in the form of Stalin's collective farm system. But in judging all things one must remember that the implementation of the domestic program of Russian Communism was interrupted, and set back roughly one decade, by the war effort of the 1940s - an effort probably unparalleled in scale in the military history of mankind. This effort would stand, alone, as one of the great historic achievements of the Russian people and as a lasting testimonial to their extraordinary capacity for heroism, endurance and sacrifice in a cause.

What exists in Russia today is, in so far as any political regime can form the character of a human community, the product of its endeavour. Russian society today is something different that no more draws heavily on historical experience and national tradition. Now it is in reality a new civilisation rather than just a national society that has thus, been created in the past.

32

Lenin

Vladimir Ilich Ul'ianov (who in 1901 began to call himself Lenin) was born on April 22, 1870, in Simbirsk, now Ul'anovsk, a provincial town on the Volga, one of the six children in an educated middle class family. When he died on January 21, 1924, near Moscow, he was acclaimed as "the greatest genius of mankind, creator of the Communist Party of the Soviet Union, founder of the Union of Soviet Socialistic Republics, the leader and teacher of the peoples of the whole world. In different measures the events of his political life, his intellectual life and his active political life contributed to this metamorphosis.

The first blow to young Ul'ianov's happy existence was the death of his father in 1886. An even worse shock was the arrest, in March 1887, of his elder brother, Alexander, whose brilliant research on worms at the university in St. Petersburg had promised a bright future but who, unknown to his family, had been active in terrorist revolutionary circles. Alexander was executed for having plotted the assassination of the Tsar. The Ul'ianov family, shunned by local society, moved to a village not far from Kazem. Ul'ianov was admitted to the university in Kazan, though only on the strength of a character reference from the director of the Simbirsk Gymnasium, father of Alexander Kerenskii, the man Lenin was latter to overthrow.

Ul'ianov was arrested in December 1887 for his part in a student demonstration against a university rule that enjoined students from forming organisations. Expelled from the university and forbidden to go abroad for study, he knew himself for preparation for external examinations and was finally permitted to take these in the spring of 1891, thus winning a first degree diploma from the Law faculty of the university in St. Petersburg. For two years he held a job in a Samara Law Office; at the same time he was studying Marxism and engaging in open criticism of the narodniki, activities which he continued in St. Petersburg, where he went in 1893 "in quest of the proletariat". By the spring of 1895 he had become well enough known to be sent by his comrades to visit Georgi Plekhanov, "the grandfather of Russian Marxism", in Geneva. Before his return he met Paul Lafargue, son-in-law of Karl Marx, and the veteran German Marxist Wilhelm Liebknecht but was unable to see the dying Friedrich Engels.

That tall young Ul'ianov joined with L. Martov (pseudonym of Lulii O. Tserderabaum) and a handful of other intellectuals to form the so-called union of struggle for the emancipation of the working class, which planned to publish an illegal, newspaper, *Rabochee delo* ("The Workers Cause"). The first issue was confiscated, and Ul'ianov was among those arrested. Imprisonment prevented him from participation in the vigorous strike movement of 1896, but with the aid of books borrowed from the leading libraries of the capital he was able to continue his study and writing. In February 1897 he was released to make his arrangements for a three year period of exile at the Siberian village of Shushenskoe in Yenisei province, near the modern coal basin of Kuznetsk. There he lived in a peasant hut, his main source of income being the government allowance of 8 rubles a month. A year later Nadezhda Krupskaia, whom he had met in St. Petersburg in 1894 arrived with her mother for a visit and was permitted to remain in Siberia on the condition that she and Ul'ianov be formally married.

In Siberia, he continued his fervish literacy activity, in particular pursuing his study of the spread of capitalist relations in the peasant villages. Aware of serious gaps in his education, he undertook a systematic study of quite diverse philosophical views, while also broadening his knowledge of the writings of Marx & Engels. He completed his first major work, 'The Development of Capitalism in Russia' in 1899.

Political Achievements

From this time on Ul'ianov's consuming passion was the organisation of a disciplined Russian Marxist Party capable of effectively combating all revisionist tendencies. To this end, he felt, it was necessary to found an all-Russian Marxist newspaper. Released from exile at the beginning of 1900 but forbidden to reside in either of the two capitals or in university or major industrial towns, he promptly applied for permission to go abroad and in July was able to leave for Switzerland. In Geneva, Plenkhanov's insistence on controlling the proposed newspaper so offended Ul'ianov that the project almost fell through. However, a compromise was reached whereby Ul'ianov was permitted to arrange for the publication of *Iskra* ("The Spark") in Munich; there Krupaskia joined him in April 1901. The first number was printed (in Leipzig) in January 1901, and a monthly periodical, *Zar,ia* ("Dawn"), followed in December. It was in the course of the year that he began to sign his articles "Lenin".

It was in 1901 also that Lenin began to write his second and most significant - major work, 'what is to be Done'? published at Stuttgart in March 1902. Meanwhile, disagreements between Lenin and his Editorial colleagues in Switzerland multiplied in particular, Lenin's insistence on emphasizing the "dictatorship" of the proletariat" in connection with the formulation of an agrarian programme irritated Plekhanov, who opposed Lenin's "polemics".

Mainly at Lenin's insistence it was decided to call the Second Party Congress to create an all Russian party, a task of which the Minsk Congress of 1898 had failed. Lenin himself devoted immense efforts, by voluminous correspondence with *Iskra* agents in Russia, to guarantee a workable majority of reliable delegates. The Congress met in Brussels in the Summer of 1903 but found it expedient to move to London. It was attended by 43 delegates, assigned 51 votes; of these 44 could be counted on to support the Iskara position. With the support of his colleagues on the Iskara editorial board Lenin won adoption of his draft programme, though two Economist delegates found hard to include a reference to class consciousness as a precondition to establishment of the "dictatorship of the proletariat". However a split developed among Iskara supporters over Lenin's effort to secure adoption of his version of the first paragraph of a party statute, embodying his conception of the dominance of a revolutionary elite. Despite the somewhat unexpected support of Plekhanov, Lenin's formulation was defeated. Martov's broader definition of party membership was adopted by a vote of 28-22, with one abstention. By vigorous canvassing Lenin was able to whip together a fairly solid bloc of 24 votes, which enabled him to carry the election of his candidates to the new editorial board of Iskara and to the new Central Committee. It was by virtue of these votes, not of the statistics of the later party allegiance that Lenin's followers for decades boasted the name bol'sheviki ("majority men").

Lenin's triumph was brief. Plekhanov soon abandoned Lenin's "hard" Iskara line, and control of the party and of its central committee passed to the men'sheviki ("minority men"). Lenin found himself doomed to years of bitter wrangling with his former colleagues. In the revolution of 1905 he was able to exercise almost no influence. He did not return to Russia until, with the October manifesto, the autocracy had apparently surrendered. In Russia, he continued to denounce all socialists who would not follow him, and all liberals. After some wavering he supported boycott of the elections in the Duma, and he gave his blessing to though he did not participate in, an abortive armed uprising in Moscow. After a few months of underground existence, of shifting from one hiding place to another, Lenin withdrew to the relatively secure of Finland. Pained by his failure to dominate the Fourth ("Unity") Congress of the Russian Social Democrats, in Stockholm (April-May 1906) he took some comfort from his success at the Bolshevik - organised fifth Congress in London (May 1907) and was considerably heartened by participation in the Stuttgart Congress of Second International (August 1907), the first International Congress he had ever attended. At the end of 1907 he abandoned his base in Finland and slipped back to Switzerland.

The next ten years were the bitterest and most difficult of Lenin's life. He became wholly occupied not with the direct struggle to combat capitalism and tsarism but with a preliminary, many faceted battle to destroy the influence of all those who professed devotion to the cause of the proletariat. Although Lenin was always ready to score a point at the expense of his rivals, he insistently denounced "opportunism" as the greatest brake on the progress of the socialist revolution. Thus he worked himself into a position of almost total isolation within the revolutionary movement. This position was ultimately to prove most advantageous to him. His name became one of the best known among the revolutionaries; but he was dissociated from all the failures of the other leading figures and thus was able, at a crucial moment, to offer fresh hope to the despairing.

In 1912, Lenin's Bolshevik adherents in Russia secured permission from the tsarist government to publish a newspaper called *Pravda* ("Truth"). Lenin at once moved from Switzerland to Cracow and then to Poronino, near the Austrian-Russian border. Here he could hope to keep in maximum contact with, and direct the policy of the new organ. He could also supervise the activities of the "Bolshevik Six" in the newly elected fourth Duma. Lenin selected Roman Malinovski to be their spokesman unaware that he was on the police payroll. Although Bolsheviks from abroad were regularly arrested on their arrival in Russia, Lenin long remained obdurately blind to this circumstance despite repeated protests from more sensitive friends.

On the outbreak of war in 1914 Lenin was arrested by the Austrian police on suspicion of espionage. The absurdity of the charge facilitated his release on condition that he return to Switzerland. There he remained in devastating impotence attending International Socialist Conferences at Zimmerwald and Kienthal, only to see the merger fruits of his vigorous efforts ruined by the subsequent defection of his allies.

At the end of January 1917, Lenin consoled himself—and all who would still heed him with the thought that the Tsar, fearing the outbreak of a bourgeois revolution in Russia, would not dare make a separate peace with Germany. Therefore the war would continue, enormously enhancing the chances that Europe (not Russia) would begin the Socialist revolution. Six weeks later, on March 15, 1917, to his surprise and delight Lenin learned from the Swiss newspapers that the Russian autocracy had collapsed and that a "provisional government" had been set up. A new danger loomed - the possibility that all elements in Russia might rally to the new regime. Lenin felt it was an urgent necessity that he reached Russia and prevent the Bolsheviks from making fools of themselves. The German government was likewise persuaded that Lenin's presence in Russia was an urgent need, though not for the same reasons. It was arranged through Swiss Intermediaries, that Lenin and other Russian exiles in Switzerland, whatever their political complexion, be permitted to travel in communicado (on the "sealed train") across Germany. Via Sweden and Finland, Lenin reached Petrograd on the evening of April 16, 1917. From that moment one might say, Lenin had no personal life for his biography and the further history of the Russian Revolution became inextricably intertwined. Lenin acknowledged that "Russia is now the freest country in the world", yet he refused to take any part in enabling the new regime to establish itself. Instead he watched for every opportunity to overthrow it in the name of a new absolutism, "the dictatorship of the proletariat". He did seize power successfully on November 7, 1917, and thereafter, notwithstanding frequent vigorous opposition from tried associates. Lenin was in fact able to guide the ever shifting policies of the new "Soviet" regime until he was incapacitated in May 1922 by a paralytic stroke. Sufficiently recovered to partially resume his duties, he was rendered wholly impotent by a second stroke and remained so for almost a year before his final, fatal stroke.

Major Writings

The explanation of Lenin's political success cannot be found in his intellectual achievements, for he was of no significance as an abstract thinker. His most scholarly work,'The Development of Capitalism in Russia' (1899), was simply a tract to prove definitively the folly of the narodnik concept of the role of the peasantry in Russia. He showed that the peasantry was ceasing to be a uniform mass and was splitting into capitalist relations on the village. Thus, the proletarian, "depeasantized", element in the countryside would strengthen the urban proletariat, whose lack of numbers was compensated for by its concentration, flooting it to lead a mass movement of the village poor to overthrow tsarism and capitalism together.

In 'What is to be Done?' directed against the Narodniki, and against the Economists as well - Lenin developed the thought that the working class, left to its own spontaneous strivings, would never become socialist. Only the conscious effort of "educated representatives of the propertied classes", i.e. the Marxists, would be able to divert the labor movement, with its spontaneous trade-unionist striving from under the wing of revolutionary social Democracy." This view point was embodied in the programme adopted by the Second Congress, in preparation for which what is to be Done? had been published. It continued to dominate all Lenin's thinking and actions and is perhaps the very essence of "Leninism" as distinct from Marxism.

Imperialism, the highest stage of capitalism, has been hailed as "the most outstanding contribution to the treasury of creative "Marxism" and as evidence of Lenin's stature as a "scholar of genius", a most conscientious researcher, and the greatest fighter for revolution."It did indeed assert as a scientific prediction that Imperialism spells the doom of capitalism and because it creates the objective conditions for world revolution also represents the eve of socialist revolution. In other writings at this time, however, Lenin suggested that the "law of uneven development" might make possible the victory of socialism in a single country.

Even less original than Imperialism was his other famous tract, *State and Revolution* (1917) written after the July uprising as a blueprint for the immediate future. He argued that the existing "hypocritically democratic" regime was merely a "dictatorship of the proletariat", a term that Lenin never ceased to think of as meaning "dictatorship of the

Bolshevikis." He was careful to emphasize the distinction between the two stages, "Socialism" (from each according to his labor) and "communism" (from each according to his abilities, to each according to his needs" a distinction that Stalin was later to include the same into the 1936 Constitution. Lenin believed that although social inequalities would persist under "Socialism", it was possible to attain to "communism " without an indefinitely prolonged period of socialism".

Political Realism

Lenin's forte was an extraordinary ability, found also in men such as Bismarck, to analyse a given practical situation and to give things an unexpected push on the general direction in which he wished them to move. He did not rely on abstract ideas as guides to policy, he attacked Trotsky for using "abstract (and therefore empty) words". Although like many other Russian middle class youths of his generation he was impressed by the grandiose aspects of Marxism, he never fully committed himself to their implications as worked out in Western Europe. On the eve of his return to Russia in 1917 he denounced, "Bolshevik" pre- revolutionary antiques" on the grounds that they failed to grasp the "incontestable truth that a Marxist must take cognizance of real life, of the true facts of reality, and not cling to a theory of yesterday ... which live on theories ...only comes near to embracing like in all complexity. Theory...is grey, but green is in the external tree of life."

His leadership of the Bolshevikis during the revolution and in the still more chaotic years that ensued involved a shrewd following of events rather than a genuinely creative initiative. With the definite goal of seizure and retention of power in mind, he showed true realism, even adopting positions that to many seemed at the moment completely unrealistic.

His initial demand, in the "April Theses" (announced to his party colleagues the day after his arrival in Petrograd (1917), for all power to the Soviet" surely seemed ridiculous, for the Bolsheviks were only a small minority in the Petrograd Soviet. Yet it turned out to be only way to save the Bolsheviks from joining the Soviet majority in support of the provisional government and thus to absolve them from responsibility in the eyes of the masses.

It was realism, too, that prompted Lenin to resist an armed uprising in November rather than wait for the certain voting at the Second Congress of Soviets. He was aware, as some of the associates were not, that the masses were not swinging to active support of the Bolsheviks. That disappointments and weariness had bred tremendous apathy and that there was no likelihood of serious opposition to any group that would act with vigour, particularly if it could wrap itself in the cloak of the Soviets and would promise speedy convocation of the long dreamt-of constituent assembly.

His extrication of Russia from the war, similarly was not the realization of a plan throughout in advance; it was the result of realistic yielding to facts as they gradually became obvious to him. The initial "Appeal to the peoples and Governments of all warring countries" (1917) simply called for a general armistice and conclusion of the "democratic peace" that had been proposed by the provisional government. When it became clear that the central powers would not make a separate peace on the basis of no annexations and no indemnities, Lenin addressed pointed questions to a Congress of army representatives: if negotiations were broken off would the Germans despite the winter weather, launch an offensive? If they did, could the army fight or would it flee in panic? Lenin was attempted by Wilson's Fourteen Points' address of January 8, 1918, to contemplate renewal of the war with practical assistance from the Allies. Even in the face of a German ultimatum, Lenin advised dragging out the negotiations in the hope that the expected German revolution would break out and save Russia. Only when Trotsky's defiant "no war, no peace" declaration precipitated the final rupture of the negotiations did Lenin begin to insist on immediate acceptance of the German terms, arguing that no matter how onerous the Brest-Litovsk terms were, they would leave the Bolshevikis in control of an amputated Russia.

This same realism showed in his handling of the peasant question. Rejecting as irrelevant the criticism that the original Bolsheviki decree on the land program in favour of the policy advocated by the Socialist Revolutionaries, Lenin had exclaimed,"we must follow Life". If the Bolshevikis were to remain in power, the peasant masses must be acquiescent otherwise there would be no food for the towns. When the peasants had clearly tired of accepting worthless Bolsheviki paper in exchange of their surplus grain, Lenin promptly abandoned his principle that "general and basic source of any right to the use of agricultural land is individual labour". He called for a crusade - not of course, against the peasantry but against the "Village bourgeoisie" to carry the class war into the countryside" with the aid of the "village poor".

His attitude towards the Constituent Assembly also reflected keen appraisal of the realities of the moment rather than any previously elaborated ideological position. At the moment of the seizure of power when the Bolshevikis still needed the semblance of democracy and there was at least some hope that the Bolshevikis and their Left Socialist Revolutionary allies might win a slender majority. Lenin had been willing to gamble on permitting the election of a Constituent Assembly, when, however, despite Bolsheviki control of the power centres, the elections went overwhelmingly against the Bolshevikis and their allies. He flatly declared,'The Soviets are superior to any Parliament, to any Constituent Assembly'. After it had been met for one night Lenin announced,"We will not give up Soviet power for anything in the world," and the assembly was dissolved.

Whenever one turns in examining the various policies for which at various times he fought so vigorously, the same theme recurs. Never did Lenin argue for action on the basis of ideas he had advanced in his major theoretical works. In combating the "Left Communists" (April 1920), he wrote them off as "doctrinaires of revolution", adding that "God himself has ordained that for a time the young should talk such nonsense". In advocating the abandonment of the policy of confiscating all surplus grain, the basic step in the introduction of the New Economic policy, he argued: "We know that only agreement with peasantry can save the socialist revolution in Russia unless Revolution begins in other countries."

It is individual incentive that raises production; we need increase in production above all and no matter what.

This "lesson in tactics" far more than his so-called testament penned in the interval between his first and second strokes, was the real guideline Lenin left to his successors.

33

Rise of Soviet Russia

"While the Communist International (Comintern) whose headquarters were at Moscow, worked through its local branches to overthrow the capitalist governments of other countries, the Soviet Government, whose directors were also the directors of Comintern, endeavoured to establish normal diplomatic relations with these same governments. This dual policy seriously embarrassed the Soviet authorities in their dealings with foreign powers during the whole of this period."

E.H. Carr.

Introduction

The seizure of supreme power in Russia by the Bolshevists led by Lenin was one of the most significant event of the post-war period. This event left deep impact both on the internal and international politics. Internally it put a violent end to the entire order represented by the Tsarist autocracy. The new rulers inaugurated the reign of *'pure communism'* by expropriation of the landlord, nationalisaion of the land and banks, the repudiation of foreign obligations of the Tsarist government and disenfranchising all *'non-working'* people. The new rulers, in spite of protests of the Allies, withdraw Russia from the war and concluded the Treaty of Brest Litovosk (March 1918). In the sphere of international politics, the revolution sponsored a great ideological struggle. It struck terror in the minds of the ruling class of other capitalist states. The establishment of the Third International confirmed suspicion of the capitalists of other countries that the revolution was not going to confine itself within its national boundaries. As a result of the revolution the class struggle in other countries was intensified and they tried to intervene to nip the revolution in the bud. The efforts of the Allied army of intervention and the White Generals who acted as their agents could not gain the desired collapse of the red regime. Inspired by the slogan *'Socialist Fatherland in danger'* the Red army achieved marvelous success and beat back all these armies. In short, by the end of 1920 the Soviet Union had successfully terminated all foreign and civil wars.

The Soviet Foreign Policy between 1917-1945

The foreign policy of Soviet Russia, like that of any other country, has been aiming at the enhancement of the security and welfare of the state. It has been to a great extent been determined by the country's location, climate, economic interest, historic traditions, ideology as well as the relative strength of the other centres of powers. At the initial stages the Soviet foreign policy was also influenced by suspicion towards Western Europe. This attitude stemmed out of the continuous aggression and attempt to crush the Russian revolution during the years 1917-21, as well as their refusal to give recognition to the communist government of Russia.

Thus the foreign policy of Soviet Russia during the period from 1917 to 1935, was not a continuation of the Czarist foreign policy. It was to a great extent influenced by the Communist ideology.

For the sake of convenience the foreign policy of Soviet Russia may be divided into following phases:

Western Intervention (1917-1921)

The foreign policy of a country is an extension of her internal policy. The Foreign Policy of Russia during the period 1917-21 was to a great extent shaped by two events - Russia's attempt at creating a world communist revolution and the counter revolution in Russia with the support of the Western powers. During this period the relations of Russia were strained with the Western powers because after the revolution Russia started propagating the inevitability of a conflict between the Communist and the non-Communist countries. (2) Russia's withdrawal from the war and conclusion of peace treaty (Brest-Litovosk) with Germany further embittered her relations with the Allies. The Allies alleged that Soviet Government had deliberately concluded peace with the Germans to enable her to concentrate all her forces in the west. They were in favour of Russia continuing the war with Germany. (3) Russia's repudiation of the Tzarist debts and nationalisation of foreign industrial enterprises created further friction. This was further aggravated when she nationalised foreign trade in 1918. (4) The military intervention of western state in favour of the counter-revolutionaries further embittered the relations of Soviet Union with Western powers. But Russia was able to thwart all attempts of the Western nations and the Bolshevik government emerged stronger.

Defensive Isolation (1921-1934)

Realising that the Soviet Union was hopelessly weak as compared to the Western nations, the Russians followed a policy of concluding non-aggression pacts. She was particularly keen that Germany should not fall in the fold of the Western powers and concluded the Treaty of Rapallo with her in 1922. The other measures in this direction were the pacts with Turkey (1925), Germany (1926), Poland, Finland, Latvia and Estonia (all in 1932). However, in the economic sphere she aimed at a sound economic base and for that purpose she was willing to cooperate even with capitalist countries. This explains her trade agreements with Britain in 1920-21. With a view to expand her trade and to secure foreign loans, during this period (1921-1932) Soviet Russia tried to establish friendly relations with all countries indiscriminately. But due to the activities of the Comintern, the European powers continued to be distrustful of Russia as before. *Schuman* has summed up the position thus: *"Soviet diplomats offered co-operation, but comintern agents preached revolution."*

Another outstanding feature of her policy during this period was that she always stood for total and universal disarmament, gave unqualified support to the Pact of Paris (1928), sponsored the Litninov Protocol in 1929, and concluded innumerable bi-lateral and multi-lateral agreements to build a security system based on neutrality and non-aggression. During this period Soviet Russia expressed her desire, more than once, to join the League of Nations, provided it would preserve peace and security in the world.

In short, during this period, Russia wanted to live in peace and amity and avoid all sorts of international tension and war. But in spite of her best intentions and efforts the Western powers were keen to restore capitalism in the Soviet Union. At Locarno (1925) the Western powers made a bold bid to bring Germany back into its orbit. That naturally estranged Soviet Russia and forced her to live in defensive isolation.

Co-operative with the West (1934-1938)

During this period the Soviet foreign policy underwent a further change. She abandoned her policy of *'defensive isolation'* and instead adopted the policy of co-operation with the West. She was forced to adopt this policy because of the aggressive policy of Japan in the Far East culminating in her occupation of Manchuria (1932) and the rise of Hitler and his Nazi party in Germany. This created a danger of two-front attack on Russia. For this reason Soviet Union felt increasingly the need for the cooperation of the Western countries. Besides, with the success of the five year plans in Russia not only the living standard of the people improved, the liberal principles also gained currency. This led to the policy of rapproachment with the West. She also became keen to conclude treaties of non-aggression, neutrality and friendship with the socialist and liberal powers to protect the Communist movement against the Fascist powers.

In 1933 Russia concluded non-aggression pacts with Afghanistan, Estonia, Latvia, Persia, Poland and Turkey. In that year she also resumed diplomatic relations with China and recognised the territorial settlements of the Treaty of Versailles. After the withdrawal of Japan and Germany from the League she not only joined it as a permanent member but also become one of the staunch supporter of collective security through the League.

This period also marked the beginning of co-operation between France and Russia. The rise of Hitler in Germany had posed threat to both Russia and France, who decided to cooperate with each other as a matter of expedience. The first beginning in this direction was made before the rise of Hitler when the two countries had concluded a non-aggression Pact. In 1935, a mutual assistance pact was concluded between France and Russia, and between Russia and Czechoslovakia. By this pact these countries were to *'aid and assist'* each other in case of unprovoked aggression by any European state.

During this period not only diplomatic relations were established between U.S.A. and Soviet Russia, but a treaty was also concluded by which both the governments agreed to preserve the territorial integrity of each other, and to prohibit subversive activities and propaganda against each other. This treaty was made possible by the rise of Japan, a common foe, in the Far East.

Dangerous Isolation (1938-1939)

The Munich Pact marked a turning point in the foreign policy of Soviet Russia. As she was not invited to the Munich Conference, it raised suspicion in her mind about the sincerity of her allies. When Austria was occupied by Germany, Russia proposed to the Western powers to take a firm stand against her, but the same was not accepted. To guard against the possible aggression of Germany and Italy, Russia also proposed a triple alliance between Russia, Britain and France, but that too was rejected by the Western powers. Under the circumstances, to preserve her security and interests, Russia concluded a non-aggression pact with Germany. By this pact Russia got the right to remain neutral in the war between Germany and Western states, and also retained the right to receive help from the Western powers in case of Germany's aggression on Russia.

Collaboration with Germany (August 1939 to June 1941)

During this phase of her foreign policy, Soviet Russia reverted to aggressive policy and violated treaties with Finland, Estonia, Latvia Lithunia, Poland, Rumania and all the Baltic states. The fall of France in June 1940 and the possibility of collapse of the British armies before the German armies, prompted Soviet Government to maintain association with Germany and Japan. Consequently she continued her co-operation with Germany and concluded a non-aggression pact with Japan in April, 1941.

The Period of War (June 1941 to 1945)

Although Soviet Russia had entered into a non-aggression pact with Germany she knew it fully well that a clash with Germany was inevitable. Therefore, she continued to prepare for her defense at a pretty fast pace.

The apprehensions of Soviet Russia came out true when Germany mounted an attack against Soviet Russia in August, 1941. Thus the Soviet Russia was also involved in the Second World War. Prime Minister Churchill immediately declared "The Russian danger is, therefore, our danger. Russia on her part signed the Atlantic Charter and all other Declarations in relation to the war-policy of the Allied powers in the hope of getting co-operation of the West. Although co-operation began between Soviet Union and the Allied powers yet none could completely rely upon the other. The Soviet victory in the battle of Stalingrad perplexed the Allies. It convinced them that Russia was capable of winning the war without the support of the Allies. Consequently from November 1943 onwards U.S.A. concluded a treaty with France and England and opened negotiations for an armistic with Bulgaria without the knowledge of Russia. It became evident at the conference at Yalta, San Francisco and Potsdam in 1945 that an unbridgeable gulf had been created between Russia and the Allies. The cold war, which started between Soviet Union and the Western powers after 1945, was to a large extent the extension of the distrust which had prevailed between Soviet Union and the Western powers right from the year 1917.

We find from the above survey that it is very difficult to have a clear idea about the foreign policy of Soviet Union because of lack of frankness on the part of Soviet Russia as well as the allies. On the whole Russian relations with Western powers remained unfriendly. This bitterness was mainly due to the influence of the Communist ideology on the Soviet foreign policy. This ideology preached the inevitability of conflict between the communist and non-communist world and regarded imperialism as the last stage of capitalism. It thus created fear, violence and hatred and posed a threat to the world peace. The Soviet policy along with the American policy throughout this period was opportunistic. It was based on changing strategy and tactics. In fact all the talk of peace, peaceful co-existence, disarmament and non-aggression by Soviet Russia during this period was a tactical manoeuvre. During this period she tried to draw a wedge in the capitalist camp by playing one country against the other. Along with it she tried to create her own spheres of influence in international politics by the system of alliances. She used Comintern for interference in the internal affairs of the other countries. All these activities of Soviet Russia caused bitterness and led to what came to be called 'cold war' in the post World War II period.

34

The Soviet Economic Reforms

The rapid rate of Soviet economic development, begun in 1921-1922, was based upon Lenin's theory that socialism and communism could be built in Russia if public ownership of the means of production was established and the economy was centrally planned.

Lenin conceded that the period of so-called "military communism" (1918-1921) had represented an attempt to establish socialism without market relations or trade, but on the basis of direct exchange of commodities between town and countryside, and that this attempt had been necessitated by the foreign military intervention. Lenin felt that the attempt could succeed if enthusiastically supported, but it would have to be based on economic accountability and personal material incentives for the working people.

Thus was laid the cornerstone for the building of socialist society, as a new, planned form of commodity production based on the law of value and commodity monetary relations. It is important to bear in mind, however, that in the USSR the law of value does not operate spontaneously but within the framework of proportions and rates fixed in the overall economic plan. This is why the operation of the law of value never did and does not lead to economic anarchy, unemployment or crises and depressions. Just as the means of production could not be privately owned for the gain, so the operation of the law of value under socialism has not led to the polarisation of poverty and wealth and the creation of antagonistic class contradictions.

But the law of value leads to the formation of profits. Many persons in the West cannot understand how profit can be compatible with socialism. Here, too, we may cite history. At one time Lenin demanded that all Soviet enterprises shift to economic accountability. They should operate on a "commercial basis", as he put it. Lenin urged that commercial accounting not be ignored and that battle be joined against the prejudices that hindered it and against adverse recollection of the past.

Lenin's comment about the view advanced in Bukharin's "The Economy of the Transitional Period" is quite characteristic. Bukharin had written that production under capitalism was production for the sake of profit, while production under proletarian rule was production to meet the needs of the public. Thus, to acknowledge the necessity of commercial operations and profit-making is to acknowledge the operation of the law of value and of the commodity-monetary mechanism in the process of building socialist society.

Actually, these principles have operated throughout the history of the Soviet state, but in World War II and in the post-war reconstruction, the operation and requirements of the law of the value were restricted. These periods demanded the utmost concentration of resources and centralised rationing of them. Moreover, since the Soviet Union was not receiving long-term financing and credits from outside, it had to restrict consumption of the available resources in order to make the necessary huge investments.

The above values were, moreover, supported by the enthusiasm and heroically selfless efforts of the majority of the soviet people. Sacrifice and enthusiasm are an immense force in the development of society (just as of the individual) at critical moments of life. They can provide the foundation for a massive daily and continuous improvement in the sphere of production, distribution and trade.

The essential principle of the reform, now in operation for more than a year, is that what is advantageous for society as a whole should be advantageous for each industrial enterprise. Towards this end a number of measures are being adopted, including: increasing the independence of enterprises; appraising their work by the criterion of profitability introducing payment for production assets; raising the material incentives for personnel, in ratio to the enterprise's performance, out of profits; increasing the enterprises' direct contracting with one another for the supply of goods and establishing economically based, as opposed to arbitrarily set, prices.

The reforms have thus far brought much that is advantageous. The pleasing aspect is that the amount of supervision by superior agencies has been reduced and the possibilities of showing initiative have increased. Practically speaking, the manager now requires supervision only in settling and gaining approval of key goals in his factory's plan; he must also be provided with up-to-date information on technical and economic developments, and most important, must be helped in solving the practical problems of obtaining supplies for major construction and the introduction of new equipment and machinery. In principle, the manager settles all day-to-day questions independently and directly with his suppliers, clients and transportation agencies.

As for the manager's cares, they have multiplied, for under the old system, though he had far less freedom of action, his task was essentially simpler, since everything was decreed from above. His responsibility consisted merely in carrying out instructions. Now he has to search, experiment and take risks; and this is not easy.

Most questions are now decided at the enterprises themselves and with the broad participation of the workers. It has become much easier to apply proposals for rationalisation, since the needed resources are available at the enterprises themselves, out of their own profits. Finally, the wages and bonuses received by the workers have increased substantially.

The question of profit has been widely discussed in recent times in the USSR. Profit was only one of many required indicators which were set as goals. These indicators established as targets for the enterprise included gross volume of output, an excessively detailed list of the items to be produced, cost reduction, number of employees, output per employee, average wage, etc.

Much of this can be explained by the fact that for a long time the Soviet Union was the world's only socialist country. It was faced with the task of creating industry as far as possible and providing for the country's defence. No thought was given at that time to the quality or attractiveness of goods, not even to production cost or profit. This was entirely justified, for the Soviet Union not only withstood the war of 1941-1945 but played a decisive role in ridding the world of fascism. This was worth any price. It was our "profit" and, if you please, the "profit" of the whole civilised world.

But, as Lenin said more than once, our virtues, if carried too far, can turn into faults. This is what happened in that country when the practices of management by administrative fiat were continued into the period after Soviet Union entered the stage of peaceful economic competition with the developed countries of the West.

Profit sums up all the aspects of an enterprise's work, including quality of output, since the price for better goods is correspondingly higher than for outmoded or relatively inefficient items. But it is important to note that profit is neither the only nor the chief goal of production. Profit is used as the chief index of, and incentive to, efficiency of production, as a mechanism for appraising and stimulating the work of an enterprise and also as a source of accumulation and investment.

What is the difference between "capitalist" and "socialist" profit ? The difference will be best understood if we consider: (1) how the profit is formed; (2) what it indicates; and (3) how it is spent.

From the viewpoint of private enterprise, all profit belongs to the capitalists alone. To justify this, there was long ago devised a theory that three factors—capital, land and labor—create value. Joseph A Schumpeter, in his "Theory of Economic Development," wrote, "profit is the excess over production cost". But this "cost" includes "payment" for the entrepreneur's labor, land rent and interest on capital, as well as a premium for "risk". Over and above this, profit should reward the entrepreneur if, by a fresh combination of production elements, he reduces the production cost below the prevailing average level of expenditure.

The nature of this "combination of elements " can be perceived from the fact that in the private enterprise system most profit is now derived from redistribution of income in the market in the process of exchange. It is common knowledge, for instance, that big profits are most easily obtained by the advantageous purchase of raw materials, by a monopoly-controlled rising of retail prices, by unequal exchanges with underdeveloped countries, by the export of capital to countries with low wage levels, by a system of preferential duties and tariffs, by the increase in stock-market prices through capitalisation above profit, and finally, by military orders.

All these sources of profit are precluded by the very nature of socialism, under which there is neither private ownership of the means of production nor holding of stock (and hence no stock market).The level at which labour is paid depends on the productivity of the labour and is regulated by law. Prices of raw materials and supplies are planned; the market cannot be taken advantage of in purchasing raw materials or hiring labour. Nor is it possible to take advantage of market conditions to raise the prices of finished goods. Exchange with other countries is conducted on a basis of equality and by long-term agreements.

In the Soviet Union, by virtue of the very nature of the mode of production and distribution, profit indicates only the level of production efficiency. Profit is the difference between production cost and the factory sale price. Higher profits in the Soviet Union are based solely on economised hours of working time, economised tons of raw materials and supplies and fuel, and economised kilowatt-hours of electricity.

Profit here belongs to those who own the means of production; that is to say, to society, to all the working people as a whole. All profit goes first of all into the planned expansion or improvement of social production, and next into providing free social services to the public, such as education and science, public health services, pensions and stipends. A part is spent on the administrative apparatus and, unfortunately, quite a large part on defence requirements.

The law of value is not a law of capitalism, but is a form of production for the market. The difference from câpitalism is that ends and means are reversed. Under capitalism, profit is the basic aim, whereas satisfaction of the needs of the public is secondary. Under socialism, on the contrary, the aim is to satisfy the needs of the public, and profit is the means toward that end.

The first stage of the economic reform has confronted with certain difficulties in realising its basic principles which appeared inherent in this period of the reform. The transfer of the first 704 enterprises to the new system was not immediately accompanied by substantial changes in their relations with the superior agencies, with other enterprises, with agencies supplying materials and equipment, etc.

Necessary changes had not been fully put into effect in the methods of planning production at the level of the ministries and industry administrations—particularly in the method of setting goals for enterprises. Due to lack of experience, sometimes the same old sharply criticised targets were simply made the new ones. For example, output has been considered as being the same as sales volume; and the assortment of items produced has not always been determined in consultation with the consumer or clients on the basis of direct contract arrangements.

The 1966 experience of working by the new method did show that, on the one hand, enterprises are becoming more dynamic and independent in their economic life, but, on the other hand, that the superior agencies frequently have been incapable of freeing themselves from old habits and from superfluous regimentation of the work of plants and factories. The inertia of thought, views and ideas which was so characteristic of some executive agencies over a long period has proved more persistent than had been expected.

The recent radical reforms put the old established relationships in industry to a severe test. The enlargement of the rights of enterprises is an important condition of the reform. In many cases, however, the superior agencies have proved insufficiently prepared for this development.

Perhaps one of the most significant consequences of the recent economic reforms is the growing influence of private industrial enterprises on the superior agencies. The reform is destroying and will continue to destroy many established patterns.

Unquestionably, the reform has strengthened the tendency of enterprises to strive for independence. To strengthen and intensify central planning of production by combining it with the initiative and full economic accountability of enterprises is to realise the principle of democratic centralism.

The recent reforms have sufficiently permeated the administrative interrelationships between enterprises and superior agencies. This is indeed a complicated process of many steps.

35

British Foreign Policy

"Geography, sea power, trade, balance of power, imperial interests - these have been the traditional bases of British foreign policy, and every British statesman of the past few centuries has been conscious of them. On the whole British diplomacy has sought to promote the interests of Britain in the light of these underlying realities, and it has done so with a continuity that is one of the outstanding characteristics of British foreign policy."

Palmer and Perkins

Introduction

Since the middle of the 17the century it has been the cardinal principle of British foreign policy to prevent the domination of Europe by any one single power. That is why during this period she intervened in the continental affairs again and again, usually in support of the state or coalition of states, which was prepared to resist the dominant power of the day. This attitude has been the outcome of the British desire to keep her sea lanes open so that the people of England may carry on their trade with other countries and import the necessary raw materials and the foodstuffs, without which they could not survive. Palmer and Perkins have observed: "Trade is indeed the life blood of Britain, and it is no mere coincidence that its promotion and protection have always been major concerns of British policy."

Although England has always considered herself as the holder of balance in Europe, she has not been an active participant in the European power politics. She intervened only when the balance of power was threatened, otherwise she followed the policy of splendid isolation. At the beginning of the present century when Britain felt that the policy of *'splendid isolation'* was not in her larger interests she gave up this policy and concluded a number of alliances with Japan (1902) Entente Cordiale with France (1904). Triple Entente consisting of Great Britain, France and Russia (1907), consequently when Russia and France declared war against Germany and Austria-Hungary, Great Britain fought the war on their side.

British Foreign Policy During 1920-1939

The preservation of *'Balance of Power'* and *'mastery over the seas'* have been the two outstanding objectives of British Foreign Policy in the pre-World War I period. After First World War it was not possible for her to continue her foreign policy on the basis of these principles due to: (1) emergence of U.S.A. and Japan as strong rivals of Great Britain. The emergence of Japan gave a serious blow to the British interests in Far East, and U.S.A. destroyed the well-accepted British principle of a two navy standard by forcing her to relinquish it at the Washington Conference. (2) The war resulted in decline of trade, depreciation of the currency and increase in unemployment figures. This effected her exports and production. (3) The people of Asia and the Middle East became violent against imperialist countries and freedom movement was gaining ground in these countries. (4) The desire on the part of the Commonwealth countries to play their own role in the world politics further weakened British hold on these countries. (5) The problem of reparation created a vicious economic reaction and led to the depression of thirties. This led to adoption of preference Empire trade at the Ottawa Conference.

All these factors brought about a change in the foreign policy of Great Britain. Henceforth the chief aim of the British foreign policy was to secure cooperation of the Commonwealth countries, strengthen friendship with U.S.A., make disarmament policy effective, which was essential for her world-trade and economic revival, and support to the world organisation for regulating international relations peacefully.

Relations with France

Although Great Britain and France had fought together during the First World War, soon differences cropped between the two. At the time of the Peace Settlement England and U.S.A. had persuaded France to give up her claims to the Rhineland by promising her a guarantee against possible German aggression. But as U.S.A. could not accept the Treaty of Versailles, due to Senate's refusal to ratify the Treaty, she backed out from this guarantee. England also felt that she was not in a position to give this guarantee alone, followed suit. France naturally felt aggrieved and the relations between the two countries were strained.

The attitude of the two powers towards Germany was also different. While France wanted to completely crush Germany so that she may not be able to attack her again, Great Britain considered a prosperous Germany essential for civilization. As Germany was a good customer of British goods she was keen to restore Germany to her normal conditions in the interest of her trade. In 1923 when the French and Belgium troops entered the Ruhr Valley, Great Britain did not approve of the action.

During the years 1924 to 1929, Great Britain tried to meet almost all the demands of France. She met the French demand for security by guaranteeing the *status quo* in the Rhineland against possible aggression from Germany. Germany renounced all designs to recover Alsace-Lorraine and was even welcomed into the League of Nations as a member. However, the public opinion in England did not feel happy over his subordination of British Foreign Policy to the interests of France. The Englishmen particularly did not like the prestige enjoyed by France in the League of Nations. They expected their Government to play the role of an impartial arbiter between France and Germany, and not that of *'shining second'* to France. Consequently, in 1929 the British Government violated the truce of Locarno.

When Hitler came to power in Germany, England did not feel perturbed and continued her old policy of isolation. England felt to check France from gaining predominance, the revival of Germany was essential. That is why Great Britain two months after the Stress Conference of April 1935 (where England along with France and Italy had denounced Nazi rearmament and the implied threat to peace in Europe), entered into the Anglo-German Navy Treaty with Germany, by which Germany was permitted to have a navy to the tune of 35% of the British naval strength. This open recognition to the illegal German rearmament by Great Britain, was greatly resented by France who described it as *'a stupid'* and *'perfidious'* betrayal of the Stressa Front.

During the Abyssinian war also the two powers took opposite stands. While England favoured stiff attitude towards Italy, France did not want to annoy Mussolini. Therefore, France refused to support Great Britain wholeheartedly. France enforced the economic sanctions recommended by League also half-heartedly. As a result, Italy succeeded in achieving her objectives.

A little later, on the occasion of the Munich Crisis (September 1938) the two countries acted together and gave a guarantee to Poland, Greece and Rumania. After this France began to lean more and more on England. When Hitler attacked Poland in 1939, the two declared war against Germany on the question of Danzig.

Relations with Russia

Although Great Britain and Russia entered the First World War as allies, after the Bolshevik Revolution of 1917, she started negotiations with the Central Powers and signed an armistice at Brest Litovsk in March 1918. After the war England entered into a trade agreement with Russia with a specific understanding that she would stop all propaganda against Great Britain. However, Soviet Russia did not keep her word and continued to follow a policy inimical to the British interests and encouraged general strike in England. This greatly offended the sentiments of the British people.

On the occasion of Munich Crisis, Soviet Russia offered to join hands with Britain to fight against Hitler but the offer was not accepted by Great Britain. After the annexation of Czechoslovakia by Hitler in March 1939, efforts were made to bring Great Britain and Soviet Russia together but these efforts did not yield any result. Commenting on this attitude of England and other Western powers towards Soviet Russia *D.N. Pritt* says, "the Western democracies were not in earnest either in desiring the friendship and cooperation of the Soviet Union ... that they had no genuine resolve to resist Fascism, which they preferred to the spread of Socialism; that they had a very strong desire to maintain the strength of Hitler and Mussolini, to save them from internal collapse, and to keep on friendly terms with them ... and that they were also pursuing with more or less consistency a policy of diverting by one mean or another the force and aggressiveness of Hitler eastwards against the Soviet Union, in order to save themselves from having to face his aggression in the West."

Realising this Soviet Union entered into a non-aggression pact with Germany for ten years on August 23, 1939. As a result of this pact the relations between Soviet Union and Great Britain remained cold till Soviet Union was attacked by Germany in 1941. Then the two countries became partners in a common war with Germany.

Relations with Italy

England's relations with Italy in the years immediately following the Peace Agreement were quite cordial. In fact the two became the guarantors of the provisions of Locarno Pact of 1925. The two countries joined hands at Stressa Conference in April 1935 to denounce Germany's programme of rearmament. But after the Abyssinian war the relations between the two became bitter. The British condemnation of the Italian action was greatly resented by Mussolini. This drove Italy into the arms of Germany. During the subsequent years Great Britain made many efforts to win back Italy but with little success. Even on the outbreak of the Second World War England sent Chamberlain and Lord Halifax to Rome, but without any result. When the war broke out Italy fought on the side of Germany.

Relations with Germany

The attitude of Great Britain towards Germany in the post-world war period was one of sympathy. England wanted Germany to be strong to check the French hegemony, and to secure a market for British goods. England pleaded fixation of reparations according to German capacity of payment. When France occupied the Ruhr Valley, the British Government expressed its disapproval of the action. England even tried to bring Germany into the League of Nations. It was mainly due to the efforts of Great Britain that Germany was admitted to the League Council. This sympathetic attitude of Great Britain towards Germany continued even during the initial years of Hitler's rule. Great Britain considered Hitler's dictatorship in Germany as an insurance against Communism. That is why England preferred to develop friendly relations with Germany rather than Soviet Russia.

In 1935 England concluded Anglo-German Navy Treaty with Germany by which Germany was permitted to have navy to the extent of 35% of the British naval strength. This implied recognition of Germany's right to rearm herself in violation of the Peace Settlement.

This policy of appeasement towards Germany continued from 1935 to 1939. After Munich Pact and occupation of Prague by the Germans (March 15, 1939), a dramatic change took place in the foreign policy of Great Britain. On March 17, 1939 Chamberlain promised British resistance "to the utmost of its power to any power which attempted to dominate the world by force." On August 25, 1939 Great Britain signed a treaty of mutual assistance with Poland. It was in fulfilment of the obligations imposed by this treaty that England entered the war.

England and Disarmament

During the inter-war period Great Britain sincerely supported all efforts for disarmament. She not only summoned a number of Disarmament Conferences but took an active part in making them a success. By the Locarno Pact signed in 1925, not only the frontiers of Belgium and France with Germany were guaranteed, but Germany agreed to refer all disputes that might arise between her and other parties to the pact. Great Britain was one of the signatories to the Four Power Pact of 1933 which enjoined on the members the duty "to consult together on all questions pertaining to them and, within the framework of the league of Nations, try to maintain peace to safeguard the decision which may be taken by the League."

In the Naval Conference of London (1930) England was one of the three powers who agreed to restrict the size of their submarines and battleships (others two being U.S.A. and Japan). Even Rhineland was evacuated by the Allies in 1930 under the influence of Great Britain, though they were entitled to keep the same upto 1935.

England and the League

Though England had taken an active part in the establishment of the League, she did not take any active part in its work. That was probably because League was dominated by France and her allies and England became indifferent towards it. Further, she embarked on policy of isolation from European politics as far as possible. Even at the time of Abyssinian war England was forced to adopt a stiff attitude towards Italy by the pressure of public opinion. At that time the economic sanctions imposed by the League of Nations were enforced mainly at the insistence of Great Britain.

From the above discussion it is evident that during the inter-war period England adopted a policy of shameful escape from war. Chamberlain, the British Prime Minister admitted the failure of British Policy and observed: "This is a sad day for all of us, and to none is it sadder than to me. Everything that I have believed in during my public life, has crashed into ruins. There is only one thing left for me to do: that is to devote what strength and powers I have to forwarding the victory of the cause for which we have to sacrifice so much."

The Policy of Appeasement followed by Great Britain During 1930-1939

The foreign policy of Great Britain, which had undergone slight changes in the years following the Peace Settlement, underwent further changes after the emergence of Hitler in Germany. This changed foreign policy of Great Britain is described as *'policy of appeasement'*. Under this policy Great Britain pursued a policy of concession to the Italian and German dictators. This policy of appeasement is specially associated with the name of Chamberlain. During this period Great Britain felt that Italy and Germany had genuine grievances, and if their grievances were removed an eternal peace will prevail in Europe. Britain felt that peace would ensure her greater trade and profits. The main causes for adopting policy of appeasement were as follows:

Fear of Communism

First reason for the adoption of policy of appeasement by Great Britain was that she was scared of Communist danger. The British clash of interests with Russia in the Middle East, China and Europe and Russia's policy of encouraging general strike and labour unrest in England, made her hostile to Russia. Britain was willing to support any country fighting against Russian danger. Germany, Japan and Italy fully exploited this attitude of Russophobia.

Balance of Power

England followed the policy of appeasement because she was keen to preserve her traditional policy of 'balance of powers'. Great Britain felt that Japan, U.S.S.R. and Germany would check each other and their mutual conflicts will exhaust all of them. Britain was sure that Germany and her partners would be able to liquidate the Communist danger, the greatest threat to the British bourgeoisie. With this view Great Britain allowed Germany to rearm herself in violation of the Treaty of Versailles and Locarno Pact. Likewise Great Britain did not oppose German aggressions in Austria and Czechoslovakia, and encouraged Japan to occupy Manchuria. She did not adopt any stiff attitude towards Italy's occupation of Abyssinia either. As a result of British attitude the Axis powers destroyed the 'balance of power' which Great Britain so earnestly wanted to maintain.

Anglo-French Differences

Anglo-French differences also prompted Great Britain to adopt the policy of appeasement. After the war sharp differences had cropped up between the two countries on questions pertaining to German recovery, disarmament, reparations, security etc. England from the very beginning was sympathetically disposed towards Germany because she felt that a weak Germany would be an open invitation to Communist expansion. Great Britain, therefore, favoured the idea of strengthening Germany by relaxing provisions of the Peace Treaty. This attitude of Great Britain towards Germany was dictated both by sympathy and self-interest. But after the emergence of Hitler British continued this policy of appeasement towards Germany on grounds of expediency. It was on this ground that Great Britain concluded the Anglo-German treaty in 1935. After 1937, this policy of appeasement was continued to gain time for war preparations.

Internal Weakness

Finally, Britain followed the policy of appeasement because of her internal weakness. The ever-deteriorating economic conditions in Britain created the danger of Communism in her mind, and to check that danger she supported Germany, Italy and Japan.

Policy Towards Hitler

As noted earlier, during the initial period of Hitler's rule in Germany, Great Britain adopted very sympathetic attitude. In fact, in the dictatorship of Hitler, Great Britain saw an insurance against the Communist threat of Russia. *Hitler* had clearly stated in Mein Kampf: "If we speak today of new territory in Europe, we can primarily think only of Russia and the border states." Therefore, Great Britain preferred to develop friendly relations with Germany.

In 1935 England concluded the Anglo-German Navy Treaty by which Germany's right to have navy to the extent of 35% of the British navy was accepted, in violation of the Treaty of Versailles and the Locarno Pacts.

In 1936 when Germany and Italy jointly intervened in the Spanish Civil War on the pretext of liberating Spain from the influence of the Communist Russia (who was supporting the Government of Spain), Great Britain did not intervene. She even did not make any effort to check the war through the League of Nations. Instead, a 'Committee of Non-Intervention' was formed in London in 1936 for the maintenance of peace in Europe. This Committee instead of settling the issue complicated it and thus provided time to Germany and her ally Italy to establish Franco Government in Spain. When Soviet Union suggested the withdrawal of foreign volunteers from Spain, the proposal was not supported by Great Britain. Thereby Great Britain approved the foreign intervention in the Spanish Civil war.

Similarly when in 1938 Hitler decided to occupy Austria and Czechoslovakia. England helped the cause of Germany by making Eden resign from the Cabinet because of his anti-Fascist views. Again when the President of USA (Roosevelt) proposed a Conference of neutral states for the preservation of world peace, Great Britain opposed the proposals and thereby foiled an important attempt at maintenance of world peace. Again when Schuschnigg, the Austrian Vice-Chancellor appealed to Britain for help against German attack, England was not willing to take any course of action which might expose his country to dangers. Similarly when Germany undertook an expedition against Czechoslovakia, Great Britain rendered no assistance to Czechoslovakia. On the contrary when Russia proposed to call a Conference of the Western States against Hitler, the proposal was summarily rejected by Chamberlain. England during the Czech crisis, however, tried everything possible to preserve the peace. It pleaded to Germany to be less rigid in her demand regarding Sudetenland, it put pressure upon Czech Government to accept the German demand so that she may not go ahead with her plan of Czech attack, and impressed on France to adopt a less rigid attitude on Czechoslovakia so that Czechs may not go to war on the basis of Franco-Czech Treaty.

The Munich Pact was drafted almost on the basis of what had already been decided at a Conference by England, France and Germany. The Czechoslovakian episode marked a remarkable change in the British Foreign Policy. For the first time Great Britain after World War I, undertook a commitment to Central Europe by accepting the obligation to guarantee to protect the remnant of Czechoslovakia. This responsibility devolved on Great Britain as a member of the International Commission which was set up under the Munich Pact.

The Czech episode was an outstanding example of the British policy of appeasement towards Germany. In the first instance England along with France, forced Czechoslovakia to cede the portions demanded by Germany. But when Chamberlain met Hitler with the letter of consent from the Czech Government, Hitler increased his demands and wanted occupation of Sudetanland by 1st October, 1938, and refused to give German security for the rest of Czechoslovakia unless demands of Poland and Hungary were accepted. For the time being Chamberlain felt quite embarrassed. But ultimately on the intervention of Mussolini, a meeting of the representatives of Britain, France, Italy and Germany was arranged at Munich, which resulted in the Munich Pact.

The Munich Pact instead of establishing peace gave impetus to the aggressive designs of Hitler. Britain kept isolated because she was not in favour of going to war over the fate of a country (Czechoslovakia) which did not directly concern her. Further, Hitler's demand for self-determination of the sudetans did not appear unjust to the British.

Within one year of the Munich Pact the German armies captured Prague, the capital of Czechoslovakia in violation of the Pact of Munich. Chamberlain for the first time denounced Hitler's adventurism, and proceeded to accord guarantees to Poland against Germany and Greece and Rumania against Italy, Britain also started negotiations with Russia, but these negotiations could not make much progress due to certain demands of Russia closer to Germany and resulted in a Non-Aggression Pact between the two.

Even at this stage Chamberlain continued British policy of appeasement towards Germany. As late as July 1939, Britain attempted to conclude a twenty-five year defense pact with Germany and offered to provide large loans and return her colonies to Germany in return for a promise that Hitler would not invade Poland. But all these efforts failed. In September 1939, when Hitler invaded Poland, England declared war against Germany in fulfillment of her obligations.

Thus the British policy of appeasement towards Germany failed to prevent war and secure peace in Europe. Chamberlain in his speech before the House of Commons on September 3, 1939 said: "This is a sad day for all of us, and to none is it sadder than to me. Everything that I have worked for, everything that I hope for, everything that believed in during my public life, has crashed into ruins. There is only one thing left for me to do; that is to devote what strength and powers I have to forwarding the victory of the cause for which we have to sacrifice so much. I cannot tell what part I may be allowed to play myself; I trust I may live to see the day when Hitlerism has been destroyed and a liberated Europe has been established.

From the above, it is evident that the policy of appeasement persued by Great Britain towards Germany destroyed the European balance of power, annihilated the framework of security and led to the Second World War. If the British Government had been able to act with more vigour and strictness, Hitler's designs would have been checked. But Britishers were duped in by clever tactics of Hitler, who always posed himself as a crusader of Communism. Again, if England had concluded an alliance with Italy, Germany would not have raised her head. An alliance with Italy could not be concluded because of the arrogance of Anthony Eden, the Foreign Minister of England.

36

The Main Objectives of French Foreign Policy in the Inter-war Period

Out of the important and persistent single factor which determined the foreign policy of France in the inter-war period was 'search for security'. Although France had emerged victorious out of Word War I, she was aware of the potential danger from Germany. This feeling persisted because, as Langsam puts it *"twice within the living memory of men had the pounding of German military boots been heard on the French soil and the citizens of Third Republic were fearful of still another incursion."* During the peace settlement of Paris, France had insisted on physical guarantees against Germany but failed to secure the same.

Military Alliances

Left to herself, after World War I France concluded a number of alliances to strengthen her position against Germany. She first proceeded to conclude alliances with countries which were afraid of Germany. In September 1920 France signed a Military Convention with Belgium. Belgium was as much exposed to the German threat as France herself. In February 1921 France signed the Franco-Polish Treaty of Alliance. These countries were also brought together by the danger of common enemy—Germany. Poland had been created out of Germany and consequently she was also afraid of Germany. By these treaties France was able to secure help from Poland in the East and Belgium in the West.

In 1924 France concluded an alliance with Czechoslovakia which was located so near the German frontier that it could be occupied by German troops within days, or perhaps within hours. In 1926 Fance concluded a treaty of friendship with Rumania and in 1927 a similar treaty was concluded with Yugoslavia. As Czechoslovakia, Rumania and Yugoslavia were created by the Peace Treaty, they eagerly defended the Peace Settlement. The policy of these countries fitted in well with the French policy of maintaining *status quo* in Europe. France agreed to strengthen these countries by providing them with war materials and military exports. France by these treaties promised to help the Czechs against Magyars and the Yugoslavs against Italy. In short, as *Carr says, "It became a recognised French interest to support Poland against Lithuania, Czechoslovakia against Hungary and Yugoslavia and Rumania against Bulgaria, and even to save her friends from the inconvenience of a too rigorous interpretation of their obligations towards their minorities."*

Locarno Pact

In 1925 Germany made an offer of Rhineland Pact, whereby France, Germany, Great Britain and Italy were to jointly guarantee the Franco-German border. France, realising that Germany was reaffirming her acceptance of the loss of Alsace and Lorraine as well demilitarization of Rhineland, welcomed the offer. However she insisted that her allies

Poland, Belgium and Czechoslovakia, should also be invited to participate. In October 1925, delegates from seven states (England, France, Germany, Italy, Czechoslovakia, Poland and Belgium) met at Locarno in Switzerland and concluded a number of agreements which are popularly termed as Locarno Pact.

By this treaty Germany, Belgium and France agreed to renounce war against each other and settle their differences by peaceful methods. (2) Franco-German and Belgo-German frontiers as determined by the Treaty of Versailles were guaranteed and Rhineland was demilitarized. (3) England and Italy agreed to act as guarantors. (4) In case of flagrant aggression, the guarantors agreed to act at once.

The Locarno Pact was a turning point in the foreign policy of France. By yielding to the British demand to evacuate the Ruhr and by bringing in the Britishers as the guarantors of Franco-German frontiers, France agreed to give up her independent foreign policy and in future could not act independent of Great Britain. After Locarno both England and America began to put pressure on France to agree to disarmament.

Emergence of Hitler

With the emergence of Hitler French security was rendered weak. In January 1934, Poland entered into a non-aggression pact with Germany and thereby weakened the position of France *vis-a-vis* Germany. In 1936, Belgium also terminated her military alliance with France. Germany also succeeded in wining over Yugoslavia to her side.

Treaty of Mutual Assistance Between France and Russia

To strengthen her position in 1935 France entered into a Treaty of Mutual Assistance with Soviet Russia. By this treaty France and Russia agreed to consult each other in the event of threat of an aggression by any European state. In case of unprovoked aggression by any European state the two countries agreed to aid and assist each other. The treaty was to last for five years from the date of its ratification. However, in actual practice the treaty remained a dead letter because France did nothing to implement it.

Franco-Italian Treaty 1935

In 1935 France also concluded an Alliance with Italy. Ever since the Paris Treaty, the relations of France with Italy had been bitter. The rivalry between the two expressed itself in the struggle for pre-dominance in the South Eastern Europe. With the emergence of Hitler France adopted more compromising attitude and agreed to readjustment of colonies in Africa in favour of Italy. The rapprochement between the two became easy when in 1934 the Austrian Chancellor Dollfuss was assassinated by the Austrian Nazi party, and the anti-German attitude of the two countries brought them together in January 1935 when the Franco-Italian treaty was signed. By this treaty the two powers agreed to discuss their differences and to encourage the neighbours of Austria to conclude non-aggression treaties with Austria, to check Germany's efforts to remilitarise herself.

Thus at the end of 1935 France stood in a very peculiar situation. Gamelin, the Chief of the General Staff of France, summed up her position thus: "If France commits herself definitely in Russia, Germany will reply by occupying the left bank of the Rhine; if Italy emerges weakened from her current difficulties in Abyssinia that means Anschluss; if there is war between Britain and Italy in the Mediterranean and we come in, Germany is prepared to move against us. Only the closed understanding between France and Britain can keep the peace from now on."

Spanish Civil War

From 1936 to 1938 France was involved in her domestic problems and could not take an active part in the foreign affairs. The policy of peace and non-intervention followed by France during the Spanish Civil War of 1936, drove more nails into the coffin of France's Eastern alliances and left France completely discredited.

Franco-British Alliance

In April 1938 the famous Franco-British Alliance was concluded, which was one of the most sweeping engagements of its kind since World War I. By this Alliance the two powers not only agreed to accord complete diplomatic cooperation but also agreed to establish a unitary command of the British and French military, naval and Air Forces.

Issue of Czechoslovakia

In September 1938 when Hitler committed aggression against Czechoslovakia France was willing to go to war. She even tried to win over the British government to her point of view. But Lord Halifax, the Foreign Minister of England, counselled pressure on the Czechs. Ultimately the French followed the British lead and agreed to put pressure on the Czechs to make maximum concessions to Hitler. On September 29-30, 1938 the representatives of Germany, France and England met at Munich and decided the area of Czechoslovakia to be handed over to Germany. It may be noted that at the Munich Conference neither Czechoslovakia nor Russian representatives were present.

Munich Pact

The Munich Pact was one of the greatest follies of French diplomacy. She lost not only the defence advantage of 35 well-equipped divisions in Czechoslovakia but also her alliance and prestige in Eastern Europe. Commenting on Munich Pact *Churchill* observed: "France and Great Britain had to choose between war and dishonour. They chose dishonour. They will have war."

Churchill proved right because soon after Hitler seized the rest of Czechoslovakia, Memal and even attacked Poland. France was thinking in terms of establishing peace through conference even when the German troops embarked on Polish aggression. However, Lord Halifax took the stand that there could be no conference without cession of hostilities in Poland. Ultimately France was forced by Britain to declare war against Germany on September 3, 1939.

37

Italy and Rise of Fascism

"From the longer perspective of times past and times to come, Italy was doomed to remain a lesser power with no independence of action - unless the coalition of West should dissolve into a new multipower constellation in which free manoeuvering and bargaining would again become possible for every sovereignty whose support might be valued, or enemity might be feared by others."

Schuman

Introduction

Though Italy fought on the side of the victorious Allies during World War I, she emerged from the war a defeated nation. She was not happy at the Peace Settlement because she was not given what had been promised to her by the Treaty of London. As the interests of Italy and Yugoslavia conflicted, the Allies decided to favour Yugoslavia to the entire discontent of Italy. She failed to secure anything tangible at the Paris Peace Conference. As a result, Italy felt dissatisfied, disappointed and considerably wounded in her self-esteem. *J. Hampden* Jakson beautifully summed up the position in the following words: "Italians felt themselves disgraced in the eyes of the world, swindled by their own politicians. War had cost Italy dear, draining her of money, saddling her with a budget deficit of over twelve thousand million liras, rising up the cost of living. The political party in power in 1919 was pacifist, its leaders old and cynical. It is little wonder that Italians turned to violence."

The general public felt that Italy had failed to secure favourable terms at the Peace Conference due to the incapacity of its leaders. They therefore favoured the rise of Fascism in Italy.

Rise of Fascism in Italy

In the post war period the Government was faced with problems which were beyond its capacity to solve. Demobilization after the war increased the army of unemployed, the country faced bankruptcy, starvation and inflation. Strikes, lock-outs and riots of the hungry people were the order of the day. National currency fell steadily and the cost of living rose very high. The uneasiness of the government to tackle these huge problems is evident from the fact that between 1919 and 1922, six governments and most of them of heterogeneous character, were formed in Italy. All this gave rise to Fascism.

Gathrone Hardy has remarked that "the circumstances under which Fascism developed in Italy, though in a sense peculiar to that country, confirmed the thesis that this form of autocracy is the product of situation when democratic sentiment proves incompatible with effective parliamentary government."

The rising discontent in the country was exploited by Mussolini, who formed the Fascist party and invited all the anti-government forces to join the revolution. Failing to capture power through elections in late October, 1922, Mussolini ordered his followers to 'march to Rome' in order to terrify the king into appointing him the Premier of Italy. Thus Mussolini came to power in the constitutional manner.

Soon Mussolini embarked upon a ruthless policy of suppression of opposition parties, censorship of press, suspended local autonomous units and democratic institutions. The election laws were modified in favour of Fascist party, the chapter of Deputies was dissolved and a council of 22 was set up. Thus dictatorship of the Fascist Party was established in Italy by Mussolini.

Role of Italy in International Relations During 1920-1945

The failure of Italy to secure lands promised, to her in 1919, at the Paris Peace Conference had caused much bitterness and dissatisfaction in Italy. Consequently Mussolini followed a forward foreign policy. This policy became necessary partly because he was determined to raise the prestige of Italy in the eyes of other powers. This could be possible only if he was able to demonstrate to the world that Italy had enough strength, not only to protect herself, but also to attain the lands she had been promised by the London Treaty in 1915, but which had actually not been given to her in 1919. An aggressive foreign policy was also helpful to him in diverting the attention of the people from domestic politics. This policy was also essential to provide an outlet to her excessive and continuously increasing population. Italy needed colonies to provide an outlet to the "hundreds of thousands of her children deprived of work in the fatherland and no longer enabled to emigrate abroad on account of limitations imposed on immigration by foreign countries. *Mussolini* openly declared "We are hungry for land, because we are prolific and intend to remain so." Italy was also keen to regain her Roman inheritance by establishing a Mediterranean and African Empire. *Katharine Duff* has depicted the objectives of Italy's foreign policy thus: "As things were, the Mediterranean far from being an empire, was her prison; Corsica, Malta, Tunis and Cyprus formed their prison's bars while Gibraltar and Suez guarded its gates and Greece, Turkey and Egypt were ready to complete the chain encircling her. Determined first to break her prison bars, and then to march to the Ocean without access to which she must be considered only half-independent. Italy might push towards the Indian ocean by linking Libya with Ethiopia through the Sudan towards the Atlantic through French North Africa."

Thus Italy was keen to have control in South-Eastern Europe, Africa and, if possible, further ahead.

First of all, Mussolini concentrated his attention on South Eastern Europe. By the Treaty of Laussane (1923) Italy got back the Dodacanese Islands, which she had surrendered to Greece in 1920. In the same year the Italian army bombed the island of Corfu and occupied it. Greece lodged a protest with the League of Nations on whose intervention Italy left Corfu after receiving compensation from Greece. This gave a fillip to the prestige of Mussolini at home. In January 1924 Italy concluded Treaty of Rome with Yugoslavia by which the free state of Fiume was divided between the two. While the city o Fiume proper went to Italy, Yugoslavia got the neighbouring town of Porto Baros.

In 1926, Mussolini concluded a treaty with Albania at *Tirana* by which Albania became practically a dependency of Italy. Later on Albania was annexed to Italy (1939), without much opposition. In 1928, Italy was invited to participate in the administration of the Free City of Tangier on the West Coast of Morocco. This was looked upon in Rome as a great diplomatic triumph for Mussolini. In 1930, at the London Naval Conference Mussolini demanded naval parity with France. In 1931, he advocated the revision of the peace treaties.

By these steps Mussolini was able to strengthen Italy's hold on the Adriatic, increase her prestige in the Mediterranean, and extend her diplomatic and commercial influence in the South Eastern Europe.

Italy's Seizure of Abyssinia

The next victim (target) of the expansionist policy of Mussolini was Abyssinia. Italy was prompted to undertake this project because (1) she needed some territory for the surplus population of Italy; (2) she needed raw materials for her industries and markets for her finished products; (3) It was essential to distract the attention of Italian people for their miserable economic conditions; (4) The area was of strategic value to Italy. It could link the Italian possessions in Somaliland, Eritrea and South East Africa; (5) A war against Abyssinia could arouse patriotic spirit of the Italians who had suffered a defeat at the hands of the Abyssinia in 1896.

Although Mussolini had nourished design against Abyssinia for a long time, he did not actually undertake this project till he was sure of a military victory. The attitude of League of Nations and other great powers towards conquest of Manchuria by Japan, convinced Mussolini that in spite of the principle of collective security, nobody was going to stop him from conquering Abyssinia. Further due to the economic depression, 'the statesmen of Europe were pre-occupied with their domestic problems. In the international sphere the Statesmen were also occupied with the problem of Hitler's rise to power and the pursuit of an aggressive policy by him.

Consequently the Italian troops entered Abyssinia in October 1935. Immediately the Council of the League of Nations declared that Italy had "resorted to war in disregard of its obligation under Article 12 of the covenant." Two days later the League Assembly recommended the appointment of a Committee to co-ordinate the work. The Co-ordinating Committee asked the members of League of Nations to prohibit, all loans or credits to Italy and place an embargo on exports to Italy. But France was not happy about these economic sanctions because she feared that it might plunge the whole of Europe into a war. In the meanwhile the Italian forces continued to penetrate into Abyssinia and ultimately occupied it in May, 1936.

The conquest of Abyssinia, according to *Gathorne* Hardy "makes a crucial turning point in post-war history. The triumph of Italian aggression, naked and unashamed, affected the whole world with fundamental consequences. To England it meant the virtual destruction of the institution which successive Governments of different parties had proclaimed to be the keystone of their foreign policy. To France, it meant that the enemy of whom she stood most in terror was encouraged to fresh audacity and rescued from his previous isolation.

During the inter-war period Mussolini opposed the Union of Austria with Germany, because such a union was likely to put a stop to the Italian influence in Europe. In 1931, he opposed the tariff union between Austria and Germany. In 1934, when the Nazis revolted in Austria and fatally wounded the Austrian Chancellor Dollfuss, Mussolini ordered Italian mobilization to help Austria. Thus Austria was saved from German annexation.

In South-Eastern Europe Italy tried to steel a march over France by impressing on the states of the region to form alliances with Italy rather than France. As far as the lesser states of the region were concerned they were eager to make alliance either with France or with Italy but they were not at all willing to accept the supremacy of either. Initially Italy was able to outwit France by forming alliances with both Yugoslavia and Czechoslovakia. France, however, succeeded only to have an alliance with Czechoslovakia. But later on, France was able to increase her influence over the states in the region. Italy made efforts to destroy French political influence by the dissolution of the Little Entente and substituting it with a combination directed from Rome. But once she was unable to have a monopoly of these alliances she encouraged Germany against French plans of reconstruction.

In the matter of disarmament, Italy supported German's stand of 'parity between German and French strength. Italy was convinced that it would give the Italian army balance of power on the continent. Italy was right in her assessment. When Germany rearmed herself to the French level, Italy was able to defy Great Britain in the Abyssinian war.

Though Italy was keen to secure German co-operation Italy's stand on Austria against Germany made it practically impossible for the two to come close for the time being. Consequently on January 7, 1935, Italy signed a pact with France at Rome. By this agreement France met the main demands of Italy in Africa in return for concessions by Italy in Central and Eastern Europe. France gave to Italy 44,500 sq. miles of territory bordering on the Anglo-Egyptian Sudan and a strip of French Somaliland giving Eritrea an outlet to the Gulf of Aden. The two parties also undertook to respect their mutual frontiers and abstain from meddling in the internal affairs of each other. Both the parties also agreed to oppose any unilateral revision of the Treaty of Versailles particularly in respect of German re-armament.

But as France participated in the economic sanctions enforced against Italy on account of her intervention in Abyssinia, the friendly relations suffered a setback.

After the rise of Hitler, Italy started improving her relations with Britain also. Realising that Great Britain was a great naval power of Europe and had influence in the Mediterranean sea, Italy could not afford to neglect her. At the Stresa Conference Italy had aligned herself with France and Great Britain. In January 1937, Great Britain and Italy issued a declaration that they had agreed to preserve the *status quo* in the Mediterranean. Another agreement was concluded by the two countries in April 1938 by which they regulated a number of issues in the Mediterranean and the Near Eastern area arising out of Italy's conquest of Abyssinia. While Italy agreed to withdraw a substantial number of her volunteers from Spain, England recognised Italy's African Empire. In 1939 Chamberlain and Halifax went to Rome to have further negotiations with Italy but the mission did not yield much results.

Mussolini by philosophy and attitude was more close to Germany. It has been rightly said that while the attitude of Italy towards Great Britain and France was one of hesitation and reserve, her advance towards friendship with Germany seemed to be smooth and steady. In 1937 Italy joined the anti-Comintern Pact (concluded by Germany and Japan in 1936) and thus the *Berlin- Rome-Tokyo axis* came into existence. *Hitler* referred to this Axis as "a great world political triangle, which "consists not of three powerless images but of free states which are prepared and determined to protect decisively their rights and vital interests.

In March, 1938 Hitler occupied Austria. Mussolini had assumed the self-imposed role of protector of Austria in July, 1934 could not do anything in view of Italy's estrangement with the Western democracies after the Abyssinian affair. He on the other hand made a bad job of the issue by informing Hitler that "Austria did not interest him at all." No doubt, he was able to earn the gratitude of Hitler but lost his cherished dream of following an independent policy and establishing protectorate over Austria.

In 1939, the supporters of Britain's policy of appeasement made another effort to win over Italy. This effort resulted in an agreement on April 16, 1939, by which both the parties agreed to stop mutually hostile propaganda, *status quo* in the Mediterranean and some concessions in Lake Tsana for Britain. Italy also agreed to withdraw volunteers from Spain. But Italy did not comply with any of the terms of the settlement. Though the agreement did not prove of any avail, it certainly enhanced Italy's prestige, which had sunk so low after Hitler's annexation of Austria. She could tell Hitler that Italy had no dearth of friends.

Though the Second World War started in September 1939, Italy remained neutral. Her plan was to attack when the Allies were almost exhausted, because that would save Italy from the destruction of war and would entitle her to share in the spoils of the victory. Such an occasion came in June 1940, when France was on the verge of collapse. Italy declared war against Britain and France on June 10, 1940. She formally joined the Tripple Alliance with Germany and Japan on September 27, 1940. Italy declared war against Soviet Russia in June 1941 and against USA in December 1941.

After 1942, the course of the war began to change and fall of Mussolini and Italy became imminent due to the continuous defeats of the Italian army, of the people and internal economic crisis. In July 1943, the Allies attacked Sicily. The king immediately ordered for the arrest of Mussolini. However, a little later the German army freed Mussolini and put him back into power. But when the Allies attacked North Italy in 1945, Italy unconditionally surrendered the Allies. This marked the fall of Fascist Italy.

38

Foreign Policy of United States (1920-1945)

> "The foreign policy of the United States of America, like that of any State is shaped largely by geographical and historical considerations, by her political and social system, by her economic strength and military power, by her relative power position, by the policies of other States and by the World environment in which now she lives."
>
> **—Palmer and Perkins**

Introduction

The entry of the United States in the First World War marked an epoch in the history of American Foreign Policy. Before the outbreak of War, USA had followed a policy of *'isolation'* for centuries. This policy of isolation was first advocated by President Washington, who in his famous farewell address warned his countrymen to avoid *'entangling alliances'* with the governments of Europe. The American people were psychologically inclined towards a policy of neutralism and non-alignment because they felt that a common man gained nothing from the war and had to pay heavy price. Further, USA was keen to develop herself economically. The wars and the large armies that were essential to conduct the war, involved huge manpower and resources which could be provided at the cost of constructive activities. Therefore, it became one of the objectives of the U.S. government to promote maximum economic development at the cost of political glory and power.

In 1823 with the enunciation of the 'Munro Doctrine' the American foreign policy moved a step further in the direction of non-intervention. *President Monroe* declared: "In the wars of the European Powers, in matters relating to themselves we have never taken any part, nor does it comfort with our policy to do so." "The United States had not intervened, and never would intervene, in wars in Europe; but they could not, on the other hand, in the interest of their own peace and happiness, allow the allied European powers to extend their political system to any part of America, and try to intervene in the independence of the South American Republics ... We should consider any attempt on their part to extend their system to any portion of this hemisphere as dangerous to our peace and safety." America continued to base her foreign policy on this doctrine for about a century.

When the First World War broke out USA adopted an attitude of 'watchful waiting'. But German policy of destroying enemy ships found in the waters about the British Isles without regard to the safety of those abroad provoked US protests. In May 1915, the Lusitania, an English unarmed liner was destroyed by the German submarines. This incident resulted in death of 1200 men, including 128 American men. The American public opinion was greatly shocked by this barbaric act and pressed President Wilson to declare war against Germany. However, President Wilson was satisfied with a guarantee from Germany that in future "Liners will not be sunk by our submarines without warning and without safety of the lives of non-combatants." Nothing untoward happened during the next nine months.

In January 1917, the German Government declared that 'it would sink at sight all ships, neutral as well as belligerent, in certain waters about the British Isles and in the Mediterranean Sea.' *President Wilson* at once cut off diplomatic relations with Germany and on April 2, 1917, declared: "The world must be made safe for democracy; its peace must be planted upon the foundations of political liberty. We have no selfish ends to serve. We desire no conquest, no domination. We seek no war indemnities for ourselves, no material compensation for the sacrifices we shall freely make. We are but one of the champions of the rights of mankind." Four days later USA joined war against Germany.

The entry of United States titled the balance in favour of Allies because she placed at their disposal not only an unplumbed reservoir of man-power but also unlimited money, food-stuffs, minerals, manufactures, shipyards and material resources of every kind. As a result the Allies came out victorious from the war.

The success of the Allies in the First World War was largely due to the American money and war materials. As a result, after the War America emerged as the economic leader of the world and played a very important role at the Paris Peace Conference. The League of Nations was created largely by the efforts of the American President. But the American Senate felt that the treaty of Versailles was not in keeping with the declared war aims of USA and would involve constant American intervention not only in European politics but also in world politics. In short, the Americans felt, as Walter Lippmann says 'for what we were asked to give to our Allies, we were to receive nothing from them." Consequently the American Government refused to give the promised guarantee to France against Germany. In the elections of 1920 the Democratic Government was ousted and the Republic Government came in office.

In 1921, *Harding*, the Republican President, enunciated the foreign policy of USA in these words: " We seek no part in directing the destinies of the world... We are ready to associate ourselves with the nations of the world, great and small, for conference and counsel for the suggestion of mediation, conciliation and arbitration; but every commitment must be made in the exercise of our national sovereignty." It would be wrong to say that Republicans adopted the policy of complete isolation. Their policy can more appropriately be described as one of 'cooperation without entangling alliances'. Though USA had not ratified the treaty of Versailles, she was not averse to assisting in the settlement of the question of German reparations known as Dawes Plan (1924). She even participated in various non-political activities of the League. For the sake of convenience the American Foreign Policy during the inter-war period may be studied under the following headings.

Attitude Towards League

Although the United States could not become a member of the League due to rejection of the Treaty of Versailles by the American Senate, she continued to co-operate with the activities of the League. After some time, the American Government began to appoint observers to attend the meetings of the League. These observers represented the American views before the League, though they were not permitted to vote. Such observers were specially attached with the Committees of the League concerning traffic in women and children, the opium trade and health. Similarly she co-operated with Conferences held for disarmament and betterment of Labour conditions. In short by March 1930, The American delegates had taken part in 22 such gatherings. During the Manchurian crisis an American representative was deputed to work with the League

Council. A number of distinguished American judges served on the Permanent Court of International Justice as judges.

Attitude towards Disarmament

During the inter-war period Americans showed great interest in the various efforts for disarmament. She was specially interested in naval disarmament. She took a lead in this direction and called a Disarmament Conference at Washington, which fixed ratios for the great powers in capital ships and aeroplane carriers. In 1927 President Coolidge called another conference at Geneva to extend the principle of limitation to smaller crafts such as cruisers, destroyers and submarines. However, the conference failed to achieve any results. USA also participated in Naval Conferences held at London in 1930 and 1932.

Simultaneously United States cooperated with the work of the Preparatory Commission for the Disarmament Conference set up by the League Council. The American representative also took part in the General Disarmament Conference held at Geneva in February 1932. In 1933, USA offered to cooperate with the League in the adoption of a general plan for disarmament. Similarly USA attended the London Economic Conference of 1933, which though mainly an economic conference also examined the possibilities of mutual understanding of the different countries regarding restriction of armaments.

United States and Neutrality

After the World War, America once again adopted her traditional policy of neutrality in the European affairs. This policy particularly became pronounced after the emergence of Hitler. In August,1935 a Neutrality Act was passed which forbade export of arms, ammunition and implements of war from any place in USA to any part of a belligerent state. In 1937, USA took another step in this direction by adopting the principle of*'cash and carry basis'* for the sale of armaments. By another Neutrality Act of 1939, in case of war between two foreign states the President could name the states through proclamation. After the proclamation it was unlawful for the US vessels to carry any passengers or articles or materials to any state named in the proclamation. Similarly, it was unlawful for the citizens of USA, to travel on any vessel belonging to the state named in the proclamation. Even foreign loans were forbidden to belligerent governments.

War Debts and Reparations

Though USA displayed lack of interest in the political affairs of Europe, she followed a policy of close co-operation with the nations of the Continent in the economic field. During and after the war US had lent out huge amounts to the various Governments in Europe. At the Peace Conference of Paris, an effort was made to settle the question of war debts and reparations, but no agreement could be reached. Majority of the states promised to repay debts after getting the war indemnity. Naturally USA became interested in the fate of Germany. With a view to put Germany on her feet USA participated in the Dawes Plan and Young Plan. Lot of American loans were advanced to Germany to enable her to recover from economic chaos. During 1931, when world was in the throes of worst type of economic depression, President Hoover of USA adopted a sympathetic attitude and imposed one year Moratorium on both debts and reparation payments. After the expiry of the moratorium, Germany declared that she would not pay any reparations. As a result the other Governments stopped payments to USA. By 1933, all states, except Finland had stopped payment of war-debts. In 1934 the US Congress passed an Act forbidding American financiers to advance loans to the defaulter governments.

Faith in Peaceful Settlement of International Disputes

America believed in solving the international disputes peacefully through arbitration, conciliation or such other methods. To achieve this objective she played a leading role in negotiating the Kellogg-Briand Pact or Paris Pact which was signed in August, 1928, by fifteen States. Under the Pact the signatories declared in the name of their people that they condemn the recourse to war for the solution of international controversies and took a vow to renounce war as an instrument of national policy.

Attitude Towards Pan-American Countries

During the inter-war years USA adopted attitude of sympathy towards the Latin American states. In 1922, Secretary of State *Hughes* declared, "We sincerely desire the independence the unimpaired sovereignty and political integrity and the constantly increasing prosperity of the people of Latin America." In 1925 the American sovereignty and integrity and the constantly increasing marines were withdrawn from Nicaragua, but the next year they were again despatched there on the plea of establishing peaceful conditions and protection of American lives and property. This intervention of America was condemned at the Pan-American conference held at Havana. During the economic crisis of 1929-30 the relations of US with the Latin-America deteriorated because US raised tariffs on imports to protect its own industry. During 1930-33, a number of Latin American countries became debt defaulters but US did not take any action.

In 1933 Roosevelt enunciated the policy of good neighbours. America even gave up her treaty right to intervene in the Latin American Republics. In 1935 a number of Treaties and Conventions were concluded for the purpose of constituting a purely American system tending towards the preservation of peace, proscription of war, and the harmonious development of their commerce. In 1934-35, as a result of Italian rape of Ethiopia and Hitler's repudiation of the Versailles Treaty the international situation was fast deteriorating. The Pan American states at the Buenos Aires Convention adopted a resolution pledging mutual consultation in the event of the threat to the peace.

In 1937-38 President Cardenas of Mexico' nationalised rail-roads which led to the expropriation of 13 American and 4 Brazilian companies. But President Roosevelt continued the policy of moderation. It was due to this policy of moderation that at the Lima Conference of December, 1938 it was agreed that "in case of possible aggression or threat to peace the foreign ministers of the American states would meet in the various capitals in turn at the request of any one of them. Any such threat was to be considered a matter of common concern by all states.

In the Panama Conference of Pan-American States, which was held in September-December, 1939 need for unity in the American hemisphere was emphasised and Neutrality Zones (extending to 300 to 1000 miles in the sea) were set up. In 1940, the Pan American Conference at Havana definite shape was given to the principle of regional collective security and the states were obliged to take common action to meet a common threat. When Japan attacked the Pearl Harbour the Latin American countries demonstrated their solidarity with USA and declared war against Japan. After the Rio De Janeiro Conference the Latin American states decided to sever diplomatic relations with the Axis powers. During the war these American Republics gave to the USA highly important and useful war materials and temporary naval and air bases.

On June 26, 1945 all these states became the Charter members of the United Nations.

America and the Far East

The basic principle of US policy in the Far East was to prevent the emergence of a great power in East Asia, which could threaten American interests. That is why America followed a policy of open-door in China. She had also opened up Japan to foreign commerce.

During the war Japan became more aggressive towards China and took possession of Germany's leased territory of Kiaochow and presented 21 demands to the Chinese government. But the United States was in no position to hamper the Japanese programmes, because she was engaged in great struggle.

When the war came to an end, USA realized that the increasing power of Japan was becoming a menace to her interests in the Pacific. Therefore, President Wilson made an attempt to restrain Japan at the 1919 Peace Conference. With utmost reluctance USA acquiesced in the transfer of Germany's economic rights in Shantung to Japan. The relations between USA and Japan were further embittered by the serious naval rivalry between the two. The Washington Conference put a check to the naval race and constituted a great victory for American diplomacy. During 1920s relations between Japan and USA on the whole remained friendly.

However, when in September 1931, Japan attacked Manchuria US Government sought a peaceful solution of the issue. Japan was reminded of her obligations under previous treaties and when these warnings fell on deaf ears in Tokyo, USA announced the policy of non- recognition of territorial changes brought out by force. Japan unmindful of these warnings continued to penetrate deeper into China. In July, 1937 an undeclared war started between China and Japan. In August, 1937 US offered its good offices to settle the controversy peacefully but Japan did not show any interest in an amicable settlement. During the next few years the US Administration remained a silent spectator of Japanese conquests.

This attitude of non-intervention on the part of the US Government encouraged Japan to occupy Hainan and Sprately Island. In 1940, however, USA resorted to successive economic measures against the aggressive policy of Japan. In 1940 Roosevelt placed an embargo on the export of scrap steel and iron to Japan.

While the US government took a number of economic steps to restrain Japan from further aggression, it also tried to resolve the dispute through diplomatic negotiations. But in the year 1940 Japanese alliance with the Axis powers and the occupation of Southern Indo-China in the summer of 1941 ultimately led to the severance of trade by the United States. The futile negotiations over the Chinese question led to the Japanese attack on Pearl Harbour in December, 1941. Thus America had to take up arms against Japan.

From the above discussion it is clear that America did not follow the policy of *'isolationism'* during the two world wars. She did take active part in the various international matters.

It is clear that the American Foreign policy during the inter-war period was not one of isolation, because she took active part in various activities of the League as well as played leading role with regard to disarmament, reparations, collective security etc. It would also not be wise to designate this policy as *'policy of internationalism'* because USA avoided unnecessary entanglements in Europe. She no doubt took interest in Far East and Latin America, but this was necessitated and guided mainly by national considerations. In short, the American foreign policy between the inter-war years alternated between isolationism and internationalism.

39

Problem of Reparation and Economic Crisis

> "The Allied and Associated Powers affirm and Germany accepts the responsibility of Germany and her allies for causing all the loss and damage to which the Allied and Associated Governments and their nationals have been subjected as a consequence of the war imposed upon them by the aggression of Germany and her allies."
>
> **—Treaty of Versailles, Article 231**

Introduction

The practice of demanding reparation from the defeated powers for the losses involved during the war has been vogue for a long time. Such reparations were demanded after the Napoleonic war the Franco-Russian war and the Russo-Japanese war. The term 'reparations' connoted "compensation either in money or in materials, commodities, capital equipment, merchant vessels, and the like, payable by a defeated nation as war indemnity for direct damages and for loss from war expenditures, occupation costs, etc. " sustained as a result of aggression by the defeated nation." (Webster) After the First World War also the victorious powers demanded indemnities from Germany and her allies. As it was not possible to determine the actual damage done by Germany and her capacity to pay, the amount of Reparation was not fixed by the Treaty of Versailles. E.H. Carr has observed in this connection that "the important difference between the Versailles Treaty and previous peace treaties providing for a payment to be made to the victors by the defeated power was that, on this occasion, no sum was fixed by the treaty.

It has been a common practice to demand indemnity from the defeated powers for the losses involved during the war. The Treaty of Versailles demanded reparations from Germany on the basis of the 'guilt-clause'. Although Germany was held responsible for causing all the loss and damage to the Allied and Associated Governments, under the impact of Wilson's declaration the Allies agreed to realise reparation only for the loss of the civilian and government property. They agreed to waive the demand for the total cost of war. Thus Germany was to pay reparation for (a) the loss of civilian property; (b) destruction of the merchant-men; (c) pension to the retired officials of the Allies. However, an exception was made in case of Belgium, who was required to pay all the costs of the war.

Reparation Commission

Although the item under which reparation was to be realised from Germany were decided, the total amount could not be determined in 1919. The job of drawing up a bill and a schedule of total reparation was entrusted to a Reparation Commission which consisted of two members each from U.S.A., England, France and Italy and one ordinary member each from Belgium, Japan and Yugoslavia. However, pending the Commission's report Germany was required to pay to the Allied Powers a sum of one million pounds. The Commission was expected to make its report by 31st May, 1921.

Spa Conference

Before the Reparation Commission could submit its report, the Allies met at Spa, a place in Germany, in July, 1920 for the distribution of the realised amount of reparation among themselves as per Article 237 of the Treaty of Versailles. As per an agreement reached on July 16, 1920 the powers agreed to distribute the receipts in the following ratio. France 52%, British Empire 22%, Italy 10%, Japan 75%, Belgium 8%, Greece, Rumania, The Serb-Croat-Slovene-State and other powers 6.5%, Portugal 0.75%.

At the Spa Conference Germany was also invited to decide a lump sum for the settlement of Germany's reparation payment. At the Conference for the first time the German Chancellor and Minister for Foreign Affairs met the leading Allied ministers round a table on terms of equality. As there was wide divergence between the views of German Government and the Allies about lump sum, no agreement could be reached at. In March, 1921, on the plea of Germany's failure to complete the preliminary reparation payment, the Allied troops occupied the three towns of Susseldorf, Duisberg and Ruhrort on the East of Rhine.

The London Schedule

The Reparation Commission submitted its report in April, 1921 and fixed Germany's total liability at £660 millions plus interest. On this basis the Allied Supreme Council at London issued a schedule of payments. The German reparation payment were divided into three classes 'A', 'B' and 'C', The 'C' class bonds accounting for £4,000,000,000, which constituted approximately two-thirds of payments, were to be held by the Reparation Commission until such time as Germany's capacity to pay was established. For the rest of the amount Germany was to pay £100,000,000 annually plus 25% of the value of her exports. The Schedule was communicated to the German government with an ultimatum that failure to accept it by May 12 would be followed by the Allied occupation of the Ruhr. Germany conveyed acceptance of the Schedule on May 11, 1921 and the first instalment of £50 million was paid on August 31, 1921.

In the meanwhile, Germany was in the throes of financial collapse. The war ravages, the loss of assets and drawing of wealth owing to payment of debts and the flight of capital due to the uncertainty in Germany resulted in the fall of Mark's value. Thus Germany's capacity to pay the reparation charges, even if she had the will to do so, was completely exhausted. The German government therefore, asked for a moratorium for three years, as she was unable to pay according to the London Schedule. While Lloyd George of England was willing to concede the request, Poincare of France refused to grant the concessions and allow Germany to evade payment as France had already spent a huge amount on pensions and economic reconstruction schemes in anticipation of the reparation.

The Ruhr Occupation

The French politicians were obsessed with the idea of 'French Security' and wanted to gain a productive guarantee. When the German deliveries of timber fell short of an agreed schedule, French insisted on the Reparation Commission to declare it a 'voluntary default' on the part of Germany. On December 26, 1922, in spite of the British protests, the Reparation Commission declared Germany in voluntary default. As per terms of the Treaty of Versailles the Allied power had the right to take any step in case of voluntary default. Thus a way was paved for France to fulfill her long cherished desire.

On January 11, 1923 the French, Italian and Belgium troops occupied Ruhr and an International Commission was set up to carry on the administration.

The occupation of Ruhr proved to be a blunder for France and disaster for Germany. It was a blunder for France because she not only lost one of her important allies—Britain, but also created a lasting bitterness in the minds of the German people towards France. It was disastrous for Germany because her economy was bound to collapse when her most important industrial areas passed under foreign occupation.

Germany started a passive resistance movement in Ruhr. All reparation payments in the form of coal and iron were stopped. The mines reduced their production of coal. The people withheld payment of taxes and refused to take orders from the foreigners. Nearly all communication services including telegraph, telephone and railway came to a standstill. The French attempt to work the mines and factories themselves proved a failure. In short the occupation of Ruhr proved to be a costly proposition for France. Therefore, when the German government withdrew its resistance in 1923, the French heaved a sigh of relief.

Dawes Plan

In view of the loss of industries, the currency crisis, internal movement in Rhineland and the fall of Cuno government in Germany, the passive resistance movement was called off Germany in September, 1923. The new Chancellor of Germany, Stresemann once again adopted the policy of fulfilment and sought foreign help for the recovery of Germany. Powers like USA, Britain, Belgium, Italy and France came forward to rescue Germany from economic ruin. The Reparation Commission appointed a Committee of experts, consisting of the representatives of above countries, under the Chairmanship of USA's representative General, Charles G. Dawes. This Committee is popularly known as Dawes Committee. The Committee was expected to propose methods of balancing the German budget and to settle her currency crisis.

The Committee met in Paris from January 14 to April 9, 1924 and submitted the following recommendations. (1) The introduction of a new currency, the Reichsmark at the old parity. The control of this new currency was handed over to a Central Bank of Issue called the Reichsbank. A board of seven German and seven foreigners was formed to supervise the Reichsbank, which controlled the issue of paper money and acted as a depository for reparation payments. (2) Germany's currency being stabilized, she was expected to pay fifty million pounds for the first five years. This amount was to be later raised to a maximum of £ 125 million, depending on the index of her prosperity. (3) The reparations were to be paid from railway bonds, transport taxes, industrial debentures and proceeds of revenues of alcohol, tobacco, beer and sugar. (4) Appointment of Foreign Agent-General for reparation payments as well as the foreign commission to execute the plan. (5) To check collapse of exchange due to transfer difficulties the payments were to be made in German currency and the operations of transfer were to rest with the creditors. (6) Evacuation of the Ruhr in order to restore Germany's economic sovereignty and to permit the new plan to operate without delay. (7) A loan of £ 40,000,000 was to be given to Germany by the creditor nations to enable her to stabilise her currency and to pay her first instalment.

The recommendations of the Dawes Committee were discussed at a Conference held in London on July 16, 1924. At the Conference Britain and America tried to persuade France to accept the recommendations. It was also decided by the Conference that hence-forth Germany could not be declared in default without the unanimous decision of the Reparation Commission.

The Dawes Plan was probably the first attempt to solve the reparation problem purely on economic basis. The Plan provided a breathing spell to Germany by fixing the amounts of annual instalments and by arranging foreign loans for her. It resulted in general economic recovery of Germany and both England and America henceforth began to invest their capital in Central Europe. The Allies were also assured of reparations. The Plan also went a long way in removing tension that had existed in Europe since the signing of the Peace Treaties. It thus paved the way for 'Locarno Spirit' which created in future an atmosphere of peace and security.

In spite of these merits, the Dawes Plan suffered from serious draw-backs. Although the Plan provided for annual payment of reparations by Germany, it failed to specify the time limit, and was silent about the total amount to be paid by Germany. This implied that the sum fixed by the Reparation Commission in 1921 was still in force. This provision of payment of huge amounts for an indefinite period crushed the German incentive to accumulate savings and improve her financial well-being because she felt that all her savings would merely enrich the foreigners. During the period from 1924 to 1929. Germany was able to pay the reparations smoothly not because she had developed the capacity or will to pay, but because she was able to secure huge loans from foreign countries, specially USA In fact during this period Germany borrowed more from foreign countries than what she paid in reparations. Thus the prosperity of Germany during these years was a borrowed one.

The Young Plan

As the Dawes Plan had improved the foreign relations of Germany and created an atmosphere of cordiality, Germany was keen to further improve the reparation problem and the settlement of the Rhineland problem. Moreover, she was keen to gain control over finances which under the Dawes Plan suffered from many restrictions. Circumstances from all sides favoured this attitude of Germany. While US capital in Germany roused her interest, France wanted a permanent settlement of her accounts with Germany so that she may be able to fulfil her obligations to USA. Britain was also keen to have a final and permanent solution of the problem.

Consequently the representatives of the concerned powers met at Geneva and decided to call a Committee of experts to suggest a final settlement of the reparation problem. The Committee came to be known as 'Young Committee', after the name of its President Owen D. Young of USA. The Committee, held its first meeting at Paris on February 11, 1929 and continued to work till June 7, 1929 when it finally submitted its Plan.

(1) The Plan considerably reduced the amount of German debt and laid down that she would pay thirty seven annual instalments of £ 100,000,000. Besides, she was also required to pay small war debt of the Allies to the Americans, in twenty-two annual instalments. (2) The Reparation Commission along with the other controls established by the Dawes Plan were abolished. (3) The Young Plan imposed the responsibility of transfers on Germany, instead of creditor countries, as envisaged under the Dawes Plan. (4) The realisation and distribution of the amount of reparation was to be arranged through an international bank. The International Bank was to be administered by a Board composed of the representatives of Germany and the creditor powers. (5) To save German currency against possible landslide and dislocation, provision was made for

postponement of a part or whole of the rest of the annual payments for a period of two years. (6) Allies were directed to evacuate the Rhineland by June 30, 1930.

The Young Plan was placed before the Hague Conference consisting of the representatives of France, Italy, Japan, Great Britain and Germany, and was accepted by it on January 20, 1930. The Hague Conference also settled the question regarding payment of non-German reparations. Agreements were concluded with Austria, Hungary and Bulgaria. While Austria was completely exempted from reparation payments, Hungarian reparation payments were to be utilised for the relief of Hungarian occupants till 1943. Bulgaria was, however, to continue the payment of reparation.

The Young Plan had certain merits. It not only reduced but also fixed the German debts. The establishment of the Bank of International Settlement and the progressive scale of annuities reduced the problem of payment and disbursement. It reduced the uncertainty for both the debtor and the creditors. The Young Plan also separated the question of reparations from political and diplomatic questions.

Impact of Depression and Hoover Moratorium

The Young Plan was put into operation in May, 1930. But at the same time the world was engulfed with a terrible economic depression, which not only stood in the way of Germany securing further foreign loans but also stood in the way of balancing her budget. The foreign investors began to withdraw their capital and deposits from Germany. As a result the economic structure of Germany practically collapsed and it was not possible for her to pay reparations. The problem of unemployment further made the situation explosive. Under the circumstances, President Hindenburg of Germany appealed to President Hoover of USA for moratorium. President Hoover asked all states to suspend their mutual payments of reparation for one year from July, 1931. Germany was however, asked not to utilise the money released from reparation payment for military purposes. The unpostponable annuities were to be paid by Germany to the Bank of International Settlement which was to buy German railway bonds and to have the railway turn the money over to the Government so that the latter may use the money for economic purposes.

End of Reparation

In spite of one year's moratorium Germany's economic conditions did not improve. In 1932, the Bank of International Settlement declared that it would be impossible for Germany to pay her reparations. Consequently the representatives of Britain, France, Belgium, Italy, Japan and Germany met at Lausanne on June 1932. In view of Germany's economic debacle and worldwide economic crisis, they offered to reduce the remaining German liability to an almost invisible figure and also to cancel their war debts to each other provided the USA agreed to a cancellation of all debts owned to her. Germany was given the option to make a total payment of £ 150,000,000 in the form of five per cent redeemable bonds.

It may be noted that it was not a gesture of philanthropy towards Germany on the part of these countries. It was a desperate attempt on the part of these countries to save their own countries from economical ruin. As USA refused to cancel the war debts, the decisions of Lausanne Conference were automatically nullified. As Germany was neither in a position nor willing to pay anything, the reparation payments automatically came to an end. The debtors of America on similar grounds also refused to make full payments to USA. However, all of them, with the exception of Finland which kept on paying instalments in full, agreed to make token payments. Subsequently even these token payments were also stopped.

The chapter of reparation was finally closed with the rise of Hitler in Germany in 1933. He officially repudiated the reparation pledges. In the words of E.H. Carr. "The year 1932 saw the last act in that confused drama of reparation and inter-Allied debts which had tormented the world for more than ten years. The Lausanne Conference burried them both in the same unhonoured grave."

40

World Depression (1929)

When President Hoover was ushered in March 1929, the future appeared bright for a prosperous America. The triumphs of a business civilization were thought to be secure. Throughout his campaign the Republican candidate had reiterated his confident prediction that by continuing to follow the policies of the previous eight years, the United States should be able to abolish poverty.

He was prepared to summon Congress into special session to meet the imperative demand of the farmers for some form of agricultural relief and to reconsider tariff policy. Hoover proposed to help the farmer through a program whereby the government would hold surplus crops off the market and thus stabilize prices. The one serious defect in the functioning of the industrial system would be eliminated, and the nation would enjoy an even better-balanced economy.

Hoover declared, "By adherence to the principles of decentralised self-government, and freedom to the individual, our American experiment in human welfare has yielded a degree of well-being unparalleled in all the world."

It was just half a year after the inauguration of the new President, however, that the sudden crash of the New York stock market in the fall of 1929 heralded an economic collapse more widespread, more prolonged, more devastating in its nationwide consequences, than anything the country had ever experienced. Business and industry were prostrated, trade and commerce almost completely dried up, agriculture was laid waste. Millions of men and women were thrown out of work. As unemployment mounted steadily in the ensuing years, the long dreary lines of people waiting sullenly at food stations and soup kitchens became a tragic commentary on the hopeful promise of poverty abolished. The bands of frustrated men and boys eking out inexistence in the tumble-down, tin-roofed shacks of tramp jungles, ironically known as Hoovervilles, were doleful evidence of the future Hoover's economic policy.

Causes of the Depression

There were few economists who foresaw or even dimly realised at the beginning of the Hoover administration that the country was headed for hard times. The experts generally agreed with the President that the economy was on a more stable basis than ever before and that there was no longer need to fear the recurrent cycles of depression which had heretofore characterized the nation's history. The report of the President's Commission on Recent Economic changes emphasized in 1929 the new "dynamic equilibrium" in the country's industrial structure, happily stating that "our situation is fortunate, our momentum remarkable." But with the advantage of hindsight, those widening cracks in the economic structure that made for collapse are readily apprarent. There will never be full agreement in evaluating the causes of the depression, but certain of them have become very clear.

The gradual decline of agriculture is a case in point. As the foreign market for staple crops contracted with increased production of wheat and cotton in other lands, and domestic consumption was restricted by changing dietary habits and new clothing styles, the agricultural surpluses forced prices downward. The farmer was again experiencing the troubles of the 1890s, caught in the old squeeze of having to sell his products in an open market while he bought his machinery, tools, and equipment in a protected market. This meant reduced buying power for a large segment of the population whose purchases of manufactured products were essential for full industrial production.

The existence of certain "sick industries" within the framework of otherwise general business prosperity was also a dangerous factor. Coal mining was in the doldrums throughout the greater part of the 1920s; the immensely important construction industry began gradually to decline in the mid-1920s, and the textile trades were never able to keep pace with the advances made on other sectors of the industrial front. In another sphere of economic activity, foreign trade was buoyed up very precariously by loans and credits, often advanced on a very insecure basis, which alone enabled European importers to obtain the exchange to pay for their purchases of American goods.

A more general and more important consideration was the fact, realized in later years as it was not realized in the 1920s, that the unequal distribution of the national income severely restricted the over-all purchasing power of the nation in terms of the continued growth of productive capacity. Too much money was being diverted into corporate investment or savings, too little going into the hands of consumers. This meant that excess funds were being used not only for enlarging the industrial plant beyond effective needs, but for unrestrained speculation in the security markets, while the public lacked the resources to buy, at prevailing prices, the expanded output of factor and mill. Purchasing power, it is true, was increasing. A growing volume of consumer goods was being absorbed, but not at the rate necessary to assure a balanced economy.

Innumerable statistics might be cited to illustrate this unequal distribution of income. One or two comparisons may suffice. While corporate dividends had increased, between 1923 and 1929, by 65 percent, the real income of workers had gone up by only 11 per cent. At the close of the decade, 36,000 families in the upper income brackets received a share of the national income approximately that of 11,000,000 in the lowest group. Over half of those in the latter category had earnings of less than $1,000 a year. Entirely apart from the effect upon individual families of such relative poverty, industry needed their purchases to maintain full production and a high rate of employment.

Once the influence of such adverse factors began to make itself felt, a chain reaction was set off in bringing industrial advance to a halt. As the demands for goods slackened, manufacturers necessarily cut production schedules. This meant the progressive lay-off of workers, and a still further decline in consumer income. Industry was then forced to curtail operations even more substantially; additional workers were dismissed and wages severely cut. The cumulative effects of such general economic dislocation steadily intensified the depression. And at that time there were no wage laws to provide a floor under the workers' earnings, no unemployment insurance to help sustain the purchasing power of the jobless.

The real significance of the warning implicit in the break in the stock market was not at first understood. The illusion of prosperity had too strong a hold upon the imagination—the imagination of economists as well as of poliltical leaders and the general public - for the dangers in the situation to be properly appreciated. Not until nationwide wage cuts, the rising tide of unemployment, and the lengthening bread lines starkly revealed that something much more fundamental was wrong with the country than an overinflated security market did the American people fully realize what had happened.

The Stock Market Crash

The sudden and spectacular collapse in security prices nevertheless shook the entire country. Speculation had become the order of the day as the paper value of common stocks spirated upward. Prices were already high in 1927, but in the next two years General Electric rose from 128 to 396, American Telephone and Telegraph from 179 to 335, Montgomery Ward from 132 to 466, and Raadio from 94 to 505. Bank presidents and college professors, midwestern dirt farmers and urban factory workers, clerks, stenographers and office boys appeared to be following the tip to invest in common stocks that John J Raskob, vice-president of General Motors and Al Smith's campaign manager, had graciously given the public in an inviting article in the *Ladies' Home Journal* entitled "Everybody Ought to be Rich". There seemed to be no limit to the speculative frenzy in1929 and every hint of caution was brushed aside in those feverish, hectic days of the great bull market.

A few premonitory qualms cast their shadow in September; then came "Black Thursday" - the twenty-fourth of October. A tremendous wave of liquidation inexplicably hit the stock market on that particular day, and within a few hours the precipitate downward plunge of stocks swept away hundreds of millions of dollors in paper profits. Complete collapse was narrowly averted by the hurried organisation of a banking pool, but five days later the market crashed again. Selling orders swamped the brokers, the tickers could not keep pace with market transactions, and over 16,000,000 shares changed hands amid the widest confusion the stock exchange had ever known. The liquidation was not even then halted. It continued spasmodiclly until November 13. By that date the recorded loss in stock values was over $30,000,000,000 with the average price of leading securities more than halved.

Solemn statements from every possible quarter sought to reassure a nervous public that panic on Wall Street was not a matter of fundamental concern. President Hoover summoned a meeting of business employers to win their promise that there would be no wage cuts or dismissal of employees, and upon its conclusion stated his firm conviction that this move had re-established public confidence. In comparable reassuring statements the Secretary of the Treasury forecast a complete revival of business activity in the spring, and the Secretary of Commerce said that there was nothing in the situation to be disturbed about. Again and again public officials declared, in a phrase which would haunt men's minds for a decade, that "conditions are fundamentally sound."

The promised recovery failed to materialize; economic conditions grew steadily worse. There could be no blinking the harsh fact that prosperity was not just around the corner and that the country faced a dire domestic crisis. In every previous period of depression the forces making for recovery had in time automatically asserted themselves. It had not proved necessary for government to intervene in helping to restore economic stability. But the situation that developed in the early 1930s gave little hope for such natural readjustments. There was forced upon a reluctant administration the unhappy realization that the powers of government had somehow to be invoked to try to stem the tide of economic disaster. Confident reliance upon a laissez faire philosophy and the spirit of rugged individualism was no longer possible when forces seemingly beyond men's control threatened the paralysis of business, trade, and agriculture, and unemployment figures were rising upward as rapidly as prices, production, and wages were plunging downward.

President Hoover recognized and accepted the new responsibility of government under these circumstances. The policy of drift that had appeared for a time to mark his attitude was abondoned, once it was clearly seen that nationwide depression rather than a stock market panic confronted the country. A series of measures carefully designed to restore economic stability were gradually adopted. In so doing Hoover broke with all past precedent and pioneered in entirely unknown areas of governmental activity. By acknowledging that under existing circumstances the reserve powers of the federal government had to be used for the protection of its citizens, this conservative Republican president in many respects laid the basis for the New Deal.

Nevertheless, the steps that Hoover took did not adequately meet the national emergency. In the phrase used on the occasion of later war crises, they were "too little and too late". The backward pull of nineteenth century economic and political concepts, at least partly blinding the President to the realities of the changed society of the twentieth century, prevented him from implementing his policies with sufficient vigor or on an adequately broad front. Hoover continued to think almost exclusively in terms of assistance for business, largely ignoring the need for direct aid to distressed farmers, impoverished workers, and the army of unemployed.

41

Economic and Political Reactions to the World Economic Crisis of the 1930s

In this article economic and political responses to the Depression in Germany, Austria, Belgium, the Netherlands, France, and Britain are analyzed. Each country applied a specific mixture of deflationary policies coupled with important restrictions, subventions and—later on—some active employment measures. At best these measures contributed to the recovery of the economy when it was already on its way back. Like the measures of economic crisis, electoral volatility, and government stability, economic policy did not introduce sufficient variation between the six countries to "account for" the collapse or survival of the polity under the impact of the Depression. The political, economic, and social cleavageas separating major actors such as labor, business, agriculture, and the state from each other and the strategies pursued in forging a compromise along different class lines are of particular importance here.

The world economic crisis of the 1930s and the political repercussions it led to, bringing about the collapse of the majority of European democracies in the interwar period, have been among the most underresearched areas in political science, at least in terms of cross-national analysis.

Economic policies had little direct effect on the survivability of democratic political systems in the 1930s. Neither the economic crisis alone nor the economic measures taken suffice to explain the different political outcomes, in particular the victory of national socialism in Germany and Austria as opposed to the maintenance of liberal democracies in Britain, France, Holland, and Belgium. Clues must rather be sought in the processes of national consensus formation that made political and economic elites join forces rather than combat each other or unite in fighting against other political elites still adhering to the rules of a democratic polity. In Germany and Austria, but not in Belgium, the rapidity of economic decline contributed to further elite polarization, providing the final element in the collapse of the political system.

Germany experienced the greatest economic downturn, but also the fastest economic recovery, albeit then under a totalitarian regime. France was affected only later and more gradually, but never fully recovered from the economic crisis, thus considerably undermining the position of the Third Republic in international relations since 1930s. The highest rate of unemployment occurred in the Netherlands in1936 three or four years later than in most of the other countries, leaving room for political manoeuvring that was effectively used by the prosystem parties. On some economic indicators e.g., industrial production, Austria exhibited patterns like those in Germany, although with lower amplitudes. Races of negative economic change are also remarkably strong in Belgium, in particular with respect to unemployment, industrial production, and money wages in industry.

In terms of electoral volatility all six polities experienced a marked increase in those elections held near the trough of the economy. However, only in Germany did a vast polarization to the political extremes occur, whereas in Britain in 1935 the Labour party quickly recovered from its crushing defeat after the national government was confirmed in the October 1931 general elections. In absolute terms, the effects of volatility were even greater in Britain than in Germany, but with the electorate concentrated in the political center, not at the extremes. Though a highly effective force in bringing about the collapse of the democratic polity in Weimar Germany, electoral polarization was not the decisive factor. Thus, neither with respect to the economy nor with respect to electoral volatility nor in terms of government instability (which was high in all countries with the exception of Britain and the Netherlands) could any necessary and unavoidable link be established between the worsening of the economy and the collapse of the polity. After all, the Nazi vote went down by 4.2 per cent in the November 1932 elections and economic indicators were pointing upward again. Thus, there was no"necessity" to bring the Nazis to power.

It is in the political realm, in the processes of national political consenses formation, that we expect major differences to emerge that will broaden our understanding of how democracies survived the economic and political challenges of the Depression or failed to do so.

The economic crisis of the 1930s led to increased volatility in all six countries. Electoral polarization, however, operationally defined as more than 20 per cent of the votes given to a single anti-system party, took place only in Germany. In September 1930, the National Socialists (NSDAP) received 18.5 per cent of the seats in the Reichstag; in July 1932, 37.8 per cent. In Austria, where the last national election was held in 1930, this electoral polarization can be observed at the provincial and municipal level. In 1932 the National socialists received 20.6 per cent of the votes cast in Salzburg and 17.4 per cent in Vienna. Electoral polarization in turn contributed to elite polarization in those two countries. Elite polarization is defined as active or verbal support for an unloyal, anti-democratic opposition by leading politicians (including leaders of major interest groups). The dashed lines in Fig. 1 indicate that of the six countries, only Germany and Austria experienced those developments, whearas the solid lines indicate that all respective countries were (positively or negatively) affected by the same processes. The economic crisis increased electoral volatility in all six countries, but led to electoral polarization and elite polarization only in Germany and Austria. Both countries failed to form a democratic national political consensus and, as a consequence, experienced a collapse of their democracies.

Two features of this model deserve special emphasis. First, elite polarization is a necessary condition for the collapse of the polity. There is no direct link from either economic crisis or electoral volatility to the ultimate dependent variable. Both economic crisis and electoral volatility may be sufficient conditions for elite polarization but they do not necessarily bring about electoral polarization and elite polarization, as the four democratic cases in our sample indicate. Second, economic responses to the Depression by democratic governments are of little discriminating value and therefore are omitted from figure. The economic responses, in particular the total failure of deflationary policies in Germany, had something to do with the collapse of the democratic polity. Yet, similar policies were pursued in other countries which, nonetheless, survived the challenge to democracy. Since the *explanandum* consists of a dichotomous rather than a metric variable, one might have thught of setting up two models, one for the polities persisting and one for those collapsing. In Figure these various theoretical links (implicitly) have been considered in one model.

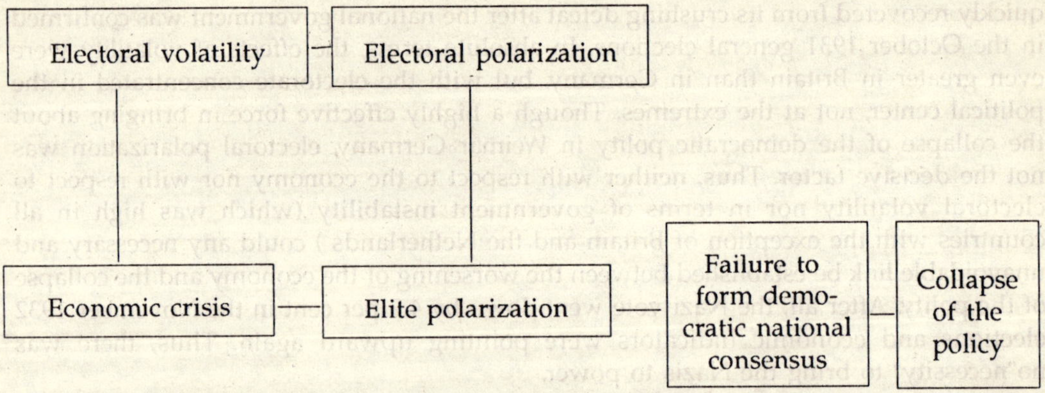

By and large, the German cabinets under Bruning, Papen, and Schieicher reacted to the Depression within the framework of traditional economic policy. Despite a certain moderation after April 1931, monetary policy was tight and interest rates remained relatively high, especially if compared to the United Kingdom. In terms of currency policy, Germany—unlike Britain or the Scandinavian countries—did not opt for depreciation when confronted with the international credit and currency crisis of the summer of 1931. According to the agreement of the Hague (January 1930), changes in the German bank law had to be approved by the Bank for International settlements in Basel. More important, most of the German political and financial leaders feared the risk of another hyperinflation once the gold standard had been abandoned.

In spite of considerabale continuity in terms of monetary and currency policies, there were important policy changes in the governments' responses to the crisis. A *first phase,* that began under Reichs-Chancellor Bruning (March 1930- May 1932), was dominated by rigorous deflationary policies. Existing taxes were increased and new direct and indirect taxes introduced. Public investment was greatly reduced.

In the second half of 1931 the cabinet approved minor public works programmes, which were largely financed out of the existing budget. When unemployment had reached the figure of 6 million, or more than 30 per cent of the workforce, in the first half of 1932, the government decided on an employment programmes (May 1932) of 135 million reichsmark. Yet, before this modest employment programmes could be implemented, President Hindenburg withdrew his backing from the Reichs-Chancellor. Since his cabinet did not enjoy the support of a solid parliamentary majority, Bruning had to resign in May 1932.

The *second phase* of economic policy, albeit very short- lived, began under Bruning's successor, Franz von Papen, and his "Cabinet of barons" who, even more than Bruning, lacked parliamentary support.

Kurt von Schleicher with his government of eight weeks put more emphasis on direct employment measures. He continued the employment programmes initiated under Bruning and Papen and turned to measures stimulating the economy as directly as possible. The compulsory wage reductions imposed by the Papen cabinet in September 1932 were repealed. Nevertheless, Schleicher failed to consolidate his position. Like Bruning and Papen before him, he lost President Hindenburg's confidence and—after political intrigues once again involving Papen—was replaced by Hitler. The Nazi Government, in a *third phase,* could draw on the recovery schemes developed since 1931. Hitler vigorously enforced existing plans.

In many respects, Austria's economy faced the most serious structural problems among the six countries concerned. The collapse of the Austro-Hungarian dual monarchy in 1918-19 had left the country with an extremely unbalanced national economy which, according to numerous contemporary observers, was unable to survive on its own. The first spectacular sign of the Depression in Austria was the crisis of the Creditanstalt, the largest Austrian bank, whose balance for 1930 showed a deficit of about 140 million shillings. In 1931 it turned out that the real deficit was more than one billion shillings. Given the bank's international importance and its very close ties to Austria's industry, the government had to grant it a credit Austria's industry, the government had to grant it a credit of 500 million shillings, i.e. nearly one-fifth of central government's total 1931 budget. The shrinking of economic activity and the dramatic rise in unemployment put additional pressure on the budget and the government policy (e.g. high interest rates), (2) maintenance of the gold standard, (3) protectionism, and (4) agricultural subsidies.

In its attempt to balance the budget, the government cut its expenditures by about one-fifth in the fiscal year of 1932. Until 1938, central government's expenditure remained significantly below its 1930 level. Wages and salaries in the public services were reduced substantially in 1931 and 1932. Public investment was cut down by 95 per cent.

Due to the weak liquidity of the government and the permanent withdrawal of loans and hard currency from the country, no active employment policies could be pursued. Even the modest Lausanne loan of 1932 brought no positive stimulus to the economy.

The absence of any improvement of the economy exacerbated the latent civil-war mentality and convinced Chancellor Dollfus, the leader of the Fatherland front and former minister of agriculture in the Ender and Buresch cabinets, as well as many other political leaders in Austria that the country's economic problems could be overcome only by authoritarian government.

France

France was affected by the Depression, but not before the spring of 1931. The late timing of the slump was mainly due to the undervaluation of the franc, the comparatively low integration of the French economy into the world economy, and the country's extreme protectionism. The overall effects of the Depression in France were not as harsh as in Germany, Austria, Belgium, or the Netherlands. This particularly true with regard to the level of unemployment. The rate of unemployment in the mining, construction, and industrial sectors rose from 1.0 per cent in 1929 to 15.4 per cent in 1932.

There were three different phases of French economic policy during the Depression. The *first phase,* lasting until June 1936, was dominated by deflationary policies. The center-left coalition governments which were in office until February 1934, as well as the subsequent center-right coalitions, concentrated their efforts on balancing the budget and defending the gold parity of the franc. Both the budgetary balance and the franc had come under pressure. A large balance of payments deficit built up, aggravated by capital shortness in the wake of financial straits in Austria and Germany and the flight of (French) capital from the country. Like the other gold bloc countries (the Netherlands, Belgium, Luxemburg, Switzerland, Italy, and Poland). France had a choice only between further deflationary policies and devaluation, the latter a barely acceptable alternative. Under Doumergue's ministry (February to September 1934) government salaries and pensions were cut and the number of civil servants reduced. Another set of deflationary measures, comprising cuts in public expenditure by 10 per cent as well as the reduction of rents and prices for gas, coal, and electricity, was introduced by the Laval government

(July to October 1935). Compared to Germany or Austria, the cuts in central government expenditure were fairly moderate. Between 1932 and 1934 central government expenditure was reduced by 9.1 per cent.•Nevertheless, the "governments arising out of the February 1934 change of majority completely failed in their efforts to restore the political and economic situation." Not only was there another rise in the level of unemployment, but the major goal of the government, a marked reduction of the price level, was not met, since costs for transport and raw materials remained virtually constant. In reaction to the currency changes caused by the devaluation of sterling (1931) and the dollar (1933), the government imposed tariffs and import restrictions on agricultural products and manufactured goods.

As the economic situation deteriorated and in response to the unsuccessful coup d'etat of the fascist *Ligues* in February 1934, the leftist political forces emerged as the winner of the election of 1936. The left majority in Parliament enabled the *Front Populaire* to initiate a *second phase* of economic policy. The far reaching measures of the Popular Front were fueled by the underconsumption theory. The leaders of the left believed that "the capitalists" squezzing of the surplus prevented workers from having enough money to buy the output.

In September 1936 the franc was devalued by about 35 per cent. However, the beneficial effects of the devaluation of 1936 as well as of the 1937 and 1938 depreciations were soon eroded by the internal rise in prices. "just as the increase in wages had been neutralized in the summer of 1936". The increase of industrial production in 1937 was followed by another setback in 1938. Capital continued to disappear the country. The deficit in the balance of payments increased from about 10 francs between 1935 and 1937. Facing the failure of his economic policy and widespread labor unrest, Prime Minister Blum resigned in June 1937.

France was caught by policy discontinuities and bad timing. It experienced increasing unemployment and declining production when Germany and Britain had already made it past the trough. Moreover, the low level of production pesisted for four or five years, weakening the French economy to such an extent that the change to active employment policies and mass demand under the Popular Front government took place under highly unfavourable economic and political circumstances. The partial repeal of many of those measures under Daladier between 1938 and 1940 is evidence of this.

Belgium

In the *first phase* of Belgian economic policy, which lasted until early 1935, government policy was dominated by the belief that sustained growth could be achieved only through market processes. State intervention was considered an impediment to recovery. The Catholic-Liberal cabinets in office largely constrained their activities to (1) maintain a stable currency by adhering to the gold standard, (2) balance the budget, and (3) impose import duties. As in France and the Netherlands, government officials believed they had no other choice but to compensate for the competitive disadvantages resulting from an overvalued currency by pursuing deflationary policies (reduction of interest rates and cuts in wages, prices, old-age pensions, and public expenditure). However, the government's economic policy was by no means consistent during this period.

In March 1935 after the low point of the Depression had been overcome, a more active *second phase* of government policy commenced with the new coalition government under Van Zeeland that brought the Social Democrats back to power. Shortly before Van Zeeland took office, the Belgian franc had been taken off the gold standard and devalued by 28 per cent against sterling.

In Belgium, "government policy [of cutting expenditure until 1934-35] was positively detrimental".

The Netherlands

In spite of increasing external and internal pressure, the Dutch government refused to depreciate the guilder until September 1936. The resulting competitive disadvantage of the Dutch economy against those currencies that had been devalued earlier was to be compensated by a comparatively rigorous deflationary policy, the "policy of adaptation." The level of domestic prices was reduced "by lowering costs such as wages, interest rates, rents, leases, expenditure of the social services and taxation. Yet, given the logic of deflationary measures, these efforts failed. Thus, drastic cuts in the salaries of public employees as well as reductions in government expenditures for social services, education, and defense became necessary between 1930 and 1936. Central government expenditures were cut by 6.1 per cent in the fiscal year of 1934 and did not recover to their 1933 level until 1938.

Although the Netherlands experienced the highest and most persistent level of unemployment (32.7 per cent in 1936; in the six-nation sample, the government refrained from large-scale employment programmes.

Great Britain

Britain witnessed a lower level of unemployment and less oscillation in its unemployment rate than the other five countries. Moreover, government stability was preserved in spite of economic crisis. Unlike the other five countries, which experienced frequent change of government coalitions, Britain was dominated by the Conservatives throughout the 1930s. The British answer to the challenges of the Depression could be summed up as follows: (1) tight fiscal policy, (2) an early devaluation and continuous management of the currency, (3) cheap money through low interest rates, and (4) protection of the home market.

In his emergency budget of September 1931, Chancellor of the Exchequer Snowden introduced most of the measures that had been suggested by the May committee on National Expenditure in February 1931: a substantial rise in income tax and reductions in public employees' salaries. Between 1931 and 1934, central government expenditure declined from 17.3 to 14.6 per cent of the GDP: in "absolute" terms it was cut by 11.1 per cent during this period. Faced with dramatic losses of gold and a persistent balance-of-trade deficit, Britain departed from the gold standard on September 21, 1931. In April 1932 the government introduced the Exchange Equalisation Account as an instrument to keep the exchange rate of sterling down.

In the budgets of 1934-35 and 1935-36 the income tax as well as indirect taxation were reduced. The cuts in the salaries of public employees were revised. Unemployment benefits were restored to their pre- 1931 level. However, the shift in domestic policy was far from radical. Fiscal policy "remained remarkably orthodox ... and therefore provided no leverage to the economy. From 1936 onward the drastic increase in rearmament expenditure compelled the chancellor to incur budgetary deficits.

A Brief Overview

None of the governments had a coherent programmes. All trusted to a large extent in the "self-healing" forces of the market economy. Thus, governments in the six countries at first did nothing to stop the deepening econome crisis, and when they started to do something they did it either halfheartedly or at a time when the onset of economic recovery made such programmes more or less unnecessary. Germany again is an extreme case in all three respects; it faced the strongest economic crisis among the six countries, with a government (Bruning) concentrating primarily on settling the question of reparation payments and in pursuit of this goal assigning the economy the strictest of all deflationay cures. After the breakdown of democracy, there was a massive government intervention in the economy, unmatched by the other five nations. The totalitarian form of government further contributed to these developments. Britain provided the most contrast. The government refrained from interference in the economy through at least the first half of the thirties. It also deepened the crisis through deflationary measures, but not to the extent that Germany did. France demonstrated how halfhearted solutions, the postponement of measures from one cabinet to the next, and contradictory policies contributed to create a weak economy and a vulnerable society. Thus, all six countries made economic mistakes, but Germany and Austria coupled these mistakes with grave political errors as well.

42

The New Deal

It is doubtful whether any modern democratic government going to the polls can survive a catastrophic economic depression. And in the presidential election of 1932 it seemed inevitable that President Hoover, although won in 1928 by the huge majority of 444 to 87 electoral votes would be defeated by almost any Democratic candidate. In fact his opponent, Franklin Delano Roosevelt, Governor of New York, was described by so perceptive and experienced a commentator as Walter Lippmann as 'an agreeable man who without any important qualifications for the office, wants to be President.' The American people showed, as they were to do on three subsequent occasions. They elected him in November by 472 votes to 59. Although this was a slightly lower percentage of the whole vote than Hoover had got in 1928, he had a popular plurality of over 7 million votes and took 42 states. The Democrats captured the Senate by 59 to 37 and the House by 312 to 123.

Thus began the presidential career of the remarkable man who was to dominate the history of the United States for a longer period than perhaps any American had done. His great power of decision making and his infinite patience sometimes alternated with procrastination and what looked like an excessive subtlety. He was an episcopalian gentle man with progressive, in rare instances almost socialistic, ideas. But he stood squarely in the radical tradition of Jefferson, Jackson and Wilson, and he restored to the Democratic party an ascendancy it had enjoyed since before the Civil War, by wielding the workers of both the city and country for the first time into a really effective voting force.

Yet he was essentially a pragmatist, not welded indissolubly to a particular political or economic programme and ready to try any course of action which showed promise of results. Perhaps the most acute judgement, quoted by his biographer J.M. Burns, is that of Oliver Wendell Holmes, after meeting FDR when the great Justice was 92: 'A second-class intellect. But a first-class temperament'. And politically it was the temperament that provided the often irresistible magnetism, from the moment when in his dramatic and unprecendented personal acceptance of the Democratic nomination at the Chicago Convention in 1932 he declared, 'I pledge you, I pledge myself, to a new deal for the American people.' His hold upon people came at bottom from his warmth—which was perhaps increased by his sufferings during the poliomyelitis which left him a permanent cripple. One of the common people explained his power and wrote his epitaph: 'Roosevelt is the only president who ever cared for poeple like us.'

The Democratic platform on which he had been elected was cautious and conservative, though dominated by the economic crisis except for its espousal of the repeal of prohibition. In the three months between the election and Inauguration Day the situation continued to deteriorate, despite more desperate efforts by Hoover to halt the decline. Farm and other prices sank further, as did factory production; unemployment rose to almost 15 million; and so many banks failed that two-thirds of them were closed by state action throughout the country on the eve of 4 March. It was perhaps the most dramatic Inaugural scene in American history, even including 1861. Putting into practice the idea he had uttered earlier, that the Presidency is ' pre-eminently a place of moral leadership'. He went on to express the hope that normal constitutional means of action would suffice, but declared that if they did not, he would not hesitate to 'recommend the measures that a stricken Nation in the midst of a stricken world may require... I shall [in that event] ask the Congress for ... broad Executive power to wage a war against the emergency, as great as the power that would be given to me if we were in fact invaded by a foreign foe.'

Action did indeed follow. And his biographer writes, 'It *was* like a war'; and appropriately enough they called the first three months of his Administration 'The 100 Days'. The hectic activity of the New Deal era also in fact recalled the First World War and the unheard-of-scale of intervention by the Federal government during that crisis in almost all branches of economic life. Rather as Wilson had built on the precedents created by Lincoln for the exercise of the war power by the President and Commander-in-Chief, so F.D.R. was able to attempt all he did because of the popular consciousness that so many such things had been done. The huge extension of the powers and functions of the Federal government during these years is vividly illustrated not only by the proliferation of agencies of administration and by the increase in the number of Federal civil servants from some half a million in 1933 to 850,000 in 1938 (and to 3 million in 1943 during the war, remaining at some 2-1/2 million recently), but also by the vast expansion of the government in Washington DC, which was now to grow for the first time into a great metropolis.

The eyes of the nation were, to a degree previously unknown in time of peace, focused on the national capital on 4 March 1933, and the drama did not disappoint them. The President immediately proclaimed a 'bank holiday' and checked withdrawals of gold and silver; he then called Congress into special session on 9 March (the earliest possible date in the pre-airline age), on which day, in a quite unprecedented burst of speed, both Houses passed an Act giving the President emergency powers over banking and currency which he signed at 9 p.m. that evening. Next day he asked for wide powers to effect economies in government spending. Even a call on the 12 March for an amendment to the Volstead Act permitting the manufacture and sale of beer and light wines was answered by the 16th. And he maintained his momentum in the ensuing weeks in a way quite new to American government even in time of war.

On 16 March he asked for the most far-reaching agricultural bill in American history aimed at raising farm prices and agricultural purchasing power. The Agricultural Adjustment Act (AAA) was signed in mid-May. On 21 March he proposed a Civilian Conservation Corps (CCC) to put 250,000 young unemployed men to work by the early summer. It was passed by voice vote ten days later. On the same day, in a complete break with Hoover's policy, he requested Federal grants to the states for direct unemployment relief, and Congress swiftly passed the Federal Emergency Relief Act (FERA) by a large majority. The increasingly favoured method of Federal influence over the states was used in FERA, by promising to 'match' every $3 produced by a state with $1 from Washington, thus stimulating the states to action and aiding them in it while $500 million available to the Reconstruction Finance Corporation (RFC), created under the Republicans. Further measures, passed by June, included one giving power to the Interstate Commerce Commission to supervise the stock market, one creating a Home Owners Loan Corporation, and another including emergency railroad legislation and extending ICC control.

Most drastic in the short-term was the National Industrial Recovery Act, setting up the National Recovery Administration (NRA). This envisaged an expenditure of more than $3 billion on public works and set up machinery for 'a great cooperative movement throughout all industry in order to obtain wide re-employment, to shorten the working week, to pay a decent wage... and to prevent unfair competition and disastrous overproduction.' It was passed almost intact despite some radical opposition. Most important, perhaps, in the long run was the creation of Tennessee Valley Authority (TVA), authorised to develop the navigability of the river and its hydro-electric potential, using the public power so produced as a yard-stick by which to measure the efficiency of private utilities. It was nothing less than a revolutionary concept, the development of the valley and its resources, both human and material, as a whole. It was ' National planning for a complete river watershed.

This ended the 100 Days. It was an extraordinary legislative achievement and it was the President's. He veritably seemed, as an admirer called him, 'the Andrew Jackson of the Twentieth Century, championing the rights of the people.' How successful he was to be in effecting a permanent cure of the body economic remained to be seen.

The great psychological effect of this rush distracted attention from the fact that Roosevelt was playing his favourite political and administrative game of riding a number of different horses—or advisers—at the same time. In practice this often meant, in one of his favourite sayings, to put holders of antithetical or differing views 'in a room together and tell them no lunch until they agree', thus nicely leaving the final decision in the hands of the President. It could be criticised as excessively Pragmatic and as producing just some kind of agreed action rather than the right action. But at a deeper level, it was an effort, as F.D.R. himself put it, 'to find among many discordant elements that unity of purpose that is best for the Nation as a whole.' He did thus make during his first term a real attempt to be President of all the people. By his dynamic leadership in Congress, he got during this term more action out of the legislative arm to attempt to grapple with the great crisis than any other President has ever done. Despite his growing unpopularity with some of the business community, he commanded very wide support indeed in the nation at large.

By mid-January 1934 the United States was off the gold standard and the dollar had been devalued by just about 40 per cent. The Gold Reserve Act of 30 January at last gave some real control of the United States currency to the government.

There were further developments in the New Deal in succeeding months, such as the replacement of FERA in 1935 by a new Works Progress Administration (WPA) under Harry L. Hopkins (not to be confused with the Public Works Administration—or PWA. PWA employed some 2 million Americans annually until the war on everything from road building to theatrical performances. Other extensions of the role and powers of the Federal government included the Federal Communications Commission (FCC) and the Civil Aeronautics Authority (CAA), but perhaps the most influential programme economically was that under the Agricultural Adjustment Act (AAA), organised by Henry A.Wallace as Secretary of Agriculture. Its objective was to raise agricultural returns to a 'level that will give agriculture commodities a purchasing power with respect to articles farmers buy equivalent to the purchasing power of agricultural commodities in the base period August 1909-July 1914.'

But the most dramatic manifestation of the New Deal was the National Recovery Administration (NRA), under its flamboyant head General High Johnson. So headlong was the pace of this attempt to organise co-operative measures in industry under the supervision of the state that it was scarcely under his control, let alone that of the

Administration. Its biggest project was to develop industrial codes of fair competition, which it did for 500 industries. Its first was for cotton, where it laid down a fourty hour week, abolished child labour, and enjoined a minimum wage of $12 or $13.

A Soil Conservation and Domestic Allotment Act was rushed through in February and (in 1938 a much more carefully considered AAA was to reach the statute book).

In pursuit of his policies and in preparation for the forthcoming presidential election, Roosevelt stepped up his pressure on Congress for further action, and thus found himself, when the campaign opened, in a decidedly radical posture. There was a growing bitterness in business opposition to 'that cripple in the White House' fundamentally perhaps because he had undermined the self-esteem of those who had but recently offered the American people a new heaven and new earth on business principles—only to find themselves faced with what seemed to that people like utter national ruin. In fact, F.D.R. was far from the socialist his enemies called him. In a quite unparalleled victory, Roosevelt in the 1936 election carried every state except Maine and Vermont (523 to 8 electoral votes) with a popular majority of 27 million to 16 million. His enormous majority in Congress, 334-89 and 75-17, made him appear invincible.

Roosevelt planned a flank attack upon the conservatism of the Supreme Court. He promoted a bill laying down that for every Supreme Court justice who failed to quit the bench within six months of reaching the age of seventy the President was empowered to appoint a new member of the Court, up to a total of six additional justices (that is, of 15 in all). But the plan misfired. Despite the huge Democratic majority in Congress, it failed to get the necessary support, partly because the attempt to avoid the cumbersome mechanism of constitutional amendment was so transparent that it looked almost very difficult.

Some achievements, such as the establishment of the U.S. Housing Administration for slum clearance and of the U.S. Maritime Commission to encourage a merchant fleet worthy of the nation, were developments of the New Deal in the post-1936 era, but most attention had to be concentrated on the second slump. It is possible that it was precipitated by the over-anxiety of the Administration to revert, to ideas of economic and orthodox finance, and its readiness to fear a premature boom, but unemployment which had briefly sunk to its lowest point since the 1920s in July 1937—below 5 million—rose to 11 million by January 1938. This had a very adverse effect on national morale, particularly in view of the Administration's claims to government planning in the economy. The conservatives cried loudly that the New Deal had failed. By the spring the President, under pressure from the left was convinced that the natural forces of recovery were again proving inadequate and launched the so-called Second New deal.

But one development of the President's term of office was of the utmost importance, the exceedingly rapid growth in the power of labour. This revolution, with its resultant raising of wages (which was in the long run probably the most significant single reflationary factor in national economic life), was perhaps the most important long-term result of the New Deal. At first the President had been only a lagging supporter of labour, but by his second term he had, despite the vicissitudes of his relationship with a number of their leaders, became increasingly warm towards them and increasingly dependent on their political support. The National Industrial Recovery Act had given the right of collective bargaining to labour and set up the Labor Advisory Board.

The Wagner-Connery Act of 1935 was very favourable to labour and set up a permanent National Labour Relations Board (NLRB). This was followed by the formation of the Congress of Industrial Organisations (CIO), the first large industrial—as opposed to craft—federation of unions, under the leadership of John L. Lewis, the Mine Workers leader, in 1936. By the begining of the Second World War labour had become powerfully entrenched in the life of the United States.

But the New Deal must not be underestimated. The problems of the Economic Blizzard were very grave and very difficult to understand, let alone to remedy. The New Deal gave power, or the promise of power, to the Federal government; more than that, it gave hope to the American people. F.D.R.'s contribution was a determination to go on experimenting until poverty was alleviated. He restored America's belief in its own democracy, and this was of inestimable value when the Second World War came. Even if the New Deal Programme brought forth a lot of protest for critics felt that the government was turning socialistic. In reality, the popularity of the programme can be seen from the fact that Roosevelt was the only American President to be elected four times.

43

Rise of Nazi Germany

"The continuing hostile attitude of France, the quarrels over the Ruhr and Rhineland occupation, the Saar and the reparation, the wrangling over disarmament—all these fed the anger of many Germans."

Langsam

Introduction

The collapse of Germany in the First World War led to political turmoils in the country. Kaiser William II was held responsible for the reverses of the German army and the miseries of the people. A country-wide anti-monarchist revolution compelled Kaiser to abdicate the throne, and along with his family he took shelter in Holland. With his abdication, a parliamentary democracy was established in Germany. The Democratic National Assembly was entrusted with the responsibility of drafting a democratic constitution for German Republic. This constitution came into effect on August 11, 1919 and is known as 'Weimer Constitution'.

The Weimer Republic, which bridged the years between the Hohenzollerns and the Nazis, had a number of outstanding achievements to its credit. Due to the introduction of the Dawes Plan (1924), Germany witnessed unprecedented prosperity. Industrial production recorded an enormous increase. The huge amounts advanced by the foreign countries to Germany enabled her to re-establish the currency and the rationalisation of the German Industrial and business life prevented ruinous competition. The establishment of branches of foreign firms in Germany not only led to the utilisation of German raw materials but also provided employment to the German labour.

In the sphere of foreign policy Germany during this period pursued three aims (1) to induce the Allies to evacuate those areas of Germany which they had occupied; (2) to restore the sovereignty of the *Reich* and recovery of Danzig and correction of the frontiers in Upper Silesia; (3) settlement of the reparation problems as per Germany's capacity. In short, through these aims Germany wanted to make her own decisions.

For the achievement of the above objectives Germany signed the Locarno treaties, by which her frontiers with France were settled. In 1922 she concluded the Treaty of Rapallo with Soviet Union by whilch both the states renounced their respective demand against each other and agreed to cooperate in the commercial sphere. In 1926, Germany was admitted to the League of Nations with a semi-permanent seat in the Council. She succeeded in getting a promise of withdrawal of foreign troops from the Ruhr in 1924, and the valley was freed in 1930. In 1930 Britain, France and Belgium agreed to withdraw their troops from the Rhineland region. The problem of reparation was largely settled by the Young Plan. In June 1932, the Lausanne Conference further cut down Germany's obligations of reparation to $750 million. Even this amount was not paid. With the economic and diplomatic revival, Germany began to rearm herself. She started equipping her army with new weapons and anti-tank defence. In 1931, when economic depression was at its worst, Germany was spending $700 million on her army. The amount was $250 million more than what she was spending in 1925, the first year of her prosperity. In early 1933, the affairs of Germany passed under Hitler.

Circumstances that Led to the Rise of Adolf Hitler

Adolf Hitler, the leader of the Nazi movement in Germany was an Austrian citizen. He began his career as a political agitator after the war. In 1920 he joined the German Workers Party, which later came to be known as the National Socialist German Workers Party (popularly known as Nazi Party). Soon he succeeded in ousting Drexter, the leader of the party and assumed supreme power in the party. In 1923 he made an unsuccessful attempt at a *coup d'etat* which brought him in clash with the authorities. During his trial he made the remarks "There is no such thing as high treason against the traitors of 1918" which attracted much attention. He was awarded five years imprisonment, but was actually released after nine months. During his imprisonment Hitler wrote *'Mein Kampf'* in which he repudited the parliamentary practice of majority rule and foreshadowed the future programme of Germany's territorial ambitions.

During the imprisonment of Hitler, the Nazi party was proscribed and its disintegration set in. In the election of 1924 the number of its supporters considerably fell down. In 1925 after the reorganisation of the Nazi party, its popularity increased. In the election of 1932 the Nazi party captured 230 out of 608 seats in the Reichstag. As Hitler was restless to capture power, in 1932, he contested the Presidential elections. However, he lost to Hindenburg by a narrow margin. In 1933 Hindenburg dismissed the former Chancellor Schleicher and appointed Hitler as Chancellor. Hitler dissolved the Reichstag and ordered an election on March 5,1933. Six days before the balloting the Reichstag building was burnt. Hitler at once accused the Communists of arson and bloody revolution. He ordered the arrest of thousands of Communists and Social Democrats, suppressed the campaign activities of the anti-Nazi parties. Nazi party was able to secure only forty-four per cent of votes polled. However, Hitler soon managed majority in the Reichstag by putting all the Communist Deputies behind the prison. Within three months, all opposition was suppressed. In August 1934 Hindenburg died and Hitler himself became the President of Germany. By 'The Enabling Act' Hitler got dictatorial powers.

Factors for the Growth of Nazism or Rise of Hitler

Hitler, who was comparatively unknown till 1929, all of a sudden emerged the unchallenged leader of Germany in 1934. The following factors contributed towards the rise of Hitler to power.

Treaty of Versailles

The humiliating treatment meted out to Germany by the Peace settlement of 1919, was the first major factor which Hitler exploited to win popular support. As *Dr. Langsam* says, "The continuing hostile attitude of France—the quarrels over the Ruhr, the Rhineland occupation, the Saar and the reparation, the wrangling over disarmament—all these fed the anger of many Germans."

Danger of Communism

The success of the Bolsheviks in Russia and the growing strength of Communists in Germany, was also exploited by Hitler. The Communists who had 77 members in the

Reichstag in 1930 were able to increase their strength in the first and second elections of 1932 to 89 and 100 respectively. As the Germans were much afraid of Communists, the Nazis fully exploited this weakness and raised the slogan "If the National Socialist Party collapses there will be another ten million Communists in Germany." A large number of industrialists and wealthy people, who were afraid of Bolshevik ideals, also helped the Nazi party. *Schuman* has correctly analysed these causes when he writes,"Industrialists and Junkers subsidized the brown shirt Nazi storm troopers hoping to make use of them against Communists, socialists, the trade unions and other threats real or imaginary to prosperity and privilege."

The Economic Crisis

The Nazi party also fully exploited the economic crisis in post-war Germany. Due to inflation the condition of the farmers and shopkeepers became desperate. Mass unemployment reduced the purchasing power of the Urban population. The condition of agriculture was no better. The National Socialists made lavish promises to the peasants and small tradesmen. In short, like Italian Fascists, the National Socialists promised heaven to all. Fortunately for the Nazis, when they came to power the world began to recover from the economic blizzard. "If their summons to office had been delayed by a few months", says *Lipson*, "the decline in popular support evinced in the general election of 1932, would probably have been greatly accelerated."

Resurgence of Militant German Nationalism

Germans by nature and temperament have a weakness for prestige and glory. They were in the look-out of a 'strong man' who could bring peace and prosperity to the country. When they found such a man in Hitler, they welcomed him with open arms. The Germans wanted a strong man to check the expansion of communism, which was winning millions of discontented workers into its ranks.

Leadership of Adolf Hitler

The personality of Hitler was one of the major factors in the rise of Nazism. Hitler was in the words of *Benns*, "an adept psychologist, a clever demagogue and a master showman', he was a resourceful agitator, a tireless worker and an able organiser." He was convinced that a political revolution must be preceded by a psychological revolution. He tried to create this psychological revolution through his *Mein Kampf*, and mentally prepared the young Germans to avenge the wrong done to them by the victors of 1918.

Other Factors

The other factors which helped the Nazi rise were the anti-semitic propaganda and lack of unity among the opposition parties. The Nazis pleaded that the Jews who formed the wealthier sections of the German society belonged to a different race and as such were foreigners. The Nazis succeeded in creating a feeling among the Germans that their hardships were due to the Jews. The opposition parties, which lacked unity, also failed to pose any check to the authority of the Nazis.

Thus Hitler came to power through constitutional machinery. He fully exploited the desire of the German people to secure for themselves a place in the sun.

The Foreign Policy of Germany under Hitler

"It was natural that the appearance of a Germany supposed to be animated by the ideals of Mein Kampf and the Nazi programme should produce immediate relations in Europe."

Gathrone Hardy

The principles of German foreign policy after Hitler were laid down in the Nazi Programme of the National Socialist German Workers' Union (later known as Nazi party), and Hitler *Mein Kampf*. The National Socialist German Workers' Union in its three-point programme of foreign policy had laid down its objectives as (1) the Union of all people of German race by the right of self-determination in one great Germany. (2) The cancellation of the Peace Treaties of Versailles and St. Germain; and (3) Acquisition of further territory for the support of the people and the settlement of the surplus German population.

Hitler in *Mein Kampft* emphasised the following principles of German foreign policy. He wrote: "The German frontiers are the outcome of a chance and are only temporary frontiers that have been established as the result of political struggles which took place at various time... State frontiers are established by human beings and may be changed by human beings. The winning back of the lost territories of a country is, in the first place, the question of winning back the political independence and power of the mother country. To make this possible and to secure it through an adroit policy of alliance is the first task for a vigorous direction of our foreign policy." He pleaded for putting a final stop to "the colonial and trade policy of pre-war times and pass over to the territorial policy of the future. But when we speak of now territory in Europe today, we must principally think of Russia and the border states subject to her. Today, there are eighty million Germans in Europe and our foreign policy will be recognised as rightly conducted only when, after barely a hundred years, there will be 250 million Germans living on this Continent, not packed together as coolies in the factories of another continent but as tiller of the soil and workers whose labour will be a national assurance for their existence."

Giving reasons for acquisition of greater living space Hitler wrote: "Germany within her existing frontiers could attain only a very limited self-sufficiency in raw materials and none at all in foodstuffs. The only remedy lay in the acquisition of greater living space. If then, we accept the security of our food situation as the principal question, the space necessary to insure it can only be sought in Europe, not, as in the liberal view, in the exploitation of colonies. It is not a matter of acquiring population but of gaining space for agricultural use. Moreover, areas producing raw materials can be more usefully sought in Europe in immediate proximity to the Rich than overseas."

He further wrote: "If we speak today of new territory in Europe, we can primarily think only of Russia and the border states .... If the Urals with their immeasurable wealth of raw materials, Siberia with its rich forests, and the Ukraine with its limited cornfields lay within Germany this country under National Socialist Leadership would swim in plenty. We would produce so much that every single German would have more than enough to live on."

From these observations of Hitler it was obvious that Germany could expand in the South and East of Europe because that region alone could give more space to the German population. The region was economically complementary to Germany and possessed huge stocks of coal,oil and wheat which Germany required badly. As the region was divided into a number of small states, none of the states was able to profitably exploit the natural resources of the area. Austria had coal but no grain. Hungary had grain but no factories, Rumania had ores and invaluable oil but she had no markets. The best results could be achieved only if one political power was established in the whole region. Germany with its industrial techniques, and its factories crying for raw material techniques, and its factors crying for raw materials and markets, was most fit to assume this responsibility.

As regards the methods to be observed for the fulfilment of the objectives of German foreign policy, Hitler stated "reliance on force and the rejection of compromise should be the keystone." The new regime preferred to take rather than receive; to tear up treaties by a unilateral repudiation of its obligations rather than to modify them by amicable negotiations; to spring its measures suddenly upon the world without any warning; and to keep the nerves of Europe on edge by creating an atmosphere of tension. *Bullock* has observed, "Hitler had only one programme; Power, first his own power in Germany and then the expansion of German power in Europe. The rest was window dressing."

But the pursuit of such an aggressive policy would have created troubles for Germany by uniting all enemies of Germany. Sensing this difficulty Hitler proceeded very diplomatically and declared "The German Government and the German people are united in the will to pursue a policy of peace, reconciliation and understanding, as the foundation of all decisions and negotiations." He stopped condemnation of the Versailles Treaty and directed his hostility against Bolshevism. This move proved quite helpful to Germany because USA, France and Britain took no immediate steps against Germany.

Withdrawal from the League

Hitler wanted to reduce the Treaty of Versailles to a scrap of paper and took the first step in this direction by withdrawing from the League of Nations in October 1933. Hitler was convinced that the League stood for perpetuation of the political settlement of 1919 and was the greatest hindrance in the way of achieving his objectives. After this withdrawal Germany was relieved of all the international obligations imposed by the Government.

Polish-German Non-aggression Pact (January 1934)

To give a show of Germany's peaceful intentions, in January 1934 Hitler concluded a Non-aggression Pact with Poland for 10 years. Hitler realised that if Germany wanted to advance southward, she must make peace with her eastern neighbours. As Soviet Union could not be won over due to the prosecution of the Jews and Communists in Germany, and Czechoslovakia was too small a country, Poland was the natural choice.

Poland at that time was feeling distrustful of her ally France, because she had subordinated the Polish interests to her own security during the Locarno Pact of 1925. Further Poland felt that a treaty with Germany would silence the German minorities, who had been a source of headache for her since 1919.

Recovery of Saar (March 1935)

The Treaty of Versailles had vested France with the right to occupy and exploit the Saar for a period of 15 years. After the lapse of this period, the people of Saar were to decide through a plebiscite (to be held under the auspices of the League of Nations) whether they would like to go back to Germany or not. In 1935, the plebiscite was arranged and 90% of the voters voted in favour of Germany. On March 1, 1935 the territory of Saar was united with Germany.

Austro-German Agreement (July 1936)

Ever since the conclusion of World War I, Germany had been looking for a union with Austria. In 1931, her efforts to venture a customs union between Germany and Austria was foiled due to intervention of the Western powers. Hitler after assuming power in Germany made it chief aim of his foreign policy to complete the Anschluss (union with Austria). He openly encouraged the subversive elements in Austria to bring about the fall of Austrian Chancellor Dollfus, who was opposed to Anschluss. On July 25, 1934 Dollfus was killed by the terrorists, which created great stir in Austria. Mussolini sent Italian troops to help the Austrian Government. Hitler felt discredited and did not intervene in the Austrian affairs. However,two years later a pact was signed by which Germany agreed to respect the Austrian independence and German trade and with Vienna was reopened. But as Hitler was bent upon annexation of Austria, he befriended Italy and ultimately annexed Austria in 1938. The Western powers remained silent spectators and did nothing. It has been well said that like wincere widows, they moaned and shouted but otherwise did nothing.

Accord with Italy (October 1936). Hitler realised that a war could not be successfully fought without allies. Realising that France and Soviet Union could not be befriended and Great Britain, though conciliatory could not be relied upon. Hitler, looked towards Italy. Italy's thrust into Ethiopia in 1934-36 created a wedge between Italy on the one hand and France, Great Britain and Russia on the other. Therefore, Mussolini saw in German friendship the only way out. Germany and Italy came closer to each other because both of them wanted to undo the Peace Settlement of 1919. During the Spanish civil war when Mussolini was sending men and munitions to General Franco, Hitler supported Mussolini and won him over. In October, 1936 the two countries concluded an agreement for mutual cooperation. Thus was created, what came to be known as*'Rome-Berlin-Axis'*

Berlin-Rome-Tokyo Axis

In 1936, Germany entered into an Anti-Comintern Pact with Japan, by which the parties agreed to inform each other regarding the activities of the Comintern. They also agreed to consult each other regarding the measures to combat their activities. In November 1937, it also joined the anti-Comintern Pact, and thus was created the famous "Berlin-Rome-Tokyo Axis".

Remilitarization of Germany

Hitler also took up the work of rearming Germany. On the day when Germany withdrew from the League of Nations, she also withdrew from the Disarmament Conference being held at Geneva. In March 1935 Germany told the world that a German Air Force was in existence. On March 16, 1935 Germany announced the *Law for the Reconstruction of National Defence Forces,* in complete violation of the treaty of Versailles. Hitler took the next step in the direction of rearmament in March, 1936 when he sent his troops to remilitarize Rhineland, in violation of the freely negotiated treaty of Locarno.

Intervention in Spanish Civil War

A civil war broke out in spain following rebellion by General Franco. While Soviet Union helped the Government of Spain, Hitler and Mussolini helped General Franco. As a result of this help General Franco was able to overthrow the Republican Government. Great Britain and France, through their policy of neutrality helped Hitler and Mussolini. The Spanish Civil war like the Ethiopian crisis, brought Italy and Germany closer to each other.

Attack of Czechoslovakia

The state of Czechoslovakia was created by the Treaty of Versailles. But certain German minorities were left in the country. These minorities in spite of nice treatment by the Czechoslovakian government continued to have their affinity for Germany. Inspired by the Nazi propaganda, this minority raised a slogan that they should be allowed to join their motherland Germany. Hitler took advantage of this appeal and intervened.

But the real cause for Hitler's interest in Czechoslovakia were quite different. (1) Chechoslovakia belonged to anti-revisionalist group consisting of France and Russia, and was strong supporter of the League of Nations. (2) The strategic importance of Czechoslovakia, was another factor. It was this territory that retarded the expansion of Germany to the South occupation of Czechoslovakia meant occupation of the land through which the Germans could march against Russia.

Consequently Germany started instigating the Sudetan-Germans (the German minority in Czechoslovakia) to launch a violent struggle. The Sudetan-Germans rose up in armed revolt on September 10, 1938 and Germany started mobilisation of her forces and threatened to go to war. Hitler even entered into a pact with Italy and Japan. In the meantime the British government proposed a peaceful settlement of Czechoslovakian crisis. The British and French governments advised the Czech government also to transfer the Sudetan area to Germany. Czech government immediately agreed. This came as a complete surprise to Hitler, who started insisting that the transfer of the territory must be effected before October 1,1938. Mussolini advised Hitler to settle things amicably.

Munich Pact

A conference was held at Munich on September 29,1938 and was attended by Great Britain, Italy, France and Germany. It may be noted that the Soviet Union and Czechoslovakia were not represented in the Conference.

After a good deal of discusssion a pact was signed on September 30, 1938. This pact is popularly known as Munich Pact. It was stated in the pact."Germany, the United Kingdom, France and Italy taking into consideration the agreement which has been already reached in principle for cession to Germany of the Sudetan Germans territory, have agreed on the following terms and conditions governing the cession and measures, consequent thereon and by this agreement they each themselves held responsible for the steps necessary to secure its fulfilment."

Under this Pact the evacuation was to start on 1st October, and to be completed by 10th of October, 1938, without any existing installations being destroyed. The occupation of the predominantly German territory by German troops was to begin on 1st and be completed by 10th October. The Sudetan-Germans were to be released by Czech government from her military and police force within four weeks. A five-power

Commission was set up to determine the territories in which a plebiscite was to be held and till then the territories were to remain under an international force.

This Pact was a clever act of diplomacy on the part of Hitler. He duped Chamberlain by giving him an assurance that if his demand of Czechoslovakia was met, he would follow a policy of peace.

Dismemberment of Czechoslovakia

Once the claim of the German minorities was established, Poland and Hungary also came out with their respective claims. While Poland demanded 'Teschen' an area which had some ethnic affinity with Poland, Hungary—demanded an area inhabited by the Magyars. Both these countries ultimately succeeded in getting these areas and Czechoslovakia became a thin strip of land.

On March 14, 1939 at the instance of Hitler, Slovakla and Ruthenla declared their independence from the Czech government. Hitler intervened and invited Dr. Hacha to Berlin where he was forced to sign the document by which Czechoslovakia was placed under the protectorate of Germany. On March 15, 1939 Nazi troops occupied Czechoslovakia.

War was now inevitable because both the camps were making fervent preparations. But Hitler felt that before the next major turn of events took place, an understanding with USSR was essential. Soviet Union was completely disgusted with the Western powers after the Munich Pact. Taking advantage of this Hitler concluded a non-aggression pact with Soviet Union on August 23, 1939. This pact was a masterpiece of Hitler's diplomacy because he was able to ward of Germany against a possible attack by the Soviet Union if he carried out his designs against Poland.

In the meanwhile Hitler had annexed Memel and demanded the Polish corridor. On September 1, 1939 Hitler attacked Poland and the second world war started.

Reaction against Rise of Hitler or Impact of Nazism

The rise of Hitler in Germany and the various measures he adopted to make Germany a totalitarian state produced mixed reactions. In some countries the predominant feeling was one of moral indignation at the cruelties and excesses of the dictatorship. In England the United States there was a feeling of indignation, not of fear, and there was no marked change in the policy of these two countries towards Germany. In other countries there was a feeling of profound anxiety at Hitler's open challenge to the peace settlement of 1919. Further Hitler openly expressed hostility towards France Soviet Russia and the least powers in Central and South-Eastern powers took steps to ensure that if Hitler started war against them, they were not alone.

Let us examine the impact of Hitler's foreign policy on the foreign policies of some of the major countries.

Impact on Soviet Russia

One of the immediate effect of Hitler's rise in Germany was the rapproachment between the Soviet Union and France, based on a common fear of Germany. The two countries signed a non-aggression pact as well as a conciliation convention with each other. In January 1934, the two signed a trade agreement for one year. In May 1935 Soviet Union signed a five year pact of mutual assistance with France as well as Czechoslovakia.

It also led to Russian membership of the League of Nations. This step was taken by Russia on the insistence of France because France felt the common interests in defence against German aggression must be expressed by common membership of the League.

In the Baltic littoral the danger of Pan-German expansionism induced both the Soviet Union and some of the Baltic states (Estonia, Latvia and Lithuania) to prolong their mutual non-aggression pacts till 1945. Similarly the Soviet Polish non-aggression pact which was concluded in July 1932 was prolonged until 1945.

Soviet Union signed a non-aggression pact with seven of its neighbours—Afghanistan, Estonia, Latvia, Persia, Rumania and Turkey, on July 3, 1933. On the following day she concluded a similar pact with the three Little Entente states—Rumania, Yugoslavia and Czechoslovakia.

In June 1934 Soviet and French governments prepared broad outlines for an Eastern Pact of Mutual Assistance. This Pact was designed on the lines of the Locarno Pact of October 1925. The first part of the proposed pact was to be concluded between Poland, Russia, Germany, Czechoslovakia, Finland, Estonia, Latvia and Lithuania. The chief provisions of this part were that in the event of crisis these states were to hold Joint consultations and render immediate military assistance to the country attacked by one of the contracting parties. This pact was to be supplemented by an additional treaty between France and Russia, by which they were to assume the same obligations as devolved on England and Italy as guarantors of the Rhine Pact of 1925. Commenting on this *Pact* Carr says: "The plan seemed somewhat artificial; for it was difficult to imagine any circumstances in which Germany would obtain the help of France against the Soviet Union or of the Soviet Union against France."

The draft was approved by Britain in February 1935. But the German government raised certain objections which tantamounted to her refusal.

Impact on the Foreign Policy of Italy

The rise of Hitler had far reaching impact on the foreign policy of Italy. Mussolini saw in it the victory of Fascism, though he showed little eagerness to conclude political agreement with Nazi Germany. Though Italy, like Germany favoured revision of Peace Treaty, Mussolini was strongly opposed to the Austro-German Union on the ground that it would bring Germany on the borders of Italy and threaten South Tirol. He accordingly supported the government of Dollfuss, against the wishes of Hitler. In March 1934 a series of political-cum-economic agreements were concluded by Italy, Austria and Hungary which led to the establishment of a sort of Italo-Austro-Hungarian bloc. But Hungary while negotiating with Italy kept the door open for collaboration with Germany.

Impact on the Foreign Policy of France

The rise of Nazi Government in Germany greatly alarmed France because Hitler had openly advocated the scrapping of the Versailles treaty and changing of *status quo*. As France was not quite sure of the attitude of Great Britain, her ally, in case of German aggression, she sought to strengthen her security by concluding agreements with countries who felt equally perturbed by the rise of Nazi Government. She turned her attention to Italy first. Italy was equally afraid of Hitler after his intervention in Austria. In January 1935 a series of agreements were signed between the two countries by which they ironed out their mutual differences, and agreed to concert upon the attitude to be adopted in the event of Germany pursuing a policy of aggression.

With regard to Central Europe, the two countries agreed to recommend to Austria and all her neighbouring states to enter into a pact undertaking not to intervene in each other's sphere. In case of a threat to the Austrian independence, they agreed to consult together with Austria and such other of her neighbours as might be willing to a concerted action. France ceded to Italy, in settlement of her claims a strip of French equatorial Africa adjacent to the Italian province of Libya and a small triangle of French Somaliland adjoining Eritrea. The status of the Italians in Tunis was regulated. France also showed her disinterestedness in any concession which Italy might obtain from Abyssinia.

France also sought co-operation of Soviet Russia and concluded a five year mutual Assistance Pact with her in 1935. By this pact the two agreed to come to each other's assistance if attacked by any European power. France concluded a pact with Czechoslovakia almost on the same lines.

Impact on Little Entente States

The establishment of Nazi Government greatly perturbed the little Entente States (Yugoslavia, Rumania and Czechoslovakia) because the German had fixed their aim at the inclusion of all German speaking peoples in the Third Reich. The divergences of interests which had existed among the Little Entente States were further increased as a result of Nazi Revolution in Germany. Rumania was afraid of Russia, but Yugoslavia and Czechoslovakia were too far from the enemy of Rumania. Likewise Czechoslovakia was afraid of Germany but was not affected by strength of Italy.

The Entente States overcome all these differences and by a pact of reorganisation signed at Geneva on February 16, 1933. They agreed to have a permanent council composed of the foreign ministers of the three countries, for the purpose of conducting a common foreign policy. An economic council was also set up for the coordination of their economic interests.

Impact of Balkan Nations

The rise of Hitler to power, and the withdrawal of Germany from the League of Nations had its repercussions in the Balkan Peninsula, who felt greatly nervous. On the initiative of Greece and Turkey, an organisation on the line of the Little Entente was formed on February 9, 1934 between Turkey, Yugoslavia, Rumania and Greece. This entente came to be known as *Balkan Entente*. By this Pact, the signatories agreed to guarantee other's frontiers. The Pact also applied to any of the signatories if it joined an outside power that committed aggression against one of the signatories. Thus, the Balkan Entente was more a defensive alliance rather than a mere non-aggression pact.

Impact on the Foreign Policy of England

The rise of Hitler and the various measures adopted by him, apparently annoyed Great Britain, though inwardly she felt happy that Germany was recovering from her downgraded position. She, therefore. adopted an attitude of reconciliation towards Germany but at the same time she did not annoy France.

In March 1935, when Hitler introduced conscription and started remilitarisation in violation of the Treaty of Versailles, Great Britain neither lodged any protest with Hitler nor used the machinery of the League to restrain him from doing so. Instead Britain accepted Hitler's offer to limit German naval strength in all categories of ships to 35 per cent of the British strength. A formal agreement (Anglo-German Naval Agreement) was signed to the effect on June 18, 1935. This implied that Great Britain openly recognised Germany's right to flout the treaty of Versailles. This gave encouragement to Hitler to go ahead with his programme of aggression, which ultimately led to war. However, when Hitler undertook an invasion of Poland in violation of his declared principles, and contrary to the assurance given to Great Britain at Munich, England abandoned her policy of appeasement towards Germany. Instead she embarked on a policy of resisting foreign aggression.

In short the rise of Hitler in Germany and the aggressive policies which he pursued, encouraged the revisionist sentiments in certain states and alarmed those states who stood for the *status quo*.

44

Adolf Hitler, Nazism and Ideology

The National Socialist movement began as one of the many tiny nationalist political and cultural groups that sprang up like mushrooms in Germany immediately following the close of World War I. In these groups demobilized soldiers, political and economic malcontents, romantic and earliest adventurers, immature idealistic youths, and designing political intriguers joined forces to fight the new Weimar democracy and the West. The National Socialist Germany Workers Party was the offspring of the Deutsche Arbeiter Partei, founded on January 5, 1919, by the soon to be forgotten Anton Drexler. In September 1919, Adolf Hitler became member Number Seven of the political committee of the party, and in March, 1920, this party became officially known as the Nationalso-zialistische Deutsche Arbeiter Partei, or N.S.D.A.P.

Drexler, a wood turner by profession, who had been thrown out of his trade-union, developed a violent hatred of Marxism, and combined it, as was usual, with antisemitism. He also preached the by no means novel doctrine of the need to unite German national interests with the "German socialism. His autobiography, *Mein politisches Erwachen* (1st ed. Munich,1919; 3rd ed., 1923), is the work of an autodidact who dabbled just enough in history to be able to create garbled versions of it. It is dull and undistinguished, but it is also not especially violent nor aggressive in its appeal. Drexler attracted to his party the anti-semitic writer Dietrich Eckart, whose weekly *Auf gut Deutsch* (first issue, December 7, 1918) came to be regarded as the first paper of the Nazi movement, and an economic writer Gottfried Feder, who offered as a panacea for the solution of Germany's troubles his theory of the *"Brechung der Zinsknechtschaft"* the destruction of the interest bondage. To these was soon added Ernst Rohm, who came from the Freikorps Epp and who brought into the party many of his military friends.

Drexter's and Hitler's party maintained from the start close and intimate relations with German racialist parties in Silesia, Austria, Czechoslovakia, and Poland. The Pan-German character of the movement is apparent from the start. Elements of the Pan-German League and the Vaterlandspartaei came in. The influence of the Austrians Walter Riehl of Vienna and Rudolf Jung of Tropau was especially marked in these early days. Jung supplied a more theoretical dressing for the movement. His book *Der nationale Sozialismus* (1st ed., Munich, 1920; 2nd ed., 1922), with its theoretical antisemitism and attacks upon the Old Testament, its anti-clericalism and anti-materialism, its program of the Pan-German union of all *Volksdeutsche,* and his economic radicalism, which likewise attempted to fuse the concepts of "national" and "social", was considered to be the most authoritative presentation of national-socialist doctrine until superseded by the gospel according to Adolf. The N.S.D.A.P also absorbed the Deutsch-Socialistche Partei, founded by Julius Stretcher in Franconia, and allied itself with the racialist movement led by General Ludendorff and his wife.

The Hitler-Ludendorff alliance reached its crest in the Putsch of November 9, 1923, which sent Hitler for a short term to the fortress of Landsberg and which marked a turning point in the tactics of Hitler's ride to power. Hitler realised that putschism could not arouse the enthusiasm of the German masses nor win the support of the more influential and respectable circles. His way now was to be that of "legality". On numerous occasions he repeated the promise that he would not use violence to secure power. In a strictly technical sense, too, he kept his word. His accession to power on January 30, 1933, came in strictly legal fashion, in accordance with the provisions of the Weimar Constitution and without the aid of violence or insurrection.

Up to September 1930, the N.S.D.A.P. was still a negligible factor on the political scene. For most Germans the term Nazi was still associated more or less with something like inmates of a lunatic asylum. The elections of September, 1930, which brought 107 Brown Shirts into the Reichstag instead of the previous twelve, changed the entire picture. From then on they became the worst dynamic factor in German political life, until their dynamism became the ruling power of Germany.

The person of Adolf Hitler, the central figure in world history from 1933 to 1945, has by now become the subject of a huge literature, but the problems of his biography will undoubtedly continue to haunt historians, and psychologists for many years to come. The phenomenon of Hitler is one that defies all rational analysis. That this individual was responsible for effecting a profound transformation in the history of Germany and in that of the world at large can be denied by no one. That this problem defies rational analysis, however, comes not from the complexity of character or profundity of mind and spirit of Adolf Hitler - he had neither - but from the much more unfathomable and fateful question of how an individual with such a combination of mediocrity could find sufficiently wide support to make himself the idolized leader of Germany and then come close to being the master of all Europe.

Mediocrity was Hitler's most distinguishing characteristic. Perhaps it was precisely this quality which, in an age of mass appeal, attracted so many to his standard. The average German saw himself mirrored in Hitler's person and could identify himself with him. Hitler was semi-educated and sufficiently cultured to make a pretense of profound interest in art and music, but he was a diletante in everything from art and architecture to politics and military strategy.

National Socialism, while primarily and in its essential features a typically German movement, was indebted to influences from countries, especially Italy, Russia, and the United States. The very success of Italian fascism served as a model and a source of inspiration to the Nazi leaders. They also learned from the experiences of Mussolini what to avoid and how fast they could proceed in their consolidation of power. From Italian fascism they borrowed the Nazi salute, the models for youth organisations, for the labor front, and for the recreational *Kraft durch Freude,* the parallel of *Fuhrer to Il Duce,* and other such symbols. The relationship between the two dictators passed through various stages of trust and admiration. In earlier days, before Hitler's conquests, it was Hitler who looked up in admiration to the Italian dictator, while Mussolini gave condescending attention to the "vulgar" and "uneducated" German rabble rouser. Serious differences between the Fuhrer and the Duce appeared in 1934-35 on German designs in Austria and in connection with the Nazi assassination of Dollfuss. From the period of their joint action in Spain, however, the two dictators established a close personal relationship that placed them shoulder to shoulder against the other Western powers. Now, however, it was Hitler who called the tune, and Italy ultimately became but a vassal state of the Third Reich. Hitler always had nothing but contempt for the Italian people, and especially the Italian soldiers, but his personal loyalty to the Duce persisted to the end, as evidenced in the breath-taking and hazardous venture carried out at his command in order to set Mussolini free after he had been ousted and jailed.

Nazi borrowings from Russia were of a dual character. From the Russian monarchist emigres who swarmed into Germany after the Bolshevik revolution and who hovered close to the Nazi movement in its early Munich days, the Nazis received additional fuel for their antisemitism. Most important of all was the diffusion in Germany of the *Protocols of the Elders of Zion,* which was translated into German and which as an "authoritative" guide to Nazi antisemitism. Violent anti-Bolshevism was likewise fed into the Nazi movement by these emigres. Alfred Rosenberg, himself an emigre from Russia, acted as the liaison officer between these anti-semitic Russian reactionaries and the Nazi movement.

There was also within the N.S.D.A.P. a marked admiration and affinity for the Bolshevik dictatorship. The so-called "socialist" elements in the party found a certain affinity with Russian communism except for the "internationalism" of the Bolsheviks, which they rejected. The saying current in Germany, that a Nazi was like a beefsteak - brown on the outside and red on the inside - was not far-fetched. The Nazis admired the Soviet system of repression from the use of the concentration camp to the centralized power of Stalin, the dictator. Goening, in his interrogation at Nurnberg, related how he had conferred with Marshal Stalin and that he "had the impression that something very strong was there ... because I saw how this one man had these 200,000,000 Russian people in his hand like that." Hitler, always referred admiringly to Stalin as Ghenghis Khan. He told his generals on August 22, 1939: "On the whole there are only three great statesmen in the world: Stalin, myself and Mussolini. Mussolini, the weakest, has not been able to break with either the power of the crown or of the church. Stalin and I are the only ones that see only the future." It was this kind of reasoning that was used on both sides, by Ribbentrop and Molotov, in negotiating the non-aggression pact of 1939. Much of it was of course artificially fabricated; but there was enough of the truth in the analogies of the two systems to make fabrication not too difficult.

From the United States the Nazi movement borrowed a few German-Americans, individuals like Ernst Ludecke and Ernst "Puzzy" Hanfstangel, a Harvard alumnus who was one of the first larger financial contributors to the movement and who became chief of the Foreign Press Division of the party and "court pianist" to the Fuhrer until he fell into disgrace. More important was the influence of American advertising on the techniques of propaganda developed by the Nazi machine. "What would one think of a soap ad which also recognised the value of other soaps? wrote Hitler in *Mein Kampf,* and the same, he concluded, must also be true for political pronouncements. American revisionist literature on the causes of World War I and on the ills of the Treaty of Versailles was translated into German and became important and weighty grist for the mills of Nazi propaganda. Most important of all was the dissemination of Henry Ford's *The International Jew* Baldur von Schirach, former Nazi Youth leader, told psychologist Dr. Gilbert in Nurnberg how at the age of seventeen someone made him read Ford's antisemitic tract. "You have no idea," said von Schirach, "what a great influence this book had on the thinking of the German youth, who did not have the maturity to think for itself." And he told the court at Nurnberg: "I read Henry Ford's book *The International Jew* ... and became antisemitic." Not that antisemitism in Germany had to be imported from the outside - the antisemitic tradition in Germany was much older than contacts with either Russia or the United States, and Nazi antisemitism would, of course, have developed without the stimulus from abroad. But Ford's tract, like the *Protocols* imported from tsarist Russia, nevertheless served to provide "literary" food as well as authority and prestige for Nazi doctrine.

The question as to the role of ideology in the history of National Socialism has been the subject of interesting speculation. Official Nazi spokesmen always vaunted their *Weltanschauung,* and the word Geist was one that fell most frequently from their lips. Hitler's *Mein Kampf* devotes a substantial part of its contents to what might be called "ideology". The works of Feder, Rosenberg, Darre, and Count von Reventlow were intended to provide the movement with an official ideology, and these were supplemented by regular publications like the *Nationalsozialistische Monatshefte* and the *Nationalsozialistische Bibliothek* that served as the ideological organs of the party. On the other hand, one of the keenest interpreters of Nazism, Hermann Rauschning, insists that ideology meant little to the Nazi movement. According to Rauschning the so-called "doctrine" of National Socialism was intended only as a facade for the masses. The elite of the party made use it just for their own purposes. He points out, and rightly so, that *Mein Kampf* was a dull book and difficult to plod through and that while it sold in millions of copies - largely through official pressure—it was merely a symbol and a literary ornament in the home, and was little read. The same held true even more so in the case of the works of Rosenberg and Darre. According to Rauschning the leaders of the Nazi movement did not have slightest idea of what they were going to do after they were in power. All they had was boundless confidence. They had "an open mind and no program at all," says Raunschning. The National Socialist philosophy was mainly the "grafting of all sorts of different fruits on the stem of the common crab-apple planted at the time of its first meetings in ... the beer house in Munich." These fruits came from the Vaterlandspartei, from Pan-German racialism, socialism, traditionalism, nationalism, Prussianism, and so on. And the programs always abounded in generalities so that any and every group could read into it whatever it wanted - farmers, workers, industrialists, small shopkeepers, youth, and so on. "Concrete promises divide, generalities unite." Hitler was the man with the authoritarian panacea that was cut to fit all malcontents. Such too is the interpretation held by another ex-Nazi, Ernst Niekisch.

Every movement which exercises power by means of naked force is bound sooner or later to sacrifice whatever ideology it possesses to the needs of maintaining itself in power. This was true of communism in the U.S.S.R. and this also was true of Nazi ideology. To take but one instance: the doctrine of racialism - considered to be the pivot of the entire movement, in which the element of constancy and permanence was the very core of the doctrine. It was subjected to compromise from almost the very beginning of the Nazi movement. It was only in tiny islets of uncontaminated population between the Elbe and the Wester rivers that "racially pure" Nordics were to be found. It was to be the purpose of Nazism to create the elite leadership for the rule of Germany from these "Pure Nordic Germans " and to breed them to become eventually the sole population of Germany. But as the Nazi party grew into a mass party it became impossible to ten millions of followers that they were racial mongrels and inferior. This highly "refined " form of racialism, therefore, was abondoned and the terms "Aryan " and "Nordic" were applied to all Germans as the superior race. In the same way the term "Non- Aryan" soon came to be identified exclusively with "Jew", and honoured positions were found in Nordic racialism first for the Mediterranean Italians and then for the yellow race of Japan.

Despite all of Hitler's scorn for the multi-national empire of the Hapsburgs and despite his repeated declarations that he wanted Germany only for Germans, yet when his aggressive designs demanded it in March 1939, he marched into Prague and made Bohemis and Moravia with their Czech population not a puppet state like Slovakia, but an integral part of the Greater German Reich. Furthermore, when the long years of war created a serious crisis in the supply of labor the racial doctrine was thrown completely to the winds and thousands of Ukrainian and Russian women were brought into Germany to be mated with German men in order to replenish the German labor supply. A document of September 4, 1942, introduced in the Nuremberg trial, tells of an order by Hitler to import 400,000 to 500,000 domestic workers between the ages of 15 to 35 from the Ukraine. The criteria of selection was to be their "conduct and physical appearance." The Fuhrer had explained that "we have to review our school knowledge about people's migrations." The Germans, he declared, had spread far into the East, hence the great number of blond-haired and blue-eyed individuals in the Ukraine." These "descendants of Germans" were to be "re-Germanized" and to receive the same treatment as Germans.

It is, therefore, true that Nazi ideology was always subject to being sacrificed to the needs of power. It is also true that its program was of such a general character as to permit the most diverse groups to read into it their own interests. Within the framework of a supreme devotion to the cause of militant nationalism and a lukewarm regard for other things, it was possible to read many things into the program. But it was not possible to read anything and everything into the party ideology. One could not find place in Nazi ideology for the humane virtues of the Sermon on the Mount, for the principles of the French and American resolutions, for democratic parliamentary government, for the principles of toleration and humanity, for the ideas of international co-operation and the dreams of world peace, for their economic or political liberalism, for Locke's rights of the individual, for scientific ridicule of racism, for modern art, for advanced views on education and for Freudian theories of sex. There was no room at all in the Nazi movement for Jews, Freemasons, Jehovah's Witnesses, pacifists, liberal democrats or futurists. On the other hand Nazi literature showed a fairly constant stress on antisemitism, on nationalism, on the glory of the soldier, on authority, and on the supreme place of force in social relations. The Nazi collection of villains in German history included Erzberger, Kurt Eisner, Rathenau, the *Frankfurter Zeitung*, Feud, and Magnus Hirschfeld. The Nazi roster of heroes in German history almost always listed Arminius and Widukind, Luther, Frederick the Great and Bismarck, Fichte, Friedrich List and Adolf Wagner, Legarde, Houston Chamberlain, Nietzsche and Spengler, Schlageter and Horst Wessel.

Thus it can be seen that ideology was much more developed and occupied a much more significant role in German National Socialism than in Italian fascism. But it did not occupy the same position of dogmatic authority nor did it receive the same degree of technical and scholarly implementation that Marxism received in the Communist dictatorship in Russia. And Nazi ideology was always subservient to the dynamic character of the movement. Rauschning is altogether on sure ground when he points to this dynamic nihilism as being the essential core of the Nazi movement. In the fundamental mainsprings of the movement it was "action pure and simple, dynamics *in vacuo*, revolution at a variable tempo, ready to be changed at any moment." There was the nihilistic destructionism driven by an insatiable dynamism and a thirst for extension of spheres of action and power that knew no bounds or end. This was what Neville Chamberlain and the Munich apologists never understood. They thought they were dealing with diplomats who had certain aspirations which, even though exaggerated and far-reaching in character, could nevertheless be negotiated and eventually satisfied. They did not understand that they were dealing with a movement that was bent on first revolutionizing the world and then conquering it. Nazi demands could never be satisfied because "being satisfied" ran counter to the entire spirit of the movement. This is what the psychiatrist rightly terms the paranoid character of the movement. For it is of the very essence of the paranoiac to be possessed of desires for power that are limitless and insatiable. This is what the conventional diplomats could not understand and why they thought they could stop German expansionism by making concessions, usually at the expense of the smaller nations. It did not work. One Nazi triumph only started a chain of new desires and new demands. The twelve years of Nazi rule saw a succession of hopes and expectations pinned upon the more "respectable" elements to tame and contain the Nazi revolution. First it was Hugenberg and von Papen and the conservative nationalists who engineered the delivery of power to Hitler on January 30, 1933, that were to hold Hitler in check then it was Hindenburg and the Reichswehr then Gergor Strasser and the "socialist" Nazis, or Goering and the "moderate" Nazis. All these hopes proved to be illusory. The dynamism of the Nazi movement overwhelmed all these attempts.

National Socialism represented the most extreme manifestation of the twentieth century revolt against reason. Its basic psychological character was anti-intellectualism. Instead of reason, it founded its entire ideological structure on the appeal to emotion and the appeal to force. "We suffer today from over-education," declared Hitler. "What we need is instinct and will". And in the *Mein Kampf* elaborating his approach toward mass propaganda, he wrote:

"It is more difficult to undermine faith than knowledge, love succumbs to change less than [to] respect, hatred is more durable than aversion, and at all times the driving force of the most important changes in this world has been found less in a scientific knowledge animating the masses, but rather in a fanaticism dominating them and in a hysteria which drove them forward."

The language used by Nazi orators and writers was permeated with words and phrases intended to evoke stirring and violent emotional reactions - *Sturm, rasen, erwache'. Kraft, Glaube, Opfer,* and above all *Schicksal* - the vocabulary of religious revivalism turned political. "*What* does it mean to be a National Socialist? asked Goebbels in his little catechism *Der kleine ABC des Nationalasozialismus*. And his answer was: "To be a National Socialist means nothing else but *Kampf, Glaube, Arbeit, Opfer*" (struggle, faith, work, sacrifice). National Socialist speeches were usually very long, sometimes lasting as much as four to five hours. It was necessary to develop ways of maintaining the hearers in a fever pitch. Symbols like the Swastika, banners, medals, uniforms, and parades, were used profusely to stimulate emotional reacations. Such emotional appeals were especially effective in winning over a large section of the German women voters. The girls and women flocked in droves to see and admire the Nazi formations in uniform more than to listen to the oratory.

National Socialism, with all its moral nihilism, also knew how to appeal to the idealistic impulse for sacrifice. It was, as a matter of fact, the only large political movement in Germany that gave evidence of genuine idealistic, even though perversely misguided, sacrifice. "The monarchy", declared Hitler in one of his early speeches, "died because not one of its monarchs ... was ready to die fighting on the steps of the throne. Hitler was right. No one was ready to die for democracy in Germany. All the idealistic will to sacrifice seemed to be concentrated on the Right. This not only gave the movement internal strength but also served to attract a wider and larger following.

With the rejection of reason as the instrument of social action, the only alternative was the acceptance of force. This was not only put into practice by the Nazis but also made an essential element of their doctrine. It was not power (*Macht*), but concrete physical force (*Gewalt*) that they accepted in true Machiavellian style." The first condition for success", wrote Hitler, "lies in the constant and uniform application of force". Force, he said, following Machiavelli, must be used consistently and with perseverance in order to prevent the suppressed group from reviving and drawing new sustenance from its persecution.

The Nazi dictatorship can be understood in its deeper meaning only if it is realised that this was not a dictatorship of a small clique, but one that rested on a wide mass basis. The question as to whether or not the masses involved constituted a majority of the German population, whether they were 49 per cent or 51 per cent, is not too significant. What is significant is that the Nazi dictatorship, even more than its fascist counterpart in Italy, rested on the following and support of millions of people who represented a true cross section of the German population. It was, in the deeper historical sense of the term, a product of the mass democratic society of the twentieth century.

The Nazis, therefore, displayed a sort of ambivalent attitude toward the masses. On the one hand they concentrated their propaganda on winning over the masses. This was what Goebbels called the "conquest of the streets". The street, wrote Goebbels, "is the characteristic feature of modern politics. Whoever conquers the street can also conquer the masses, and whoever conquers the masses thereby conquers the state." This was the task that Goebbels set himself when he became Berlin gauleiter. With the aid of the S.A. and the Nazi press he did indeed carry out his task with a great measure of success. The appeal for mass support continued to be used most effectively after the seizure of power in the demagogic plebiscites that were staged after decisions on major aspects of home and foreign policy had already been carried out.

Parallel with this appeal for mass support, however, Nazi ideology displayed an open disdain for the masses. It attacked political democracy and popular government, heaped ridicule on majority rule and presented instead the conception of the rule of an elite, capped by the dominant position of the Fuhrer. The very masses that were cajoled and wooed were told in the same breath that they were incapable of deciding for themselves what they wanted and what was to be done. And the amazing fact was that the Nazi masses accepted this role with approbation. The belief inculcated in the German people since the debacle of 1848, that they were incapable of governing themselves, now bore monstrous fruit.

The organisation of the S.A. and the S.S. served to gather the elite during the period of the party's struggle for power, and the special Adolf Hitler schools and other S.S. institutions were set up to train the new elite after the Third Reich came into being. "Energy", wrote Hitler in his first published article, "like everything great, slumbers only in the minority of men." The Germanic principle of leadership, without the help of parliamentary majorities but with the Fuhrer's intuitive perception of the will and needs of the people, was set up in contradiction to the "Western" conceptions of popular government derived from Locke and the French revolution. De Tocqueville's clairvoyant prediction in 1835 of the way in which industrialized and technological democracy would result in the establishment of a new type of despotism came to be realized a century later in Nazi Germany.

Propaganda, next to physical coercion, was thus necessary for the appeal to and the control of the masses. Propaganda, wrote Hitler in *Mein Kampf*, was not intended for intellectuals but for the masses. It should be designed to influence the feelings rather than the understanding. People react to feelings, and feelings, said Hitler, are not complex but simple. There is always one positive and one negative, love or hate, right or wrong, true or false, never half and half. Two things impressed Hitler: the failure of imperial Germany to use propaganda effectively during World War I as compared with British propaganda, and the effective techniques for influencing the masses developed modern advertising. From these he learned to cultivate the most diabolical methods for mass suggestion. Goebbels later became the master propagandist and the first minister for propaganda in the cabinet of the Third Reich.

Nazi propaganda technique also made it necessary to set up enemies and scapegoats on whom to heap abuse and ridicule and especially on whom to place the blame for all of Germany's troubles. The entire world was Germany's enemy, and the geography books continued to define Germany as "a country surrounded on all sides by enemies." But propaganda required more specific and more concrete objects of hatred. A whole series of "enemies" was discovered or manufactured. There were the "November criminals" and the perpetrators of the "stab in the back", there were the Marxists and the international capitalists; there were the pacifists and the internationalists; there were the Freemasons and the Papist clericals and there were, above all, the Jews. The Jews became the scapegoat par excellence of the movement; they were responsible for anything and everything that worked counter to Nazi ideals, and antisemitism became the pivot of the whole totalitarian structure of the Third Reich. Antisemitism served as the vehicle not only for the consolidation of power at home but as the instrument of Nazi foreign policy by means of which it was able to stir up discontented elements abroad and find a basis for support in all parts of the world. Antisemitism as an old, deeply rooted and ubiquitous phenomenon in the Western world could serve better than anything else to galganize and diffuse pro-Nazi sentiment throughout the world. The Nazi slogan "without a solution of the Jewish problem there is no salvation for mankind" could find sympathetic ears among unscrupulous malcontents everywhere.

The Jew, in Nazi ideology, was the embodiment of all their enemies, all rolled into one. He was the "November criminal" and the traitor; he was both a Marxist and an international capitalist; he was a pacifist and an internationalist; he was a Freemason and, if not a clerical himself, the ally and partner of the clericals. He was above all the debaser of the purity of the German race.

Nazi antisemitism received alleged "Scientific" foundation and was biologically grounded in Nazi racialism. This meant two things: a premium placed upon"purity" of race and dogmatic belief in the undisputed superiority of the so-called Nordic or Aryan race. All civilizations of the past, according to Nazi doctrine, decayed and disappeared because of race mixture. All that is creative in all phases of human endeavor is the product of the Aryan race, the "Prometheus of humanity" and the "founder of culture", as Hitler called it. The cultivation of racial purity, therefore, was, according to Hitler, the real end and purpose of the state. It is a common error to suppose that Nazi ideology followed Hegel in setting up the power of the state as an end in itself and for itself. The Nazi *Weltanschauung*, wrote Hitler in *Mein Kampf*, "sees in the state principally only a means to an end and conceives this end to be the preservation of the racial existence of man." The mission of the German state was to gather and preserve the "most valuable of the original racial elements and gradually and securely to bring them up to the dominant position in the state." The state "must place race as the central point of the life of the community and must guard the preservation of its purity."

Almost all of the Nazi racial doctrine was taken bodily from the writings of Gobineau, Schemann, and in particular from Houston Stewart.

45

Civil War in Spain (1936)

"The Spanish Civil War might not, in other circumstances have been an international event. The causes which made it one were of two kinds. In the first place, Italy fresh from her Abyssinian victory, which had thrown into relief the strategic importance of the Mediterranea, welcomed an opportunity to strengthen her position in Western Mediterranean waters. Secondly the notion had grown up since the first world war that a country whose internal organisation was based on a certain political theory was expected to encourage and assist the triumph of that theory in other countries."

E.H. Carr

Introduction

Spain formed a part of the Roman Empire before it was conquered by the barbarians in 406 A.D. In 720 A.D it passed under Arab Muslims and remained under their domination till 1492. By 16th century she developed into a first rate power and became a rival of England in the race of colonisation. But due to her internal conflicts and convulsions her decline started and during the next three hundred years she remained a third-rate power. With the dawn of the present century Spain began to consolidate herself. When the war broke out Spain remained neutral, though the population was divided in its support of the two parties. While the clergies, army, bureaucracy, etc. had pro-German leanings, the intellectuals and the working classes were pro-Allies. The policy of neutrality during the First World War proved beneficial for Spain.

Issues Involved in the Spanish Civil War

Spain has a peculiarly unfavourable soil for the growth of parliamentary institutions because she lacked a strong middle class which traditionally formed the backbone of representative institutions. Though Spain remained neutral during the First World War, political corruption, illiteracy and revolutionary conspiracies made the parliamentary institutions unworkable in Spain, and prospects of democratic regime became slender. The crisis was further aggravated when the Spanish army was defeated by the Riff tribes in the battle of Anual in 1921. The people of Spain held King Alfonso XIII responsible for this defeat. In 1923 General de Rivera, the military governor of Catalonia, staged a military *coup d'etat* and seized power as President of the Military Directorate.

In 1931, Rivera's rule became unpopular and in the municipal elections of April 12, 1931, the Socialist Republican Party gained majority and its leader Zamora demanded abdication of the King. In the face of mounting demand King Alfonso abdicated the throne on April 14, 1931 and a democratic republic was established. But as Spain never had a strong democratic tradition, from 1931 to 1936, democracy was able to maintain itself by a somewhat precious balance between royalists and other reactionaries on the Right and anarchists and Communists on the left. During this period the finances of the country were in chaotic condition and the public order was very frequently threatened.

Taking advantage of the internal dissensions in July, 1936, General Franco, the commander of the troops in Spanish Morocco, raised the banner of revolt against the government, and crossed into Spain with an army. The army was mainly composed of the Moorish troops. He overran the extreme south and the whole of western Spain without much opposition. In October, 1937 the capital of Spain was moved from Valencia to Barcelona which implied that the fall of the government seemed imminent. In January, 1937 even Barcelona fell to the rebels. During the war thousands of loyalists were done to death and the whole of spain passed under the authority of Franco. By April, 1939 the civil war came to an end.

Before examining the attitude of the various powers towards the Spanish war, it is desirable to know its significance. In the words of *Carr*, "The Spanish Civil War might not in other circumstances, have been an international event. The causes which made it one were of two kinds. In the first place Italy, fresh from her Abyssinian victory, which had thrown into relief the strategic importance of the Mediterranean, welcomed an opportunity to strengthen her position in Western Mediterranean waters. Secondly, the notion had grown up since the first world war that a country whose internal organisation was based on a certain political theory was expected to encourage and assist the triumph of that theory in other countries."

Attitude of Italy and Germany

Italy and Germany treated the Spanish Civil War as a struggle between communism and Fascism and decided to support the rebels. Soon after Franco's rebellion Italian soldiers poured into Spain to fight on the side of the rebels. Italian aeroplanes assisted him in the transportation of his troops from Morocco. Likewise Germany contributed thousands of aviators and technicians to France. In short they did everything within their power to overthrow the democratic government.

But it would be wrong to assume that Italy and Germany decided to support Franco solely on ideological grounds. Their self-interests also warranted this action. As Italy wanted to consolidate her position in the Mediterranean, a friendly Spain could be of much help to her in eliminating the British and French control of Western Mediterranean. The Spanish promise of bases in Europe, Africa, Spain, and the Canaries Islands was also helpful to Italy to weaken the grip of Britishers on the straits of Gibraltar. Germany saw in the emergence of Spain under Franco, the problem for France of keeping watch on all her frontiers. This would reduce her position. Germany also expected to get bases from where she could check the British fleet in the Atlantic.

Attitude of Great Britain and France

While Italy and Germany did everything possible to establish Fascist regime in Spain, France and England were keen to follow the policy of neutrality and localise the Spanish conflict. Both these powers treated the Spanish war an internal matter of Spain and set up an "International Non-Intervention Committee" consisting of UK, France, Germany, Italy and Portugal. The Committee was to ensure that powers did not supply war material to either side. But this agreement proved ineffective. While Italy and Germany continued, more or less openly, to send arms to the insurgents, Soviet Union sent the same to the government.

The attitude of 'neutrality' on the part of England and France was also dictated by their national interests. Both these countries had started feeling that Fascism alone could counter Communism and therefore, favoured the rise of Franco to power. Further, England sought to safeguard her control over Gibralter by appeasing Franco. As France wanted to win over Italy's friendship against Germany and Italy was supporting Franco, France was left with no other choice but to follow the policy of non-interference.

Attitude of Soviet Union

Of all the Big powers, Soviet Union alone supported the Spanish government. She did this not because she had much sympathy for the Spanish Government but because she was dreadful of the rise of Fascist regime in Spain. Further, she wanted to baffle the designs of Hitler and Mussolini. But Russia, unlike Italy and Germany, did not send any regular troops to Spain to fight on the side of the government. She only offered to sell arms for "cash on the board". But as Spanish government had not much of money, it could not procure sufficient arms from Russia. But it cannot be denied that on many occasions the Spanish government was able to smash the plans of the rebels only with the support and equipments of Russia.

Attitude of USA

America adopted an attitude of isolation in the Spanish war. But as a rich capitalist country America welcomed the emergence of Fascist states in Europe, which could counter the Communist menace. This attitude of USA is evident from the incident of 1938 when the Italian bombers aided the Spanish capital, Patrick Cardinal Hayes publicly prayed for the success of General Franco.

Attitude of the League of Nations

The attitude of the League of Nations was as unhelpful to the Spanish government as that of England and France. In fact League could not be anything more than what London and Paris would make of it. On a number of appeals from the Spanish Government, the League adopted a resolution on December 12, 1936 calling upon all Members to refrain from interference in the internal affairs of another state. Not where a reference was made to Spain, although it could be implied so. However, the Assembly of the League adopted a resolution on October 2, 1937 which declared that there were 'veritable foreign corps on Spanish soil' and urged upon the members to immediately and completely withdraw them. This resolution of the Assembly had no effect because Italy and Germany refused to withdraw their volunteers, and the rebels continued their conquest of Spain. The volunteers of Italy and Germany left Spain only few weeks after Franco and his rebels had won a decisive victory.

Recognition of New Regime

Italy and Germany had accorded recognition to the Franco government as back as November 18, 1936. Subsequently these powers had also pleaded for grant of belligerent status to the rebels, with a view to impose an effective blockade upon Loyalist ports and deprive the Spanish government of all assistance from abroad. The Franco regime was recognized by England and France on February 27, 1939 and USA on April 1939. Soon after these democratic powers rushed with aid and loans to the Franco regime.

Consequences of Spanish Civil War

The Spanish Civil War had far-reaching consequences. In the first place, the attitude of the Western Democracies convinced Hitler and Mussolini that the western countries were scared of Communism and war. This encouraged Italy and Germany to go ahead with their programme of conquests. Secondly, the failure of the League to deal with the Italian and German interference in the internal affairs of Spain, not only undermined the prestige of the League but also gave a blow to the system of collective security.

From the above it is evident that the Spanish Civil War *"assumed many of the aspects of a European Civil War fought on Spanish territory"*, Carr. While considerable number of Italians and German troops were fighting on the side of the insurgents, the contingents of Russians, anti-Fascist Italians and anti-Nazi Germans, as well as volunteers from other countries were fighting on the side of the Spanish government. The participation of Italy, Russia, Germany and Portugal in the Spanish Civil war was not dictated by ideological motives alone. The interests of these powers were the main motivating force. While Italy saw in a friendly Spain the possibility of checking British naval power in the Mediterranean, Germany saw in it the reduction of French forces on the Franco-German frontiers. Russian motives are less implicit. The chief reason for the Russian support of Spanish Government was that Franco was being supported by the Germans. The policy of neutrality followed by France and England, and the policy of isolation followed by USA in this war, were also dictated by self-interests of these countries. But the results of the war demonstrated that all these powers had miscalculated the future and wasted their energies. Though Spain sympathised with the Axis powers during the Second World War, she on the whole observed neutrality.

However, it would not be wrong to say that Spanish Civil War of 1936 was a trial baloon of international power politic which was to usher in the thunderous outbreak of the Global War of 1939.

46

Japan Since the Advent of the West

The early history of Japan cannot be separated from legend and mythology. These legends are contained in the two chronicles Kojiki and Nihongi or Nihanshoki. They reveal that the Japanese Islands were created by the Heavens. The Japanese particularly attribute it to the Sun Goddess, Ametersau and her brother Susanoo. The latter is said to have descended to Silla in Korea and sailed to Izumo in Japan. In Japan he initiated his line of kings, according to the legend.

The eminent scholar Will Durant states that according to the oldest historical records of Japan their ancestors were Gods. The two Gods Izanagi and Izanami, brother and sister, were commanded by the senior Gods to create Japan. So they stood on the floating bridge of Heaven and thrust down into the ocean a jewelled spear and held it aloft in the sky. The drops of water that fell from the spear formed into the sacred Islands. Izanagi and Izanami mated and as a result Ameterasu, the Sun Goddess was born. "From her grandson Ninigi sprang, in the divine and unbroken lineage, all the emperors of Dai Nippon." Hence Japan came to be described as the land of the Rising Sun. From that day there has been the only imperial dynasty in Japan. However the historical period of Japan may be dated from 400 A.D. Many historical events of this period have also been testified by the Chinese annals and Korean records. Thereafter chronology of the Japanese history becomes exact. The Emperor ruled Japan with the help of the feudal war lords and the subjects reverted their emperor as the lineal descendent of the Gods.

For a long time the Japanese remained in seclusion. No doubt their culture was influenced by that of the Chinese. Confucianism and Buddhism spread into Japan through Korea. But the Japanese maintained their own social and political institutions in a distinct manner. They did not welcome the foreign elements all through their history until the advent of the West.

The Advent of the West

By the middle ages Japanese administration was controlled by several powerful clans. Among them the Satsuma, Choshu and the Tokugawa clans were the most powerful. There were the Daimyos or the Feudal lords, who controlled the agricultural economy. The Samurai were the military class and they exercised sufficient force. There were also the Bakufu who formed the court of the Shogun and were practically managing the entire Japanese trade. Under these conditions the Tokugawa clan became powerful and created its Shogunate or the military dictatorship in the name of the Emperor. The Shogun was the supreme military dictator who guided the destiny of the nation. Yedo, modern Tokyo, became the seat of the Government of the Shogun and that of the Bakufu or the Court of the Shogun. The Mikado or the Emperor had his court nobility called the Kuge at Kyoto. Thus the Japanese society under the Tokugawa Shogunate was composed of three important classes: (1) The Kuge or the Court nobles, (2) the Samurai or the military class, and (3) the Heimin or the common people. The Tokugawa clan remained supreme in the political arena of Japan from 1637 to 1854. During this period the Emperor was reduced to the position of a presiding deity. Though the imperial seal was affixed to the ordinances and laws were promulgated in the name of the Emperor, the Shogun was the de facto ruler in Japan. The Tokugawa Shoguns followed a very rigid isolation policy. However, as pointed out by Professor B.R. Chatterji, "the Tokugawa Shoguns gave the Japanese people a sense of discipline and of unity which would prove to be a very valuable asset during the period of transition in Meiji times (1868 to 1912)."

Thus the feudalistic Japan confronted the advent of the West which contributed considerably to the fall of the Shogunate. The Dutch were perhaps the first European traders to maintain contacts with the Japanese. Their influences prevailed at Nagasaki. Some of the Japanese were able to learn through them about the western civilization. There were attempts on the part of other European powers to obtain access to the shores of Japan.

The American shipping activity increased in the North Pacific after they discovered gold in California from where the American ships were steaming towards the treaty ports of China. In 1853 an American squadron was sent under Commodore Party to the Uraga Bay near Yedo. The American steamships demonstrated their superiority to the Japanese. Commodre Perry handed over a letter from the American President to a Japanese high official and returned after warning that he would be back the next year for the Japanese reply. This produced a great conservation in Japan. Both the Shogun and the imperial court were alarmed. Finally, the Shogun concluded a treaty in 1854, which was ratified by the emperor later on.

This treaty, however, did not provide for the opening of the Japanese mainland for USA. It was agreed for the repatriation of the shipwrecked sailors and supplying the provisions for the ships of USA. According to this treaty Japan opened the two ports of Shimoda near Yedo and Hakodate on the northern Island. It was also agreed to set up an American consulate at Shimoda. The American trade was to be governed by the local regulations and supplies for vessels were to be purchased through the Japanese officials only. By 'the most-favoured-nation clause' the Japanese guaranteed to the Americans any concessions that might be extended to other countries. England, Russia and Holland also obtained similar treaties two years later. After this Townsend Harris, the US Consul-General succeeded in securing another full-fledged treaty in 1857. According to if the American citizens were privileged to reside in the treaty ports. Nagasaki was opened for the Americans. Japan also granted the right of extra-territoriality to the Americans. The customs duties on the foreign goods were to be regulated by the treaty of 1858.

Anti-foreign sentiments developed very soon in Japan. The Satsuma and Choshu Daimyos who were powerful among the western feudal groups fomented these feelings. They did not endorse the action of the Tokugawa Shogun regarding the admission of the foreign elements. They attacked the American, Dutch and French ships in the Straits of Shimonoseki obeying-an Edict issued by the Emperor without the knowledge of the Shogun. On this the combined foreign squadron bombarded the forts at Shimonoseki. The ships of the Daimyos were destroyed.

Though this incident cowed down the most powerful Daimyos who opposed the foreign intervention, it produced far reaching consequences in the history of Japan. The Tokugawa Shogunate was terribly shaken by the rising anti-foreign sentiments. The nationalists demanded the Shogun to renounce his powers in favour of the Emperor. Accordingly the Tokugawa Shogunate came to an end when the last of the Shoguns resigned on 14 October 1867. The Emperor by an imperial decree declared the office of the Shogun abolished. Thus the dual government came to an end and the real power was transferred from the Bakufu to the Emperor. This was a conspicuous milestone in the history of modern Japan.

The MEIJI ERA

The end of the Shogunate was achieved in a dramatic manner. The Emperor Komei died in 1867. He was succeeded by his son Mutsuhito, a boy of fifteen years. All the clans opposed to the Tokugawa Shogunate united themselves under the leadership of the Satsuma chief. The Satsuma Choshu and Hizen clans supported an enlightened Daimyo of Tosa to submit a memorandum to the Shogun demanding him to restore the administration to the Emperor. The memorial stated that "the cause of our trouble lies in the fact that the administration proceeds from two centres... You should restore the governing power into the hands of the sovereign and so lay a foundation on which Japan may take its stand as the equal of other countries." Accordingly the last of the Shoguns, Keiki summoned the important Daimyos and declared that "the laws cannot be maintained in face of the daily extension of our foreign relations unless the government be conducted by one head, and I propose, therefore, to surrender the whole governing power into the hands of the Imperial Courts." This was followed by his resignation in November 1867. Though some of his followers revolted, they were suppressed. But it may be noted that the overthrow of the Tokugawa Shogunate, however, did not expel the foreigner. It only resulted in the restoration of the Emperor in Japan. All the Daimyos and the Samurai renounced their age old feudal privileges in the interests of the nation. This demonstrated the fact that the Japanese always stood for sacrifice in the interests of their nation.

The Emperor Mutsuhito, who inaugurated the new era, came to the throne on 25 January 1868. He was an enlightened monarch. Therefore, his reigning period from 25 January 1868 to 30 July 1872 came to be called 'The Meiji era' (Enlightened peace) in the history of Japan. Under him Japan achieved political and constitutional development. Close relations were maintained with the foreigners. Progress was achieved in the economic, intellectual, educational and literary fields. The administrative machinery was reorganised. Formerly the Emperor had delegated all the administrative powers to the Bakufu. Now a ministry was set up to act as an advisory council. An attempt was made to create an assembly composed of the Samurai and the Kuge nobles.

The Emperor, Mutsuhito, shifted his capital from Kyoto to Yedo (Tokyo) in 1868. The Emperor took the 'Charter oath' before his court and an assembly of the Daimyos. By this oath Mutusuhito promised a deliberative assembly, and to consult public opinion. But the young Emperor took every care to see that political confusion is not created by introducing the democratic set up all in a haste. Instead His Government sent the promising young men abroad to learn about the secret of the might of the advanced nations. These young men were to form the future national intelligentsia.

Foreign experts were invited to assist the Japanese Government in modernising the various departments. British Naval advisers, French and German officers to reorganise the Japanese army, French legal experts to codify the laws, German agricultural experts and American educationists were employed by Japan. Japanese delegates were sent to obtain a first hand knowledge about the European way of life. Many distinguished students were sent abroad to secure higher education and expert training in different fields.

As already pointed out there were different clans in Japan. They represented the feudal character of the Japanese social and political life. The most powerful among them were the Satsuma, Choshu, Hizen and Tosa clans. The chiefs of these clans demonstrated their patriotism by surrendering the fiefs held by them to the Emperor along with their feudal privileges. They appealed to the Emperor to reorganise these territories under national law and establish unifirmity. The Daimyos of the other clans also followed this noble example in the larger interests of the nation. The Samurai or the warrior class who were serving under different Daimyos encouraged their chiefs in this direction. The Daimyos who sacrificed their fiefs were granted compensation. They invested this money in trade and industry and formed the new capitalist class. Thus feudalism was replaced by a centralised Government both in theory and in practice.

The Emperor Mutushito was only fifteen years old when he came to the throne. But he was endowed with a remarkable personality. The political leaders of the Meiji era were drawn from the 'Satchchito' or the Satsuma, Choshu, Hizen and Tosa clans. These leaders were young and enthusiastic patriots. Their objective was to achieve political stability and military glory. Some years later they came to be divided into two political groups on the basis of their political ideology. One group regarded militarism as their national tradition. They advocated an aggressive foreign policy. Korea, Formosa and some parts of China were coveted by them. They were to be acquired by conquest. The militarists were led by Saigo. The second group staunchly opposed militarism on the ground that Japan was not in a position to risk for the time being. They stood for economic reconstruction at home and consolidating their strength by exploiting the available resources at their disposal. They were for the introduction of social reforms, industrial development and progress of trade and education. In 1870, the Japanese Government sent Saigo and Yamagata to study the various aspects of the military system of the west. By the rich experience he obtained in Europe Yamagata was able to plan the reorganisation of the army on the German model. The Universal Conscription or military training was introduced in Japan. Iwakura, Kido, Okubu and Ito toured Europe and America. In the meantime they had obtained a promise from the leaders at home not to introduce any major reforms. But, it was not kept up.

This resulted in a permanent breach between the two political groups. One was led by Saigo and the other by Kido. Saigo insisted that Korea should be made to open commercial relations with Japan. Russia was interested in Korea. But, Saigo did not hesitate to involve Japan in a war with Russia. By 1873 Iwakura and the other members returned from abroad. They recommended internal reforms. The Emperor accepted them. The imperial designs of Saigo were frustrated and he retired. Later on he was assassinated. In order to avenge his death Okubu, the Home Minister, of the Satsuma clan was assassinated. These developments produced a consternation in the Imperial Guard which formed the National Militia. At this juncture Yamgata, the war minister, of the Choshu clan intervened and the Imperial Guard was brought under control. Henceforth the Choshu occupied a conspicuous place in the Japanese army. The Navy was controlled by the Satsuma clan. The most significant feature in the modernisation of Japan was that the new leaders in their zeal for reforms did not ignore the time honoured traditions. The new reforms did not interfere with their national heritage. The authority of the Emperor as the supreme head of the state was respected.

When the Mikado Mutsuhito attained proper age he evinced greater interest in the affairs of the State. He was known for his excellent discipline and extraordinary common sense. The Meiji Emperor maintained high dignity and integrity.

The Meiji Constitution

The Meiji Era witnessed the constitutional reforms. In the new regime provincial assemblies were advising the Governors. But constitutional changes were not introduced at the centre. Therefore, there was popular agitation demanding constitutional reforms. At this stage Itagaki, a liberal leader came to prominence. He always opposed the influence of the Satsuma and the Choshu clans. He organised a liberal party which aimed at the establishment of representative government. A delegation was sent abroad under Ito in 1882 to study the constitutions of the western countries. Accordingly this delegation found in the German constitution a model to be adopted in Japan. It was their intention to maintain the Emperor as the entire source of authority, while the actual administration was to be carried on by the experienced statesmen.

On these lines the Japanese constitution was promulgated in 1889. The Emperor was at the apex of the government. The new constitution provided for a legislature with two chambers. The Upper chamber was called the House of Peers, constituted by the members elected and nominated by the nobility and the highest tax-payers. The Lower House was constituted by the members elected by a limited male franchise. The Japanese Parliament was to meet at least once in a year. It was to be in session atleast for three months. Provision was also made for summoning a special session to discuss certain important matters. The members of the Parliament enjoyed the privileges of freedom from arrest and freedom of speech. The Parliament was empowered to initiate legislation and no laws were to be passed without its vote. The Emperor as the supreme executive head acted through the Cabinet and the Privy Council.

The Constitution granted by the Emperor was sacred and was not to be amended as it affected the sanctity of the imperial authority. The legislature could exercise such powers as to reject the budget. But the government was authorised to carry on the new budget limited to the sanctions made in the previous year. New taxes could not be levied without the approval of the Parliament. The Parliament was not competent to discuss or vote the expenditure of the Imperial Household. The Emperor exercised the power of veto to suppress any legislation. Imperial ordinances could be promulgated which had the force of Law.

Religious and Economic Conditions

The Meiji Era was known for remarkable progress in the religious, economic and intellectual fields. In the new regime Shintoism was revived. It was the ancient cult of the Japanese. Confucianism and Buddhism which came from China and India in the ancient times also wielded considerable influence in the Meiji Era. However, Buddhism was excluded from ceremonies in the palace. But Shintoism came to be emphasised more vigorously by the state. It was categorised into two. One was the sect Shinto which came to be recognised as only a religion, to be supervised by the Department of Religion. The State Shinto was not a religion but the manifestation of Japanese patriotism. It was under a separate Department. The State Shinto advocated the sanctity of the Imperial Shrines of Ise, the imperial ancestors and the Emperor. It also held the national heroes in high esteem.

There were Confucians, Buddhists and the Roman Catholics in Japan. Though the Japanese persecuted the Christians they had to give up the anti-Christian activities due to the protests from the treaty powers. Evidently the Christian institution rendered invaluable service in educating the Japanese on western lines.

The advent of the west brought about the industrial revolution in Japan. They introduced various factories and westernised the industrial system. Foreign capital helped the industrial agencies of Japan. Some of the families like the Mitsui, Mitsubishi, Sumitomo and Yasuda became the most powerful industrialists. In fact, they were described as the 'Zaibatsu'. The Zaibatsu practically controlled the entire commerce of

Japan. In order to control the flow of foreign capital into Japan the industrial production was so designed that they would be able to effectively compete with the foreign products. The needs of the army and the navy were given priority in the Japanese industrial production. Mining industry, textiles, paper, chemical and ceramic industry progressed remarkably. The Japanese Commerce was greatly expanded. The Japanese products attracted foreign markets very soon.

The growth of commerce and industry was followed by the reforms in currency and banking. During the Meiji period the age old feudal character of the Japanese currency was abandoned and it was completely reorganised to bring about uniformity. Paper currency and the decimal system was introduced on the basis of the American system. Thus the currency system came to be nationalised. The creation of the Bank of Japan resulted in the centralisation of the Banking system. The Bank of Japan alone was authorised to issue notes. This was followed by the establishment of the Yo Kohoma Specie Bank, which was intended to assist foreign exchange and foreign trade. These developments in the banking system promoted the Japanese trade and commerce.

These developments needed an efficient system of the means of communication and transportation. In 1872 the first Government owned railway line was built between Tokyo and Yokohoma. It also aided private companies to construct other railways. In course of time these private owned railways were nationalised. Telephone was introduced in 1877. By 1886 the posts and telegraphs system was very well organised. The earliest steamships were introduced by the foreigners. But the Japanese themselves built the steamers very soon through private companies with the assistance of the state. This helped the growth of naval power of Japan.

In the intellectual field also Japan achieved quick progress. They adopted the western system in their education. A law was passed in 1872 introducing universal compulsory primary education. The next stage in education was secondary schools leading to the University education. Along with the educational institutions run by the State there were also the private schools. Some of them were maintained by the Christian missions. For sometime scholars from abroad were employed in teaching. Valuable works of the western writers on various subjects including science, technology, history and other humanities were translated into Japanese language. Many Japanese western educated gentlemen replaced the foreign teachers in course of time.

The intellectual progress helped the codification of the Japanese laws on western lines. The commercial laws were totally reformed to suit the new conditions. Law courts were reformed and legal luminaries were appointed as judges. The Japanese civil code was promulgated in 1890, the Code of Civil Procedure in 1892 and the Commercial Code in 1899.

JAPAN BECOMES A WORLD POWER

In the history of Modern Japan the revision of the 1858 treaties, concluded with the foreign powers, may be regarded as the first step towards becoming a world power. Japan was in a position to compel the treaty powers to renounce the various concessions she had granted to them. The public opinion in Japan strongly agitated for the withdrawal of all the concessions. A Japanese political mission was sent under Iwakura in 1872 to negotiate a settlement with the west. Among the western powers America was willing to revise its treaty. But the intention of Japan was to convene a conference of all the treaty powers in Europe so that modifications may be effected commonly in all the treaties. This was not agreeable to the United States. However, The Iwakura mission impressed upon the west that Japan has undergone a remarkable change.

At the time of the revision of the Japanese Criminal Code in 1880 an attempt was made to remove the provision of extra-territoriality from the treaties. Several conferences were held to settle this issue. But except the United States no treaty power was willing to surrender this very important privilege. They demanded that provision should be made for the foreign judges to adjudicate the cases in the Japanese courts. In principle an increase in the tariffs was accepted. But they insisted that the rate of tariff be fixed by a treaty. Japan did not agree for these conditions. She came to the conclusion that nothing could be achieved by bringing together all the vested interests to ask them to renounce the privileges which they enjoyed in common. Instead she now followed a policy of negotiating with the different powers separately to effect the revision of the treaties. She concluded a treaty with Mexico in 1889 on the basis of tariff autonomy. It did not contain the provisions regarding the privileges like extra-territoriality, reciprocal freedom of travel, trade and residence as contained in the previous treaties. This was to become the basis for other treaty powers to change their attitude. When the new constitution was promulgated in 1889 some of the foreign powers volunteered to agree for the revision of the conventional tariffs and extra-territoriality. In spite of this diplomatic victory achieved by the minister Okuma by his negotiations he was attacked by the Japanese public opinion.

England had the largest Interests and there were large number of English citizens resident in Japan. She agreed to revise her treaty. Thereby provision was made to end the consular jurisdiction and foreign settlements in Japan by 1899. England was followed by the United States. She agreed to omit the conventional tariff. By this the other powers also were compelled to give up their respective treaties. Thus by 1899 extra-territoriality came to an end in Japan. However, these changes brought about by the revision were not effected on account of the Victory won by Japan in the Sino-Japanese war.

The Sino-Japanese War (1894-1895)

The economic growth and the military development of Japan encouraged her to initiate a policy of territorial expansion after 1894. This was also prompted by the growth of Japanese population. She required the markets for the goods produced by her industries. She was very eager to take a more active part in the international politics. This desire was strongly supported by the intense partiotism of the Japanese.

To start with Japan selected the issue of Korea. There was some agreement between China and Japan regarding Korea. However, when the Russian designs in Korea became patent Japan could not restrain herself any longer. She considered the presence of Russia in Korea a source of constant danger both militarily and commercially. Russia coveted a foothold in southern Korea to maintain a safe passage from Vladivostok to the Pacific. It was always an advantage for Russia to secure the ice-free ports in Korea or North-China which would serve as best outlets to Siberia. The railways and trade routes could be thereby controlled for the Russian commerce in the Far East. By now she had established her influence in the Chinese court. As against these designs of Russia Japan initiated a policy to encourage the reformist party in Korea to strengthen her position. Thus in Korea the reactionary group was supported by China while Japan took sides with the reformists.

Friction arose on the status of Korea whether she was a tributary of China or an independent state. China held that from a very long time Korea was a tributary state under her. Japan argued that Korea enjoyed an independent status. When a rebellion broke out China sent her troops into Korea to suppress it. It was announced to Japan later. According to the convention of 1885 China should have notified her intention to send her troops before hand. Therefore, Japan resolved to send her troops to Korea which was notified to China in advance. In spite of the fact that the said rebellion ended neither Japan nor China withdrew their forces from Korea. Japan proposed a joint effort to reorganise the Government of Korea and to remove the Chaos. This proposal was rejected by China by claiming Korea was her tributary state and not independent.

In spite of the severe warnings from Tokyo China continued to send more troops into Korea. In July 1894 there was an armed clash between the Japanese naval forces and the Chinese reinforcements. This resulted in the outbreak of the Sino-Japanese war.

The intense patriotism of the Japanese prompted them to set aside their internal differences and to consolidate their war efforts against China. This unexpected solidarity of the Japanese frustrated the designs of the Chinese. They were defeated both on land and sea. The Chinese navy, consisting of modern ships, was destroyed. The Japanese captured Port Arthur and Talien. These ports occupied a strategic position on the Liaotung peninsula which commanded access into Manchuria. The Manchurian capital Mukden was threatened by the Japanese. Wei-hai-wei was captured. It was the most important harbour-fortress of Shantung. In this manner Japan came to control the naval approaches to North China and Peking. She also sent an expedition to Formosa and the Pescadores Islands. This successful expedition compelled China to negotiate for peace.

The treaty of Shimonoseki concluded in April 1895 brought the Sino-Japanese war to a close. According to this treaty China formally recognised the complete independence of Korea. She ceded the Liao-tung peninsula in southern Manchuria, Formosa and the Pescadores Islands to Japan. China also agreed to pay a huge war indemnity to Japan. Above all these, she also agreed to open five new ports under the 'most-favoured-nation' clause, including the Yangtze river. By concluding a new treaty China was to concede the status of a 'most-favoured nation' to Japan. Thus Japanese gains in the Sino-Japanese war were extensive which produced great apprehension in the minds of the west.

The European powers, particularly Germany, Russia and France became jealous of Japan's gains. Russia considered that her designs of southern expansion were frustrated and her influence in North China checked. Germany feared that a new era of Asian militarism has begun to replace that of the Europeans. Therefore, Russia and her ally, France protested in Tokyo. They contended that the terms of the Shimonoseki treaty "threatened the peace of the Far East." Germany also sent a protest note to Japan. These factors made Japan to behave cautiously as she had no ally to fall back.

The Japanese public opinion sharply reacted against the treaty of Shimonoseki which was regarded as very mild. When the Liaotung peninsula was taken back by force they felt their national prestige was insulted. However, it strengthened the Japanese desire to claim equality with the west by developing their military supremacy. Therefore, immediately after this the war minister insisted on an extensive naval development programme and reorganisation of the army on the western lines. Japan levied more taxes to secure money to equip the army with the most sophisticated arms and equipment. This new development in Japan strengthened the Satsuma and Choshu groups. All these compelled Japan to follow a policy of imperialism. The world also came to feel the superiority of the Japanese military and their skill in using the arms they obtained from the west. Even then Japan had to wait for the western powers to recognise her as a major power to be reckoned with.

The Russo-Japanese War

Though Japan was forced out of the Liaotung peninsula by the intervention of Germany, France and Russia by 1898 they themselves made slices of the Chinese possessions and shared them. Accordingly Russia secured for herself the Liaotung peninsula along with port Arthur. Kiaochow Bay was taken away by Germany and France obtained a leasehold in the flourishing regions of South China. In order to make the western powers feel the importance of the Japanese military development she accepted the responsibility of protecting the foreign legations in China from the Boxer rebels. This task she completed effectively and won the admiration of the west. This enhanced her prestige in the international level. But the western powers had no mind to equate Japan with themselves.

Japan could not bear this attitude and she became anxious about her boundaries touching Korea where Russian influence became dominant. Two alternatives were left for her now to adopt. One was to enter into partnership with Russia in the Far East. The other course open for her was to give up her policy of 'splendid isolation' and negotiate an alliance with some foreign power. The latter was found to be more suitable. So Japan found her western friend in Britain which was also looking forward for a friend in the East. This was supported by the great military man like Yemagata and Katsura, the Prime Minister of Japan. In 1902 the Anglo-Japanese Alliance was concluded. By this treaty Japan recognised the British interests in China while Britain reciprocated by recognising the position of Japan both in China and in Korea specially. This treaty made a provision for the neutrality of one party when the other was at war with a third power. But in the event of another power joining the hostile camp the neutral power was to join the ally. Japan could now depend upon Britain for help if France or Germany joined Russia with whom Japan was contemplating a war.

Russia had promised that she would withdraw from Manchuria and Korea. But in 1903 she suggested to Japan that Russia would allow Japan to develop her commercial and industrial interests in Korea provided Japan allowed Russia free hand in China. This implied that Japan is denied of her political interests in Korea. At this stage the English statesmen including the Prime Minister Balfour, Admiral Sir John Fisher and Foreign Secretary Lord Lansdowne discussed the possibilities of Japan suffering a crushing defeat in the hands of Russia. The American President Theodore Roosevelt issued a warning to Germany and France that in the event of a combined attack on Japan America would go to the help of Japan. This certainly boosted the morale of the Japanese. Their war efforts were stabilised.

The Russian armies crossed the Yalu River to enter into Korea in February 1904. This was promptly replied by Japan. Her Torpedo boats effectively attacked the Russian warships which were protected by the Guns stationed at port Arthur. Japan declared war against Russia two days later.

Dramatic events followed successively. The Russian flagship was sunk along with its Admiral by a Japanese mine. General Kuroki reached Seoul and the battle of the Yalu River was fought on both the sides vigorously. General Nogi attacked port Arthur which was defended by the Russians desperately. When they were driven out of South Manchuria and Marshall Oyama successfully advanced northwards, the Russian defence broke down. Port Arthur was captured on 1 January 1905 by the Japanese General Nogi at the cost of 20,000 men. In the famous battle of Mukden Russia lost about 150,000 men. This brilliant victory clearly demonstrated the military supremacy of Japan.

These disasters forced Russia to order her Baltic Fleet to move to the Far East in order to obtain the control of the sea. The Japanese Admiral Togo sighted the Russian fleet in the Korean straits on 27 May 1905. He successfully forced the Russian admirals to surrender. One of the three admirals were killed while fighting. This naval engagement has been called the battle of Tsushima. Having found Russia in a miserable position France came out with her proposal to mediate between Russia and Japan on condition that Japan did not insist on the ceding of territory or payment of indemnity from Russia. But Japan invited the American President Theodore Roosevelt to negotiate peace. Accordingly the US President Roosevelt brought about the treaty of Portsmouth in September 1905. Though the Japanese had won brilliant victories on the battle field, diplomatically they lost the battle.

The Japanese who had heard of the glorious victories of their armies were disappointed by the terms of the treaty of Porstmouth. The war time Katsura ministry fell in Japan after this treaty. But evidently the Russo-Japanese war produced far reaching consequences so far as the military prestige of Japan was concerned. The European of powers certainly felt the astonishing military development of Japan as a serious threat to their own military supremacy.

Internal Politics after the Russo-Japanese War

It may be recalled that during the Sino-Japanese war an ordinance was promulgated by the Privy Council of Japan that the Ministers of war and Marine be selected from among the army and naval officers. This strengthened the hands of Yamagata and the Choshu generals and Satsuma admirals who supported him. Yamagata himself was a staunch militarist. It became impossible to form a Cabinet without his consent. Marquis Ito who pioneered an ambitious foreign policy found himself in trouble when the militarists were not agreeable to join the Cabinet unless the budget is military oriented. To get rid of the militarist influence in the Government Ito organised the 'Seiyukai' or the Constitutional Government party. With the support of the Progressive Party Chief Okuma Ito became the Prime Minister. The international situation made Britain to feel the Japanese friendship essential and the Anglo-Japanese alliance was extended in 1905. However, at the instance of America the same was revived again in 1911 which exempted England from aiding Japan in the event of a conflict between America and Japan. At the same time Japan expanded her industry and achieved a remarkable progress economically.

The enlightened rule of the Emperor Mutsuhito came to an end with his demise in 1912. He was a man of great commonsense. By his policy of perseverance Mutsuhito was able to balance the conflicting political forces in Japan. His magnetic personality often influenced the political decisions. For his wisdom the reign period of Mutsuhito came to be called the 'Meiji Era' or the rule of the 'englightened'. He was succeeded by Yoshihito.

Japan During and After First World War

On the death of the Meiji Emperor in 1912 the Japanese oligarchical groups had to disappear from the political arena. Emperor Mutsuhito was succeeded by his son Yoshihito. His reign period came to be called the 'Taisho Era'. But the new Emperor was not fortunate to inherit the brilliant qualities of his father. There was also a gradual move towards a parliamentary constitution. However, there were no effective political parties to command popular support in Japan. Therefore, the militarists had to depend upon the support of the people.

In the reign of Yoshihito the 'Genro' or the 'Elder Statesman' gradually died out. It was mainly due to the assassination of Ito and Yamagatu, who were known for their extraordinary ability. The Emperor gradually became a tool in the hands of the ambitious men who controlled the political and military affairs. However, in the field of industry and commerce Japan derived an advantage over her western counterparts. The Japanese industry was westernised, both in technique and means of production. The Japanese labour was cheap. As such cost of production was very less. This helped the Japanese goods to compete effectively in the eastern as well as western markets. The new trends were responsible to push Japan in the direction of expansion and imperialism.

When the First World War broke out Japan was a developed nation. Her imperial designs had already been well formed. She was powerful enough to maintain her control in her dependencies of Formosa and Korea. In Manchuria also she had developed her interest. As such on the outbreak of the War Japan demanded from Germany in her ultimatum, issued on 15 August 1914, to withdraw from the Sino-Japanese waters and handover all her lease holds to Japan. Thereby Kiaochow Bay and the Shantung province were to be left in the control of Japan.

Under these circumstances the English ambassador met the Japanese Foreign Minister Kato to request the Japanese to destroy the German ships on the Chinese coast. Meanwhile France and Russia also made their intention clear to join the Anglo-Japanese Alliance. These developments resulted in the entry of Japan into the First World War on the side of the Allies on 23 August 1914.

The events of the war in the Far East reveal that Japan conquered the strongholds of Germany in Kioachow Bay. She also captured the German bases Marshalls, Marianas, Carolines and other Pacific islands. A Japanese destroyer force was also sent to the Mediterranean to aid the allies and prevent the submarine activity of the Germans. During the course of the war Britain, France and Russia successively pledged themselves to support the claims of Japan to the Shantung province and the islands north of the equator conquered from Germany. Japan in her turn was to support the claims of England for the German islands to the south of the equator. France desired Japan to pressurise China to declare war against Germany.

Keeping in view her obligations to the Allies Japan prepared the grand plan as to how China could be forced to declare war against Germany. Accordingly in January 1915 Japan presented her Twenty- one Demands to China. Though these demands were classified into five categories the fifth group was not pressed. The other demands purported to give Japan all the rights and concessions enjoyed by Germany in Shantung, Southern Manchuria and Inner Mongolia. The Chinese President Yuan Shi-kai tried to arouse public opinion against these demands of Japan. But he was forced by circumstances to concede them.

The status of Japan in South Manchuria and Inner Mongolia was recognised by Russia by concluding an agreement in 1916. This was followed by the Lansing-Ishii Agreement concluded in 1917. By this USA recognised the special interests of Japan in China. Though doubts were expressed about the implication of "the special interests" for America it was nothing but the reaffirmation of the 'Open Door' policy without prejudice to the integrity of China. But Japan meant entirely something different.

Japan and the Treaty of Versailles

In the earlier discussion it is observed that Japan rose to prominence only by her victories in the Sino-Japanese war and the Russo-Japanese war. Her position in the international level came to be admired for the brilliant work turned out as the protector of the foreign interests in China against the Boxer rebels. When the First World War came to an end Japan got herself ready to participate in the Peace Conference as a major power. It may be pointed out that the Japanese industrial and military advancement was carefully noted by the USA. The American President Woodrow Wilson was very particular to see that China's economic dependence on Japan is reduced by advising the American traders to increase their investments in China. The USA also tried to restrict the Japanese influence by Diplomatic means. But she was forced to invite the Japanese representative Viscount Ishii Kikujiro to Washington in 1917. This was followed by a meeting of Ishii Kikujiro and the American Secretary of State Robert Lansing. They signed the Lansing-Ishii agreement. This recognised the special position of Japan in China. However, after the war America tried to interpret this treaty in a different tone to prevent Japan from gaining special privileges in East Asia. Despite the fact that America was serious in this matter it became evident that Japan was a great power at the peace conference.

So far as Japan was concerned her representatives Baron Makino Nobuaki and Viscount Chinda Sutemi put forward three demands at the Versailles Conference. Firstly, Japan asked for the cession of the Marianas, Carolines, and Marshalls islands in the North Pacific ocean which belonged to Germany formerly. She also demanded the confirmation of her claims to the former rights of Germany in the Shantung province. The third demand of Japan was to issue a declaration regarding the acceptance of the "principle of the equality of nations and the just treatment of their nationals" to ensure racial equality among states as a basic principle of the League of Nations that was in formation. These demands were based on the principle of conquest and possession. It was also backed by the secret treaties signed by the European powers with Japan and also with China in May 1915. However, when China consented to transfer Kiaochow to Japan on condition that Japan would return this leasehold to China by reserving for herself the right for the German economic rights there, all these had legalised Japan's claims for the possession of the Kiaochow province. During the discussions Australia, New Zealand, South Africa, France, Italy and Belgium also demanded for the inclusion of these provinces in their own. China herself desired to possess them. Ultimately the Mandates were created to settle the issue to the satisfaction of the American President. The German islands in the North Pacific came under class 'C' Mandate to Japan while England was to hold the Mandate over the German South Pacific Islands. As regards the 'declaration of racial equality' the vote was divided and not unanimous. Therefore the proposal was defeated. It was followed by a demand of the Chinese delegates for the abrogation of all the treaties of 1915. Thereby "the special position" of Japan in South Manchuria and Eastern Mongolia were affected. Even Shantung was also to be lost. At this stage Japan threatened that she would withdraw from the conference if the demand for Shantung was not met with. Though the gains of Japan were very meagre it may be pointed out that she emerged as one of the Big Five Powers from the Treaty of Versailles. Her prestige was greatly enhanced in the international politics.

JAPAN BETWEEN THE TWO WORLD WARS

The period between the two world wars was momentous in the history of the Japanese people. The Japanese leadership aimed at a positive continental policy to make Japan emerge herself as a great military power in Asia. Her relations with the West during this period clearly reflect her ambition to compel them to accept Japan as their equal in the international politics with particular reference to the Asian continent. To achieve this end and obtain the recognition of the West, Japan launched a policy of military aggrandisement and commercial monopoly with her neighbours. Her activities in Siberia and Manchuria testify this. During this period she also incurred the displeasure of America which passed anti-Japanese immigration laws to restrict the flow of Japanese population into the American mainland. As a result anti-American feeling increased in Japan. It gave a new impetus to their glowing patriotism.

Japan and Siberia

It was the long cherished desire of Japan to establish her influence in Siberia. But Russia was in occupation of it as a strategic area. During the World War Russia was obtaining arms and other equipment of war from Japan. But she was finding it difficult to pay for them often. Therefore, Russia had transferred her railway assets extending from Chang-chun to Harbin. This approached very close to the Siberian frontiers. However, the Russian revolution of 1917 influenced the affairs in Siberia also. When the interim Government summoned the Constituent Assembly Siberian delegates were sent to demand autonomy. But very soon the Bolshevists overthrew the provisional government and they tried to establish Communist influences in Siberia also.

At this stage the foreign powers paid attention to the developments taking place in Siberia. The American Rear-Admiral Knight tried to influence the different groups at Vladivostok and he also suggested an allied action. His suggestions were not implemented. The allies took a serious note of it only when they found Communism establishing its influence. In 1918 Mr. Balfour, in the British House of Commons, called for inviting Japan to intervene in Siberia and prevent the German influences. This was not decided due to the doubts expressed by the American President. On 16 May 1918 Japan entered into an agreement with China in which it was provided for cooperation in mobilising the troops. Accordingly Japan obtained passage for the mobilisation of troops by means of the Chinese Eastern railway. This concession helped an allied intervention in Siberia in the later stages. Though America was disinclined earlier she too endorsed this policy finally. The Japanese armies were sent to Siberia in 1918 following those of America, Britain and France. The allied armies overran up to Lake Baikal in the Eastern Siberia. By 1919 the Russians were defeated. Though in 1920 the troops of America, Britain, Canada and France left Siberia the Japanese War Minister Tanaka resolved to send reinforcements to Siberia. The Japanese Diet vehemently criticised this adventure which involved heavy expenditure. The Japanese had to engage 75,000 troops in this. Russia felt offended and her relations with Japan further deteriorated. However, in 1922 the Japanese troops were finally withdrawn from Siberia. The militarist Terouchi ministry became unpopular in Japan. At the same time her support to the Anfu Clique in Peking and the huge loan advanced to them created suspicion in the international circles. Moreover by the Japanese support to the Anfu Clique, with sinister designs, Japan antagonised the popular opinion in China.

Japan and Manchuria

The rapid growth of the Japanese population posed a serious problem to Japan. Though attempts were made to effect continuous emigration to the neighbouring islands like Chosen, Taiwan and Karafuto it was not possible to meet the problem of rehabilitating millions of Japanese. When Japan established a sort of semi-colonial control in Manchuria the Japanese migrated into this island in large-scale. Along with the rapid growth of population Japan also confronted the problem of securing the markets for the goods produced in her industries. After the First World War the demand for the Japanese products greatly declined. Therefore, Japan had to search for new markets where she could establish her own trade monopoly. These factors forced Japan to turn herself into an imperial power. Her foreign policy, therefore, was reshaped to suit these trends after 1931. Though politically there were divergent opinions among the leaders regarding internal and external policy, it became inevitable to develop a new trend which obtained the shape of a capitalist society. In this, both, the state and the capitalists took interest. The state was interested in developing the new trade for enabling the population to migrate and to obtain markets for the Japanese industrial products. The capitalists were interested in increasing their fortunes. Among them the Sumitomo Company, the Mitsui Company and the Mitsubishi Company were the most flourishing industrial capitalists which even controlled the State to a great extent. By 1932 the Japanese Government came to be supported by the majority political party.

In the meantime the old element in the Army and Navy was replaced by that of the young men belonging to the lesser clans or families of Japan. They were opposed to the policy of a capitalist monopoly. Towards 1930 these elements gained control of the supreme powers. Their success was also due to the fact that the people were fed up with the corrupt old elements. As such the patriotic societies established by the younger generation attracted the masses who expected something radical to happen in Japan. At the very outset, to promote their interests the new societies identified themselves as terrorists. They openly proclaimed 'the policy of military expansion' as their objective. This was a direct blow against the weak foreign policy adopted by the capitalist interests earlier. Therefore, the new elements found an excellent opportunity to force the Government to follow a vigorous foreign policy. Their first act was to point out to the growth of Nationalism in China and to emphasise the need for counteracting the Japanese interests in Manchuria. The assassination of Prime Minister Hamaguchi in 1930 was to serve as the signal for ushering in a new era in the Japanese foreign policy. The supporters of this new trend contended that the return of the Army into power would root out corruption and carry out the policy of territorial expansion in the best interests of the nation. In their view the Army and the Navy was not corrupt. The supporters of the Army leadership employed the Manchurian question as an effective means of propaganda. Thus the Manchurian issue tremendously influenced the Japanese politics.

It may be recalled that in the Washington Conference Japan was compelled to accept the American interpretation of the 'open door policy' and at the same time she signed the League Covenant swearing to respect the independence and integrity of the League members. Article 10 of the league Covenant was deliberately intended to prevent Japan from attempting to take advantage of the internal political situation in China so as to enable the Kuomintang regime to establish itself firmly.

But the post-war economic situation in Japan was adverse. She had to depend upon the foreign markets for the disposal of the goods produced in her industries. In fact the Japanese Foreign Minister, Baron Shidehara openly proclaimed that the Japanese foreign policy should be characterised by the acquisition of foreign markets and not the territory to achieve economic stability. China and the USA were the two important foreign markets with whom Japan traded earlier. But America was no longer interested in the Japanese products after the war. In the case of China the Kuomintang regime was disinclined to oblige Japan. The Peking regime negotiated with Japan for a settlement of their old treaties. However, Japan resolved not to yield to these requests of China. Japan was firm to maintain the rights she enjoyed in Manchuria. For an industrialised Japan Manchuria was found to be indispensable from the economic point of view. The attacks directed by China against the Russians in northern Manchuria were taken to imply that a similar policy to exclude Japan in southern Manchuria would follow. The increasing movement of the Chinese population into Manchuria further confirmed this belief of the Japanese. In China there was an effective propaganda against imperialism to promote national solidarity. After 1929, the situation in Manchuria began to change rapidly. The Nationalist activities of the Chinese produced anti-Japanese feelings. The two incidents pertaining to the status of Koreans in the case of Wanpaoshan and Nakamura further aggravated the situation when the Japanese Consular Police intervened to defend the rights of the Koreans in 1931. A Japanese Army Officer Captain Nakamura was killed by the Chinese in June 1931. The Japanese held that the Chinese showed disrespect to the Japanese army and nation by killing Captain Nakamura. After this incident the Japanese antagonism against China gained greater intensity. The Japanese public opinion favoured a settlement of all the outstanding disputes in Manchuria by applying force, if necessary. At this stage a bomb explosion caused damage to the South Manchurian Railway line. Japan held that it was the work of Chinese soldiers. Though China disowned the onus of having exploded the bomb the Japanese army stationed at Kwantung to protect the Japanese controlled Railways in the three eastern provinces occupied Mukden and the surrounding areas. By successive stages Japan drove out the Chinese from Manchuria by the end of 1931.

The Japanese aggression in Manchuria produced far reaching consequences. China appealed to the League of Nations in this behalf. The League Council despatched the Lytton Commission in 1932 to investigate the entire matter on the spot. When the Lytton Commission arrived in Japan in February 1932 there was a political change. The militarists had been in power in Japan. In spite of the fact that the negotiations were going on at Geneva Japanese armies continued the work of occupation in Manchuria. They set up the local governments in Manchurian provinces and cities. The puppet central government of Manchuria controlled by the Japanese army declared Manchuria an independent republic. Henry Pu-yi, the dethroned Manchu Emperor of China, was invited to head the new regime. They declared that the new state was created by the "will of the liberated people of Manchuria now renamed Manchukuo." Even before the Lytton report could be submitted to the Council of Geneva Japan recognised the new state as a sovereign power in September 1932.

The American Secretary of State Mr. Stimson notified Japan and China that the USA would not recognise the new developments which might prove contrary to the provisions contained in the League Covenant. This was endorsed by the League Assembly in a similar resolution. The efforts of America to make Britain to cooperate in this direction were a failure. This attitude of Britain encouraged Japan to pursue her aggressive policy. However, the Lytton Report submitted in October 1932 held the claims of Japan that "China was not entitled even to titular sovereignty over Manchuria or that the Japanese occupation of the country was an act of defence to protect the life and property of the Japanese resident in that region and to safeguard the South Manchurian Railway as false. The report attributed the establishment of the new state entirely to the Japanese army. The Lytton Report recommended that the existing treaties be respected. The sovereignty of China and the legitimate interests of Japan in Manchuria be recognised. China was to concede autonomy to Manchuria and to safeguard the Japanese interests by concluding treaties between the two countries. The Report further recommended that foreign advisers be appointed by the League to undertake the work of reconstruction in Manchuria. To facilitate their work the area was to be demilitarised. In other words the occupation forces were to be withdrawn by Japan. The League Assembly considered this Report in February 1933 and Japan was censured by a Resolution. But it was not pursued by any of the member Nations. The

League of Nations had already shown the signs of breakdown. Its weakness was patent. As such Japan declared her intention to withdraw from the League on 17 February 1933. In 1935 she also repudiated the Washington agreement which had fixed the Naval ratio of 5:5:3. Thus the Manchukuo was proclaimed an independent state on 18 February 1932.

Domestic Affairs in Japan

The Japanese military adventure in Manchuria produced a sharp reaction in Japan. The entire adventure was planned and executed by the Kwantung army which was no doubt blessed by the Army High Command in Japan. At the very outset the action of the Government was vehemently condemned which resulted in the fall of the Minseito Government in December 1931. The Seiyukai leader, Tsuyoshi Inukai formed the new Government. He was an advocate of a stronger foreign policy. But the same old party politics continued. In the February 1932 elections the Seiyukai party was returned with a considerable majority to the Diet.

The militarists who were unhappy over the reestablishment of party Government in Japan resumed their attempts to overthrow the same. Political murders and assassinations produced a chaotic situation. Many young military officers and students were involved in these terrorist acts. Atlast the premier Inukai was killed on 15 May 1932. It was followed by a non-party Cabinet formed by Admiral Saito with three ministers representing the Seiyukai party and two representing the Minseito party. General Araki was made the War Minister while Korekiyo Takahashi became the Finance Minister. This ministry fell in 1934. Admiral Okada formed the next ministry. He was a staunch believer in the organisation of a strong navy. Naturally, as already pointed out, he repudiated the Washington Agreement, which purported Naval limitation, in 1935. There was a brief respite in Japan until 1936. But the leaders of the Army and Navy were also found joining hands with the capitalists. This favoured the Minseito party to return to power with 205 members in the Diet. The next strong party was the Seiyukai with 174 seats.

The political instability and the influence of the capitalists on the one hand and the militarists on the other, hampered agricultural development in Japan. The capitalists aimed at the industrial prosperity while the militarists stood for a strong foreign policy. This made the agricultural indebtedness to increase to 6,000 million yen in 1936 as against 4,800 million yen in 1932. The farm income amounted to only 2,182 million yen. Though the Government subsidised the farming adequate financial provisions were not made to relieve the peasants from their difficulties. The five year wheat plan was, however, successful. It resulted in the 60 per cent increase in wheat production which enabled Japan to become self-sufficient in wheat. On the other hand there was serious fluctuation in the agricultural income.

No doubt the Japanese industry flourished and the capitalist class invested their wealth to develop the new industrial concerns. The Japanese products obtained a great demand even in the western markets. There was a marked increase in the exports. The Japanese textiles, silk and cotton goods had established monopoly in the western countries like Netherlands, Central America, South America and Latin America until 1936. However, after that Latin America imposed trade restrictions. Moreover the withdrawal of Japan from the League of Nations had made USA and also Britain to isolate Japan gradually. This resulted in an adverse trade balance of Japan. And in fact all of a sudden Japan lost vast markets for her finished goods. Japan was not only affected economically by her aggressive Foreign Policy but also in her relations with her erstwhile allies like Britain and the USA. Therefore Japan had to go in search of new markets for her goods and new allies as well for her political survival. She therefore, gradually moved towards the camp of Central European powers. The militarists who held power in Japan realised in Mussolini and Hitler their allies.

Japan and the Second World War

Before discussing the participation of Japan in the Second World War it is necessary to know something about her activities in China after establishing the Manchukuo. It is needless to point out that there was a civil war in China between the Kuomintang armies led by Chiang Kai Shek and the war lords. There was also the hatred between the Kuomintang regime and the newly founded communist party of China. Under these circumstances Japan tried to exploit the situation and even to grab the entire China. Some of powerful war lords were won over in the provinces of Chahar and Hupei. These areas were brought under the Japanese sphere of influence by 1935. This extended the Japanese influence up to the frontiers of Inner-Mongolia and North-West China. Japan was practically at war with China. But Chiang Kai Shek was busy in suppressing the Chinese Communists rather than terminating the Japanese enemy. Therefore, his own followers who anticipated a major military aggrandisement of Japan in China kidnapped Chiang in 1936 to a secret place where he was made to understand the importance of National defence and solidarity. He was made the Generalissimo or the Supreme Commander of the combined, Nationalist and Communist, armies of China against the Japanese aggression.

It is significant to note that Japan was experiencing a dangerous isolation after her withdrawal from the League of Nations. When Hitler and Mussolini joined hands together and concluded the famous Rome-Berlin Axis, a military treaty, the army leaders in Japan suggested the entry of Japan into this western military treaty to end her isolation. Accordingly, after prolonged negotiations, Japan and Germany concluded the Anti-Commintern Pact in 1936. By this pact the signatories were to act jointly against the progress of Communist International. After this Japan followed a forward continental policy to fulfil her ambitions in the Asiatic regions. To begin with she fought the Second Sino-Japanese war with China. The Japanese and Chinese troops clashed at Marco Polo bridge on 7 July 1937. This war was fought for eight years and ended only when Japan surrendered unconditionally at the end of the Second World War in 1945.

The Second-Sino-Japanese conflict was not expected to result in a major war. The USA tried to intervene and bring about a peaceful settlement. But the Japanese army leaders rejected the US intervention as unwarranted. The conflict spread to Shanghai by 15 August 1937. The Sino-Japanese conflict very soon became an international issue. The League of Nations denounced Japan for having violated the treaty obligations. China was assured of the moral support of the League. The USA even went to the extent of suggesting to the nations to declare a quarantine against Japan.

The Japanese armies obtained control of important places. Shanghai was captured. The Chinese followed a policy of defence and withdrew into the interiors. They concentrated on the defence of their capital Nanking. However, by the end of 1937 Nanking also fell. The Japanese fired at the British and American ships, stationed there, in contempt. They set up a provisional Government of the Chinese Republic in the areas conquered. As the Japanese advanced the Chinese withdrew themselves in a systematic manner. In 1938 Japan obtained control of the China Coast and the Treaty ports were all captured one after another including the most strategic city of Shantung. The Chinese followed a policy of 'scorched earth' to exhaust the enemy and then to attack him. They also adopted Guerilla tactics. After the fall of Nanking Chiang Kai Shek had set up his capital at Hankow. It was also captured by the enemy. The most important city, in the south, Canton was lost. Thereafter Chiang retreated towards Chunkiang which was considerably safe. However, the Chinese were practically blockaded. The Chinese ports and the Railway system came to be controlled by the invader. Having found the Guerilla activities of the Chinese a serious menace the Japanese founded the Chinese 'People's Renovation Party'. It proclaimed its faith in the three principles of the San Min Chu-i enunciated by Dr. Sun yat-Sen who founded the Kuomintang party in China. At this stage Japan offered peace to China and invited her to cooperate in the work of rehabilitation of China. The terms of peace were that Manchukuo was to be recognised by China. Japanese troops were to be permitted to remain in certain areas as a protection against the communists. China was to join the Anti-Commintern Pact. Evidently the peace proposal never intended a settlement. Chiang Kai Shek also knew it. Therefore, he rejected the offer. But an influential top Kuomintang leader Wang Ching-wei held that this proposal could be taken as the basis for initiating negotiations. When Chiang turned down it Wang Ching-wei left Chunkiang for Hong Kong from where he issued a statement favouring a settlement with Japan. For this treacherous act Wang Ching-wei was expelled from the Kuomintang party. Therefore, he escaped into the Japanese occupied China in January 1940. But so far as the Japanese fortunes were concerned it produced no effect. In the meantime the Government in Japan was preparing to launch an extensive military operation as the champion of the Asiatics against western imperialism. This was considered to be the mission of Japan. The new policy came to be described as "A Greater East Asia Coprosperity Sphere".

The Rome-Berlin-Tokyo Axis and the War

Following the Anti-Commintern Pact a tripartite Pact was concluded in 1940 by Italy, Germany and Japan. This expanded the Rome-Berlin-Tokyo Axis. At the same time Japan obtained the long needed allies to end her dangerous isolation.

There are divergent views regarding the circumstances that compelled Japan to enter into the Rome-Berlin axis. Some authorities attribute it to the American delaying tactics in finalising a treaty with Japan. There are others who hold that the growing desire of Japan to establish her imperialism in the Far East encouraged her to enter into an alliance with the European military blocs. The latter argue that the outbreak of the Second Sino-Japanese War brought about a remarkable political change in Japan. The militarists, having gained political control in Japan initiated a totalitarian regime. They diverted all the energy for the success of the China war. The new legislations enacted in Japan transferred all the powers of the Diet to the Cabinet. The National General Mobilisation laws passed in 1938 were conspicuous among them. Military training was made compulsory. The naval authorities arranged demonstrations for training the youth of Japan aboard the ships. In addition to this the Air Force was reorganised and every attention was paid to expand it. General Tojo was appointed head of the Military Aviation Department.

It has been further pointed out that the leading political groups gave up their differences and the 'Federation for the prosecution of the Holy War' was formed by them. It was intended to promote a new order in East Asia under the leadership of Japan. Communism and liberalism were to be destroyed to promote national sentiments. All the political parties were voluntarily dissolved to merge themselves in what was called the Imperial Rule Assistance Association. Some of the elderly army officers set up the 'Current Affairs Discussion Society' and the 'East Asia Research Institute' and others practically to supplant all the opposition to the totalitarian trends by indoctrinating the Japanese youth with the fascist ideals. Prince Konoe who became the President of the 'Imperial Rule Assistance Association' tried to bring the army under control through this organisation. He also aimed at the setting up of one party rule and end the China War. But the army became so powerful that it established effective control over the Government. There was a growing anti-American feeling among the Japanese.

These trends in Japan were further encouraged by the developments in Europe. Germany committed aggression against Holland in 1940. The Japanese Foreign Minister Arita snatched this opportunity to announce that 'the destiny of the Dutch Indies (Indonesia) was a matter of graver concern for Japan which was the stabilising force for East Asia. Japan's task of establishing a new order in East Asia was an attempt to form a regional sphere of coexistence and coprosperity by the peoples who are closely related to each other geographically, racially, culturally and economically.' This view was also endorsed by many leading army men in Japan.

The military success of Germany in Europe resulted in the collapse of France very soon. England was also very badly hit. Watching these developments Japan made herself bold to serve an ultimatum to the French Governor-General of Indo-China demanding air bases. East Indies was the main source of Japanese rice imports. Therefore, such a strategic area was to be protected against anarchy on the collapse of the Dutch in Europe. The French authorities in Indo-China yielded to these demands. Further, Japan supported Siam or Thailand in a boundary dispute with the French Indo-China or Cambodia. Thereby she obtained commercial facilities from Siam. This foothold was a great help for the southward movement of Japan.

So far as the USA was concerned premier Konoe had been able to maintain his stand and prevented Japan entering into the war. But when the US President Roosevelt announced that "there could be no compromise with the forces of aggression" the situation became tense. Though the supporters of Prince Konoe were even prepared to negotiate with America the Foreign Minister Matsuoka was away in Europe. Therefore, a settlement with the USA was not possible. In fact the Japanese Foreign Minister while in his European tour was impressed by the brilliant victories that the Nazis were scoring. He was assured of German cooperation by Hitler if Japan was involved in a war with America. This stabilised the Rome-Berlin-Tokyo Axis. On his way back Matsuoka concluded the Soviet-Japanese Neutrality Pact in April 1941 at Moscow. According to this Pact Japan and Russia agreed that if Japan and Russia were involved in war with a third party, the party not at war would remain neutral. Russia agreed to respect the inviolability of Manchukuo while Japan agreed to respect the status of Outer Mongolia where Russian interests were involved. It is needless to point out that during the European tours of the Japanese Foreign Minister Matsuoka the assurances of Hitler and the Moscow Pact with Stalin encouraged Japan to enter into the Second World War. By the time he reached Japan Hitler violated the "mutual Non-Aggression Pact" concluded earlier with Stalin. The Germans invaded the Russian territory on 22 June 1941. The implications of the Rome-Berlin-Tokyo Axis were explained to the Emperor by Matsuoka, and advised that Japan was under obligation to join Germany in the war. A serious rift developed between Matsuoka, the Foreign Minister and Konoe, the Premier. The latter resigned.

The primary objective of Japan was territorial expansion in the pacific and in South-East Asia. By the entry of Japan into the war the hostilities so far confined to Europe and the Mediterranean regions were spread into the pacific, the Far East and the South-East Asia. As such it converted the Eurpoean war into a world wide conflagration. Japanese troops had already over run the French Indo-China. On this the USA became anxious that her interests in the Philippines might suffer. As a warning the American President ordered the freezing of all the Japanese assets in the USA. This action of America amounted to the declaration of an economic war against Japan. Therefore, Japan was constrained either to submit to the USA or to launch an extensive military conquest in the regions of Dutch East Indies, Malaya and Burma to procure oil, rice, rubber and other products to stabilise her economy. Though the Japanese Emperor was in favour of negotiations, in the Imperial Conference held on 6 September 1941 it was resolved to wage a war against the USA, England and Netherlands if an amicable settlement was not reached by October 1941. The US Secretary of State Mr Cordek Hull handed a draft proposal to the Japanese Ambassador in Washington, Admiral Nomura in November. This was to be the basis for negotiations. It contained that "no government except the Nationalist Government of Chunking was to be recognised. All Japanese forces were to be withdrawn from China and Indo-China. The Tripartite Pact with Germany and Italy was to be virtually nullified. A non-aggression pact should be entered into by Japan, the USA, Britain, Russia and Holland. The Japanese premier Tojo considered this proposal as nothing short of an ultimatum and he declared that further negotiation for a settlement with USA is ridiculous. It appears that USA was under the impression that these threats would Cow down Japan and may not risk a war with America. This was a wrong calculation of the Statesmen of the USA. It was proved when the entire world was shocked by the news that the American naval base at Pearl Harbour in Hawaii Islands was attacked by Japan. On 7 December 1941, the Japanese bombers and torpedo planes struck the American stockpiles of war equipment and huge battle ships at 7 a.m. An untold devastation was effected by the Japanese. The mighty American Nation was taken by surprise. This practically put the American pacific Fleet out of action which enabled Japan to move about freely in the pacific region. Thus Japan entered the Second World War. It was denounced by the USA as highly treacherous. But it went unheard in any part of the Eastern World as the Japanese action enhanced her military prestige.

After the Pearl Harbour adventure, in quick succession, the Japanese overran the Philippines and Hong Kong. They also reached the east coast of Malaya. The Japanese aircraft effectively hit the British battleships the 'Prince of Wales' and the cruiser 'Repulse'. Many other large vessels of Britain which tried to prevent the Japanese landing in Malaya were destroyed. They forced the Americans to withdraw to the Hawaii Islands. After having encircled the Malayan Coast the Japanese forced the British to retreat from Malaya to Singapore by the end of January 1942. The most strategic naval base of Britain, Singapore, fell on 15 February 1942.

In the east Borneo and the smaller islands were conquered. When the Japanese occupied South Sumatra the Dutch retreated to Java. The Dutch surrendered after a naval disaster suffered by the British and the Dutch in February and March 1942 in the hands of the Japanese. In Philippines Manila fell in January 1942. However, the American General MacArthur held his position effectively in the Bataan Peninsula. When he was ordered by the American President Roosevelt to get away from Philippines in order to take up the command of the Allied forces in the South Pacific, 40,000 American troops commanded by him in Bataan surrendered to the Japanese in May 1942. General MacArthur evacuated Philippines along with President Quezon and Vice-President Osmena of the Commonwealth Government of Philippines. These victories of Japan gave her the supreme control over the vast regions extending from the borders of India to the northern coast of Australia. After having effectively crippled the American navy in the East Japan was in a position to free South East Asia from the western influence. Thus the Greater East Asia coprosperity sphere extended from Manchukuo to Manipur embracing in its wide sweep the richest portions of China, the whole of Indo-China, Burma, Malaya, and all the islands great and small in the South-West Pacific." The dramatic events and their perfect execution displayed the efficiency of the Japanese army.

It is appropriate to make a reference here to the activities of the Indian soldiers (British army) who were captured by the Japanese in East Asia and some of the Indian patriots resident in East Asia in different capacities as journalists and domiciles. Among the leading men Rash Behari Bose was well-known even in the Japanese circles. These Indians were inspired by the Japanese success. A speck of hope sparked in them that in collaboration with Japan they can organise an Indian National Army to liberate their motherland. Their object was to organise the Indian Independence movement in East Asia and then to wage a war against Britain in which they were assured of Japanese support. Rash Behari Bose was elected the head of the Indian Independence League. In the meantime Subhash Chandra Bose (Netaji) was in Berlin on the same mission. He reached Saban Island in a Japanese submarine on 6 May 1943 from there he was flown to Tokyo on 11 May. When he took over the leadership of the movement in East Asia, an armed force of 12,000 strong was at his disposal. Later on a Provisional Government of Free India *(Arzi Hakumat-e-Azad Hind)* was set up on 21 October 1943 with Singapore as its Headquarter. "The Provisional Government of Free India consisted of five Ministers with Bose as the Head of the State, Prime Minister and Minister for War and Foreign Affairs, eight representatives of the INA and eight civilian advisers representing the Indian community of East Asia. The provisional Government was recognised by the Axis powers and their allies. The first decision of importance which the provisional Government took was its declaration of war on Britain and America, which was decided in the night of 22-23 October." The INA was organised into a Revolutionary Army to liberate India, of course, with the help of Japan. However, it does not mean that it was to serve as a puppet regime. This fact has been clearly established by the legal luminary Bhulabhai Desai who defended the INA in the Red Fort trials. Though several problems, like finance and equipment, confronted Netaji he was able to obtain the necessary funds from the Indian merchants and domiciles in East Asia. No doubt the Japan Government also provided him necessary funds only on the basis of a loan to be redeemed when India became free. Thenceforth the INA and the Japanese armies fought together against the western imperialism until Japan surrendered in 1945. The same spirit was also found among the peoples of the French Indo-China and Thailand who readily cooperated with the victorious Japan. They extended every help for the easy movement of the Japanese troops. Thus Japan was almost accepted as the champion of the Asian cause. The slogan 'Asia for Asians' became popular.

In May 1942 Japan experienced the first check off the Bougainville and Guadelkanal islands in the Coral Sea after the Pearl Harbour adventure. The naval battle fought near Midway Island in the pacific was the first serious discomfiture of Japan. In this battle four Japanese aircraft-carriers were sunk. The year 1943 began with a series of reverses for Japan. She had to withdraw from the areas occupied by her in South-West Pacific regions. However, these reverses were concealed from the Japanese public.

Japan's Reverses

The Allies selected Australia as their base in the public zone to carry on the operations effectively. General MacArthur was holding the Supreme Command of the Allied Forces.

Admiral Nimitz commanded the American Navy with New Zealand as his headquarters, New Guinea, Australia and New Zealand were carefully guarded against a possible Japanese invasion. The Submarine and the aerial attacks of the allies cut off the communications of the different units of the Japanese forces. Japan suffered heavily both in men and material. If Japan's resources were strained in the pacific, in Europe the Germans suffered a disastrous failure in Russia. Even China began to recover when the American aid was rushed constantly to supply the most sophisticated machinery to the Chinese. The Chinese soldiers were trained by the American officers. All these factors reduced the fighting ability of Japan. She was running short of the aircraft, the necessary ammunition and the manpower to meet the Allied forward movement in the pacific.

The Allies gradually advanced into the central pacific where they conquered the Gilberts, the Marshalls, the Carolines and the Marianas Islands from Japan between 1943 and 1944. The occupation of the Okinawa and the Ryukyu Islands in April 1945 by the Allies secured for strategic land bases. These conquests gave the Allies an advantage to attack the Japanese islands. From these bases they directed a dreadful air attack and strategic places and cities of Japan were bombarded. It destroyed the industrial production and agricultural system of Japan.

The arrival of fresh American forces in 1944 in the Marshal Islands and the Marians compelled Japan to move her entire fleet for the defence of Saigon, its most vital defence system. The American warships inflicted heavy loss on the Japanese fleet. At the same time there was no coordination between the Japanese Army and Navy. It affected the Japanese defence greatly. The public opinion in Japan was mounting against premier Tojo. They felt that the Emperor could bring the war to a close and save the nation from a total disaster. Under these conditions in July 1944 General Tojo fell from power in Japan. But it may be noted that the 'Liaison Conference' which controlled the war affairs became more powerful after the fall of Tojo and naturally there was no change in the war policy of Japan. In the following months a vigorous campaign was launched in the Imphal sector in Manipur. It was the aim of Japan to enter India after conquering Imphal. She employed an army of about 270,000 in this adventure. But this entire army suffered a serious setback in September 1944 and thousands of them perished.

The Japanese naval power was crippled in the battle that took place in the Leyte Gulf (Philippines) in October 1944. The Allied submarine activities cut off all the means of communication of Japan. Thereby she was practically blockaded. The American fleet successfully covered the landing of their troops in the Philippines. The Japanese navy and air forces suffered a crushing defeat. This naval disaster destroyed all hopes of Japan

Added to this the Japanese hopes were further shattered when Stalin denounced Japan as an aggressor on the anniversary of the Bolshevik Revolution on 7 November 1944. On 10 November the Nanking head, Wang Ching Wei died. The Allies began the first air-raid on Tokyo on the New Year's day of 1945. Several main islands like Iwojina were attacked. By April the American forces successfully landed in Okinawa. Premier Koiso who succeeded General Tojo resigned and an eighty years old Admiral Suzuki, became the Prime Minister of Japan in April 1945. He was only to hear that the Japanese naval fleet was devastated near Kyushu. On 5 April 1945 Stalin denounced the Neutrality Pact (concluded with Japan in April 1941). In June 1945 the 'Wartime Emergency Measure' was passed. This vested the executive with all powers so as to enable the Government to prosecute the war.

47

The Second World War: Causes and Consequences : 1939-1945

After twenty years of the end of the First World War (1914-19), the world had to see another global war, in which practically whole of Europe got involved. This war proved to be more dangerous, destructive and devastating than the First World War. The second global war renewed the wounds of the First World War which had hardly started healing. It also had its impact on socio-politico-economic, foreign, military and diplomatic life of the then world.

The seeds of Second World War had been sown during the Paris Peace Conference (1919). Germany had been much humiliated and it was impossible for self-respecting German people to tolerate humiliation. The treaty of Versailles based upon the idealism of President Wilson's (America) Fourteen Points through its territorial readjustments and other clauses sought to cripple Germany. German army was reduced to the size of less than the armed forces of Belgium. The major terms of the 440 articles of the treaty of Versailles aimed to prevent Germany from ever again becoming a Great Power. Germany accepted the Peace Treaty as long as she was weak. But as soon as she managed to raise her armies, she decided to recoil. On January 30, 1933, Hitler became Chancellor of Germany and some time later he was accepted by the people of his country as their President. He set up Nazism in the country and monopolised all powers. He undertook the task of rebuilding the nation. He refused to accept the Treaty of Versailles. He became so powerful that European nations now thought in terms of their security. They signed pacts with each other. Since Germany had been insulted at Paris and was now prepared to take revenge. This proved one important cause responsible for the outbreak of World War II.

Another cause was that the victors at Paris so distributed the territories that the people belonging to a race and culture were placed under the charge of a nation which possessed entirely different culture. Thus cultural development came to a stand still. These people were clamouring for coming together. The Balkanisation of South—Eastern Europe proceeded apace and in the newly created states were included German minorities—a factor which accounted for German aggression in future. Then another cause was that Germany decided not to pay money to European nations which she was required to pay as war reparations. This gave great setback to their economic programme and activities. These nations were in no mood to forgive Germany for this offence.

When Germany decided that in violation of all treaties she will re-arm herself, this alarmed all European nations. Heavy amounts began to be spent on defence. In addition, in every country factories began to produce war material. Strength of armed forces tremendously increased and every nation began to build forts. In France a chain of forts called Maginot Line was built. This was countered by Germany, who built her own chain of forts called Seigfried Line. When both Germany and France built chain line of forts all other nations got worried and these too started building forts and thus accelerated their war preparations.

Saar was an industrially advanced area and a vital part of Germany's economic development. Without this Germany's economy was practically bound to collapse. After World War I, this had been taken away from Germany and placed under the League of Nations for 15 years. Thus, whereas on the one hand Germany was required to pay heavy amounts as war losses to European nations, on the other her wealth producing Saar had been taken away from her. She was now keen to get back Saar, so that her economy was put on sound footings.

When Germany began to re-arm herself, each European nation got alarmed and preparations began to be made both for individual security, as well as collective security of Europe. Each European nation began to align herself with the other nations. Two powerful blocks thus emerged. One such block was headed by France and claimed itself as the defender of democracy and other was led by Germany and Italy which believed in Nazism and Fascism. Thus bloc and group formation divided whole of Europe and each nation was keen to join either one group or the other to save her future.

After the first world war was over, feelings of nationalism developed in every nation. The international tensions which culminated in the Second World War were in part due to ideological conflicts and in part to conflicts of national interests. The combined operations of these two factors produced a cleavage between nations and led to their alignment in rival groups.

Besides, after the First World war there was an apparent triumph of liberal democracy all over Europe. With the fall of the three old royal dynasties in Europe—the Hohenzollern, the Hapsburg and the Romanoff, democratic constitutions were adopted by almost all nations of Europe. It was only in Russia that the democratic movement became entangled with Bolshevism. But within a decade of this triumph of Democracy, due to the impending socio-economic crisis of 1920s and 30s, the democratic experiments failed. Two types of dictatorship sprang up viz: the Communist as in the Russia and the Fascist as in Italy, Germany, Japan, Spain and Portugal. The new radical ideologies like Fascism, Nazism and Communism engulfed the whole world. The people were now attracted by these ideas. The old philosophy that the democracy is the best form of government did not attract the people. Rise of Hitler in Germany and that of Mussolini in Italy, with immense powers in their hands on the one hand and their touching speeches and policies about nationalism, nation's self-respect etc. on the other very much created war atmosphere.

Paris Peace Conference had fixed armed strength of each nation. The idea was that with reduced armies, the world will be safe from wars. But that did not happen. German, as she grew strong, decided to withdraw from the League of Nations. She also decided not to abide by the provisions of the 1919 Peace Treaty. She captured Austria and Czechoslovakia. European nations instead of checking Garmany tried to expand their areas of influence. They were divided nations and could not take any united action against Germany. Suit was followed by Italy and Japan and these nations also captured territories. Thus race for capturing territories started and versailles treaty became meaningless for all practical purposes.

League of Nations had been founded in the hope that it would provide a forum where the nations of the world would sit together to solve their differences. It will also help in checking aggressive designs of a nation, if any. But in actual practice it miserably failed. It found itself helpless in checking Japan's occupation of Manchuria, Italy's riding rough shod over Abbysinia and Germany's occupation of Czechoslovakia and Austria.

During 1929-30, the whole world witnessed economic depression which caused economic miseries. Germany was the sufferer but in the country the feelings were that this could have been avoided had European nations behaved properly with Germany.

Besides the World Economic crisis, in the post-Versailles era the policy-makers of Europe demonstrated a strange lack of appreciation of the dangers that threatened the world peace. Their Pacific policy of appeasement to Dictators led them to think that, that would help the Dictators satisfied and others would be left alone. They were also induced to follow this policy of appeasement due to their desire to drive German aggression eastward towards the hated citadel of communism or Bolshevism. Thus the dictators were allowed to re-arm and occupy the areas they liked.

At Paris Peace Conference, Poland had been treated as an independent nation. In order to connect Poland with sea a way was made through Germany which ran into the Port of Danzing. Since Danzing had German population therefore, Hitler demanded that it should be annexed to Germany. He also demanded that Poland should have no passage through Germany, but for this Poland was not ready. Though some efforts were made to solve the problem by peaceful means, but these failed and on September 1, 1939, German forces attacked Poland and this was the beginning of the world war II. Thereafter all the European nations joined the war and it became global in nature.

Impact of War

Impact of the Second World War was much more than the First World War. It was much more devastating than the first one. The losses in material and manpower were far more than what the world had already seen. This created many social problems. There was shortage of essential commodities. Control had to be introduced which resulted in hoarding and black marketing. Prices of essential commodities went very high. Education, art and culture received great setback. All economic and developmental activities came to a standstill. Besides, on both the sides 1.5 crore people were killed and more than one lakh crore rupees were lost. It is estimated that about 2 crore people were either killed or wounded and 50% of them were civilians.

After the war was over many Asian nations which were under colonial rule were awakened and fought for their national independence. Mention among others may be made of India, Burma, Malaya and Egypt. In fact, European supremacy over Asia received a great setback.

Before war began Great Britain was leader of Europe but as the war ended that leadership got transferred from Great Britain to Russia and America. After getting many colonies liquidated from her control, Britain no more remained the biggest power of the world, but a big power.

During the war many destructive weapons were produced which still kept the world frightened. These have resulted in arms race and each nation was required to spend heavily on defence. In this way developing countries were the worst sufferers.

Since Asian and African countries got awakened and many successfully won their freedom from colonial powers, which were big European nations, therefore, need was felt for keeping contacts with these new born States and this gave birth to neo-colonialism.

It was during world war that the nations got themselves divided into two blocs. The seeds sown were still giving fruits and the world has been so far in a position to give up power bloc tendency. This tendency had got deeper roots till recent times because of ideological differences between the two powers, namely the USA and former Soviet Union.

In order to increase their hold over Asian and African nations, power blocs had started giving economic aid to these countries, which have developing economies. In this way whereas economic dependence on big powers has increased on the one hand, on the other in many cases so much economic aid has been poured that economies of these nations were overburdened. This has resulted in inflation and economic instability throughout the developing and underdeveloped world.

One good effect of the war has been the establishment of UNO (United Nations Organization) which is till today considered as the only hope of the world for saving it from third world war. Though the world body has its own problems, yet it is the only agency to which every nation today looks with hope.

The world war resulted in so much of devastation and destruction that even 45 years after the war is over, its horrors, horrify every living being.

48

The United Nations Organisation

The United Nations arose on the ashes of the League of Nations. Although the League of Nations had failed to provide security, the idea of an international organisation to prevent war and promote peace was not abandoned. Throughout the world, there was persistent demand for an effective system of collective security to prevent a third world war and to realise the ideal of one 'world state' in which all nations may dwell together in unity. It is this ideal which gave birth to the United Nations Organisation (U.N.O.).

Meaning and Principles

The United Nations may be defined as an organisation of independent states (about 181 in number), which have accepted the obligations contained in the United Nations Charter signed at San Francisco on June 26, 1945, effective since October 24, 1945. The principles stated in the Charter were derived from the conception and plans of the war time Allies, which first found expression in: (a) The Atlantic Charter (August 1941), (b) The United Nations Declaration signed by twentysix nations on New Year' s Day, 1942, (c) The Moscow Declaration of October 1943, and (d) The Dumbarton Oaks Conference of 1944 in which the representatives of Great Britain, Russia, America and China drew up draft proposals for the structure of the contemplated world organisation.

The fundamental aims and purposes as set forth in the United Nations Charter are as follows: to maintain international peace and security; to develop friendly relations among states based on respect for the principle of equal rights and self-determination of peoples; to achieve international cooperation in solving problems of an economic, social, cultural or humanitarian character; and to harmonise the actions of states in the attainment of their common ends. The organisation is not to intervene in matters which are essentially within the domestic jurisdiction of any country.

Organs

The headquarters of the UNO was originally located in Paris but later on shifted to New York. To carry out its aims and objectives, six principal organs of the United Nations Organisation (now referred to as the United Nations or simply the UN) were created. These were viz., the General Assembly, the Security Council, the Economic and Social Council, the Trusteeship Council, the International Court of Justice and the Secretariat. Besides, there is a group of subsidiary and specialised agencies which operate under the general coordination of the Economic and Social Council.

The original members were those states who had signed the United Nations Declarations or taken part in the San Francisco Conference. New membership has been thrown open to all other peace-loving states. Admission is effected by the General Assembly on the recommendation of the Security Council. Applicants must accept the obligations contained in the Charter and must satisfy the organisation that they are capable of carrying out these obligations. Any of the Big five can veto an application and so there is ample room for dispute and diplomatic bargaining.

The UN Organs at a Glance

General Assembly

The General Assembly is composed of the United Nations' 179 members, each of which has one vote. It controls the organisation's finances, makes non-binding recommendations on a variety of issues and oversees and elects some members of other UN organs. The General Assembly meets in plenary session, for three to four months, beginning on the third Tuesday in September. It can also meet in emergency session to address immediate threats to international peace and security and in special session to deal with specific issues such as disarmament. Fifteen organisations have been created by the assembly and report to it, including the United Nations Environment Programme (UNEP), the United Nations Children's Fund (UNICEF) and the Office of the United Nations High Commissioner for Refugees (UNHCR).

Security Council

The Security Council has primary responsibility within the UN system for maintaining international peace and security. It may determine the existence of any threat to international peace, make recommendations or take enforcement measures to resolve the problem, and establish UN peace-keeping forces. The Council has 15 members; five permanent members designated by the UN Charter (Britain, China, France, the Soviet Union and the United States) and 10 others elected for two-year terms. Decisions on substantive matters require nine votes; a negative vote by any permanent member (a "veto") defeats the motion. Security Council resolutions are binding on all UN member states.

Economic and Social Council (ECOSOC)

Under the authority of the General Assembly, ECOSOC coordinates the economic and social work of the United Nations and its large family of specialised and affiliated institutions. ECOSOC meets in plenary session twice a year for a month at a time, once in New York and once in Geneva. The 54 members of ECOSOC are elected by the General Assembly for three-year terms.

Trusteeship Council

The five members of the Trusteeship Council—Britain, China, France, the Soviet Union and the United States—are also the five permanent members of the Security Council. When it was created, the Trusteeship Council administered 11 trust territories, most of which later became independent or joined neighbouring countries. Today, only the United States still administers a trust territory—the Trust Territory of the Pacific Islands (Micronesia).

International Court of Justice (World Court)

The World Court, which meets in the Dutch city of The Hague, hears cases referred to it by the states involved and provides advisory opinions to the General Assembly and the Security Council at their request. It is made up of 15 judges representing 15 member states, who are elected by an absolute majority of both the Security Council and the General Assembly for nine-year terms.

Secretariat

The Secretariat administers the programmes and policies established by the other UN organs. It is headed by the secretary-general, currently Dr. Boutros Boutrous-Ghali of Egypt, who is elected by the General Assembly on the recommendation of the Security Council for a five-year term. The secretary-general is authorised by the UN Charter to bring to the attention international peace and security and may use his office and authority to attempt to resolve international disputes. He leads an international civil servant staff of 14,000, 5,000 of whom are at UN headquarters in New York.

Specialised Agencies

Food and Agriculture Organisation of the United Nations (FAO), Rome. Works to increase food production, raise rural standards of living and help countries cope with emergency food situations.

International Civil Aviation Organisation (ICAO), Montreal

Works to facilitate and promote safe international air transportation by setting binding international standards and by recommending efficient practices. ICAO regulations govern international flights.

International Fund for Agricultural Development (IFAD), Rome

Lends money on concessional terms for agricultural development projects, primarily to increase food production for the poorest rural populations.

International Labour Organisation (ILO), Geneva

Formulates international labour standards and provides technical assistance training to governments.

International Maritime Organisation (IMO), London

Promotes international cooperation on technical matters related to shipping and provides a forum to discuss and to adopt conventions and recommendations on such matters as safety at sea and pollution control.

International Monetary Fund (IMF), Washington DC

Provides technical assistance and financing to countries that are experiencing balance of payments difficulties.

International Telecommunication Union (ITU), Geneva

Promotes international cooperation in telecommunications, allocates the radio-frequency spectrum and collects and disseminates telecommunications information for its members.

United Nations Educational, Scientific and Cultural Organisation (UNESCO), Paris

Pursues international intellectual cooperation in education, science, culture and communications and promotes development by means of social, cultural and economic projects.

United Nations Industrial Development Organisation (UNIDO), Vienna

Serves as an intermediary between developing and developed countries in the field of industry and as a forum for contacts, consultations and negotiations to aid the process of industrialisation.

Universal Postal Union (UPU), Berne

Sets international postal standards and provides technical assistance to developing countries.

The World Bank, Washington DC

Made up of the International Bank for Reconstruction and Development (IBRD), the International Finance Corp. (IFC) and the International Development Association (IDA). IBRD lends funds to governments, usually for specific projects. IFC lends to private corporations without government guarantees. IDA provides interest-free "credits" to the world's poorest countries for a period of 50 years, with a 10-year grace period.

World Health Organisation (WHO), Geneva

Conducts immunization campaigns, promotes and coordinates research, and provides technical assistance to countries that are improving their health systems. It is currently coordinating a major effort to control and cure AIDS.

World Intellectual Property Organisation (WIPO), Geneva

Promotes the protection of intellectual property (patents and copyrights). It encourages adherence to relevant treaties, provides legal and technical assistance to developing countries, encourages technology transfers and administers the International Union for the Protection of Industrial property and the International Union for the Protection of Literary and Artistic Works.

World Meteorological Organisation (WMO), Geneva

Promotes the exchange and standardisation of meteorological information through its World Weather Watch and conducts research and training programme.

Other Autonomous Affiliated Organisations : General Agreement on Tariffs and Trade (GATT), Geneva

Sets out norms and rules for international trade and provides a multilateral form for their further elaboration.

International Atomic Energy Agency (IAEA), Vienna

Promotes the peaceful uses of nuclear energy, establishes standards for nuclear safety and environmental protection and carries out inspections to safeguard against diversion of nuclear material to military uses, by agreement with parties to the Non-Proliferation Treaty.

Achievements of the UNO

Ever since its inception (1945), the UNO has been performing the most strenuous task of maintaining peace and security in the world. Year after year she is called upon to manage crisis which otherwise would threaten world peace and security. The first problem which was brought to its attention was that of Iran. She complained of the non-withdrawal of the Red Army from her soil. The Red Army had set up a puppet communist regime in the north. The Security Council took up the case and appealed to Russia to withdraw her forces from Iran.

The next issue which came up before UNO was the Greek complaint. The Security Council of the UNO received a complaint from Greece that the communist guerillas were operating in her state with the aid of some neighbouring communist countries. She was afraid that conditions may worsen and a civil war on her soil may break out. The U.N. General Assembly passed the resolution condemning the subversive activities of the communist countries in the neighbourhood of Greece. The USA rendered help to Greece under the garb of Truman Doctrine and prevented the menace of the communist guerillas on the Greek soil.

Soon after World War II, the Japanese vacated their occupation of the East Indies held by the Dutch. The natives of the Dutch Indies declared their independence and established a republic under the presidentship of Sukarno. But the Dutch wanted to recover their colonies and a war broke out. The dispute between Indonesia and the Dutch was referred to the Security Council by India and Australia. The UNO intervened in this dispute and brought about a compromise which included the recognition of the independence of Indonesia on certain conditions by the Dutch government in 1949.

The Balfour declaration of 1917 envisaged the creation of a separate state for the Jews called Israel. Unfortunately, the state of Israel was forcibly created in the midst of all the Arab countries. The setting up of Israel resulted in the expulsion of the native Arab-Palestinians from their place of residence. To fight for the sake of Palestinian (Arab) cause the Arab League was formed. It was founded by Egypt, Jordan, Syria and Iraq. They invaded Israel and fought for the Palestinian cause. The UNO intervened and arranged for a cease-fire. The Arab states which were defeated by Israel not only demanded from the UNO their territories back but also insisted on the resettlement of 600,000 Arab-Palestinian refugees who fled their homeland during the war.

The British had given option to all the 562 princely states in India to join either India or Pakistan. Before India's independence, Sardar Vallabhbhai Patel was able to persuade all but three states to join India. One of the three states which hesitated to join India was the state of Kashmir. Kashmir was ruled by a Hindu ruler (Hari Singh) which had a majority of Muslim population. Meanwhile Pakistan-supported tribals invaded Kashmir. Fearing a large scale invasion, the Hindu ruler of Kashmir signed the instrument of accession with India and sought India's help to expel the intruders. The Pakistani Army was actively involved in its assistance to the tribals with the hope of the final military takeover of Kashmir by herself. The conflict between India and Pakistan was referred to the UNO by India's Prime Minister, Jawaharlal Nehru. The UNO brought about a ceasefire which resulted in the retention of a part of Kashmir by Pakistan. A solution to the Kashmir problem now depended upon the attitude of Pakistan towards India. The Kashmir problem has embittered the relations between India and Pakistan for the last 44 years. The Shimla agreement signed between the late Prime Minister Indira Gandhi and the late Pakistan Premier Bhutto may provide for better understanding between the two parties.

After the World War II Japanese forces vacated the Korean peninsula. Unfortunately, this country was divided into two parts—North Korea and South Korea. North Korea came under communist control. The invasion of North Korean troops on South Korea created a serious problem. South Korea complained to the UNO about North Korea's invasion. The UNO passed a resolution to the effect that South Korea should be saved from North Korea's aggression. A number of nations led by the USA sent troops to help South Korea to expel the North Korean communists. The Korean war continued for about two years. After that there was the ceasefire and mutual exchange of prisoners of war. Despite heavy losses, South Korea was saved from North Korea's aggression.

When President Abdel Gemal Nasser of Egypt nationalised the Suez canal company which was in control of the international waterway, Israel encouraged by France and Britain attacked Egypt. It was followed by the Anglo-French invasion of Egypt in 1956. Both these powers would have won the war but for the restraint exercised by the USA. If the war had continued, there was a likelihood that it would have turned into another world war. The UNO played its role in bringing about a settlement of this dispute.

The British continued to rule Cyprus, an island in the Mediterranean even after the second World War despite the opposition of the Greeks there. There was Turkish minority on that island. The Greeks on the mainland eagerly waited to annex that island but it could not be since the Turkish minority opposed it. But the *Enosis* (Union with Greece) movement on that island became strong under the leadership of Archbishop Makarios. The armed struggle against the British continued with full vigour and the British found it difficult to suppress the movement. The British forced the Greek leader on that island to go into exile. When the Greek majority and the Turkish minority leaders agreed on the new constitutional set up for that island, the British granted independence to the natives of Cyprus in 1960. But in practice the agreement between the Greek Cypriots and the Turkish Cypriots did not work out smoothly and there was an armed conflict. The UN peace keeping force was sent there to maintain the ceasefire. Relations between the two communities have since then embittered, however, the actual partition of the country has not taken place.

When the third Arab-Israel War broke out in 1967, Israel fought the Arabs in what is known as the, six days war'. She forcibly seized both the West Bank and the Gaza Strip. The UNO also sent its peace-keeping force to prevent a conflict arising out of the abrupt departure of the Belgians from Congo. But the civil war continued and the UN peace-keeping mission could not work satisfactorily.

The UNO had been the venue of many disarmament talks. The purpose of these meetings was to make the world safer by urging the big powers to reduce the size of their armed forces and expenditure on armaments. A new round of talks which began after 1955 with Russia's cooperation gave new hopes to mankind.

The United Nations in the recent times is emerging once again as a viable instrument for maintaining world peace and security. Long the scene of bitter exchanges between the United States and the Soviet Union, and often the focus of heated criticism for its inefficiency and waste in the 1970s and 1980s, this 181 member body is enjoying a quiet revival on its 48th birthday.

The revival is possible because of the easing of tensions between the superpowers. "The Cold War [was] probably the major impediment to a realisation of the UN as people thought about it in 1944-45", says Donald F. McHenry, US ambassador to the United Nations during the Carter administration and now a professor of diplomacy and international relations at Georgetown University's School of Foreign Service. When the organisation was founded, he says, people believed that countries would cooperate in peace as they had cooperated in war. "Of course, they did not. They immediately started fighting. Now, with the Cold War practically over and countries having exhausted themselves in regional conflicts, there is once again a [useful role for] the UN to get people out of the problems they are in."

Signs of the United Nations' resurgence can be seen around the globe.

In Afghanistan, UN mediators finally were able to end the conflict to some extent between the Soviet-backed government and the US-supported Islamic rebel forces. In 1988, nearly a decade after the conflict began, the belligerents signed the Geneva Accords, the first UN-brokered agreement with the superpowers as co-guarantors. A UN peacekeeping mission was then sent to Afghanistan to monitor the withdrawal of Soviet forces, which was completed in February 1989, and the return of refugees from Pakistan. Although the civil war continues, the UN presence has allowed the Soviets a face-saving way out of a costly and protracted war.

In Africa, the former UN Secretary-General Javier Perez de Cuellar was instrumental in negotiating the independence of Namibia and the withdrawal of foreign forces from neighbouring Angola. The UN Security Council had demanded free elections in Namibia since 1976, but the issue was not resolved until 1988, when Angola, Cuba and South Africa accepted a UN-backed peace settlement that opened the way for Namibia's independence. The UN Transition Assistance Group, a combined military and civilian mission, has overseen the withdrawal of troops from the occupied territories and monitored the elections that led to the installation of an independent government in Namibia on March 21,1990.

In the Middle East, the United Nations was instrumental in ending the Iran-Iraq war. The war, which began in September 1980, dragged on for nearly eight years, until the two sides agreed to a UN-sponsored ceasefire in 1988. Since then, an unarmed UN Military Observer Group has been monitoring the ceasefire.

In the recently concluded Iraqi-US led Kuwaiti war, the UN could not play an important role. Here the US took the initiative to enhance its military capability in the oil rich Middle East region. It felt important to reduce and control the capability of regional powers to challenge not only the US but also pro-US regimes in the area. Here the US efforts were directed both within the UN and outside it. US sponsored UN Security Council Resolution 687 of 3 April 1991 imposed conditions for a comprehensive ceasefire on Iraq and the destruction of the Iraqi society, both men and material, and evoked an anti-western wave in large parts of the Islamic world. The UN Security Council was denied any say in the conduct of the US-sponsored war against Iraq. The Security Council remained on the sidelines without a meeting for nearly four weeks.

Apprehensions that what happened to Iraq is sought to be projected as an example are growing because of the latest US campaign to target Libya for its alleged involvement in international terrorism. Moreover, in the case of the Palestine problem, the UN has failed miserably. Despite the prolonged efforts of the Arab-Palestinians, there seems to be not much progress in the Arab-Israeli Peace negotiations. The last series of peace talks ended inconclusively without taking into account the basic issues of the rights of Arab-Palestinians, the return of Israeli-occupied Arab territories to Arab-Palestinians and establishment of an independent Palestinian state.

In Central America, the United Nations has set up its first peacekeeping operations. The world organisation first got involved in the region in 1982 at the request of the leftist Sandinista government of Nicaragua, which charged the United States with intervening in its affairs by funding and supporting the " contra" rebels. The United Nations later helped broker agreements among five Central American countries that ultimately led to free elections in Nicaragua and the dismantling of the US- backed contra operations based in neighbouring Honduras. A UN observer mission monitored the Feb. 25 elections, whose victor, President Violeta Chamorro, had the support of the United States. Contra rebels also are turning over their arms to the UN peace-keeping forces there. The UN is still playing an important role in the crisis-ridden areas like Somalia, Cambodia, former Yugoslavia and Western Sahara.

Of course, the United Nations has not acted alone in implementing its recent missions. UN peace-keeping operations owe their success to the superpowers' decisions in the late 1980s to de-escalate the arms race. Mikhail S. Gorbachev, who rose to the Kremlin leadership in 1985, has moved to reduce Soviet military and economic presence in the developing world. More concerned with improving his country's economy Gorbachev had undertaken a vast programme of economic and political reform that has redirected Soviet resources away from military spending and overseas commitments and toward domestic needs.

Although it has yet to shake its image as the world's chief UN-basher, the United States has tempered its hostility toward the organisation. George Bush, who is the first president to have served as special representative, or ambassador, to the United Nations (1971-1972, under President Richard M. Nixon), has asked Congress to restore full funding to the organisation, which was interrupted during the Reagan Administration. The present UN Secretary-General Dr. Boutros Boutros-Ghali urged all UN members to pay their dues promptly to the cash poor world body.

The easing of East-West tensions is reflected in the General Assembly, where all member nations have equal votes. The United States has for years criticised the assembly as little more than a forum for the Soviet Union and its allies in the Third World to denounce capitalism and the United States.

The question that remains for the United Nations, then, is not whether the world organisation is needed, but whether its members, particularly the US—the only imperialist superpower and its allies—have the political will to make it work.

A general sentiment is emerging in some parts of the Afro-Asian world that they are being treated harshly by the United States and its western allies on every issue or question. Indeed all over the world, there is increasing evidence of an advancing *Pax-Americana* which is hard to resist within the Parameters of unipolar world politics.

49

Nationalism in Indonesia

The spice trade attracted the Europeans to the East Indies from a very long time. The Portuguese merchants were the earliest to arrive in these islands. The Dutch followed the Portuguese. The Dutch East India Company which was initially carrying on trade after 1750 found the local political situation favourable for setting up their Government. However, they did not establish direct rule. When the Dutch East India Company's fortunes suffered a serious setback, the Netherlands Government stepped into the possessions of the company in 1798. Thus Dutch Colonialism was confirmed in the East Indies. Therefore, this Island came to be known as the Netherlands Indies. Though the British also held the Islands for a short period during the Napoleonic wars they were returned to the Dutch again after the Congress of Vienna.

Under the Dutch resources of the Islands were exploited for the advantage of Dutch throughout the nineteenth century. In the 20th century the Dutch apprehended other foreign influences in these Islands. Therefore, they gradually spread their control all over. The Dutch created a centralised administration under a Governor-General and the different provinces were administered by Governors subordinate to him. Batavia (Jakarta) was made the seat of the imperial Government. The Governor-General was directly responsible to the Government of Holland (Netherlands).

These developments awakened the national sentiments of the Indonesians. The earliest of the national organisations was Boedi Octomo, the glorious endeavour. Its first congress was convened in 1908. The main objective of this organisation was to achieve economic and educational progress. The next major political organisation was Serekat Islam. It mainly comprised of Moslems. The initial programme of this Society was to achieve economic independence by excluding Chinese trade monopolies. However, politically it aimed at the establishment of an Islamic State. Its first convention was held in 1913. Very soon the Sarekat Islam became a powerful organ and gradually attracted the trade unions also into its fold. The Indonesian communist party was another important political force which began to operate against the Dutch rule. It was founded in 1920. The programme of the Indonesian communist party was to establish a secular state. The nationalist party founded in 1927 followed a more liberal policy and aimed at the establishment of a free Republic. It was led by Sukarno. These organisations trained the young men for political activity. But it did not gain momentum as it was not organised as a mass movement. Only the intelligentsia was attracted and not the masses and the laymen.

In spite of the fact that the Indonesian national movement was not mass oriented it did attract the attention of the Dutch. There were political disturbances organised by the communists. Though the communist insurrections were later suppressed the Dutch had to introduce certain reforms to weaken the growth of vigorous nationalism. Accordingly, they announced a policy of gradual introduction of self-government and associating the Indonesian intellect in the administration. But there was only a negligible percentage of educated among the Indonesians. As such the larger section of the Society remained ignorant. A few educated were trapped into the Civil Service. This thwarted the progress of Indonesian nationalism. After 1927 when the communist uprisings were enacted the national societies were suppressed. The nationalist leaders like Achmed Sukarno, Soetan Sjahrir and Mohammed Hatta were imprisoned. After 1930, the nationalists followed a policy of cooperation. They entered the legislatures.

Though the Dutch were not prepared to concede independence there had been a proposal to grant self-government. But such ideas remained to be shelved for, after 1941, the International situation was tense due to the outbreak of the Second World War. Moreover there was an economic crisis. The export trade fetched very poor profits while the prices of imported finished products were generally increasing. This trade policy was advantageous for Holland and adverse to the Indonesian. Therefore, as a compromise, a quota system was introduced on a reciprocal basis. When the Second World War broke out the Dutch were little worried so far as the Indonesians were concerned and they also did not anticipate the sudden collapse of their colonial Government. Japan invaded Indonesia in 1941 and completed the occupation of the Islands by 1942. This marked the end of Dutch colonialism. They obtained support of a section of the nationalists. Anti-Dutch feelings developed among the Indonesians. They were led to believe that the end of the Dutch rule would bring them political freedom if they collaborated with the Japanese. But, it is needless to point out that the Japanese exploited the resources of Indonesia and caused further deterioration in the Indonesian economy. Politically, the Japanese occupation enabled the Indonesians to declare their independence. Sukarno and Mohammed Hatta joined the Japanese invaders. They declared the independence of Indonesia on 17 August 1945 while the Japanese were still in occupation. The late arrival of the Allied troops after the surrender of Japan helped the nationalists to consolidate their authority and set up a stable Government. Moreover, the Japanese on their surrender had left vast arms and ammunition for the use of the nationalists against the Dutch. When the British troops arrived on 29 September 1945, the Indonesian Republic was firmly established. The Dutch remnants in the Islands were put to brutal suffering and when the Dutch troops arrived along with their exile colonial Government they found that they cannot re-establish sovereignty over their former colony.

These circumstances forced the Dutch to reach a political settlement with the Indonesian Republic. Though negotiations were upset in the beginning due to the hesitation of the Dutch to have parleys with Sukarno, as he was a collaborator with the enemy, it became inevitable. Formally, the Indonesian Republic was recognised by the Dutch when the Linggadjati agreement was signed on 15 November 1946. The *de facto* sovereignty of Indonesia over Java, Madura and Sumatra was recognised. It was also agreed to cooperate in the establishment of democratic United States of Indonesia as a Federal Union composed of the entire Netherlands Indies to be constituted into the three states of the Republic of Indonesia, Borneo and the Great East. The Union was to consist of the Netherlands, the Netherlands West Indies, Surinam Curacao and the Federated States of Indonesia. This arrangement did not last long. Differences arose very soon. The Dutch made it clear to employ force in the Republican territory to settle the outstanding issues. There was a rupture and the situation became grave. However, India and Australia invoked the Security Council of the United Nations on 1 August 1947, to intervene. Accordingly the first cease-fire order was issued by the UNO after it came into being. The United States, Australia and Belgium used their good offices in the negotiations and helped the signing of the truce on 18 January 1948 which came to be called the Renville agreement. It ended the hostilities and paved the way for a political settlement. According to the principles enunciated in the agreement a sovereign, democratic, federated United States of Indonesia was to be recognised vesting sovereignty in the Dutch until Netherlands transferred it to the United States of Indonesia at a stipulated time. But other issues could not be easily settled. Therefore, once again the Republicans and the Dutch entered upon the path of hostilities. In the meantime the Indonesian communists attempted to give the situation an international complexion and they rose in revolt. But the nationalists carried on a vigorous campaign against them. Many of their top leaders were captured and shot dead. Among them Muso and Sjarifuddin were also included.

Taking advantage of this the Dutch accused the Republicans as terrorists. They overpowered the Republican armies. The Republican capital Jakarta was captured. Sukarno and Mohammed Hatta were imprisoned. In order to control the situation the UN adopted the cease-fire resolution. The delegates of Asian nations met in New Delhi to take united action to preserve the independence of Indonesia. Due to international pressure the Dutch evacuated the Republican capital and freed the nationalist leaders. It was agreed to convene a Round Table Conference at the Hague to grant complete independence to the Indonesians.

The Hague Conference

The Hague Round Table Conference was intended to reach a final settlement regarding the political relations between Holland and Indonesia. It was also to settle the other associated issues like the trade, debts and the economic readjustment. Moreover, the different territories to be included in the United States of Indonesia was also to be settled. After protracted deliberations a final agreement was reached on all the issues and it was signed on 2 November 1949. According to this the United States of Indonesia became a Sovereign Federal Republic of sixteen States with the status of an equal partner with the Netherlands. This union was not to affect the status of either party as an independent sovereign state. It recognised the fundamental human rights and freedom. Further, Her Majesty the Queen Juliana was recognised head of the Union. Several other issues were also settled by this conference. On 27 December 1949 Netherlands transferred sovereignty to the United States of Indonesia. However, shortly after this the Federal structure was destroyed by popular movements. In its place the Unitary Republic of Indonesia was set up on 15 August 1950. The new state of Java was also included into the Republic. In the same manner the Union of Netherlands and Indonesia also collapsed by 1955. With this the Republic of Indonesia included all the territories of Netherlands Indies except western New Guinea or West Irian. Later on President Sukarno made every effort to include this territory also into the Republic through the UNO. He repudiated all obligations of Indonesia to Netherlands under the Hague settlement and denounced the claims of Netherlands to Irian.

President Sukarno and the 'Guided Democracy'

From the beginning the Republic of Indonesia was not provided with a permanent constitution. The Unitary Republic under Sukarno possessed a simple constitutional structure. At the centre there was a single-chambered parliament. Its members were to be nominated by the political parties on the basis of proportional representation. Sukarno was elected by the parliament as the President and titular head of the state. Mohammed Hatta was appointed Vice-President by the President.

The President was vested with wide powers. Availing these powers he introduced a new political system which he described as 'Guided Democracy'. He found the political parties unstable and were, therefore, causing internal troubles. In order to avoid political strife Sukarno proclaimed martial law in February 1957. Thereby he assumed supreme powers and the army was to exercise control under the guidance of the President. He dissolved the Constituent Assembly in July 1959 and revived the 1945 constitution. He then suspended the parliament. He filled the different branches of administration with men of his choice who could support his regime. The different political parties like the Nationalists, the Moslem conservatives, the communists and the army cooperated with him in carrying through the experiment of Guided Democracy under his personal control.

By exercising supreme power for over a decade President Sukarno managed to control internal troubles. He also succeeded in reshaping the economy of the nation. He followed a policy of economic nationalism and put an end to foreign capitalism. This helped the State to successfully carry through economic planning and achieve the welfare of the people. But the economic growth was not commensurate with the growth of population. Moreover the personal rule of Sukarno began to loose its charm gradually. It was also affected by the communist insurrections.

Though Sukarno was influenced by western democracy in his early days, when he assumed supreme powers he transformed the democratic concepts as a national ideology. The national interests became more dominant. His philosophy laid emphasis on the national traditions. According to him the party system resulted in political antagonism which affected the national interests. The concept of Guided Democracy was based on the principle of deliberation, unanimity and strong leadership. The President represented the aspirations of the people in this system. The system, established by Sukarno kept the communists away from the Governmental machinery. The people were commended not to slander, not to render disrespect to the Government and not to act against the established ethical standards. His moral code was explained in the famous 'Panch-Sheela' or the five ethical principles. These concepts were to be practised by all implicitly. It aimed at the development of national character among the people. The army was entrusted with the work of enforcing these ideals.

The critics of President Sukarno felt that his regime was tending towards the personal dictatorship of the President. He was overthrown by a military coup. After the successful military coup Suharto succeeded him in 1967.

However, Socialism was newly interpreted by Sukarno. He presented it to his people in the form of Guided Democracy. According to the new interpretation Socialism for him was anti-imperialist, anti-capitalist and it was spiritual rather than a materialistic philosophy. He emphasised the need for 'Indonesian identity', 'human values', 'economic democracy', and eradication of exploitation. His successor Suharto practically altered the policy of Sukarno and gradually inclined to encourage western capital investments in Indonesia. The slogans of anti-capitalism and anti-imperialism were lost in wilderness.

Foreign Policy

At the very outset President Sukarno and his people denounced imperialism in any form. He shaped the Indonesian foreign policy on the basis of mutual cooperation and respect for independence. He maintained neutrality and remained away from the power blocs. He had no hesitation to conclude treaties of friendship with China and Japan which did not involve military alliance. He strived to promote international peace and end colonialism. Under him Indonesia played an important role to bring the Asian-African States together at the conference table to understand their common problems, as the host at the Bandung Conference in 1955. The achievements of the conference are discussed elsewhere. Indonesia joined the Asian-African states in the United Nations whenever their common interests were involved. After the Bandung Conference Indonesia was able to settle the issue of Chinese nationals in Indonesia. Thus the policy of peaceful coexistence was cultivated and he tried to prepare the nation to face the more serious problems with greater vigour.

50

Indo-China Liberation Movement

The earliest western contacts of Indo-China may be traced to the sixteenth century when the Portuguese traders entered the regions. As usual trade was followed by the Jesuit missionaries in search of new following to compensate the loss suffered by the Christian Church, due to the schism, after the Reformation. The Portuguese were followed by the French in the seventeenth century. The French remained powerful in Indo-China from 1747 to 1858. The French opened diplomatic relations with the different states in Indo-China to secure a foothold in order to spread their factories and compete with the Dutch and the British traders. Accordingly in 1787 France and the King of Cochin China signed a commercial treaty. Thereafter the French trade and missionary activity spread into Cochin China. This was resisted both by the native rulers as well as the people in the nineteenth century. Emperor Napoleon III also tried to conclude a treaty with the king of Annam, but failed. It was followed by a French naval attack in 1858. Both France and Spain joined together in this adventure. Da Nang and Saigon were successfully attacked. As a result of this naval expedition France acquired Saigon in 1859 which was formally ceded by Annam along with the three southern provinces. Annam concluded a costly peace with France agreeing to guarantee religious toleration and opening three ports for the French and Spanish trade. An indemnity of about $4,000,000 had to be paid by Annam. Very soon Cambodia became a protectorate of the French. Later on the other provinces were also brought under the French control.

It may be noted that Indo-China comprised of five political divisions. They were Cochin China, a possession of the French, Tonkin, Annam, Laos and Cambodia, which formed the French protectorates in the twentieth century. After having established mastery over Indo-China France interfered with the Siamese possessions to the east of Mekong. By taking away these areas from Sian Laos and Cambodia were made French protectorates by 1907.

Unlike the other Europeans in Asia the French aimed at the establishment of close political relations as though the colony was an integral part of France. The local administration of the French possession was subordinate of the Home Government. The Governor-General and his councils were just nominal bodies. However, in the protectorates, the four provinces, the native officials administered the territories under the supervision of the French officials. As already pointed out, the people of Indo-China did not submit without offering any resistance to the French imperialism. Their national sentiments were always active. But the cultural, racial and linguistic divergence of the population affected their solidarity to a great extent.

The French people were always cautious in their administration not to awaken nationalism among their subjects. But the patriotism of the nation was enkindled by the very political ideals and the institutions the French themselves had. Further, the Japanese victory in the Russo-Japanese war made the intellectuals in Indo-China to realise their humiliating position under the French. They were seriously affected when the French employed the Indo-Chinese for forced labour during the First World War in

Europe. At the same time the commercial interests of the Chinese in Indo-China were also considered to be disadvantageous by the nationalists. There was an anti-Chinese movement in 1919 and 1920 when the communist movement developed vigorously. But the nationalism in Indo-China suffered a setback in the initial stages itself. It was due to the racial distinction that was always maintained by the Annamese. They generally disregarded the people of the Laos and Cambodia as inferior. Above all these the Annamese nationalists were not united and were lack of a certed programme. It helped the French in suppressing the national movement in Indo-China before the Second World War.

During the Second World War colonialism in Indo-China was terribly shaken by the Japanese invasions. By 1940 France suffered a disastrous defeat in Europe. It affected the colonial government in Indo-China. The Vichy regime in Indo-China was possessing hardly 50,000 French troops and 120 Planes. All the efforts to obtain help from America futile. As such all the resources of Indo-China had to be placed at the disposal of Japan for promoting the Greater East Asia Co-prosperity sphere designed by Japan. During the regime of Decoux which extended until March 1945 Indo-China was practically handled as a puppet state. Under the Japanese supervision Bao Dai united Tonking and Annam. He declared the independence of the empire of Annam renaming it as Viet Nam. Similarly the king of Cambodia and Luang Prabang in Laos declared their independence.

Bao Dai inspired the nationalists by giving the empire its old name and Ngo Dinh Diem, who held office as premier under the French but laid down the same, also joined him against the Japanese and the French. But they were not supported by the other nationalists and revolutionaries. By 1941, the Viet Nam Doc Lap Dong, Minh Hoi or the Viet Nam Independence League (Vietminh) was founded in South China by the Vietnamese revolutionaries and Communists. Chiang Kai Shek's Government encouraged their activities on the Chinese mainland against Japan. The work of Ho Chi Minh was remarkable during this period.

The rich experience of Ho Chi Minh was reflected in his ideals explained to the masses. They appealed to the intellectuals, working class as well as to the farmers. He declared that "the battle that we fight is not directed against honest French men but against the cruel domination of French colonialism... Corvee, gabelle, forced consumption of opium and alcohol, crushing taxes, absolute lack of liberty, permanent terror, moral and material misery, and shameless exploitation." He worked with Vo Nguyen Giap, who organised the Viet Nam Communist guerrillas. With the help of the Allies they were able to mobilise the Vietnamese resistance against the Japanese. Under their leadership the Vietminh obtained a definite programme aiming at the establishment of a republican constitution which guaranteed democratic rights and privileges and promoted the national economy and welfare of the people. The events in the pacific forced Japan to surrender in August 1945 and the war came to an end. In the same year the national congress was convened by the Vietminh in Tonking. It elected Ho Chi Minh as President. The local administration was to be entrusted to the committees set up by the new regime. Bao Dai renounced his throne and accepted the office of the Supreme political adviser of the provisional government of Ho Chi Minh. By constituting Annam, Tonking and Cochin China into a Democratic Republic of Viet Nam, Ho Chi Minh declared its independence on 2 September 1945 at Hanoi.

However, the French were not ready to give up sovereignty over this vast empire in South East Asia. General De Gaulle had proposed a plan for the organisation of an Indo-Chinese Federation as an integral part of France. The Potsdam declaration provided for the French and Chinese occupation of Indo-China north of the sixteenth parallel. The British and the French troops were to occupy south of the sixteenth parallel. When the final settlement was arrived the French alone were left in control of Indo-China so that necessary political agreements were reached with Viet Nam, Cambodia and Laos. As a result of the different agreements concluded in 1946 Cambodia and Laos became protectorates of France once again. But the Vietnamese resisted the French return. While the French Government was busy in making preparations for resuming control Ho Chi Minh consolidated his forces. The Chinese were able to extend timely assistance to Ho Chi Minh. They prevented French entry into Tonking. At this juncture the three political factions, the old Viet Nam Nationalist party, the Viet Nam Revolutionary League and the Vietminh were brought together in the elections of January 1946. These three groups were represented in the national cabinet formed by Ho Chi Minh. This was followed by the recognition of the Democratic Republic of Viet Nam by France as a "free state with its own government, parliament, army, and finances, forming part of the Indo-Chinese Federation and the French Union." A referendum was to be held to ascertain whether the provinces of Annam, Tonking and Cochin China should be united. The Vietnamese agreed for the returning of the French troops to Tonking. But its size was limited to 25,000, out of which 15,000 were to be French and the rest Vietnamese. These troops were to be under French command and to be withdrawn by 1952.

In spite of these accords popular uprisings broke out all over in Viet Nam, Cambodia and Laos. They demanded "Unity and Independence." Ho Chi Minh visited France to negotiate a settlement. But anti-nationalist officials in Indo-China made every effort to upset negotiations of the French with the Vietminh leaders.

A settlement was reached when Ho Chi Minh and the French Minister for Overseas signed an accord in Paris on 14 September 1946. But major issues like unity and independence remained unsettled.

The French cooperated with the Vietminh in suppressing political parties of Viet Nam National Party and Viet Nam Revolutionary League. Ho Chi Minh was ably assisted by Vo Nguyen Giap in organising the Viet Nam Army. Very soon differences arose between the French and the Vietminh on the question of control over the customs at Haiphong. It resulted in a Civil War. The French bombarded Haiphong on 23 November 1946,while the Vietnamese retaliated by attacking the French in Hanoi on 19 December 1946. The French began a political campaign against Ho Chi Minh and brain-washed Bao Dai and his supporters. Even the religious elements were approached by the French against Ho. Due to French pressure the supporters of Bao Dai group proclaimed the new provisional Central Government of Annam. Nguyen Van Xuan was named President. The French recognised the new regime by signing an agreement on 5 June 1948. The Bao Dai Government came to be described as Viet Nam and that of Ho Chi Minh as Vietminh.

The issue assumed an international dimension for the French, Vietnamese and Cambodians sought for the support of the different powers in solving the question. It also involved ideological forces. The United States supported anti-Communist forces in South Viet Nam and the Soviet Union tried to influence the Vietminh.

Bao Dai visited France and concluded agreements with French Government which included Viet Nam in the French Union enjoying the status of an Associate State. Similar status was also extended to Laos and Cambodia. On his return to Saigon Bao Dai became the chief of the Viet Nam Government on 30 December 1949. The USA, Britain and other powers recognised Bao Dai's Government in February 1950. However, USSR,

China, Yugoslavia and other powers continued diplomatic relations with Vietminh headed by Ho Chi Minh. After the establishment of communist Republic in China Ho Chi Minh inclined more and more towards the Chinese. These developments only increased the military tension. The French obtained aid from America. The Vietminh forces fought desperately for obtaining control of important cities. The delta areas of Red river and Meking river and Dien Bien Phu witnessed the deadliest fight. The fighting capacity of the French was affected on the outbreak of the Korean War in June 1950. However, the United States came to the rescue. Even amidst these difficulties the Vietnamese did not ignore their demand for independence. Therefore, the French President made a declaration on 28 April 1954 regarding the total independence but within the French Union. This was opposed by the Viet Nam nationalists and they insisted complete independence without any limitations.

On the other hand, Ho Chi Minh successfully organized the Democratic Republic of Viet Nam. Law and order was maintained. Though the National United Front constituted the government the policies of the government were dictated by the Lao Dang or the Communist Party. He obtained every equipment and help from Russia. No doubt Cambodia and Laos were not Associate States within the mainland. But they were in a similar position as that of Bao Dai's Viet Nam with France. The Cambodian Prince Sihanauk insisted absolute independence for Cambodia. By signing several protocols in 1953 with France he obtained full sovereignty for Cambodia in military, judicial and economic matters. Laos also signed a treaty in the same year declaring it to be fully independent within the French Union. Both Cambodia and Laos were to fight against the Vietminh invaders. When the hostilities were thus mounting and human blood was split indiscriminately in Indo-China an international conference met at Geneva on 26 April 1954. When the conference ended in July 1954 series of agreements and declarations were recorded to end hostilities in Indo-China.

Among them the agreements regarding simultaneous cease-fire, temporary demarcation line above the seventeenth parallel along the Ben Hai River and withdrawal of French troops were important. For the cessation of hostilities in Laos and Cambodia separate treaties were concluded. The cease-fire was to be supervised by an international commission consisting of India, Poland and Canada. Thus the unification of North and South Viet Nam was permanently marred and the different international power blocs contributed for this division.

The Vietminh in the North Viet Nam introduced several reforms both in the administration and the economic fields. Ho Chi Minh who headed the North Viet Nam Government consolidated all the resources to employ the same for the economic reconstruction and establishing political stability. The Lao Dang or the workers party and the Communist Party introduced the programme of land reforms to increase agricultural production. In the industrial system heavy industry was given priority and all the business came to be owned by the State. Though the implementation of these reforms was opposed, it was effectively crushed in the national interest. Soviet Russia and Communist China gave necessary aid for the development of North Viet Nam. Factories were established and Railways were developed. The Railway lines that were closed formerly were reopened connecting North Viet Nam with Southern China. All these helped the rapid economic growth of Viet Nam under Ho Chi Minh. By 1960 there was a stable government and a well developed economic system enabled the communists to bring about further political changes.

The provisional Government of Ho Chi Minh successfully controlled the entire administrative machinery. It gave confidence to the leaders of the Lao Dang to introduce a new constitution as a permanent feature. In the new set up provision was made for the dictatorship of a single party. The Lao Dang was to control the political authority through its leaders. This was ratified by the people by a mandate in the elections. Ho Chi Minh was to continue to head the government as President. Phan Van Dong was made the Premier and Foreign Minister. Vo Nguyen Giap became the Minister of Defence and Commander-in-Chief. They were assisted by Truong Chinh by leading the National Assembly. This team worked remarkably for the all round progress of North Viet Nam. Amidst strain and stress they waded through successfully. The death of Ho Chi Minh in 1969 was a national loss. However, his colleagues continued the policies and programme of work initiated by him.

On the other hand, in South Viet Nam political factions affected progress. The Bao Dai's Government did not enjoy whole-hearted cooperation of the different groups. Saigon became the hot bed of political intrigues. This political chaos enabled the two adventurous brothers to emerge successfully to lead the Government of South Viet Nam. They were Ngo Dinh Diem and Ngo Dinh Nhu. Ngo Dinh Diem was popular as the premier of the South Viet Nam Republic from 1955 and also became its President. He obtained American help to maintain his authority. The different political groups were played against one another so that they may be ultimately weakened. The Communists were crushed by Diem. In spite of it political opposition for him could not be totally stamped out. The communists in South Viet Nam organised insurrections and guerilla activities. The lack of consolidation in the local administration greatly helped the communists to establish administrative control in the rural parts through the National Liberation Front. They also collected taxes from the people in utter disregard to the Diem regime. Ngo Dinh Diem branded these communists as the Vietcong. The Diem's regime was brought to an end by a military coup in 1963 and he was killed.

The American administration resolved to destroy the Vietcongs so that the communist progress in South East Asia was prevented. At the same time they contended that Ho Chi Minh and his Government should be defeated to achieve this objective. What followed next was the long drawn tragedy of Viet Nam War.

The Geneva Conference of 1954 brought independence to Laos. But the international interests often fomented political strife in Laos. However, it was ended in 1962 when the United States and Soviet Union brought about the fourteen nations declaration contemplating "independence, neutrality, and peace for Laos." According to this all foreign control was to be withdrawn from Laos. An International Control Commission was to be set up to see that the Royal Laotian Government is established. For the time being affairs in Laos were settled. But the issue of Pathet Lao dragged Laos into the war.

In Cambodia the Prince Sihanouk was able to establish political stability. His personal interest in the matters of administration attracted the masses towards him. But the administrative machinery was not based on firm foundations to obtain the unifying force. His attitude was vehemently criticised by the intellectuals and some of the political factions obtained aid from the American administration against the Prince. Sihanouk ended diplomatic relations with the USA in 1965, instead he inclined towards Haoi and Peking for friendship and aid. Later developments resulted in political confusion and economic distress. Prince Sihanouk's regime was overthrown in April 1970, when he was away in Europe, by General Lon Nol. The Communist China proclaimed her support to the exile Government of Cambodia headed by Prince Sihanouk. And the Viet Nam war spread into Cambodia also.

51

The League of Nations

Introduction

Although the League of Nations was directly an outcome of the First World War, yet a considerable amount of influence was exercised by the pre-war movements like the Concert of Europe, the Hague Conferences and the public international unions, in the modelling of the different organs of the League of Nations. However, it cannot be denied that the League provided for the first time a comprehensive system with the union in one institution of a number of separate elements which had previously existed in a piecemeal fashion.

The horrors of the First World War convinced the people that war was not an effective method of settling disputes. It helped neither the conqueror not the conquered. Therefore, in almost all quarters of world a need was felt for an international organisation, strong enough to ward off the recurrence of war, capable of ensuring peace and security in the war-weary world. The League of Nations was the outcome.

The idea of having a league of states was being canvassed even before the out-break of the war. In 1905, Sir Henry Campbell proposed the creation of 'a League of Peace'. In 1911, Sir Edward Grey emphasised the need of establishing some sort of a comity or concern of Nations. After the out-break of the war, frantic efforts were made to find out the basis of a lasting world peace. Prof. Rappard of Switzerland took a lead in this regard, followed by a group of English men under the leadership of Lord Bryce in USA also an organisation known as 'The League to Enforce Peace, was formed under the leadership of ex-President Traft in 1915. Proposals were also submitted by Sweden, Denmark, Norway, England, France etc. for organising an international body which could effectively dispense with war and establish peace. The establishment of League of Nations received special impetus when President Woodrow Wilson announced his historic fourteen-point programme in January 1918. The last point of President Wilson's programme emphasised that "a general association of nations must be formed under specific covenants for the purpose of according mutual guarantees of political independence and territorial integrity to great and small states alike."

The Covenant of the League of Nations was drafted by a very small and compact group. Originally the commission consisted of only ten members—two from each of the five great powers. But later on, after protests were received from small states, nine additional members were added. President Wilson of USA served as the Chairman of the Commission. Subsequently the covenant was incorporated in Treaty of Versailles as Part I and was signed on June 28, 1919. Likewise the Covenant was included as part I of other peace treaties concluded between 1919-1920. The Covenant actually came into force on January 10, 1920, after obtaining the ratification of the requisite number of states.

Chief Objectives of the League of Nations

The League of Nations was the direct outcome of the horrors of World War I, and was established to ward-off the recurrence of war and to ensure peace and security in the war-weary world.

Membership

There were two types of members of the League of Nations—the original and non-original. The original members of the League of Nations were those states and dominions who were the signatories to the Treaty or Peace or those states who were invited to accede to the Covenant and actually acceded before March 20, 1920. As regards the non-original members, the Covenant provided in Article 1(2) that "any fully self-governing state, dominion or colony not named in the annex may become a member of the League if its admission is agreed to by two-thirds of the Assembly, provided that it shall give effective guarantees of its sincere intention to observe its international obligations, and shall accept such regulations as may be prescribed by the League in regard to its military, naval and air forces and armaments". There were 42 original members of the League of Nations. Seventeen states were subsequently admitted as members. Certain states were refused membership on numerous grounds, viz. the application was not in order, the states applying for admission were having unstable governments and unsettled frontiers, the past record of the state with regard to discharge of its international obligations was not good etc.

The membership of a state could be terminated by voluntary withdrawal, by expulsion and by lapse consequent upon dissent from amendments under Article 26. Article 1(3) provided that "any member of League may, after two years' notice of its intention so to do, withdraw from the League, provided that all its international obligations and all its obligations under the Covenant shall have been fulfilled at the time of its withdrawal." During the lifetime of the League 16 states withdrew from its membership. USSR was the only country to be expelled from the membership of the League for violating Article 16 of the Covenant, when she committed aggression on Finland in December, 1939. Though 62 states were members of the League of Nations, their total strength at any one time never exceeded 58.

Organisation of the League

The League of Nations had three main organs—the Assembly, the Council and the Secretariat. However, in addition to these three two other organisations, viz., the Permanent Court of International Justice and the International Labour Organisation, also existed.

The Assembly

Every member of the League of Nations automatically became a member of the Assembly. Although each state was permitted to send three representatives to the Assembly, it had only one vote. The Assembly thus closely resembled a diplomatic conference; it certainly was not an international legislative body. As a rule, all important decisions could be taken by the Assembly by the unanimous agreement of the members present at the meeting. The Assembly was expected to meet at least once a year. However, special sessions of the Assembly could be convened as and when necessary. The Assembly elected its own President at every new session by a majority of votes.

Usually the President was taken from some small state not at that time represented on the Council.

Functions of the Assembly

The Covenant had not drawn a clear line of demarcation between the functions of the Assembly and the Council. The powers of the two organs were defined in identical language, viz., each had the power to "deal at its meetings with any matter within the sphere of action of the League or affecting the peace of the world" (Articles 3(3) and 4(5). However, the Covenant also conferred on both the bodies a number of special or exclusive functions. The exclusive functions assigned to the Assembly included (i) the right to admit new members to the League of Nations by a two-thirds majority; (ii) election of the non-permanent members of the Council; (iii) apportioning the expenses of the League among the member states; (iv) advising reconsideration by members of the League, of the treaties which had become inapplicable; (v) consideration of international conditions whose continuance might endanger the peace of the world; (vi) supervising the work of the Council; (vii) election of fifteen judges of the Permanent Court of International Justice every nine years by majority vote; (viii) amendment of the Covenant; and (ix) approval of the nomination of the Secretary General by the Council.

In short, the functions assigned to the Assembly made it a dominant organ of the League, though in actual practice due to its nature and size it could not make effective use at these powers.

Council

The Council was designed to be a small body to serve as the executive organ of the League. It consisted of five permanent members (the USA, the British Empire, France, Italy, and Japan) and four non-permanent members, mostly lesser powers. Due to failure of the United States of America to join the League, the membership of the Council stayed at eight until two non-permanent seats were added in 1922. The Council could increase the number of permanent and non-permanent members with the approval of the majority of the Assembly (Art. 4(2)). It was in pursuance of this power that Germany was given a permanent seat in 1926, and USSR was made a member in 1934. The number of the non-permanent members was also eventually increased to eleven.

The Council was expected to meet at least once a year. It met either at the seat of the League or at such other place as was decided upon. Emergency meetings of the Council could be summoned during the emergency arising out of war or threat of a war. Every member of the Council had only one vote. When a state was not represented on the Council, and a matter pertaining to that state came up for consideration, a special invitation was to be extended to the state concerned.

Functions of the Council

The Council was assigned as extensive functions as those of the Assembly. It could deal with all the matters within the sphere of the League or affecting the peace of the world. In addition the Council was specifically entrusted with the following functions : (i) nomination of additional permanent members of the Council; (ii) formulating plans for the reduction of armaments, taking into account the geographical situation and circumstances of each state; (iii) to advise how the evil effects of manufacture of munitions and implements of war by private enterprise can be prevented. However, due regard had to be given to the necessities of those members of the League which were not able to manufacture the munitions and implements of war necessary for their safety; (iv) advise upon the means which the members of the League were to preserve, as against external aggression, the territorial integrity and existing political independence of their fellow members; (v) to define the scope of authority or control to be exercised by the Mandatory powers under the Mandate System; (vi) to direct the work of the Secretariat and receive reports from the subsidiary organs of the League; (vii) to recommend to the several governments effective military sanctions and expulsion of any member who had violated any of the covenants of the League. The Council also prepared plans for disarmament and nominated the Secretary-General, subject to the approval of the Assembly. " Because of its small size and its more frequent meetings" hold Vandenbosch and Hogan. "The Council did develop into something like an executive body, while the role of the Assembly was more restricted to primary action and the determination of the principles".

The Secretariat

The Covenant also provided for a permanent Secretariat, headed by the Secretary General, at Geneva. It was to consist of such Secretaries and Staff as may be required. The Secretary-General was appointed by the Council with the approval of the Assembly. The Secretary and other staff of the Secretariat was appointed by the Secretariat-General with the approval of the Council. The expenses for the maintenance of the Secretariat were contributed by the member states in proportion decided by the Assembly. Unlike the Assembly and the council which held periodical meetings, the Secretariat worked throughout the year. The officials of the League while on duty were entitled to diplomatic privileges and immunities. The members of the League were in no way responsible to their respective governments.

Functions of the Secretariat

The chief functions of the secretariat included (i) co-ordinating the widespread activities of the League carried on by its various organs ; (ii) providing a source of continuity and follow-up for League work ; (iii) keeping the records of the League agencies ; (iv) furnishing information and analysis to organs and delegates ; (v) registration of treaties and international engagements entered into by the members of the League ; (vi) arrangement of the meetings and the like ; (vii) indirectly influencing in a limited manner the settlement of disputes and formulation of League policy.

The Permanent Court of International Justice

Article 14 of the Covenant had entrusted to the Council the responsibility of formulating and submitting to the members plans for the establishment of a Permanent Court of International Justice. Accordingly in 1920, the Council appointed a Commission of Jurists. The Commission prepared a statute of the proposed Court, which was submitted for approval to the Council, Assembly and the members of the League. After the statute was ratified by the member states, a Court was set up at the Hague. By 1939, fifty-one states had become the member of the Court.

Composition

Originally the International Court of Justice consisted of 11 judges and 4 deputy judges. The strength of the judges was increased to 15 through an amendment in 1930. In 1936, the offices of deputy judges were abolished. All these judges were elected for a term of 9 years by the Council and the Assembly. However, the candidates were nominated by the national groups of the Hague Permanent Court of Arbitration, each group having the right to name 4 candidates, only 2 of whom were to be of its own nationality. The Secretary-General of the League prepared a list of the persons so nominated and transmitted it to the Council and the Assembly. These two bodies concurrently elected the judges.

Jurisdiction of the Court

The Court gave its judgements on questions involving the interpretation of International law, treaties and other mutual obligations. However, it had jurisdiction only over such disputes as members were willing to submit to it. A few countries, however, agreed in advance to submit all their disputes to the court for settlement. Others reserved the right to submit only those cases to the Court which they liked. The establishment of the Permanent Court of International justice was, in the words of Schuman, "the most important and successful effort thus for made to establish an international judicial tribunal for the adjudication of controversies between States". During it existence "the Court tried sixty-five cases and handed down thirty-two judgments, "twenty-seven advisory opinions and severals hundred orders". Thus it created a body of legal precedents of great utility for the solution of future international cases of justicable character.

International Labour Organisation

The International Labour Organisation was set up as a part of the organisation of the League and was an integral part of the League. All members of the League also became the members of the International Labour Organisation.

The main objective of the I.L.O. was to promote international peace through the promotion of social justice by regulating working hours, labour supply, prevention of unemployment, providing adequate living wages, protection of workers against sickness, disease, injury, etc. protection of children and women, vocational and technical education, freedom of association and technical assistance to underdeveloped countries and protection of the interest of workers when employed in foreign countries. In short, the chief objective of the I.L.O. was "to gain recognition for workers as human social beings rather than as mere commodities to be brought cheaply and to be exploited in the process of industrial and agricultural production".

The International Labour Organisation worked under the control of a Governing Body consisting of 32 persons. While 16 of these members represented the governments, 8 each represented the employers and workers. The term of the Governing body was fixed at three years.

The Organisation provided an international forum for the discussion of labour legislation, prepared the way for the formulation of international standards of labour legislation and worked as a useful agency for the collection and publication of labour statistics. The I.L.O. continued to work even during the Second World War and ultimately became a specialised agency of the UN in December, 1964.

Functions of the League of Nations

The main functions of the League of Nations have been specified in the Preamble to the Covenant, which reads : "The high contracting parties, in order to promote international co-operation and to achieve international peace and security by the acceptance of obligations not to resort to war by the prescription of open just and honourable relations between nations by the firm establishment of the understandings of international law as the actual rule of conduct among governments and, by the maintenance of justice and a scrupulous respect for all treaty obligations in the dealings of the organized people with one another, agree to this Covenant of the League of Nations."

In pursuance of the objectives laid down in the Preamble the League of Nations was expected to formulate plans for "the reduction of national armaments to the lowest point consistent with national safety" (Art.8). Another important function assigned to the League was to 'undertake to respect and preserve as against external aggression the territorial integrity and existing political independence of all members of the League'. In case of any such aggression, the Council was expected to advise the means by which this obligation was to be fulfilled (Art. 10). The Senate of USA refused to ratify the treaty of Versailles mainly on the grounds of Article 10, and consequently USA could not become a member of the League of Nations.

The third important function of the League was settlement of international disputes. Under Article 12 the members were obliged to submit their disputes, likely to cause rupture either to arbitration or judicial settlement or to the inquiry by the Council, and they had not to resort to war until three months after the awards by the arbitrators or the judicial decision or the report by the Council. The members were expected to comply with the award or decision. In case the members failed to carry out the award or decision, the Council could propose the necessary steps to give affect to the same. (Art. 13(4). If a state resorted to war in violation of the covenant it was *ipso facto* considered to have committed an act of war against all other members of the League, which were expected to severe all trade and financial relations and prevent all financial, commercial or personal intercourse between the nationals of the covenant breaking state and the nationals of any other state. For the protection of the covenant the Council could also demand from several Governments concerned necessary contribution of armed forces. In extreme cases members violating the Covenant of the League could be expelled from the membership of the League (Art. 16). Russia was actually expelled from the membership of the League in 1940 following her invasion of Finland.

In fourth place, the League of nations was expected to take steps to bring about peaceful changes. For the purpose, the Assembly could from time to time advise the reconsideration by members of the League of the treaties which had become inapplicable, and the consideration of international conditions whose continuance could endanger the peace of the world (Art. 13).

Apart from the above functions the League was also expected to exercise supervision over the mandate territories.

The League was also expected to take the necessary steps for the promotion of human welfare.

Thus, the League helped to make the people aware of the existence of world conditions and world problems and to dispel ideas concerning purely national and isolated difficulties.

The Work and Achievements of the League of Nations

During the two decades of its existence the League of Nations worked on various fronts. While it was successful in certain areas, it had to face failure in others. The activities of the League of Nations during its existence may be conveniently studied under the following headings.

Political Achievements

One of the chief objectives for the creation of the League was to promote international co-operation and achieve international peace and security. During its existence the League was called upon to examine about 40 political disputes between different states. Most of these disputes were handed by the Council, although some of them were also referred to the Assembly or the Permanent Court of International Justice. Some of these disputes were really of a serious nature which could threaten the peace of the world, while certain other disputes were of minor importance. The success of the League was also not uniform. However, one thing can easily be observed that League was able to assert its authority more effectively against small nations, alone. The big and strong powers however did not submit to the authority of the League and retarded its investigations on the plea that it infringed their sovereign rights. Let us examine some of the important disputes handed by the League.

Asland Islands

Asland dispute was one of the first disputes brought to the attention of the League Council. This island lay between Sweden and Finland, both of which once belonged to Sweden. These were acquired by Russia in 1809. During the Russian Revolution of 1918 Finland declared her independence, which was recognised by Swedish, began to agitate for union with Sweden. Though the Swedish Government remained indifferent, the people of Sweden wanted their government to help the islands. As a result, there was a possibility of war. Great Britain, exercising her rights under the Covenant, brought the case to the attention of the Secretary-General. The matter was referred to a Committee of Jurists, which decided that the dispute was not a matter of domestic jurisdiction as claimed by Finland. The Council gave its decision in June 1921 by which Finland's sovereignty over the islands was recognised. The resident of the islands were to be guaranteed autonomy and protection of political rights. Use of Swedish in schools was to be preserved. The archipelago was to be neutralized and unfortified. In April, 1922 an international convention guaranteed the neutrality of the Islands and gave them the requisite international protection.

Eupen and Malmedy

In 1920-21 Germany protested to the Council against the attribution of Eupen and Malmedy to Belgium. In September 1920, the Council decided to recognise as final the transfer of the districts of Eupen and Malmedy to Belgium. On February 22, 1922 Germany was informed by the Secretary-General that the decision was final.

Mosul Boundary Dispute

As per terms of the Treaty of Lausanne (1923) a mutually acceptable boundary line was to be drawn between Turkey and Iraq. As both the parties failed to draw a mutually acceptable boundary line and claimed Mosul Vilayet, an area rich in oil, the matter was referred to the League in 1924. As the situation was grave, an emergency session of the League Council was called at Brussels, which drew a provisional boundary line pending final judgement. Ultimately, the same line was made permanent line between Turkey and Iraq. Though Great Britain (as Mandatory Power) and Iraq accepted the award, Turkey refused to do so. By a compromise treaty concluded between Turkey and Great Britain in 1926, a small part of the Vilayet was given to Turkey. Some royalties from the Mosul oil fields were also given to Turkey.

Greco-Italian Dispute or the Corfu Incident

In August 1923, certain military officers were murdered on Greek soil. The Italian government demanded apologies and full reparations for the crime from the Greek government. As the later failed to comply with the demands of Italy, she occupied the island of Corfu. In September, 1923 the Greek Government referred the matter to the League Council. Later the League Council notified that communisation had been received from the Conference of Ambassadors informing the settlement of the dispute as a result of diplomatic negotiations.

The Greco Bulgarian Crisis

In October, 1925 a border incident led to flagrant invasion of Bulgarian territory by forces. To repair the breach of Covenant obligations, the Bulgarian government requested an immediate meeting of the Council of the League. The Acting President of the Council ordered that until the Council had heard both the sides, all troops must be withdrawn to their respective frontiers. The belligerents acceded to the demand. Military attaches of Great Britain, France and Italy went to the scene of action to verify the position. Within nine days of the aggression calm was restored on both the sides.

War in Gran Chaco

In 1928 trouble started in Gran Chaco, situated between Bolivia and Paraguay. As soon as the matter came to the notice of the Council, it sent a telegram to both the parties, urging both the parties to reach an amicable settlement. As a result the immediate quarrel was resolved. However, in 1932 fresh troubles started, which could not be checked by the efforts of the neighbouring states. Impelled by the circumstances the League sent a Commission of Inquiry. Although the war between the two states ended in 1936 by the exhaustion of both the belligerents rather than by the concerted efforts of the Inquiry Commission, the incident certainly demonstrated the interest which the League was taking in the preservation of peace everywhere.

Manchurian Dispute

In 1931, a serious dispute arose between Japan and China over Manchuria. In September 1931 Japan occupied Central Manchuria on the plea that China had destroyed her railway properties. China appealed to the League Council, which called upon the disputants to withdraw their troops. But as the Japanese failed to withdraw their troops, the Council appointed a five-men Commission to study the situation. In the meanwhile Japan attacked Shanghai and China once again appealed to the assembly, which adopted a resolution on March 4, 1932 calling on Japan to evacuate Shanghai. Tokyo did quit Shanghai under the Armistic of May 5, 1932 but she continued to hold on to Manchuria. The League could not do anything except that some of the powers of the League refused to recognise Manchukuo.

Italian Attack of Ethiopia

In October, 1935 Italy attacked Ethiopia and Ethiopia asked the League to take action under Article 16 of the Covenant. The League Council appointed a ' Committee of Six' which reported that the Italian Government had resorted to war in utter disregard of its obligations under Article 12. On October 9, 1935, the Assembly adopted the report and decided to apply economic sanction met with very favourable response and by November 18, 1945 'the economic siege' of Italy was completely enforced. But Italy did not bother about the resolutions of the League and continued bombing. Addis Ababa fell to the invaders and the whole country lay at the mercy of Mussolini. On May 5, 1936 Italy declared that the war is over and Abyssinia is Italian. Thus the League sanctions failed to stop the invading Italian armies. By July 1936 the measures taken in execution of Article 16 were withdrawn and Ethiopia was left to her fate.

German Aggression and the League

But the most serious challenge was posed to the League by Germany. On October 14, 1933 Germany withdrew from the League; on March 16, 1935 she ordered conscription in violation of the Treaty of Versailles. On March 7, 1936 the Rhineland was remilitarized in violation of the Locarno treaties, in March 1938 Austria was occupied and in March 1939 Czechoslovakia was invaded and seized. The League took no effective action against Germany for all these violations except adopting resolutions and giving warnings. In September, 1939 Germany invaded Poland and the World War II started. By this time the League had become almost defunct.

Other Disputes

In addition to the above cases the League also handled the case of city of Vilna between Poland and Lithunia (1920-22), the case of Hungarian optants between Hungary and Rumania (1923-30), Dispute over Faworzina District between Poland and Czechoslovakia (1923-24). Demir Kapur case between Bulgaria and Greece (1925-26), Austro-German Customs Union case between Great Britain, France and Austria in 1931.

It may be noted that League was effective during the years 1924 to 1930 because during this period not only Germany was also included as a member in the League, but members attached great importance to the activities of the League. This is evident from the fact that prior to 1924 the member states were not represented at Geneva by their Foreign Ministers. In 1924 when MacDonald and Herriot came to Geneva for the Assembly of 1924, they set a precedent of far-reaching importance. Soon the foreign ministers of most other European powers also started attending nearly every session of the Council and Assembly. In course of time Geneva came to be recognised as the meeting, place for the statesmen of Europe. This development accorded strength to the League and she was able to settle almost all the cases referred to her during this period.

Besides maintaining international security, the other political activities of the League were also important. The Mandates Commission, a body composed of eleven experts in colonial government, received annual reports from the Mandatory Powers on the territories administered by them. The Commission submitted these reports to the Council with its comments and recommendations to the Mandatory Powers.

The League also looked after the problem of the minorities and appointed a Committee of three members of the Council, for this purpose. The Committee would receive complaints from the minorities and discussed the matter with the Government of the concerned state, and generally succeeded in obtaining an undertaking from the government to remedy the grievance complained of. However, if the committee failed to obtain satisfaction it could refer the petition to the Council. In short, the League worked through the method of persuasion and consent.

The League also successfully administered the Saar territory through a Governing Commission from 1920-35, till a plebiscite was conducted there in January 1935. It also guaranteed the constitution of the free city of Danzig and appointed a High Commissioner to arbitrate on disputes between the Free City and Poland. However, both the parties were given the right to appeal to the Council against the decisions of the High Commissioner.

Economic Achievements

In the economic sphere the League provided for a new and elaborate machinery for international co-operation. It set up financial and economic committee composed of experts from various countries. These committees met annually at Geneva and directed the work of the financial and economic sections of the League. The Financial Committee of the League helped in tackling the problem of counter-feiting, falsification of commercial documents, double taxation and fluctuating value of gold. The Economic Committee also did the preliminary work on a number of major international conferences, viz., the World Economic Conference of 1927 and the Monetary and Economic Conference of 1933.

For the implementation of Article 23 of the Covenant "to make provision to secure and maintain freedom of communications and of transit and equitable treatment for the commerce of all members of the League", the League created an autonomous Communications and Transit Organisation. The organisation was concerned with the freedom of international transit, the collection of transit statistics, press facilities and accuracy of reporting, the simplification of passport and other travel documents, discrimination against foreign shipping in ports, the use of inland waters, the uniformity of highway traffic regulation, coordination of the national public works programmes, etc.

Social Achievements

In the social sphere also the League did a remarkable job. In 1925, a Slavery Convention was concluded at Geneva and in 1932, the League decided to set up a Permanent Slavery Commission. It tried to improve the lot of the working people through the International Labour Organisation, though the various conventions concluded by the I.L.O. were generally not ratified by the member states.

In terms of Article 23 of the Covenant, the League set up in 1923 the Health Organisation with a Health Committee and Secretariat. It closely collaborated with the governments in organising action against malaria, small-pox, leprosy, rabies, cancer, tuberculosis, syphilis, heart disease, etc. With a view to improve the national health, the Health Organisation held technical conferences and helped researches in medicine. The League co-operated with China to organise relief work in flood areas. The League also did notable work in combating infant mortality, collecting statistics, fixing dietary standards and controlling plagues.

The League also successfully solved the problem of the care and resettlement of millions of war prisoners and refugees. Dr. Nansen played an important role in the settlement of refugees under the aegis of the League. The chief contribution of the League in this regard was mainly that of co-ordination with the help of funds provided by the states and private charitable institutions.

To assist the intellectuals in the war devastated areas the League appointed an International Committee on Intellectual Cooperation in 1922. In 1926, The International Institute of Intellectual Co-operation was set up at Paris to co-ordinate "international collaboration with a view to promoting the progress of general civilisation and human knowledge and notably the development and diffusion of science, letters and arts". This was achieved through conferences, lectures, published materials to urge collective security, support of the League, elimination of inflammatory material from text books and radio broadcasts, etc.

The League also did useful work in the field of control of traffic in dangerous drugs, promotion of child welfare, prison reform, prohibition of traffic in women, suppression of trade in obscene publications, etc.

Impressed by the humanitarian work of the League Cordell Hull, the Secretary of State remarked in 1939 : " The League of Nations has been responsible for more humanitarian and scientific endeavour than any other organisation in history".

Estimate of the League

According to Walters the establishment of the League was a 'revolutionary step'. It involved " changes of principles, changes even in the general conviction which form the basis of public opinion. Before the League it was held both in theory and practice that every state was the sole and sovereign judge of its own acts, owing no allegiance to any higher authority, entitled to resent criticism or even questioning by other states." With the establishment of the League " the belief that aggressive war is a crime against humanity and that it is the interest, the right, and the duty of every state to join in preventing it is now everywhere taken for granted." Although the League as a working institution is dead, but the ideals which it sought to promote and the agencies it created have become an essential part of the political thinking of the civilised world.

"If measured by what other international organisations had accomplished in the past," holds Potter, "the League's performance even in the security field rates very high, indeed higher than that of any other international institution, with the exception of a very few highly special and limited agencies". Probably, the greatest contribution of the League was the influence it exercised in spreading the idea of international co-operation.

From the above discussion it is evident that though politically a failure, the League of Nations had much to its credit in the social, economic and educational fields. Even in the political sphere it was able to reduce tension on many a occasions and resolve disputes.

The Failure of the League of Nations

In spite of its best intentions and efforts the League of Nations failed to save the succeeding generations from the scourge of war and the world was involved in yet another fierce war. The failure of the League of Nations can be attributed to the following factors:

Covenant was Incorporated in the Peace Treaties

If was unfortunate that the Covenant of the League of Nations was made a part and parcel of the peace treaties. As a result, it came to be regarded as instrument of the victorious states to maintain status quo. It would have been better if the Covenant had been kept separate from these peace treaties. There were a number of states who were not satisfied with the peace treaties and were unwilling to ratify the same. By refusing to ratify the treaties, these states were automatically debarred from the membership of the League. For example Germany looked at the Treaty of Versailles as a symbol of her national humiliation and was always in the look out to wreck it at the earliest opportunity.

All the Great Powers were not Associated with the League

Another important factor responsible for the failure of the League was that it was not broad-based. A number of states like Russia, Germany, Austria and Turkey were not invited to join the League at the initial stages which gave them the feeling that the League was not a gathering of free nations but an assembling of the victorious imperialists. Even those major powers who joined the League of Nations were unwilling to co-operate. The United States of America, which had played a dominant part in the birth of the League could not join it as a result of us Senate's refusal to ratify the treaty of the Versailles. In the absence of USA even England became less enthusiastic. In fact she had accepted the obligations of the League Covenant in the hope that the USA, with her vast resources, would be by her side in the new enterprise.

Structural Defects

The failure of the League was also partly due to the inherent defects in the structure and constitution of the Covenant of the League. According to Prof. Morgenthu a grave constitutional weakness of the League was that it permitted the states to resort to war under certain conditions. The Covenant made a distinction between the offensive and defensive war and permitted the latter. By permitting exception to the prohibition of war, the Covenant seemed to assume that war was the normal solution of international disputes.

Another defect of the Covenant was that it insisted that all decisions should be taken by a unanimous vote of the members of the Council, except the parties to the dispute. This rule proved unworkable and ultimately the Assembly moved towards the rule of simple majority.

The League also lacked teeth, because no international force was provided to enforce its decisions. It could merely request the member states to act in a particular manner in a given situation, but its request was not binding on them. Further the Covenant did not make any provision for immediate action on the part of the League. League did not intervene until a crucial stage had been reached. Usually by that time the major powers would commit themselves and it was not possible for them to recede without loss of prestige.

The Attitude of Great Powers

The failure of the League was not so much due to constitutional weakness as to the absence of the will on the part of the powers to work it. In the absence of a spirit of co-operation even the best organisation is bound to fail. Potter has rightly observed that "The ultimate culprits in the failure of the League were the member states. It was not the League of Nations but the Nations of the League which failed in so far there was failure. The legal obligation or the legal theory of the Organisation was defective on this side, but this did not preclude action by the members for effective promotion of security and welfare."

The various members of the League wanted to use the League for the furtherance of their own ends. France was more interested in security against Germany than anything else. For this reason she supported Italy in Ethiopia to win her over as against Germany. Similarly, England viewed the League as "a valuable organ for the chanalization and settlement of international disputes, for the promotion of economic recovery and social co-operation and for the preservation of an international balance." Even USSR did not sincerely support the efforts of the League and in 1940 undertook aggression in Finland in violation of the Covenant of the League. This action led to her expulsion from the world body. Likewise, Germany, who was in the beginning excluded from the League, used the League to change some of the abnoxious features of the Treaty of Versailles. Later she left the League because it clashed with her ideal of 'world-hegemony'. Italy and Japan had also similar attitude towards the League.

Thus the League failed because the major powers of the world were not genuinely interested in the effective working of the League. They used the League as an instrument to safeguard their national interests. This certainly undermined the basis of the League.

Small Nations had no Faith in League

As a result of the attitude of the major powers, the small nations lost faith in the capacity of the League to save them from any aggression. The principle of Collective Security was not applied in actual practice. Had all the states joined hands against Japan and Italy on the questions of Manchuria and Abyssinia respectively aggression would have been checked and the prestige of the League increased. As each state decided to follow its own policy and the League could not take any concerted effort the principle of collective security was weakened. This gave rise to a feeling in the minds of smaller nations that they could not depend much on the League.

Equal Status of Members

The equal status which was granted to all the members of the League irrespective of their size and status was not a proper basis of representation in the international organisation. Anothony Eden says the idea of 'one nation, one vote' led to Liberia being treated as important as the Soviet Union and Costa Rica as important as the United Kingdom. This was not fair to big nations who had to bear the major responsibility.

Narrow Nationalism

The spirit of narrow nationalism which prompted every country to save itself at the expense of the rest of the world was another important factor which contributed to the failure of the League. Prof. Potter has brought out this point thus : "The League of Nations failed in so far as it failed because of the people of Germany, Japan and Italy preferred to support their governments in careers of imperialistic conquest and because the people of England, France and the United States discouraged their governments from taking effective action early enough to stem the tide of axis aggression. The peoples and governments of totalitarian states were more responsible for the destruction of international collaboration under the League auspices than those of the liberal states, but the latter must bear a large share of negative blame."

Lack of Sanction

The lack of force at the command of the League was another factor responsible for its failure. The League was not provided with any independent force to effectively deal with the states threatening the peace and security of the world. All the forces to be used against such states were under normal circumstances, left under the national governments concerned. Only during the time of crisis these forces were put under international control. This implied that the states were free to contribute such forces to the international authority or refuse to do so.

No doubt, the League possessed an effective weapon in economic sanction but it was never applied effectively in actual practice. Economic sanctions were applied against

Italy in a half-hearted manner and they naturally failed to achieve the desired results. Even the member states were reluctant to apply the economic sanctions because it hit their economy in turn.

Formation of League Ahead of Time

Some critics feel that the League of Nations failed because it was formed ahead of its times. The people of the world were given to the habit of thinking in terms of national interest and never realised that the interest of the world was greater than their national interest. Further the ideas of 'sovereignty' and 'freedom of action' were too deeply entrenched in their minds that it was not possible to replace them with the ideas of internationalism. As a result even when the League took a decision they never felt it binding on them.

Unanimity Rule Made the League Ineffective

Yet another factor responsible for the collapse of the League of Nations was the defective procedure of voting in the Council and the Assembly. Under the Covenant a decision in all matters, other than procedural, was to be taken by a unanimous vote of all the members. However, in actual practice, due to power rivalries this unanimity of vote could not be achieved and the League could hardly take any action in the face of a crisis.

League Suffered from Imbalance

To the above factors of League's failure Prof. Vendenbosh and Hogan have added the factor of League's imbalance. According to them the League of Nations rested upon three or four main pillars. These were the provision for the reduction of armaments (Art. 8) the guarantees against aggression (Articles 10 and 16), the settlement of disputes (Articles 12 to 15 and 17) and the provision for peaceful change (Art. 19). The last two dovetailed into each other somewhat, as the settlement of a dispute may involve a considerable revision of existing treaties. Because these pillars were not of equal strength, the League suffered from imbalance. The drafters of the Covenant attempted to make the guarantees against aggression very strong, while the provisions for the reduction of armaments and for peaceful change were made relatively weak. Not only was the provision for peaceful change weak, but it seems to be taged on as an after thought."

Though the League failed to preserve the security and peace of the world, we must not lose sight of the excellent work done by the League and its agencies in various fields. The League's greatest achievement was that it did not die but merged with the UN. As Lord Cecil said "The League is dead, Long Live the United Nations".

52

The League of Arab States

A major repercussion of World War II has been the spawning of innumerable regional organisations, reflecting the changing geographical, social, political, economic, diplomatic and ideological order. Many of these were military alliances formed in support of one or the other of the two Super Powers embroiled in the cold war. But the first of these formations - the League of Arab States - was unique in several respects. On 22 March 1945 the League of Arab States (more generally known as the Arab League) came into existence. It was born out of Arab nationalism and a general Arab desire for unity. This phenomena developed during the later part of the nineteenth century and early part of the twentieth as a reaction against Ottoman domination and against the centralisation policies of the contemporary system.

The Arab League was a stage in a series of developments which was by no means ended. In relation to particular historical events, it may be regarded as the first important step in the dual process of Arab unification and liberation since the great Arab revolt of 1915. It was to a large extent a continuation of that unfilled revolution. The Arab unity movement, or the Arab awakening, as it has sometimes been called, may be defined as an effort to recreate and to reintegrate the Arab community. It was essentially a movement of synthesis. While on the one hand it seeks the liberation of Arab territories and states from foreign external domination, on the other it seeks unification on all levels within the Arab domain. The struggle for unity among the Arabs can not be dissociated from their struggle for independence. Throughout the four hundred years in which they formed part of the Ottoman Empire, the Arabs, nevertheless preserved the sense of a community. They had a common past in which all Arabs shared and took pride. They had a common religion i.e. *Islam,* which shaped the main outlines of Arab society and character. They had a common language, a common framework of society and law, and a common way of life. These above factors preserved the common identity of the Arabs, and gave them both distinctness and the power of resistance to external pressure and disintegration.

At the beginning of the nineteenth century, when the forces of nationalism in the world came into their own, the Arabs had retained sufficient identity and self-consciousness to create their own movement for national independence. The different phases of its evolution have often been told: all that is necessary to point out is that the Arab League was only the latest in a chain of developments, the links of which include the creation of modern Egypt by Mehmet Ali; the rise of Wahabism in Central Arabia; the literary activities of the Syrians; the Egyptians, and the Lebanese, the movement of Islamic modernism since Muhammad Abdou; the Pan-Arab Conference of 1913 in Paris; the Arab Revolt of 1915-16, the Iraqi revolt of 1920; the Syrian revolt of 1925-26; the Arab-Palestine revolt of 1936; the Pan-Arab Conference of 1937; the Inter-parliamentary Conference in Cairo in 1938, and the 1939 Palestine Conference in London in which all the then Arab governments participated.

Besides, the Balfour Declaration of November 2, 1917, which called for the establishment of a national home for the Jewish people in Palestine, created dismay and frustration among the Arabs and this led to a mutual sympathy and the aspiration for Arab unity. The post-World War I political division of the Arab world cut the Arabs off from each other physically, administratively, and economically. Arab youth was subjected to a variety of outside influences. To many Arab nationalists it appeared that the independence of a number of small Arab states was bought at too heavy price.

Moreover, the need to unify the Arab world under one international organisation was felt in the early forties even though most of the Arab world was still not free from colonial and Imperial clutches. Furthermore, the need to confront the growing pressure of international Zionism by an Arab Front also necessitated the urge for a Pan-Arab organisation. The British too, for their long-term interests as a major foreign external power in the region, decided to promote the idea and hoped that they would be able to influence it through the pro-British regimes in the region. Thus, the creation of the Arab League was a natural expression of the trends which were already present and which gathered momentum during the Pre-and Post-first world war period.

The immediate impetus for the formation of the Arab League may be found in the initiative taken by Prime Minister Nuri Pasha al- Said of Iraq. In the outcome the Arab League was formed, not as Nuri al-Said had at first envisaged it, but on a more general pattern and with Egypt taking the lead. This was due to the fact that during World War II Cairo had become internationally most important of the Arab capitals. Accordingly the next step in the creation of the Arab League was taken by Mustafa Nahas Pasha, then Prime Minister of Egypt. The Alexandria Protocol of 1944, which was the preparatory character of the proposed Arab League, incorporated the Palestinian question in its Part V. Among other things it said, "Palestine constitutes an important part of the Arab world and that the rights of Arabs in Palestine can not be infringed without prejudice to peace and stability in the Arab world."

The Arab League Pact was formally signed on 22 March 1945. There were seven founder members: Egypt, Iraq, Jordan, Lebanon, Saudi Arabia, Syria and Yemen.

This League was to encourage progress towards regional cooperation and unity and to formulate a joint Arab response to the Zionist colonisation of Palestine. The Charter for the League of Arab States was adopted and signed on 22 March 1945 set forth the following objectives viz.: to strengthen the existing close relations and multiple ties between Arab States; to consolidate and reinforce ties based on respect for the independence and sovereignty of Arab States and to direct efforts towards the interest of all Arab countries with a view to improving their situation, guaranteeing their future and realising their hopes and aspirations. There were seven former members (as mentioned above). Membership has since expanded to include 21 independent states and Palestine, which is represented by the PLO at League meeting. Today among the various officials of the League there is a post of an Assistant Secretary General for Palestine affairs.

According to the provisions of the Article one (The League constitution has twenty articles), all independent Arab states shall be entitled to join the League. Accordingly, 15 states that subsequently became independent joined the League in due course: Libya, 28 March 1953; Sudan, 19 January 1956; Tunisia, 18 January 1958; Morocco, 1 December 1958; Kuwait, 20 July 1961; Algeria, 16 August 1962; the Democratic Yemen, 12 December 1967; Baharain, 11 September 1971; Qatar, 11 September 1971; Oman, 29 September 1971; The Emirates, 6 December 1971; Mauritania, 26 November 1973; Somalia, 14 December 1974; Palestine, 9 August 1976 and Djabouti. 4 September 1977. In March 1979 Egypt' s membership of the Arab League was suspended and it was decided to make Tunis (previously Cairo, i.e. since 1945) the temporary headquarters of the League. Its Secretariat and its permanent committees.

Palestine is considered an independent state as explained in the charter, Annex on Palestine, as follows: since the termination of the last great war, the rule of Ottoman Empire over the Arab countries, among them Palestine, which has become detached from that Empire has come to an end. She has come to be autonomous not subordinate to any other state.

However, even though she was as yet unable to control her own affairs the covenant of the League (of Nations) in 1919 made provision for a regime based upon recognition of her independence. Her international existence and independence in the legal sense cannot, therefore, be questioned any more than could the independence of Arab countries.

Although the outward manifestations of this independence have remained obscured for reasons beyond her control, this should not be allowed to interfere with her participation in the work of the Council of the League.

The states signatory to the peace of the Arab League are, therefore, of the opinion that considering the special circumstances of Palestine and until that country can effectively exercise its independence the council of the League should take charge of the selection of an Arab representative from Palestine to take part in its work.

Relations between member states are regulated by the principle according to which each member undertakes to respect the systems of government of the other members. Member states which desire to enter into a closer relationship may conclude agreements to that effect. In all disputes, threatening to lead to war, the League Council is to act as a mediator. In case of aggression or threat of aggression against a member state the Council may be convened at the request of that state and will then determine the measures to check the aggression.

The Arab League's main achievements have been the convening of Summit meetings, the adoption of resolutions at and outside these Summits, mediation in inter-Arab conflicts and creation of Pan-Arab institutions to foster unity and cooperation among these countries. The Arab summits have been convened following specific developments related to the West Asian conflicts. The League's most important resolution—taken at these summits and otherwise concerned Palestine. The League decided to boycott " Zionist Products" made in Palestine (1945), rejected the Palestine Partition Plan (1946), decreed that no member country could negotiate or conclude a separate peace treaty with Israel (1950), decided the Palestine question (1964), ratified the PLO's decision to create the Palestine Liberation Army (PLA, 1964), drew up three-fold refusal to recognise, negotiate with or make peace with Zionists (1967), demanded a " just" peace, approved the opening of the international conference at Geneva, recognised the PLO as the representative of the Palestinian people (1973), affirmed their right to establish an independent national authority (1974), suspended Egypt's membership in the League (1979), and demanded an independent Palestinian state under the PLO leadership on the West Bank and Gaza strip with Arab Jerusalem as the capital (1982).

As laid down by the pact the structure of the League is relatively simple. It consists of a Council, the special permanent committees, and the permanent Secretariat General. The supreme organ of the Arab League is the Council. It consists of representatives of the 21 member states each of which has one vote, and a representative for Palestine. It generally meets, at foreign ministers' level every March and September. The Council has 16 committees including the political committees and those dealing with communications, health information, youth, women and social affairs.

The Arab League maintains permanent office at the United Nations in New York and has observer status at the UN General Assembly. A general secretariat responsible for implementing Council decisions and for providing financial and administrative services for the personnel of the League. The Secretary General, presently Dr. A.I. Abdel Meguid is appointed by a two-thirds majority of Council members, and holds the rank of ambassador. And the Assistant Secretaries (about 8) have the rank of ministers plenipotentiary.

Besides, the League's three principal organs established under the pact, a number of secondary organs have been created over the years by League Council resolutions to carry out specific purposes of the organisation. In 1950 a joint defence and economic cooperation treaty was concluded to complement the Arab League charter and bodies established under this include a joint Defence Council comprising foreign and defence ministers, and an Economic, linking Economic ministers or their deputies. Other specialised agencies include the Arab organisation for Education, Science and Culture and Arab Civil Aviation and the Council for Arab Economic Union.

Egypt was said to be the most influential member of the Arab League. It hosted the Arab League's headquarters and the offices of its specialised agencies and provided most of the permanent staff. Besides, the first three Secretary Generals were also Egyptian: Abdel Rahman Azzam Pasha (1945-52), Abdul Khaliq Hassouna (1952-72) and Mahmoud Riad. However Egypt's peace treaty with Israel, concluded on 26 March 1979, caused a major crisis in the Arab ranks.

The Arab League Council meeting in Baghdad (27 March 1979) passed the following resolutions, viz: (i) to withdraw Arab ambassadors from Egypt; (ii) to recommend severance of political and diplomatic relations with Egypt; (iii) to suspend Egypt's membership of the League on the date of the signing of the peace treaty with Israel; (iv) to make the city of Tunis the temporary headquarters of the League; (v) to condemn the United States' policy regarding its role including the Camp David Agreement and the Peace Treaty; (vi) to halt all financial and technical aid to Egypt; and; (vii) to prohibit trade exchanges with the Egyptian state and with private establishments dealing with Israel.

Egypt's expulsion from the League scene has led to the decline of Arab League's political influence. Along with this the Arab's lack of a united policy reflects the divisions in the League. Inter-Arab frictions have also contributed to the League's comparative eclipse in recent years. Besides, the Arab Summits that have taken place under the League's auspices since 1964 didn't achieve any concretees success. The challenge of Israel has divided the Arab states on both intention and strategies more than it has united them. Added to this, the participation in Arab Summits was seen as an instrument to strengthen state power against internal opposition.

The disunity among the Palestinians is another indicator of the League's declining role. The split within Fateh, which is the largest of the bodies grouped within the PLO (Palestine Liberation Organisation), ensured that moves towards a resolution of the Arab-Israeli conflict and the Palestine problem would be put on the back burner. Starting with the Lebanese civil war as early as April 1975 and Egyptian-Israeli second disengagement treaty in September 1975 culminating in the Egyptian-Israeli treaty in 1979 each Arab state become more concerned with its own security than the more urgent Palestine problem. As a matter of fact inter Arab conflict increased a great deal in the decade that followed.

Syria intervened in Lebanon after 1975, Libya and Egypt entered into a small border war in July 1977, Algeria and Morocco have great differences concerning the Palestine issue. Jordan and Syria experienced periods of tense relations with their military being put on alert at least twice. Syria and Iraq never developed cooperative relations during this time. Their split continue to be the most damaging aspect of the Arab system's over-all cohesiveness. Each country created its own way of exerting influence. And thus the Arab League became more involved in debating intra-Arab tension and contributed to their frustration with their own paralysis.

Renewed fighting between Lebanese factions, and the continued Iran-Iraq war taking a dangerous turn with the successive American attacks in Gulf were further factors which undermined the scope for effective Arab League in the subsequent years. Indeed intra-Arab differences over the Palestine question intensified and events in Lebanon, Western Sahara, Persian Gulf, the Israeli brutalities in West Bank and Gaza and in killing the PLO Commander Abu Jihad and their tragedy culminated as further major sources of tensions. The Arab League summits till early 1988 strongly condemned Iran for its insistence on continuing the Gulf war and declared its resolve to mobilise all efforts in order to put a speedy end to the fighting. It has succeeded in this pursuit. But the League couldn't play an important role in the recently concluded Gulf crisis, i.e. the Kuwait crisis. Moreover, in the recent times, Arab-Israeli relations were influenced more by Super powers i.e. U.S. mediation in which the Arab League is isolated and side-tracked. Finally, the League is not only constrained in its function by US policy of intervention and forced diplomacy but also by the fact that it is working on a diminished staff and low finances.

Despite its eventual failure the Arab League still survives as an important pioneering venture for peace, cooperation and unity in the Arab region. Apart from the Arab League there is no other unified Arab institution which can act as a mechanism for evolving a common Arab consensus on the various burning issues in international affairs.

53

Rise of Egyptian Nationalism

Egyptian Nationalism is one of the most frequently studied movements in modern Middle Eastern History. As a matter of fact, Egypt's unique position of being situated at the crossroads of Asia, Africa and Europe, the stories of her magnificence and splendour as also the fact of most convenient trade routes lying across her lands, have always fascinated the great empire builders and conquerors of the world. In the 671 B.C., the Assyrians were the first to annihilate the Pharoes and their successors, the Persians, the Greeks, the Romans, the Byzantians, the Arabs and the Turks, were all irresistibly drawn to the valley of Nile for the single reason i.e. of its vital strategic situation and resources. The European powers also recognised that the possession of Egypt was of great advantage in any contest of supremacy in the world.

Motivated by his desire to obtain mastery over the Mediterranean, Napoleon's army encountered no serious resistance and easily overran the country. Because Egyptians were sick and tired of misrule, corruption and cruelty of Mamelukes. Though lasted only a few years, the French occupation proved to be a turning point in Egypt's history. It initiated a chain of events and ideas which in totality constitute Egyptian Nationalism.

First of all, the door for the penetration of western modernity was swung open. Another and most important contribution was the introduction of printing press and newspapers in Egypt. It led to the interaction of the Europe and European civilization and Muslim Egypt. Therefore, we find that very soon after his return to France, classical works and translations of European books on a variety of subjects began to be printed in Egypt. The result was introduction of the idea of nationality.

Soon after Napoleon's departure, Muhammad Ali seized power in Egypt. He took six years (1905-11) to consolidate his own position in Egypt and put an end to the prevailing anarchy there. He put Egypt on the road to modernization. Sending Egyptians to France for studies, opening modern schools, introducing non-religious subjects into the educational curricula, generously patronizing the translation of Eurpoean books, building up a strong modern army and improving the administration of country all go to his credit.

Change began taking place not only in civilisation but also in culture. Apart from the physical aspects of life, change was taking place due to the intrusion of new ideas from across the Mediterranean. Even the group of students who studied in France began to write about previously unknown subjects as the French Revolution and constitutional monarchy of British pattern.

Among the new ideas that came to Egypt from abroad was the idea of Watan (Fatherland) and watanivah (patriotic nationalism). Watan denoted one's birthplace - the particular village or town in which one was born, rather than the whole country. Rita'ah al- Tahtawi (1801-73) was one of the thinkers who were affected by European way of life. But he also used watan in the sense of birthplace. By and by, the boundaries of watan expanded, until it came to mean the whole of Egypt.

Several factors were responsible for the growth of a sense of national consciousness among the people of Egypt. Improved means of communication, one language and Mohd. Ali's policy of separation and independence from the Ottoman Empire were important among them. In addition to these, geographically the frontiers of Egypt were well-defined by natural factors, as the country is surrounded by desert and sea and it had always remained under centralized governments.

The successors of Mohd. Ali did not leave a profound mark on the mind of Egypt. Their policies plunged deeper and deeper into debt and allowed foreigners more and more say in the running of the country. Khedive Ismail (1863-79) fostered a sense of national pride by prescribing Mariette's History of Egypt from earliest times of the Muslim Conquest for Egyptian high schools. But his financial stocklessness ended in European intervention, which in a sense sharpened the nationalism of educated classes.

It was around this time that al-Sayyid Jamal al-Din al-Afgani visited Egypt and remained there for about eight years (1871-79). His magnetic personality, his dauntless courage and extraordinary eloquence drew around him a large number of young Egyptians, who later played a major part in shaping the destiny of modern Egypt. Al-Afgani's main concern was the problem of European expansion at the expense of Islam. His solution was to unite the Muslim world in some manner to check Western expansion and to revive Islam. Among his political activities, he helped in the establishment of the first organized nationalist group in 1879, al-Hizb al-Watni.

Al-Afgani was expelled from Egypt by the Khedive Taufiq in 1879. Perhaps he was scared of the liberal-constitutionalist movement which was growing up around al-Afgani. Around this time, the nationalist ideas found expression through secret societies like Misr al-Fatat, al-Jamiyyah al-Wataniyyah or National Society.

During the years 1879-82, this growing Egyptian consciousness found violent and confused expression in a series of military uprisings led by Orabi in collaboration with Mohammad Abduh. Both were disciples of Al-Afgani. However, this popular uprising was forcibly suppressed and purposely termed as 'rebellion'. But it developed into a genuine national movement of 'Egypt for Egyptians'. This incident led to the occupation of Egypt by the British in 1882. This occupation proved to be a blessing in disguise for the development of Egyptian nationalist feeling. It gave Egyptian nationalism a definite objective - the evacuation of Egypt by British.

In January 1893, less than a year after his accession Khedival Abbas Hilmi II wanted to exercise his prerogative as a ruler. The same year Latif Salim organized a secret society, which he called *Nationalist Party.* Its purpose was to work for the independence of their country and present its cause to European, especially French, public opinion. Abbas became a catalyst for activities of the Watan Party led after 1895 by Mustafa Kamil. Kamil's role in the development of Egyptian nationalism was that of a pioneer. He came forward with the old idea that all Egyptians - Muslims as well as Copts - constituted one nation and shared fatherland equally. He won the support and cooperation of Copts for his nationalist movement. He only took up the theme of British withdrawal and made it the main demand of the nationalist movement. "Egypt for Egyptians became a popular catchword." He was talented in articulating popular feelings and in organizing a mass movement. His party might possibly have become the vehicle whereby Egypt attained her independence.

Another current of thought during this time was represented by Muhammad Abduh. He was much more concerned with the inner reform of Islam and unification of Muslims while Kamil stressed Egypt's independence and necessity of driving away British from Egypt.

During this time newspapers also spread views of Muslim modernists (Salafiyya). *Al-Manar* was published by a Syrian disciple of Abduh named Rashid Rida. These Muslim modernists were significant in upholding Egypt's Islamic and Arabic heritage and identity.

In addition to this Egyptians were severely affected by economic crisis in 1907-1909. Over-exploitation of Egypt's soil led to decrease in productivity of cotton. This depression undoubtedly fueled peasant discontent and receptivity to nationalism.

Egyptian nationalism started to change its orientation at the beginning of this century, when Ahmed Lutfi al-Sayyid began to expand his concept of Egyptian nation through *al-Jaridah* (founded in 1907). It opposed the infiltration of Pan-Islamic ideas into Egyptian nationalism. Together with this there went on in Egypt the agitation for independence.

On the eve of first World War, Egypt was placed in a unique position. Though occupied by British since 1882, it was still under the technical sovereignty of Ottoman Sultan, in 1914, Great Britain announced that the suzerainty of Turkey over Egypt is terminated and Britain extended a protectorate over Egypt.

Soon Egypt began to seethe with discontent. Defeat of Turkey in the First World War destroyed last centre of hope for any effective support for Egyptian independence. Immediately after the end of first World War, Egyptian liberation movement gained momentum. After the armistice, Egyptian leaders were amazed to find that they were not granted the privilege to attend the Paris Peace Conference in 1919. Hence, Saad Zaghlul placed himself as the head of delegation (al-Wafd) to embark for Paris to present Egypt's case for independence. He was arrested and shipped to Malta. It inflamed Egyptians with resentment. Finally, Milner mission was completely boycotted and this was a manifest testimony of the strength of the nationalist movement. It was followed by other disorders until in early 1922, Egypt was proclaimed as an 'an independent sovereign state'. Britain reserved to its own government four points: the defense of Egypt, protection of communications, protection of foreign and minority interests. In 1923 a constitution was promulgated and parliamentary elections were held. The Wafdists were overwhelmingly victorious at the polls and Zaghlul became premier. But Egypt remained under the thumbs of the British for over thirty years.

King Fuad's acceptance of the reservations made him a British collaborator and created rivalry with the nationalist forces. Egypt's politics came to be characterized as a three-way struggle between the King with the minority parties, British officialdom, and Egypt's Wafdist leaders, who refused to compromise on independence.

After the Ist world war nationalism had spread from Egypt to Sudan, in 1924, Sir Lee Stack, Governor-General of Sudan was murdered in Cairo. It resulted in the resignation of Zaghlul. Zaghlul's contribution to Egyptian nationalism was two-fold. He aroused patriotic zeal and brought Muslims and Copts together to struggle jointly for the national cause. Hence in the inter-war period parliamentary life enjoyed a rocky existence. Although Wafd would win the elections, the King usually appointed the prime minister from among minority party politicians. On occasions when a Wafdist served a premier he was soon dismissed due to some conflict with the King or British. Throughout the interwar period denial of power to Wafd enhanced its popularity, but it also made the Wafd impede resolution of difference between Britain and Egypt.

Around this time there flourished in Egypt the movement known as Pharaonism, led by Salamah Musa. It meant that Egypt was essentially Pharaonic and Egyptians still retained the heritage of their forebears. Further in 1928, the Ahrar government led by Muhammad Mahmud dissolved parliament and then instituted direct monarchical rule, aided by cabinet. Thus began the constitutional crisis that culminated in the Sidqui dictatorship of 1930-33. During this time, restraints on political behaviour were dropped in favour of greater activism and violence, especially on the part of students. In 1933 the Young Egypt Society (Green Shirts) was founded, Egypt's first para-military organization. It was closely linked with the Ahrars and the Watan Party. Wafd regarded it as a serious challenge and it was indicted by the foundation of its own paramilitary group called the Blue Shirts. Wafd after coming to power in 1936, also tried to suppress Young Egypt.

The Muslim Brothers (al-Ikhwan al-Muslimun) won a larger popular following than Young Egypt. They established paramilitary groups called Rovers and Bablis. They viewed themselves as the heirs of the Salafiyya movement. Because of their belief in the universal applicability of Islam, the Brothers openly proclaimed that theirs was not only a religious, social or political organization but also one involved in culture, education, business and athletics.

In 1933, Sidqui resigned due to illness and interference of King in administrative affairs. After 14 months, Mohammed Taufik Hassim came to the helm. In 1935, situation became dangerous due to the Mediterranean crisis precipitated by Italy's Ethiopian venture. Wafdists warned Great Britain to expect no help from Egypt except on a basis of cooperation between equals. In 1935, anti-British riots broke out in several cities and late in 1935 all Egyptian political parties formed a United Front. The death of King Fuad in 1936, gave an opportunity to Wafdists to reassert its influence in Egypt's politics. Growing menace of Mussolini in the surrounding areas, Tripolitan and Abyssinia, enhanced Wafd's bargaining position regarding modification in the British Policy. In 1936, the long awaited Anglo-Egyptian Treaty of Alliance was signed in London, followed in 1937 by the admission of Egypt into the League of Nations.

While the Wafd was changing the political scene without much a break with the tradition that believed in the validity of Islam for the modern world, two young men from al-Azhar were ushering in a revolution of different kind. Ali Abd al-Raziq argued cogently that the unity brought about by the Prophet was basically one of faith, not politics. It was an open attack on the corpus of opinion that thought of Egypt as a unit in an Islamic empire under the Caliph. However, by the time the book was published the Wafd had already won the day for Egyptian nationalism.

The British Protectorate system gave the country a certain independence but not enough to satisfy all Egyptians, as Britain still retained the responsibility for the defence of the Suez Canal. But the general public had long lost faith in the Wafd's competence and was now beginning to question its integrity. Several groups, radicals, army officers, students, the Muslim Brothers, continued to work for full independence.

In the meantime, King Farouk ascended the throne and Montreaun Convention was signed on May 8, 1937 which abolished capitualarty rights for foreigners in Egypt. In 1942, the British had forced Egypt, under the threat of tanks and cannon, to join war on the side of Allies. Egyptian public opinion was against participation and felt that its national self-respect had been violated by British coercion. Egyptians started feeling intensely indignant about the presence of British troops which, they realized, could reduce violent opposition. The years 1945-46 were, therefore, years of constant nationalist strife and struggle in Egypt. Mass demonstrations took place frequently either against the policies of the British Government or against the men-in-power in Egypt itself, who were criticized for following weak policies.

Egyptian nationalist struggle during the period was all along focussed on two immediate objectives, the evacuation of British forces from the Suez Base and the unification of Nile Valley. Devotion of these objectives was not confined to those who might be designated as 'Egyptian nationalists'. But all sections of Egypt's public opinion were unanimous in supporting them. The Ikhwan, the Ulama of al-Azhar, the Arab nationalists, the Socialists and the Communists.

In May 1948, Britain terminated its mandate in Palestine and Egypt sent troops into Palestine to try to expel the Jewish settlers. Although the King and Public opinion were in favour, the army was ill prepared and had no plan of coordination with other Arab states. Thus began the nightmare of Egypt's relationship with Israel. The Egyptian army was defeated by Israel. There were scandals over inferior equipment and the King and government were blamed for treacherously letting down the army, in which there developed an intense feeling of shame. The ground was immensely fertile for the growth of a resistance movement.

The defeat of Palestine had a profound impact upon the Arab world including Egypt. It was among the several causes that led to the army *coup d'etat* in July 1952. The post-1952 period gave rise to a more militant form of Egyptian nationalism under the dynamic leadership of President Nasser. The military organizers of the July 1952 coup were fired essentially by the same ambiguous nationalism that had motivated the traditional elite groups they had overthrown. Undoubtedly their primary purpose in taking power had been to realize the main ideals of Egyptian nationalism,—the building of strong independent nation-state. The military incorporated the inherited Egyptian nationalism into the nebulous "Six Principles" of the revolution published in January 1953 and reiterated by Abdal-Nasser at Bandung. Two of these principles—the liquidation of imperialism and the building of a strong army—were pursued almost immediately as a part of the Officers' nationalistic creed. The remaining four—the ending of feudalism and capitalism, and the establishment of social justice and democratic life—represented the bare outlines of an internal ideological programme, the implementation of which was postponed. Subsequent shift in revolutionary action from the domestic to the international stage was accompanied by a parallel redirection of ideological development whereby Egyptian nationalism evolved into Pan-Arabism. That is to say that Egyptian nationalism had been supplemented by another nationalist ideology Pan-Arabism, which lacked a creed of internal change. Thus this socialization did not touch more immediate day-to-day social and economic needs of Egyptians.

The 1956 defeat in the Sinai demonstrated that, as in 1948, the Egyptian soldier still lacked the spiritual preparation necessary for effective combat. But the slowly advancing Anglo-French campaign on the heels of Israel's attack strengthened the people's identification with the charismatic leader. In order to seek reform, it laid emphasis on constitutional form of government, land reform, and social, economic and political values. Besides, 'Nasserism' believed that the state had to ensure that the fruits and burdens of development were equally distributed and that the haves did not exploit the have-nots.

However the death of President Nasser in 1970 led to a gradual shift in Egypt's policy. Egypt's Pan-Arab and nationalist policy reflected a change. A major debate ensued between the 'aspirationists' who adhered to Arab nationalism and the 'pragmatists' who emphasised state nationalism (e.g. Egyptian as opposed to Arab) and prescribed domestic consolidation.

Nasser was succeeded by Vice-President Anwar al-Sadat. In 1971, Sadat consolidated his position by removing many of Nasser's political lieutenants from positions of influence. While steadfastly claiming to have extended, indeed improved the Nasser revolution, Sadat, in fact, began to pull in another direction. "Egypt first" became the emphasis in regime propaganda. As such, Nasser's adherence to the policy of Arab unity and nationalism had now become limited to the value of 'Egyptian Patriotism'.

In the sphere of foreign policy even, Nasser's anti-western orientation had been almost totally reversed. This was particularly true in the case of the United States, which had constituted the major focus of Nasser's anti-imperialist campaign, but which now seems to have replaced the Soviet Union as Egypt's trusted ally.

In the economic sphere, Sadat pledged to reform the existing system by allowing freer enterprise and encouraging investment from abroad. He initiated the policy of *Infitah* (Open Door) which actively sought foreign investment and encouraged the establishment of private enterprise. However, *Infitah* as a policy was not well thought out. There were no guidelines, either stated or implied, about what the nature of involvement of these domestic partners should be and how Egypt would expect to benefit from these activities. Sadat opened the door to Egypt and invited foreigners to make money at her expense.

In the conclusion it can be said that the dramatic steps which Sadat took in the implementation of his new policy including his visit to Jerusalem in November 1977 and the signing of the Egypt-Israel Peace Treaty (Camp David) on 26 March 1979, resulted in the virtual break up of the League of Arab Sates and the severing of diplomatic relations with Egypt by several Arab states. Egyptian identity without the Arab connection lost its own significance. Egypt which had championed the cause of nationalism and Arab unity, had been rejected by the Arabs themselves.

54

Arab Nationalism and the Gulf Crisis

The Iraqi thrust into Kuwait can not be viewed in isolation as a case of Iraq's nascent sub-imperialist desire in the Gulf region. The Iraqi move has its wider ramifications—which ultimately led to the resurgence of Arab Nationalism and Palestine question. The Iraqi effort to arouse Arab Nationalism through its action in Kuwait is a new attempt to challenge the Western or US Imperialism. Before one comes to the present-day crisis one has to take into account what Arab nationalism actually means. Arab Nationalism or Arabism is said to be a concept based primarily on emotional and sentimental attachment to a nationalist entity called 'the Arab Nation'. Nationalism is a social concept that expressed the bond existing between individuals of one nation.

It is the bond which relates the individuals of one nation in a common *Patrie.* Arabism in this context presupposes a high level of homogeneity among the inhabitants of the Arab States based on mutual perceptions of a common historical, cultural, linguistic and religious heritage. It is also identified with the Arab existence, its past, present and future.

Arab Nationalism is an attitude of mind which almost all Arabs share. It is unique in the two important respects. First, it is linked to memories of past glories. It recalls a golden age of Arab greatness which is said to be the true image of the Arab genius. The second is its pan-Arab aspiration.

The Arab Nationalists argue that all Arabic-speaking people from the Persian Gulf to the Atlantic constitute one nation. They conceive of the Arab World as a single homogeneous whole and of the Arab people as a single nation"qaqm" bound by common titieses of language, territory, economic life, religion and history. The kinship Arabs feel is far stronger than among English speakers of North America, Britain, Australia and New Zealand or Spanish speakers of Middle and South America.

To the radical Arab Nationalists, Arab nationalism is the outcome of excessive fragmentation, under development, exploitation and subjection. It represents the motorforce of the Arab Nation in its struggle. Besides, it gives rise to awareness of the link welding together the Nation's past, present and future and the personality common to all Arabs.

Evolution

Today, the term "Arab" generally designates the Arabs as a cultural entity. The cultural evolution which the Arabs set in motion was the resultant of two processes, viz: the religious and social. The first was the process of Islamisation whereby the new faith preached by Prophet Muhammad, transformed their spiritual life. It is essential to consider Islam which had outgrown its Arab origin and spread far beyond the Arab peoples. That God chose, to reveal His most perfect word to Arabs, in Arabic, and that by God's will or historical circumstances it were the Arabs who spread Islam throughout the world is of great significance to Arabs. Moreover, it permeates the daily life of the individual with its ritualistic obligations. It is an important part of socialisation and serves to integrate the Arab society by inculcating a sense of the Arab special relationship with God.

The other result was the process of *Arabisation* which had two aspects: *Linguistic Arabisation,* i.e. the process by which the conquered people gradually acquired Arabic as their mother tongue; and *racial Arabisation,* caused by entry into those countries of masses of immigrants of pure Arab stock, whose absorption gave the conquered races a predominant admixture of Arab blood.

In formulating the postulates of Arab nationalism, Arab writers have drawn upon *two principal sources.* The first one (mentioned above) is the *legacy of the past.* The community of language, of tradition, and of historical experiences have all been stressed as common denominators of an Arab nation. The second source of inspiration is *the cultural impact of the West* (the term west stands for modern European civilisation in its totality).

Arab Nationalism

The principal factor that binds all Arabs together is said to be the *language.* A language is important because it is the medium through which people express their minds and emotions. It is linked to the national idea and acts as a symbol of Arab unity.

The second most important factor among the constituents of Arab nationalism is *historical tradition.* It is said to be the living memory of the nation. The unity of Arab history generates uniform sympathies, leads to a sharing of pride in the glories of past and creates identity of aspirations for the future.

The third factor constituting Arab nationalism, is said to be the *community of interest.*

The major ideological currents during the early phase of Arab Nationalism (1800-1945) were *Westernisation, Islamic revivalism,* combining nationalism, reformism, revolutionary activism and *constitutionalism* inspired by the winds blowing from Europe.

From the nineteenth century onward, western concepts have been incorporated into Arab nationalist thought and seems to have formed an integral part of the Arab tradition. The conquest of Egypt by Napoleon Bonaparte of France in 1789 initiated a chain of events and ideas. The above, in its totality constitute Arab nationalism. The first and foremost result of this was the *general Arab awakening.* A second result was the introduction of the *Printing Press,* which gave impetus to Arab classics and hence to national consciousness. A final result was the introduction of the *European idea of nationality,* which among other, led to the reaction against Ottoman tyranny.

Next in line it was Mehmet Ali (1805-1849) who was instrumental in sowing the seeds of intellectual awareness, and the belief in the freedom of all peoples, and their right to national self-determination. Mehmet Ali's conquest of Egypt (1805), strove to serve his own ends by building up a strong modern army on the lines of Napoleon's renowned forces. Having learned from his French advisers that he would ultimately have to rely on Egyptian recruits, Mehmet Ali turned his energies to an educational movement designed to provide the military institutions with the educated elements amongst Egypt's indigenous population. As part of such a campaign, he sent a number of Egyptians to further their education in France, to assimilate western ideas, and to master the French language.

However, Mehmet Ali and his successors' projection of carving out an Arab empire for themselves was never realised. It crashed on the rock of British hostility, contemporary economic crisis, moral decline and above all the absence of Arab national consciousness.

The story of the rise of a specifically Arab national movement, writes George Antonius, "opens in Syria in 1847, with the foundation in Beirut of a modest literary society under the American patronage". The first organised effort in the Arab national movement can be traced back to the year 1875, when five young men who had been educated at the Syrian protestant college in Beirut formed a secret society. They established branches in Damascus, Tripoli and Sudan. The main points of their programme were: (i) the grant of independence to Syria in union with the Lebanon; (ii) the recognition of Arabic as an official language; (iii) the removal of censorship; (iv) the employment of local recruited units on local military service only. Whatever may be, the society's appeals were the first trumpet-call emitted by the infant Arab movement. It was the earliest organisation to be founded with a primarily political object. One of the earliest representatives of Islamic revivalism was *Jamal al-Din al-Afghani* to whom goes great credit for disseminating a new and vigorous nationalist spirit. He was the founder of the modern Pan-Islamic movement combining a nationalist interpretation of Islam with modernism and reformism. Another leading representative of Islamic *revivalism* was *Muhammad Rashid Rida,* a Syrian living in Egypt whose book The Caliphate is the most systematic exposition of the Islamic theory of government. To him, the authority of the people is meant the authority of those who represent the people. The third leading representative of modern Islamic revivalism was *Abdul Rahman al-Kawakabi.* He combined the four principal ideological currents which prevailed in his era: Islamic revivalism, Arab nationalism, westernisation and constitutionalism.

The distinguished representatives of the school of constitutional reform were *Francis Fatuallah Murrash al-Halabi* and *Shibli al-Shumayyil* who believed in the eventual triumph of popular sovereignty.

Modern Arab Nationalism

Modern Arab nationalism owes its birth to a movement, which had, as its principal aim, the overthrow of autocratic rule. It started as a protest against centralisation and as a plea for the introduction of democratic processes. One of the most important exponents of Arab nationalism was Adib Ishaq (1856-1885), a Christian (born in Damascus). He was also one of the staunchest advocates of liberalism and constitutionalism. Ishaq was conscious of the obstacles which stood in the way of a free democratic society. Besides, he gave emphasis on equality which he considered indispensable to the success of democratic system of government.

The other prominent exponents of Arab nationalism were Mustafa Kamel, and Sheikh Mohammed Abdou of Egypt representing the radical and moderate school of thought. The British occupation of Egypt (1882) led to the growth of a separate and intense feeling of nationalism. Abdou believed in reform as the ideal method to achieve national aspiration whereas Kamel (the leader of the Nationalist Party) believed that reform would be of no avail until the complete evacuation of the occupying forces. Kamel was an ardent supporter of popular sovereignty. He believed that participation of the people in their own government was a prerequisite to progress.

In Egypt, the Ottoman empire was viewed by both nationalists and Ulema as Egypt's natural ally against British domination. Ever since the British occupation of Egypt the wave of nationalism, demanding the evacuation of the country continued. Every Egyptian nationalist leader was working towards the aim of putting an end to the foreign domination with which the country was afflicted. The Arab nationalists in Syria and Iraq moved further away from the concept of Islamic solidarity, which the Ottoman caliphate represented, and towards independent Arab nationalism. The Arabs in these countries, with their sincere love of independence, had been showing symptoms of a budding Arab national consciousness.

The first World War (1914-18) indeed offered opportunities to the Arab nationalists and led to the collapse of the Ottoman empire. Five new states were created from the ruins of the Ottoman empire—Iraq, Syria, Lebanon, Transjordan and Palestine. However the net result of the war, was the transformation of the Arab peoples from the status of citizens to that of subjects. No sooner was the war terminated than most of the Arab countries found themselves occupied by their wartime allies. A system of colonial rule in the guise of mandatory trusts, was imposed on them against their wishes.

Besides, the Balfour Declaration of 2nd November 1917, which called for the establishment of a national home, for the Jewish people in Palestine, created frustration and dismay among the Arabs. It was during this time that a new basis for mutual sympathy and the aspiration for Arab unity in the struggle against foreign domination was established. It was accompanied by national uprisings in Egypt, Iraq and Syria.

In the 1920s, and still more in the 1930s, there began to grow up a new sort of nationalism, more thorough going and revolutionary than that of the pre-first world war generation. As late as the second world war Arab nationalism really had two important centres, Damascus and Baghdad. However, Egypt played a major role in the movements of literary intellectual revival. During this period the aim of all political action was to gain independence from Britain and France. Unity was the goal to be achieved after foreign domination had been brought to an end. To secure independence and make proper use of it, help was looked for from Europe. Mustafa Kamel of Turkey hoped that in its own interest the French government would check the growth of British Power. Said Zaghlul Pasha (a moderate leader of Egypt) appealed to the liberal conscience of England.

In Egypt this was the period when 'pharonic' nationalism was at its height, and Egyptians were concerned primarily with their own problem of independence from the British. The influence of monarchy was declined. The 1936 Anglo-Egyptian Treaty gave her comparative freedom in foreign policy. Besides, some Arab leaders were looking to her as a possible source of help in the complicated problem of Palestine. At the Bludan conference, the then Vice-President stated that a Jewish state in Palestine would be a danger to Egypt as much as to its neighbours.

In the 1930s Arab nationalism had taken the shape of a secular movement. The Arab leaders wished to state their opposition to Zionism in national terms, i.e. in terms of Christian and Muslim Palestinians alike. In the 1940s, political changes in the Arab world took place which were more radical than those occurring after the end of the First World War. Efforts were initiated to establish some concrete manifestation of Arab unity and cooperation. The result was the *Arab League*, which came into being on 22nd March 1945.

The Arab League was created to promote cooperation and coordination among Arab states. It aimed at encouraging a joint Arab response to the Zionist colonisation of Palestine (1948). It represented the Arab movement of synthesis aiming at the liberation of Arab territories and states from foreign domination. There were seven founder members: Egypt, Lebanon, Iraq, Syria, Jordan, Yemen, and Saudi Arabia. Membership has since expanded to include 21 independent Arab States plus Palestine, which is represented by the PLO or the State of Palestine at League meetings.

The end of Second World War shattered the European dominance in the Arab world and led to the emergence of the United States and the Soviet Union as the world's two super powers. In 1945, France was forced to evacuate the republics of Syria and Lebanon, and by the end of the following decade, to grant independence first to Tunisia and then to Morocco. The Algerian revolution, which broke out in 1954, brought about Algeria's independence in 1962. Libya, which had been put under United Nation's trusteeship after the war, achieved independence in 1951.

Britain's withdrawal from the Arab world was carried out gradually and without bloodshed except in Palestine where the mandate was formally terminated in 1948. Transjordan was recognised as an independent monarchy in 1946; Sudan was granted the right to self-determination in 1953 and became independent in 1956. Iraq, already declared independent in 1952, became fully sovereign after the Baghdad Pact in 1955 stipulated Britain's evacuation. In 1961 the oil-rich Sheikhdom of Kuwait was declared independent and became the state of Kuwait.

In the post-war period another radical change took place: the domination of the old-guard nationalist leaders came to an end and was replaced in most Arab countries by a new type of nationalist leadership. The post-1952 period gave rise to a more militant form of Arab-nationalism and Arab unity under the dynamic leadership of President Nasser in Egypt. He was said to be the Paladin of Pan-Arab Nationalism and was identified by many in the west as well as in the east as the personification of the quest for Arab unity.

It was from this time that Nasser began to assume the stature of the hero of the Arab Nationalism. Most Arabs felt that here at least was the leader they had been waiting for who could stand upto the imperialist powers. Some looked further ahead to see him recovering Palestine for the Arabs. It was Nasser's Egypt that breathed life into the Palestine Liberation Organisation (PLO), and it was Ismail Fahmy, the Egyptian foreign minister at the 1974 Rabat Summit, who proposed the PLO as the "sole legitimate representative of the Palestinian people". It was since Nasser's time that the struggle for Arab unity and Arab Nationalism symbolised the quest for Arab unity and Arab Nationalism.

However, the death of Nasser in 1970 led to a gradual shift in the rapid movement of Arab unification. After the death of Nasser, this nationalism manifested through Palestinian revolution in the seventies and eighties. Palestinian *intifedah* is also a new dimension which, since November 1987, has been added to the Arab Nationalism. *Intifedah* in fact is Arab nationalism of the oppressed Arab-Palestinian people. When this four-year old Resistance Movement went unheeded by the US Iraq had to take a step to put an end to the West Asian impasse. Nationalism is now manifested in a different way.

The questions and the issues raised by President Saddam Hussein of Iraq have not been answered by the US and other western countries. The US finds itself in the most uncomfortable position when Saddam Hussein linked up the Kuwait issue with the central question of Palestine. If Israeli occupation on the Arab Palestinian territories is supported by the US then why is this occupation of Kuwait being actively opposed by it? Saddam Hussein's declaration that Iraq would withdraw from Kuwait if Israel withdraws from the Arab territories and Syria from Lebanon is the central point raising once again the Arab Nationalism which has more or less dominated the major part of this century revolving around the question of Palestine.

Though the Iraqi action has cost much consternation and insurmountable difficulties for the Arabs and foreigners in the Gulf the time has come to solve the major West Asian problems once for all. Iraqi action has generated the tremors of Arab Nationalism among the Arab masses which is crystal clear from the demonstrations in various Arab capitals in support of Saddam Hussein. This is ostensibly because relatively a small country like Iraq without the support of any big power has defied the world's biggest Super Power the US. This has definitely raised the prestige of the Arabs and has given a new direction to the Arab Nationalism. Unless the Palestine problem, which is the crux of the West Asian crisis, is solved and the Palestinians get back a state of their own on their native soil west Asia will continue to endanger the world peace.

The Palestine problem is, to put it in modern lexicon, a problem created by the North against the South. As Professor K.R. Singh (JNU) pointed out in a recently held seminar on the Gulf crisis, "It's a problem (Kuwaiti occupation by Iraq and Palestine Question) of exploitation of South by the North." Kuwait was used by the US to promote its own interests. The US depends on the Arab oil for two-third of its oil requirements. By deploying military forces in Saudi Arabia it has not only hurt the ego of the Arab people but also taken the entire area to the brink of war. Iraqi thrust into Kuwait is an internal conflict of the Arabs which could have been solved within the framework of Arab nationalism. Instead of US directly intervening in the area the Arab peace-keeping forces under the aegis of Arab League should have been deployed. The matter could have been settled amicably without causing tension and war psychosis. The rash action of the US will do much harm to its interests in the long run as the Arab masses in general have woken up from their slumber to express solidarity with President Saddam Hussein. The Iraqi thrust is not considered by them as an invasion but as a challenge to the US or the dominance of the North. It is as if Saddam Hussein is avenging the age-old humiliation of the Arabs at the hands of the West. The present Gulf crisis and the *Intifedah* are originally linked with each other as the latest manifestation of Arab nationalism.

A Chronology of the Arab-Israeli Conflict (1882-1993)

1882 Beginning of Zionist immigration to Palestine, then part of the Ottoman Empire. Population of Palestine: 500,000 (95% Arabs). First signs of Arab nationalism

1897 First World Zionist Congress in Basel, Switzerland. Decision to promote Jewish settlement in Palestine and found the World Zionist Organization.

1904 Najib Azoury's book *Revil de la Nation Arabe* warns of Zionist political aims.

1916 The British McMahon Letters are understood by the Arabs to pledge British support for the unity and independence of Arab lands, including Palestine, at the end of World War I.

1917 The British conquer Palestine and issue the Balfour Declaration, favouring "the establishment in Palestine of a national home for the Jewish people".

1920 Britain is assigned the Mandate for Palestine. Jewish immigration to Palestine steps up.
Anti-Jewish riots by Arabs protest Jewish immigration and settlement (similar outbreaks. Arabs of violence occurred in 1921 and 1929).

1922 British separates Transjordan from Palestine.

1936-39 Three-year Arab rebellion against British rule and Zionist settlement, eventually crushed by the British.

1937 The British Peel Commission proposes the partition of Palestine into Jewish and Arab states. Arab rejection, conditional Jewish approval.

1939 British White Paper conditions future Jewish immigration to Palestine on Arab consent, and limits Jewish land purchases.

1939-45 World War II and Nazi Holocaust increase Jewish demands for Immigration and a Jewish state. The Grand Mufti of Jerusalem supports Hitler and is exiled by the British.

1942 The Zionist Biltmore Conference in New York calls for a Jewish Commonwealth in Palestine.

1945 The Arab League is established in Cairo and emphasizes the Arab character of Palestine.

1946 British refusal to admit Jewish war refugees into Palestine unleashes a wave of Jewish terrorism. The King David Hotel in Jerusalem is blown up.

1947 British turns over the Palestine problem to the United Nations.

The U.N. (Resolution 1881) votes in November for the partition of Palestine into a Jewish and an Arab state, linked by an economic union, with Jerusalem internationalized.

Population of Palestine: 1,933,673—77% Arabs, 33% Jews.

1948 The British Mandate is ended. The State of Israel is proclaimed on May 15. Six Arab armies invade the new state and are defeated in what the Jews call the "War of Independence" and the Arabs call *Al Nakba* (the Disaster). Hundreds of thousands of Palestinians are uprooted and become refugees. U.N. Resolution 194 recognises their right to return to Palestine or receive compensation. About 150,000 Arabs remain (and become citizens of the State of Israel)

An All-Palestine government is formed in Gaza.

1949 Israel is admitted as the 59th member of the United Nations. Armistice agreements between Israel, Egypt, Syria, and Jordan mark the end of the war, and give one-third more territory than allocated by the U.N. in 1947. Israel declares Jerusalem as its capital. Jordan takes control of the West Bank and East Jerusalem. Egypt administers the Gaza Strip. The proposed Arab state in Palestine never materializes.

1950 UNRWA (U.N. Relief and Works Agency) is established to provide for Palestinian refugees.

The Israeli parliament (Knesset) expropriates over a quarter of a million acres of land owned by Arabs living outside Israel or by "present absentees".

1951 Israel passes the Law of Return, granting automatic citizenship to all Jewish immigrants.

1953-56 Palestinian infiltrators, mainly from Egypt, continually attack Israeli population centers. Israel conducts reprisal raids into neighboring Arab countries.

1956 Israel invades Sinai in collusion with the British and French, who try to wrest the Suez Canal from Egyptian control. Israel withdraws under pressure from the U.S. and USSR.

1964 The Palestine Liberation Organization (PLO) is founded. The PLO Charter calls for the liberation by force of the whole of Palestine.

1967 The June War breaks out between Israel, Egypt, Jordan, and Syria. Israel conquers Sinai, the Gaza Strip, East Jerusalem, the West Bank, and the Golan Heights. 250,000 Palestinians flee from the West Bank, including many refugees of 1948.

Arab Summit in Khartoum declares: no recognition of Israel, no peace, and no negotiations.

UN Resolution 242 is passed calling for: withdrawal of Israeli troops from territories occupied during the war, termination of the state of belligerency: recognition of the right of all states in the region to live in peace within secure and recognized borders.

1969 A war of artrition begins between Israel and Egypt along the Suez Canal.

1970 Palestinian military attacks increase in Israel and abroad.

Black September: King Hussein wipes out the PLO presence in Jordan. The remaining Palestinian guerrillas move to Lebanon.

1973 Yom Kippur or Ramadan War: Egypt and Syria launch a military offensive in an attempt to regain territories lost in 1967.

1974 Disengagement agreements in Sinai and the Golan Heights.

Palestine National Council calls for a Palestinian state in any part of the occupied territories evacuated by Israel. An 'independent Palestinian state' replaces the goal of a 'secular democratic state' in all of Palestine.

The seventh Arab Summit in Rabat recognizes the PLO as the sole representative of the Palestinians. The UN recognizes the PLO as the representative of the Palestinian people. Arafat addresses the General Assembly.

First unofficial talks between representatives of the Israel peace forces and the PLO.

1975 UN resolution defines Zionism as a form of racism.

1977 Israel's first right-wing nationalist government is formed by Likud party leader Menachem Begin, who promotes settlement in the occupied territories.

President Anwar Sadat of Egypt flies to Israel for talks with the Israeli government.

1978 The Israeli peace movement 'Peace Now' is formed.

1978-79 The Camp David Accords between Egypt and Israel lead to the first peace treaty between Israel and an Arab state. Israel agrees to return the whole of Sinai to Egypt and to enter autonomy negotiations over the occupied territories.

1979 UN Security Council calls on Israel to dismantle all settlements in the occupied territories and East Jerusalem.

1980 The Israeli Knesset annexes East Jerusalem

1981 Israeli planes destroy the Iraqi nuclear reactor outside Baghdad.

Israel annexes the Golan Heights.

1982 Arab Summit in Fez, Morocco produces the Fez Peace Plan, which talks of a political solution with Israel and International guarantees for all states in the region.

Israel invades Lebanon.

Lebanese Christian troops allied with Israel massacre close to a thousand Palestinians in the Sebra and Shatilla refugee camps outside Beirut. 400,000 people demonstrate in Tel Aviv against the massacre and the war in Lebanon.

1985 Most Israeli forces withdraw from Lebanon. Israel establishes a "security zone" in Southern Lebanon.

1987 The Palestinian intifada against the Israeli occupation erupts in December and continues to this day. In its first three years, 715 Palestinians, including 161 children, were killed by Israeli troops.

1988 Arafat's deputy and PLO military commander, Abu Jihad, is assassinated in Tunisia. Israel is presumed responsible.

The Islamic Resistance Movement, Hamas, is founded. Its covenant rejects negotiations with Israel.

— The Palestine National Council (PNC) meets in Algiers in November and declares the establishment of an independent Palestinian state (soon recognized by some 60 countries including the USSR and China and India). The PNC endorses the 1947 UN resolution on the partition of Palestine and recognizes UN Resolution 242 as a basis for peaceful negotiations between Israelis and Palestinians.

— In a special UN session in Geneva in December, Arafat recognizes the State of Israel and renounces militarism. The US decides to open official contacts with the PLO for the first time. Peace now calls for negotiations with the PLO.

1989 The Israeli government initiates a peace plan in May calling for elections in the occupied territories. The plan, intended to bypass the PLO, founders and leads to the break-up of Israel's national unity government.

1990 The US suspends its dialogue with the PLO after Yasser Arafat refuses to condemn a terrorist attack against Israel planned by Abul Abbas, a member of the PLO Executive.

— Iraqi thrust into Kuwait in August. The PLO supports linkage between the Gulf crisis and the Palestinian question.

1991 The US-led coalition attacks Iraq. Saddam Hussein attacks Israel with missiles. Under the cover of Kuwaiti liberation, the United States has quietly moved to step up its military presence in the Arab homeland. The brutal US led Imperialist coalition's bombardment of the thousands of Iraqi and Kuwait civilians in the recent times has again highlighted the dangers facing the Afro-Asian or Third World.

1992 The Palestinian *intifada* in the Israeli occupied Arab-Palestinian territories went on amid unsuccessful American led efforts to bring Arab-Israeli place closer

— Africa began the new decade of 1990s in a mixture of hope and frustration. Along with the independence to Namibia, the release of *Nelson Mandela*, the great South African nationalist leader had brought hopes for peace, stability and transformation in Africa.

1992- Mr. Bill Clinton (Democrat) became the new President of United States of America.

1993 South Africa's most popular militant, nationalist leader and chief of Communist Party Mr. Chris Hani was assassinated.

— The Middle East Peace talks reconvened this April after a break of five months due to Israeli's forcible deportation of nearly 400 Arab-Palestinians.

— Mubarak's Egypt faces the crisis of extreme Islamic militantism.

— Turkey's 66 years old charismatic President Turgot Ozal died of heart failure.

55

Apartheid

Today the African National Congress (which has its office in Delhi and is recognised by the Government of India) of South Africa is leading the fight against the most vicious form of racialism since the destruction of Hitlerite fascism. Africa remains very much the victim of a colonial mentality, a relic of an age in which Africa frequently appeared on the pages of school atlasses as though it was the same size, as say, France.

Apartheid is said to be the most brutal and violent form of human exploitation in the contemporary world. It is a serious blot on human civilisation and a moral challenge confronting all humanity.

Apartheid is a fatal cancerous disease which had infected the minds of white South Africans to such an extent that they do not consider blacks as human beings but as the beasts of burden. It has poisoned race relations in South Africa so much so that the whole of the Southern African region is today threatened with a racial conflagration. The operation of apartheid laws, rules and regulations are so wide that no sphere of human life—political, economic, social, cultural and psychological has been spared.

The policy of apartheid is practised in all the spheres of human activity. White South Africans do behave as they though are imperial masters of a distant colony. They also perpetuate archaic social forms among the colonial population, inhibit its spontaneous development, and impose autocratic methods of government. While settlers monopolise the sources of power, all key positions and maintain a wide cultural gap between themselves and the native black people.

Whatever may have been the strength of the native population during the past few decades, the application of the policy of apartheid, is bound to effect the day-to-day life of the natives. For apartheid as a policy is disastrously different from 'apartheid' as a theory. It is very closely associated with the evil of serfdom.

In action, the policy of apartheid denies to them all those rights which they are, or could be, entitled to as human beings. In reality, it is based on the colonial principle of inequality, and its object is to keep the non-whites as the servile appendages of the whites for ever. To understand apartheid in practice here it is necessary to go into some of the pillars of this practice: Master and servant laws. For instance here, the laws make it a criminal offence for an African to refuse or fail to enter into service after having signed a contract of employment or to render himself unfit for work.

The pass laws (recently scrapped but still in practice): Africans in South Africa do not enjoy, the freedom to move about and reside in any part of the country according to their wish. According to the provisions of the pass laws, every African who is above 10 years, must carry with him all the time a notebook which is a type of booklet containing a set of documents. The pass-book has to be produced on demand by a police man or any other authorised official.

An African who is unable to do so either because he has left it at home or lost it, is guilty of criminal offence with a heavy fine or imprisonment of one month.

The Bantustan scheme was said to be the climax of apartheid. The entire African population, under this policy, has been relegated to areas totalling roughly 13 per cent of the total land in South Africa. It is in the semi-fertile or barren areas which are the poorest of the poor, and economically unavailable Units, that the entire African population is supposed to live, while the rest of the territory comprising of the best agricultural and mining areas belongs to the whites.

The women are also forced to go to white areas to work there as domestic servants or as agriculture labour but not necessarily in the same city where their husbands are already working. The women also can not carry their children with them. Thus the Bantustan scheme resulted in complete destruction of family life. One can just imagine the effect of this policy upon children who have to grow up in the absence of the love and care of their parents. Ex-President Jimmy Carter of United States has rightly said that, 'In South Africa, even children—many hundreds of little children—have been imprisoned and tortured by a government whose cruel apartheid policies have justly earned it worldwide condemnation.

The basic feature of the labour system is that all skilled work is reserved for the Whites unless, as a special case, an African is permitted to do it. Employers wanting to employ Africans to do jobs must take prior permission to do so from the Minister of Labour.

If a white worker suffers total disability as a result of some disease or accident, he is entitled to a monthly pension based on his earnings, but an African suffering in the same way or dying in the process is entitled to a limited sum based on his earnings but not to a monthly pension. So far the wages are concerned, black workers are paid much less than whites.

In the social sphere, there were separate facilities for whites and Non-whites. There were separate entrances to post offices and railway stations, separate carriages on trains, separate hospitals, public pools and conveniences.

Africans did not enjoy the normal freedom in the sphere of religion either. The minister of Bantu Administration and Development was empowered to prohibit the attendance of Africans at a church service in a town if he thinks that that is undesirable.

In the cultural sphere as well expressions of the culture of resistance and unity are suppressed. It is very difficult for different racial groups to come together.

Inadequate and inferior education system: One of the most rigid aspect of the system of apartheid was the determined effort to bring education under full government control, to segregate the educational system on the basis of race and tribe, and to train the non-whites for the inferior position assigned to them by government policies.

Political rights under apartheid system: In the political arena, apartheid ensured that state power was firmly entrenched in the hands of the white minority and that Blacks do not have any political rights. They did not have the right to franchise and their political organisations were ruthlessly suppressed. In short, nonwhites exercised no political rights in South Africa.

In the economic arena, as stated by an author (Sigugudwane Mashele's, 'Apartheid,—what is it?' *Ethiopian Herald* (Addis Ababa), 28 January 1982, 'All the seemingly inexhaustible mineral wealth is concentrated in the hands of a few white capitalists. While blacks are forced to cough their lungs out literally in the bowels of the earth for a pittance'. Besides, the gap between the wages of white and African miners were wider than it was about thirty years ago. African pay a high price in fines, imprisonment and loss of wages for their individual defiance of the detested laws. Again, the average wage of a white worker is more than five times that of the African in manufacturing industries, £ 119 a month as against £22), and more than fifteen times that of the African in the gold mines (£ 5.17s a shift as against 7s.5d). The difference in status and living standards instilled a sense of superiority in white and dispelled any notion of unity or cohesion with the black workers. In the courts and in the legal profession also, white domination is clearly visible. There were special courts for trying cases under láws applicable only to Africans. African magistrates had jurisdiction over Africans only and could not hear charges against Whites.

In the sphere of freedom of opinion and expression the South African government had enacted a series of laws to restrict the freedom of opinion and expression. Under the existing laws, it is deemed to be a punishable offence if a newspaper writes that apartheid is unjust to the African people.

South African women were the worst victims of apartheid, first on account of black colour and then on account of being women. This racial system accorded the meanest social status to the women. The fate of children under apartheid system was hardly better. As soon as a child is born in South Africa his race is determined by the doctors who certify it on his birth certificate. This certificate sets a seal on his future, whether he would be leading a life of privilege as all white children do or he would be leading a life of frustration and poverty like all black children.

From the above presentation, it is clear as to how apartheid in theory and practice affected the lives of the non-whites of all categories in South Africa. Although in recent years in order to adopt to the changing situation and increasing pressures from within and without the South African Government has introduced certain changes in the apartheid system. Under these changes, the government claims to have given certain concessions to the non-whites of South Africa in social, economic and political spheres. In fact these changes are only superficial which retain the vigours of apartheid. In other words, these changes have been made to indirectly strengthen the essential characteristics of apartheid and is only a process of remodelling the system to meet the exigencies of the time.

The white rulers are not prepared to share authority with Non- whites. They still insist upon the political, social, industrial and residential segregation of Europeans and Non-Europeans. Therefore these so-called changes or reforms must be set against the cold realities of the apartheid system which is firmly rooted in the country and is effectively backed by the peaceful military and police and a totally biased judiciary. It is very unfortunate that the Africans and other non-whites have been made aliens in their own land of birth like the Palestinians in Israel.

56

The Rise of African Nationalism

The period after the Second World War saw the emergence of most countries of Asia and Africa as independent nations. One country after another in these continents became independent. They won their independence through long and hard struggles against colonial powers. In some countries independence was won only after long and bitter armed struggle against the colonial powers. In some it was won without much bloodshed but not without a long period of struggle. Generally, the colonial powers were not willing to give up their hold on the colonies and left only when they found that it was not possible to maintain their rule any more. During the Second World War, many imperialist countries had been ousted from their colonies, but after the War they tried to reestablish their rule. For sometime they succeeded in doing so but were ultimately forced to withdraw.

The achievement of independence was primarily the result of the struggles of the peoples of the colonies. However, the changes in the international climate which followed the Second World War helped the peoples struggling for independence. Imperialism as a whole had been weakened as a result of the War. The economies of many imperialist countries had suffered. Forces within the imperialist countries which were friendly with the peoples struggling for independence also had grown powerful. Freedom and democracy were the major aims for which the Allies had fought against the fascist countries and these aims had been made the bases for arousing peoples all over the world against fascism. The fulfilment of these aims could no longer be confined only to Europe, as had been done after the First World War. In many colonies which fascist countries had occupied by ousting the older colonial powers, the freedom movements had played an important role in the struggle against fascist occupation. For example, Japan had to face the resistance of the freedom movements in the countries of South-east Asia which she had occupied. It was not easy to restore the rule of the former colonial powers over these countries.

Another major international factor which facilitated the end of imperialism was the emergence of the Soviet Union and other socialist countries as a major force. These countries were inimical to imperialism and often gave aid and support to the freedom movements in the colonies. Similarly the movement of socialism which had grown powerful the world over, including in the colonial countries, also supported the movements of freedom in the colonies.

The entire international context in which the freedom movements were launched had changed after the Second World War. At the international forums, particularly at the United Nations, the cause of the independence of colonies began to gain popularity. The international opinion was clearly against the continuation of imperialism. Imperialist countries resorted to various means to maintain their rule. They tried to create divisions in the freedom movements. They resorted to the use of terror. In some countries they tried to install governments which were nominally free but were in fact their puppets. However, most of the freedom movements were able to defeat these methods of weakening them.

An important role in the achievement of independence by the countries of Africa was played by the unity which freedom movements in various countries achieved. The freedom movement in one country supported the freedom movements in other countries. The role of countries which had achieved their independence was very crucial in this regard. These countries not merely supported the cause of those peoples who were still under colonial rule at the United Nations and other international forums. They also gave active help to the freedom movements. Besides the movements in the colonies for independence, there were also movements in African countries to oust outdated political systems, to modernise the social and economic systems and to assume control over the resources of one's country which had remained under foreign control even after freedom. These movements expressed the resolve of the peoples of Africa to become fully independent as well as to launch programmes of rapid social and economic development. Within two decades of the end of the Second World War, the political map of Africa had been completely changed.

A Glimpse into the Past

Africa's first contact with the West began when the Portuguese, five hundred years ago, arrived in Africa for trade, plunder and colonisation. Other European nations including the Dutch, English and the French arrived in the sixteenth century. The Arabs and the Turks began to cause increasing troubles for Portuguese in the Eastern coast from the end of the sixteenth century. The European rivals of the Portuguese first invaded West Africa which became the springboard for penetration into the hinterland. The religious, political and economic contact of the West resulted in the destruction of native institutions and customs.

Among the European explorers who discovered Africa for the West mention should be made of Mungo Park, the famous eighteenth century explorer, David Livingstone (1813-1873) and H.M. Stanley, the American newspaperman who went in search of him and met him in October, 1871 at Ujigi on Lake Tanganyika. John Speke and Richard Burton, Livingstone and Stanley were only few among the scores of European travellers and missionaries who went to the African continent as spearhead of the commercial civilisation of the West. Then came the trader and the African began surrendering his personality and eventually became so dependent upon the coloniser that he accepted foreign domination. The West began to exploit the Africans who were completely dispossessed, trampled and desecrated by the usurper.

The partition of Africa, inhabited by nearly 200 million people, started in earnest at the end of the nineteenth century. Between 1880 and 1890 Africa was almost entirely divided up between different European powers. France, Britain, Italy, Spain, Belgium and Portugal gained the lion's share in the partition of colonial Africa. Thus the scramble for Africa among European nations resulted in the parcelling out of the continent. The major actors in the drama were king Leopold II of Belgium and Bismarck of Germany. The division was settled in a conference held at Berlin in 1884 which accepted the theory of spheres of influence.

For four centuries the blood, toil and tear of Africa enriched the civilisation of the Westerners on the other side of the continent. The Europeans distinguished themselves by "avarice, treachery, hypocrisy and brutality". The African personality was crushed and the African received inhuman treatment at the hands of the slave traders. The slave trade was continent-wise and centuries long. Nearly one crore of Africans were sold out in slavery and more than six times that number were eliminated by the white slave traders. The slave trade of the Arabs and others accounted for the expatriation, death or banishment of as many more. Africans protested and faced the cannon with spear. They failed in their attempt but yet they preferred to die in the defence of liberty.

In Angola, Mozambique, Congo, South-West Africa, Rhodesia, in short, all over the African continent thousand of Africans small and great, men, women and children have manured the tree of liberty with their blood. It would not be out of place here to enumerate, for instance, some of the barbarities practised by the European nations to uphold their colonial rights in Africa. In 1952 alone the British soldiers killed nearly 11 thousand Africans in Kenya for their association with the Mau Mau movement. Nearly forty thousand Africans were murdered in cold blood in Madagascar (now independent Malagasy) in 1947. Portuguese barbarity has reduced the whole of Angola and Mozambique into one vast concentration camp. As a result in the post-Versailles era techniques of launching movement have undergone change. A strong African labour movement developed in the post-war era. The Africans also developed farmers' union like the 'Syndicate Agricole African' in the Ivory Coast and the Uganda African farmers' union.

Factors Contributing the Growth of Nationalism

Africa's freedom struggle took the form of nationalism as a result of her contact with Western ideas. In Africa, as in Asia, the leaders of the national movement were naturally the Western educated youth. Everywhere in Africa the same sentiment operated though the technique differed. Mr. R.M. Rawawa, the Vice-President of Tanganyika, in his address to the university students at Dar-es Salem on December 28, 1963 has rightly pointed out that "The freedom movements of the different parts of Africa were—and are—simply the local organisation of a continent-wide people's movement. They had to operate separately and adopt different tactics only because of the colonial organisation. Basically, they were all part of one movement.

But the beginning of a strong national movement for liberation goes back to post-Versailles era. The First World War gave a tremendous momentum to African nationalism. The Anglo-French powers recruited 650,000 soldiers and 238,000 labourers from Africa to win the war. It broadened the horizon of the Africans and made them realise that their services to the Allied powers were as much needed as they were valuable. The metropolitan powers in order to gain willing cooperation made concessions to the Africans and the economy of all the colonies of the belligerents was put on a war footing. This meant that the Africans had a greater insight into the economic system. In the post-Versailles era the war veterans were promised compensations. Whether these promises were fulfilled or not the African's claim to a better sharing to the benefits of his country was recognised. The end of the First World War, therefore, saw the growth of the movement for Pan-Africanism.

The impact of the Second World War was more farreaching than that of the first. The war set the stage for Africa's liberation. During the war the strategic importance of the African continent made the Allied powers eager to gain the willing cooperation of the Africans in their war efforts. Africa became not only an important source of war materials but also the 'bread basket' of Europe. The war spread ideas about human rights and loosened Europe's hold over Africa. It forged a new and more radical African leadership and sparked off the possibility of the notion of African independence.

The impact of the two world wars created ferment in the African continent and to this was added social dissatisfaction arising out of the contrast between the status, the wealth, the standard of wages, the housing and living condition of the white minority and the native majority. This contrast became more and more unacceptable with the spread of political consciousness and education.

Pan-Africanism

African unity is the logical development of the freedom struggle in which Africa is still engaged. Each country has had its own nationalist movement. But the basic purpose has been the same everywhere. Pan-Africanism aims at achieving the freedom of all Africans.

Pan-Africanism owes much to two outstanding Africans-Marcus Aurelius Gravey and William E. Dubois. The First Pan-African Conference was called in London in 1900. In 1909 that uncompromising enemy of imperialism and father of Pan-Africanism Dr. William Dubois founded the National Association for the Advancement of the coloured people and it was he who wrote "most men in the world are coloured". Dubois's efforts received a staunch support in the person of the Jamaican Marcus Aurelius Gravey. Gravey lifted his call of wake up Africa and started his "Universal Negro Improvement and African Communities League".

The stimulant of African nationalism began to gather momentum and assume new significance with the outbreak and outcome of the First World War. Dubois presented a petition to the Allied Powers to adopt a Charter of Human Rights for the Africans. The meeting of Pan-African Congress called in 1919 demanded that the former German colonies should be placed under international trusteeship as a step towards future self-government. The Congress also adopted a Charter of 'the Rights of the Negro people of the World'. Subsequent meetings of the Pan-African Congress were held at Lisbon in 1923 and at New York in 1927.

The African Scene After World War II

The era following World War II set the stage for African liberation. The Bandung Conference of 1955 saw for the first time the participation of independent African states in equal footing in an international gathering. The Conference forged the unity of two-thirds people of the world. Liberated Africa shook hands with independent Asia and condemned Western imperialism in no unmistaken terms. The spirit of Bandung inspired the gathering of free African states called at Accra in 1958. It was the first gathering of independent African states in the African soil. Egypt, Ghana, Libia, Liberia, Morocco, the Sudan, Tunisia and Ethiopia met together at Accra to discuss matters of common interest to Africa and the relation of the continent to the rest of the world. This meeting was an event of utmost importance because it signified that Africa is determined the break the bond of imperialism in near future. The Accra Conference passed resolutions condemning colonialism. Such principles as equality of all races and non-interference in the domestic affairs of all nations were accepted at Accra. The Conference resolutions were in conformity with the U.N. Charter.

The need for economic unity in Africa and economic cooperation among African states was keenly felt. The Conference also passed resolutions approving the investment of foreign capital in Africa without political strings. The Conference stressed the need for African unity through consultation of the Heads of the States.

The Pan-African movement set in motion at Accra received a new impetus in the Addis Ababa Conference of May, 1963. This Conference crystallized the principle formulated in the earlier conferences. It signified the birth of a new Africa determined to forge unity among all African peoples and to drive out imperialism, racialism and colonialism from the African soil.

The supreme importance of the Adis Ababa Conference lies in the fact that none of the earlier conferences held at Monrovia, Lagos, Accora or Cassablanca had been so impressive numerically or in scope. The Monrovia Conference held in 1961 was attended by representatives of twenty African and Malagasy states. It discussed the problem of inter-African cooperation. The Lagos Conference of Foreign Ministry was held in May, 1962 and the Cassablanca Conference was held later the same year. Both Lagos and Cassablanca charters condemned colonialism and affirmed the solidarity of the African peoples.

The Addis Ababa Conference adopted a charter for African unity and declared the following as the aim of the organisation set up for the purpose—(a) to promote African unity; (b) to defend the sovereignty of the African states; (c) to eradicate colonialism; (d) to promote international cooperation; (e) to promote cooperation to achieve a better life for the peoples of Africa.

The Conference in an unanimous resolution declared "the urgent necessity of coordinating and intensifying their efforts to accelerate the unconditional attainment of national independence of all African territories still under foreign domination." The Conference condemned the policy of apartheid and racial discrimination pursued by the Union of South Africa. The Conference reiterated its faith in the United Nations as an instrument for the maintenance of peace and security among nations and its desire to strengthen and support the United Nations. Other items of the agenda included disarmament and problem of economic cooperation. The Conference passed resolution for general disarmament under strict and effective international control and demanded that Africa should be declared a 'denuclearised zone'. The resolution on economic problem urged cooperation in the economic field and rapid industrialisation of African countries. The Addis Ababa Conference gave lie to the old theories viewing Africa in terms of 'Muslim Africa' and 'Negro Africa', 'Mediterranean Africa' and 'Africa South of Sahara'. The Pan-African Conferences displayed a striking solidarity of outlook among the representatives who gathered from different parts of Africa.

The Addis Ababa Conference did not establish African unity; sovereignty was not surrendered to any one. But it did state quite clearly the African objectives and it established an All-African machinery for cooperation and for the settlement of disputes between African nations. It also laid down the principles which should be observed by all states in their relation with each other and the outside world. It laid the foundation for the edifice of a United Africa.

Achievement of Freedom by African Nations

The countries of southern Africa or Black Africa began to gain their independence after the mid-1950s. Within the last three decades or so, almost every country in Africa, with the exception of South Africa and South-West Africa (Namibia), has become independent.

The freedom movements in Africa, as in other parts of the world, were the consequence of the growth of nationalism and the increasing resentment against the exploitation and oppression by the colonial countries. The international situation further strengthened these movement. The Second World War had resulted in the general weakening of imperialism. It had also shattered the myth of the invincibility of some major colonial powers in Africa such as France and Belgium which had suffered defeat in Europe during the War. The collapse of colonialism in Asia within a few years after the war also had a tremendous impact on freedom movements in Africa. The question of Africa's freedom gradually became one of the major issues in the world.

The first country in Black Africa to gain independence was Ghana. The British had conquered a colony in this region to which they gave the name Gold Coast. The most prominent leader of the people of the Gold Coast colony was Kwame Nkrumah who in 1949 had organised the Convention People's Party. A strong trade Union movement also had emerged in Gold Coast. The Convention People's Party and the trade unions joined together to demand independence from Britain. However, most of their leaders were arrested and attempts were made to suppress the demand for freedom. After 1950, the British government started introducing certain constitutional reforms. Under pressure from the People's Party which had won a resounding victory in elections, the British government agreed to the independence of Gold Coast. The new independent state which came into being on 6 March 1957 called itself Ghana, after the name of the old West African kingdom. The part of Togoland which had been under British control also joined Ghana.

The next country to achieve her independence was the French colony of Guinea in West Africa. In 1958, while embroiled in the war in Algeria, France held a referendum in her colonies which had been grouped together as French West Africa and French Equatorial Africa. The people of Guinea voted almost unanimously for complete independence and Guinea was proclaimed a republic on 2 October 1958.

The year 1960 is generally regarded as the Africa Year. In that year, seventeen countries in Africa gained their independence. These included all the French colonies in French, West Africa and Equatorial Africa, and Nigeria and Congo (former Belgian Congo) now called Zaire.

Between 1961 and 1964 a number of countries in East and Central Africa became independent. These were Kenya, Uganda, Tanganyika, Zanzibar, Nyasaland, Northern Rhodesia and Ruanda-Urundi, Sierra Leone, Gambia, Basutoland and Bechunaland also gained their independence.

Before the end of the 1960s, almost all of Africa with the exception of Portuguese colonies of Angola, Mozambique and Guinea-Bissau and Cape Verde Island, and South Africa, South-West Africa and Rhodesia and become free. Powerful freedom movements had arisen in the Portuguese colonies. They had organized their liberation forces and had secured the help of many countries in their struggle for freedom. In April 1974, the Portuguese army, much of which had been used to suppress the freedom struggles in the colonies, with the support of the people overthrew the 50-year old dictatorship in Portugal. The communists, socialists and other radical elements in the armed forces and the new government of Portugal were opposed to the continuation of the Portuguese rule in Africa. They entered into negotiations with the freedom movements in the Portuguese colonies and by 1975 all the former Portuguese colonies in Africa became independent. Zimbabwe became independent in April 1980.

The last two major countries in Africa yet to achieve independence are the Republic of South Africa and South-West Africa. Of these, South Africa is militarily the most powerful. The government of South Africa is the most oppressive regime in the world today. The white minority in that country rules over the vast majority of the African population. It practises the policy of *apartheid* which means the separation of black and white communities. This policy is used to maintain the rule of the white minority over the majority of the population which comprises black and coloured people. In the name of separation of the communities, it is really a policy of denial of human rights to the majority of the population. The South African government depends on the use of terror to maintain its rule. The people have been subjected to massacres when they organized peaceful protests. The United Nations has condemned the policies of South Africa. Many Western countries maintain close economic and military relations with South Africa and thus have helped in sustaining the oppressive government there. The main organization of the South African people is the African National Congress (ANC) which for many years has been fighting for the liberation of South Africa.

Another major country which is still to become independent is South-West Africa or Namibia. This was a German colony before the First World War and handed over to South Africa as a 'mandate' after the defeat of Germany in that war. South Africa has always treated South-West Africa as her colony and has refused to withdraw from there in spite of the resolutions of the United Nations. The freedom movement in South-West Africa has gained momentum in the recent years under the leadership of the South-West Africa People's Organisation (SWAPO). The governments and peoples of independent nations of Africa actively aid the freedom movements in these countries. They also played an important role in bringing about the end of the white minority rule in Zimbabwe.

Thus within the last two decades, most of Africa has become independent and the independence of the remaining part cannot be deferred for long. Many African countries have changed their names. The colonial powers had given them names which had little to do with their past history and culture. Some countries and cities had been named after colonial adventurers, for example Rhodesia, Leopoldville, Stanleyville, etc. The African peoples are trying to overcome the damage caused to them during the colonial rule. Renaming their countries and cities after their original names is a part of their effort to establish and assert their independence and national identity. The need to unite in the face of common tasks and for the achievement of common aim has led to the emergence of the unity of all African peoples. These aims include the safeguarding of their independence and to help the liberation movements in those countries in Africa which are still fighting for their independence. The most significant step taken in this direction was the formation of the Organization of African Unity (OAU) in 1963.

The Problems to be Overcome

The vestige of traditionalism and tribalism still persists in Africa. The lack of literacy among large section of people and their loyalty to tribalism stands in the way of Africa's liberation and offers opportunity for outside intervention. There are among Africans some thoroughly westernized well-do-so leaders like Tshombe. They provide the disintegrating factors in African politics. The miseries of Congo is a classical example of the dangers from which the newly independent states of Africa are threatened.

The African states have inherited artificial boundaries. These boundaries were created by the imperialist powers in their scramble for Africa. Within Africa there is not a single border which has been drawn on the basis of dividing different races, tribes or peoples. Neither are there many border lines which run along the natural geographical divisions of the land. The danger of such border line existing between two states have been already demonstrated by several border conflicts including the clash between Morocco and Algeria, Kenya and Somali. Such conflicts did not arise before independence because boundaries then were unimportant; they were administrative divisions. The boundary disputes provide a stumbling block in the way of African unity and create the danger of neo-colonialism.

Africa is too valuable a prize in the eyes of the imperialist powers to be given up without an attempt to retain the substance. No doubt the acceleration of national liberation movement has forced imperialism to strike a hasty retreat in the post-World War II era, yet the colonial powers are ever on the look out to re-enter Africa through the backdoor taking advantage either of an internal or international dispute. If an outside power is interested in selling armaments, destroying a government, diverting a particular economic policy or anything of this sort, then conflict or internal disunity would give the opportunity to intervene. Such an eventuality is fraught with much danger for African unity. Africa in that case may become involved in the global power conflict and cold war and African countries may find themselves in opposing camps. Africa is, therefore, eager to follow a policy of non-alignment. The problem of African unity is that each of the separate nations has the fear that in a United Africa it might become a backward and neglected area, exploited for the benefit of another part. There is also the problem of time and opportunity. The African peoples must be allowed to develop their national outlook and learn how to bring it in line with continental outlook before they are asked to take steps for African unity.

The African peoples have attempted to forge not only an all African unity but also Afro-Asian unity. This is evident from the different Afro-Asian Conferences held at Cairo in 1957, in Guinea in 1960 and at Mosi in Tanganyika in 1963. The unity and solidarity of the Afro-Asian states has been amply demonstrated by their co-operation in the UN. Outside the UN most of the Afro-Asian states have adhered to a policy of non-alignment.

THE AFRICAN REGION

State	*Area (in sq. kms.)*	*Population (in millions)*
Algeria	2,381,741	23.84 (1989)
Angola	1;246,700	9.20 (1989)
Benin	112,622	4.30 (1989)
Botswana	582,000	1.21 (1989)
Burkina Faso	274,200	8.30 (1989)
Burundi	27,834	5.15 (1989)
Cameroon	475,442	10.70 (1989)
Cape Verde Islands	4,033	0.36 (1989)
Central African Republic	622,984	3.00 (1989)
Chad	1,284,000	5.40 (1989)
Comoros	2,171	0.42 (1989)
Congo	349,650	2.00 (1989)
Cote d'Ivoire	322,463	11.60 (1989)
Djibouti	23,310	0.50 (1989)
Egypt	1,101,490	55.00 (1989)
Ethiopia	1,780,450	47.90 (1989)
Gabon	267,667	1.09 (1989)
The Gambia	11,295	0.81 (1989)
Ghana	239,460	14.10 (1989)
Guinea	245,957	6.50 (1989)
Guinea Bissau	36,125	0.92 (1989)
Kenya	582,646	23.90 (1989)

(Contd.)

State	Area (in sq. kms.)	Population (in millions)
Lesotho	30,355	1.70 (1989)
Liberia	111,369	2.50 (1989)
Libya	1,761,132	4.30 (1989)
Madagascar	587,041	10.90 (1989)
Malawi	118,484	8.40 (1989)
Mali	1,240,192	8.70 (1989)
Mauritania	1,030,700	2.00 (1989)
Mauritius	1,865	1.08 (1989)
Morocco	711,000	23.30 (1989)
Western Sahara	Yet to be independent	3.00 (1987)
Mozambique	783,030	14.70 (1989)
Namibia	822,620	1.70 (1989)
Niger	1,267,000	6.80 (1989)
Nigeria	923,768	105.00 (1989)
Rwanda	26,338	6.80 (1989)
Sao Tome and Principe	964	0.11 (1989)
Senegal	196,192	7.00 (1989)
Seychelles	443	0.07 (1989)
Sierra Leone	72,325	4.00 (1989)
Somalia	725,541	5.70 (1989)
South Africa	1,221,037	33.80 (1989)
Sudan	2,505,813	23.10 (1989)
Swaziland	17,363	0.70 (1989)
Tanzania	945,087	23.20 (1989)
Togo	56,785	3.30 (1989)
Tunisia	164,150	7.80 (1989)
Uganda	236,036	17.20 (1989)
Zaire	2,345,409	34.00 (1989)
Zambia	752,614	7.50 (1989)
Zimbabwe	391,109	8.90 (1989)

57

African National Congress

Today the African National Congress of South Africa is leading the fight against the most vicious form of racialism since the destruction of Hitlerite fascism.

White settlement in South Africa dates back to the beginning of the second half of the seventeenth century. On 6th April, 1652, employees and servants of the Dutch East India Company, a mainly Holland concern, arrived at the Cape to establish a half-way house or station for supplying their ships going to Asia with fresh provisions. At first the settlement did not appear to have been conceived as a base or a bridgehead for the conquest of the country. Not long after, however, it turned out to be such. Soon a struggle began between the inhabitants of the territory and the new settlers. The causes of the dispute were the questions of:-

labour supply;
livestock; and
land ownership and control.

In these struggles the Nama who were called the Hottentots and the Khol Khoi Khoi who were called Bushmen were practically wiped out in a similar manner as the so-called Red Indians in America. The White colonial usurpers actually organised hunting expeditions to track down and kill off the Khoi Khoi like wild animal. Possessing superior weapons, the Whites shot down these relatively unarmed people, deprived the survivors of their land and drove them out of the area, took away their livestock, and forced those whom they had captured to work for them as slaves.

Long before the time of White settlement, as far back as the second half of the 15th century, there had been several bloody clashes in which lives had been lost on both sides. Those clashes had been between the Khoison and other African people on the one hand, and the would be Portuguese colonisers on the other hand. One such clash took place in November-December, 1947, at a place named "Bay of Cows" by one Portuguese explorer, Vasco da Gama. The "Bay of Cows" is our present day Mossel Bay. It is said that the place was so named "because many cattle grazed near the shore".

The Portuguese had landed at the "Bay of Cows" under the pretext of distress, to repair their ships and to get supplies of fresh water and food. These Portuguese sailors were treated as guests and lavishly entertained by the local inhabitants.

Whereas the Africans welcomed the new arrivals from Europe with open arms, the latter, however, harboured evil designs. The colonists soon spread rapidly over a wide area and violated the boundaries which had been fixed with the indigenous people. They rode rough-shod over the prior rights of the original inhabitants to hunting, grazing and arable land.

Because of the intrusion and the predatory and aggressive policies of the Whites, disputes which soon led to wars, ensued. In the Cape alone there were nine such wars of resistance against encroachment on the part of the Whites. These wars were waged almost continuously for nearly a hundred years. The Boer forces and later both the Boer and British forces were checked. But because of superior arms which the Whites possessed, the Africans were slowly pushed back beyond the Great Fish River.

Wherever the Boers went they met still resistance and were routed in some dramatic battles. For example, the Zulu section of people thoroughly outmanoeuvred, outgenerated and completely wiped out to a Boer marauding force headed by the iniqutous, racist Piet Relief, the architect and author of the racist Great Trek Manifesto of 1836 on which present day apartheid policies are based. To this day they have not forgotten the defeat at the hands of the Zulu King, Dingaan. On the other hand every African in Southern Africa vividly remembers Dingaan's battle-cry on that occasion when he ordered: "Bula L' Abathakathil" (Kill the evil men). Today this very very battle-order is being reechoed by young guerillas who are locked in battle with the racist forces in Southern Africa.

The arrival in South Africa of the British military forces towards the end of the eighteenth century brought about quantitative and qualitative changes in the resistance struggle of the people; they immensely strengthened the forces of colonisation and national oppression. The British were the foremost reactionary power in Europe and were at that time allied with Holland in the war against Republican France. With their overwhelming superiority in arms, their economic might and above all their long experience at intrigue, they were able to eventually subdue all opposition offered by the African people to their grand design for the colonisation of the country and the subjugation and exploitation of the people.

There are various reasons which brought about African people's military defeat and political humiliation. These are political, economic, military and historican reasons. Let us list these briefly as follows:

This was a confrontation between an advanced, commercial capitalist Europe personified by Britain and Holland. Whereas Africa was only emerging out of communalistic social organisation and no modern industrialised development had emerged. Therefore the ganging up of a powerful combination of British and Holland proved difficult for the people to withstand.

The industrial development of Europe placed powerful up-to-date weapons of destruction in the hands of the colonialists which they did not hesitate to use against ill-armed people.

There was lack of co-ordination and united struggle on the part of the people against the common enemy. Attempts were made by the various tribal leaders to achieve a grand alliance of the African people against the White invaders, but these did not succeed.

On January 8th, 1912, an unusual and truly remarkable conference assembled at Bloemfontein. Present were a few professional men and intellectuals: a large number of chiefs and tribesmen, workers and peasants. They came from all parts of South Africa, which only two years earlier was constituted into a Union; they came from the rural areas of the Transkei and Zululand and from the urban areas of Johannesburg, Kimberley, Durban, Port Elizabeth and Cape Town. They came from far as Botswana, Lesotho and Swaziland.

The most astonishing feature of that conference was the number of tribes who sent representatives. There were Zulus, Exhosas, Tswanas, Sothos, Vendas, Shongaans, Tongas, and others. These tribes, some of them only recently locked in feuds, had looked upon each other with suspicion. Each was proud and could only, with difficulty look upon others as equals. For two years before they had seen the bitter fruits of their disunion and division when, at the formation of the Union, they had all been ignored when Boer and Briton met to form the so-called Union of South Africa. As Dr. Pixley ka Isaka Seme, prominent leader and lawyer, stated at the Conference:

> "We are one people. These divisions, these jealousies, are the cause of all our woes and all our backwardness and ignorance today."

The assembly conferred and at the end of their deliberations emerged the AFRICAN NATIONAL CONGRESS.

In some ways the thoughts and ideas of those pioneers reflected the different strata from which the conference participants were drawn. For example, they had a House of Chiefs and a House of Commoners. But basically they were far-sighted. They saw the need for a United National Struggle of all the oppressed. They also saw as their most important demands, the demand for universal franchise and land. In matters of foreign policy the conference advocated the freedom and unity of the whole of Africa.

Since its formation, the African National Congress (ANC) has gone through various phases. It has been in the vanguard of innumerable struggles. Today there is no doubt about its supreme position as the spearhead of revolution in South Africa.

The ANC is not only the oldest liberation organisation in South Africa, but, unquestionably the only body with a mass base; with the organisational framework; with a dedicated leadership; and above all a highly-trained People's Army - Umkhonto we Sizwe (The Spear of the Nation) - capable of leading the National Liberation struggle to ultimate victory in South Africa.

The ANC realised from the outset that the problems of forging unity among Africans was the key to their freedom struggle. The formation of the ANC, therefore, marked the birth of a nation whose foundations were laid in a stirring call by Dr. P. I. Seme, later to become its Treasurer-General, when in an article written in 1911 he declared:

"The demon of racialism, the aberrations of Exhosa-Fingo feuds, the animosity that exists between Zulus and the Tongas, between the Basuto and every other Native, must be forgotten... We are one people."

Throughout the years, the ANC patiently and tirelessly preached the doctrine of African Nationalism and African Unity. On the other hand successive White minority regimes and particularly the regime of Apartheid did their utmost to foster tribal divisions among the Africans. They incited and continue to incite inter-tribal faction fights, ethnic grouping of Africans at school and residential areas along tribal lines.

Britain, in 1910, granted "independence" to the White minority and the Union of South Africa, which excluded Africans and other non-Whites, was established in the place of four existing Provincial regimes. Soon after assuming power, the White minority regime passed the notorious Land Act in 1913. This law robbed the Africans of their remaining land and created a state of affairs whereby 87% of the land passed into the hands of the Whites whilst the Africans retained only 13%. This particular piece of legislation was designed to impoverish the African people and thus compel them to work in the mines, industries and large White-owned farms for miserable wages.

So far-reaching were the implications of the Land Act on the economic well-being of the African people that the ANC decided to launch a campaign against this measure. At that time Great Britain still retained powers to disallow discriminatory measures passed by the South African Parliament. The ANC, therefore, sent a delegation to Britain to obtain British intervention for the repeal of this iniquitous measure. But using the excuse of the outbreak of the War in 1914, Britain refused to help the African cause.

The year 1913, also saw the great ANC-inspired antipass struggle of the African people. That year the pass laws, long regarded as a badge of slavery by the African people, were extended to women as well. A bitter campaign of defiance by the women ensured. Many women were jailed and beaten. They persevered and finally the Government was forced to retreat and repeal the section of the law compelling women to carry passes.

At the end of World War I in 1919, the ANC sent another mission abroad to champion the cause of people and to put more pressure on Britain to use her constitutional powers and intervene in favour of the Black man. The delegation attended the Peace Congress in France in 1919. There they demanded freedom for people and bitterly resisted the handing over the South West Africa as a mandated trust territory to South Africa. Whilst in Paris the ANC delegation also attended the first Pan-African conference sponsored by Dr. W. du Bois and other Pan-Africanists.

However, the delegation's mission to London met with failure. Instead Whitehall referred them to the White racist minority regime against whom the Africans had sought British protection and assistance in the first place.

During the twenties with rapid industrialisation taking place in South Africa and with hundreds of thousands of African workers being drawn into secondary industry the struggle of African people shifted largely into the economic plane. Trade union activity was stepped up and a great deal of industrial struggles and economic strikes took place. The Industrial Commercial Union, led by Clements Kadalie, played a prominent role in rallying the masses of the African workers. But the ANC played an equally significant political role in supporting strike action by the African workers. The ANC vigorously denounced the massacres by South African military forces on striking African workers.

During the mid-thirties, exploiting the upsurge of Nazi and Fascist reaction in Western Europe, the South African White ruling circles executed their grand design of taking away the vote from the Africans of the Cape Province and Natal, the last remaining areas where Africans "enjoyed" the right to elect White representatives to Parliament. By ruse and intrigue the South African "Whites Only" Parliament trumped up the two-thirds majority required to remove from the constitution the entrenched clauses which supposedly guaranteed the vote of the Cape Africans. Much later, the Coloured people were disenfranchised by similar intrigues. So much for the constitutional guarantees pledged for Africans by the White men of Whitehall. The entire African population was outraged by the disenfranchisement of the Cape Africans.

To meet this crisis, the African National Congress, convened a special Convention which embraced Africans from all walks of life in Bloemfontein in 1936. It is regretable that the action emanating from this Convention amounted to nothing much more than the sending of a deputation to the South African regime. But the struggle for the franchise had received a serious setback.

The period of the Second World War and after saw a new upsurge of National Liberation Movements in Asia and Africa. In South Africa, this upward wave of anti-colonial struggle gripped the ranks of young African intellectuals and there were political disturbances in education centres like Fort Hore, Lovedale and elsewhere. In 1943, the ANC formed a Youth League. The ANC Youth League played a prominent part in getting the mother-body to adopt a militant programme of action.

The Programme of Action adopted by the ANC conference in 1949 proclaimed that the main content and principal vehicle of the struggle against the racist regime must be mass action. The programme set out various tactics to be employed flexibly, depending on the prevailing situation. These tactics of struggle included the use of boycotts, passive resistance, strike action and other forms of mass action.

The adoption of the Programme of Action in 1949 ushered in a new era of mass struggles. Thus, in 1950, the ANC in the Transvaal Province participated in the launching of a one day strike on May Day. On June 26 the same year, the ANC together with the South African Indian Congress called a national day of mourning in the form of a nation-wide strike to mourn the victims of police shootings during the May Day strike and to protest against new repressive legislation.

In 1951, the ANC National Conference in Bloemfontein resolved to embark upon a massive Campaign of Defence of Apartheid laws. On June 26, 1952 together with the South Indian Congress, the ANC launched the Defiance of Unjust Laws Campaign. The Defiance Campaign Carried on through 1953 covering all major centres in South Africa. Over 8,000 volunteers belonging to the ANC and its allies defied Apartheid and were jailed. in 1954, the ANC launched a struggle against the imposition of the inferior Bantu Education System calculated to reduce African youth into 'hewers of wood and drawers of water' for the White man. Massive agitation took place among the parents and teachers and a boycott was organised against Bontu Educational schools.

In the meantime, the question of unity among all genuine democratic forces which has always consumed the serious attention of the ANC was beginning to take a more concrete shape.

Cooperation between the Indian Congress and the ANC had already been tested in action. Steps for this co-operation were taken in 1947 when the late Dr. Xuma, then President- General of the African National Congress signed a pact with Dr. Y.M. Daddo and Dr. G.M. Naicker, Presidents of the Transvaal Indian Congress and National Indian Congress respectively, in which they agreed to cooperate on matters of common interests. This agreement was subsequently endorsed by the then African People's Organisation. Since then a firm basis of solidarity and joint action in the struggle among Africans, Indians and Coloureds was firmly established. Later, during the Defiance campaign of 1952 some progressive Whites joined the struggle on the side of the oppressed people, and the Congress of the Democrats was formed.

The alliance was further strengthened with the South African Congress of Trade Unions actively joining in.

Having succeeded substantially in mobilising the various African tribal groupings into a single fighting nation, the ANC, in keeping with its overall strategy, to lead a united front of all anti-racist and democratic forces, hammered out a common programme with the representatives of the various racial groups and the trade union movement.

This programme was further crystallised when early in 1955 the ANC called for 50,000 volunteers of all sections of the South African people to go among the people and collect freedom demands to be incorporated into a common programme for South Africa.

Thus began one of the greatest campaigns in the history of the South African liberation movement. Demands flowed into the offices of the ANC from every corner of South Africa; from Africans, Indians, Coloureds and Whites; from workers and peasants; from shop-keepers and intellectuals.

On June 26, that year at the historic Congress of the People, the fighting demands of the people were enshrined in The Freedom Charter.

The success of this campaign and the widespread support the Charter received from the people did not go un-noticed by the racist regime in South Africa.

In 1956, the political police swooped and arrested 156 leaders of the ANC and its allies and charged them with High Treason using the Freedom Charter as the basis of its charge. It was alleged that the ANC planned a revolutionary overthrow of the regime. In 1957, the ANC together with local residents' associations organised the Great Rand and Pretoria bus boycott. In April 1958, the ANC organised another one day national strike. In 1959 at its national conference in Durban, the ANC resolved to conduct the following year a massive nation-wide struggle against the Pass Laws. This campaign was under way when the P.A.C. sought to wreck it by launchint its passive resistance campaign only ten days before the National Anti-Pass Campaign was to begin on 31st March, 1960. When the police shot the people of Sharpville and PAC was in disarray the ANC called a national one day strike on March 28, 1960 and ordered massive burning of passes. The South African regime, alarmed by the powerful wave of mass action declared the African National Congress illegal. The ANC refused to accept the order of the powers that be, and decided to continue the struggle as an underground and illegal organisation.

The ANC leaders did not stand behind and merely command the people into action. They were in the fore-front at all times. The very first banning orders imposed in 1950 by the regime victimised ANC and S.A. Indian Congress leaders like Moses Kotone, J.B. Marks, Dr. Yusuf Dadoo and others. In 1953, ANC leaders and other leaders of the Defiance Campaign were arrested; in 1956, a total of 156 ANC and allied leaders were arrested and charged with High Treason. Numerous ANC leaders at the national and local levels were either arrested, banned, banished, restricted, or victimised in one way or another. Thousands of local leaders and rank and file members fearlessly faced the bullets of the forces of tyranny.

In South Africa, the ANC flexibly applied all the non-violent means of action at its disposal. It brushed aside armchair dogmatists.

Having dealt a death blow to tribalism and having forged a fighting alliance of all democratic and oppressed forces in South Africa the ANC followed up on its earlier efforts to work for broader African unity embracing the whole continent of Africa. The slogans of the ANC clearly reflected this. Their slogan "Moyibuye i' Africa" (Africa must come back to us) is an example. The ANC thumb up salute signified the unity of Africa; the fist stands for the continent and the protruding thumb, the Ethiopian horn of Africa while the bent elbow formed South Africa.

The actions of the ANC in the struggle against White domination, not only at home but on a Continent-wide scale clearly showed the belief of the ANC that a stable unity of all the countries of Africa was an essential prerequisite for the defeat of Imperialism on the Continent and the destruction of White domination.

58

Afghanistan

The later part of 1970s contained important pointers to the future of peace and war in the South-West Asian region. It was marked by increasing domestic tensions, political confusion, power rivalries, (coup d' etat) and superpower competition for spheres of influences and intervention. To a world used to seeing more sources of conflict and tension, the Soviet action in Afghanistan witnessed a series of civil military wars and events moved close to provoking a direct military and diplomatic clash between the superpowers.

The impact of the Soviet presence was greater because it occurred against a background which had looked particularly unpromising. The increasing importance of the Persian Gulf oil and the revolution in Iran led to the growth of Islamic radicalism throughout the Gulf and West Asian and North African regions. Afghanistan has been the focus of worldwide attention for more than a decade now. It is situated in South-West Asia and occupies an area of approximately 6,55,000 square kilometres. Afghanistan shares a border with the Soviet Union (2,384 kilometres long) in the north, with the People's Republic of China (75 kilometres) and India (120 kilometres) in the north-east with Pakistan (2,180 kilometres) in the east and south, and with Iran (820 kilometres) in the west. With a rural population of about two million, Afghanistan is a highly traditional, and tribal-oriented state. It was only around the later part of the 1940s and 1950s that the superpowers aid began to make perceptible inroads, in the form of schools, hospitals, highways connecting the far-flung provinces and air-fields, together with the expansion of the military technology and army.

During the inter-war period (1919-1945), following the consolidation of its rule in India, Great Britain persistently strove to make Afghanistan its protectorate and intervened in the internal affairs of that state. Since 1948 when the partition took place with the British withdrawal from India, a new vacuum was created. This vacuum was filled up with the United States taking the position of Great Britain against the Soviet Union. The US efforts to make Afghanistan sign a pact with Iran and Pakistan in 1953, providing facilities for the US airfields, did not succeed. The US failed in having an equation with the Soviet Union in Afghanistan.

The US military designs and the subsequent closure of the Pakistani-Afghan border over the issue of the future of the Pushtun tribe forced Afghanistan to re-route its trade through the Soviet Union and seek assistance to modernise its army.

Afghanistan passed through a period of uncertainty during the regime of Lt. Gen Muhammad Daud, who came to power after overthrowing King Zahir Shah in a bloodless coup on July, 17, 1973. Daud, who became the head of state on August 23, 1973, seemed in full control of the situation and on good terms with his Soviet neighbours. In the act of crushing the left-wing opposition, Daud was himself overthrown in a military coup (April 1978) which was led by army and air force officers who released the imprisoned Leftist leaders to form a new government. The Soviet Union recognised the new regime.

The new government was dominated by civilians of the Peoples Democratic Party of Afghanistan (PDPA), founded in 1965, and its Secretary-General, Nur Muhammad Taraki, succeeded as Prime Minister. He floundered quickly as his party split into two rival factions, and the country drifted into civil war. In quick succession, the chief figures of PDPA became President, each after the murder of his predecessor- Taraki replacing Daud (as mentioned), Hafiz-ullah Amin replacing Taraki and, after the Soviet intervention in December 1979, Babrak Karmal stepping into the shoes of Amin and Maj. Gen Najibullah replacing Karmal in May 1986.

Since 1979, there has been an almost complete breakdown of the Central Government's administration over its 28 provinces. The Soviet intervention in Afghanistan since December 1979 was defended on the basis of the November 1978 Treaty of Friendship and Article 51 of the UN Charter. It was claimed that Amin, who was accused of plotting to partition Afghanistan with foreign imperialist powers had been overthrown by an internal revolution, and that military support from the Soviet Union had been requested by the new regime. World opinion however, was sceptical of such claims, and a Soviet withdrawal was demanded by the UN General Assembly, the Islamic Conference Organisation (OIC) the Association of South-east Asian Nations (ASEAN), the Non-Aligned Movement as well as by Western powers.

Since the spring of 1979 the Soviet Union began to play a greater role in Afghanistan. Evidently alarmed at the extent of the hostility to the regime and the prospect of being drawn into a protracted civil war, and concerned about the possible international complications of Afghan disputes with Pakistan and Islamic Iran, she began to argue for less radical policies, conciliation of the opposition, and the formation of a broad-based government. But at the same time, a steady build-up of Soviet military presence in Afghanistan had been felt.

The US State Department issued a series of diplomatic warnings and protests since then.

However, for the first time since they intervened in Afghanistan in 1979, the Soviets have made determined diplomatic efforts to try and bring about a peace settlement there in 1987. The year 1987 also saw widespread intensification of the war between Soviet and Kabul government troops and the Afghan guerillas (operating from Pakistan and Islamic Iran). The war and unrest in Afghanistan has largely wiped out three decades of development progress there, schools, medical clinics and farmers' access to fertiliser and improved seed from the state agencies have suffered in the general destruction. Besides, the costs to the Soviet Union of this war were considerable and mounted rapidly, both in casualties suffered and losses incurred in military hardware.

Moreover, foreign interference in the region took a serious turn with the US's espousal of the theory of an "arc of crisis" in the wake of the fall of the Shah of Iran. The developments in Afghanistan came as a blessing in disguise for the then Pakistan President, General Zia-ul-Haq, who used the pretext of a "Soviet threat" to obtain enormous US military and economic aid. The Soviet Union and Babrak Karmal and Najibullah regimes in Kabul repeatedly expressed their readiness to pull out the Soviet troops the moment an international agreement was concluded on cessation of foreign interference in the internal affairs of Afghanistan. India supported this position.

By intensifying the war (militarily) Moscow aimed to push the guerillas back across their borders in to Pakistan and Islamic Iran. It wanted to create a no-man's land along the Afghan border to ensure Afghanistan's internal security. At the same time, Moscow attempted to stabilise Maj. Gen Najibullah's regime. Both the above steps were taken with a background of intense diplomatic activity by the Soviets to convince the US administration and Pakistan that the key to the success of Soviet leader Mikhail Gorbachev's glasnost or perestroika policy was a quick end to the war and the withdrawal of Soviet troops. Accordingly, the Great Geneva Agreement reached on April 14, 1988, the Soivet troops started pulling out from Afghanistan and completed the same recently, that is on February 15, 1989, after eight turbulent years of undeclared war there.

Internationally, the Geneva Accord gave the US first time an equation with the Soviet Union in the region. The Soviets lost even if they had everything in their favour in Afghanistan. They could not afford to continue as they realised the cost is higher in terms of international goodwill. By one action alone in Afghanistan the Soviet Union lost its prestige. All US allies in Europe, West Asia and South Asia condemned the Soviet position. Hence the new Soviet leadership under Gorbachev assured Western Europe that there will be no threat to them from the Soviet Union in future. Gorbachev agreed to certain terms and conditions in the Geneva Accord.

With the last of the Soviet troops gone fundamentalist Mujahidin factions, operating from Pakistan and Islamic Iran, insisting on pulling down the Najibullah regime in Kabul by force, Afghanistan is heading for a long bloodbath and uncertain future. It is time for the United Nations to send a strong UN peace-keeping force to Afghanistan to ensure that the civil war there ends, a dialogue begins and relief, rehabilitation and reconstruction measures are undertaken. Moreover, urgent steps must be taken to end US arms deliveries to the warring factions there. India's and the entire South-West Asia's security is closely linked to the restoration of permanent peace in Afghanistan and the resumption of its status as a sovereign and Non-aligned nation.

In the wake of recent changes in the disintegrated Soviet Union and international sphere, whatever, President Najibullah's fate, there is at least a possibility that the US-Soviet detente could open the door to UN sponsored talks in Afghanistan. After more than one million dead, 5 million living as refugees in Pakistan and Iran, and their country in ruins, it is high time Afghanistan's warring parties put down their guns and restore peace and stability in their state.

59

The Palestinian Imbroglio

The question of Palestine became a symbol of Arab unity. Egypt's commitment to the Palestine cause has become a historical part of her strategy in seeking the resolution of the Arab-Israeli conflict. Nasser's policy has been characterised as adhering to the strategic goal i.e. the establishment of an independent Palestinian entity.

No one can fail to recognise Egypt's contribution which is greater than that of any other Arab state in sustaining Palestinian entity. It pursued that policy through the establishment of the Provisional government of Palestine under Mufti al-Husseini which existed in Gaza till 1956 and which shifted its headquarters to Cairo after the 1956 war. In 1964 Egypt took a major part in the establishment of the PLO. It was also a major step towards its recognition as the sole and legitimate representative of the Palestinian people. The achievements of the PLO would be inconceivable without Egypt's initiative, support and ongoing activity especially during the Nasser's era.

To start with the Egyptian-Palestinian relations have a background of their own. The Arab struggle against Zionist designs and British policies in Palestine can be said to be the most important of all factors which had contributed to the sense of Arab unity. The Palestine Arab Revolt of 1936 was the most serious expression of Arab discontent made so far, and had its repercussions all over the Arab world.

Palestine was held by Britain as a League mandate. Her task was to prepare the People of Palestine for self-government. Since 1936, the question of Palestine began to intrude into the Egyptian domestic politics. Being Arabs, the Egyptians had a natural sympathy for the Arabs in Palestine. The Islamic organisations were attracting an increasing number of disenchanted youths and were using the Palestine issue to embarrass the contemporary WAFD government. Nahas Pasha, the Wafd Party leader saw the benefit to himself and to Wafd in championing the Arab cause in Palestine. The maiden speech of the Egyptian Minister of Foreign Affairs after Egypt's admission to the League of Nations in 1937 dealt entirely with the Palestine question.

Egypt played an important part in the Arab League on the Palestine question. It was under Egypt's insistence that the Arab League had taken over the conduct of Arab cause on Palestine. Egypt being a founder member of the Arab League, and being its leader was honour bound to defend the cause of Palestine.

On 29 November 1947, the General Assembly of the United Nations passed the resolution recommending the partition of Palestine. The Arabs including Egypt totally rejected the recommendation, but the Zionists accepted it. Britain announced its decision to relinquish its mandate for Palestine on 15 may 1948.

Partition

The partition of Palestine was a staggering blow to Egypt's prestige. So, on 15 May 1948 Egypt sent her armies into Palestine to forestall the establishment of a Jewish state. When the war broke out in Palestine, Egypt contributed the largest single contingent of Arab troops. It played a significant role in this 1948 war. But the Arabs were defeated.

The humiliating defeat of Egypt in Palestine had a profound and immediate effect on Egypt's public life. Prime Minister Nokarashi Pasha tried to conceal from public the disastrous course of the war but failed. The government's inefficiency, corruption and cowardice was exposed. Frustration, humiliation and anger caused the outbreak of violence and destruction.

The post-1948 period gave rise to the new factors; the creation of a provisional government of Palestine in Gaza and the Refugee problem. Egypt was interested in keeping in tact the legal point of a Palestinian government especially after the absorption of the West Bank by Transjordan. Hence a government of Palestine was set up in Gaza with Egyptian assistance under the leadership of Mufti Haj Amin al-Husseine. It was formed in October 1948.

The Palestinians were frustrated by the half-hearted attitude of the Arab countries towards their problem. The Husseini group decided to launch on FEDAAYEEN raids, and by 1951 they started active operations. The increase in the encounters between the groups of the Palestinian FEDAYEEN and the Israelis forced the latter to adopt a policy of massive armed retaliation. In 1955, largescale Israeli raids on Fedayeen bases in Gaza were engineered. They involved Egypt directly in military confrontation with Israel for Gaza was under Egypt's patronage. The Fedayeen raids and Israeli retaliations became a pretext for the war of October 1956.

After the war of 1956 the Palestine government in Gaza moved to Cairo and continued to operate from there till Mufti Husseini moved to Beirut in 1959. In the sixties the Government in exile ceased to be of any relevance and its place was taken by the PLO in 1964.

The military elite that came to power after the 1952 *coup d'etat* in Egypt was influenced by the events in Palestine and their repercussions in Egypt. Gamal Abdel Nasser who emerged as the leader of Egypt was an Arab nationalist who was committed to the Palestinian cause. Nasser had fought in Palestine in 1948 and it was a significant factor in galvanising his Arab policy. He felt that a great injustice was committed against the millions of Palestinian Arabs who were now refugees.

After the Arab defeat in Palestine in 1948, the only Palestinian organisation tolerated in the Arab world was the Palestinian Students' Federation in Cairo. It was founded and led by Yasser Arafat, Abu Iyyad Farouk Kaddoumi and also by the members of the Baath Party. Parallel to this, Palestinians in Gaza Strip now began to form underground groups. They were led by Khalid Wazir (Abu Jihad) and Abu Youssef El-Najjar, who was killed in an Israeli Commando operation in 1973. The aim of these groups in the Gaza strip was to form a common front of all Palestinians. They were no longer content to pin their hopes on Arab armies or UN resolutions. Accordingly, they formed the National United Front (Al-Fatah) in 1955.

Nasser's rise to Arab leadership and popularity among Arab masses had in large part rested on his promise to act in restoring Arab rights in Palestine. The Palestinian problem occupied a key element in Nasser's policy of Arab unity. Radio Cairo was developed into a powerful instrument through which 'Nasserism could be communicated throughout the Arab world, and by 1954 the Palestine Service of Radio was on the air daily. That represented something of a commitment to the Palestinian cause. Radio Cairo expanded its Palestine Service greatly in the early 1960s and by January 1962 was broadcasting two hours in the morning and thirty minutes in the afternoon.

At the Arab League Council session of March 1959 Egypt initiated a discussion on Palestinian entity. From the outset Egypt laid the stress on the creation of institutions, or representative bodies, which would speak in the name of Palestinians.

Arab League Council

The Arab League Council deliberated Egypt's proposals for the adoption of operative resolutions on the establishment of such institutions. Egypt's plan for reviving the Palestinian entity was thus a turning point in its process of solving the Palestine problem.

Under Egyptian influence the Arab League Council Session of September 1963 decided to appoint Ahmad Sheqeiri as representative of the Palestinians in the League until the Palestinian people were able to choose their own representatives. Thus seeds were sown for the creation of the Palestine Liberation Organisation (the PLO). The first Arab Summit held in Cairo on 16 January 1964 at Nasser's initiative resolved that Ahmad Sheqeiri as Palestinian representative, would continue his contacts with Palestinians. It led the way for Sheqeiri to establish the Palestine Liberation Organisation (PLO) in May 1964, following the first meeting of the Palestinian National Council (PNC) held in East Jerusalem.

The Second Arab Summit Conference, held in Cairo in September 1964, formally welcomed the creation of the PLO as the basis for the Palestinian entity. The setting of the PLO marked the fulfilment of the Egyptian initiative for the establishment of and the Arab recognition of the formal Palestinian entity. The Summit also affirmed the decision of the PLO to establish the Palestine Liberation Army (PLA).

For Nasser, the establishment of the PLO was the turning point in the Arab effort to liberate Palestine. Cairo allowed Sheqeiri to use Gaza and its inhabitants to conduct the PLO's political and organisational activities. Moreover, in March 1965, Radio Cairo began broadcasting the Voice of Palestine Programme.

Egyptian Decline

Defeat of Egypt in 1967 June war resulted in the decline of Egypt's role in the Arab world though from the Khartoum Summit of September 1967 to the Casablanca Arab Summit of 1969, Nasser had sought to win Arab support for a policy of confrontation with Israel. Besides the Arab defeat in the 1967 war completely discredited the traditional leadership of the PLO. On 24 December 1967 Shequeiri resigned as chairman of the PLO and as representative of Palestine in the Arab League. He was succeeded by Yahya Hammouda as PLO chairman for the time being. In February 1969, Yasser Arafat, the leader of al-Fatah was elected chairman of the PLO.

Nasser's support for the Fedayeen organisation was reflected in his declaration that the standing of every Arab country determined in terms of the struggle (with Israel) and by its relations with the Palestinian resistance movement. He described the Palestinian organisation as a national liberation movement and both he and his spokesman Mohammad Hussein Heikal referred to the West Bank and Gaza as occupied Palestinian territories. He lobbied with the countries of the Eastern Bloc and the Third World for the recognition of the PLO and to project it as the legitimate representative of the rights of the Palestinians. It was he who introduced Arafat the PLO leader to the Soviet leadership in July 1968 which paved the way for Soviet military aid to that organisation.

Nasser played an important role as a mediator between the Palestinian guerrillas and the Arab governments. Lebanon was in the grip of civil war in 1969 on the question of the Palestinian presence there. The Cairo agreement was signed between the Lebanese government and the Palestinians on 3 November 1969 following Nasser's mediation which recognised the presence of Palestinian guerrillas in Lebanon.

Besides, when the civil war broke out in Jordan between the Palestinians and Jordanian army, resulting in the massacre of 3,000 Palestinians in September 1970 Nasser played his last role as a peace keeper. An agreement was signed in Cairo on 26 September 1979 between Yasser Arafat and King Hussein of Jordan in the presence of President Nasser.

However, the death of President Nasser in 1970 led to a gradual shift in Egypt's Palestinian policy. Nasser might have failed to do much for the Palestinians yet he was a father figure who always provided protection for them. Palestinians mourned his death.

Palestine Question After Nasser

With the death of President Nasser on September 28, 1970 an entire page of Egypt's Arab history came to an end. It ended an era on contemporary Egyptian history. Within less than a year after his death, his political lieutenants were ousted from all positions of power by his successor Anwar al-Sadat. The policy of Egypt under President Sadat underwent significant change.

In the Arab sphere, the policy of President Sadat, while seemingly similar to that of Nasser during 1967-70, has exhibited subtle differences in emphasis which indicate basic shifts in the underlying elements of the policy. He tended to keep a low profile in Arab politics. His Arab Policy as also his policy towards the great powers underwent a total reversal. Egypt's ties with the PLO and the Fedayeen organisation reached the lowest point during the Sadat period.

By July 1972, Sadat had removed thousands of Soviet military advisers signalling an about-face in Egyptian foreign policy. At the same time he moved closer to the United States and the oil rich and conservative Arab State of Saudi Arabia. The paralysis in Egyptian-Soviet relations has deprived Egypt of the capability to manipulate the competitive nature of the bipolarised global system. Besides, while gaining the support of the conservative Arab elements, Sadat's anti- Soviet orientations have equally alienated the radical and 'leftist' forces inside Egypt and in the Arab world generally. These trends truly projected Sadat's policies as a flagrant reversal of the Nasserite socialist pro-Arab, anti-imperialist crusade.

As his domestic power and authority increased, Sadat began to gradually modify the Nasserite principles. Indeed, Nasser's vehement anti-western orientation had been reversed. This is exemplified in the case of the United States, which had constituted the major focus of Nasser's anti- imperialist campaign, but which now replaced the Soviet Union as Egypt's trusted ally. Similarly, as Egyptian attitudes towards the Eastern bloc grew more ambivalent, Egypt's relations with the Western community as a whole became warm and cordial.

Egypt's Arab or Palestinian involvement also reflected a change. Sadat began to gradually shift Egypt's position regarding the Arab world towards an increasing emphasis on Egyptian affairs. Sadat's earlier adherence to Arab Unity in the period following Nasser's death had by 1972, become subordinate to the value of Egyptian patriotism. In his speech made in July 1972, Sadat declared that in the forthcoming 'battle' with Israel, 'Egyptian Patriotism and Arab nationalism will, if necessary, be alone in the field. This imposes on us an organised programme of action regarding Egyptian patriotism, and to safeguard it with domestic unity.' Such a statement was indeed a far cry from Nasser's often repeated assertion that his, and Egypt's responsibility was to the Arab nation and Palestinians as a whole.

Sadat's relative success in the 1973 war did not permit him to regain the Arab position which Nasser had held in the past. In any case, under Sadat, Egypt rapidly moved towards a settlement with Israel in spite of the objections of other Arab states. It began with the two agreements on troops disengagement signed in 1974 and 1975, under US mediation. Replying to Syrian accusation that he had abandoned the Arab cause by signing the interim agreement with Israel, Sadat asserted that his first responsibility was to Egypt. Thus Sadat's indignation at Syrian and Palestinian hostility to Egypt's interim agreement with Israel indicated that the Egyptian leadership had expected their policies to be met with whole-hearted and unequivocal support.

US mediation between Egypt and Israel was later followed by the visit of President Sadat to Jerusalem between 19-21 November 1977 and his address to Knesset. It was followed by the summit meeting in America in September 1978, and the Camp David accords leading to the signing of the Egypt-Israel peace treaty in March 1979. This visit of Egyptian President Anwar Sadat to Jerusalem between November 19 and 21, 1977 marked a turning point in the history of the Arab-Israeli conflict. It reversed Egypt's earlier policy of commitment to Pan-Arabism and a total support for the Palestinians. For half a century since the meeting between Emir Faisal, son of Sherif Hussein of Mecca and Zionist leader Chaim Weizmann in June 1918, no Arab leader had publicly met with any Zionist or Israeli official.

Sadat's visit to Israel stirred angry reactions in the Arab world as a whole. It undermined Egypt's role as leader of the Arab world. It found expression in noisy demonstrations in various Arab countries and cities, especially Beirut, Damascus, Baghdad, Aden, Tripoli and Algiers. Popular disgust reached its apex in Damascus, Baghdad and Tripoli.

The day Sadat arrived in Israel, a "Day of National Mourning" in Syria was declared. Flags were flown at half-mast, citizens stopped working at noon for five minutes, church bells rung and muezzins sounded the call to prayer throughout the mosques of Syria.

In Iraq, celebrations of the Al-Adha feast, which coincided with the day of Sadat's visit were cancelled in protest. Libya withdrew its recognition of the Sadat Government and severed diplomatic relations with Egypt, and imposed upon it the terms of Arab boycott against Israel, calling upon other countries to follow suit. Besides, several Arab newspapers and broadcasting stations, both official and semi-official, described Sadat a "traitor", a "capitulator", a "conniver with the enemy" and an "agent of imperialism". The visit was seen as an indication of a desire to abandon the Palestinian cause in particular and the Arab cause in general.

Arab opposition to Sadat's visit manifested in Egypt itself. In protest to this, Egypt's foreign minister Ismail Fahmy submitted his resignation, declaring that "Arab sovereignty over their lands is not subject to compromise". Sadat then appointed Mahmoud Riad, Minister of State for Foreign Affairs, as Foreign Minister, but he too resigned. These events marked a turning point not only in the history of the Arab-Israeli conflict but also the end of Nasser's policy of Pan-Arabism and total support for the Palestinians.

Outside Egypt, the Palestine National Liberation movement, Fateh, also condemned Sadat for his visit. On November 17, 1977, Fateh issued a statement calling upon Sadat to forge that step as it would be a dangerous turning point and a gain for Zionism and its Imperialist allies. In its statement, Fateh maintained that the visit would place the Palestinian people and the PLO in a dangerous position in the face of an aggressive

Israel which is waxing more intransigent and is declaring on every occasion that the people of Palestine have no rights, that there can be no independent Palestinian state, and no total withdrawal from occupied Arab land.

Besides, a meeting of the Syrian and Palestinian leadership resulted, in a Syrian-Palestinian communique, stating that the visit "along with the Sadat-Begin plan, has no other aim but to impose a fait accompli on the Arab nation and thereby invalidate all genuine efforts to achieve a just peace based upon total Israeli withdrawal from all the occupied territories' and the safeguarding of the rights of the Palestinian Arab people to return, to self-determination and to establish an independent state". For the Palestinians in general and the PLO in particular, Sadat's visit to Jerusalem represented a grave threat to their independence struggle. In reaction to Sadat's visit, a conference was held in Libya. It was attended by Syria, the PLO, South Yemen, Libya and Algeria. The five leaders accused Sadat of attempting to create "an alliance between the Zionist enemy and the present Egyptian regime with the object of liquidating the Arab and Palestinian cause, fragmenting the Arab nation and endangering its national interests. The Tripoli conference also adopted sanctions against the Egyptian regime. The conferences announced their refusal to take part in any Arab league meetings held in Cairo and also discussed about the relocation of League headquarters located in Cairo.

Moreover, what Sadat did in going to Jerusalem was to recognise Israel de facto without anything in return. He also violated the basic Arab position regarding Jerusalem itself. By going to Jerusalem he recognised Israel's claim to that city as its capital.

The Camp David talks which began on 5 September 1978 under the auspices of US ended with the signing of documents, on 17 September 1978 between Egypt and Israel. These documents: (i) A framework for peace in the Middle East; (ii) A framework for the conclusion of a peace treaty between Egypt and Israel. The first of these documents contains the Egyptian-Israeli declaration of their intent to reach an agreement covering all aspects of the Middle East problem on the bases of the UN resolution 242 and 338. It called for an Israeli withdrawal from the Sinai, including the dismantling of the air bases. The second document envisioned a five-year period of autonomy for the Palestinians of the West Bank and Gaza. An administrative body, or authority, would be elected. And at the end of the first three years, negotiations would begun over the question of eventual sovereignty. But there was no mention of Palestinian self-determination nor did Israel commit itself to eventual withdrawal.

The peace treaty between Israel and Egypt was formally signed on 26 March 1979 under the auspices of the United States. The treaty guaranteed normal relations with full diplomatic recognition, economic and cultural relations, an end to the state of war between two countries. Far from achieving the much-promised honourable and comprehensive peace based on total Israeli withdrawal from Arab lands occupied in 1967 and Palestinian self-determination, the Camp David agreements provided the grounds for a separate Egyptian-Israeli peace treaty. In the light of the Camp David framework these following observations can be made.

To start with, all the basic decisions relating to the procedures to be followed in seeking solution have been made at Camp David in the absence of Palestinian representatives and without regard for the known wishes of the Palestinian people. Besides, the Camp David Framework divides the Palestinian people into separate categories and offers different formulae for dealing with their respective situations. The dismemberment of the Palestinian people, which is itself a feature of this tragedy, has been transformed at Camp David into a permanent feature of the proposed Egyptian-American-Israeli final solution to the Palestine problem. Moreover, the Camp

David formula excludes the three basic rights of the Palestinian people which have been recognised and affirmed by the United Nations as the foundation of a just and lasting solution of the Palestine problem viz. - the right of the Palestinian people to self-determination and independence in Palestine; right to designate its own national representative and to participate through the PLO—its sole representative—in all efforts aimed at achieving a settlement of the problem.

Arab criticism of the Camp David agreement came also from the inhabitants of the Occupied Territories themselves. The announcement of the signing of the agreements was met with an uprising. On 1 October 1978 a national Congress attended by 150 West Bank figures and political representatives met 'officially to give Begin, Carter and Sadat a definite response : an absolute rejection and a formal condemnation of the Camp David agreements. The PLO too rejected the agreements categorically. In April 1979, a distinct hardening of attitude of the whole of the Arab world was perceptible; the Arab countries broke their relations with Egypt, and decided on an economic boycott of Egypt and the transfer of the Arab league headquarters to Tunis.

Sadat also faced criticism at home. Opposition newspapers sharpened their attacks; Friday sermons in the mosques raged against the "separate peace"; and Police were called out to control public protests. By September 1981, Sadat had lost his nerve and cracked down on the dissidents in Egypt, jailing hundreds of people from all walks of life and thus alienating virtually every element of Egyptian society. All these factors culminated in Sadat's assassination at the hands of his own soldiers on 6 October 1981. Ironic that he was mourned mainly in the West. Begin managed to isolate Sadat even in death. By insisting on attending his funeral, Begin kept other Arab leaders except Sudan's former President Numeiri away.

There are lessons to be drawn from Sadat's odyssey. As far as Camp David is concerned, it has been a complete disaster for the Arab world. Sadat's peace initiative could only have succeeded if he had been able to get the minimum that other Arabs would accept. What the Americans and Sadat seemed to forget was that while the Arabs could not make war without Egypt, neither could Sadat make the peace he desired without the rest of the Arabs. During the year since Sadat's assassination, tensions in the Middle East have multiplied. Most are a direct result of Camp David.

The Egyptian-Israeli talks on Palestinian autonomy were destined to go nowhere. The war between Iraq and Iran created new divisions within the Arab world and drained billions of dollars from the economies of the region. Arab disunity, exacerbated by Egypt's isolation had made the Arab states individually vulnerable to foreign enemies. The Israeli invasion of Lebanon in June 1982 was another direct outcome of the Camp David. The tragedy in Lebanon give Arab States and others new cause for anger at the United States and a new sense of their own helplessness.

Several peace initiatives have been put forward since the Islraeli invasion of Lebanon. There is the Arab Fez plan, the Reagan plan, and the PLO-Jordanian peace initiative. All have been rejected outright by Israel.

The key lesson of Camp David for the Americans to ponder lies in what happened to Sadat. None of the promises made to him were kept. Besides, the Palestinian issue has been deliberately made into an obstacle by the Americans and the Israelis. The Israelies use it to buy time, further absorbing the territories, while the Americans use it to justify their own inaction.

Arafat on several occasions has said that he accepts all UN resolutions pertaining to Palestine. The importance of this has been both overlooked and downplayed. By accepting all UN resolutions pertaining to Palestine, Arafat has for the first time also accepted the 1947 UN partition resolution, which called for the creation of a Jewish and a Palestinian state in Palestine.

Now it is time that the Americans and the Israelis fulfilled the promise made to the Palestinians in that same resolution. The Palestinian problem is not one of terrorism as the Americans and Israelis see it but of a people deprived of their homeland.

The Americans must pressurise Israel for accepting independent Palestinian representatives at the *International Peace table* and find a solution to the West Asian crisis. West Asia will continue to be unstable politically, militarily and diplomatically until the Palestine problem is resolved at the earliest time possible.

India's policy should not be dictated by the pro-Israeli lobby. We should depend on our independent foreign policy initiated since the time of Prime Minister Nehru. It is our moral duty to support the Palestinians all the way. Satisfaction in the sphere of Palestinian question should precede India's Israeli policy. India should have nothing to do with Israel till there is a satisfactory solution to the Palestine problem. For all practical purposes, India has got good political, economic, cultural, diplomatic and historic ties with Arab countries. We must not look at the problem from any other point of view either Arab or West. There is no morality observed here. India must think of its own perspectives. The only solution to the West Asian crisis lies in the establishment of a Palestinian State in West Bank and Gaza Strip with its capital at Jerusalem. The establishment of the Palestinian state would be good for Israel from the political, economic and military point of view. This would cut Israel's excessive defence spending, because Israel is spending 89% to 90% of its GNP on Defence. Moreover, this would also reduce Israeli insecurity.

60

Iraq-Iran War (1980-1988)

The war between Iran and Iraq ranks as one of the most serious and dangerous wars between states in the world since World War II. It is said to be most tragic because the warfare, reminiscent of the first world war in Europe, caused high casualties for no obvious advantage to either side.

The Islamic Revolution in Iran followed by this inhuman war have produced unforeseen results and developments, the course of which cannot yet be fully assessed.

One consequence of this prolonged war is to strengthen the standing of the regimes in Iran and Iraq. In both the countries the war helped to consolidate the domestic political scene and enabled the government to gain massive support for a vigorous confrontation of the invader. The determined, uncompromising attitude of Iran and Iraq has paid ample dividends as demonstrated by the failure of the UN Secretary General's peace initiatives and the direct US military intervention in this area. Iran and Iraq have emerged as the two most destructive powers in the Arab (Persian) Gulf by holding the key to the solution of the war.

In the Arab sphere, this war has shifted attention from the Arab-Israel conflict and diluted the efforts of the Palestinians to sustain their struggle for an independent state of Palestine. Besides the war has relieved much of the pressure from Egypt which had been isolated from the general Arab scene. As the tide of war turned against the Baghdad regime, the Iraqis found it necessary to seek Egyptian support. This had led to a complete reversal of the Iraqi position from being one of the major sponsors of Egypt's isolation to becoming the main advocate of Egypt's readmittance to the Arab family.

The impact of the war on Egyptian foreign policy has been the increase of its importance for the Gulf Arab States. Of equal significance are the economic benefits that Egypt derived from cash sales of arms to Iraq and from the remittances of so many Egyptians working there. Besides, the war provented Iraq from achieving hegemony in the Arab Gulf by slowly exhausting its strength. It also forced the Baghdad government to look towards the West for material assistance. Agreements were reached with France, US and other West European countries providing for deliveries of war material and related technology.

Again, the war increased the threat of direct US involvement (as realised in the US helicopters attack on Iranian ship, which killed atleast four Iranian crewmen and seized the Iranian vessel and destroyed the same) in the region. It soon became obvious that the United States would increase its existing military involvement in the region at least as the so-called protector of the Gulf Arab friendly states, and to protect its vital interests in the region. The US assistance and direct military action would be accepted by the Gulf States as long as they felt threatened.

Another important consequence of this war had been the creation of plans by the oil-producing countries to protect their oil exports from war operations. These measures indicated that the oil producers want to be prepared not only for the eventual spread of this conflict throughout the area but also for other kinds of emergency situations in the future. The plans envisaged a gradual shift of oil shipments from the Arab (Persian) Gulf.

For the Soviet Union the outbreak of the war was an unwelcome development. Given the mood of intense hostility in Iran towards the US military intervention and President Reagan's idea of imposing sanctions on Iran, there appeared to be good prospects for greater Soviet influence. The Soviet Union had warned that the deployment of an American atomic cruiser in the Gulf "is a step along the dangerous path". In the words of the then Soviet Foreign Minister, Mr. Shevardnadze remarked, "The safety of navigation in the Gulf can and must be ensured by the entire world community, on whose behalf the United Nations will be acting. If necessary, appropriate and sufficient forces should be made effectively available for it. The Soviet Union would agree to such a decision".

It was here that for the first time Moscow had supported the idea of a UN force in the Gulf. Besides the Soviet Foreign Minister suggested that an "impartial body" should be formed to "investigate responsibility for the outbreak of the war within a clearly etablished timeframe".

Unlike its rival, the United States continues to face fundamental questions about its political, military and strategic posture in this area. In spite of the revelations of secret US-Iranian arms deals in November 1985, US strategy towards the Gulf war had consisted primarily of three interrelated strands, viz. repeated public commitments to freedom of navigation in the Gulf; the reassurance of local allies like Saudi Arabia and Kuwait; and the maintenance of the regional balance of power. Underlying these strands is an awareness of the need to limit potential Soviet gains without, at the same time, provoking a Soviet response.

The strategic situation in the Gulf seems to have changed since the early part of the year 1987. The US was given no real cause for anxiety, nor incentive to alter the direction of its policy. The declared rationale behind the arms deal operation was said to be to bolster the position of 'moderates' in Iran who favoured closer relations with the United States. Even if this had been a primary motive, it was clear that the arms deal had become inextrically linked to an attempt to persuade Iran to use its influence to free a number of American hostages being held by Lebanese extremists.

Washington is now in an unenviable position. Its policy in the Gulf has got very badly mixed up with its commitment to take on the Soviets everywhere. Its commitment to defend the contemporary rulers in the Gulf does square up with a burning desire to keep the Soviets out but it does not square up with its long-term interests in Iran. In the war, the US seems to be on the wrong side. The coming weeks are likely to be critical for the gulf and so present a tough challenge to American intentions in the gulf.

Referring to the case of middle powers, the interests of western industrialised nations in the Gulf were largely commercial in the early years of the war. These nations have distanced themselves politically from both sides and have neither affected nor been affected by the war (except in placing themselves along with the United States, to a certain extent, in a dangerous position where the options seemed limited to humiliation).

In the domestic sphere, the war had come to involve the nations to a greater and greter extent calling upon them to sacrifice not only their sons but also to mortgage the countries' future. The war had taken its toll in less obvious ways. The combined cost to the belligerents' economies, in terms of lost oil revenues, may have been as high as $50 billion in the first year alone. Thus its economic losses can be measured in the hundreds of billions of dollars. More important the cumulative effects of the fighting dominated the planning and the pattern of government expenditures for many years to come. Indeed the war left permanent scars on both the countries' development prospects. It had become a political and economic liability to both the countries. Even, with an early end to the war, it may take as much as a decade for these two countries to rebuild and restore what has already been destroyed.

In the social sphere, the war had been used (as mentioned) to consolidate the regime, unite and divert people's attention and repress the opposition in both the countries. Besides it had affected the institutions of society, extending the reach of the government in the countries. A large element of coercion had been used to mobilise the people. Moreover, the dictates of the war have accelerated the concentration of absolute powers in the hands of the rulers in both these countries.

At the international level both the countries have militarily weakened and consequently left the field of confrontation to the super powers, particularly the United States. Besides, the Palestine cause had receded in the world's crisis into a secondary position.

The Iran-Iraq war had not yet revealed what new regional balance of power will emerge in the Gulf. Neither Iran nor Iraq did manage to establish itself as a "regional caretaker". The dangers posed by the war and failure of the peace initiatives have under-scored for us the conclusion that we cannot develop a workable strategy for establishing peace in the Gulf unless we give as much energy to dealing with the socio-economic and political problems of the area as we devote to military gains.

A disorganised Gulf is unlikely to play a major role in West Asia. Its very instability tends to make the area more unstable and more unpredictable. The one possible solution in the present state of atmosphere is the voluntary US military withdrawal from the Gulf.

61

Lebanese Crisis*

We, in India, are well aware that, the search for peace in Lebanon is perhaps a more complex task than in other crisis ridden areas in the Middle East. Lebanese scene today presents a conflict between the different religious communities. But it has become embroiled in the Israel- Palestinian conflict by the fact that the Syrians (in 1975) and the US and Israelis (covertly from 1978 on, overtly in 1982) and the Iranians, and the French in the recent times intervened in Lebanon, and all of them now have the country divided between themselves by constituting formal and informal Zones of occupation and influence.

Today's Lebanon is a microcosm of a multitude of conflicts and contradictions. Its war, which started in 1975, reflects the features of a civil war, a war by proxy, and a direct regional confrontation. In a country of 10,452 square kilometres and with a population of 3 million, military forces loyal to Syria, Israel and Iran face each other, in addition to host of private militias reflecting the religious divisions of Lebanese society. Lebanon is both the battleground and the meeting point where the Security policies of a number of above-mentioned key regional actors come into dreadful and dangerous play. These powers follow a number of tactics. They organise friendly local military groups : they intervene and send troops; and they occupy and/or neutralise areas perceived as crucial to their security. The local web of relations is complex. Alliances change and hostilities shift focus depending on the current military balances and politics-military interests. Ultimately, Lebanese problem has proved to be beyond the ability of any single actor to control or overcome.

The aim of this paper is to outline the features and policies of the key players in Lebanon and to summarise some conclusions derived from what is now approaching 14 years of civil war.

Evolution of the Lebanese Politics

Historically, the diverse communal-religious composition of Lebanese society and the conflicting identities and aspirations of its communities have led to tension, infighting, and foreign intervention. Each major group has sought the support and protection against the domination of the other. The Christians, especially the Maronites have depended upon Western powers; the Muslims, upon the Arab-Muslim sources. The post-world war I French creation of Lebanon (Le Grand Liban) as a country was

---

* The Lebanese civil war, unleashed by Maronite reluctance to share power and resources with the Muslim majority, completed its 15th year last April. Together with the perennial problem of Palestine, Cyprus, Kampuchea and Afghanistan, it is one of the oldest problems that eludes settlement due to interventions by foreign powers. This ongoing civil war took a terrible toll of Labanese life and economy. By the end of 1991, the casualties of the civil war, both dead and injured, had reached an estimated 311,626 people—very substantial number considering the country's total population of only three million. The numbers of the handicapped have exceeded 850,000, which includes about 1,700 children and 4,400 women.

designed to preserve the "special identity" and to institutionalise the supremacy of the Maronite community. Prior to the French, in 1841 Bashir III (1788-1941) organised a Confessional Council of ten members (three Maronites, three Druse, one Greek Catholic, one Greek Orthodox, one Shi'i and one Sunni) who represented the country's divergent political identities.

In 1860, after Maronite Peasants rose up against their Druse land-lords as many as 11,000 Maronites were killed. After the 1860 massacres and under pressure from the British, Russians, French and the Austrians —each of which had its own Lebanese political client, the *Reglement organique* of 1861 was acceded to by the Ottomans, the real Imperial masters in Lebanon. The *Reglement organique* (an organic statue) provided for the establishment of a representative council to consist of two representatives of each major community (Maronite and Druse) for Lebanon. The latter system was revised in 1864 to give greater numerical representation to the Maronites, Druse and Greek orthodox. The period from 1864 to 1914 was one of increasing prosperity, especially among the Christian elements.

Lebanon and the French Mandate

The privileged position of Lebanon ended when the Turks entered the first world war (1914-1918) and by 1919 the coastal areas of Lebanon were occupied by British and French Forces. In September 1920, the French created the State of Greater Lebanon, which included not only the former autonomous province (of 1864) but also Tripoli, Sidon, Tyer and Beirut, some of which had in earlier times been under the control of the Emirs or the feudal Lords of Lebanon.

The period from 1920 to 1936 was for Lebanon one of peaceful progress.

A constitution was devised in 1926, which proved unworkable and was suspended in 1932, from which time the president of the Republic carried on the administration. Hex was, by convention, a Christian, while the Prime Minister was a Muslim, and both worked towards the achievement of a careful balance between the various religious communities of the new state. In November 1941 the French Commander, General Cartoux, formally proclaimed Lebanon as a sovereign independent state.

Demographic Reality and the Civil War

In September 1943 a new parliament which had a strong nationalist majority soon came into conflict with the French authorities over the transfer of administrative services. However, the Republic of Lebanon was established in 1943, at the end of the French Mandate.

The country's politico-demographic system is confessionally based, under an unwritten national pact (mentioned above) which divided power between Christians (Maronites, Greek orthodox, Greek catholics, Armenian orthodox, Catholics and Protestants) and Muslims (Sunnis, Shia and Druse) on a ratio of 6 : 5, reflecting the demographic situation at the time of the last census in 1932. This politico-demographic system has been at the heart of Lebanon's protracted civil war four times, in 1975-76, 1982 and in the recent times.

The Muslims now outnumber the Christians, but the latter have been reluctant to give up their privileged position, guaranteed by the national pact. Precise demographic data are impossible to obtain in the present circumstances, but the skilful manipulation of limited data by demographers indicates that the Christians have long since ceased to enjoy the previous 6 : 5 population advantage over the Muslims (Shia, Sunni and Druse) who probably represent 60 per cent of Lebanon's population. The current 90-seat chamber of Deputies, elected in 1972, includes seates for 19 Shi's and 30 Maronite Christians. Yet recent population estimates would justify 29 or 30 seats for the Shia and only 19 or 20 for the Manorite community.

Lebanon and the Palestinians

Another important politico-demographic factor has been the influx of Palestinian refugees to Lebanon. Perhaps as many as 100,000 Palestinian civilians moved to Lebanon between 1948 and 1967. Although the earliest influx of Palestinians was in large part assimilated, the second wave of refugees began in 1967 (after the June Arab-Israeli war) proved harder to absorb for an already fragile Lebanon. By the beginning of the 1970s, the Lebanese found themselves faced with a human infusion that constituted 10 per cent or more of the country's population. Besides, since most of the Palestinians were Muslims, they were viewed by many Maronite Christians as a dangerous threat to Maronite supremacy in Labanon.

Lebanon, Syria and the Civil War (1975-76)

By the 1970s, as noted above, Lebanon's Muslims outnumbered the Christians but the national pact prevented any political reflection of this demographic reality. Lebanon was ripe for civil war, and this was triggered in April 1975 when right-wing Maronite militiamen murdered a busload of Palestinian civilians in Beirut. Soon the country was embroiled in fighting, between Maronites and Muslims, Maronites and other Christians and between rightists and leftists. The Palestinians (PLO) led by the Chairman Yasser Arafat sought neutrality but was soon sucked in on the side of the leftists and Muslims. The Lebanese army fell apart along sectarian lines.

By 1976 the Muslim/Leftist alliance had gained the upper hand. Neighbouring Syria, fearing the establishment of a destabilising state on its western flank, intervened militarily at the request of the then Lebanese government and imposed a fragile truce. 100,000 people were killed and at least 500,000 displaced in the 1975-76 civil war. Lebanon as a unified state, no longer existed. Later, the Arab League established the Arab Deterrant Force (ADF) to keep the peace in Lebanon. Units from several countries were included, but the 30,000 strong Syrian element was always the largest.

Syria's policy towards Lebanon has two major objectives. The first is to avoid isolation among Arab states by remaining in the centre of Arab attention. A major policy aim in this respect is for Syria to establish itself as the dominant power in the Arab East. The ingredients of this dominance include : control of the PLO; a privileged position in Lebanon; and evolving policies towards the moderate Arab states, particularly Egypt and Jordan. The second objective is to enhance its military power to reach a strategic balance of parity with Israel

Israeli Invasion of Lebanon (1978-1982)

In March 1978 Israel launched a massive US inspired invasion of South Lebanon to contain the PLO militarily. The UN Security Council called on Israel to withdraw, and the 4,000 strong UN Interim Force (UNIFIL) was formed to police the evacuated zone. Israel did eventually withdraw, but handed over a good portion of border territory to a local Israeli-backed rightist militia, headed by Sa'ad Haddad, a renegade Lebanese Army Major.

Israeli intentions in Lebanon are primarily geo-strategic : to secure its northern borders from incursions and rocket bombardment by creating a 25-kilometre security zone. This was achieved through raids on Palestinian bases in Lebanon, direct military presence or military patrols there and the creation of the South Lebanon Army (SLA), an Israeli agent force. Another Israeli interest is economic, that is, the need for water from the Litani river.

In the next four years (1978-1982) little changed in Lebanon. East Beirut and a region stretching north from Beirut to Jounich was controlled by the Christians, headed by the phalangists. West Beirut and the areas to the north, east and south of the Christian heartland were dominated by the Leftist Lebanese militias and the PLO, although the Syrians, in the form of the ADF, were the ultimate power. The Syrians kept out of the South, where Israel was having its influence. Skirmishes between PLO and Gen. Haddad's Israeli-backed forces, accompanied by Israeli raids, were frequent. In Beirut, firece artillery duels often raged between the Muslim West and Christian East of the fractured city. An important development in this period was the growing influence of the Shia Muslims. Their militia, Amal, became a major force, operating in a frequently strained alliance with the Muslim-Leftist and PLO militias.

In early 1982, Israel completed its evacuation of Egypt's Sinai Peninsula under the Camp David accords (1978), and was free to strike against the PLO and Muslim militia in Lebanon without retaliation from Egypt. The then Israeli Premier, Menachem Begin, and the defence minister, Ariel Sharon, nursed grandiose plans to engineer the establishment of a right wing pro-Israeli Maronite regime in Lebanon which would expel the Syrians and PLO militias from Lebanon. Besides, in the view of Begin and Sharon, this was to pave the way for the annexation of the West Bank into greater Israel.

In June 1982 Israel launched a full-scale invasion of Lebanon and, in August (1982), after a siege of Beirut, PLO militia fighters were forced to evacuate from the city by sea. This Israeli invasion of Lebanon, known as (Operation Peace for the Galilei), represented an Israeli attempt radically to alter in its favour both the security situation and the politico-strategic equation in Lebanon. This (June-August) 1982 Israeli invasion of Lebanon resulted in Israeli occupation of most of Lebanon and the forced withdrawal of PLO forces under the supervision of a multinational force (MNF: consisting of the US, France and Italy). During this siege, Israel secured the election of Phalangist leader Bashir Gemayel as President of Lebanon. In September 1982, Bashir was assassinated and his brother, Amin Gemayel, succeeded him. The political fruit of Israeli invasion and victory in Lebanon was the agreement of 17 May 1983 whose main points included ending the state of war between the two countries, Lebanese recognition of Israel, and the withdrawal of Israeli troops (provided Syrian and Palestinian forces also withdrew).

Israel's occupation army became the target of a sustained resistance campaign. Increasing Israeli brutality accompanied by human casualties and the absence of a clear objective for the continued occupation of Lebanon led to one of the most bitter security debates in Israel. Later the debate developed in a way that divided both the country and the cabinet. Eventually on 14 January 1985, the Israeli cabinet voted (16 to 6) to withdraw unilaterally from Lebanon. In 1986 the return of some PLO elements to the south and the increasing power of *Hezbollah* '(Party of God' an agent force for Iran) renewed Israeli intervention in Lebanon. However, this time Israel supported Amal militia faction led by Nabih Berri.

Iranian Involvement in Lebanon

Islamic Iran's main instrument in Lebanon is *Hezbollah* whose military presence is centred in the South and which has the objective of turning Lebanon into an Islamic republic. It competes with Amal, the largest and most influential Shiite militia, for the loyalty of the Shiite community. Islamic Iran also supports a number of small military groups such as *al-Jihad al-Islami* and *Monazamat al-Adala al- Thwriya* (Revolutionary justice organisation). Iran's influence became evident in 1986, when Iranian diplomats negotiated a cease-fire between Amal and the PLO militias in the southern villages of Maghdoushah. Recognising that their interests were not identical, Syria grew uneasy about Iranian involvement in Lebanon. An early signal came in 1985, when Syria started a campaign against the Sunni *Harakat al-Tawhid al-Islam* ('Movement for Islamic Unity'), Iran intervened on the movement's behalf.

Lebanon in the Recent Times

More than fifteen years after the outbreak of the Lebanese civil war, more than two years after Elias Hrawi's election to the Lebanese Presidency the Lebanese crisis seems no nearer to solution. Lebanon is still divided into several virtual autonomies. Violence has become the dominant order of things in Lebanon : between Maronite and Maronite, between Sunni Muslims and Shiite Muslims, between Shiites and Palestinians and between religious and secular groups. Lebanon's political system is totally paralysed and its political institutions and state bureaucracy are functioning on a part-time basis.

The civil war in Lebanon has resulted in a *de-facto* partition of the country generated by the involvement (massive in the case of US, Israel and Syria, less massive in the case of PLO, Islamic Iran, Iraq and France in the recent times)—of external actors in the Lebanese crisis and their interplay with domestic Lebanese forces. The recent incidents in Lebanon starting since the expiry of President Amin Gemayel's term in September 1988, the illegal succession of Michael Aoun, the unsuccessful Taif Agreement on Lebanon brokered by Saudi Arabia, Algeria and Morocco, the assassination of the new President Rene Mouwaad (64) just after 17 days in office and the election of Elias Hrawi (59), 77 hours after his predecessor, President Rene Mouwaad's assassination has dealt a devastating blow to the already fractured Lebanese state.

Conclusions

The civil war in Lebanon is not likely to last for a long period. Today no more a malaise hangs over Lebanon, that is, a palpable sense of hope is reflected in people's faces, in a ruined economy. Perhaps it is in socio-economic terms that Lebanon's sad state is most starkly exposed.

Foreign powers will continue to exert considerable influence over events inside Lebanon. US, Israel, Syria, Islamic Iran and France still continue to shop for suitable Lebanese clients. Even with a healthy skepticism, it is overtly cynical to claim that the Lebanese do not want peace. The Lebanese do want peace, but each faction wants it on its own terms. Leadership struggles within the Sunni, Shiite and Maronite or Christian communities are likely to end soon.

62

Mohandas Karamchand Gandhi

Introduction

Mahatma Gandhi (1869-1948)was not a systematic academic thinker in the field of metaphysics and political philosophy. He was an inspired teacher and prophet. He was neither a Shankara nor a Kant. Instead he is akin to Socrates and Buddha pouring forth the results of his deepest feelings and his most sincere realisations of truth. His Autobiography has at times a Biblical ring and is more revealing than Tolstoy's confessions although not as shockingly revealing as Rousseau's confessions. Mahatma Gandhi always emphasised his role as a citizen of the world. The South African and Indian politics has been the laboratory in which he experimented with his formulas of truth and non-violence. The Malthusian-Darwinian-Nietzschean emphasis on the biological victory of the strong over the weak has set the political pattern of the modern world and hence the modern intellectual initially finds it difficult to accept the message of Gandhi which is the quintessence of the Vedantic-Buddhistic stoic Christian conception of the final victory of truth (as contrasted with the survival of the fittest. In an age full of sickening horror and secrecy and espionage carried to perfection, the gospel of truth and creative non-violence as advocated by Gandhi sounds anarchonistic but at the same time it is a terribly tragic commentry on the transfer of the loyalty of the modern man from Buddha, Mahavira and Christ to Lamarck, Darwin and Heeckel. Gandhi appears as another Plato and Cicero vindicating the cause of the spiritual and moral approach to political problems.

From 1893 to 1914 Gandhi rendered great services to the cause of racist equality in South Africa. From 1915 to 1948 Mahatma Gandhi worked in India for the sake of the country's freedom. He was much more than a liberator of a country. Although as a patriot he will be ranked with Washington, Mazzini and Sun Yat-sen, his achievements are not confined to bringing Independence to four hundred millions. His stand on truth and the persistent resolute attempt at the crystallization and concretization of the perfectionist dreams of humanity in his own person and his society impart to him a place all unique and beyond the grasp of a parochial patriot or a power politician.

His message for the unification of emotions and a coherence of personality through the realization of creative non-violent spiritual life is very significant for millions of disturbed, exasperated and unhappy persons throughout the world. The life of Gandhi was a manifestation, a vindication of the noble truth of the Bhagvadgita and the other great scriptures of humanity that one grain of truth is infinitely more powerful than mountains of falsehoods.

Metaphysical Idealism

The fundamental basis of Gandhism is the conception of God or an omnipresent fundamental spiritual reality, on all embracing living light which could be called Sachchidananda or Brahman or Rama or simply turth.

The spiritual truth, according to him, was not to be realized by dialectical skill or conceptual cognition but by spiritual experience, pure and disciplined holy life and by the persistent endeavour to concretize the norm of Ahimsa in one's action and motivation. "Reason is a poor thing in the midst of temptations... Faith that transcends the reason is our only rock of ages". There is a note of radical Individualism in Gandhian thought because great stress has been laid on the sanctity of personal experience of truth. His faith in a fundamental truth was not born out of arguments and external observations but out of spiritual apprehension and intuition. Prayer was the essence of Gandhi's personality. He said that he could live without food but not without prayer. "The only weapon of the satyagrahi is God". A living faith in God as the unfailing protector makes one fearless.

Gandhi was not a philosopher of History. His whole life was full of ceaseless actions, all inspired by the vision of a spiritual whole which imparted a higher meaning to his diverse actions as a social worker, a journalist, a political leader and a moral prophet. Thus Gandhi combined a faith in the supremacy of God with the insistent on constant actions.

Ethical Absolutism

Gandhi accepted metaphysical idealism and hence he believed in the supremacy of ethical values and Sarvodaya (the good of all). The philosophy of Sarvodaya is based on the concept of the unity of existence. It implies a perpetual fight against cruelty to human beings and animals.

The Gandhian theory of ethical absolutism can be traced to the Vedic concept of the Gita - the doctrine that there are all-encompassing, cosmic and moral ordinances which govern both men and gods. Buddha also had faith in the existence of a moral order. The great Hindu philosopher Patanjali also accepted that the cardinal concepts of ethics were beyond the relativism of space and time. Gandhi accepts these insights. His own experience in life completely convinced him of the superior efficacy of the moral norm.

He interpreted history in terms of the progressive vindication of the superiority of Ahimsa. "It is by firm faith that man is by nature going higher", he wrote. Ahimsa was a demonstration of the resolute strength of the heroic soul which refuses to hurt anybody because every living creature is essentially spirit and fundamentally one with himself. Gandhi considered truth and non-violence to be absolutely binding. "Non-violence is the first article of my faith. It is also last article of my creed". It was the imperative duty of the Satyagrahi to make endless endeavours for the realisation of truth through non-violence. Jesus Christ and Harish Chandra are examples of the practice of this law of pure suffering. Non-violence is the strongest force known. It is a force of the subtlest kind. Real non-violence is a mighty force and can be used against the most powerful government.

Religion as a Factor in History

Since Gandhi believed in truth and non-violence he accepted the creative force of religion in human history. Religion, signified, to him, belief in the ordered moral governance of the world. He condemned the godlessness and violence associated with Bolshevism. Like Buddha and Ramakrishna he was above the bounds of creeds, cults, rituals and ceremonies. He accepted the spiritual and moral essence of Hinduism which according to him was the essence of all the great religions of mankind as Judaism, Christianity, Islam and Zoroastrianism. Hinduism signified a relentless search after truth. True religion, according to Gandhi, implored an emphasis on the moral values of man as spirit. All religions are founded on the same moral laws. My ethical religion is made up of laws which bind men all over the world. Religion provided the dynamic impetus to his actions and life. He said that he was essentially a religious man in quest of *Moksha*—redemption and emancipation of the soul from the clutches of *Maya*. But emancipation to Gandhi did not signify isolation. It did not mean the negation and repudiation of the claims of the society and the human kind.

This true religious attitude to Gandi, meant the voluntary acceptance and enthusiastic fulfilment of the duties that naturally came one's way—*Swadharma.* In the spirit of the Gita he felt that living with a sense of detachment and disinterestedness the life of Karmayoga could lead to the attainment of *Moksha* . A life of dedicated service to one's kind does not generate an attitude of aggressive or self-righteous altruism but will lead to a progressive expansion of the human self till it came to comprehend almost the whole of human kind. Karmayoga means disinterested pursuit of one's obligations and duties and that signified a cosmic and spiritual awareness. In the human heart an eternal battle was raging between the forces of good and evil and Karmayoga signifies the elimination of the latter and the victory of truth, good and virtue. The victory of Rama over Ravana is a symbol of the conquest of physical power by spiritual strength. Religions are meant to tame our savage nature and they bind man to God and man to man when Gandhi talked of the religious basis of politics he was not preaching primitivism but inculcated the superiority of a life of strenuous dynamic activity in quest of the good of one's soul and mankind. He pointed out that the lives of Buddha and Christ were inspired by the synthesis of active work and deep love. Gandhi accepted the Biblical precept that it is far better to lose the world than to lose one's soul. In the present materialistic, sensate phase of human civilisation Gandhi's conception of Karmayoga, as established on the basis of the teachings of the Gita is a fundamental contribution. It is this concept of Karmayoga or religion as a dynamic altruism that Gandhi wanted to make the basis of transformed social and political action.

Religion, according to Gandhi, was not merely a means for personal purification but it was an immensely powerful social bond. Religion in the sense of philanthropy forbearance, justice, fraternity, peace and all-embracing love can alone be the basis of the existence of the world. Hence Gandhi said : "To try to root out religion itself from society is a wild-goose chase. And were such an attempt to succeed it would mean the destruction of socity.

Sociology and Economics

Gandhi challenged the foundations of modern civilisation. The sophisticated, technological, seculatristic, aggressive and lustful aspects of modern western civilisation repelled him. He provided a return to nature like Plato, Rousseau and Tolstoy and said that true civilisation consists not in the accumulation of commodities but in a deliberate and voluntary reduction of wants. Earlier than Spengler, Gandhi prophesied the decline and doom of western civilisation but he had tremendous faith in the rejuvenating power of the human spirit and firmly held that non-violence could provide a healing tonic to modern civilization.

Gandhi accepted the spiritual orientation to politics, sociology and economics. He said that truth and Ahimsa must incarnate in socialism because "the first condition of non-violence is justice all around in every department of life". The western theory of socialism was, however, born in an atmosphere full of violence. Satyagraha was the only means to bring about true socialism.

The central evils against which Gandhi fought were racialism, imperialism, communalism and untouchability. In South Africa, he fought against the racially discriminatory policies of the Whites. In India, as a reformer, he fought against social injustices, tyrannies and oppressions. He was primarily engaged in abolishing the unjust economic and political exploitation of India. He condemned British imperialism because it resulted in the political and economic prostration of India.

Gandhi preached a return to simplicity and the absence of pretensionsness and luxury. In the context of modern India he apeared a ruralist. He stood for safeguarding the integrity and foundations of the villages. His heart bled to see the disintegration and utter ruin of Indian countryside. Like some of other western sociologists, Gandhi felt that a strengthened and economically sound village economy would revitalise our democracy. Gandhi condemned the nineteenth century doctrine of *laissez faire.* He advocated the revolutionary doctrine that 'Land belongs to him who tills it'. In the charkha he found not the symbol of crudeness but the means and instrument of helping our people in at least getting the barest morsel of food. It symbolised the dignity of labour.

Gandhi accepted the concept of economic equality. All persons should be supplied with the necessaries to satisfy their natural needs. He subscribed to the Marxian formula : "to each according to his need". The constituent elements of economic equality were a balanced diet, a decent house to live in, medical relief and facilities for the education of children for every family. Both Socialism and Gandhism want to establish a society oriented to economic equality. But the transcedental, ascetic and secularistic ideal of modern socialism which accepts the cult of the accentuation of production.

Gandhi advocated a return to simplicity and plainness of nature. In the *Hind Swaraj* he opposed large-scale Industrialism and mechanisation, and condemned western commercialism, imperialism and secularism as 'disease'. But he was not a complete ruralist advocating an unmitigated return to Village Arcadianism. Later on, he advocated a reconciliation of large-scale and small-scale industries, the nationalisation of key industries, and the organisation of urban centres not as lopsided outgrowths but functioning as catering to the interests of the village where the real soul of India lay. He was not even opposed to rural electrification. But his attachment to village industries and khadi was intense and deep. He had a strong fear and suspicion that India might become a highly militarised and industrialised country that might result in the submergence or even elimination of village industries and khadi which to Gandhi, were symbols of non-violence.

Gandhi was a moral but not an economic individualist. He emphasised the dignity and sanctity of the conscience of the Individual. The Individual seeking to better his character by moral techniques is the starting point of Gandhian ethics. Gandhi also inculcated the revolutionary doctrine of equality of wages for the lawyer, the doctor, the teacher and the scavenger as the panacea for socio-economic evils. The individualistic propensity towards the acquistion of wealth is the central devil. Hence Gandhi advocated a wise regulation of riches and absolute social justice. The rich men should recognise the immanence of God in all creatures and should take the initiative in dispossession with a view to the diffusion of universal contentment.

In the Gandhian conception of Socialism the prince and the peasant, the poor and the rich, the employer and the employee were to be treated equally. But this socialism was not to be attained by conquest of political power by an organised party. It was of the utmost importance that socialists should be truthful non-violent and pure-hearted. The spiritual socialism which Gandhi wanted was to begin with the moral regeneration of the individual. He believed in a change in human nature and behaviour. There should be no cooperation with evil, but there should be no hatred against the evil doer. The omni presence of God has to be realised even in the thief, the robber and the scoundrel. Like Buddha he believed that the enemy has to be converted into a colleague and helper. Just as Aristotle in his critique of phaleas of Chalcedon and Hippodamus pointed out that man's moral faculties have to be ennoble and that the sole reliance should not be placed on surface external changes in the outward organisations, so also Gandhi wanted not only the end of the British regime and of the Indo-British capitalistic and feudal exploitation of society, but the final elimination of the desire to exploit. He was inclined to bring about a psychological regeneration of man since he sincerely believed that there was something inherently divine in man's nature. He thought during the Second World War that the active non-violence of the Jews could melt the stoniest German hearts.

A really equalitarian society based on mutual active love and harmony was his goal. He accepted the sociology of the Varnashrama but he refused to acknowledge any sense of distance and superiority between the Varnas. He took an evolutionary approach to history. Gandhi was a reformer through and through but he did not like to give a rough handling to social patterns for the sheer delight of novelty and experimentation. He wanted to demonstrate the rationality of some social institutions which has been almost immanent in the historical evolution of the country.

Gandhi was a critic of capitalism because the institution of capital was a negation of Ahimsa. But he would not sanction the forcible overthrow of capitalism. He championed the revolutionary doctrine of equal distribution. This implied that each man should have the wherewithal to supply all his natural needs. There should be no accumulation and no useless possession. The rich should become trustees of their surplus wealth for the good of society. In case they would not become willing trustees, satyagraha was to be resorted to against them.

Philosophy of Politics

Gandhi wanted like Gokhale, a spiritualisation of politics. Gokhale stressed the incorporation of moral values in politics. But Gandhi's attachment to the concept of non-violence was far deeper and more extensive than that of Gokhale. Gandhi wanted to bring religion into politics. "For me the road to salvation lies through incessant toil in the service of my country and of humanity. I want to identify myself with everything that lives. In the language of Gita, I want to live at peace with both friend and foe. So my patriotism is for me a stage on my journey to the land of eternal freedom and peace. Thus it will be seen that for me there are no politics devoid of religion. They subserve religion. Politics bereft of religion are a death trap because they kill the soul". But by this he did not mean the establishment of my theocracy. Religion means the assertion of unity with God. It is a dynamic force. Hence the incorporation of religion in politics meant a progressive movement towards justice and truth, because a man of religion will never tolerate any kind of oppression and exploitation.

Gandhi condemned bitterly western democratic politics because they were infected with threefold contradictions. They believed in limitless expansion of capitalism and this resulted in exploitation of the weaker peoples. "Western democracy as it functions today is undiluted Nazism or Fascism. At best it is merely a cloak to hide the Nazi and Fascist tendencies of imperialism". Gandhi stressed that non-violence alone could lead to true democracy. Politically, democracy implied scrupulous exactness in dealing with opponents. Economically, it meant that the weakest should have the same opportunity as the strongest. Democracy and violence could not be reconciled. He wanted India to evolve 'True Democracy'. He was a realist and hence he did not cherish the utopian dream that the India of the future will do away with the army and accept complete independence and non-violence.

Gandhi's Sarvodaya has its roots in the Vedantic concept of the spiritual unity of existence and the Gita. Buddhist concept of Sarvbhutabita or the good of all living beings. Its wide comprehensive idealism, is opposed to the Lockean theory of majoritarianism, the Marx-Gumplowicz concept of class and racial struggle and the Benthamite formula of the greatest good of the greatest number. Just as in Plato's writings his ethereal idealism is brought out in the Republic while the statesman and the laws show concessions to the realistic demands of human nature and the social structure, so also in Gandhi there is a realistic theory which was meant for immediate application for winning the freedom of India and for possible application in the near future as well as a more transcendent theory which postulates a radical transformation of human nature and a more perfect incorporation of the moral technics in the corporate life of mankind. Gandhi considered the state as an organisation of violence and force. Being an apostle of non-violence he was repelled by the coercive character of the state. He postulated that in the ideal state of Ramarajya or the Kingdom of God upon Earth there will be sovereignty of the moral authority of the people, and the state as a structure of violence would be extinct. But he was not for the immediate ending of state power. The increasing perfection of the state should be the immediate goal although the ultimate aim is philosophical and moral anarchism. In an article in the *Young India* (9th March 1922) Gandhi draws a distinction between the ideal society and swaraj. In the ideal society there will be no railways, no hospitals, no machinery, no army and navy, and no laws and no law courts. But he emphatically states that under swaraj these five categories will function. Under swaraj laws and law courts will, be the custodians of people's liberty and not the bureaucratic instruments of oppression. These following are the possible factors which have generated the hostility towards the state in Gandhi's mind : (a) Brutalities perpetrated by the South African Government upon the poor defenceless Zulus, (b) Betrayal by Smuts during the South African Satyagraha movement; (C) Atrocities perpetrated by British imperialistic power in India. He, however, did not contemplate the deliberate destruction of the state machine, but visualised the final end of coercive state by increasing observance of non-violence in political action. He visualised that in the future independent Indian state soldiers will form a national militia and would be used not for offensive but defensive and protective purposes.

The Gandhian philosophy of satyagraha is a natural outcome from the supreme concept of truth.

Satyagraha means the exercise of the purest soulforce against all injustice, oppression and exploitation. Suffering and trust are attributes of soul force.

Satyagraha is an inherent birthright of a person. It is not merely a sacred right but it can also be a sacred duty. If Hampden and Wat Taylor would not have been able to bear suffering, they could not raise the standard of revolt.

Mahatma Gandhi referred to the teachings of Thoreau in this connexion. But Gandhi stated that Thoreau was not a complete champion of non-violence. During the various battles and wars, after the thirties of the present century, Gandhi wanted that the Abyssinians, the Spaniards, the Czechs, the Chinese and the Poles could have offered non-violent resistance against the aggressors.

There are different technics of satyagraha. Fasting can be one form of satyagraha. Voluntary migration can be another form of satyagraha.

Satyagraha as conceived by Gandhi is not a formula of social and political disintegration. A satyagrahi must have first rendered willing obedience to the laws of the state.

A satyagrahi while resisting the laws of the government should see that the social structure is not subverted.

Gandhi laid down strict canons of moral discipline for the satyagrahi. He must have an unshakeable faith in God, otherwise he will not be able to bear calmly the physical atrocities perpetrated on his person by authorities with superior force of violence at their command. He must not hanker after wealth and fame. He must obey the leader of the satyagraha unit. He should strengthen his body by physical exercises like Hathayoga. He should practise Brahmacharya and should be absolutely fearless and firm in his resolve. He must have patience, single-minded purposefulness and must not be swayed from the path of duty by anger or any other passion. Satyagraha can never be resorted to for personal gains. It is a 'Love process' and the appeal is to the heart and not to the sense of fear of the wrong-doer. Thus satyagraha is on personal purification. This Gandhian stress on purity as a criterion of political power is a great contribution to political thought. It is essential to employ pure means for serving a righteous cause. Plato also prescribed physical, mathematical and dialectical training for the guardians, but Gandhi goes beyond Plato in stressing Brahmacharya. It is true that Gandhi does not put much emphasis on rigorous intellectual training in sciences and philosophy. Satyagraha does not require scholastic learning but it does require the stout heart that comes from suffering and faith. There are different forms of satyagraha. Non-cooperation with the evil doer is a mild form. Civil disobedience of the laws of the government is a strong and extreme form of satyagraha. Gandhi meant by civil, in the concept of civil disobedience, a sense of discrimination, discipline, civility and non-violence.

There can be individual as well as mass civil disobedience. The latter means spontaneous action by masses. Complete civil disobedience implying a refusal to render obedience to every single state-made law can be a very powerful movement.

Gandhi was a believer in the superiority of the soul. He would never sanction any submission to any law if it conflicted with the sense of higher duty of a person. If it did, it has to be resisted. Gandhi had no special attachment for the forms of parliamentary democracy. He did not accept that the axiomatic superiority of the majority will be represented in parliament as Locke did. The basic problem, according to him, was life in accordance with the canons of truth. The ethics of satyagraha, is certainly never synonymous with the ethics of democracy based on the counting of numbers. Satyagraha is independent of numbers participating in it. A democracy can be swayed by all types of passions, prejudices and petty considerations. But a devotee of truth would not tamely accept this.

The Gandhian philosophy and sociology of satyagraha is a spiritualised and moralised form of the concept of resistance. In western political thought resistance has been advocated. John Calvin advocated partial resistance by 'inferior magistrates'. Thoreau was an arch champion of civil disobedience. During the Swadeshi movement Tilak, Aurobindo and the extremist school also advocated passive resistance. Sometimes the Gandhian satyagraha is confused with the passive resistance advocated by the Quakers. But there are vital differences between them. To begin with, satyagraha is a dynamic force because it contemplates action in resistance of injustice. Passive resistance is compatible with internal violence towards the enemy but satyagraha stresses continuous cleansing of the mind. It emphasises even inner purity. Passive resistance is mainly contemplated at a political level. Satyagraha can be practised at all levels — domestic, social and political. Satyagraha goes beyond passive resistance in the stress on a spiritual and moral teleology because the final source of hope and consolation for the satyagrahi is God. The Gandhian theory of satyagraha is far more comprehensive than the passive resistance as advocated in India in 1906-1908. Tilak and Aurobindo would not condemn violence on moral grounds. But Gandhi accepted the absolutism of Ahimsa. The passive resistance of 1906-1908 was a political technic of limited application. Sometimes it meant only Swadeshi and boycott, while sometimes it was extended to cover disobedience of unjust laws and decrees. The Gandhian theory of satyagraha is a philosophy of life and politics, and it contemplates stupendous mass action for paralysing the total structure of a despotic government.

Gandhi was an arch champion of the moral conscience. He stressed the religious basis of politics. He would never have sanctioned that famous maxim of expediency according to which religion is a matter of private life having nothing to do with one's public life. Such a divorce between private and public is un-Gandhian. To Gandhi there must be unity between the inner and outer life of a man. But although Gandhi wanted to strengthen the religious basis of politics he would not tolerate any privilege to any particular group or sect, neither would be discriminate against any group. He advocated the theory of Ethical Religion. He categorically rejected the concept of coercion in the field of religion.

Gandhi was intensely attached to the concept of nationalism. But he was also an Internationalist. He wanted that before Internationalism could become a reality, those countries which are still suffering under feudal overlordship and colonial dependence should have the political freedom to determine their own future. Nationalism was a stage to Internationalism. But Nationalism would not mark the climax of political evolution. It was not an end but a stage. Like Mazzini, and Aurobindo, Gandhi accepted that nationalism is the logical step to cosmopolitanism. Although not enamoured of a world federation, Gandhi was prepared to accept it, if it were built on an essentially non-violence basis. He agreed that 'there may be a world police to keep order' so long as the belief in non-violence was not a vital force among the nations.

Philosophy of Freedom

With intense devotion of the concepts of moral and spiritual freedom, in Mahatma Gandhi we find also a tremendous urgency for political freedom. Swaraj for him is part of truth which is God. Political freedom or swaraj could be attained only by intense suffering and struggle. Gandhi accepted the truth of the famous Mantra given by Tilak that Swaraj is the birthright of Indians. He said : "For me every ruler is alien that defies public opinion". The Swaraj of Gandhi's conception was to champion the interests of the downtrodden and starving millions. He pleaded that all useful labour should bring the same and adequate wages to the worker. But until that ideal was realised, every labourer should get enough remuneration to feed and clothe himself and his family. It was the imperative duty of the government to ensure this much to all. "A government that does not ensure this much is no government. It is anarchy. Such a state should be resisted peacefully.

Gandhi pleaded for freedom in the sense of national independence. He dedicated his own life to secure the freedom of governing themselves rightly through a government imposed from without; even as the fabled jackdaw could not walk like a peacock with feathers borrowed from his elegant companion". Gandhi also pleaded for personal freedom and civic freedom.

He never accepted the theory of freedom as arbitrariness or License. Freedom results in self-denial for the sake of society, license means the desire to enjoy exclusive privileges even by resort to violence. Moral freedom for him did not lay in the egoistic assertions of the claims of the individual ego but in identification with the spiritual being. To Gandhi freedom was a whole. Moral freedom as emancipation from the slavery to passions, national freedom as emancipation from the bondage of alien rulers and exploiters, and spiritual freedom as emancipation and realisation of truths were all phases of freedom. To one whose life was permeated by the belief in the presence of a higher spiritual reality, any compromise with evil, lust and slavery was wrong.

Gandhi's life was a vindication, a supreme concretisation of the great Vedantic gospel that a man of realisation transcends not only hate and sorrow but also all separatist differences and the consciousness of finite claims and the just apportionment of his dues. This sentiment of cosmopolitan and universalism and fraternity give a deeper human touch to Gandhian political thought than can be found in the idealism of Green and Bosanquet.

Conclusion

Gandhi was a saint and a moral revolutionary. He believed that violence interrupted the real revolution of the social structure and ideals. He was a moral realist with occasional touch or the celestial prophet and the ethereal mystic in him.

Gandhism is not a systematic well-worked out political philosophy in the western sense. He provides empirical suggestions. He did not have either the requisite time or the philosophical competance to work out mature academic expositions of his sociological, economic and political insights.

Gandhi's fusion of the teachings of the Gita and Buddhism, with the teachings of Thoreau, Ruskin and Tolstoy points to a cultural synthesis of the East and the West.

Gandhi did not view economic problems as isolated departments of man's activity. To him a moral, simple and devout life was central and hence along with Ruskin and Tolstoy, he sponsored a psychological approach to economics. He regarded the villages as the center of Indian economic organisation. He was keen on mitigating evils of a growingly disproportionate and hierarchical economic structure.

Marx constructed his philosophy of dialectical materialism on the basis of Hegelian dialectics and the Greek and French materialistic philosophy. Bergson's Vitalism, Alexander's emergent evolution and Whitehead's philosophy organism repudiated the thesis of old nineteenth century materialism on which dialectical materialism was based. The philosophy of Gandhi, on the other hand, is based on the concept of the unity of existence. It traces itself to the Yajurveda. Both Gandhi and Marx have been colossal giants in modern history and thought. Gandhi is a philosophical idealist, and Marx a scientific materialist. Gandhi believes in faith and spiritual experience. Marx accepts a dialectical rationalism. Satyagraha is the way of Gandhi, revolution even by armed violence, that of Marx. Gandhi is an ethical absolutist. Instead of these differences we find some similarities between Gandhi and Marx. Both are reactions to the western civilisation. To Gandhi the west symbolised imperialism, to Marx it was equivalent with capitalism. Both Gandhi and Marx are essentially agreed in their concept of transcending petty interests for a higher cause and for establishing liberty and justice for exploited mankind.

He stressed peace, modesty, gentleness, philanthropy and a sense of devout respect for the religious views of others. Gandhi had an invincible faith in the nobility of human nature. Perhaps man will be compelled by sheer necessity to become noble because the alternative to goodness is immanent peril and possible destruction.

Gandhi's Views on State

Gandhi was not a systematic political philosopher in the sense of speculative type and he cannot be said to have developed a coherent and systematic political philosophy. What we call Gandhism is not a set of doctrines, rules or regulations, injunctions or inhibitions but it is a way of life. Gandhiji did not make any direct suggestion as to the nature of the state. He considered the state as an organisation of violence and force. He did not regard state as necessary or divine creation. He was repelled by the coercive character of the state.

In short, Gandhiji had a hostile-attitude towards the state. For such an attitude the brutalities committed by South african Government, betrayed by Smuts during the South African Satyagraha movement, the atrocities committed by England in India were responsible. From these incidents Gandhiji came to regard the entire sturcture of the state with deep suspicion and hostility.

Gandhi's conscience revolted against the very idea of state sovereignty. Any concept of the exaltation of the absolute, uncontrolled and unlimitable power was according to him an attack on the moral fibre of civilisation. He regarded the state as a instrument of coercion and compulsion which goes against the free moral development of the world. According to him, what can be sovereign is not the state but the moral will of the community. This view of moral will of the people being sovereign was based upon three considerations :

Firstly, Gandhi was a spiritual being and so regarded spiritual authority as higher than the state authority. According to him no ruler could set himself against God.

Secondly, being a Satyagrahi he preached right of inner conscience to oppose an unjustified law for order of the state.

Thirdly, he stood as the prophet of the moral authority of the people.

However, Gandhiji did not contemplate the destruction of the state; he, in fact, wanted a non-violent state.

He was more concerned with the immediate rather than the future. According to him, the non-violent state must be based on the willing allegiance of an intelligent body of citizens. The government in such a state will represent the will and the ideals of the overwhelming majority of the people.

His immediate concern was to free India from the subjection of the British. He thought it desirable that the details of a non-violent state should be determined by the people according to their moral level and their preferences.

But as a realist he was not very hopeful of the immediate acceptance of non-violence as a principle of state policy. He was a philosophical anarchist and he rejects the state outright and in any of its form. The establishment of a non-violent state was the goal of his ideology. He was not in favour of the immediate ending of the state power. In his concept of the state what Gandhiji had in mind was the vision of perfection of mankind and hence he was hostile to the modern state which to him represented organised violence. He refused to see in the state the manifestation of any superior reason. He was opposed to the western idealists. His ideal was the establishment of a society based on non-violence. He was a sort of religious anarchist who wanted to establish 'Ram Rajya' or the 'Kingdom of God' on earth. It can be called as an enlightened anarchy.

The state tries to standardise human conduct and as such it becomes an impediment in the way of evolution and progress of the individual since state cannot be completely done away with it therefore should continue to perform only negative functions.

Gandhiji was not an anarchist of Bakunin type. He laid stress on cultivation of moral strength and discipline. Thus he did not believe in any deliberate and violent destruction of the state but on the truth and non-violence through which alone a stateless society could be brought about. He wrote : "A society organised and run on the basis of complete non-violence would be the purest anarchy."

63

Jawaharlal Nehru (1889-1964)

Like Lenin, Nasser, Tito and Washington, it fell to Jawaharlal Nehru's lot not only to become a leading figure, next only to Mahatma Gandhi, in India's struggle for freedom but also to become the architect of a new nation. At an early stage of his life, he rose in the hierarchy of the Indian National Congress, the main instrument of the Independence movement, to become the general secretary of the Congress. There was only one such secretary then and it was indeed a recognition of his eminence. Within five years, while not yet fourty, Nehru was chosen the President of the Congress at the historic Lahore session (1929) which adopted complete Independence as the goal of the struggle.

No doubt, he had a flying start, being the only son of Motilal Nehru, one of the leading lawyers of his time who was also a leader of the Congress and a man of many parts. Motilal had his son educated in the best institutions in England but, unlike many Indians of his generation, he did not return a Brown Sahib. While acquiring the best in the British liberal tradition, Nehru was imbued by the desire to do something for the country. He studied the contemporary socio-economic, political and international trends of Europe which was to stand him in good stead later in life and give him world view which some of the other leaders of the freedom movement lacked.

It was natural that Jawaharlal would enter the legal profession for which he had been trained and for which his father's flourishing practice and great reputation would have acted as a launching pad. By temperament, however, young Nehru was not attuned to the profession, and events on the political horizon were moving so fast that he was drawn into the *Vortex* straightaway and had little time to spare for the courts. Mahatma Gandhi had already arrived on the Indian scene after his great success in leading the Indian community in South Africa in its struggle for self-respect in that racist country.

Nehru hitched his wagon to the Gandhian star. He was greatly attracted to the Mahatma's direct ways and readiness to fight the British Government. By 1920 when Mahatma Gandhi was completely dominating the Congress, even Motilal Nehru, used to the ways of affluence and high living with which he also combined high thinking. He was a willing associate of Mahatma Gandhi. But he shuddred at the thought that his only son would have to court imprisonment and undergo the hard life of a jail inmate. Motilal Nehru, as Nehru has recorded, tried sleeping on the floor in his palatial house of Allahabad to realise how hard would be jail life for his son and possibly himself.

Soon, both father and son were by the side of the Mahatma and although there were differences between the elder Nehru and Mahatma Gandhi over entry into legislatures which then had little power. A great bond of affinity sprang up between father and son and Mahatma Gandhi. The Mahatma saw in the young Nehru a leader who could fire the imagination of the youth, full of idealism, new ideas and a world consciousness, yet pragmatic. For Nehru had realised early in his career that the only man who could move the Indian masses, in the cities, towns and villages, was Mahatma Gandhi and, however, much he differed from him, and some of the Mahatma's notions which he could not readily accept, he always remained attuned to Mahatma Gandhi.

In good time, Mahatma Gandhi called him his political heir. Despite long periods of imprisonment, which he utilised for his extensive writings, Nehru remained surprisingly free of bitterness towards the British as a people. He also retained his taste for the good things of life, although he had completely identified himself with the poor and the weakest in the land — the hewers of wood and drawers of water, as Mahatma Gandhi called them, or the "Daridranarayan". The people also felt instinctively drawn to him, as someone who loved them, one who had abandoned a life of luxury for their sake. The Indian people always admired the man who gave up something, and one who was so close to Mahatma Gandhi.

As Independence dawned, Nehru was the natural choice to lead the newly independent nation, with Sardar Patel, another stalwart of the freedom struggle, as his deputy and senior colleague. The two together handled the complex problems of the partition of a huge country, the migration of some 20 million people in both directions and soon settled down to the gigantic tasks of nation building. While Sardar Patel busied himself with the unification of the country and gave us a much bigger India than we had inherited from the British, by peacefully merging some 550 princely States with free India, Nehru began the process of development.

Within months of freedom he laid the foundation of several major development projects like Hirakud in Orissa and other railway and industrial schemes. The gigantic Bhakra Project which tansformed the face of Punjab and made it the granary of India, was taken up early and while laying its foundation Nehru called the development projects the "new temples" of India. Today much of our energy is wasted over disputes over temples and mosques and the people lack direction, but Nehru had told us that we should look forward rather than backward.

In just three years after Independence the first Prime Minister set up the Planning Commission and the First Five Year Plan was launched in 1951. He was himself the Chairman of the National Planning Committee set up by Netaji Subhas Chandra Bose, as president of the Indian National Congress, in 1939. Now as Prime Minister, he assumed the Chairmanship of the full-fledged Planning Commission of free India.

The Planning era began and while some fruits were realised quick enough, others like the Green Revolution were reaped after his death. But he had sown the seeds and nursed the plants through the difficult early years. Foundations of a large public sector were laid, an iron and steel industry was built up and expanded, oil discoveries were made and refineries were founded. He predicted that the refineries will 'beget children', meaning there would be petrochemical and other industries based on their products and by-products. He was proved right by events. He also launched community development for the villages and later ushered in Panchayati Raj.

Almost within the first year of Independence, he had set up an Atomic Energy Commission, under the great nuclear physicist Homi Bhabha, and it was his constant encouragement and recognition of the scientists' role that Yielded results in later years, making India a member of the exclusive nuclear club. Nehru repeatedly emphasised the scientific temper. While ensuring that all religions in a secular India had equal treatment. Yet he had reverence for the Indian traditions and willed that his ashes be scattered over the Himalayas and immersed in the Ganga for which he had a great affinity.

As the leader of the first country in Asia and Africa to wrest its freedom from the colonialists, Nehru knew India must play an important role in helping others gain their freedom and preserve it. When Indonesia was in trouble in 1949 and the Dutch were refusing to hand over power to Dr. Sukarno and his colleagues, who were imprisoned, Nehru convened a 19 nation conference in Delhi which utimately resulted in the Dutch being forced to leave Indonesia. Likewise, when Nasser's Egypt was attacked in 1956 by the Anglo-French forces in collusion with the Israelis, Nehru thundered and mobilised world opinion against such neo-colonialist acts. The invaders had to beat a hasty retreat.

Non-Aligned Movement was born out of Nehru's will that India would not take sides in the Cold War of the power blocs and would not be dictated to by either. India, he laid down, would pursue an independent foreign policy, a policy of peace and friendship for all, but without sacrificing India's honour and her right to decide every issue on its merits, whether it pleased one bloc or the other. India, he also laid down, would align itself with the nations still struggling for their freedom and with the people of South Africa and Palestine fighting for their just right against *apartheid*, Zionism and Imperialism. There were difficult situations both in domestic and foreign policies and some resulted in serious consequences, like the 1962 Chinese War. But Nehru pursued his course of developments at home and peace in the world, without sacrificing India's honour or interests steadfastly.

To India he also gave the gift of a great Constitution which was fashioned by great minds and people of wisdom and forethought, among whom he was the leader. Not only was he one of the principal architects of India's secular and democratic constitution, while all around countries were opting for fundamentalist, one religion dominated and dictatorial regimes, he gave a unique example of his democratic temper. He was a great parliamentarian and treated the rather weak Opposition with much respect. He made it a point to participate in as many debates as possible and was the moving spirit behind the Hindu reform law which laid the foundation of the liberation of Indian women by statute, completing the task begun by Gandhiji of breaking the shackles of Indian women.

Nehru was a prolific writer not only of books, which are well known, but in his 17 years as Prime Minister of India, he wrote a plethora of memoranda.

He stood for human progress and happiness, a stand which emanated from his deep love for human dignity and unflinching faith in the human potential.

64

Some Important Dates and Events in History

A.D.

527-65 : The reign of the Emperor Justinian.
570-632 : The Life of Mohammed.
732 : Charles Martel defeated the Mohammedans at Tours.
771-814 : The reign of Charles the Great.
800 : Charles the Great crowned Emperor at Rome - the beginning of the holy Roman Empire.
1066 The Norman Conquest of England.
1095 The First Crusade.
1198-1216 : Innocent III, Pope.
1215 : Magna Carta signed by the English King John.
1226 : Death of Francis of Assisi.
1227 : Death of Cenghiz Khan.
1271-95 : The travels of Marco Polo.
1309 : The Papacy shifted from Rome to Avignon.
1348 : The Black Death.
1378-1417 : The Great Schism in the Papacy, ended by the acknowledgement by all Roman Catholics of the Pope, whose headquarters were to be at Rome.
1348 : The Death of John Wycliffe.
1415 : John Huss burned at Constance.
1453 : Constantinople captured by the Ottoman Turks.
1492 : Columbus's first voyage to America.
1498 : Vasco da Gama and sea route to India.
1519 : Leonardo da Vinci died. Magellan's expedition started to sail round the world. Cortez entered the city of Mexico.
1521 : Luther at the Diet of Worms.
1526 : The Moghul Empire founded in india.
1539 : The Jesuit Order founded.
1546 : Death of Martin Luther.
1547 : Ivan the Terrible took the title of Czar of Russia.
1556-1605 : The reign of Akbar the Great in India.
1564-1616 : The Life of William Shakespeare.
1609 : Dutch independence secured.
1618-48 : The Thirty Years' War.
1620 : The Pilgrim Fathers left England in the *Mayflower*.
1642-60 : The Great Rebellion in England.
1643 : Louis XIV of France began his long reign of 72 years.
1644 : The beginning of the Manchu Dynasty in China.

1688	:	The 'Glorious Revolution' in England.
1689-1725	:	Peter the Great Czar of Russia.
1707	:	End of the Mogul Empire in India.
1727	:	Death of Sir Issac Newton.
1740	:	Frederick the Great became King of Prussia.
1756-63	:	The Seven Years' War. England and France fought for supremacy in North America and India.
1775-83	:	The American War of Independence.
1776 (4 July)	:	The American Declaration of Independence.
1789-94	:	The Great French Revolution.
1705	:	Napoleon became commander-in-chief of the French troops in Italy and so embarked upon his career of conquest.
1805	:	The Battle of Trafalgar.
1812	:	The Retreat from Moscow.
1814	:	Napoleon sent to Elba.
1815	:	The Battle of Waterloo and the final overthrow of Napoleon.
1821-29	:	The War of Greek Independence.
1830	:	The First Passenger Railway (Liverpool to Manchester).
1832	:	The First Reform Bill passed by the English Parliament.
1840	:	China begins to attract the serious attention of Europeans.
1848	:	The great year of revolutions.
1853	:	Japan opened to foreign nations.
1859	:	The beginning of the struggle for Italian Independence.
1871	:	William I of Prussia became German Emperor. The Third French Republic established.
1912	:	China became a republic.
1914-18	:	The Great War.
1917	:	Establishment of the Soviet Republic of Russia.
1920	:	The first meeting of the League of Nations.
1921	:	Creation of the Irish Free State.
1922	:	The Fascist March on Rome.
1923	:	Proclamation of the Turkish Republic.
1931	:	End of the Spanish Monarchy.
1934	:	Hitler became head of the German State.
1935-36	:	Italian Conquest of Abyssinia.
1936	:	Accession (January) and Abdication (December) of Edward VIII, King of Great Britain.
		Civil War in Spain.
1937	:	Franklin Roosevelt re-relected President of the United States of America.
		The Japanese ventures in China led to the first campaigns of the Second World War.
1938	:	The *Anschluss* i.e. the Austrian Union with Germany took place. It was followed in autumn by the German invasion and seizure of part of Czechoslovakia.

1939 : With the German attack on Poland began the Second World War on 1 September 1939.

1940 : In December 1940 planning began for a German invasion of Russia.

1941 : The German attack on Russia launched on 22 June 1941. Vast numbers of prisoners were taken.

1942 : The battle of Atlantic took place. President Roosevelt of the United States and Premier Winston Churchill of Great Britain agreed on an active military alliance.

1943 : Italy, the weakest of three Axis Powers, was defeated.

1944 : On June 6, 1944, an allied expedition force under General Eisenhower landed in Normandy. It was the greatest attack by sea ever made and is considered one of the biggest gambles in the history of warfare.

1945 : It resulted in the collapse of Germany. During the battle of Berlin the Germans announced the death of Hitler, who committed suicide. The Second World War came to an end.

The *San Francisco Conference* led to the birth of the United Nations as an International Organisation.

1946 : The first meeting of the United Nations General Assembly was held in London.

1947 : U.S. Secretary of State George *Marshall* proposed American aid for a European recovery plan.

: *Rio de Jeneiro Conference* : A Conference of American Republics for mutual security and cooperation.

: The partition of Indian subcontinent followed in August.

1948 : The forcible establishment of Zionist State of Israel in 1948 led to the disintegration of the Arab State of Palestine and the first Arab-Israeli war broke out.

This period also witnessed the coming of the cold war and the Western and American exploitation of the Arab oil.

1949 : North Atlantic Treaty Organisation (NATO)

An Imperialist alliance against possible Russian aggression backed by the United States of America and including also Belgium, Canada, Denmark, France, Great Britain, Greece, Iceland, Italy, Luxemburg, Netherlands, Norway, Portugal and Turkey.

1950 : The outbreak of cold war became a reality as the world was divided into two major blocs - the United States and Western European countries forming one bloc and the Soviet Union and the Socialist countries of Eastern Europe forming the other. The formation of military alliances was accompanied by the race for weapons of destruction.

1952 : Egyptian Revolution under Nasser's leadership. This revolution symbolised the real end of foreign domination and colonial exploitation of Egypt since a long.

1955 : The central treaty organisation (CENTO), originally known as the Baghdad Pact came into being. The members included in this were Great Britain, Turkey, Iraq, Iran and Pakistan.

The first meeting of Afro-Asian Latin American leaders at Bandung.

1956	:	The French relinquished Tunisia and Morocco.
		The Second Arab-Israeli war or Suez crisis resulted due to the Anglo-French, Israeli invasion of Egypt.
1957	:	Ghana became independent of British colonial rule.
1958	:	Another French colony, Guinea became the next part of French West and Equatorial Africa to gain independence.
1960	:	The Belgian Congo gained its independence.
	:	British colony of Nigeria also achieved independence.
1962	:	French President de Gaulle proclaimed Algerian independence after a referendum.
		China attacked India.
1963	:	The Organisation of African Unity (OAU) was established.
1964	:	The Palestine Liberation Organisation (PLO) came into being.
1965	:	Indo-Pak war broke out in January.
1967	:	The Six Day (5-10th June) third Arab-Israeli war broke out.
1968	:	Mr. Yasser Arafat became the Chairman of PLO.
1969	:	American military invasion of Vietnam.
1970	:	President Nasser of Egypt died on 28 September.
1971	:	The Second Indo-Pak or Bangladesh War.
		The new State of Bangladesh came into being.
1972	:	The opening of the European Common market summit conference in Paris.
		The visit of American President Richard Nixon to Peking in a "Journey of peace" led to the re-establishment of contacts between China and the US, the erstwhile enemies.
		In May 1972, shortly after his visit to Peking, President Nixon visited Moscow and concluded the first Strategic Arms Limitation Treaty (known as SALT -I) with the USSR.
1973	:	The Fourth Arab-Israeli or October War broke out.
		The sharp rise in oil prices by the OPEC and Arab States.
		Algeria supported the Polisario national movement in Western Sahara.
1975	:	Establishment of the Socialist Republic of Vietnam.
1977	:	Anwar Sadat, President of Egypt was the first Arab leader to visit Isreal unexpectedly.
		In July, a military coup deposed Pakistani Prime Minister Zulfiqar Ali Bhutto (1971-77). General Mohammad Zia ul-Haq seized power and pursued a policy of ruthless repression.
		In March 1977 elections Mrs. Indira Gandhi, Prime Minister of India, suffered a shattering defeat and the Janata Party (People's Front) headed by Morarji Desai took over the reins of Indian Government.
1978	:	The Camp David Accords between US, Egypt and Israel signed.
		The election in 1978 of a Pole, John Paul II, as the first non-Italian Pope for four centuries and the tremendous enthusiasm with which he was greeted, infused a new energy into the Roman Catholic Church.
1979	:	Islamic Revolution in Iran.
		Soviet military intervention in Afghanistan.

A Second SALT Agreement was signed in Vienna by Presidents Jimmy Carter of US and Leonid Brezhnev of Soviet Union in June 1979. Its ratification by the American Senate was delayed.

Mrs. Margaret Thatcher became the United Kingdom's first female Prime Minister by leading the Conservative Party to a decisive victory.

1980 : The Iraq-Iran war broke out with the Iraqi announcement of its abrogation of the Shatt-el-Arab agreement with Iran on 16 September.

In July the US and many of its allies boycotted the Olympic games which were held in Moscow.

1982 : The Falkland war broke out on 2 April.

Britain invaded Argentina.

Israeli full-scale invasion of Lebanon.

Palestinians still survived.

Egypt and Israel agree on final withdrawal of Israeli forces from Sinai and Egypt officially gets back Sinai Peninsula, 15 years after Israeli occupation.

Soviet President Brezhnev (75) dies in Moscow. Yuri Andropov succeeds Brezhnev as General Secretary of the Soviet Communist Party.

Lech Walesa, leader of Poland's outlawed Solidarity free trade union is released after 11 months of internment.

1983 : Seventh Non-Aligned Summit opens at New Delhi. Mrs. Indira Gandhi, Chairperson, appeals for reversal of arms race.

US invasion of Greneda, a small Caribbean country.

Philippines' opposition leader Benigno S. Aquino Jr. returns from voluntary exile and is shot and killed when he touches homeground.

US notifies withdrawal from UNESCO.

1984 : Soviet President Yuri Andropov dies, Konstantin Chernenko becomes new Soviet Communist Party chief.

2,500 persons killed due to inhalation of poisonous gas from the Union Carbide plant at Bhopal.

On 31 October Mrs. Indira Gandhi, Prime Minister of India was assassinated by two of her security guards at her residence in New Delhi. Mr. Rajiv Gandhi is sworn in as Prime Minister.

1985 : Mr. Hun Sen elected as Prime Minister of crisis-ridden Kampuchea or Cambodia.

on 2 July, Mr. Andrei Gromyko elected President of the Soviet Union.

Mr. Robert Mugabe voted back to power in Zimbabwe. He was elected Chairman of the Non-Aligned Movement.

Mikhail Gorbachev took over the reins of leadership in the Soviet Union. With his reform policies of Perestroika and Glasnost, he is in the process of leading the Soviet Union from a Command economy to a market oriented one.

1986 : US bombs Tripoli, the capital of Libya. The UN and the NAM condemn US attack on Libya.

Eighth Summit of Non-Aligned Movement begins in Harare, Zimbabawe. Dr. Robert Mugabe takes over as the chairmanship from Prime Minister Rajiv Gandhi of India.

1987 : Campus demonstrations in China for greater democracy strengthens.

400 pilgrims (mostly Iranians) die in Mecca when they clashed with Saudi police.

The Arab Summit in Amman adopts a resolution giving Arab states right to individually restore relations with Egypt severed in 1979 following the Camp David Agreement with Israel.

1988 : President Yassar Arafat of Israeli-occupied Arab State of Palestine made the historic declaration of an independent Palestine comprising West Bank of river Jordan and Gaza strip at the 1988 Novemeber Algriers Session of the Palestine National Council.

Mr. George Bush, Vice-President for eight years in Reagan Administration, elected President of the US.

PLO Chairman or President Arafat addresses the special session of the UN General Assembly, convened in Geneva in his honour.

1989 : France celebrated the bicentennial of its great revolution (1789) that changed the history of mankind.

Namibia became independent on April 1.

Mikhail Gorbachev emerges as the most powerful leader in Soviet Union combining the offices of General Secretary of the Communist Party and President of the country.

Egyptian writer, Naguib Mahfouz wins 1988 Nobel Prize for literature (the first Arabic language writer to win it).

Latin America has been considered as the nearest laboratory for US Imperialist experiments towards decolonised Third World. This is very well proved by the US naked military intervention in Panama.

1990 : Germany is united. Since October 3, 1990 unified Germany has for the first time since the end of Second World War enjoyed full sovereignty over its domestic and foreign policies.

Cold war comes to an end with the disintegration of Soviet Union. The US emerges as the single most powerful power at the world state.

The Kuwaiti crisis or the Second Gulf War rightly projected the US concept of New World order, i.e. re-establishing its political, economic and military hegemony over the Gulf region more fully than at any time since the cold war period.

1991 : A crisis in Yugoslavia. Civil war situation holds sway there.

President George Bush of US spoke of a New World Order. Such a new world order does not take into account the realisation of the inalienable Arab-Palestinian human rights, does not bother about the economic and social development of the underdeveloped world, does not believe in giving independent role to the united Nations.

The opening of the historic West Asia Peace Conference (on 30 October) in Madrid (the capital of Spain) - sponsored jointly by the US President, Mr. George Bush and the Ex-Soviet President, Mr. Mikhail Gorbachev and attended, significantly, by both Israeli and Palestinian-Arab delegations.

In this era of 1990s we are facing dynamic and worldwide challenges to which, in many cases, we have not yet found responses.

Bibliography

Abdel-Malek, A., ed. *contemporary Arab Political Thought* (London: Zed Books, 1989).

Ake, C., *Revolutionary Pressures in Africa* (London: Zed Books, 1989).

Ali, B. Sheikh, *Islam : A Cultural Orientation* (Delhi, Bombay, Calcutta, Madras: MACMILLAN India Ltd., 1981).

Allison, Roy and Williams, Phil (eds.), *Super-power Competition and Crisis Prevention in the third World* (New York, Cambridge University Press, 1990).

Amin, S., *The Arab Nation: Nationalism and Class Struggle* (London: Zed Books, 1989).

——, *Eurocentrism* (London: Zed Books, 1989).

Aruri, N., *Occupation: Israel Over Palestine* (London: Zed Books, 1989).

Astrow, A., *Zimbabwe: A Revolution that Lost its Way? (London: Zed Books, 1989).*

Ball, W. Macmahon, *Nationalism and communism in East Asia* (Victoria: Melbourne University Press, 1952).

Barber (M.J.), *Europe in a Changing World: Some aspects of twentieth-century history* (London: Macmillan, 1969).

Barch Jr., Oscar Theordre, Blake, Nelson Manfred, *Since 1900: A History of the united States in our Times* (New York: The Macmillan Co., 1959).

Barlow (Frank), *Feudal Kingdom of England 1042- 1216* (London: Longman, 1974).

Belloc, *The French Revolution* (London, 1929).

Beloff (Max), *Europe and the Euresseans : An International Discussion* (London; Chatto and Windus, 1957).

Bennis and Cassidy, *The Palestinian Intifada: From stones to Statehood* (London: Zed Books, 1989).

Berberoglue, B., *Turkey in Crisis: From State Capitalism to Neo-Colonialism* (London: Zed Books, 1989).

Berberoglu, B. (ed.), *Power and Stability in the Middle East* (London: Zed Books, 1989).

Bianco, Lucien; *Origins of the Chinese Revolution* (1970).

Blum, W., *The CIA: A forgotten History: US Global Intervention Since World War II* (London: Zed Books, 1989).

Bodde, D; *Peking Diary* (1950)

Boulger, Demetrius Charles, *The History of China*, Vols. I & II (London, Calcutta: W. Thacker & Co., 1898).

Brabdy, *A Shorty History of the French Revolution* (Oxford, 1926).

Brecht, A; *Prelude to Silence* (1945)

Bulletin of CAS (ed.), *China From Mao to Deng: The Politics and Economics of Scolialist Development* (London: Zed Books, 1989).

Bullock, A; *Hitter* (1964).

Cambridge Modern History, Vols. X and XI (Cambridge, 1938).

Cardri, *Saddam's Iraq: Rovolution or Reaction*: New Edition (London: Zed Books, 1989).

Carr. E.H., *International Relations Between the two World Wars 1919-1939* (London: Macmillan, 1952).

——, *What is History?* (Middlesex, New York, Victoria, Ontario, Auckland: Penguin Books Ltd., 1961).

——. *Internatioal Relations Between the Two World Wars* (London: Macmillan Co., 1965).

Carrie, Rene Albrecht, *A Diplomatic history of Europe Since the congress of Vienna* (New York: Harper and Brothers Publishers, 1958).

Carter, E.H., and Mears, R.A.F., *A History of Britain* (Oxford: clarendon Press, 1960).

Chaytor, *The Making of Modern Europe* (Vol. Vi of Gresham's European History) (London, 1914).

Cheng, Sih gung, *Modern China: A Political Study* (Oxford: Clarendon Press, 1919).

Choueiri, Youssef M., *Arab History and the Nation- State: A Study in Modern Arab Historiography 1820-1980* (London and New York: Routledge, 1989).

Churchill, Winston S., *The Second World War: Triumph and Tragedy* (New York: Bantam Books, 1953).

Churchill (Winston S.), *History of the English- Speaking Peoples*, V. 4 (London: Cassell, 1956).

Cimade, Inodep, Mink, *Africa's Refugee Crisis* (London: Zed Books, 1989).

Cole (G.D.H.) *Europe, Russia and the Future* (London: Victory Gollancz, 1941).

Craig (G.A.I.), *Europe Since 1815* (New York: Holt, Rinehart and Winston, 1962).

Cranshaw, Edward, *The New Cold War: Moscow V. Peking* (Middliesex, Baltimore: Penguin Books Ltd., 1963).

Crombie, A.C., *Augustine to Galileo* (London, 1952).

Curtis, Michael, *Religion and politics in the Middle East (Boulder, Colorado: Westview press,* 1981).

Davies, H.A., *An Outline History of the World* (London: Oxford university Press, 1928).

Davies, R. et al., *The Struggle for South Africa, Vol. I A Reference Guide New Edition* (London: Zed Books, 1989).

Davies R. et. al., *The Struggle for south Africa, Vol. 2 A Reference Guide New Edition* (London: Zed Books, 1989).

Davis, U., *Israel: An Apartheid State* (London: Zed Books, 1989).

Deane, Phyllis; *The First Industrial Revolution.*

De Braganca & Wallerstein, *The African Liberation Reader, Vol. 1 (London: Zed Books, 1989).*

——, *The African Liberation Reader*, Vol. 2 (London: Zed Books, 1989).

——, *The African Liberation Reader*, Vol. 3 (London: Zed Books, 1989).

De Porte (A.W.), *Europe between the Super Powers: The enduring balance* (New Haven: Yale University Press, 1979).

Eaford & Ajaz, *Judaism or Zionism? : What Difference for the Middle East* (London: Zed Books, 1989).

Easton, Stewart C., *The Twilight of European Colonialism* (New York: Holt, Rinehart and Winston, 1960).

Edquist, C., *Capitalism, Socialism and Technology: A Comparative Study of Cuba and Jamaica* (London: Zed Books, 1989).

Edwards, William, *Notes on European History* (London: Rivingtons, 1925).

Elliott (J.H.), *Europe divided, 1559-1598* (London: Collins, 1968).

Ellwood, David W., *Italy: 1943-1945* (New York: Holmes and Meier, 1985).

El-Sheikh, Dr. Khalid, *Zionism: A tale of Terror* (New Delhi: League of Arab States & Embassy of the State of Palestine).

Elton (G.R.), *England under the Tudors*, Ed. 2 (London: Methuen & Co., 1974).

Elton, Godfrey; *The Revolutionary idea in France, 1789-1871*, 2nd edition, (London, 1931).

Encyclopaedia Britannica (Chicago, London, Toronto, Geneva, Sydney, Tokyo, Manila: Encyclopaedia Britannica, Inc.)

Engels, Frederick; *The condition of the working class in England in 1844* (London, 1892)

Fisher (H.A.L.), *History of Europe* (London: Edward Arnold, 1941).

Fisher, *Bonapartism* (Oxford, 1928).

Fitt, Y. et. al., *The World Economic Crisis: US Imperialism at Bay* (London: Zed Books, 1989).

Footman, David, *The Russian Revolution* (London: Faber and Faber, 1962).

Ford (Franklin L.), *Europe 1780-1830* (London: Long mans, 1970).

Foster, William z., *Outline of Political History of the Americas* (New York: International Publishers, 1951).

Foucault, Michel; *The order of things* (New York, 1970).

Frenaye, Frances, *The Death of Hitler's Germany* (New york: Macmillan Company, 1954).

Friedman, Wolfgang, *An Introduction to World Politics* (London: Macmillan, 1952).

Frangi, A., *The PLO and Palestine* (London: Zed Books, 1989).

Fyffe, *History of Modern Europe* (London, 1924).

Gathorne-Hardy, G.M., *A Short History of International Affairs 1920-39* (London: Oxford University Press, 1950).

Gay, Peter; *The Enlightenment: An Interpretation 2 Vols.* (New York, 1966-69).

Genound, Francois (eds.), *The Testament of Adolf Hitler*, Translated by Colonel R.H. Stevens (London: Cassell, 1959).

Gershoy, The French Revolution and Napoleon (Allahabad, 1960).

Gilbert, Martin, *Atlas of Russian History* (Great Britain: Dorset Press, 1972).

Gordon Wright, *France in Modern Times.*

Gottschalk and Lach, *Europe and the Modern World*, VOL. I (Bombay, 1962).

Grant (A.J.) and Temperley (H.W.U.), *Europe in the Nineteenth and Twentieth Centuries* (London: Longman, 1984).

Green, J.R.; *Short History of English People* (ed. 1874).

Gresh, A., *The PLO: The Struggle Within*, New Edition (London: Zed Books, 1989).

Gunther, John, *Inside Europe Today* (New York: Pocket Books Inc., 1962).

Gupta, parthasarathi, *Adhunik Paschim Ka Udaya* (Delhi: University of Delhi, 1983).

Hall, D.G.E., *A History of South-East Asia* (London: Macmillan and Co. Ltd., 1964).

Halliday, Jon and McCormack, Gavar, *Japanese Imperialism Today: Co-Prosperity in Greater East Asia* (New York and London: Monthly Review Press, 1973).

Hampson, *A Social history of the French Reovlution.*

Hassal, *The Balance of Power* (London, 1947).

Hayes, *A Political and Cultural History of Modern Europe, vols. I and II (New York, 1932).*

Hayes & Cole, *A History of Europe*, Vol. II (New York, 1949).

Hazard, Paul; *The European Mind: The Critical Years, 1680-1715 (New Haven, 1953).*

Hazen, *Europe Since 1815* (Calcutta, 1955).

——, *Modern European History* (New York, 1938).

——, *The French Revolution*, 2 Vols. (New York, 1932).

Hearder, Harry, *Italy in the Age of the Risorgi-mento*: 1790-1870 (London and New York: Longman, 1983).

Hearnshaw, *Main Currents of European History* (London, 1925).

Hill (Christopher), *Century of Revolution, 1603- 1714* (London: Nelson, 1967).

Hill, Norman, *Contemporary World Politics* (New York: Harper, 1954).

Hitler, Adolf, *MEIN KAMPF*, Translated and edited by john Chamberlain, Sidney B. Fay (Etc.) (New York: Reynal and Hitchcock, 1941).

Hobsbawm, E.J.; *The Age of Revolution: Europe 1789-1848* (London: Weidenfeld and Nicolson 1962).

Holevi, I. *A History of the News: Ancient and Modern (London: Zed Books, 1989).*

Holland Rose, *Life of Napoleon.*

Hansen, E. (ed.), *Africa: Perspectives on Peace and Development* (London: Zed Books, 1989).

Heltine, B. (ed.), *Europe: Dimensions of Peace* (London: Zed Books, 1989).

Howard, J.E., *Letters and Documents of Napoleon*

ICHI, *Refugees: Dynamics of Displacement* (London: Zed Books, 1989).

——, *Modern Wars: The Humanitarian Challenge* (London: Zed Books, 1989).

Ikle, Frank William, *German-Japanese Relations* (New York: Bookman Associates, 1956).

Irving, R.E.M., *The First Indo-China War: French and American Policy 1945-54* (London: Croom Helm, 1975).

Issawi, Charles, *The Washington Papers: Oil, The Middle East and the World* (New York: The Library Press, 1972).

Jackson (J. Hampden), *Europe Since the War: A Sketch of Political Development, 1918-1932) (London: Victor Gollancz, 1933).*

Jaffe, H., *A History of Africa* (London: Zed Books, 1989).

Jansen, M., *The Battle of Beirut: Why israel invaded Lebanon* (Lonon: Zed Books, 1989).

Jazani, B., *Capitalism and Revolution in Iran* (London: Zed Books, 1989).

jerrold (Douglas), *England: Past, Present and future* (London: J.M. Dent, 1950).

Jervis, Robert, *Perception and misperception on international politics* (Princeton: Princeton University Press, 1976).

Joll (James), *Europe Since 1870: An international history* (Hammondsworth: Penguin, 1976).

Jordan (Donaldson) and Pratt (Edwin J.), *Europe and the American Civil War* (Lodnon: Oxford University Press, 1931).

Kalijarvi, T.V., *Modern World Politics*, 3rd ed., (New York: Crowell, 1953).

Kautsky, John H.; *Political Change in Underdeveloped Countries* (New York, 1962).

Keeton, G.W. and George Schwartzenberger (eds.), *Year-book of World Affairs* (New York: Praeger, 1947).

Keynes, J.M. (Lord) *The Economic Consequences of Peace* (1919).

Ketelbey, *A History of Modern Times* (London, 1951).

Khomsin, *Palestine : Profile of an Occupation* (London: Zed Books, 1989).

Kornilov, Alexander, *Modern Russian History from the age of Catherine the Great to the end of the Nineteenth Century* (New York: Alfred A. Knopf, 1948).

Kukushkin, Yu, *History of the USSR: An Outline of Socialist Construction* (Moscow: Progress Publishers, 1981).

Langsam, W.C. and Mitchell, Otis C., *The World Since 1919* (Delhi: Surjeet Publications, 1981).

Laski, H.J.; *Liberty in the Modern State* (1930).

Laqueur, Walter, *Europe Since Hitler: The Rebirth of Europe* (Pelican Books, 1981).

Leang-Li, T'ang, *The Inner History of the Chinese Revolution* (London: George Rottledge & Sons, Ltd., 1930).

Lecky (William Edward Hartpole), *History of England in the eighteenth century* (London: Longmans, Green & Co., 1890).

Lefebvre, Georges; *The French Revolution From its origins to 1793* (New York, 1962).

Lefebvre, *The Coming of the French Revolution.*

Levy, Jack S., *War in the Modern Great Power System* (Lexington: University Press of Kentucky, 1983).

Lewis, Bernard, *The Emergence of Modern Turkey* (London, New York, Toronto: Oxford University Press, 1961).

Lietaer (Bernard A.), *Europe, Latin America and the multinational: A Positive sum game for the exchange of raw materials and technology in the 1980s* (New York: Praeger, 1980).

Lincon, W. Bruce, *Nicholas I: Emperor and Autocrat of all the Russians*(Bloomington and London: Indiana University Press, 1980).

Lipson (E.), *Europe in the 19th and 20th centuries, 1815-1939*, Ed. 2 (London: Adam and Charles Black, 1944).

Lippmann, W., *The Good Society* (1939).

Littlefield (Henry W.), *History of Europe Since 1815*, Ed. 18 (New York: Narnes and Noble, 1955).

Lockhart, *The History of Napoleon Bonaparte* (London, 1916).

Lodge, *A History of Modern Europe* (London, 1942).

Lovell, C.R.; *English Constitutional and legal History* (1962)

Ludwig, *Napoleon* (New York, 1924).

Mackerras, Colin (eds.) *China: The Impact of Revolution: A Survey of Twentieth Century China* (Hong Kong: Longman, 1976).

Modelin, *The Revolutionaries.*

Madelin, *Consulate and the Empire*, 2 vols.

Mantoux, P.; *The Industrial Revolution in the 18th Century.*

Marcussen & Torp, *Internationalization of Capital: Prospects for the Third World* (London: Zed Books, 1989).

Marlowe, John, *Anglo-Egyptian Relations: 1800- 1956* (London: Frank Cass and Co., 1965).

Marriott, Sir J.A.R., *History of Europe: From 1815 To 1923* (London: Methuen & Co., 1931).

Marriott, *The Eastern Question* (Oxford, 1924).

Marriott, *The Remaking of Modern Europe* (London, 1928).

Marriott, *Makers of Modern Italy.*

Marshall (Dorothy), *Eighteenth Century England* (London: Longmans, 1962).

Moumba & Naisser, *Namibia in History* (London: Zed Books, 1989).

Mcmaster, John Bach, *A History of the People of the United States: From the Revolution to the Civil War* (New York: Dr. Appleton and Co., 1891).

Meiklejohn, J.M.D., *A new history of England and Great Britain* (London: Edinburg University Press, 1893).

Middle East Review 1990 (Essex: World of Information, 1989).

Miliband, R.; *The State in Capitalist Society* (London, 1970).

Mills, Wright; *Power Elite* (New York, 1959).

Monroe, Paul, *China: A nation in Evolution* (New York: The macmillan Company, 1928).

Morgenthau, H.J., *Politics Among Nations* (New York: Knopf, 1954).

Morton, A.L., *A People's History of England* (London: Victor Gollancz Ltd., 1938).

Mowat, R.B., *History of European Diplomacy, 1914-1925* (Calcutta: World Press, 1961).

Mowat, *The States of Europe, 1815-71* (London, 1932).

Muir, *A Short History of the British Commonwealth*, Vol. II (London, 1934).

Muir, *British History* (London, 1929).

Mujeeb (M.), *World Hsitory: Our Heritage* (Bombay: Asia, 1960).

Musto (Setan A.) and Pinkele (Carol F.), ed., *Europe at the Crossroads: Agenda of the Crisis* (New York: Praeger, 1985).

Nabudere, D., *The Political Economy of Imperialism* (London: Zed Books, 1989).

Namier, L.B., *Europe in Decay: A Study in Disntegration* (London: Macmillan and Co. Ltd., 1950).

Niess, F., *A Hemisphere to Itself: A History of US-Latin American Relations* (London: Zed Books, 1989).

Nores & Turner (eds.), *Oil and Class Struggle* (London: Zed Books, 1989).

Ogg (Frederic Austin), *English Government and Politics*, Ed. 2 (New York: Macmillan, 1947).

Oadmore, George, *Pan-Africanism or Communism*: The Coming struggle for Africa (London: Dennis Dobson, 1956).

Osmanczyk, Edmund Jan; *Encyclopedia of the United Nations And International Agreements* (Philadelphia, London, 1985).

Palmer, *A History of Modern World* (New York, 1961).

Palmer, N.D. and H.C. Perkins, *International Relations* (Boston: Houghton Mifflin, 1953).

Parker, Geofrey, *The World: An Illustrated History* (ed.) (New York: Harper Row Publishers, 1986).

Parker (R.A.C.), *Europe 1919-45* (London: Weidenfeld and Nicolson, 1969).

Parker, Richard B., *North Africa: Regional Tensions and Strategic concerns* (New York: Praeger Publisers, 1984).

Phillips, *Modern Europe* (London, 1924).

Pole, J.R., *The Revolution in America 1754-1788: Documents on the Internal Development of America in the Revolutionary Era* (ed.) (London: Macmillan 1970).

Pollard, A.F.; *Factors in Modern History* (1907, 1926).

Pollard; *Political History of England*. (1912).

Postgate, R.W.; *Revolution from 1789 to 1906* (London, 1920).

Proceedings of the Indian History Congress (Delhi: Dept. of History, University of Delhi).

Proctor, J. Harris, *Islam and International Relations* (London: Dunmow: Pall Mall Press, 1965).

Rann (Agatla), *Europe in twentieth century 1905- 1970* (London: Longman, 1984).

Rauch, Georg Von, *A History of Soviet Russia* (London: Pall Mall Press, 1967).

Rees, J.F.; *A Social and Industrial History of England, 1815-1918.*

Rene Arnaud, *The Second Republic and Napoleon III* (London, 1930).

Revolution of 1911 (Peking: Foreign languages press, 1976).

Richter, Werner, *Bismarck*, Translated by Brian Battershaw (London: Macdonald, 1962).

Riker, T.W., *A Short History of Modern Europe* (New York: The Macmillan Co., 1935).

Roberts (Clayton), *Growth of responsible government in Stuart England (London: cambridge University, 1966).*

Roberts (Clayton) and Roberts (David), *History of Engalnd*, Ed. 2, v. I (Engleweed Cliffs: Prentice-Hall Inc., 1980).

Roberts, J.M., *The Pelican History of the World* (Middlesex, New York: victoria, Ontario, Auckland: Penguin books, 1976, 1980).

Robertson, *Bismarck* (London, 1947).

Robertson, Priscilla, *Revolutions of 1848: A Social History* (New York and Evanston: Harper and Row, 1960).

Robertson, R.T., *The Making of the Modern World: An Introductory History* (London: Zed Books, 1989).

Robinson, Richard D., *The First Turkish Republic: A Case Study in National Development* (Cambridge, Massachusetts, 1963).

Robinson and Beard, *The Development of Modern Europe*, Vol. II (New York, 1908).

Robinson and Cossali, *Stateless in Gaza* (London: Zed Books, 1989).

Ropp, Theodore, War in the Modern World (London: Duke University Press, 1959).

Rothchild (Joseph), *East Central Europe between the two world wars* (Seattle: University of Washington Press, 1974).

Royal Institute of International Affairs, *Survey of International Affairs* (London: Oxford University 1925).

Rude (George), *Europe in the eighteenth century: Aristocracy and bourgeoisie challenge* (London: Weidenfeld and Nicolson, 1972).

Sakamoto, Y. (ed.), *Asia: Militarisation and Regional Conflict* (London: Zed Books, 1989).

Saraste, L., *For Palestine: War in Beirut* (London: Zed Books, 1989).

Saul, Norman E., *Russia and the Mediterranean 1797-1807* (Chicago and London: The University of Chicago Press, 1970).

Saul and Gelb, *The Crisis in South Africa: The Struggle against Apartheid* (London: Zed Books, 1989).

Saunders, Harold H., *The Other Walls: The Politics of the Arab-Israeli Peace Process* (Washington D.C.: American Enterprise Institute for Public Policy Research, 1985).

Sayigh, R., *Palestinians: From Peasants to Revolutionaries* (London: Zed Books, 1989).

Schleicher, Charles P., *Introduction to International Relations* (New York: Prentice Hall, 1955).

Scherer, Paul, *European Diplomacy: From 1914 to the present* (Meerut, Review Publications, 1966).

Schuman, F.L., *International Politics*, 5th ed. (New York: McGraw-Hill, 1953).

Schwarzenberger, George, *Power Politics*, 2nd rev. ed. (New York: Praeger, 1951).

Schevill, *A History of Europe* (New York, 1946).

Siegel, P., *The Meek and the Militant: Religion and Power Across the World* (London: Zed Books, 1989).

Shapiro, *Modern and Contemporary European History* (Cambridge, USA, 1953).

Sharabi, Hisham, *The Next Arab Decade* (ed.) (Boulder, London: West View Press and Mansell Publishing Ltd., 1988).

Sharma, J.P., *The Arab Mind* (Delhi: H.K. Publishers, 1990).

Singh, K.R., *The Indian Ocean: Big Power Presence and Local Response* (Columbia: South Asia Books, 1978).

Slosson, Pretson, *Europe Since 1815* (New York: Charles Scribner's Sons, 1954).

Smellie, K.B., *Great Britain Since 1688: A Modern History* (Ann Arbor: University of Michigan Press, 1962).

Smith, G.B., *Outlines of British History* (London, 1920).

Somervell, D.C., *Modern Europe 1871-1950* (London: (Methuen and Co. Ltd., 1940).

Stearns (Peter n.), *World History: Patterns of change* and countinuity (New York: Harper & Row Pub., 1987).

Stephens, *Revolutionary Europe* (London, 1924).

Stoddard, Lothrop, *The New World of Islam* (New York: Charles Scribner's Sons, 1921).

Strachy, *Queen Victoria* (London, 1948).

Stromberg (R.N.), *Europe in the Twentieth Century*, Ed. 2, (Engleweed Cliffs: Prentice Hall, 1988).

Strong, *Dynamic Europe* (London, 1945).

Strong, C.F., *Dynamic Europe: A Background of ferment and change* (London: University of London Press Ltd., 1945).

Sumner, B.H.; *A survey of Russian history*(n.d.)

SWAPO Dept. of Information, *To Be Born a Nation: The Liberation Struggle for Namibia* (London: Zed Books, 1989).

Taine, *Journeys though France* (London, 1897).

The Encyclopaedia Americana: The International Reference Work (New York, chicago, Washington D.C.: Americana Corp., 1924).

Thompson, (David) *The French Revolution.*

Thompson, *Europe Since Napoleon* (London, 1960).

Thompson, *Napoleon Bonaparate, His Rise and Fall.*

Thomson, *Europe Since Napoleon* (Harmondsworth: Penguin, 1975).

Thornton, Ricard C., *China: A Political History, 1917-1980* (Boulder: Westview, 1982).

Tomquist, O., *Dilemmas of Third World Communism: The Destruction of the PKI in Indonesia* (London: Zed Books, 1989).

Trevelyan, *British History in the Nineteenth Century and After* (London, 1948).

Trevelyan, *Garibaldi and the Thousand* (London, 1936).

Treveyan (G.M.), *History of England* (London: Longman, 1974).

Tsoukalis, Loukas (ed.), *Europe, America and the World Economy* (Oxford: Basil Blackwell for the College of Europe, 1986).

Troiner, F., *Abandon Affluence: Sustainable Development and Social Change* (London: Zed Books, 1989).

Turok, B., *Revolutionary Thought in the 20th Century* (London: Zed Books, 1989).

Turok, B., *Africa: What Can Be Done?* (London, Zed Books, 1989).

Turok B., *Development in Zambia* (London: Zed Books, 1989).

Twitchett (Kenneth J.), ed., *Europe and the World: The external relations of the common market* (London: Europa Pub., 1976).

Theimer, Walter, *An Encyclopaedia of Modern World Politics* (New York: Rinehart, 1950).

Thomson, David; *World History from 1914 to 1950* (London, New York, Toronto: Oxford Univ. Press, 1954).

Usher, A.P.; *A History of Mechanical Inventions* (1929)

Vercruisse, E., *The Penetration of Capitalism* (London: Zed Books, 1989)

Verdadsky, *History of Russia* (Philadelphia, 1944).

Vuknanonic, Svetozar, *Struggle for the Balkans*, Translated by Charles Bartlett (London: Martin Press, 1980).

Wakeman, *The Ascendancy of France* (London, 1927).

Walker, R., *One World/Many Worlds: Struggle for a just World Peace* (London: Zed Books, 1989).

Wallace (Kennett E.), *Eurasian Problem: Constructively Approached* (Calcutta: Thacker, Spink, 1930).

Warner and Martin, *The Groundwork of British History* (London, 1931).

Waterlow (Charlette) and Evans (Archibald), *Europe: 1945 to 1970* (London: Methuen Educational, 1973).

Wells. H.G.; *The Outline of History* (1950).

Wilkins, Frances, *Let's Visit Egypt* (London: Burke Publishing Co., 1977).

Wiskemann, Elizabeth, *Europe of the Dictators: 1919- 1945* (London and Glasgow, Collins Clear-Type Press, 1966).

Wood, Anthony; *Europe 1815-1945* (Longmans, 1964).

Young, G.M.; *Victorian England: Portrait of an age* (Oxford, 1936).

Zoolouk, M., *Power, Class and Foreign Capital in Egypt* (London: Zed Books, 1989).

INDEX

Present Day World

*CAS : Central Asian States * KAZAKHASTAN * KIRGIZIA * UZBEKISTAN * TADZAKISTAN etc.